In C...

Beloved Osho, we love you.

Your pioneers in the marketplace

osho

Glimpses of a Golden Childhood

The Rebellious Childhood of a Great Enlightened One

Contents ...

———————————————————————————— . . .

Introduction

Introduction to the revised and expanded second edition.

THE BOOK YOU HOLD IS a uniquely true story. It is a story of truth.

Once upon a time in the city of Rajneeshpuram, Oregon, in that insanity we call America, the living Master Osho went to his dentist.

This in itself is not unusual. (Even the enlightened ones have teeth). What is unique is that the Master turned this seemingly ordinary occasion into an event, another chance to share his being with us. The dental work was fairly routine and, near the end, Osho said a few quiet words as if to himself. Devageet wrote them down.

Devageet had no idea then what he was doing. Little did he know that these few words were the first sparks that would ignite a great fire. But the Master knew. He had seen the words written and later that morning he called a meeting.

Four attended the mysterious meeting: Devageet, the dentist; Devaraj, Osho's personal physician; Ashu, the dental nurse; and Vivek, Osho's caretaker.

At the appointed time they were shown into Osho's room and those who had not yet seen it received a bit of a shock. Instead of the much publicized luxury, their Master was sitting in an almost bare linoleum-tiled room. There was no marble, no gold fittings, no trappings of any kind. The room was empty except for his chair and three plastic buckets.

The Oregon rain, which every winter reduced the land around to a sticky valley of mud, had penetrated the roof, and these three supermarket buckets had been strategically placed to catch the water dripping steadily through the trailer ceiling.

Osho, of course, was totally relaxed and to the rhythm of the drips motioned them to be seated. He told them that the words spoken at the dental sessions were to be taken down and made into books. Devageet was to be the notetaker. Devaraj was to edit, Ashu was to assist and type, and Vivek was to take some beautiful new photographs for the books.

Of all the recorded words of Osho, this small series of gossips from the dentist's chair were to prove the most intimate so far. It was a special kind of communion. Therefore, these words have a special flavor.

It is said the esteemed notetaker had a little trouble at first actually hearing Osho's words. They were almost a whisper. One small step from silence. They seemed to come from far far away, as though he were calling from the great height he has reached down to this earth. Yet these soft words have all the strength, all the waking power, of a lion's beautiful roar of freedom.

In the first session, Osho simply talked of this and that, weaving words of beauty and silence into a delightful tapestry of jokes and mischief. Then he began to go deeply into the source of the ancient Tibetan mantra Om Mani Padme Hum. Osho takes all the seriousness out of this usually lofty subject and these passages are wonderfilled with energy, lightness and much laughter. These first two series are contained in a single volume called *Notes of a Madman*.

Osho has read an amazing number of books in his lifetime and in the third series he spoke about some of the most treasured in his library. The series is called, simply, *Books I Have Loved*. It invites us to also savor these books, to be inspired and nourished by their poetry and beauty.

The fourth series he called *Glimpses of a Golden Childhood*. Suddenly Osho had begun to speak of his early years, something he had hitherto not done. Now he began to unveil a rare and wondrous gift to his disciples and to the world. He spoke of the years when his buddhahood was still a bud.

Osho is the ultimate nonconformist. He bows to no creed, no doctrine. He is this way as a man. He was this way as a child.

He took nothing at face value: the flame of rebellion against the juiceless traditions, the dried out religions and values, was already burning brightly. He was never afraid of consequences. He went his own sweet way, fearless of danger, diving into the deepest, most dangerous rivers, staying alone in the darkest night.

Even his parents, his schoolteachers, came to respect this roguish rascal of a child. It is said that while other children went outside to play, Osho went inside – in the truest sense – to find his playground.

Osho had no master in this lifetime, yet he encountered many great beings who recognized even then who this boy was. They saw his potential, the seed ready to burst into flower. This book is filled with stories of these men, their love and deep respect for Osho and, in return, his love and respect for them.

Although this series is about the Master's early life, it is in no way a conventional autobiography. Osho has more than grown up, he has grown upwards. When he speaks of his childhood, he is not giving us a personal history lesson. He has no masks, no persona; there are no boasts of what he has 'done', no regrets. The stories in this book are not in chronological order; they are a stream of pure, spontaneous consciousness, direct from the timeless ocean. You cannot put the life of a Master into the framework of time.

When Osho relates a story it is not nostalgia. When he speaks with such love for his parents, his grandparents, those crazy characters he met along the way, he brings them to life, full of laughter, energy. It is alive here and now. You can feel it, share it.

It is sometimes hard to imagine, but everything Osho does is for us. He has long ago reached his own fulfillment. He has long ago found that deepest realm of silence. There is no reason for him to speak, it is *all* for us.

This book, these glimpses of his truly golden childhood, is just another invitation, a little more encouragement for us also to find that space in which to blossom. The pure love in these pages is simply to give us a taste, a fragrance of this miracle, this mystery of enlightenment.

This is the second edition of this book. The first was changed in a few subtle and less subtle ways by its first publisher. But the original diamond remained flawless, the changes she made are gone, and it is now back in its original form.

This edition is richer. Since the original series of talks given in 1981 Osho has spoken many times of his childhood. These stories and anecdotes have now been added in an appendix to the book – a few extra spices for this already superb banquet.

If the reader detects a few changes in style in this appendix it is due to the fact that in the original text Osho was simply relating a childhood narrative. In these additional passages, mainly from discourses, he uses stories to illustrate specific points.

Much has happened in the last few years to Osho and his people. It hasn't always been easy. He never said it would be. He has been chained, imprisoned, poisoned. This beautiful individual has been treated by the unconscious world like a criminal, and his health destroyed. For more than four years after he was poisoned and expelled from America, Osho managed to keep his body together so that he could continue to work with his people. He left his body in January, 1990 in Poona, India. There, the commune which has grown up around him continues to expand and flourish.

Much has happened, yet nothing has happened, for it is still happening, moment to precious moment.

Osho says in this book: "Many times I am surprised at how the body has grown old. But as far as I am concerned, I don't feel old age or the aging process. Not even for a single moment have I felt different. I am the same; so many things have happened but only on the periphery.

"So I can tell you what has happened. But remember always, nothing has happened to me. I am just as innocent and as ignorant as I was before my birth."

And a few months before he left his body, he dictated this inscription for the crypt containing his ashes:

OSHO

NEVER BORN – NEVER DIED

ONLY VISITED THIS

PLANET EARTH BETWEEN

DECEMBER 11, 1931 – JANUARY 19, 1990

If you come to this book expecting logic, you will not find it. Masters are not logical men. What you will find is life, in all its craziness, all its love, all its laughter!

If you can read this book with an open heart, if for a few moments you can put aside your serious "grown–up," you too may have a few glimpses of your own inner child. You too may begin to play inside.

Swami Deva Abhinandan

Session 1

I T IS A BEAUTIFUL MORNING. Again and again the sun rises and it is always new. It never grows old. Scientists say it is millions of years old. Nonsense! Every day I see it. It is always new. Nothing is old. But scientists are grave-diggers, that's why I say they look so grave, serious. This morning, again the miracle of existence. Each moment it is happening, but only very few, very very few ever encounter it.

The word 'encounter' is really beautiful. To encounter the moment as it is, to see it as it is, without adding, without deleting, without any editorial work – just to see it as it is, like a mirror…. The mirror does not edit, thank God; otherwise no face in the world would be able to fit its requirements, not even the face of Cleopatra. No face at all would be able to fit the mirror, for the simple reason that if it starts cutting you, editing you, adding to you, it will start destroying you. But no mirror is destructive. Even the ugliest mirror is so beautiful in its undestructiveness. It simply reflects.

Before coming into your Noah's Ark, I was standing looking at the sunrise…so beautiful, at least today – and who cares for tomorrow? Tomorrow never comes. Jesus says, "Think not of the morrow…."

Today it is so beautiful that for a moment I was reminded of the tremendous beauty of the sunrise in the Himalayas. There, when the snow is surrounding you, and the trees are looking like brides, as if they have flowered white flowers of snow, one does not care a bit about the so-called bigwigs, the prime ministers and the presidents of the world, the kings and queens. In fact kings and queens are going to exist only in playing cards; that's where they belong. And the presidents and the prime ministers will take the place of the jokers. They don't deserve anything more.

Those mountain trees with their white flowers of snow...and whenever I saw the snow falling from their leaves I was reminded of a tree from my childhood. That kind of tree is possible only in India; it is called *madhumalti* – *madhu* means sweet, *malti* means the queen. I have never come across any fragrance that is more beautiful and more penetrating – and you know that I am allergic to perfume, so I immediately know. I am very sensitive to perfume.

Madhumalti is the most beautiful tree one can imagine. God must have created it on the seventh day. Relieved of all the worries and hurries of the world, finished with everything, even men and women, he must have created madhumalti on his day off, a holiday, a Sunday...just his old habit of creating. It is difficult to get rid of old habits.

Madhumalti flowers with thousands of flowers all at once. Not one flower here and there, no, that is not the way of madhumalti, nor is it my way. Madhumalti flowers with a richness, with luxury, with affluence – thousands of flowers, so many that you cannot see the leaves. The whole tree becomes covered with white flowers.

Snow-covered trees have always reminded me of madhumalti. Of course there is no perfume, and it is good for me that snow has no perfume. It is unfortunate that I cannot hold the flowers of madhumalti once again. The perfume is so strong it spreads for miles, and remember, I am not exaggerating. Just one single madhumalti tree is enough to fill the whole neighborhood with immense perfume.

I love the Himalayas. I wanted to die there. That is the most beautiful place to die – of course to live too, but as far as dying is concerned, that is the ultimate place. It is where Lao Tzu died. In the valleys of the Himalayas Buddha died, Jesus died, Moses died. No other mountains can claim Moses, Jesus, Lao Tzu, Buddha, Bodhidharma, Milarepa, Marpa, Tilopa, Naropa, and thousands of others.

Switzerland is beautiful but nothing compared to the Himalayas. It is convenient to be in Switzerland with all its modern facilities. It is very inconvenient in the Himalayas. It is still without any technology at all – no roads, no electricity, no airplanes, no railroads, nothing at all. But then comes the innocence. One is transported to another time, to another being, to another space.

I wanted to die there; and this morning, standing and looking at the sunrise, I felt relieved, knowing that if I die here, particularly on a day as beautiful as this, it is okay. And I will choose to die on a day when I feel I am part of the Himalayas. Death for me is not just an end, a full stop. No, death for me is a celebration.

Remembering the snow falling from the trees, just like flowers falling from madhumalti, a haiku flashed....

> *The wild geese*
> *Do not intend to make their reflections.*
> *The water has no mind*
> *To receive their images.*

Ahhh, so beautiful. Wild geese not intending to make their reflections, and the water not intending to receive them either, and yet the reflection is there. That is the beauty. Nobody has intended, and yet it is there – that's what I call communion. I have always hated communication. To me communication is ugly. You can see it happening between a wife and a husband, the boss and the servant, and so on and so forth. It never really happens. Communion is my word.

I see Buddha Hall with all my people...just for a moment like a flash, so many moments of communion. It is not just a gathering; it is not a church. People do not come to it formally. People come to me, not to it. Whenever there is a master and a disciple – it may be only the master and just one disciple, that does not matter – communion happens. It is happening right now, and there are only four of you. Perhaps with my eyes closed I can't even count, and it is good; only then can one remain in the world of the unaccountable...and tax-free too! If you can count, then taxation comes in. I am unaccountable, nobody has ever taxed me.

I was a professor in a university. When they wanted to raise my pay, I said no. The vice-chancellor could not believe it; he said, "Why not?"

I said, "Beyond what I am getting now I would have to pay taxes, and I hate taxation. I would rather remain with the pay I am getting right now than get more and be bothered by the income tax department." I never went beyond the limit which was allowed to remain tax-free.

I have never paid any income tax; in fact there is no income. I have been giving to the world, not taking anything from the world. It is outcome, not income. I have given out of my heart and my being.

It is good that flowers are allowed to be tax-free, otherwise they would stop flowering. It is good that snow is allowed to be tax-free, otherwise it would not snow, believe me!

I must tell you that after the Russian Revolution something happened to the Russian genius. Leo Tolstoy, Fyodor Dostoevski, Turgenev, Maxim Gorky – they all disappeared. Yet in Russia today, the writer, the novelist, the artist, is the most highly paid and honored person. So what happened? Why don't they create any more books like *The Brothers Karamazov, Anna Karenina, Fathers and Sons, The Mother,* or *Notes from the Underground?* Why? I want to ask a thousand times, why? What happened to the Russian genius for writing novels?

I don't think any other country could compete with Russia. If you count only ten novels of the world, just out of necessity you will have to include five Russian novels, leaving only five for the whole remaining world. What happened to this great genius? It died! – because flowers cannot be ordered, there are no ten commandments for them. Flowers flower, you cannot order them to flower. Snow falls – you cannot issue a commandment, you cannot make a date with it. That is impossible. And that is so with the buddhas. They say what they want to say, when they want to say it. They will say, even to a single person, something which the whole world would have liked to hear.

Now, you are here, perhaps only four. I say "perhaps" because my mathematics are poor, and with closed eyes…you can understand …and with tears in my eyes, not because only four are present but for this beautiful morning, for the sunrise.

Thank God. He thinks of me – although he does not exist, still he thinks of me. I deny him, and yet he thinks of me. Great God.

Existence seems to take care. But you do not know the ways of existence; they are unpredictable. I have always loved the unpredictable.

My tears are for the sunrise. Existence has taken care of me.

I had not asked.

Nor did it reply.

But still the care has been taken.

The wild geese do not intend to cast their reflections.

The water has no intention to reflect their images....

That's how I am speaking. I do not know what the next sentence is going to be or whether it is going to be at all. Suspense is beautiful.

I am reminded again of the small village where I was born. Why existence should have chosen that small village in the first place is unexplainable. It is as it should be. The village was beautiful. I have traveled far and wide but I have never come across that same beauty. One never comes again to the same. Things come and go, but it is never the same.

I can see that still, small village. Just a few huts near a pond, and a few tall trees where I used to play. There was no school in the village. That is of great importance, because I remained uneducated for almost nine years, and those are the most formative years. After that, even if you try, you cannot be educated. So in a way I am still uneducated, although I hold many degrees. Any uneducated man could have done it. And not any degree, but a first-class master's degree – that too can be done by any fool. So many fools do it every year that it has no significance. What is significant is that for my first years I remained without education. There was no school, no road, no railway, no post office. What a blessing! That small village was a world unto itself. Even in my times away from that village I remained in that world, uneducated.

I have read Ruskin's famous book, *Unto This Last*, and when I was reading it I was thinking of that village. *Unto This Last*...that village is still unaltered. No road connects it, no railway passes by, even now after almost fifty years; no post office, no police station, no doctor – in fact nobody falls ill in that village, it is so pure and so unpolluted. I have known people in that village who have not seen a railway train, who wonder what it looks like, who have not even seen a bus or a car. They have never left the village. They live so blissfully and silently.

My birthplace, Kuchwada, was a village with no railway line and no post office. It had small hills, hillocks rather, but a beautiful lake, and a few huts, just straw huts. The only brick house was the one I was born in, and that too was not much of a brick house. It was just a little house.

I can see it now, and can describe its every detail...but more than the house or the village, I remember the people. I have come across millions of people, but the people of that village were more innocent than any, because they were very primitive. They knew nothing of the world. Not even a single newspaper had ever entered that village. You can now understand why there was no school, not even a primary school...what a blessing! No modern child can afford it.

I remained uneducated for those years and they were the most beautiful years.

Yes, I must confess I had a private tutor. That first tutor was himself uneducated. He was not teaching me, but trying to learn by teaching me. Perhaps he had heard the great saying, "The best way to learn is to teach," but he was a good man, nice, not like a nasty schoolteacher. To be a schoolteacher one has to be nasty. That is part of the whole business world. He was nice – just butterlike, very soft. Let me confess, I used to hit him – but he would not hit me back, he would simply laugh and say, "You are a child, you can hit me. I am an old man, I cannot hit you back. When you are old you will understand." That's what he said to me, and yes, I understand.

He was a nice villager with great insight. Sometimes villagers have insight which civilized people lack. Just now I am reminded....

A beautiful woman comes to a beach. Seeing nobody around she undresses. Just before she steps into the ocean an old fellow stops her and says, "Lady, I am the village policeman. It is prohibited to swim in the ocean from this beach." The woman looks puzzled and says, "Then why did you not prevent me from getting undressed?" The old man laughs and laughs, with tears in his eyes. He says, "Undressing is not prohibited, so I waited behind a tree!"

A beautiful villager...that type of people lived in the village –

simple people. It was surrounded by small hills and there was a small pond. Nobody could describe that pond except Basho. Even he does not describe the pond, he simply says:

> *The ancient pond*
> *Frog jumps in*
> *Plop!*

Is this a description? The pond is only mentioned, the frog too. No description of the pond or the frog…and plop!

The village had an ancient pond, very ancient, and very ancient trees surrounding it – they were perhaps hundreds of years old – and beautiful rocks all around…and certainly the frogs jumped. Day in and day out you could hear "plop," again and again. The sound of frogs jumping really helped the prevailing silence. That sound made the silence richer, more meaningful.

This is the beauty of Basho: he could describe something without actually describing it. He could say something without even mentioning a word. "Plop!" Now, is this a word? No word could do justice to the sound of a frog jumping into the ancient pond, but Basho did it justice.

I am not a Basho, and that village needed a Basho. Perhaps he would have made beautiful sketches, paintings, and haikus…. I have not done anything about that village – you will wonder why – I have not even visited it again. Once is enough. I never go to a place twice. For me number two does not exist. I have left many villages, many towns, never to return again. Once gone, gone forever, that's my way; so I have not returned to that village. The villagers have sent messages to me to come at least once more. I told them through a messenger, "I have been there once already, twice is not my way."

But the silence of that ancient pond stays with me. Again I am reminded of the Himalayas – the snow…so beautiful, so pure, so innocent. You can only see it through the eyes of a Bodhidharma, a Jesus, or Basho. There is no other way to describe the snow; only the eyes of buddhas reflect it. Idiots can trample it, can make snowballs out of it, but only the eyes of the buddhas can reflect it.

Although...

The wild geese
Do not intend to cast their reflections.
The water has no mind
To reflect their images....

And still the image happens.

The buddhas do not want to reflect the beauty of the world, nor does the world in any way intend to be reflected by the buddhas, but it is reflected. Nobody wills, but it happens, and when it happens it is beautiful. When it is done, it is ordinary; when it is done, you are a technician. When it *happens* you are a master.

Communication is a part of the world of the technician; communion is the fragrance of the world of the master.

This is communion.

I am not speaking about anything in particular....

The wild geese and the water....

Session 2

I JUST HAD A GOLDEN EXPERIENCE, the feeling of a disciple so lovingly working on his master's body. I'm still out of breath because of it. And it also reminds me of my golden childhood. Everybody talks of his golden childhood, but rarely, very rarely, is it true. Mostly it is a lie. But so many people are telling the same lie that nobody detects it. Even poets go on singing songs of their golden childhood – Wordsworth for example, not a worthless fellow at all – but a golden childhood is extremely rare, for the simple reason: where can you find it?

First, one has to choose one's birth. That's almost impossible. Unless you have died in a state of meditation you cannot choose your birth; that choice only opens for the meditator. He dies consciously, hence earns the right to be born consciously.

I died consciously. Not in fact died, but was killed. I would have died three days later but they could not wait, not even for three days. People are in such a hurry. You will be surprised to know that the man who killed me is now my sannyasin. He came to kill me again, not to take sannyas...but if he sticks to his game, then I stick to mine. He himself confessed later, after seven years of being a sannyasin. He said, "Beloved Master, now I can confess to you without fear: in Ahmedabad I had come to kill you."

I said, "My God, again!"

He said, "What do you mean by 'again'?"

I said, "That's another matter, go on...."

He said, "In Ahmedabad, seven years ago, I came to your meeting with a revolver. The hall was so full that the organizers had allowed people to sit on the dais."

So this man, with a revolver to kill me, was allowed to sit at my side. What a chance! I said, "Why did you miss your chance?"

He said, "I had never heard you before, I had only heard about you. When I heard you I thought I would rather commit suicide than kill you. That's why I became a sannyasin – that's my suicide."

Seven hundred years ago this man had really killed me; he poisoned me. Then too he was my disciple...but without a Judas it is very difficult to find a Jesus. I died consciously, hence I had the great opportunity to be born consciously. I chose my mother and my father.

Thousands of fools are making love around the earth, around the clock. Millions of unborn souls are ready to enter into any womb whatsoever. I waited seven hundred years for the right moment, and I thank existence that I found it. Seven hundred years are nothing compared to the millions and millions of years ahead. Only seven hundred years – yes, I am saying only – and I chose a very poor couple but a very intimate one.

I don't think my father ever looked at another woman with the same love he had for my mother. It is also impossible to imagine – even for me, who can imagine all kinds of things – that my mother, even in her dreams, had another man...impossible! I have known both of them; they were so close, so intimate, so fulfilled although so poor...poor yet rich. They were rich in their poverty because of their intimacy, rich because of their love for each other.

Fortunately, I never saw my mother and father fighting. I say "fortunately" because it is very difficult to find a husband and wife not fighting. When they have time for love only God knows, or maybe he doesn't know either. After all, he has to take care of his own wife ...particularly the Hindu God. At least the Christian God is in a happier state of affairs: he has no wife at all, no woman at all, what to say of a wife! Because a woman is more dangerous than a wife. A wife you can tolerate, but a woman...you are a fool again! You cannot tolerate a woman, she "attracts" you; a wife "distracts" you.

Look at my English! Put it in inverted commas so nobody misunderstands me – although whatsoever you do everyone is going to misunderstand me. But try, put it in inverted commas: the wife "distracts," the woman "attracts."

I have never seen my father and mother fight, not even nagging.

People talk about miracles — I have *seen* a miracle: my mother did not nag my father. It is a miracle, because for centuries woman has been bossed so much by man that she has learned underhand practices — she nags. Nagging is violence in disguise, masked violence. I never saw my mother and father in any fighting situation.

I was worried about my mother when my father died. I could not believe that she would be able to survive. They had loved each other so much, they had almost become one. She survived only because she also loves me.

I have been continuously worried about her. I wanted her to be near me just so that she can die in utter fulfillment. Now I know. I have seen her, I have seen into her, and I can say to you — and through you it will one day reach the world — she has become enlightened. I was her last attachment. Now there is nothing left for her to be attached to. She is an enlightened woman — uneducated, simple, not even knowing what enlightenment is. That's the beauty! One can be enlightened without knowing what enlightenment is, and vice versa: one can know everything about enlightenment and remain unenlightened.

I chose this couple, just simple villagers. I could have chosen kings and queens. It was in my hands. All kinds of wombs were available, but I am a man of very simple tastes: I am always satisfied with the best. The couple was poor, very poor. You will not be able to understand that my father had only seven hundred rupees — that means thirty dollars. That was all he possessed, yet I chose him to be my father. He had a richness which eyes cannot see, a royalty which is invisible.

Many of you have seen him and must have felt the beauty of the man. He was simple, very simple, you could even call him just a villager, but immeasurably rich — not in the worldly way, but if there is an otherworldly way....

Thirty dollars, that was his sole possession. I would not have known it. I came to know only later on when his business was going bankrupt...and he was very happy! I asked him, "Dada" — I used to call him that; dada means father — "Dada, soon you are going to be bankrupt, and still you are happy. What is the matter? Are the rumors false?"

He said, "No, the rumors are absolutely true. Bankruptcy is bound to happen – but I am happy because I have saved seven hundred rupees. That's what I started with. And I will show you the place...."

Then he showed me the place where he had hidden the seven hundred rupees and said, "Don't be worried. I started with only seven hundred. Nothing else belongs to us – let it go to hell. What belongs to us is hidden here, in this place, and I have shown it to you. You are my eldest son, remember this place."

This I know...I have not said anything to anybody about that place, and I am not going to either, because although he was generous in showing me his secret, I am neither his son, nor is he my father. He is himself, I am myself. "Father and son" is just a formality. Those seven hundred rupees are still hidden somewhere under the earth, and will remain there unless found accidentally by someone. I told him, "Although you have shown me the place, I have not seen it."

He said, "What do you mean?"

I said, "It is simple. I don't see it, and I don't want to see it. I don't belong to any heritage, big or small, rich or poor."

But from his side he was a loving father. As far as my side is concerned, I am not a loving son – excuse me.

He was a loving father. When I left my university post, only he was worried, nobody else. None of my friends were worried. Who cares? – in fact, many of my friends were happy that I had vacated the chair; now they could have it. They rushed. Only my father was worried. I told him, "There is no need to worry."

But my saying it was not of much help. He purchased a big prop-erty without telling me, because he knew perfectly well that if he had told me, I would have hit his head. He made a beautiful little house for me, exactly as I would have liked it to be. You will be surprised: it was even air-conditioned, with all modern facilities.

It was near my village, with a garden on the bank of the river, with steps leading down so that I could go swimming...with ancient, old trees and absolute silence surrounding, no one else for miles. But he never told me.

It is good that my poor father is dead; otherwise I would have given him trouble. But he had so much love, and so much compas-sion for a vagabond son.

I am a vagabond. I have never done anything for the family. They are not obliged to me at all. They have done everything for me. I had chosen this couple not without good reason…for their love, their intimacy, their almost one-ness. That is how, after seven hundred years, I entered into the body again.

My childhood was golden. Again, I am not using a cliché. Everybody says his childhood was golden, but it is not so. People only think their childhood was golden because their youth is rotten; then their old age is even more rotten. Naturally, childhood becomes golden. My childhood was not golden in that sense. My youth was diamond, and if I am going to be an old man then it is going to be platinum. But my childhood was certainly golden – not a symbol, absolutely golden; not poetically, but literally, factually.

For most of my very early years I lived with my mother's parents. Those years are unforgettable. Even if I reach to Dante's paradise I will still remember those years. A small village, poor people, but my grandfather – I mean my mother's father – was a generous man. He was poor, but rich in his generosity. He gave to each and everyone whatsoever he had. I learned the art of giving from him; I have to accept it. I never saw him say no to any beggar or anybody.

I called my mother's father "Nana"; that's the way the mother's father is called in India. My mother's mother is called "Nani." I used to ask my grandfather, "Nana, where did you get such a beautiful wife?"

My grandmother looked more Greek than Indian. When I see Mukta laughing, I remember her. Perhaps that's why I have a soft spot in my heart for Mukta. I cannot say no to her. Even though what she demands is not right, I still say "Okay." The moment I see her I immediately remember my Nani. Perhaps there was some Greek blood in her. No race can claim purity. The Indians particularly should not claim any purity of blood – the Hunas, the Moguls, the Greeks and many others have attacked, conquered and ruled India. They have mixed themselves in the Indian blood, and it was so apparent with my grandmother. Her features were not Indian, she looked Greek, and she was a strong woman, very strong. My Nana died when he was not more than fifty. My grandmother lived till eighty and she was fully healthy. Even then nobody thought she was going to die. I promised her one thing, that when she died I would come, and that would be my last visit to the family. She died in 1970. I had to fulfill my promise.

For my first years I knew my Nani as my mother; those are the years when one grows. This circle is for my Nani. My own mother came after that; I was already grown up, already made in a certain style. And my grandmother helped me immensely. My grandfather loved me, but could not help me much. He was so loving, but to be of help more is needed – a certain kind of strength. He was always afraid of my grandmother. He was, in a sense, a henpecked husband. When it comes to the truth, I am always true. He loved me, he helped me…what can I do if he was a henpecked husband? Ninety-nine point nine percent of husbands are, so it is okay.

I remember an incident that I have never told before. It was a dark night; it was raining and a thief entered our house. Naturally my grandfather was afraid. Everybody could see that he was afraid, but he pretended not to be, he tried his best. The thief was hiding in the corner of our small house, behind a few bags of sugar.

My grandfather was a continuous pan-chewer. Pan is betel leaf. Just like a chain smoker, he was a chain pan-chewer. He was always making pan, and the whole day long he would chew it. He started chewing pan and spitting it at the poor thief who was hiding in the corner. I looked at this ugly scene, and told my grandmother, with whom I used to sleep, "This is not right. Even though he is a thief we should behave in a gentlemanly way. Spitting? Either fight or stop spitting!"

My grandmother said, "What would you like to do?"

I said, "I will go and slap the thief and throw him out." I was not more than nine.

My grandmother laughed and said, "Okay, I will come with you – you may need my help." She was a tall woman. My mother does not resemble her in any way, neither in physical beauty, nor in her spiritual daring. My mother is simple; my grandmother was adventurous. She came with me.

I was shocked! I could not believe what I saw: the thief was a man who used to come and teach me, my teacher! I really hit him hard, more so because he was my teacher. I told him, "If you were only a thief I would have forgiven you, but you have been teaching me great things, and at night you do *these* things! Now run away as fast as you can before my grandmother gets hold of you, otherwise she will crush you."

She was a big woman, tall, strong and beautiful. My grandfather was small and homely, but they both went well together. He never fought her – he could not – so there was no problem at all.

I remember that teacher, the village pundit, who also used to come and tutor me sometimes. He was the priest of the village temple. He said, "What about my clothes? Your grandfather has been spitting all over me. He has spoiled my clothes."

My grandmother laughed and said, "Come tomorrow, I will give you some new clothes." And she really did give him some new clothes. He did not come, he did not dare, but she went to the thief's home and took me with her, and gave him the new clothes, telling him, "Yes, my husband is terrible to spoil your clothes. It is not good. Whenever you need clothes you can always come to me."

That teacher never came to teach me again…not that he was told not to, he did not dare. He not only stopped coming to teach me, he stopped coming to the street where we lived; he stopped passing that way. But I made it a point to visit him every day just to spit in front of his house, to remind him. I would shout to him, "Have you forgotten that night? And you always used to tell me to be true, sincere and honest and all that bullshit."

Even now I can see him with his eyes cast down, unable to answer me.

My grandfather wanted the greatest astrologers in India to make my birth chart. Although he was not very rich – in fact not even rich, what to say of very rich, but in that village he was the richest person – he was ready to pay any price for the birth chart. He made the long journey to Varanasi and saw the famous men. Looking at the notes and dates my grandfather had brought, the greatest astrologer of them all said, "I am sorry, I can only make this birth chart after seven years. If the child survives then I will make his chart without any charge, but I don't think he will survive. If he does it will be a miracle, because then there is a possibility for him to become a buddha."

My grandfather came home weeping. I had never seen tears in his eyes. I asked, "What is the matter?"

He said, "I have to wait until you are seven. Who knows whether I will survive those years or not? Who knows whether the astrologer himself will survive, because he is so old. And I am a little concerned about you."

I said, "What's the concern?"

He said, "The concern is not that you may die, my concern is that you may become a buddha."

I laughed, and amongst his tears he also started laughing. Then he himself said, "It is strange that I was worried. Yes, what is wrong in being a buddha?"

When my father heard what the astrologers had told my grandfather, he took me to Varanasi himself – but more of that later.

When I was seven an astrologer came to my grandfather's village searching for me. When a beautiful horse stopped in front of our house, we all rushed out. The horse looked so royal, and the rider was none other than one of the famous astrologers I had met. He said to me, "So you are still alive? I have made your birth chart. I was worried, because people like you don't survive long."

My grandfather sold all the ornaments in the house just to give a feast for all the neighboring villages, to celebrate that I was going to become a buddha, and yet I don't think he even understood the meaning of the word 'buddha'.

He was a Jaina and may not have even heard it before. But he was happy, immensely happy...dancing, because I was to become a buddha. At that moment I could not believe that he could be so happy just because of this word 'buddha'. When everyone had departed I asked him, "What is the meaning of 'buddha'?"

He said, "I don't know, it just sounds good. Moreover I am a Jaina. We will find out from some Buddhist."

In that small village there were no Buddhists, but he said, "Someday, when a passing Buddhist *bhikkhu* comes by, we will know the meaning."

But he was so happy just because the astrologer had said that I was to become a buddha. He then said to me, "I guess 'buddha' must mean someone who is very intelligent." In Hindi *buddhi* means intelligence, so he thought 'buddha' meant the intelligent one.

He came very close, he almost guessed right. Alas that he is not alive, otherwise he would have seen what being a buddha means – not the dictionary meaning, but an encounter with a living, awakened one. And I can see him dancing, seeing that his grandson has become a buddha. That would have been enough to make him enlightened! But he died. His death was one of my most significant experiences. Of that, later on.

Is there time yet?

"It's eight-thirty, Osho."

Good, just five minutes for me....

It is time to stop, but it has been beautiful, and I am grateful. Thank you.

Session 3

·····

AGAIN AND AGAIN THE MIRACLE of the morning…the sun and the trees. The world is just like a snow flower: take it in your hand and it melts away. Nothing is left, just a wet hand. But if you see, just see, then a snow flower is as beautiful as any flower in the world. And this miracle happens every morning, every afternoon, every evening, every night, twenty-four hours, day in, day out…the miracle. And people go to worship God in temples, churches, mosques and synagogues. The world must be full of fools – sorry, not fools but idiots – incurable, suffering from such retardedness. Has one to go to a temple to search for God? Is he not here and now?

The very idea of search is idiotic. One searches for that which is far away, and God is so close, closer than your own heartbeat. When I see the miracle every moment I am amazed how it is possible. Such creativity! It is possible only because there is no creator. If there were a creator you would have the same Monday every Monday, because the creator created the world in six days, then was finished with it. There is no creator, but only creative energy – energy in millions of forms, melting, meeting, appearing, disappearing, coming together and departing.

That is why I say the priest is the farthest away from the truth, and a poet the closest. Of course the poet has not attained it either. Only the mystic attains it…. 'Attain' is not the right word: he becomes it, or rather he finds that he has always been it.

People ask me, "Do you believe in astrology, in religion…in this, in that?" I don't believe in anything at all, because I *know*. That reminds me of the story I was telling you the other day….

The old astrologer came. My grandfather could not believe his eyes. The astrologer was so famous that even kings would have been surprised if he had visited their palace; and he came to my old grandfather's house. It has to be called a house, but it was nothing much, just made of mud walls, not even a separate bathroom. He visited us and I immediately became a friend to the old man.

Looking into his eyes – although I was only seven and I could not read a word, I could read his eyes: they don't need your three R's – I said to the astrologer, "It is strange that you traveled so far just to make my birth chart."

Varanasi in those days, and even now, is far away from that small village.

The old man said, "I had promised, and a promise has to be fulfilled." The way he said "a promise has to be fulfilled" thrilled me. Here was an alive man!

I said to him, "If you have come to fulfill your promise, then I can predict your future."

He said, "What! You can predict my future?"

I said, "Yes. Certainly you are not going to become a buddha, but you are going to become a bhikkhu, a sannyasin." That is the name of a Buddhist sannyasin.

He laughed and said, "Impossible!"

I said, "You can bet on it."

He asked me, "Okay, how much?"

I said, "It does not matter. You can bet any amount you want, because if I win, I win; if I lose, I lose nothing, because I don't have anything. You are gambling with a child of seven. Can't you see it? I don't have anything."

You will be surprised to know that I was standing there naked. In that poor village it was not prohibited, at least for seven-year-old children, to run around naked. It was not an English village!

I can still see myself standing there naked, before the astrologer. The whole village had gathered around, and they were all listening to what was conspiring between me and him.

The old man said, "Okay, if I become a sannyasin, a bhikkhu" – and he showed his gold pocket watch, studded with diamonds – "I will give this to you. And what about you, if you lose?"

I said, "I will simply lose. I don't have anything – no gold wrist-watch to give to you. I will just thank you."

He laughed and departed.

I don't believe in astrology. Ninety-nine point nine percent of it is nonsense, but point one percent is pure truth. A man of insight, intuition and purity can certainly look into the future, because the future is not nonexistential, it is just hidden from our eyes. Maybe just a thin curtain of thoughts is all that divides the present and the future.

In India, the bride covers her face with a *ghoonghat*. Now, it is difficult to translate this word; it is just a mask. She pulls her sari over her face. That's the way the future is hidden from us, just by a ghoonghat, a thin veil.

I don't believe in astrology, I mean the ninety-nine point nine percent of it. The remaining point one percent I need not believe in; it is true. I have seen it function. That old man was the first proof. But it is strange: he could see my future, of course vaguely, with all kinds of possibilities, but he could not see his own. Not only that, he was ready to bet against me when I said that he would become a bhikkhu.

I was fourteen, and traveling around Varanasi with my father's father. He had gone on business, and I had stubbornly insisted on going with him. I stopped an old bhikkhu on the road between Varanasi and Sarnath and said, "Old man, do you remember me?"

He said, "I have never seen you before – why should I remember you?"

I said, "You may not, but I have to remember *you*. Where is the watch, the gold watch studded with diamonds? I am the child with whom you gambled. Now the time has come for me to ask. I had declared that you would become a bhikkhu, and now you are. Give me the watch."

He laughed, and brought out from his pocket the beautiful old watch, gave it to me with tears in his eyes, and – can you believe it – he touched my feet. I said, "No, no. You are a bhikkhu, a sann-yasin, you cannot touch my feet."

He said, "Forget all about it. You proved to be a greater astrologer than I; let me touch your feet."

I gave that watch to the first of my sannyasins. The name of my first sannyasin is Ma Anand Madhu – a woman of course, because that's what I wanted. Nobody has initiated women into sannyas like me. Not only that, I wanted to initiate a woman as my first sannyasin, just to put things in balance and in order.

Buddha hesitated before giving sannyas to women...even Buddha! Only that thing in his life hurts me like a thorn, and nothing else. Buddha hesitating...why? He was afraid that women sannyasins would distract his followers. What nonsense! A buddha and afraid of business! Let those fools be distracted if they want to be!

Mahavira said that nobody in a woman's body could attain to nirvana, the ultimate liberation. I have to repent for all these men. Mohammed never allowed any woman into the mosque. Even now women are not allowed into the mosque; even in the synagogue women sit in the gallery, not with the men.

Indira Gandhi was telling me that when she visited Israel and went to Jerusalem, she could not believe that the prime minister of Israel and herself were both sitting in the balcony, and all the men were sitting downstairs on the main floor. She did not realize that even the prime minister of Israel, being a woman, could not be allowed into the synagogue proper; they could only be observers from the balcony. It is not respectful, it is an insult.

I have to apologize for Mohammed, for Moses, for Mahavira, for Buddha, and for Jesus too, because he didn't choose a single woman as one of his twelve apostles. Yet when he died on the cross the twelve fools were not there at all. Only three women stayed – Magdalena, Mary and Magdalena's sister. But even these three women had not been chosen by Jesus; they were not among the chosen few. The chosen few had escaped. Great! They were trying to save their own lives. In the hour when there was danger, only women came.

I have to apologize to the future for all these people; and my first apology was to give sannyas to a woman. You will be amused to know the full story....

The husband of Anand Madhu, of course, wanted to be initiated first. It happened in the Himalayas; I was having a camp in Manali. I refused the husband saying, "You can only be second, not the first." He was so angry that he left the camp at that very moment. Not only that, he became my enemy and joined Morarji Desai.

Later on, when Morarji Desai was prime minister, this man tried in every way to persuade him to imprison me. Of course Morarji Desai does not have that kind of courage; one can't have if one drinks one's own urine. He is an utter fool – again, sorry, utter idiot. 'Fool' I reserve only for Devageet; that's his privilege.

Anand Madhu is still a sannyasin. She lives in the Himalayas, silently, without speaking. Since then my effort has always been to bring women to the front as much as possible. Sometimes I may even look unfair to men. I'm not, I am just putting things in order. After centuries of man's exploitation of women, it is not an easy task.

The first woman I loved was my mother-in-law. You will be surprised: am I married? No, I am not married. That woman was Gudia's mother, but I used to call her my mother-in-law, just as a joke. I have remembered it again after so many years. I used to call her mother-in-law because I loved her daughter. That was Gudia's previous life. Again, that woman was tremendously powerful, just like my grandmother.

My "mother-in-law" was a rare woman, especially in India. She left her husband, went to Pakistan and married a Mohammedan even though she was a brahmin. She knew how to dare. I always like the quality of daring, because the more you dare, the nearer you come to home. Only the daredevils ever become buddhas, remember! The calculating ones can have a good bank balance but cannot become buddhas.

I am thankful to the man who declared my future when I was only seven. What a man! To have waited until I was seven just to make my birth chart – what patience! And not only that, he came all the way from Varanasi to my village. There were no roads, no trains, he had to travel long on horseback.

And when I met him on the road to Sarnath and told him that I had won the bet, he immediately gave me his watch and said, "I would have given you the whole world but I don't have anything else. In fact I should not even have this watch, but just because of you I have kept it all these years knowing that any day you are bound to come. And when I became a bhikkhu, Buddha was not in my mind, but you – a naked seven-year-old child declaring the future of one of the greatest astrologers in the country. How did you do it?"

I said, "That I don't know. I looked into your eyes and I could see that you could not be content with anything this world could give you. I saw the divine discontent. A man only becomes a sannyasin when he feels the divine discontent."

I don't know whether the old man is still alive or not. He cannot be, otherwise he would have searched for me and found me.

But that moment, in the life of the village, was the greatest. They still talk about that feast. Just recently a person from that village came here, and he said, "We still talk about the feast that your grandfather gave to the village. Never before and never after has anything like that happened."

I enjoyed so many people enjoying. I enjoyed the white horse. Gudia would have loved that horse. She used to show me the horses as we passed them on the road. "Look," she would say, "what beautiful horses."

I have seen many horses, but nothing like the horse that old astrologer had. I have seen the most beautiful horses, but I still remember his horse as being the most beautiful. Perhaps my childhood was the cause of it, perhaps I had no way to compare them. But believe me, whether I was a child or not, that horse was beautiful. It was immensely powerful, must have been eight horsepower!

Those days were golden. Everything that happened in those years I can again see like a film passing before me. It is unbelievable that I would ever be interested....

No...Ashu is looking at her watch. It is too early to look at your watch. Don't be just like Canada Dry – relax. Don't be so dry. You looked at your watch at such a moment, and you don't know what you have disturbed. It is not just a plop!

What was I saying...? Those days were golden. Everything that happened in those nine years, I can again see like a film passing before me.

Good, the film is back, despite Ashu and her watch.

Yes, it was a golden time. In fact more than golden, because my grandfather not only loved me but loved everything that I did. And I did everything that you could call a nuisance.

I was a continuous nuisance. The whole day he had to listen to complaints about me, and he always rejoiced in them. That is what is wonderful and beautiful about the man. He never punished me. He never even said a single word like "Do this," or "Don't do that." He simply allowed, absolutely allowed me to be myself. That is how, without knowing it at all, I came to have the taste of Tao.

Lao Tzu says, "Tao is the watercourse way. The water simply flows downwards wherever the earth allows it." That is how those early years were. I was allowed. I think every child needs those years. If we could give those years to every child in the world we could create a golden world.

Those days were full, overfull! So many events, so many incidents that I have never told to anybody....

I used to swim in the lake. Naturally my grandfather was afraid. He put a strange man to guard over me, in a boat. In that primitive village you cannot conceive what a "boat" meant. It is called a *dongi*. It is nothing but the hollowed-out trunk of a tree. It is not an ordinary boat. It is round, and that is the danger: unless you are an expert you cannot row it. It can roll at any moment. Just a little imbalance and you are gone forever. It is very dangerous.

I learned balance through rowing a dongi. Nothing could be more helpful. I learned the "middle way" because you have to be exactly in the middle: this way, and you are gone; that way, and you are gone. You cannot even breathe, and you have to remain absolutely silent; only then can you row the dongi.

The man who was put on guard to save me, I called him strange. Why? Because his name was Bhoora, and it means "white man." He was the only white man in our village. He was not a European; it was just by chance that he did not look like an Indian. He looked more like a European but he was not. His mother most probably had worked in a British Army camp and had become pregnant there. That's why nobody knew his name, everybody called him Bhoora. Bhoora means "the white one." It is not a name but it became his name. He was a very impressive-looking man. He came to work for my grandfather from early childhood, and even though he was a servant he was treated like one of the family.

I also called him strange because although I have come to know many people in the world, one rarely comes across such a man as Bhoora. He was a man you could trust. You could say anything to him and he would keep the secret forever. This fact became known to my family only when my grandfather died. My grandfather had entrusted to Bhoora all the keys and all the affairs of the house and the land. Soon after we arrived in Gadarwara my family asked my grandfather's most devoted servant, "Where are the keys?"

He said, "My master told me, 'Never show the keys to anybody else but me.' Excuse me, but unless he asks me himself I cannot give you the keys." And he never gave them the keys, so we don't know what those keys were hiding.

Many years later when I was again living in Bombay, Bhoora's son came to me and gave me the keys and said, "We have been waiting and waiting for you to come, but nobody came. We have taken care of the land and looked after the crops and put aside all the money."

I gave him the keys back and said to him, "Everything now belongs to you. The house, the crops and the money belong to you, they are yours. I am sorry that I did not know before, but none of us wanted to go back and feel the pain."

What a man! But such men used to exist on earth. They are disappearing by and by, and instead of such people you find all kinds of cunning people taking their place. These people are the very salt of the earth. I call Bhoora a strange man because in a cunning world, to be simple *is* strange. It is to be a stranger, not of this world.

My grandfather had as much land as one could desire, because in those days, in that part of India, land was absolutely free. You had just to go to the government office in the capital and ask for the land. That was enough – it was given to you. We had fourteen hundred acres of crops which Bhoora attended to.

When my grandfather became sick, Bhoora had said he would never be able to live without him, they had become so close. When my grandfather was dying we took him from Kuchwada to Gadarwara, because there were no facilities in Kuchwada to care for the sick. My grandfather's house was the only house in the village.

When we left Kuchwada Bhoora had given the keys to his sons. On the way to Gadarwara my grandfather died, and because of the shock, the next morning Bhoora did not wake up from his sleep; he died in the night. My grandmother, my father and mother did not want to go back to Kuchwada because of the pain it would cause us, because my grandfather had been such a beautiful man.

Bhoora's son is around the same age as me. It is only just a few years ago that my brother Niklanka and Chaitanya Bharti went back just to take pictures of the house and the pond.

The house in which I was born, they are now asking ten lakhs rupees for it, knowing that one of my disciples may be willing to purchase it. Ten lakhs! That is one hundred thousand dollars. And do you know? – it was worth thirty rupees at the time my grandfather died. Even that was too much. We would have been surprised that anybody would be ready to give us even that.

It was a very primitive part of the country. Just because it was primitive it had something which is now missing from man everywhere else. Man also needs to be a little primitive, at least once in a while. A forest, a jungle rather – an ocean, a sky full of stars.

Man should not be only concerned with his bank account. That is the most ugly thing possible. That means the man is dead! Bury him! Celebrate! Burn him! Dance about his funeral! The bank account is not the man. Man, in order to be man, must be as natural as the hills, rivers, rocks, flowers....

My grandfather not only helped me to know what innocence is – that is, what life is – but he also helped me to know what death is. He died in my lap. Of that, sometime later on.

Session 4

I WAS TELLING YOU OF THE moment when I met the astrologer who had now become a sannyasin....

I was nearabout fourteen at the time, and with my other grandfather, that is, my father's father. My real grandfather was no more; he died when I was only seven. The old bhikkhu, the ex-astrologer, asked me, "I am by profession an astrologer, and by hobby a reader of many things – lines of the hand, of heads, of feet, and so on. How could you manage to tell me that I was going to become a sannyasin? I had never thought about it before. It was you who dropped the seed in me, and since then I have been thinking only of sannyas, and nothing else. How did you manage?"

I shrugged my shoulders. Even today if someone asks how I manage, all I can do is shrug my shoulders – because I do not manage, I simply allow things to be. One just has to learn the art of running ahead of things so that everybody thinks you are managing them; otherwise there is no management, particularly in the world I am concerned with.

I told the old man, "I just looked into your eyes and saw such purity that I could not believe that you were not yet a sannyasin. You should have been already; it was already too late."

In a sense sannyas is always too late, and in another sense it is always too soon...and both are true together.

Now it was the turn of the old man to shrug his shoulders. He said, "You puzzle me. How could my eyes give the clue?"

I said, "If eyes cannot give the clue then there is no possibility for any astrology."

The word 'astrology' is certainly not concerned with the eyes, it

27

OSHO AT AGE 14

is concerned with the stars. But can a blind man see stars? You need eyes to see stars.

I said to that old man, "Astrology is not the science of the stars, but the science of seeing – seeing the stars even during the day, in full daylight."

Once in a while it happens…when the master hits the disciple on the head. Just this morning, Ashu, do you remember when you were looking at your watch, and I hit your head with a Canada Dry soda bottle? Remember now? At the time you missed it. That's what it means to know astrology. She had a little taste of it this morning – I don't think she will ever look at her watch again.

But please, look at it again and again, so I can hit you again and again. It was only a beginning. Otherwise how are you going to freak in? Forgive me, but always allow me to hit you. I am always ready to ask your forgiveness, but never ready to say that I will not hit again. In fact, the first is only a preparation for the second, and a deeper hit.

This is a strange company here. I am an old Jew. There is a proverb which says: Once a Jew always a Jew. And I was once a Jew, and I know the truth of that proverb. I'm still a Jew, and sitting by my right side is a one-hundred-percent Jew, Devageet; and there, by my side near my feet, Devaraj is sitting, partially a Jew. You can see from his nose…otherwise from where could he get such a beautiful nose?

And Gudia, if she is still here, is not English either. She has also once been a Jew. For the first time I want to make it known to you that she is none other than Magdalena! She loved Jesus, but missed him. He was crucified so early, and a woman needs time and patience – and he was only thirty-three. That is the time to play football, or if you are a little grown up at thirty-three, then to go to see a football match.

Jesus died too early. The people were too uncruel to him… I mean cruel to him. I wanted them to be uncruel, that's why the word came. Gudia, this time you cannot miss – whatsoever you do, and howsoever you try to escape. I am not Jesus, who could be easily crucified at thirty-three. And I can be very patient, even with a woman, which is hard…that I know, difficult, very very difficult at times. A woman can really be a pain in the neck!

I have never suffered from a pain in the neck, thank God, but I know pain in the back. If it is so terrible in the back, how much more it must be in the neck! The neck is the very pinnacle of the back. But with me whether you are a pain in the neck or the back, it does not matter: this time you cannot miss. If you miss this time, it will be impossible to find a man like me again.

Jesus can be found again very easily – people are becoming enlightened all the time. But to find a man like me, who has traveled thousands of ways, in thousands of lives, and has gathered the fragrance of millions of flowers like a honeybee, is difficult.

If one misses me, perhaps he misses forever. But I won't allow it to happen to any of my people. I know all the ways to cut through their cunningness, their hardness, their cleverness. And I am not concerned with the world at large; I am concerned only with my people, those who are really in search of themselves.

Just today I received a translation of a new book they are publishing in Germany. I don't know German, so somebody had to translate the part concerned with me. I never laughed so much at any joke – yet it is not a joke, it is a very serious book.

The author devoted fifty-five pages just to prove that I am only illuminated and not enlightened. Great! Just great! – only illuminated, not enlightened. And you will be surprised to know that just a few days ago I received another book from the same category of idiot, a Dutch professor. The Dutch are not very different from the Germans, they belong to the same category.

By the way, I must tell you that Gurdjieff used to divide every person according to a certain plan. He had a few categories of idiots. Now this German and that Dutch fellow, whose name I have fortunately forgotten, both belong to the first category of fools...no, not fools – that is reserved for my Jew disciple, Devageet – idiots. The Dutch idiot proved, or tried to prove, in a long dissertation, that I am only enlightened, not illuminated. Now, these two idiots should meet and wrestle and hit each other with their arguments and books.

As far as I am concerned, once and for all, let me declare to the world: I am neither illuminated nor enlightened. I am just a very ordinary, very simple man, with no adjectives and no degrees. I have burned all my certificates.

The idiots always ask the same question – it makes no difference. This is the miracle. Everything is different between India, England, Canada, America, Germany, but not the idiot. The idiot is universal, the same everywhere. You taste it from anywhere and it is the same. Perhaps Buddha would have agreed with me; after all he said: Taste the Buddha from anywhere, and he is just like the ocean: wherever you taste it, it tastes of salt. Perhaps just as the buddhas taste the same, *buddhus* – which is the Indian name for idiots – also taste the same. It is good, but only in the Indian languages, that 'buddha' and 'buddhu' are made from the same root, are almost the same word.

I am not at all concerned whether you believe me to be enlightened or not. What does it matter? But this man is so concerned that in his small book fifty pages are devoted to this question, whether I am enlightened or not. It certainly proves one thing, that he was a first-class idiot.

I am just myself. Why should I be enlightened or illuminated? And what great scholarship! Illumination is different from enlightenment? Perhaps you are enlightened when there is electricity, and you are only illuminated when there is only candlelight? I don't know what the difference is.

I am neither. I am light myself, neither enlightened nor illuminated. I have left those words far far behind. I can see them like dust, still stirring, far away on the path that I will never travel again, just footprints in the sand.

These so-called professors, philosophers, psychologists – why are they so concerned about a poor man like me, who is not at all concerned with them? I am living my life, and it is my freedom to live it as I want to live it. Why should they waste time on me? Please, it would have been better to have lived those fifty-five pages. How many hours and nights this poor professor must have wasted! He could have become illuminated meanwhile, or at least enlightened. And the Dutch one would have become enlightened meanwhile, if not illuminated. Both would have understood: who am I?

Then there is only silence
Nothing to say

> *Perhaps a song to sing*
> *Or a dance*
> *Or just to prepare a cup of tea*
> *And silently sip it....*

The flavor of the tea is far more important than all philosophy.

Remember, Ashu, that's why I say only one thing has come out of Canada that is worth mentioning: that is Canada Dry, the soda. It is really beautiful – I love it. Among all the sodas in the world, that's the best. Now you are laughing. You are allowed to look at the watch. There is no need to hide it under your sleeve, or to leave it behind in case by accident you see it. I do not bother at all what time it is. Even when I ask, I don't really mean it; it is just to console you. Otherwise I go on and on in my own way. I am not a man of time. Look how long it took me just to come back to the missing thread.

My mother's father suddenly fell ill. It was not time for him to die; he was not more than fifty, or even less, perhaps even younger than I am now. My grandmother was just fifty, at the very peak of her youth and beauty. You will be surprised to know that she was born in Khajuraho, the citadel, the ancientmost citadel of the Tantrikas. She always said to me, "When you are a little older, never forget to visit Khajuraho." I don't think any parent would give that advice to a child, but my grandmother was just rare, persuading me to visit Khajuraho.

Khajuraho consists of thousands of beautiful sculptures, all naked and copulating. There are hundreds of temples: many of them are just ruins, but a few have survived, perhaps because they were forgotten. Mahatma Gandhi wanted these few temples to be buried under the earth because the statues, the sculptures, are so tempting. Yet my grandmother was tempting me to go to Khajuraho. What a grandmother to have! She herself was so beautiful, like a statue, very Greek in every way.

When Mukta's daughter, Seema, came to see me, for a moment I could not believe it, because my grandmother had exactly the same face, the same coloring. Seema does not look European, she is darker, and her face and figure are exactly the same as my grandmother's.

Alas, I thought, my grandmother is dead, otherwise I would have liked Seema to see her. And do you know, even at the age of eighty she was still beautiful, which is utterly impossible.

When my grandmother died I rushed from Bombay to see her. Even in her death she was beautiful. I could not believe that she was dead. And suddenly all the statues of Khajuraho became alive to me. In her dead body I saw the whole philosophy of Khajuraho. The first thing I did after seeing her was to again go to Khajuraho. It was the only way to pay homage to her. Now Khajuraho was even more beautiful than before because I could see her everywhere, in each statue.

Khajuraho is incomparable. There are thousands of temples in the world, but nothing like Khajuraho. I am trying to create a living Khajuraho in this ashram. Not stone statues, but real people who are capable of love, who are really alive, so alive that they are infectious, that just to touch them is enough to feel a current in you, an electric shock!

My grandmother gave me many things; one of the most important was her insistence that I should go to Khajuraho. In those days Khajuraho was absolutely unknown. But she insisted so much that I had to go. She was stubborn. Perhaps I got that quality from her, or you may call it a *dis*-quality.

During the last twenty years of her life I was traveling all over India. Each time I passed through the village she would say to me, "Listen: never enter a train that has already started, and do not get out of the train before it has stopped. Second, never argue with anyone in the compartment while you are traveling. Thirdly, remember always that I am alive and waiting for you to come home. Why are you wandering all over the country when I am waiting here to take care of you? You need care, and nobody can give you the same care as I can."

For twenty years continuously I had to listen to this advice. Now I can say to her, "Don't be worried, at least there in the other world. First, I no longer travel by train; in fact I no longer travel at all, so there is no question of getting out of the train that has not yet stopped. Secondly, Gudia is taking care of me as beautifully as you would have liked to. Thirdly, remember that just as you waited for me while you were alive, wait for me still. Soon I will be coming, coming home."

The first time I went to Khajuraho I went just because my grandmother was nagging me to go, but since then I have been there hundreds of times. There is no other place in the world that I have been to so many times. The reason is simple: you cannot exhaust the experience. It is inexhaustible. The more you know, the more you want to know. Each detail of the Khajuraho temples is a mystery. It must have taken hundreds of years and thousands of artists to create each temple. And I have never come across anything other than Khajuraho that can be said to be perfect, not even the Taj Mahal. The Taj Mahal has its flaws, but Khajuraho has none. Moreover, Taj Mahal is just beautiful architecture; Khajuraho is the whole philosophy and psychology of the New Man.

When I saw those naked...I cannot say "nude" – forgive me. Nude is pornographic; naked is a totally different phenomenon. In the dictionary they may mean the same, but the dictionary is not everything; there is much more to existence. The statues are naked, but not nude. But those naked beauties...perhaps one day man will be able to achieve it. It is a dream, Khajuraho is a dream. And Mahatma Gandhi wanted it buried under earth so nobody could be tempted by the beautiful statues! We are grateful to Rabindranath Tagore who prevented Gandhi from doing such a thing. He said, "Leave the temples as they are...." He was a poet and he could understand their mystery.

I have gone to Khajuraho so many times that I have lost all count. Whenever I had time I would rush to Khajuraho. If I could not be found anywhere else, my family would automatically say that I must have gone to Khajuraho, look for me there. And they were always right. I had to bribe the guards of those temples to tell people that I was not there when I was. It is a confession, because that is the only time I ever bribed anyone. But it was worth it, and I don't regret it, I don't feel sorry about it.

In fact, you will be surprised, you know how dangerous I am.... The guard who I bribed became my sannyasin. Now, who bribed whom? First I bribed him to say that I was not inside; then by and by he became more and more interested in me. He returned all the bribes that I had given him. He is perhaps the only man who has returned all the bribes given to him. He could not keep them after becoming a sannyasin.

Khajuraho – the very name rings bells of joy in me, as if it had descended from heaven to earth. On a full-moon night, to see Khajuraho is to have seen all that is worth seeing. My grandmother was born there; no wonder she was a beautiful woman, courageous and dangerous too. Beauty is always so, courageous and dangerous. She dared. My mother does not resemble her, and I am sorry about that. You cannot find any proof of my grandmother in my mother. Nani was such a courageous woman, and she helped me to dare everything – I mean *everything*.

If I wanted to drink wine, she would supply it. She would say, "Unless you drink totally you cannot get rid of it." And I know that is the way to get rid of anything at all. Whatsoever I wanted she arranged. My grandfather, her husband, was always afraid – just like every other husband in the world, a mouse; a beautiful mouse, a nice fellow, loving, but nothing compared to her. When he died in my lap she did not even weep.

I asked her, "He is dead. You loved him. Why are you not weeping?"

She said, "Because of you. I don't want to weep before a child" – she was such a woman! – "and I don't want to console you. If I start weeping myself, then naturally you will weep; then who is going to console whom?"

I must describe that situation…. We were in a bullock cart going from my grandfather's village to my father's, because the only hospital was there. My grandfather was seriously sick; not only sick, but unconscious too, almost in a coma. She and I were the only other people in the cart. I can understand her compassion for me. She did not even weep at the death of her beloved husband, just because of me; because I was the only one there, and there would be nobody else to console me.

I said, "Don't worry. If you can remain without tears, I can also remain without tears." And, believe it or not, a child of seven remained without tears.

Even she was puzzled. She said, "You are not crying?"

I said, "I don't want to console you."

It was a strange group of people in that bullock cart. Bhoora, of whom I talked this morning, was driving. He knew that his master was dead, but he would not look inside the bullock cart, not even then, because he was only a servant and it was not his place to interfere in private affairs. That is what he said to me: "Death is a private affair; how can I look? I heard everything from the driving seat. I wanted to cry, I loved him so much. I feel like an orphan – but I could not look back into the cart, otherwise he would never forgive me."

A strange company...and Nana was in my lap. I was a seven-year-old child with death not just for a few seconds, but continuously for twenty-four hours. There was no road, and it was difficult to reach my father's town. The progress was very slow. We remained with the dead body for twenty-four hours. I could not weep because I did not want to disturb my grandmother. She could not weep because she did not want to disturb the little seven-year-old child that I was. She was a real woman of steel.

When we reached the town, my father called the doctor, and can you imagine: my grandmother laughed! She said, "You educated people are all stupid. He is dead! There is no need to call any doctor. Please burn him, and as quickly as possible."

Everybody was shocked by these words except me, because I knew her. She wanted the body to evaporate into the elements. It was already time...already late; you can understand. She said, "And I am not going back to that village."

When she said she was not going back to live in the village, it of course meant that I could not go back to see her there again either. But she never stayed with my father's family; she was different. When I started living in my father's village, I lived very mathematically in that town, spending the whole day with my father's family and the whole night with my grandmother. She used to live alone in a beautiful bungalow. It was a small house but really beautiful.

My mother used to ask me, "Why don't you stay home at night?"

I said, "It is impossible. I have to go to my grandmother, particularly at night when she feels so alone without my Nana, my grandfather. During the day she is okay, she is busy and there are so many people around – but at night alone in her room she may start crying if I am not there. I have to be there!" I remained there always, every night, without exception.

During the day I was at school. Only in the morning and in the afternoon I spent a few hours with my family – my mother, my father, my uncles. It was a big family, and it remained foreign to me; it never became part of me.

My grandmother was my family, and she understood me because from my very childhood she had seen me grow. She knew as much of me as anyone has ever known, because she allowed me every-thing...everything.

In India, when the Festival of Lights comes, people may gamble. It is a strange ritual: for three days gambling is legal; after that you can be caught and punished.

I told my grandmother, "I want to gamble."

She asked me, "How much money do you want?"

Even I could not believe my ears. I thought she would say, "No gambling." Instead she said, "So you want to gamble?" So then she gave me a one-hundred-rupee note and told me to go and gamble wherever I wanted, because one learns only by experience.

In this way she has helped me tremendously. Once, I wanted to go to visit a prostitute. I was only fifteen years old and had heard that a prostitute had come to the village. My grandmother asked me, "Do you know what a prostitute means?"

I said, "I don't know exactly."

Then she said, "You must go and see, but first only go to see her sing and dance."

In India prostitutes sing and dance first, but the singing and the dancing was so third rate and the woman was so ugly that I vomited! I returned home in the middle, before the dancing and singing had finished, and before the prostituting had begun. My Nani asked, "Why have you come home so early?"

I replied, "It was nauseating."

Only later when I read Jean-Paul Sartre's book, *Nausea*, did I understand what had happened to me that night. But my grand-mother even allowed me to go to a prostitute. I don't remember her ever saying no to me. I wanted to smoke; she said, "Remember one thing: smoking is okay, but always smoke in the house."

I said, "Why?"

She said, "Others may object – so you can smoke in the house. I will provide you with cigarettes." She continued to provide me with cigarettes until I said, "Enough! I don't need any more."

My Nani was ready to go to any length just to help me experience myself. The way to know is to experience for yourself; it is not to be told. That's where parents become nauseating: they are continuously telling you. A child is a rebirth of God. He should be respected, and he should be given every opportunity to grow, and to be – not according to you but according to his own potential.

If my time is over, it is good. If my time is not over, it is even better. Now it is up to you, how long you prolong it. You are not the only Jew, remember. You are only a Jew by birth, I am a Jew by spirit. It is all up to you.

Session 5

I WAS TALKING ABOUT THE DEATH of my Nana, my grandfather. Just now I remembered that he never had to go to a dentist. What a fortunate man! He died with all his teeth intact. And look at me. When you were examining my teeth I heard you say that one is missing. That may be why I am so hard: thirty-one teeth instead of thirty-two. That may be why I hit so mercilessly. Naturally, when even one tooth is missing, what else can I do but hit mercilessly this way and that, at whatsoever I can put my hands on?

That was my way during those first years when I lived with my grandfather, and yet I was absolutely protected from punishment. He never said "Do this," or "Don't do that." On the contrary he put his most obedient servant, Bhoora, at my service, to protect me. Bhoora used to carry a very primitive gun with him. He used to follow me at a distance, but that was enough to frighten the villagers. That was enough to allow me to do whatsoever I wanted.

Anything one could imagine…like riding on a buffalo backwards with Bhoora following. It was only later on, in the university museum, I saw the statue of Lao Tzu sitting backwards on a buffalo. I laughed so loudly that the museum director came running to me saying, "Is anything wrong?" Because I was holding my stomach and sitting on the floor, he said, "Are you suffering from something?"

I said, "No, and don't bother me, and don't make me laugh any more; otherwise I will start crying. Just leave me alone. Nothing is wrong with me. I am just reminded of my childhood. This is the way I used to ride on a buffalo."

In my village particularly, and all over India, nobody rides on a buffalo. The Chinese are strange people, and this person Lao Tzu was the strangest of all. But God knows, and only God knows, how I discovered the idea – even I don't know – to sit on a buffalo in the marketplace, backwards. I assume it was because I always liked anything absurd.

Those early years – if they could be given to me again, I would be ready to be born again. But you know, and I know, nothing can be repeated. That's why I am saying that I would be ready to be born again; otherwise who wants to, even though those days were full of beauty.

I was born under a wrong star. I regret that I forgot to ask the great astrologer why I was so mischievous. I cannot live without it; it is my nourishment. I can understand the old man, my grandfather, and the trouble my mischief caused him. The whole day he would sit on his *gaddi* – as the seat of a rich man is called in India – listening less to his customers, and more to the complainers. But he used to say to them, "I am ready to pay for any damage he has done, but remember, I am not going to punish him."

Perhaps his very patience with me, a mischievous child…even I could not tolerate it. If a child like that was given to me and for years…my God! Even for minutes and I would throw the child out of the door forever. Perhaps those years worked a miracle for my grandfather; that immense patience paid. He became more and more silent. I saw it growing every day. Once in a while I would say, "Nana, you can punish me. You need not be so tolerant." And, can you believe it, he would cry! Tears would come to his eyes, and he would say, "Punish you? I cannot do that. I can punish myself but not you."

Never, for a single moment, have I ever seen the shadow of anger towards me in his eyes – and believe me, I did everything that one thousand children could do. In the morning, even before break-fast I was into my mischief, until late at night. Sometimes I would come home so late – three o'clock in the morning. But what a man he was! He never said, "You are too late. This is not the time for a child to come home." No, not even once. In fact, in front of me he would avoid looking at the clock on the wall.

That is how I learned religiousness. He never took me to the temple where he used to go. I also used to go to that temple, but only when it was closed, just to steal prisms, because in that temple there were many chandeliers with beautiful prisms. I think, by and by, I stole almost all of them. When my grandfather was told about it he said, "So what! I donated the chandeliers, so I can donate others. He is not stealing; it is his Nana's property. I made that temple." The priest stopped complaining. What was the point? He was just a servant to Nana.

Nana used to go to the temple every morning, yet he never said, "Come with me." He never indoctrinated me. That is what is great...not to indoctrinate. It is so human to force a helpless child to follow your beliefs. But he remained untempted – yes, I call it the greatest temptation. The moment you see someone dependent on you in any way, you start indoctrinating. He never even said to me, "You are a Jaina."

I remember perfectly – it was the time that the census was being taken. The officer had come to our house. He made many inquiries about many things. They asked about my grandfather's religion; he said, "Jainism." They then asked about my grandmother's religion. My Nana said, "You can ask her yourself. Religion is a private affair. I myself have never asked her." What a man!

My grandmother answered, "I do not believe in any religion whatsoever. All religions look childish to me." The officer was shocked. Even I was taken aback. She does not believe in any religion at all! In India to find a woman who does not believe in any religion at all is impossible. But she was born in Khajuraho, perhaps into a family of Tantrikas, who have never believed in any religion. They have practiced meditation but they have never believed in any religion.

It sounds very illogical to a Western mind: meditation without religion? Yes...in fact, if you believe in any religion you cannot meditate. Religion is an interference in your meditation. Meditation needs no God, no heaven, no hell, no fear of punishment, and no allurement of pleasure. Meditation has nothing to do with mind; meditation is beyond it, whereas religion is only mind, it is within mind.

I know Nani never went to the temple, but she taught me one mantra which I will reveal for the first time. It is a Jaina mantra, but

it has nothing to do with Jainas as such. It is purely accidental that
it is related to Jainism....

> *Namo arihantanam namo namo*
> *Namo siddhanam namo namo*
> *Namo uvajjhayanam namo namo*
> *Namo loye savva sahunam namo namo*
> *Aeso panch nammukaro*
> *Om, shantih, shantih, shantih....*

The mantra is so beautiful. It is going to be difficult to translate it,
but I will do my best...or my worst. First listen to the mantra in its
original beauty:

> *Namo arihantanam namo namo*
> *Namo siddhanam namo namo*
> *Namo uvajjhayanam namo namo*
> *Namo loye savva sahunam namo namo*
> *Aeso panch nammukaro*
> *Savva pavappanasano*
> *Mangalam cha savvesam padhamam havai mangalam*
> *Arihante saranam pavajjhami*
> *Siddhe saranam pavajjhami*
> *Sahu saranam pavajjhami*
> *Namo arihantanam namo namo*
> *Namo siddhanam namo namo*
> *Namo uvajjhayanam namo namo*
> *Om, shantih, shantih, shantih....*

Now my effort at translation: "I go to the feet of, I bow down to, the
arihantas...." Arihanta is the name in Jainism, as *bodhisattva* is in
Buddhism, for one who has achieved the ultimate but cares nothing
about anybody else. He has come home and turned his back on the
world. He does not create a religion, he does not even preach, he
does not even declare. Of course he has to be remembered first. The
first remembrance is for all those who have known and remained
silent. The first respect is not for words, but for silence. Not for

serving others, but for the sheer achievement of one's self. It does not matter whether one serves others or not; that is secondary, not primary. The primary is that one has achieved one's self, and it is so difficult in this world to know one's self.

Just this morning I gave Gudia a car-sticker from California that says: Warning! I brake for hallucinations. This should be on every car – not only on cars, but on everybody's buttocks too. People are living in hallucinations; that's what their life is – an hallucination. They brake for ghosts which are not there – perhaps a Holy Ghost? But what does it matter whether the ghost is holy or unholy? All that matters is that it is not.

And what a stupidity! What a climax of stupidity to put a holy ghost into the Christian trinity: God, the Son, and the Holy Ghost! Just to avoid the woman they put a holy ghost in there. What un-holiness! Do you see the trick? They could not put in the mother; they have painted out the mother and written in the Holy Ghost. This Holy Ghost has destroyed the whole of Christianity, because from the very beginning, from its very foundation it depends on lies, hallucinations.

Californians can be forgiven – they are all Californiacs – but Christians cannot be forgiven for bringing this ugly fellow, the Holy Ghost, into the trinity. And this Holy Ghost did the unholy act of making poor Mary pregnant! Who do you think made the poor carpenter's wife, Mary, pregnant? Why, the Holy Ghost! Great! Great holiness! Then what is unholiness?

One thing is certain, that Christianity has been trying to com-pletely avoid the woman, to erase her completely. They even create a family. If a child paints a picture of a family – of the Father, Son and Holy Ghost – you would say, "What is this nonsense? Where is the mother?"

Without a mother how can there be a father? Without a mother how can there be a son? Even a child would understand your logic, but not a Christian theologian. He is not a child, he is a retarded child. Something is wrong with his brain. Particularly the left side of his brain is either empty or full of junk – maybe theological junk, the Bible – in short, the Holy Ghost.

I am against this fellow. Let me say it most clearly: if I meet him

...I want you to know that although I am a nonviolent man, if I meet this Holy Ghost fellow I will kill him. I will say to myself, "To hell with all nonviolence, at least for the moment, kill this fellow! Later on we will see. We can be nonviolent again later on." I would put a woman in his place. Immediately Christianity would come to its senses.

Another Californian car-sticker which I gave to Gudia to keep says: The best man for the job is probably a woman. Not probably, but certainly...a woman could do the job of being the third partner of the holy company. Without a woman it is an absolute desert: Father, Son, and Holy Ghost!

The Jainas call the person arihanta who has attained to himself and is so drowned, so drunk in the beautitude of his realization that he has forgotten the whole world. The word 'arihanta' literally means "one who has killed the enemy" – and the enemy is the ego. The first part of the mantra means, "I touch the feet of the one who has attained himself."

The second part is: *Namo siddhanam namo namo*. This mantra is in Prakrit, not Sanskrit. Prakrit is the language of the Jainas; it is more ancient than Sanskrit. The very word 'sanskrit' means refined. You can understand by the word 'refined' there must have been something before it, otherwise what are you going to refine? 'Prakrit' means unrefined, natural, raw, and the Jainas are correct when they say their language is the most ancient in the world. Their religion too is the most ancient.

The Hindu scripture *Rigveda* mentions the first master of the Jainas, Adinatha. That certainly means it is far more ancient than *Rigveda*. *Rigveda* is the oldest book in the world, and it talks about the Jaina *tirthankara*, Adinatha, with such respect that one thing is certain, that he could not have been a contemporary of the people writing *Rigveda*.

It is very difficult to recognize a contemporary master. His fate is to be condemned, condemned from all quarters, in all possible ways. He is not respected – he is not a respectable person. It takes time, thousands of years, for people to forgive him; only then do they start respecting him. When they are free of the guilt of having condemned him once, they start respecting him, worshipping him.

The mantra is in Prakrit, raw and unrefined. The second line is: *Namo siddhanam namo namo* – "I touch the feet of the one who has become his being." So, what is the difference between the first and the second?

The arihanta never looks back, never bothers about any kind of service, Christian or otherwise. The siddha, once in a while holds out his hand to drowning humanity, but only once in a while, not always. It is not a necessity, it is not compulsory, it is his choice; he may or he may not.

Hence the third: *Namo uvajjhayanam namo namo*…"I touch the feet of the masters, the *uvajjhaya*." They have achieved the same, but they face the world, they serve the world. They are in the world and not of it…but still in it.

The fourth: *Namo loye savva sahunam namo namo*…"I touch the feet of the teachers." You know the subtle difference between a master and a teacher. The master has known, and imparts what he has known. The teacher has received from one who has known, and delivers it intact to the world, but he himself has not known.

The composers of this mantra are really beautiful; they even touch the feet of those who have not known themselves, but at least are carrying the message of the masters to the masses.

Number five is one of the most significant sentences I have ever come across in my whole life. It is strange that it was given to me by my grandmother when I was a small child. When I explain it to you, you too will see the beauty of it. Only she was capable of giving it to me. I don't know anybody else who had the guts to really proclaim it, although all Jainas repeat it in their temples. But to repeat is one thing; to impart it to one you love is totally another.

"I touch the feet of all those who have known themselves"… without any distinction, whether they are Hindus, Jainas, Buddhists, Christians, Mohammedans. The mantra says, "I touch the feet of all those who have known themselves." This is the only mantra, as far as I know, which is absolutely nonsectarian.

The other four parts are not different from the fifth, they are all contained in it, but it has a vastness which those others do not have. The fifth line must be written on all the temples, all the churches, irrespective of to whom they belong, because it says, "I

45

touch the feet of all those who have known it." It does not say "who have known God." Even the "it" can be dropped: I am only putting "it" in the translation. The original simply means "touching the feet of those who have known" – no "it." I am putting "it" in just to fulfill the demands of your language; otherwise someone is bound to ask, "Known? Known what? What is the object of knowledge?" There is no object of knowledge; there is nothing to know, only the knower.

This mantra was the only religious thing, if you can call it religious, given to me by my grandmother, and that too, not by my grandfather but by my grandmother...because one night I asked her. One night she said, "You look awake. Can't you sleep? Are you planning tomorrow's mischief?"

I said, "No, but somehow a question is arising in me. Everybody has a religion, and when people ask me, 'To what religion do you belong?' I shrug my shoulders. Now, certainly shrugging your shoulders is not a religion, so I want to ask you, what should I say?"

She said, "I myself don't belong to any religion, but I love this mantra, and this is all I can give you – not because it is traditionally Jaina, but only because I have known its beauty. I have repeated it millions of times and always I have found tremendous peace...just the feeling of touching the feet of all those who have known. I can give you this mantra; more than that is not possible for me."

Now I can say that woman was really great, because as far as religion is concerned, everybody is lying: Christians, Jews, Jainas, Mohammedans – everybody is lying. They all talk of God, heaven and hell, angels and all kinds of nonsense, without knowing anything at all. She was great, not because she knew but because she was unable to lie to a child. Nobody should lie – to a child at least it is unforgivable.

Children have been exploited for centuries just because they are willing to trust. You can lie to them very easily and they will trust you. If you are a father, a mother, they will think you are bound to be true. That's how the whole of humanity lives in corruption, in a thick mud, very slippery, a thick mud of lies told to children for centuries.

If we can do just one thing, a simple thing: not lie to children, and to confess to them our ignorance, then we will be religious, and we will put them on the path of religion. Children are only innocence; leave them not your so-called knowledge. But you yourself must first be innocent, unlying, true, even if it shatters your ego – and it will shatter. It is bound to shatter.

My grandfather never told me to go to the temple, to follow him. I used to follow him many times, but he would say, "Go away. If you want to go to the temple, go alone. Don't follow me."

He was not a hard man, but on this point he was absolutely hard. I asked him again and again, "Can you give me something of your experience?" And he would always avoid it.

When he was dying in my lap, in the bullock cart, he opened his eyes and asked, "What is the time?"

I said, "It must be nearly nine o'clock."

For a moment he remained silent, and then he said,

> "Namo arihantanam namo namo
> Namo siddhanam namo namo
> Namo uvajjhayanam namo namo
> Namo loye savva sahunam namo namo
> Om, shantih, shantih, shantih...."

What does it mean? It means "Om" – the ultimate sound of soundlessness. And he disappeared like a dewdrop in the first rays of the sun.

There is only peace, peace, peace.... I am entering into it now....

> Namo arihantanam namo namo....
> I go to the feet of those who have known.
> I go to the feet of those who have achieved.
> I go to the feet of all who are masters.
> I go to the feet of all the teachers.
> I go to the feet of all who have ever known,
> Unconditionally.
> Om, shantih, shantih, shantih.

Session 6

KAY. MY OKAY IS A little sad because Ashu is sad, and the
membership of this Noah's Ark is so small that just one
person being sad is enough to change the whole atmosphere. She is sad because her lover is gone and may not be back.

Do you remember a few days ago I asked her, "Where is your
love, Ashu?" And how joyously she said, "Soon he will be here."

She may not have thought at the time why I had asked. I don't
ask anybody anything without a purpose. It may not be apparent to
you at the time, but it is always there. In all my absurdities there is a
reason. In all my insanity there is an undercurrent of utter sanity.

I had asked her because I knew she would soon be sad. Cheer up,
don't be worried. I know your lover better than you know him.

He will manage. I will manage. But in this little Noah's Ark,
don't be sad. Ah! You are laughing; that is good. And it is always
good to have a little separation from the lover; it makes you and
your longing deeper. It makes you forget the stupidities that were
happening, the conflicts. Suddenly only the beauty is remembered.
Little separations bring new honeymoons. So wait for the honeymoon. My disciples will always find a way to me, to be by my side.
They want the way. He will find a way to me.

But unfortunately the word 'sad' reminds me again of that German, Achim Seidl. My God, I was not going to speak about him
ever again in my life, and he is there, just because of your sadness....
Look what you have done! So never be sad, otherwise these people
can enter.

I was trying to find out from his book what it is he finds wrong in
me that makes him say I am not enlightened. Not that I am – just

why he feels that I am not enlightened, and why he feels that I am just illuminated. Out of curiosity I wanted to see why he had concluded in this way. What I found out is really worth laughing at. His reason that I am illuminated is: certainly what I am saying is of immense importance for the whole of humanity, but I am not enlightened because of the "way I say it."

That really made me laugh. I rarely laugh, and then only in my bathroom. Only the mirror knows it. The beauty of the mirror is that it carries no memories. I laughed because it seemed that this man had met and known many enlightened people, and does not find my way of saying things the same as theirs. I would like to use an American word for him: the sonofabitch is simply intellectually constipated. He needs to start a movement; I mean he needs to eat prunes!

I say it on authority – on my own authority, of course – that Bodhidharma, if he had known the expression, would have said to Emperor Wu of China, "You sonofabitch! Go to hell and leave me alone!" but in those days this American expression did not exist. Not that America did not exist – that again is a European myth. America was discovered by Columbus? Nonsense! It has been discovered many times but was always hushed up.

May I remind you that Mexico comes from a Sanskrit word *makshika*, and in Mexico there are thousands of proofs that Hinduism existed there long before Jesus Christ – what to say of Columbus! In fact America, particularly South America, was part of one vast continent in which Africa was also included. India was exactly in the middle, Africa below, America above. They were only divided by a very shallow ocean; you could walk across it! There are references to it in ancient Indian scriptures; they say that people used to pass from Asia to America on foot. Even marriages used to happen. Arjuna, the famous warrior of the Indian epic *Mahabharata* and Krishna's famous disciple, was married to a Mexican girl. Of course they called Mexico, Makshika, but the description is exactly that of Mexico.

In Mexico there are statues of Ganesh, the Hindu elephant god. A statue of the elephant god would be impossible to find in England! It would be impossible to find anywhere unless that country had come into contact with Hinduism. In Bali, yes, or in Sumatra and Mexico – but not anywhere else unless Hinduism had been there. In some Mexican temples there are even inscriptions in ancient Sanskrit. I am saying this by the way…if you want to know more you will have to look into the life work of the monk Bhikkhu Chamanlal, in his book *Hindu America*. It is strange that nobody pays attention to his work. Christians of course cannot pay him attention, but scholarship should be unprejudiced.

This German man, and his colleague the Dutch psychologist who wrote that I am enlightened but not illuminated, and that I am illuminated but not enlightened, should both meet to discuss matters and come to a conclusion, then let me know – because I am neither. They are so much concerned with words: 'illumination' or 'enlightenment'? Also, the same reasons are used by each of these men to reach totally opposite conclusions. The Dutchman wrote his book some time before the German, who it seems stole the theme from the Dutchman. But this is how professors behave – they go on stealing the same arguments from each other, exactly the same argument…that I don't speak like an enlightened man or like an illuminated man.

But who are they to decide how an enlightened or illuminated person should speak? Have they known Bodhidharma? Have they seen his picture? They will immediately conclude that an enlightened or illuminated person cannot look like that. He looks ferocious! His eyes are those of a lion in the forest, and the way he looks at you is such that it seems he will jump from the picture and kill you instantly. That's how he was! But forget Bodhidharma, because now fourteen centuries have passed….

I knew Bodhidharma personally. I traveled with the man for at least three months. He loved me just as I loved him. You will be curious to know why he loved me. He loved me because I never asked him any question. He said to me, "You are the first person I have met who does not ask a question – and I only get bored with all the questions. You are the only person who does not bore me."

I said, "There is a reason."

He said, "What is that?"

I said, "I only answer. I never question. If you have any question you can ask me. If you don't have a question then keep your mouth shut."

We both laughed, because we both belonged to the same category of insanity. He asked me to continue the journey with him, but I said, "Excuse me, I have to go my own way, and from this point it separates from yours."

He could not believe it. He had never invited anyone before. This was the man who had even refused Emperor Wu – the greatest emperor of those days, with the greatest empire – as if he was a beggar. Bodhidharma could not believe his eyes, that I could refuse him.

I said, "Now you know how it feels to be refused. I wanted to give you a taste of it. Goodbye." But that was fourteen centuries ago.

I could remind the German of a few later editions...of Gurdjieff, who was alive just a few years ago. He should have seen Gurdjieff and then he would have known how an enlightened or illuminated person behaves and speaks. There was not a single word that Gurdjieff would not say – and of course those words are not written in his books, because nobody would have published them.

Or, if he is only concerned with Indian enlightenment, which seems to dominate these idiots...otherwise what has India got to do with it? Enlightenment has happened everywhere. If he is concerned only with Indian enlightenment, then Ramakrishna is very close to us. His words were not reported correctly, because he was a villager and used the language of a villager. All those words which people think should not be used by any enlightened person have been edited out. I have wandered in Bengal, asking people who are still living how Ramakrishna used to speak. They all said he was terrible. He used to speak as a man should speak – strong, without fear, without any sophistication.

I have always spoken the way I like. I am nobody's slave, and I don't care what these idiots think about me. It is up to them: they can think that I am enlightened; they can think that I am illuminated; they can think I am ignorant. They can think whatever they want – it is their mind. They can write; the paper is there, the ink is there. Why should I be concerned?

Just by the way, Ashu, because you were sad, you brought this idiot in. Never be sad again – because if you are I will bring this idiot in, and you know I can bring anything from anywhere, even from nowhere.

Now we are finished with this German and sadness, right? At least giggle…good! Yes, I can understand. Even if you laugh in sadness it has a different color to it, but it is natural. My sannyasins have to learn to be a little above nature. They have to learn things which, in the ordinary world, nobody cares about. Separation has its own beauty, as does meeting. I don't see that there is anything wrong with separation. Separation has its own poetry; one just has to learn its language, and one has to live it in its depth. Then out of sadness itself comes a new kind of joy…which looks almost impossible, but it happens. I have known it. That's what I was talking about this morning. I was talking about the death of my Nana.

It was a total separation. We will not meet again, yet there was a beauty in it, and he made it more beautiful by repeating the mantra. He made it more prayerful…it became fragrant. He was old and dying, perhaps from a severe heart attack. We were not aware of it because the village had no doctor, not even a pharmacist, no medicine. So we didn't know the cause of his death, but I think it was a severe heart attack.

I asked him in his ear, "Nana, have you something to say to me before you depart? Any last words? Or do you want to give me something to remember you by forever?"

He took off his ring and put it in my hand. That ring is with some sannyasin now; I gave it to someone. But that ring was always a mystery. His whole life he would not allow anybody to see what was in it, yet again and again he used to look into it. That ring had a glass window on both sides that you could look through. On top was a diamond; on each of its sides there was a glass window.

He had not allowed anybody to see what it was that he used to look at through the window. Inside there was a statue of Mahavira, the Jaina tirthankara; a really beautiful image, and very small. It must have been a small picture of Mahavira inside, and those two windows were magnifying glasses. They magnified it and it looked really huge. It was of no use to me because, I am sorry to say, even though I have tried my best I have never been able to love Mahavira as much as I love Buddha, although they were contemporaries.

Something is missing in Mahavira, and without it my heart cannot beat for him. He looks exactly like a stone statue. Buddha looks more alive, but not up to my standards of aliveness – that's why I want him to become a Zorba too. If he meets me somewhere in the other world there is going to be great trouble. He is going to shout at me, "You wanted me to become a Zorba!"

But you know I know how to shout far better. He cannot shut me up; I am going to have my own way. If he does not want to become a Zorba, that is his own business, but then his world is finished; he has no future. If he wants a future then he has to listen to me. He has to become a Zorba. Neither can Zorba exist alone – he will end in Hiroshima – nor can Buddha exist alone. In the future there is no possibility of their being separate.

The future psychology of man needs to be a bridge between materialism and spiritualism; between East and West. Someday the world will feel grateful that my message is reaching to the West; otherwise seekers have been going to the East. This time a living buddha's message has come to the West.

The West does not know how to recognize a buddha. It has never known a buddha. It has known only partial buddhas – a Jesus, a Pythagoras, a Diogenes – it has never known a total buddha. It is not surprising that they are arguing about me.

Do you know what they are publishing in the Indian news-papers? They are publishing a story that I may be abducted by some enemies, and that my life is in danger. I am here now and they are not really concerned about me. India is a rotten country. It has been rotten for almost two thousand years – it stinks! Nothing stinks more than Indian spirituality. It is a corpse, and a very old corpse, two thousand years old!

What stories people invent! I may be "abducted by some enemies, and now my life is in danger." In fact for twenty-five years my life has been in continuous danger. It is a miracle that I have survived. And now they want to protect me! There are strange people all over the world; but the future of man does not belong to these strange people, but to a very new kind, and that new kind I have named Zorba the Buddha.

I was telling you that my grandfather, before he died, gave me his most cherished thing – a statue of Mahavira hidden behind a diamond in a ring. With tears in his eyes he said, "I don't have anything else to give you because all that I have will be taken away from you too, just as it has been taken away from me. I can only give you my love for the one who has known himself."

Although I did not keep his ring, I have fulfilled his desire. I have known the one, and I have known it in myself. In a ring what does it matter? But the poor old man, he loved his master, Mahavira, and he gave his love to me. I respect his love for his master, and for me. The last words on his lips were, "Don't be worried, because I am not dying."

We all waited to see if he was going to say something else, but that was all. His eyes closed and he was no more.

I still remember that silence. The bullock cart was passing through a river bed. I exactly remember each detail. I didn't say anything because I didn't want to disturb my grandmother. She did not say a thing. A few moments passed, then I became a little worried about her and said, "Say something; don't be so quiet, it is unbearable."

Can you believe it, she sang a song! That's how I learned that death has to be celebrated. She sang the same song she had sung when she was in love with my grandfather for the first time. This too is worth noting: that ninety years ago, in India, she had had the courage to fall in love. She remained unmarried up till the age of twenty-four. That was very rare. I asked her once why she had remained unmarried for so long. She was such a beautiful woman... I just jokingly told her that even the king of Chhatarpur, the state where Khajuraho is, might have fallen in love with her.

She said, "It is strange that you should mention it, because he did. I refused him, and not only him but many others too." In those days in India, girls were married when they were seven, or at the most nine years of age. Just the fear of love...if they are older they may fall in love. But my grandmother's father was a poet; his songs are still sung in Khajuraho and nearby villages. He insisted that unless she agreed, he was not going to marry her to anybody. As chance would have it, she fell in love with my grandfather.

I asked her, "That is even stranger: you refused the king of Chhatarpur, and yet you fell in love with this poor man. For what? He was certainly not a very handsome man, nor extraordinary in any other way; why did you fall in love with him?"

She said, "You are asking the wrong question. Falling has no 'why' to it. I just saw him, and that was it. I saw his eyes, and a trust arose in me that has never wavered."

I had also asked my grandfather, "Nani says she fell in love with you. That's okay on her part, but why did you allow the marriage to happen?"

He said, "I am not a poet or a thinker, but I can recognize beauty when I see it."

I never saw a more beautiful woman than my Nani. I myself was in love with her, and loved her throughout her whole life. When she died at the age of eighty, I rushed home and found her lying there, dead. They were all just waiting for me because she had told them that they should not put her body on the funeral pyre until I arrived. She had insisted that I set light to her funeral pyre, so they were waiting for me. I went in, uncovered her face…and she was still beautiful! In fact, more beautiful than ever, because all was quiet; even the turmoil of her breathing, the turmoil of living was not there. She was just a presence.

To put the fire to her body was the most difficult task I have ever done in my life. It was as if I was putting fire to one of the most beautiful paintings of Leonardo or Vincent van Gogh. Of course to me she was more valuable than the Mona Lisa, more beautiful to me than Cleopatra. It is not an exaggeration.

All that is beautiful in my vision somehow comes through her. She helped me in every way to be the way I am. Without her I may have been a shopkeeper or perhaps a doctor or an engineer, because when I passed my matriculation my father was so poor, it was difficult for him to send me to the university. But he was even ready to borrow money in order to do it. He was utterly insistent that I go to the university. I was willing, but not to go to medical college, and I was not willing to go to engineering college either. I flatly refused to be a doctor or an engineer. I told him, "If you want to know the truth, I want to be a sannyasin, a hobo."

He said, "What! A hobo?"

I said, "Yes. I want to go to the university to study philosophy so that I can be a philosophical hobo."

He refused, saying, "In that case I am not going to borrow money and take all that trouble."

My grandmother said, "Don't you worry, son; you go and do whatsoever you want to do. I am alive, and I will sell everything I have just to help you to be yourself. I will not ask where you want to go and what you want to study."

She never asked, and she sent me money continuously, even when I became a professor. I had to tell her that I was now earning for myself, and I should rather send her money.

She said, "Don't worry, I have no use for this money, and you must be using it well."

People used to wonder where I got all the money from to purchase my books, because I had thousands of books. Even when I was just a student in high school I had thousands of books in my house. My whole house was full of books, and everybody wondered where I got all the money from. My grandmother had told me, "Never tell anyone that you get money from me, because if your father and mother come to know they will start asking me for money, and it will be difficult for me to refuse."

She went on giving money to me. You will be surprised to know that even the month she died she had sent the usual money to me. On the morning of the day she died she had signed the check. You will also be amazed to know, that was the last money she had in the bank. Perhaps somehow she knew that there was not going to be any tomorrow.

I am fortunate in many ways, but I was most fortunate in having my maternal grandparents...and those early golden years.

Session 7

DEVAGEET, WHEN YOU SOMETIMES SAY "Okay" to Ashu, I misunderstand: I think it is okay to me. That's why she laughs. But still I say deep within me there is nothing but laughter. You can anesthetize my body, everything, but not me. That is beyond you.

That is the case with you too. Your innermost core is beyond all chemicals and chemistry. Now I can hear Devageet giggling. It is good to hear a man giggle. Men almost never giggle. Giggling has become the sole domain of women. Men either laugh or not, but they don't giggle. Giggling is just in the middle. It is the Golden Mean. It is Tao. Laughter can be violent; not to laugh is stupid. But giggling is good.

See how I can say something significant even about giggling: "Giggling is good." Don't worry even if I say something correct, it is just an old habit. I can even talk in my sleep, so it is no trouble to talk like this.

Gudia knows I talk in my sleep but she does not know to whom. Only I know that. Poor Gudia! I am talking to her and she thinks and worries about why I am talking, and to whom. Alas that she is not aware that I am talking to her just like this. Sleep is a natural anesthetic. Life is so hard that one has to go under every night for a few hours at least. And she wonders whether I really sleep or not. I can understand her wondering.

For more than a quarter of a century I have not slept. Devaraj, don't be worried. Ordinary sleep.... I sleep more than anybody else in the whole world: three hours during the day, and seven, eight, nine hours at night – as much as anybody can afford. In all, in toto,

I sleep twelve hours per day, but underneath I am awake. I see myself while asleep, and sometimes it is so lonely during the night that I start talking to Gudia. But her difficulties are many. First, when I talk in my sleep I talk in Hindi. I cannot talk in English while asleep. I never will, although I could if I wanted to. Sometimes I have tried and succeeded, but the joy was missing.

You must be aware that every day I listen to a song of Noorjahan, the famous Urdu singer. Every day before I come in I listen to her again and again. It could even drive you crazy. What do you know of drilling? I know what drilling means. I drill that song into Gudia every day. She has to hear it, there is no way to avoid it. After my work is over I again play the same song. I love my own language...not that it is my language, but it is so beautiful that even if it were not mine I would have learned it.

The song that she hears every day, and will have to hear again and again, says: "Whether you remember or not, once there was a trust between us. Once you used to tell me, 'You are the most beautiful woman in the world.' Now I don't know whether you would recognize me or not. Perhaps you do not remember, but I still remember. I cannot forget the trust, and the words that you uttered to me. You used to say that your love was impeccable. Do you still remember? Perhaps not, but I remember – not in its totality, of course. Time has done much harm.

"I am a dilapidated palace, but if you look, look minutely: I am still the same. I still remember the trust and your words. That trust that once existed between us, is it still in your memory or not? I don't know about you but I still remember."

Why do I go on playing the song of Noorjahan? It is a kind of drilling. Not drilling of your teeth, although if you continue drilling long enough it will get to your teeth too, but drilling into her the beauty of a language. I know it will be difficult for her to understand or appreciate it.

In my sleep when I speak to Gudia, I again speak in Hindi because I know her unconscious is still not English. She was only in England for a few years. Before that she was in India, and now she is again in India. I have been trying to efface all that lies between these two. Of this later, when the time comes....

Today I was going to say something about Jainism. Look at the madness of this man! Yes, I can jump from one peak to another without any bridge between. But you have to tolerate a madman. You have fallen in love: it is your responsibility, I am not responsible for it.

Jainism is the most ascetic religion in the world, or in other words the most masochistic and sadistic. Jaina monks torture themselves so much that one wonders if they are insane. They are not. They are businessmen, and the followers of the Jaina monks are all businessmen. It is strange, the whole Jaina community consists only of businessmen – but not really strange because the religion itself is basically motivated for profit in the other world. The Jaina tortures himself in order to gain something in the other world which he knows he cannot attain in this.

I must have been about four or five years old when I saw the first naked Jaina monk being invited into my grandmother's house. I could not resist laughing. My grandfather told me, "Keep quiet! I know you are a nuisance. I can forgive you when you are a pain in the neck to the neighbors, but I cannot forgive you if you try to be mischievous with my guru. He is my master; he initiated me into the inner secrets of religion."

I said, "I am not concerned about the inner secrets, I am concerned about the outer secrets that he is showing so clearly. Why is he naked? Can't he at least wear short pants?"

Even my grandfather laughed. He said, "You don't understand."

I said, "Okay, I will ask him myself." I then asked my grandmother, "Can I ask a few questions to this utterly insane man who comes naked in front of ladies and gentlemen?"

My grandmother laughed and said, "Go ahead, and don't take any notice of what your grandfather says. I allow you. If he says anything just indicate towards me and I will put him right."

She was really a beautiful woman, courageous, ready to give freedom without any limits. She did not even ask me what I was going to ask. She simply said, "Go ahead...."

All the villagers had assembled for the *darshan* of the Jaina monk. In the middle of the so-called sermon I stood up. That was forty or so years ago, and since then I have been fighting these idiots continuously. That day a war began which is only going to end when I am no more. Perhaps it may not end even then; my people may continue it.

I asked simple questions that he could not answer. I was puzzled. My grandfather was ashamed. My grandmother patted me on the back and said, "Great! You did it! I knew you were able to."

What had I asked? – just simple questions. I had asked, "Why don't you want to be born again?" That's a very simple question in Jainism, because Jainism is nothing but an effort not to be born again. It is the whole science of preventing rebirth. So I asked him the basic question, "Don't you ever want to be born again?"

He said, "No, never."

Then I asked, "Why don't you commit suicide? Why are you still breathing? Why eat? Why drink water? Just disappear, commit suicide. Why make so much fuss over a simple thing?" He was not more than forty years of age…. I said to him, "If you continue in this way, you may have to continue for another forty years or even more."

It is a scientific fact that people who eat less live longer. Devaraj will certainly agree with me. It has been proven again and again that if you feed any species more than they need, they become fat, and comfortable of course, beautiful of course, but they soon die. If you feed them only half of what they need, it is strange: they don't look beautiful, they are not comfortable, but they live to almost double the average age. Half the food and double the age – double the food and half the age.

So I said to the monk – I did not know these facts then – "If you don't want to be born again, why are you living? Just to die? Then why not commit suicide?" I don't think anybody had ever asked him such a question. In polite society nobody ever asks a real question, and the question of suicide is the most real of all.

Marcel says: Suicide is the only real philosophical question. I had no idea of Marcel then. Perhaps at that time there was no Marcel, and his book had not been written yet. But this is what I said to the Jaina monk: "If you don't want to be born again, which you say is your desire, then why do you live? For what? Commit suicide! I can show you a way. Although I don't know much about the ways of the world, as far as suicide is concerned I can give you some advice. You can jump off the hill at the side of the village, or you can jump into the river."

The river was three miles away from the village, and so deep and so vast that to swim across it was such a joy for me. Many times while swimming across the river I would think it was the end and I would not be able to reach the other shore. It was so wide, particularly in the rainy season, miles wide. It looked almost like an ocean. In the rainy season one could not even see the other shore. When it was in full flood, that was when I would jump in, either to die or to reach the other shore. The greater probability was that I would never reach the other shore.

I told the Jaina monk, "In the rainy season you can jump into the river with me. We can keep company for a little while, then you can die, and I will reach the other shore. I can swim well enough."

He looked at me so fiercely, so full of anger, that I had to tell him, "Remember, you will have to be born again because you are still full of anger. This is not the way to get rid of the world of worries. Why are you looking at me so angrily? Answer my question in a peaceful and silent way. Answer joyously! If you cannot answer, simply say, 'I don't know.' But don't be angry."

The man said, "Suicide is a sin. I cannot commit suicide. But I want never to be born again. I will achieve that state by slowly renouncing everything that I possess."

I said, "Please show me something that you possess because, as far as I can see you are naked and you don't possess anything. What possessions do you have?"

My grandfather tried to stop me. I pointed towards my grandmother and then said to him, "Remember, I asked permission of Nani, and now nobody can prevent me, not even you. I spoke to her about you because I was worried that if I interrupted your guru and his rubbishy, so-called sermon, you would be angry with me. She said to 'Just point towards me, that's all. Don't be worried: just a look from me and he will become silent.'" And strange...it was true! He became silent, even without a look from my Nani.

Later on my Nani and I both laughed. I said to her, "He did not even look at you."

She said, "He could not, because he must have been afraid that I would say 'Shut up! Don't interfere with the child.' So he avoided me. The only way to avoid me was to not interfere with you."

In fact he closed his eyes as if he was meditating. I said to him, "Nana, great! You are angry, boiling, there is fire within you, yet you sit with closed eyes as if you are meditating. Your guru is angry because my questions are annoying him. You are angry because your guru is not capable of answering. But I say, this man who is sermonizing here is just an imbecile." And I was not more than four or five years old.

From that time on that has remained my language. I immediately recognize the idiot wherever he is, whoever he is. Nobody can escape my X-ray eyes. I can immediately see any retardedness, or anything else whatsoever.

The other day I had given one of my sannyasins the fountain pen that I wrote his new name with, just for him to remember that this was the pen I had used at the beginning of his new life, his sannyas. But his wife was there. I had even invited his wife to become a sannyasin. She was willing, and not willing – you know the way women are: this way and that way; you never know exactly. Even when they show their right hand out of a car, you never know if they will really turn right. They may be feeling the wind, or nobody knows – they can be doing anything. That woman was willy-nilly, wishy-washy...a perfect woman in a way. She wanted to say yes and yet could not say it. She wanted to say no and yet could not say it – that kind of woman. And remember that is ninety-nine point nine percent of all women on the earth; only point one percent is left out. Otherwise that woman is very representative.

Still I tried to seduce her – into sannyas, I mean! I played my game a little bit, and she was coming very close to saying yes when I stopped. I am also not so simple as it may seem from the outside. I don't mean that I am complex, I mean that I can see things so clearly that sometimes I have to withdraw my simplicity and its invitation.

When she was just about to say yes, she clutched her husband's hand, who was now a sannyasin. I looked at him and could see that he wanted to get rid of this woman. She had tortured him enough.

In fact he was hoping that by becoming a sannyasin this woman would have mercy, and leave him of her own accord. I could see his puzzlement when I was trying to persuade his wife to become a sannyasin. In his heart he was saying, "My God. If she becomes a sannyasin then even in Rajneeshpuram I can't be at ease."

He wants to become part of this commune. He is a rich man and owns a multimillion-dollar business and wants to donate all of it to the commune. He was afraid.... I could see through and through this sannyasin and his wife.

There was no bridge between them, and there never had been. They were just an English couple, you know.... God knows why they married – and God does not exist. I repeat it again and again because I always feel you may think that God really knows! God does not know because he exists not.

God is a word like 'jesus'. It does not mean anything, it is just an exclamation. That's how the story goes, telling how Jesus got his name....

Joseph and Mary are taking their child back home from Bethlehem. Mary is sitting on the donkey with the child. Joseph is walking ahead holding the rope, leading the donkey. Suddenly he stumbles, hitting his toe on a rock. "Jesus!" he shouts. And you know the ways of women....

Mary says, "Joseph! I was thinking what name to give to our new child, and just now you uttered the right name – Jesus!"

That's how the poor child got his name. It is not a coincidence that when you hit your hand with a hammer by mistake, you exclaim, "Jesus!" Don't think you are remembering Jesus; just remember poor Joseph hitting his toe on the rock.

When I have stopped breathing Devaraj will know what to do. Although he is a partial Jew...but still he is a man you can trust. I know he does not believe he is partly a Jew. He thinks a part of his family may have been Jewish, but he is not! That's the way of all Jews, even part Jews. He seems to be perfect. A Jew is always a perfect Jew, to tell you the truth. Just a single drop of Jewishness in you is enough to make you a perfect Jew.

But I love Jews and I trust Jews. Just look in this Noah's Ark: there are two and a half Jews. I am a perfect Jew without any hesitation.

Devageet is not a perfect Jew, just a Jew. Devaraj is partially a Jew and making every effort to hide it – but that only makes it more Jewish. You cannot hide your Jewishness. Where will you hide your nose? That's the only thing that remains unhidden in the whole body. You can hide everything except your nose, because you have to breathe.

I was saying that Jesus, even Jesus, is not a name but only an exclamation made when Joseph hit his toe on a rock. So is God. When one says, "My God!" he does not mean that he believes in God. He is simply saying that he is complaining, if there is anyone in the sky to listen. When he says "God!" he simply means what is written on many government documents – "To Whom It May Concern." "My God!" simply means "To whom it may concern," or if there is nobody, then "Sorry, it concerns nobody. It is just an exclamation and I couldn't resist it."

What is the time?...because I am half an hour late and I don't want you to be late too. Once in a while I too can be nice. Just to remind you.... This is the best you have been up to now. Very good. Even when it is very good I know how to say "Enough"....

This is tremendously beautiful....

So beautiful.

Stop.

Session 8

I HAVE BEEN TALKING ABOUT AN incident that is absolutely important in order to understand my life and its workings...and it is
still alive for me.

By the way, I was saying I can still remember, but the word 'remember' is not right. I can still see the whole incident happening. Of
course I was just a young child, but that does not mean that what I
said is not to be taken seriously. In fact it is the only serious thing
that I have ever talked about: suicide.

To a Westerner it may seem a little rude to ask a monk – who is
almost like a pope to the Jainas – such a question: "Why don't you
commit suicide?" But be kind to me. Let me explain before you
conclude, or stop listening to me.

Jainism is the only religion in the world which respects suicide.
Now it is your turn to be surprised. Of course they do not call it
suicide; they give it a beautiful metaphysical name, *santhara*. I am
against it, particularly the way it is done. It is very violent and cruel.
It is strange that a religion which believes in nonviolence should
preach santhara, suicide. You can call it metaphysical suicide, but
after all, suicide is suicide; the name does not matter. What matters
is that the man is no longer alive.

Why am I against it? I am not against the right of man to commit suicide. No, it should be one of the basic human rights. If I
don't want to live, who has the right to force me to live? If I myself
want to disappear, then all that others can do is to make it as
comfortable as possible. Note it: one day I would like to disappear.
I cannot live forever.

Just the other day someone showed me a car-sticker. It says, "I am proud that I am an American." I looked at it, and afterwards I cried over it. I am not an American, and I am proud that I am not an American. Nor am I an Indian. Then who am I? I am proud that I am nobody. That is where my whole journey has brought me – to nobodiness, to homelessness, to nothingness. I have even renounced enlightenment, which nobody has done before me. I also renounce illumination, for the illumination of that German idiot! I have no religion, no country, no home. The whole world is mine.

I am the first citizen of the universe. You know I am crazy. I could start issuing passports for universal citizenship. I have been thinking about it. I am thinking about an orange card, which can be issued by me to my sannyasins as a passport for universal brother-hood, as opposed to nations, races and religions.

I am not against the Jaina attitude to suicide, but the method... their method is not to eat anything. It takes almost ninety days for the poor man to die. It is torture. You cannot improve on it. Not even Adolf Hitler could have conceived of such a great idea. For Devageet's knowledge, Adolf Hitler conceived of the idea of drilling into people's teeth – without anesthesia of course. There are still many Jews around the world whose teeth were drilled for no reason other than to just create anguish. But Adolf Hitler may not have heard of Jaina monks and their masochistic practices. They are superb! They never cut their hair, they pull it out with their hands. Look what a great idea!

Every year the Jaina monk pulls out his hair, beard and mustache, and all hair on the body, just with his bare hands! They are against any technology – and they call it logic, going to the very logical end of a thing. If you use a razor, that is technology; did you know that? Have you ever considered a razor a technological thing? Even so-called ecologists go on shaving their beards without knowing that they are committing a crime against nature.

Jaina monks pull out their hair – and not privately, because they do not have any privacy. Part of their masochism is not to have any privacy, to be utterly public. They pull their hair out while standing naked in the marketplace. The crowds, of course, cheer and applaud. And Jainas, although they feel great sympathy – you can even see tears in their eyes – unconsciously they also enjoy it, and without needing a ticket. I abhor it. I am averse to all such practices.

The idea of committing santhara, suicide, by not eating or drinking, is nothing but a very long process of self-torture. I cannot support it. But I am absolutely in support of the idea of the freedom to die. I consider it a birthright, and sooner or later every constitution in the world will contain it, will have to have it as the most basic birthright – the right to die. It is not a crime.

But to torture anybody, including yourself, is a crime. With this you will be able to understand that I was not being rude, I was asking a very relevant question. On that day I began a lifelong struggle against all kinds of stupidities, nonsense, superstitions – in short, religious bullshit. Bullshit is such a beautiful word. It says so much, in short.

That day I began my life as a rebel, and I will continue to be a rebel to my very last breath – or even after it, who knows. Even if I won't have a body, I will have thousands of my lovers' bodies. I can provoke them – and you know I am a seducer, I can put ideas in their heads for centuries to come. That is exactly what I am going to do. With the death of this body my rebellion cannot die. My revolution is going to continue even more intensely, because then it will have many more bodies, many more voices, many more hands to continue it.

That day was significant, historically significant. I have always remembered that day along with the day when Jesus argued with the rabbis in the temple. He was a little older than I was, perhaps eight or nine years older. The way he argued determined the whole course of his life.

I don't remember the name of the Jaina monk; perhaps his name was Shanti Sagar, meaning "ocean of bliss." He certainly was not that. That is why I have forgotten even his name. He was just a dirty puddle, not an ocean of bliss or peace or silence. And he was certainly not a man of silence, because he became very angry.

Shanti can mean many things. It may mean peace, it may mean silence; those are the two basic meanings. Both were missing in him. He was neither peaceful nor silent, not at all. Nor could you say that he was without any turmoil in him because he became so angry that he shouted at me to sit down.

I said, "Nobody can tell me to sit down in my own house. I can tell you to get out, but you cannot tell me to sit down. But I will not tell you to get out because I have a few more questions. Please don't be angry. Remember your name, Shanti Sagar – ocean of peace and silence. You could at least be a little pool. And don't be disturbed by a little child."

Without bothering whether he was silent or not, I asked my grandmother, who was by now all laughter, "What do you say, Nani? Should I ask him more questions, or tell him to get out of our house?"

I did not ask my grandfather of course, because this man was his guru. My Nani said, "You can ask whatsoever you want to, and if he cannot answer, the door is open, he can get out."

That was the woman I loved. That was the woman who made me a rebel. Even my grandfather was shocked that she supported me in such a way. That so-called Shanti Sagar immediately became silent the moment he saw that my grandmother supported me. Not only her, the villagers were immediately on my side. The poor Jaina monk was left absolutely alone.

I asked him a few more questions. I asked, "You have said, 'Don't believe anything unless you have experienced it yourself.' I see the truth in that, hence this question…."

Jainas believe there are seven hells. Up to the sixth there is a possibility of coming back, but the seventh is eternal. Perhaps the seventh is the Christian hell, because there too, once you are in it you are in it forever. I continued, "You referred to seven hells, so the question arises, have you visited the seventh? If you have, then you could not be here. If you have not, on what authority do you say that it exists? You should say that there are only six hells, not seven. Now please be correct: say that there are only six hells, or if you want to insist on seven, then prove to me that at least one man, Shanti Sagar, has come back from the seventh hell."

He was dumbfounded. He could not believe that a child could ask such a question. Today, I too cannot believe it! How could I ask such a question? The only answer I can give is that I was unedu-cated, and utterly without any knowledge. Knowledge makes you very cunning. I was not cunning. I simply asked the question which any child could have asked if he were not educated. Education is the greatest crime man has committed against poor children. Perhaps the last liberation in the world will be the liberation of children.

I was innocent, utterly unknowledgeable. I could not read or write, not even count beyond my fingers. Even today, when I have to count anything I start with my fingers, and if I miss a finger I get mixed up.

He could not answer. My grandmother stood up and said, "You have to answer the question. Don't think that only a child is asking; I am also asking and I am your hostess."

Now again I have to introduce you to a Jaina convention. When a Jaina monk comes to a family to receive his food, after taking his meal, as a blessing to the family, he gives a sermon. The sermon is addressed to the hostess. My grandmother said, "I am your hostess today, and I also am asking the same question. Have you visited the seventh hell? If not, say truthfully that you have not, but then you cannot say there are seven hells."

The monk became so puzzled and confused – more so by being confronted by a beautiful woman – that he started to leave. My Nani shouted, "Stop! Don't leave! Who is going to answer my child's question? And he still has a few more to ask. What kind of man are you, escaping from a child's questions!"

The man stopped. I said to him, "I drop the second question, because the monk cannot answer it. He has not answered the first question either, so I will ask him the third; perhaps he may be able to answer that."

He looked at me. I said, "If you want to look at me, look into my eyes." There was great silence, just as it is here. Nobody said a word. The monk lowered his eyes, and I then said, "Then I don't want to ask. My first two questions are unanswered, and the third is not asked because I don't want a guest of the house to be ashamed. I withdraw." And I really withdrew from the gathering, and I was so happy when my grandmother followed me.

The monk was given his farewell by my grandfather, but as soon as he had left, my grandfather rushed back into the house and asked my grandmother, "Are you mad? First you supported this boy who is a born troublemaker, then you went with him without even saying goodbye to my master."

My grandmother said, "He is not my master, so I don't care a bit. Moreover what you think to be a born troublemaker is the seed. Nobody knows what will come out of it."

I know now what has come out of it. Unless one is a born troublemaker one cannot become a buddha. And I am not only a buddha, as Gautam the Buddha; that is too traditional. I am Zorba the Buddha. I am a meeting of the East and the West. In fact, I do not divide East and West, higher and lower, man and woman, good and bad, God and the devil. No! A thousand times no! I don't divide. I join together all that has been divided up to now. That is my work.

That day is immensely significant in order to understand what happened during my whole life, because unless you understand the seed, you will miss the tree and the flowering, and perhaps the moon through the branches.

From that very day I have always been against everything masochistic. Of course I came to know the word much later, but the word does not matter. I have been against all that is ascetic; even that word was not known to me in those days, but I could smell something foul. You know I am allergic to all kinds of self-torture. I want every human being to live to the fullest; minimum is not my way. Live to the maximum, or if you can go beyond the maximum, then fantastic. Go! Don't wait! And don't waste time waiting for Godot.

That's why I say to Ashu again and again, "Go on, go on, and drive Devageet nuts!" Of course I cannot drive Ashu nuts; a woman cannot be driven nuts, that is not possible. She drives men nuts. That is her ability, and she is efficient. Even if she sits in the back seat, she will drive the driver. You know back-seat drivers: they are the worst! And when there is nobody to drive the driver, what freedom! Women cannot be driven nuts – even I cannot drive a woman nuts.

So it is difficult. Although I go on saying, "Go on, go on," she does not listen. Women are born deaf; they go on doing whatsoever they want to. But Devageet hears. I am not saying anything to him, but still he hears, and freaks out. That is the way of the coward. I call it the way of the minimum, the speed limit. If you go more than that, you get a ticket.

The minimum is the way of the coward. If I am to decide, then their highest limit would be the minimum limit; anybody going below it would immediately be given a ticket. We are trying to reach the stars, and they are sticking to bullock carts. We are trying, and it is the whole aim of physics, to ultimately reach the same speed as light. Unless we reach that speed we are doomed. If we can reach the speed of light, we can escape from any dying earth or planet. Every earth, every planet, every star is going to die one day. How are you going to escape from it? You will need a very speedy technology. This earth in just four thousand years will be dead. Whatsoever you do, nothing can save it. Every day it is getting closer to its death...and you are trying to move at thirty miles per hour! Try one hundred eighty-six thousand miles per second. That's the speed of light.

The mystic attains to it, and suddenly in his inner being there is only light and nothing else. That is awakening. I am for the maximum. Live to the maximum in every possible way. Even if you are deciding to die, die with maximum speed. Don't die like a coward – take a jump into the unknown.

I am not against the idea of ending life. If one decides to end it, then of course it is his right. But I am certainly against making it a long torture. When this Shanti Sagar died, he took one hundred and ten days of not eating. A man is capable, if he is ordinarily healthy, of easily lasting ninety days without food. If he is extraordinarily healthy then he can survive longer.

So remember, I was not rude to the man. In that context my question was absolutely correct, perhaps more so because he could not answer it. And, strange to tell you today, that was the beginning not only of my questioning, but also the beginning of people not answering. Nobody has answered any of my questions in these last forty-five years. I have met many so-called spiritual people, but nobody has ever answered any of my questions. In a way that day determined my whole flavor, my whole life.

Shanti Sagar left very annoyed, but I was immensely happy, and

I did not hide it from my grandfather. I told him, "Nana, he may have left annoyed, but I am feeling absolutely correct. Your guru was just mediocre. You should choose someone of a little more worth."

Even he laughed and said, "Perhaps you are right, but now at my age to change my guru will not be very practical." He asked my Nani, "What do you think?"

My Nani, as ever true to her spirit, said, "It is never too late to change. If you see what you have chosen is not right, change it. In fact, be quick, because you are getting old. Don't say, 'I am old, so I cannot change.' A young man can afford not to change, but not an old man, and you are old enough."

And only a few years later he died, but he could not gather the courage to change his guru. He continued in the same old pattern. My grandmother used to poke him saying, "When are you going to change your guru and your methods?"

He would say, "Yes, I will, I will."

One day my grandmother said, "Stop all this nonsense! Nobody ever changes unless one changes right now. Don't say 'I will, I will.' Either change or don't change, but be clear."

That woman could have become a tremendously powerful force. She was not meant to be just a housewife. She was not meant to live in that small village. The whole world should have known about her. Perhaps I am her vehicle; perhaps she has poured herself into me. She loved me so deeply that I have never considered my real mother to be my real mother. I always consider my Nani to be my real mother.

Whenever I had to confess anything, any wrong that I had done to somebody, I could only confess it to her, nobody else. She was my trust. I could confide anything to her because I have come to realize one thing, and that is: she was capable of understanding. I must have done every kind of thing a person is capable of doing, and I would tell it to her at night. This was while I stayed with her, before I went to the university.

I never slept at my mother's house. Although my grandmother had moved to the same village as the rest of the family after my grandfather's death, I would sleep there for the simple reason that I could tell her so many mischiefs that I had done during the day. She would laugh and say, "Well done! Great! Good! That man deserved it. Did he really fall into the well just as you said?"

I would say, "Yes, but he didn't die."

She said, "That's okay, but you managed to push him into the well?"

There was a well in our neighborhood without any protecting wall. At night anybody could fall into it. I used to lead people towards it, and the man who had fallen in was none other than the sweetmaker. My mother – my *grandmother*…I always forget because I consider her to be my mother. Better to call her Nani, so there is no misunderstanding. I told my Nani, "Today I managed to make that sweetmaker fall into the well." I can still hear her laughter. She laughed herself to tears.

She said, "That's very good, but is he alive or not?"

I said, "He is perfectly okay."

"Then," she said, "there is no problem. Don't be worried; that man deserved it. He mixes so many rubbishy things into his sweets, somebody had to do something about it." Later she told him, "Unless you change your ways, remember, you will fall into the well again and again." But she never said a single word to me about it.

I asked her, "Don't you want to say anything about it?"

She said, "No, because I have watched you from your very childhood. Even if you do something wrong, you do it so rightly, and at exactly the right moment, so that even a wrong becomes a right." It was she who told me, for the first time, that right in the hands of a wrong man becomes wrong, and wrong in the hands of a right man becomes right.

So don't be worried about what you are doing; remember only one thing: what you are *being*. This is a great question, about doing and being. All religions are concerned about doing; I am concerned with being. If your being is right, and by right I mean blissful, silent, peaceful, loving, then whatever you do is right. Then there are no other commandments for you, only one: just be. Be so totally that in the very totality no shadow is possible. Then you cannot do anything wrong. The whole world may say it is wrong, that does not matter; what matters is your own being.

I'm not worried about Christ being crucified, because I know even on the cross he was fully at ease with himself. He was so fully at ease that he could pray, "Father" – that was his word for God. To be exact he did not even say "Father," but "Abba," which is far more beautiful. "Abba, forgive these people because they know not what they are doing." Again emphasize the word 'doing' – "what they are *doing*." Alas, they could not see the being of the man on the cross. It is being that matters, the only thing that matters.

That moment in my life, asking the Jaina monk strange, irritating, annoying questions, I don't consider that I did anything wrong. Perhaps I helped him. Perhaps one day he will understand. If he had had courage he would have understood even that day, but he was a coward – he escaped. And since then, this has been my experience: the so-called mahatmas and saints are all cowards. I have never come across a single mahatma – Hindu, Mohammedan, Christian, Buddhist – who can be said to be really a rebellious spirit. Unless one is rebellious one is not religious. Rebellion is the very foundation of religion.

Session 9

TIME CANNOT GO BACK, BUT mind can. What a wastage – to give such a mind, which cannot forget anything whatsoever, to a man who not only has become a no-mind, but also preaches to others to drop the mind. As far as my mind is concerned – remember, my mind, not me – it is as much a mechanism as the one being used here. My 'mind' simply means the machinery, but a perfect machine given to a man who will discard it! That is why I say what a wastage.

But I know the reason: unless you have a perfect mind, you cannot have the intelligence to discard it. Life is full of contradictions. Nothing is bad about it; it makes life more tasteful.

There was no reason for man and woman to be two; they could have been like the amoeba. You can ask Devaraj: the amoeba is neither male nor female, it is one. It is also like Muktananda, and all the other idiotanandas – celibate, but it has its own way of reproducing. What a trouble it causes all the doctors in the world! It simply goes on eating, becoming fatter and fatter, and at a certain point it splits in two. That is its way of reproduction. It is really *brahmacharya*, celibate.

Man and woman could have been one, like amoebae, but there would have been no poetry, only reproduction – of course, no conflict either, no nagging, no fighting – but the poetry which has arisen is so valuable that all the conflicts and all the nagging and all the bickering are worthwhile.

Just now I was again listening to Noorjahan…. "That trust that was between us, you may have forgotten, but I have not. I still remember at least a little. Those words that you spoke to me, perhaps you don't remember them at all, but just the memory of them is enough to keep me hoping. That love that was between us...."

Wo karar, "that love"...*karar* is far more intense than the word 'love' can translate; it is far more passionate. It would be better to translate it as "that passion," or "that passionate love." And *wo rah mujh mein our tujh mein thee* – "and the way that was between you and me...."

"The way...." Only once in a while, when the hearts are open, is there a way; otherwise people communicate, they do not commune. They talk but nobody listens. They do business, but there is just emptiness between them, there is no overflowing joy. *Wo rah* – "that way," and *wo karar* – "that passionate love."

"Perhaps you have forgotten it, but I remember. I cannot forget that you once said, 'You are the queen of the world, the most beautiful woman.' Perhaps you cannot even recognize me now...."

Things change, loves change, bodies change; it is the very nature of existence to be changing, to be in a flux. I listen to that song just before I come into your cabin, because I have loved it from my very childhood. I think perhaps it may provoke some memories in me... and it certainly does.

Yesterday, I was telling you of the incident that happened between me and the Jaina monk. It was not the end of that story, because that next day he had to come again to beg for his food from my grandfather's house.

It will be difficult for you to understand why he had to come again when he had left our house in such anger. I have to explain the context to you. A Jaina monk cannot take food from anybody except another Jaina, and unfortunately for him, we were the only Jaina family in that small village. He could not beg elsewhere for his food, although he would have liked to, but it was against his discipline. So, in spite of himself, he came again.

I and my Nani were both waiting upstairs, watching from the window because we knew he had to come. My Nani said to me, "Look, he is coming. Now, what are you going to ask him today?"

I said, "I don't know. First, let him at least eat, and then conventionally he is bound to address the family and the people who have gathered." After each meal, a Jaina monk delivers a sermon of thanks. "Then don't be worried," I told her, "I will find something or other to ask. First let him speak."

He was very cautious in speaking, and very brief, which was unusual. But whether you speak or not, if someone wants to question you, he can. He can question your silence. The monk was speaking about the beauty of existence, thinking perhaps that it could not create any trouble, but it did.

I stood up. My Nani was laughing at the back of the room – I can still hear her laughter. I asked him, "Who created this beautiful universe?"

Jainas do not believe in God. It is difficult for the Western Christian mind to even comprehend a religion that does not believe in God. Jainism is far superior to Christianity; at least it does not believe in God, and the Holy Ghost, and the whole nonsense that follows. Jainism is, believe me or not, an atheistic religion – because to be atheist and yet religious seems to be contradictory, a contradiction in terms. Jainism is pure ethics, pure morality, with no God. So when I asked the Jaina monk, "Who created this beauty?" obviously, as I knew he would, he answered, "Nobody."

That was what I was waiting for. I then said, "Can such beauty be created by no one?"

He said, "Please don't misunderstand me...." This time he had come prepared; he looked more together. "Please don't misunderstand me," he said, "I am not saying that no one is someone."

Remember the story in *Alice Through the Looking Glass*? The Queen asks Alice, "On the way here, did you meet anybody coming to see me?"

Alice said, "I saw nobody."

The Queen looked puzzled, then said, "It is strange; then nobody should have arrived here before you, and he is not here yet."

Alice, just like an English lady, of course, giggled, only spiritually. Her face remained grave. She said, "Ma'am, nobody is nobody."

The Queen said, "Of course, I know nobody is bound to be nobody, but why is he so late? It seems nobody walks slower than you."

Alice forgot for a moment and said, "Nobody walks faster than me."

The Queen then said, "That is even stranger. If nobody walks faster than you, then why has he not arrived yet?"

Alice then understood her mistake, but it was too late. She again repeated, "Please Ma'am, remember that nobody is nobody."

The Queen said, "I know it already, nobody is nobody. But the question is, why is he not yet here?"

I said to the Jaina monk, "I know that no one is no one, but you talk so beautifully, so praisingly of existence that it shocks me, because Jainas are not supposed to do that. It seems that because of yesterday's experience you have changed your tactics. You can change your tactics but you cannot change me. I still ask, if no one created the universe how did it come to be?"

He looked here and there; all were silent except for my Nani, who was laughing loudly. The monk asked me, "Do you know how it came to be?"

I said, "It has always been there; there is no need for it to come." I can confirm that sentence after forty-five years, after enlightenment and no-enlightenment, after having read so much and having forgotten it all, after knowing that which is, and – put it in capitals – IGNORING IT. I can still say the same as that young child: the universe has always been there; there is no need for it to have been created or to have come from somewhere – it simply is.

The Jaina monk did not turn up on the third day. He escaped from our village to the next where there was another Jaina family. But I must pay homage to him: without knowing it he started a small child on the journey towards truth.

Since then, how many people have I asked the same question, and found the same ignorance facing me – great pundits, knowledgeable people, great mahatmas worshipped by thousands, and yet not able to answer a simple question put by a child.

In fact, no real question has ever been answered, and I predict that no real question will ever be answered, because when you come to a real question, the only answer is silence. Not the stupid silence of a pundit, a monk or a mahatma, but your own silence. Not the silence of the other, but the silence that grows within you. Except that, there is no answer. And that silence that grows within is an answer to you, and to those who merge with your silence with love; otherwise it is not an answer to anyone except you.

There have been many silent people in the world who have not been of any help to others. The Jainas call them *arihantas*, the Buddhists call them *arhatas*; both words mean the same. It is just that the languages are a little different. One is Prakrit, the other is Pali. They are neighboring languages or sister languages rather. Arihanta, arhata – you can see yourself that both words are the same.

There have been arihantas and arhatas, but although they had found the answer they were not able to proclaim it, and unless you are able to proclaim it, proclaim it from the housetops, your answer is not of much value. It is only one person's answer in a crowd where everybody is full of questions. Soon the arihanta dies, and with him his silence. It disappears as if one has been writing on water. You can write, you can sign on water, but by the time you have finished writing your signature it is no longer there.

The real master not only knows, but helps millions to know. His knowledge is not private, it is open to all those who are ready to receive. I have known the answer. The question I have carried for thousands of years, in one body, in another body, through one body to another body, but the answer has happened for the first time. It has happened only because I questioned persistently without any fear of the consequences.

I am recalling these incidents to make you aware that unless one asks, and asks everyone totally, it is difficult to ask oneself. When one is thrown out from every door – when all the doors are locked or slammed in your face – then at last one turns withinwards...and there is the answer. It is not written; you will not find a Bible, a Torah, or a Koran, a Gita, a Tao Teh Ching or a Dhammapada.... No, you won't find anything written there.

Nor will you find anyone there either – no God, no father-figure, smiling and patting you on your back, saying, "So! Good, my son, you have come home. I forgive all your sins." No, you will not find anyone there. What you will find is a tremendous, overwhelming silence, so dense that one feels one can touch it...like a beautiful woman. One can feel it like a beautiful woman, and it is only silence, but very tangible.

When the monk had disappeared from that village we laughed continuously for days, particularly my Nani and I. I cannot believe

79

how childlike she was! At that time she must have been nearly fifty, but her spirit was as if she had never grown older than a child. She laughed with me and said, "You did well."

Even now I can still see the back of the escaping monk. Jaina monks are not beautiful people; they cannot be, their whole approach is ugly, just ugly. Even his back was ugly. I have always loved the beautiful wherever it is found – in the stars, in a human body, in flowers, or in the flight of a bird...wherever. I am an unashamed worshipper of the beautiful, because I cannot see how one can know truth if one cannot love beauty. Beauty is the way to truth. And the way and the goal are not different: the way itself ultimately turns into the goal. The first step is also the last.

That encounter – yes, that's the right word – that encounter with the Jaina mystic began thousands of other encounters; Jaina, Hindu, Mohammedan, Christian, and I was ready to do anything just to have a good argument.

You will not believe me, but I went through circumcision at the age of twenty-seven, after I was already enlightened, just to enter a Mohammedan Sufi order where they would not allow anybody in who had not been circumcised. I said, "Okay, then do it! This body is going to be destroyed anyway, and you are only cutting off just a little piece of skin. Cut it, but I want to enter the school."

Even they were unable to believe me. I said, "Believe me, I am ready." And when I started arguing they said, "You were so willing to be circumcised and yet you are so unwilling to accept anything we say at all!"

I said, "That's my way. About the nonessential I am always ready to say yes. About the essential I am absolutely adamant, nobody can force me to say yes."

Of course they had to expel me from their so-called Sufi order, but I told them, "Expelling me, you are simply declaring to the world that you are pseudo-Sufis. The only real Sufi is being expelled. In fact, I expel you all."

Bewildered, they looked at each other. But that's the truth. I had gone to their order not to know the truth; I knew that already. Then why had I entered? Just to have good company to argue with.

Argument has been my joy from my very childhood. I will do

anything just to have a good argument. But how rare it is to find a really good milieu for argument! I entered the Sufi order – this I am confessing for the first time – and even allowed those fools to circumcise me. They did it by such primitive methods that I had to suffer for at least six months. But I didn't care about that; my whole concern was to know Sufism from within. Alas, I could not find a real Sufi in my life. But that is true not only about the Sufis; I have not found a real Christian either, or a real Hassid.

J. Krishnamurti invited me to meet him in Bombay. The man who brought the message was a common friend, Parmananda. I told him, "Parmananda, go back and tell Krishnamurti that if he wants to see me, he should come – that is proper – rather than asking me to come to him."

Parmananda said, "But he is years older than you."

I said, "You go to him. Don't answer on his behalf. If he says that he is older than me, then it is not worth going, because awakening cannot be older or younger; it is always just the same – simply fresh, eternally fresh."

He went and never came back, because how could Krishnamurti, an old man, come to see me? Yet he wanted to see me. This is interesting, is it not? I never wanted to see him, otherwise I would have gone to him. He wanted to see me, and yet still wanted me to go to him. You must concede that is a little too much. Parmananda never returned with a reply. Next day when he came I asked, "What happened?"

He said, "Krishnamurti became very angry, so angry that I did not ask him again."

Now, he wanted to see me; I would have loved to see him, but I had never wanted to, for the simple reason that I don't like to go to people, even though the person was J. Krishnamurti. I love what he says, I love what he is, but I have never desired – at least have never said to anyone – that I want to see him, because then it is a simple matter: I should go to him. He desired, he wanted to see me, and yet wanted me to come to him. I don't like that, and never will.

That created, at least on his part, an antagonism towards me. Since then he has been speaking against me. The moment he sees one of my sannyasins he behaves exactly like a bull. If you wave a red flag at a bull you know what will happen. That's what happens when he sees one of my sannyasins clothed in red: suddenly he becomes enraged. I say that he must have been a bull in his past life; he has not forgotten his antagonism with the color red.

This only started when I refused to go to see him. Before that he had never spoken against me. As far as I'm concerned, I am a free man. I can speak for somebody, and in the same breath against the same person, without any trouble on my part. I love all kinds of contradictions and inconsistencies.

J. Krishnamurti is against me, but I say I am not against him. I still love him. He is one of the most beautiful men of the twentieth century. I don't think there is anybody else alive I can compare him with. But he has a limitation, and that limitation has been his undoing. The limitation is that he tries to be utterly intellectual, and that is not possible if you want to rise high, if you want to go beyond words and numbers.

Krishnamurti should be beyond, just beyond, but he is tethered to the Victorian intellectuality. His intellectuality is not even modern but Victorian, almost one century old. He says he is fortunate in not having read the Upanishads, the Gita, or the Koran. Then what does he go on doing? I will tell you: he reads third-rate detective novels! Please don't tell it to anybody, otherwise he will hit his head against the wall. I am not worried about his head, I am worried about the wall. As far as his head is concerned, he has been suffering from migraine for more than the last fifty years – that's more than my whole lifetime – so much so that in his diary he says many times he wanted to hit his head against the wall. Yes, I am worried about the wall.

Why does he suffer from migraine? – because of too much intellectuality, and nothing else. It is not the same as poor Asheesh, my chair-maker. He too suffers from migraine, but his is physical. J. Krishnamurti's migraine is spiritual. He is too intellectual; just to hear him is enough to give you a migraine. If you don't suffer from migraine after hearing a lecture by J. Krishnamurti it means that you are already enlightened – or that you don't have a head. The second is more probable. The first is a little difficult.

Asheesh's migraine can be cured, but Krishnamurti's is not

terminable. He is incurable. But now there is no need either because he is so old and accustomed to living with his migraine. It has become almost like a wife. If you take away his migraine he will be left alone, a widower. Do not do that. He and his migraine are married, and they are going to die together.

I was saying that my first encounter with the naked Jaina monk started a long, long series of encounters with many so-called monks – bullshitters. They all suffer from intellectuality, and I was born to bring them down to earth. But it is almost impossible to bring them to their senses. Perhaps they don't want to because they are afraid. Perhaps not to have sensibility or intelligence is very advantageous to them.

They are respected as holy men; to me they are only holy cow dung. One thing about cow dung is good: it does not smell. I remind you of that because I am allergic to smells. Cow dung has this one good quality, it is nonallergic. What is the right word, Devaraj?

"Nonallergenic, Osho."

Right, nonallergenic.

My Nani was not really an Indian woman; even the West would have been a little less foreign to her. And remember, she was absolutely uneducated – perhaps that's why she was so perceptive. Perhaps she could see something in me of which I was not aware in those days. Perhaps that's the reason she loved me so much...I can't say. She's no longer alive. One thing I do know: when her husband died she never went back to the village, she remained in my father's village. I had to leave her there, but when I returned, again and again I would ask her, "Nani, can we go back to the village?"

She would always say, "For what? You are here." Those three simple words resound in me like music reverberating: "You are here." I also say the same to you. She loved me – and you know nobody can love you more than I love you.

It is beautiful.

You have never been here.

Alas, if only I could invite you also to this Himalayan space! "Now" is such a beautiful space. And poor Devageet – I can still hear his giggle. My God! Can no chemistry at least prevent me from hearing the giggles?

Don't think I have gone mad, I am already mad. Do you see? – your insanity and my insanity, they are totally different. Note it down. Even Rasputin, if he were alive, would be a sannyasin...I mean, he would have been a sannyasin. Nobody, without exception, can cheat me.

I am the type of person who even at the time of death will say, "Enough, enough for today...."

Session 10

I WAS LOOKING AT SOME PICTURES of the marriage procession of Princess Diana, and strangely, the only thing that impressed me in the whole nonsense was the beautiful horses, their joyous dance. Looking at those horses I remembered my own horse. I have not told anyone about it, not even Gudia, who loves horses. But now that I am not keeping anything secret, even this can be told.

I not only owned one horse; in fact I had four horses. One was my own – and you know how fussy I am...even today nobody else can ride in the Rolls Royces. It is just fussiness. I was the same at that time too. Nobody, not even my grandfather, was allowed to ride my horse. Of course, I was allowed to ride everyone else's horse. Both my grandfather and my grandmother had one. It was strange in an Indian village for a woman to ride a horse – but she was a strange woman, what to do! The fourth horse was for Bhoora, the servant who always followed me with his gun, at a distance of course.

Destiny is strange. I have never harmed anyone in my life, not even in my dreams. I am absolutely vegetarian. But as destiny would have it, from my very childhood I have been followed by a guard. I don't know why, but since Bhoora I have never been without a guard. Even today my guards are always either ahead or behind, but always there. Bhoora started the whole game.

I already told you that he looked like a European, that's why he was called Bhoora. It was not his real name. *Bhoora* simply means "the white one." Even I don't know his real name at all. He looked European, very European, and it looked really strange, especially in that village where I don't think any European had ever entered. And still there are guards....

Even when I was a child, I could see the point of Bhoora following me at a distance on his horse, because twice there was an attempt to abduct me. I don't know why anybody should have been interested in me. Now at least I can understand. My grandfather, though not very rich by Western standards, was certainly very rich in that village. *Dakaits* – now Devageet will be in real difficulty to spell the word 'dakait'....

It is not an English word; it comes from the Hindi word *daku*. But in that sense English is one of the most generous languages in the world. Every year it goes on absorbing eight thousand words from other languages; that's why it goes on growing bigger and bigger. It is bound to become the world language – nobody can prevent it. All the other languages of the world, on the other hand, are very shy; they go on shrinking. They believe in purity, that no other language should be allowed to enter. Naturally they are bound to remain small and primitive. Dakait is a transliteration of daku; it means thief – not just an ordinary thief, but when a group of people, armed and organized, plan the act of stealing, then it is dakaitry.

Even when I was young, in India it was a common practice to steal rich people's children, then to threaten the parents that if they didn't pay, then the hands of the child would be cut off. If they paid, then they could save the child's hands. Sometimes the threat would be to blind the child, or if the parents were really rich then the threat was direct – that the child would be killed. To save the child, the poor parents were ready to do anything whatsoever.

Twice they tried to steal me. Two things saved me: one was my horse, who was a really strong Arabian; the second was Bhoora, the servant. He was ordered by my grandfather to fire into the air – not at the people trying to abduct me, because that is against Jainism, but you are allowed to fire into the air to frighten them. Of course my grandmother had whispered in Bhoora's ear, "Don't bother about what my husband says. First you can fire into the air, but if it doesn't work, remember: if you don't shoot the people I will shoot you." And she was a really good shot. I have seen her shoot and she was always accurate to the minutest point. She was just like Gudia – she did not miss much.

Nani was in many ways like Gudia, very exact as far as details are concerned. She was always to the point, never around it. There are some people who go around and around and around: you have to figure out what they really want. That was not her way; she was exact, mathematically exact. She told Bhoora, "Remember, if you come home without him just to report he has been stolen, I will shoot you immediately." I knew, Bhoora knew, my grandfather knew, because although she said it into Bhoora's ear, it was not a whisper; it was loud enough to be heard by the whole village. She meant it. She always meant business.

My grandfather looked the other way. I could not resist; I laughed loudly and said, "Why are you looking the other way? You heard her. If you are a real Jaina, tell Bhoora not to shoot anybody."

But before my grandfather could say anything, my Nani said, "I have told Bhoora on your behalf too, so you keep quiet." She was such a woman that she would even have shot my grandfather. I knew her – I don't mean literally, but metaphorically, and that is more dangerous than literally. So he kept quiet.

Twice I was almost abducted. Once my horse brought me home, and once Bhoora had to fire the gun, of course into the air. Perhaps if there had been a need he would have fired at the person who was trying to abduct me. But there was no need, so he saved himself and also my grandfather's religion.

Since then, it is strange…it seems very, very strange to me because I have been absolutely harmless to everybody, yet I have been in danger many times. Many attempts have been made on my life. I have always wondered, since life will end by itself sooner or later, why anybody should be interested to put an end to it in the middle. What purpose can it serve? If I could be convinced of that purpose I can stop breathing this very moment.

I once asked a man who had tried to kill me. I had the chance to ask him because he finally became a sannyasin. I asked, "Now we are both alone, tell me why you wanted to kill me."

In those days, at Woodlands in Bombay, I used to give sannyas to people alone in my room. I said, "We are alone. I can give you sannyas, there is no problem in it. First become a sannyasin, then tell me the purpose, why you wanted to kill me. If you can convince me I will stop breathing here and now in front of you."

He started weeping and crying and holding my feet. I said, "This won't do, you have to convince me of the purpose."

He said, "I was just an idiot. There is nothing I can say to you. I was just throwing a tantrum." Perhaps that is the reason why an absolutely harmless man like me has been attacked in every possible way. I have been given poison....

Gudia goes through tantrums once in a while but even then she has not harmed me. She cannot, it is impossible for her. Once in a while anybody can have a tantrum, particularly a woman; and more so if she has to live twenty-four hours a day, or maybe more, with a man like me, who is not nice at all; who is always hard, and always trying to push you to the very edge, and who does not allow you to come back. He goes on and on pushing and telling you to "Jump before you think!"

My Nani was certainly similar to Gudia, particularly when she was in a tantrum. I have seen her in a tantrum, but I was never worried. I have seen her pull her gun out and rush towards my grandfather's room – but I continued what I was doing. She asked me, "Are you not afraid?"

I said, "You go on and do your work and let me do mine."

She laughed, saying, "You are a strange boy. I am going to kill your grandfather and you are trying to make a house out of playing cards. Are you mad or something?"

I said, "You just go and kill that old man. I have always dreamed of doing it myself, so why should I worry? Don't disturb me."

She sat down by my side and started helping me to make the palace I was creating out of playing cards. But when she had said to Bhoora, "If anyone touches my child, you are not just to fire into the air because we believe in Jainism.... That belief is good, but only in the temple. In the marketplace we have to behave in the way of the world, and the world is not Jaina. How can we behave according to our philosophy?"

I can see her crystal-clear logic. If you are talking to a man who does not understand English, you cannot speak to him in English. If you speak to him in his own language then there is more possibility of communication. Philosophies are languages; let that be clearly noted. Philosophies don't mean anything at all – they are languages.

And the moment I heard my grandmother say to Bhoora, "When a dakait tries to steal my child, speak the language he understands, forget all about Jainism" – in that moment I understood. Although it was not so clear to me as it became later on, it must have been clear to Bhoora. My grandfather certainly understood the situation because he closed his eyes and started repeating his mantra: *"Namo arihantanam namo…namo siddhanam namo…."*

I laughed, my grandmother giggled; Bhoora, of course, only smiled. But everybody understood the situation – and she was right, as always.

I will tell you another resemblance between Gudia and my grandmother: she is almost always right, even with me. If she says something, I may not agree, but I know that finally she is going to be right. I will not agree, that too is true. I am a stubborn man, I have told you again and again. I stick to whatsoever I am, right or wrong. My wrong is my wrong, and I love it because it is mine. But as far as the question of its being right or wrong is concerned…whenever there is a conflict I know Gudia is going to be right finally. For the moment I am going to decide – and I am a stubborn man.

My grandmother had the same quality of being always right. She said to Bhoora, "Do you think these dakaits believe in Jainism? And that old fool…" she indicated my grandfather who was repeating his mantra. She then said, "That old fool has only told you to fire into the air because we should not kill. Let him repeat his mantra. Who is telling him to kill? You are not a Jaina, are you?"

I knew instinctively at that moment that if Bhoora was a Jaina he would lose his job. I had never bothered before whether Bhoora was a Jaina or not. For the first time I became concerned about the poor man, and started praying. I did not know to whom, because Jainas don't believe in any God. I was never indoctrinated into any belief, but still I started saying within myself, "God, if you are there, save this poor man's job." Do you see the point? Even then I said, *"If* you are there…." I cannot lie even in such a situation.

But mercifully Bhoora was not a Jaina. He said, "I am not a Jaina so I don't care."

My Nani said, "Then remember what I have told you, not what that old fool has said."

In fact she always used to use that term for my grandfather: "that old fool" – and I have reserved it for Devageet. But that "old fool" is dead. My mother...my grandmother is dead. Excuse me, again I said "my mother." I really cannot believe she was not my mother and only my grandmother.

By the way, you will be surprised that all my brothers and sisters – and there are nearly a dozen of them excluding me – they all call my mother "Ma," mother, except me; I call her "Bhabhi." Everybody in India always used to wonder why I called my mother Bhabhi, because it means "elder brother's wife." In Hindi, the word for elder brother is *bhaiya*; the word for his wife is *bhabhi*. My uncles call my mother Bhabhi, and that is perfectly okay. Why do I still call her Bhabhi even now? The reason is, I had known another woman as my mother – that was my mother's mother.

After those early years of knowing Nani as my mother it was impossible to call any other woman Ma – mother. I have always called her my Nani, and I know she was not my real mother, but she mothered me. My real mother remained a little far away, a little foreign. Even though my Nani is dead, she is closer to me. Even though my mother is now enlightened I will still call her Bhabhi, I cannot call her Ma. To use that would be almost a betrayal of one who is dead. No, I cannot do it.

My grandmother herself had said many times to me, "Why do you go on calling your mother Bhabhi? Call her mother." I simply avoided the question. This is the first time that I have spoken about it or discussed it – with you.

My Nani has somehow become part of my very being. She loved me so immensely. Once, when a thief entered our house she fought with him barehanded, and I saw how ferocious a woman can be... really dangerous! If I had not interfered she would have killed the poor man. I said, "Nani! What are you doing? Just for my sake, leave him. Let him go!" Because I was crying and telling her to stop for my sake, she allowed the man to go. The poor man could not believe that she was sitting on his chest holding his neck with both her hands. She would certainly have killed him. Just a little more pressure on his throat and the man would have died.

When she spoke to Bhoora I knew she meant it. Bhoora knew

she meant it too. When my grandfather started the mantra, I knew he also understood that she meant business.

Twice I was attacked – and to me it was a joy, an adventure. In fact, deep down I wanted to know what it meant to be abducted. That has always been my characteristic, you can call it my character. It is a quality I rejoice in. I used to go on my horse to the woods which belonged to us. My grandfather promised that all that belonged to him would be willed to me, and he was true to his word. He never gave a single *pai* to anybody else.

He had thousands of acres of land. Of course, in those days it didn't have any value. But value is not my concern – it was so beautiful: those tall trees, and a great lake, and in summer when the mangoes became ripe it was so fragrant. I used to go there on my horse so often that the horse became accustomed to my path.

I am still the same...and if I don't like a place I never return there.

I have been to Madras only once, just once, because I never liked the place, particularly the language. It sounded as if everybody was fighting with everybody else. I hate that, and I hate that kind of language. So I said to my host, "This is my first and last visit to you."

He said, "Why the last?"

I said, "I hate this type of language. Everyone seems to be fighting. I know they are not – it is just the way they speak." I hate Madras, I don't like it at all.

Krishnamurti likes Madras, but that is his business. He goes there every year. He is a Tamil. In fact he was born near Madras. He is a Madrasi, so for him to go there is perfectly logical. Why should I go there?

I used to go to many places. Why? There is no why. I just liked to go. I like to be on the go. Do you get it?...on the go. I am a man who has no business here, or there, or anywhere. I am just on the go. Let me say it in other words: I am on the merry-go-round. Now I think you get it.

I used to go on my horse, and seeing those horses in Princess Diana's wedding procession I could not believe that England could have such beautiful horses. The queen is just homely – I don't want to say ugly, just out of politeness. And Prince Charles is certainly not a prince: look at his face! You call his type of face princely?

Perhaps in England.... And the guests! The bigwigs! In particular, the high priest – what do you call him in England?

"The Archbishop of Canterbury, Osho."

Great! Archbishop! A great name for such a dash-dash-dash; otherwise they will say that because I used such words I cannot be enlightened! But I think everybody in the world will understand what I mean by dash-dash-dash – even the archbishop!

All those people, and I could only love the horses! They were the real people. What joy! What steps! What dance! Just sheer celebration. I immediately remembered my own horse, and those days... their fragrance is there still. I can see the lake, and myself as a child on the horse in the woods. It is strange – although my nose is under this mousetrap I can smell the mangoes, the neem trees, the pines, and I can also smell my horse.

It is good that I was not allergic to smell in those days, or, who knows, I may have been allergic but unaware of it. It is a strange coincidence that the year of my enlightenment was also the year of my becoming allergic. Perhaps I was allergic before and just not aware of it, and when I became enlightened the awareness came. I have dropped the enlightenment now.

"Please," I am telling existence, "drop this allergy so that again I can ride a horse." That will be a great day, not only for me but for all my sannyasins.

There is only one picture, which they go on publishing all over the world, in which I am riding on a Kashmiri horse. It is just a picture; I was not really riding. But because the photographer wanted me to be photographed on a horse, and I loved the man – the photographer, I mean – I could not say no to him. He had brought the horse and all his equipment, so I said okay. I just sat on the horse, and you can even see from the picture that my smile was not true. It is the smile when a photographer says, "Smile please!" But if I can transcend enlightenment, who knows, I may transcend allergy to horses at least. Then I can have the same kind of world around me:

The lake...
The mountains,
The river...

OSHO ON THE KASHMIRI HORSE

Only I will miss my grandmother.

Devageet, you are not the only Jew here. Remember, you are not in a hurry; I am in the hurry. My bladder is hurting! So please...I always want to have the last word. Devageet, you would have been such a good nagging wife. Really, I mean it! Just find a nice boy and go on honeymoon. Look, you are already thinking that I have released you. Don't be in such a hurry. Your bladders are not bursting! Now....

That's good.

This is *fabulous!* I have just used this word for the first time in my life...just fabulous! I don't know what it means, but when your bladder is bursting, who cares!

Session 11

DEVAGEET...REALLY GOOD, AND AFTER being hit, you have seen stars. I too can see the stars along with you. Okay.

The village where I was born was not part of the British Empire. It was a small state ruled by a Mohammedan queen. I can see her now. Strange...she was also as beautiful as the queen of England, exactly as beautiful. But there was one good thing: she was Mohammedan, whereas the queen of England is not. Such women should always be Mohammedan, because they have to remain hidden behind a veil, called a *burqa*. She used to visit our village once in a while; and of course, in that village, my house was the only one where she could stay, and moreover she loved my grandmother.

My Nani and she were both talking when I first saw the queen without her veil. I could not believe it: a queen, and so homely! Then I understood the purpose of the burqa, the veil – what the Hindus call *parda*. It is good for ugly women; in a better world it would be good for ugly men too. At least then you can't attack anybody with your ugliness. It is an aggression. If beauty is an attraction, then what is ugliness? It is an aggression, an attack, and nobody is protected against it. No law protects anyone.

I laughed in the very face of the queen. She said, "Why are you laughing?"

I said, "I am laughing because I always wondered what was the purpose of a parda, and burqa. Today I know."

I don't think she understood, because she smiled. Although she was an ugly woman I must concede her smile was beautiful.

The world is full of strange things. I came across many people who were beautiful, but when they smiled their faces would look distorted, ugly. I have seen Mahatma Gandhi, again only when I was a child. He was ugly to the core. In fact I would say he was uniquely ugly, but his beauty was in his smile. He knew how to smile; about that I cannot be against him. About everything else I am against him, because except for his smile everything was just rubbish, rot! He was really a great Bodhigarbage. Our own Bodhigarbage is nothing compared to him.

I have heard that people call Swami Bodhigarbha, Bodhigarbage. I like it! They have added something to the name. In fact they have put him exactly where he is. I gave him the name Bodhigarbha, which can only be his future. But people can only see what is under their feet; they call him Bodhigarbage. Perhaps this name would have been good for Mahatma Gandhi.

The queen...(*Devageet stifles a sneeze.*) Now, this really distracts me. Do you know, Devageet, that in India people believe that when you sneeze, the devil enters into you? So when they sneeze, to prevent the devil from coming, they say with a click (*Osho snaps his fingers with a click*) "*Om shantih, shantih, shantih...Om shantih, shantih, shantih...Om shantih, shantih, shantih....*" Thrice you have to click with your fingers. I don't know what you call this click with the fingers; whatsoever it is, the Indians actually do it.

I don't know whether the devil is prevented or not, but whatsoever you were doing is not disturbed. Now, you are a Jew, not a Hindu, so at least you only sneezed and did not go through the whole Hindu procedure; otherwise I would really have gone sane, and I am so afraid of sanity. But I am not saying anything wrong – I *mean* sanity: I am so afraid of sanity.

I can feel your bewilderment. No need for you to be bewildered. I am an insane man afraid of being sane again – and that procedure could drive anybody sane. But you are a Jew, thank God! Like an Englishman, you tried hard to prevent the sneeze; even that I can understand. An Englishman prevents everything possible, even a sneeze, particularly when you are in the presence of someone who pretends to be holier-than-thou.

But relax, I don't pretend to be holier than you. You can sneeze joyously, then it will not distract me. It may even give me a few hints for the story I am telling you. Back to the work. Enough distraction from this sneeze.

As I was saying, my village belonged to a small state, very small, Bhopal. It was not part of the British Raj. Of course the queen of Bhopal used to visit us once in a while. I was talking about the time when I was present, and laughed at the ugliness of the woman and the beauty of her mask. Her burqa was really beautiful; it was studded with sapphires. She was so impressed by my grandmother that she invited her to the coming yearly celebration in the capital. My grandmother said, "It is impossible for me to go because I can't leave my child uncared for for so many days."

In Hindi "my child" is a tremendously beautiful phrase, *mera beta*; it means "my child, my boy."

The queen said, "There is no problem: you can bring him too. I also love him."

I could not understand why she should love me. I hadn't done anything wrong. Why should I be punished? Just the very idea of being loved by this woman was as if a monster was crawling on you. At that moment she looked exactly like a monster, full of sticky stuff. Perhaps she liked to chew gum – she was all gum. In my life I have never been afraid, except of that woman. But the adventure of going to the capital as a guest of the queen, and staying at her beautiful palace of which I had heard a thousand and one stories, was too much. Although I never wanted to see the woman again, I went with my grandmother to the yearly celebration.

I remember the palace. It is one of the most beautiful in India. It has five hundred acres of woodland and a five-hundred-acre lake – one thousand acres in all. The queen was good to us as her guests, but I confess, I avoided seeing her face as much as I could. Perhaps she is still alive, because she was not very old then.

A strange incident happened concerning that palace – I should call it a coincidence. On the day I said, "Okay, I am ready to move to the Himalayas," on that very same day the son of the queen of Bhopal phoned saying that if we were interested they were willing to offer their palace – the same palace that I am telling you about. That palace...for a moment I could not believe that they would offer it. They had lost everything; the whole state was gone, merged into India. All that was left was only the one thousand acres, and that palace. But still it is a beautiful kingdom – five hundred acres of ancient trees, and five hundred acres of a lake that was just part of the great lake of Bhopal.

In India the lake of Bhopal is the greatest lake. I don't think there is any other lake in the world that can compete with it, it is so huge. I can't remember how many miles wide it is, but one cannot see the other shore from anywhere. Those five hundred acres in the palace grounds are part of the same lake but they belong to the palace.

I said, "It is too late. Tell the prince and his mother, if she is still alive, that we are thankful for their offer but I have decided to go to the Himalayas." For seven years I have been trying to find just a few thousand acres of land, and the politicians are always interfering. Tell him, "I remember visiting your palace and your mother – perhaps she is still alive, I don't know." But tell him, "I loved the palace, and still do, even more so now that you have offered it to me. But I have decided to go to the Himalayas."

My secretary was shocked and she said, "He is offering the palace to you and not even asking for any money. It must be worth at least two million dollars."

I said, "Two million or twenty million dollars, it does not matter at all. My thank-you is far more valuable. How many million dollars do you think it is worth? Just say to him, 'He sends his thanks, but your offer came just a few hours too late. If you had offered the palace just a few hours earlier perhaps he may have accepted it. Now nothing can be done at all.'"

When he heard, the prince was shocked. He could not believe that one could offer such a palace without asking for anything in exchange and just be told, "Sorry, no thank you."

I know the palace. I was a guest there once in my childhood, and once again later in my life. I have seen it through the eyes of a child and also through the eyes of a young man. No, I was not deceived when I had seen it as a child, but it was far more beautiful than I had understood it then. A child, although innocent, has limitations; his vision cannot imply all that is possible. He sees only that which is apparent. I also visited the palace as a young man, again as a guest, and I knew that it must be one of the most beautiful structures in the world, particularly its location. But I had to refuse it.

Sometimes it feels so good to refuse, because I already knew that if I accepted, there were bound to be troubles ad infinitum. That palace could not be my palace. The politicians, who have become all-powerful – uneducated, corrupt, untalented and immoral – would be bound to jump in. Although I refused, they still jumped in, thinking that the prince was lying, because how could anyone refuse such an offer?

I have come to know that they are torturing him in every possible way to know why he offered me the palace. I did not accept it. Nothing happened in reality, just a phone call – but that was enough.

Indian politicians must be the worst in the world. Politicians are everywhere, but they are nothing like Indian politicians.

The reason is clear: for two thousand years India has been in slavery. In 1947, just by luck, India became free. I say by luck because India still does not deserve it; the whole credit goes to Attlee, the English prime minister at that time. He was a socialist, a kind of dreamer. He thought about equality and freedom and all kinds of great things. It was he who was really the father of Indian freedom. It is not that India earned it or even deserved it. It was just luck to have Attlee as the prime minister of England.

After two thousand years of slavery the Indians have become really cunning. Just in order to survive, the slave has to be cunning. The slavery has finished but the cunningness continues. No Attlee could destroy it. It is not in anybody's hands; it has spread all over India. By the end of this century India will be the most populated country in the world. Just to think of it is enough for me not to sleep.

Whenever I don't want to sleep I think of India at the end of this century. That is enough! Then, even if you gave sleeping pills they would not affect me. The very idea that India will be the most densely populated country, with all those pygmy politicians, is enough! Can you think of another nightmare to defeat it?

I refused that beautiful palace. I still feel sorry that I had to refuse the only man who has come with an offer, without even asking for money. Yet I had to. I certainly feel sorry for him…. I had to refuse because I had decided, and once I decide, rightly or wrongly, I cannot go back. I cannot cancel it; it is not in my blood. It is just a kind of stubbornness.

What is the time, Devageet?

"Ten thirty-one, Osho."

Good! Just give me ten minutes. Remembering that, I did not sleep the whole night.

Without my insistence where would you be? You would have stopped long ago. Continue – don't be a Jewish wife. Jewish and a wife, both together! Even God could not handle that, so he manages with a Holy Ghost.

Poor Devageet, no matter how hard I hit him he never takes revenge. So good. Anybody – and when I say anybody, I mean Moses, Jesus, Buddha – would be jealous of me. Gautam Buddha had his own personal physician, but no buddha has ever had his own personal dentist. They were certainly not so fortunate. At least nobody had a Devageet with them, that much is absolutely certain.

Good, now stop.

Session 12

I HAVE BEEN WORKING THE WHOLE night because of a small remark I made which may have been hurtful to Devaraj. He may not have noticed it, but it has been sitting heavy on me all night. I could not sleep. I had said, "No buddha has ever had a personal dentist, but Gautam the Buddha had a personal physician." That was not quite right so I consulted the records, the Akashic records.

I will have to say a few more things, which nobody cares about, particularly the foolish historians. I was not consulting history. I had to go in what H.G. Wells called *The Time Machine,* back into time. It is the hardest work, and you know I am a lazy man. I am still huffing and puffing.

Buddha's physician, Jivaka, was given to Buddha by a king, Bimbisara. Another thing is that Bimbisara was not one of Buddha's sannyasins; he was just a sympathizer. Why did he give Jivaka to Buddha? – Jivaka was Bimbisara's own personal physician, the most famous of those days – because he was competing with another king whose name was Prasenjita. Prasenjita had offered Buddha his own physician. He had just mentioned that, "Whenever you have need, my personal physician will be at your service."

This was too much for Bimbisara. If Prasenjita could do it, then Bimbisara would show him that he could offer his most cherished physician to Buddha as a gift. So although Jivaka followed Buddha wherever he went, he was not a follower, remember. He remained Hindu, a brahmin.

That was strange – a physician to Buddha, continuously with him, even in his most intimate moments, and still a brahmin? That shows the truth. Jivaka was still on salary from the king. He was in the service of the king. If the king wanted him to be with Buddha, okay; a servant has to follow the order of his master. Even so he was very rarely with Buddha because Bimbisara was old, and again and again he needed his doctor, so he called him back to the capital.

Devaraj, you may not have thought about it, but I felt sad that I had been a little cruel. I should not have said that. You are as unique as one can be. As far as having been a physician to a buddha is concerned, nobody can be compared to you, either in the past or in the future...because there is never going to be a man so simple, so insane that he calls himself Zorba the Buddha.

That reminds me of the story I was telling you. A great burden has been lifted from my heart. You can even see it in my breathing. I am really relieved. It was just a simple remark, but I am so sensitive, perhaps more than a buddha is supposed to be. But what can I do? I cannot be a buddha according to anybody else; I can only be myself. I am relieved of a great burden that you may not have felt at all, or perhaps deep down you were aware of it and you giggled just to hide it. You cannot hide anything from me.

But strangely, awareness becomes even more clear and unclouded by anything that helps the body to disappear. I am holding on to this chair just to remind myself that the body is still there. Not that I want it to be there, but just so that you all won't freak out. There is not enough room in here for four people to freak out. Yes, if you freak in, there is enough room anywhere.

Now we come to the story. I call it a story – not that it is, but so much in life is storylike that if you know how to read life, you won't need a novel. I wonder why J. Krishnamurti reads novels, and third-rate detective novels at that. Something is missing in him. Alas, he cannot see it, a man of such intelligence, or perhaps he sees it and is trying to deceive himself through detective novels.

He says he is fortunate not to have read the Bhagavadgita nor the Koran, nor the Rigveda...yet he reads detective novels. He should also say that he is unfortunate in that he reads detective novels; he never says that. But I know because I was also a guest in the same house where he used to stay in Bombay. The lady who was our hostess asked me, "I want to ask you only one thing: I don't see you reading detective novels – what's the matter?" She said, "I thought every enlightened person must read detective novels."

I said, "Where did you get this nonsensical idea?"

She said, "From Krishnamurti. He stays here too; my husband is his follower. I too am a lover and a sympathizer. I have seen him reading third-rate detective novels and I thought there must be something in it. Please forgive me for being curious about something very personal, but I was looking in your suitcase. I thought perhaps you were hiding detective novels in it."

I used to carry not just one suitcase, but three big ones. She must have thought that I was carrying almost a library of detective novels with me, but she could not find even a single book. She was puzzled.

Other friends from Varanasi, where J. Krishnamurti stays, have asked the same thing. Still other friends from New Delhi have asked the same question. It cannot be wrong – so many people from so many different places asking the same question again and again. Many people have seen him reading a detective novel while traveling by plane. In fact, to tell you the truth, I myself saw him by chance, on a plane traveling from Bombay to Delhi. He was reading a detective novel then. As destiny would have it we were both traveling on the same plane, so I can say absolutely that he reads detective novels. I don't need any witnesses; I myself am a witness.

But I can create a story about any small thing that happens; it just has to be brought into a proper context. This morning I was telling you about the time when the queen of Bhopal visited our village, which was part of her state, and she invited us to be her guests at her annual celebration. When she was in our village she asked my Nani, "Why do you call the boy Raja?"

'Raja' means "king," and in that state, the title of Raja was of course reserved for the owner of the state. Even the queen's husband was not called "Raja," but only "Prince" – *Rajkumar* – just as poor Philip in England is called "Prince" Philip – not even "King." Yet strangely he is the only man there who looks like a king. Nor does the queen of England look like a queen, nor does poor Prince Charles look like the proverbial Prince Charming. The only man who looks like a king is not called a king, he is only called "Prince" Philip.

I feel sorry for him. The reason is that he does not belong to the same blood line, and it is blood that determines everything, at least in their idiotic world. Otherwise blood is blood. In the laboratory, even a king or queen's blood will not show up as anything different.

Both of you here are doctors, and one is a nurse, and the fourth is, although not a doctor or a nurse, almost both together, without a certificate of course. You can all understand that blood cannot be the determining factor. Queen Elizabeth has the right blood – right, not according to the scientist, but according to the idiots. Charles is her son, at least fifty percent; he has the heritage. Philip is a foreigner, and just to console him they call him "Prince."

In the same way, in that small state at that time, the woman was the head and she was called the queen, rani, but there was no raja. Her husband was only a prince – Rajkumar. Naturally she asked my grandmother, "Why do you call this boy of yours Raja?" You will be surprised to know it was really illegal in that state to give the name Raja to anybody. My grandmother laughed and said, "He is the king of my heart, and as far as the law is concerned, we will soon leave this state, but I cannot change his name."

Even I was surprised when she said we would soon be leaving the state...just to save my name? That night I said to her, "Nani are you mad? Just to save this stupid name...? Any name will do, and in private you could call me Raja. There is no need for us to leave."

She said, "I feel in my very guts that we will soon have to leave this state. That's why I risked."

And that is what happened. This incident happened when I was eight, and after just one year we had left that state forever...but she never stopped calling me Raja. I changed my name, just because Raja – "the king" – seemed so snobbish, and I didn't like to be laughed at by everybody in school, and moreover I never wanted anyone else to call me Raja except my grandmother. It was a private affair between us.

But the queen was offended by the name. How poor these people are, the kings and the queens, the presidents, the prime ministers... what a lot! Yet they are powerful. They are idiotic to the maximum, yet powerful also to the maximum. It is a strange world.

I said to my grandmother, "As far as I understand, she is not only offended by my name, she is jealous of you." I could see it so clearly that there was no question of doubt. "And," I told her, "I am not asking you whether I am right or wrong." In fact that determined my way for my whole life.

I have never asked anybody whether I am right or wrong. Wrong or right, if I want to do it, I want to do it and I will make it right. If it is wrong then I will make it right, but I have never allowed anyone to interfere with me. That has given me whatsoever I have – nothing much of this world, no bank balance, but what really matters: the taste of beauty, of love, of truth, of eternity...in short, of oneself.

What is the time, Devageet?

"Three minutes before eight, Osho."

So good. I have been hard on you too this morning. I will not say anything about it, only this much: with whomsoever I love, I forget that I have to behave. Then I start doing or saying things which are okay if I am alone, and that's what love is – to be with someone as if one were alone. But sometimes it can be hard on the other person.

I can always say "sorry," but it is so formal. And when I hit, and I hit often, it is so loving that a formal "sorry" won't do. But you can see my tears, they say more than I can...many times more. I remind you, in the future too I will be hard, perhaps harder on you. That's my way of being loving. I hope you will understand – if not today then tomorrow, or perhaps the day after tomorrow. More than that I cannot say, because at least for these two days I am booked. I am going to be here. It remains open, but for the next two days I am certainly going to be here.

I was saying that after one year we had left that state and that village. I have told you before that on the way my grandfather died. That was my first encounter with death, and it was a beautiful encounter. It was not in any way ugly, as it more or less happens for almost every child around the world. Fortunately I was together with my dying grandfather for hours, and he died slowly. By and by, I could feel death happening to him, and I could see the great silence of it.

I was also fortunate that my Nani was present. Perhaps without her I may have missed the beauty of death, because love and death are so similar, perhaps the same. She loved me. She showered her love upon me, and death was there, slowly happening. A bullock cart...I can still hear its sound...the rattling of its wheels on the stones...Bhoora continuously shouting to the bullocks...the sound of his whip hitting them.... I can hear it all still. It is so deeply rooted in my experience that I don't think even my death will erase it. Even while dying I may again hear the sound of that bullock cart.

My Nani was holding my hand, and I was completely dazed, not knowing what was happening, utterly in the moment. My grandfather's head was in my lap. I held my hands on his chest, and slowly slowly, the breathing disappeared. When I felt that he was no longer breathing I said to my grandmother, "I'm sorry, Nani, but it seems that he is no longer breathing."

She said, "That's perfectly okay. You need not be worried. He has lived enough, there is no need to ask for more." She also told me, "Remember, because these are the moments not to be forgotten: never ask for more. What is, is enough."

Is it enough? Just ten minutes for me; I will tell you when to stop. I am more in a hurry than you are. I seduced you at last.

Now I can say, with great joy, stop it.

Session 13

OKAY, REMOVE THE TOWEL. Ashu, forgive me, because now I have to begin my business, and you can understand that two shirts together on one chest is very difficult for the poor chest, particularly for the poor heart hidden behind the chest. The heart cannot behave in a political or diplomatic way. It is not a diplomat; it is simple and childlike.

I cannot forget Jesus. I remember him more than any Christians in the world. Jesus says, "Blessed are those who are like little children, for theirs is the kingdom of God." The most important thing to remember here is the word 'for'. In all Jesus' sayings which start with, "Blessed are those…" and end with "…the kingdom of God" this is the only statement which is unique, because all the other statements say, "Blessed are the humble *because* they will inherit the kingdom of God." They are logical and they are promises for the future – the future which does not exist. This is the only statement which says, "…*for* theirs is the kingdom of God." No future, no rationality, no reason, no promise for profit; just a pure statement of fact, or rather, a simple statement of fact.

I am always impressed by this statement, always amazed. I cannot believe that one can be amazed by the same statement again and again for thirty years…. Yes, for thirty years this statement has been with me, and it always brings a tremble of joy in my heart: "For theirs is the kingdom of God"… so illogical yet so true.

Ashu, I had to tell you to remove the towel because two businesses cannot go together, particularly on one heart. And you have been so good to me every day since I have known you, and when I try to remember when it began it seems as if I have known you forever. I'm not joking. Actually when I think of Ashu I cannot remember when she entered into my world of intimates. It seems she has always been there, sitting by my side, whether as a dental nurse or not. Now she has become an associate editor to Devaraj – that is a great promotion. Now you can have two doctors under you. Is it not great? – you can make them wrestle with each other, and enjoy it!

Now I come to my story.... Before the story it is always good to have a little introductory note, as irrational as possible, because that is exactly the right introduction to the man I am. Sometimes I laugh at myself, not for any reason...because when there is reason, laughter stops.

One can laugh only without reason. Laughter has no relationship with rationality, so once in a while I put away my rationality, and irrationality too – remember they are two sides of the same thing – and then I have a really hearty laugh.

Of course nobody can hear it. It is not of the physical, otherwise Devaraj and Devageet would have detected it with their instruments. They cannot detect it. It is transcendental to all instrumentality. Look what a beautiful word I have created: instrumentality. Write it exactly that way, instru-mental-ity. Then you can understand what I am saying – at least the words, and perhaps one day the wordless too. That's my hope, my dream for you all.

You will be worried, because today I am really taking too long to begin. You know me, I know you. I will go as slowly as possible. That will help to empty you. That's my whole business, emptying: you can call it "Emptying Unlimited."

The other day I was telling you that my grandfather's death was my first encounter with death. Yes, an encounter and something more; not just an encounter, otherwise I would have missed the real meaning of it. I saw the death, and something more that was not dying, that was floating above it, escaping from the body...the elements. That encounter determined my whole course of life. It gave me a direction, or rather a dimension, that was not known to me before.

I had heard of other people's deaths, but only heard. I had not seen, and even if I had seen, they did not mean anything to me.

Unless you love someone and he then dies, you cannot really encounter death. Let that be underlined:

Death can only be encountered in the death of the loved one.

When love plus death surrounds you, there is a transformation, an immense mutation, as if a new being is born. You are never the same again. But people do not love, and because they do not love they can't experience death the way I experienced it. Without love, death does not give you the keys to existence. With love, it hands over to you the keys to all that is.

My first experience of death was not a simple encounter. It was complex in many ways. The man I had loved was dying. I had known him as my father. He had raised me with absolute freedom, no inhibitions, no suppressions, and no commandments. He never said to me, "Don't do this," or "Do that." Only now can I realize the beauty of the man. It is very difficult for an old man not to say to a child, "Don't do that, do this," or "Just sit there, don't do anything," or "Do something; why are you just sitting there doing nothing?" But he never did. I don't remember a single instance where he even tried to interfere with my being. He simply withdrew. If he thought what I was doing was wrong, he withdrew and closed his eyes.

I once asked him, "Nana, why do you close your eyes sometimes when I am just sitting by your side?"

He said, "You will not understand today, but perhaps someday. I close my eyes so that I don't prevent you from doing whatsoever you are doing, whether it is right or wrong. It is not my business to prevent you. I have taken you away from your mother and father. If I cannot even give you freedom, then what was the point in taking you away from your parents? I only took you so that they would not interfere with you. How can I interfere?"

"But you know," he went on, "it is a great temptation sometimes. You are such a temptation. I never knew, otherwise I would not have taken the risk. Somehow you have a genius for finding the wrong things to do. I wonder," he said, "how you go on finding so many things to do wrong. Either I am completely insane, or you are."

I said, "Nana, you need not get worried. If anyone is insane, then it is me." And from that day I have been telling people, "Don't be bothered by me, I am a madman."

I had said that to console him, and I am still saying it to console people who really are mad. But when you are in a madhouse and you are the only one who is not mad, what can you do except say to everybody, "Relax, I am a madman, don't take me seriously." That's what I have been doing my whole life.

He used to close his eyes, but sometimes it was too much of a temptation.... For example, one day I was riding on Bhoora, our servant. I had ordered him to behave like a horse. First he looked bewildered, but my grandmother said, "What is wrong in that? Can't you act a little? Bhoora, behave like a horse." So he started doing everything a horse is supposed to do, and I was riding him.

That was too much in front of my grandfather. He closed his eyes and started chanting his mantra: *"Namo arihantanam namo...namo siddhanam namo."*

Of course I stopped, because when he started chanting his mantra that meant it was too much for him. It was time to stop. I shook him and said, "Nana, come back, there is no need to chant your mantra. I have stopped the game. Can't you see that it was only a game?"

He looked into my eyes, I looked into his eyes. For a moment there was just silence. He waited for me to speak. He had to yield; he said, "Okay, I should speak first."

I said, "That's right, because if you had remained silent, I was going to remain silent my whole life. It is good that you spoke, so now I can answer you. What do you want to ask?"

He said, "I have always wanted to ask you, why are you so mischievous?"

I said, "That is a question you should reserve for God. When you meet him, ask him, 'Why did you create this child so mischievous?' You cannot ask me that. It is almost like asking 'Why are you you?' Now, how can that be answered? As far as I am concerned, I am not concerned at all. I am just being myself. Is that allowed or not, in this house?" We were sitting outside in the garden.

He looked at me again and asked, "What do you mean?"

I said, "You understand perfectly what I mean. If I am not allowed to be myself then I won't enter this house again. So please be clear with me: either I enter this house with the license to be

myself, or I forget about this house and just be a wanderer, a vagabond. Tell me clearly and don't hesitate, come on!"

He laughed and said, "You can enter the house. It is your home.
If I cannot resist interfering with you then I will leave the house.
You need not."

That's exactly what he did. Just two months after this dialogue
he was no longer in this world. He not only left the house, he left
every house, even the body, which was his real house.

I loved the man because he loved my freedom. I can love only if
my freedom is respected. If I have to bargain and get love by paying
with my freedom, then that love is not for me. Then it is for lesser
mortals, it is not for those who know.

In this world almost everybody thinks that he loves, but if you
look around at the lovers, they are prisoners to each other. What a
strange kind of love is this love which creates bondage! Can love
ever become a bondage? But in ninety-nine point nine percent of
cases it does, because from the very beginning love was not there.

It is a fact that ordinarily people only think they love. They
don't love – because when love comes, where is 'I' and 'thou'?
When love comes, it immediately brings a tremendous sense of freedom, nonpossessiveness. But that love happens, unfortunately, very
rarely.

Love with freedom – if you have it, you are a king or a queen.
That is the real kingdom of God – love with freedom. Love gives
you the roots into the earth, and freedom gives you the wings.

My grandfather gave me both. He gave his love to me, more
than he ever had given to either my mother or even my grandmother; and he gave me freedom, which is the greatest gift. As he
was dying he gave me his ring, and with a tear in his eye told me,
"I don't have anything else to give you."

I said, "Nana, you have already given me the most precious gift."

He opened his eyes and said, "What is that?"

I laughed and said, "Have you forgotten? You have given me
your love and you have given me freedom. I think no child ever had
such freedom as you gave to me. What more do I need? What more
can you give? I am thankful. You can die peacefully." Since then I
have seen many people die, but to die peacefully is really difficult.

I have only seen five people die peacefully: the first was my grandfather; the second was my servant Bhoora; the third was my Nani; the fourth, my father, and the fifth was Vimalkirti.

Bhoora died just because he could not conceive of living in a world without his master. He simply died. He relaxed into death. He had come with us to my father's village because he had been driving the bullock cart. When for a few moments he heard nothing, no word from the inside of the covered cart, he asked me, "Beta" – it means son – "is everything okay?"

Again and again Bhoora asked, "Why this silence? Why is nobody speaking?" But he was the kind of man who would not look inside the curtain which divided him from us. How could he look inside when my grandmother was there? That was the trouble, he could not look. But again and again he asked, "What is the matter – why is everybody silent?"

I said, "There is nothing wrong. We are enjoying the silence. Nana wants us to be silent." That was a lie, because Nana was dead – but in a way it was true. He was silent; that was a message for us to be silent.

I finally said, "Bhoora, everything is okay; only Nana is gone."

He could not believe it. He said, "Then how can everything be okay? Without him I cannot live." And within twenty-four hours he died. Just as if a flower had closed…refusing to remain open in the sun and the moon, of his own accord. We tried everything to save him, because now we were in a bigger town, my father's town.

My father's town was, for India of course, just a small town. The population was only twenty thousand. It had a hospital and a school. We tried everything possible to save Bhoora. The doctor in the hospital was amazed because he could not believe that this man was Indian; he looked so European. He must have been a freak of biology, I don't know. Something must have gone right. As they say, "Something must have gone wrong," I have coined the phrase, "Something must have gone right" – why always wrong?

Bhoora was in shock because of his master's death. We had to lie to him until we got to the town. Only when we reached the town and the corpse was taken out of the bullock cart did Bhoora see what had happened. He then closed his eyes and never opened them again. He said, "I cannot see my master dead." And that was only a master-servant relationship. But there had arisen between them a certain intimacy, a certain closeness which is indefinable. He never opened his eyes again, that much I can vouch for. He lived only a few hours longer, and he went into a coma before dying.

Before my grandfather died, he had told my grandmother, "Take care of Bhoora. I know you will take care of Raja – I do not have to tell you that – but take care of Bhoora. He has served me as nobody else could."

I told the doctor, "Do you, can you, understand the kind of devotion that must have existed between these two men?"

The doctor asked me, "Is he a European?"

I said, "He looks like one."

The doctor said, "Don't be tricky. You are a child, only seven or eight years old, but very tricky. When I asked whether your grandfather was dead, you said no, and that was not true."

I said, "No, it was true: he is not dead. A man of such love cannot be dead. If love can be dead then there is no hope for the world. I cannot believe that a man who respected my freedom, a small child's freedom so much, is dead just because he cannot breathe. I cannot equate the two, not breathing and death."

The European doctor looked at me suspiciously and told my uncle, "This boy will either be a philosopher or else he will go mad." He was wrong: I am both together. There is no question of either/or. I am not Søren Kierkegaard; there is no question of either/or. But I wondered why he could not believe me...such a simple thing.

But simple things are the most difficult to believe; difficult things, the easiest to believe. Why should you believe? Your mind says, "It is so simple, there is no complexity at all. There is no reason to believe." Unless you are a Tertullian, whose statement is one of my most beloved....

If I had to choose only one statement from the whole of literature in any language of the world, I am sorry, I would not choose from Jesus Christ; and I am sorry, I would not choose from Gautam the Buddha either; I am sorry, I would not choose from either Moses or Mohammed, or even Lao Tzu or Chuang Tzu.

I would choose this strange fellow about whom nothing much is known – Tertullian. I don't know exactly how his name is pronounced, so it is better that I spell it out: T-e-r-t-u-l-l-i-a-n. The quote that I would have chosen over all others is, *"Credo qua absurdum"* – just three words – "I believe because it is absurd."

It seems someone must have asked him what he believes in and why, and Tertullian answered, *"Credo qua absurdum* – it is absurd, that's why I believe." The reason for believing given by Tertullian is *absurdum* – "because it is absurd."

For a moment forget Tertullian. Drop the curtain on him. Look at the roses. Why do you love them? Is it not absurd? There is no reason to love them. If someone persists in asking further why you love roses, you are finally going to shrug your shoulders. That is *"Credo qua absurdum,"* that shrug. That is the whole meaning of Tertullian's philosophy.

I could not understand why the doctor could not believe that my grandfather was not dead. I knew and he knew that as far as the body was concerned, it was finished; there was no quarrel about that. But there is something more than the body – in the body and yet not part of the body. Let me repeat it to emphasize it: in the body and yet not of the body. Love reveals it; freedom gives it wings to soar in the sky.

Is there more time?

"Yes, Osho."

How much? We are going very slow, just like a poor man's celebration. Go to the extreme. Not this way, not slowly – that's not my way. Either burn or don't burn at all. Either burn both ends together or let darkness have its own beauty.

Session 14

LOOK WHAT AN ENGLISH GENTLEMAN I am! Although I wanted to interfere, I didn't. I had already opened my mouth to speak but I stopped myself. This is called self-control. Even I can laugh. When you whisper it feels so good. Although I know that you are not whispering nonsense, it still sounds nice – although it is technical and what you are saying is perfectly scientific. But between the two of you, you know, the rascal is lying in the chair.

I have not yet said okay. First go to the point where I can say okay. When the "okay" is far from me it means something. An okay from me is just far out...I'm a faaar gone guy! I don't know anybody who is so spaced out. Now, to the work....

Tvadiyam vastu Govinda, tubhyam eva samarpayet: "My Lord, this life you have given to me, I surrender it back to you with my thanks." Those were the dying words of my grandfather, although he never believed in God and was not a Hindu. This sentence, this sutra, is a Hindu sutra – but in India things are mixed up, particularly good things. Before he died, among other things, he said one thing again and again: "Stop the wheel."

I could not understand it at the time. If we stopped the wheel of the cart, and that was the only wheel there was, then how could we reach the hospital? When he repeated again and again, "Stop the wheel, the *chakra*," I asked my grandmother, "Has he gone mad?"

She laughed.

That was the thing I liked in that woman. Even though she knew, as I did, that death was so close...if even I knew, how could it be possible that she did not know? It was so apparent that just at any moment he would stop breathing, yet he was insisting on stopping the wheel. Still she laughed. I can see her laughing now.

She was not more than fifty at the most. But I have always observed a strange thing about women: the phony ones, who pretend to be beautiful, at the age of forty-five are the ugliest. You can go around the world and see what I am saying. With all their lipstick and makeup, and false eyebrows and whatnot...my God!

Even God did not think of these things when he created the world. At least it is not mentioned in the Bible that on the fifth day he created lipstick, and on the sixth day he created false eyebrows etcetera. At the age of forty-five, if the woman is really beautiful she comes to her peak. My observation is: man comes to his peak at the age of thirty-five, and woman at the age of forty-five. She is capable of living ten years longer than a man – and it is not unjust. Giving birth to children she suffers so much that a little bit of extra life, just to compensate, is perfectly okay.

My Nani was fifty, still at the peak of her beauty and youth. I have never forgotten that moment – it was such a moment! My grandfather was dying and asking us to stop the wheel. What nonsense! How could I stop the wheel? We had to reach the hospital, and without the wheel we would be lost in the forest. And my grandmother was laughing so loudly that even Bhoora, the servant, our driver, asked, of course from the outside, "What is going on? Why are you laughing?" Because I used to call her Nani, Bhoora also used to call her Nani, just out of respect for me. He then said, "Nani, my master is sick and you are laughing so loudly; what's the matter? And why is Raja so silent?"

Death, and my grandmother's laughter, both made me utterly silent, because I wanted to understand what was happening. Something was happening that I had never known before and I was not going to lose a single moment through any distraction.

My grandfather said, "Stop the wheel. Raja, can't you hear me? If I can hear your grandmother's laughter you must be able to hear me. I know she is a strange woman; I have never been able to understand her."

I said to him, "Nana, as far as I know she is the simplest woman I have seen, although I have not seen much yet."

But now to you I can say, I don't think there is any man on the earth, alive or dead, who has seen so much of women as I have. But just to console my dying grandfather I said to him, "Don't be worried about her laughter. I know her. She is not laughing at what you are saying, it is something else between us, a joke that I told her."

He said, "Okay. If it is a joke that you told her then it is perfectly okay for her to laugh. But what about the chakra, the wheel?"

Now I know, but at that time I was absolutely unacquainted with such terminology. The wheel represents the whole Indian obsession with the wheel of life and death. For thousands of years, millions of people have been doing only one thing: trying to stop the wheel. He was not talking about the wheel of the bullock cart – that was very easy to stop; in fact it was difficult to keep it moving.

There was no road – not only at that time, even now! Last year one of my distant cousins visited the ashram, and he said, "I wanted to bring my whole life to your feet, but the real difficulty is the road."

I said, "Still?"

Almost fifty years have passed, but India is such a country that there, time stands still. Who knows when the clock stopped? But it stopped exactly at twelve, with both hands together. That's beautiful: the clock decided the right time. Whenever it happened – and it must have happened thousands of years ago, whenever it happened – the clock, either by chance or by some computerized intelligence, stopped at twelve, with both hands together. You cannot see them as two, you can only see them as one. Perhaps it was twelve o'clock at night...because the country is so dark, and the darkness is so dense.

"My God," the man said to me, "I could not bring the whole family to see you because of the roads."

Perhaps they will never see me, just because of the roads. No roads existed then, and even today no railway line passes by that village. It is a really poor village, and when I was a child it was even poorer.

I could not understand at that moment why my Nana was so insistent. Perhaps the bullock cart – because there was no road – was making too much noise. Everything was rattling, and he was in agony, so naturally he wanted to stop the wheel. But my grand-mother laughed. Now I know why she laughed. He was talking about the Indian obsession with life and death, symbolically called the wheel of life and death – and in short, the wheel – which goes on and on.

In the Western world only Friedrich Nietzsche had the guts and the madness enough to propose the idea of eternal recurrence. He borrowed it from the Eastern obsession. He was very impressed by two books. One was *Manu Smriti*. It is called *The Collection of Manu's Verses;* it is the most important Hindu scripture. I hate it! You can understand its importance. I cannot hate anything ordi-nary. It is extra-ordinarily ugly. Manu is one of the men that if I see him I will forget all about nonviolence; I will just shoot him! He deserves it.

Manu Samhita, Manu Smriti – why do I call it the ugliest book in the world? Because it divides men and women – and not only men and women, but it divides humanity into four classes, and nobody can cross from one class to another. It creates a hierarchy.

You will be surprised to know that Adolf Hitler always had a copy of *Manu Samhita* on his desk, just by the side of his bed. He respected that book more than the Bible. Now you can understand why I hate it. I don't even have a copy of *Manu Samhita* in my library, although I have been presented with at least a dozen copies, but I always burned them. That was the only way to behave with it. Respectfully, of course, I burned it.

Nietzsche loved two books and borrowed from them immensely. The first was *Manu Samhita* and the other was the *Mahabharata*. This book is perhaps the greatest as far as volume is concerned; it is huge! I don't think that the *Bible*, the *Koran, Dhammapada, Tao Te Ching* can even compare with it as far as volume is concerned. You can only understand me if you put it by the side of *Encyclopaedia Britannica*. Compared to the *Mahabharata* the *Encyclopaedia Britan-nica* is just a small book. It is certainly a great work, but ugly.

Scientists know perfectly well that there have been many very huge animals on the earth in the past – almost mountainous, but very ugly. *Mahabharata* belongs among those animals. Not that you cannot find anything beautiful in it; it is so big that if you dig deep you can certainly find a mouse here and there in the mountain.

Those two books influenced Nietzsche immensely. Perhaps nothing was more responsible for Friedrich Nietzsche's work than those two books. One is by Manu, and *Mahabharata* was written by Vyasa. I must concede that both books have done a tremendous amount of work, dirty work! It would have been better if these two books had not been written at all.

Friedrich Nietzsche remembers both books with such respect that you would be amazed – amazed because this was the man who called himself "anti-Christ." But don't be amazed. Those two books are anti-Christ, in fact they are anti-anything that is beautiful: anti-truth, anti-love. It is no coincidence that Nietzsche fell in love with them. Although he never liked Lao Tzu or Buddha, he liked Manu and Krishna. Why?

The question is very significant. He liked Manu because he loved the idea of hierarchy. He was against democracy, freedom, equality; in short he was against all true values. He also loved Vyasa's book *Mahabharata* because it contains the concept that only war is beautiful. He once wrote in a letter to his sister, "This very moment I am surrounded by immense beauty. I have never seen such beauty." One would think that he had entered the Garden of Eden, but no, he was watching a military parade. The sun was shining on their naked swords, and the sound which he calls "the most beautiful sound I have ever heard" was not Beethoven or Mozart, not even Wagner, but the sound of the boots of the marching German soldiers.

Wagner was Nietzsche's friend, and not only that, but something more: Nietzsche had fallen in love with his friend's wife. At least he should have thought of the poor man…but no, he thought that neither Beethoven, nor Mozart, nor Wagner, nobody could compare with the beautiful music from the boots of the German soldiers. For him swords in the sun and the sound of the parading army were the very ultimate in beauty.

Great aesthetics! And remember, I am not a man who is against Friedrich Nietzsche as such. I appreciate him whenever he comes close to truth, but truth is my value and my criterion. "Swords in the sun" and "the sound of the marching boots" – when he goes away from truth, then whatsoever he is, I am going to hit his head with a naked sword. And how beautiful it looks: the naked sword, and the sound of the head of Friedrich Nietzsche being cut off, and the beautiful blood all around.... This is what his disciple, Adolf Hitler, did.

Hitler got Manu's ideas from Nietzsche. Hitler was not a man who could have found Manu on his own; he was a pygmy. Nietzsche was certainly a genius, but a genius gone astray. He was a man who could have become a buddha, but alas he died only as a madman.

I was telling you about the Indian obsession, and in that reference remembered Nietzsche. He was the first in the West to recognize the idea of "eternal recurrence." But he was not honest; he did not say that the idea was borrowed. He pretended to be original. It is so easy to pretend to be original, very easy; it does not need much intelligence. And yet he was a man of genius. He never used his genius to discover anything; he used it to borrow from sources which were not ordinarily known to the world at large. Who knows Manu's *Samhita*? – and who cares? Manu wrote it five thousand years ago. And who bothers about *Mahabharata*? It is such a big book that unless one wants to really go insane one would not read it.

But there are people who read even the *Encyclopaedia Britannica*. I know such a person; he was my personal friend. This is the moment when I should at least remember his name. He may still be alive – that's my only fear – but then too, there is no reason to be afraid, simply because he only reads the *Encyclopaedia Britannica*. He will never read what I am saying – never, never; he has no time. He not only reads the *Encyclopaedia Britannica*, he memorizes it – and that is his madness. Otherwise he looks very normal. When you mention anything that is part of his encyclopaedia he immediately becomes abnormal, and starts quoting pages and pages and pages. He does not bother at all whether you want to listen or not.

Only such people read *Mahabharata*. It is the Hindu encyclopaedia; let's call it the "Encyclopaedia Indiana." Naturally it is bound to be bigger than *Encyclopaedia Britannica*. Britain is just Britain – no bigger than a small state in India. India has at least three dozen states of that size – and that is not the whole of India, because half of India is now Pakistan. If you really want the full picture of India then you will have to make a few more additions.

Burma was once part of India. It was only early in this century that it was disconnected from India. Afghanistan was once part of India; it is almost a continent. So *Mahabharata*, the "Encyclopaedia Indiana," is bound to be a thousandfold bigger than the *Encyclopaedia Britannica*, which is only thirty-two volumes. That is nothing. If you collect all that I have said, it would be more than that.

Somebody else has counted. I don't know for sure because I never do such rubbishy things, but they estimated that I had written three hundred and thirty-three books, up till now. Great! – not the books, but the man who counted them. He should wait, because many are still in manuscript, and many others are not yet translated from the Hindi originals. When all that is collected it will really be the "Encyclopaedia Rajneeshica." But *Mahabharata* is bigger, and will always remain the largest book in the world – I mean in volume, in weight.

I mention it because I was talking about the Indian obsession. The whole of the *Mahabharata* is nothing but the Indian obsession written at length, voluminously, saying that man is born again and again and again, eternally.

That's why my grandfather was saying, "Stop the wheel." If I could have stopped the wheel I would have stopped it, not only for him but for everybody else in the world. Not only would I have stopped it, I would have destroyed it forever so that nobody could ever turn it again. But it is not in my hands.

But why this obsession?

I became aware of many things at that moment of his death. I will talk about everything that I became aware of in that moment, because that has determined my whole life.

Session 15

    . . .

I HAVE ALWAYS LOVED THE STORY told of Henry Ford. He had made his most beautiful car, and he was showing it to a prosperous, very prosperous and promising customer. It was his latest model, and he took the customer for a ride. After thirty miles the car suddenly stopped.

The customer said, "What! A new car and it stops after just thirty miles?"

Ford said, "Excuse me, sir. I forgot to put petrol in it."

In those days, even in America, it was called petrol, not gas.

The customer was amazed. He said, "What do you mean? Are you saying that this car was running without petrol for thirty miles?"

Ford said, "Yes, sir. For thirty or forty miles just my name is enough: no petrol is needed."

Once I am off, just I am enough – nothing else is needed. I could not sleep the whole night. It was not a trouble to me – it was a beautiful night in a way. The moon was so bright...perhaps the beauty and the brightness of the moon did not allow me to sleep. But no, that cannot be the cause. I think the cause was that I was a little too hard on Devageet. Yes, I can be very hard. I am not hard, but I can be very hard, particularly at certain moments when I see a possibility of some opening in you. Then I really hit! – not with a small hammer, but with a sledgehammer. When one has to hit, why choose a small hammer? Be finished in a single hit! Sometimes I am very hard, that's why sometimes I have to be very soft – just to compensate, to bring balance.

When I left the room, although you were smiling it was a little sad. I could not forget it. It is very easy for me to forget anything;

but if I have been hard, then it is not easy. I can forgive anyone in the world except myself. Perhaps that was the reason that I could not sleep. My sleep anyway is just a thin layer. Underneath I am always awake. The thin layer can be very easily disturbed, but only by me, not anybody else.

The moment I left the room and saw you looking a little sad... maybe for many reasons, not only that I had hit you. But whatsoever the reasons for your sadness, I had in some way deepened the darkness in you. And I am here to enlighten you, not to endarken you – if that word is allowed. In fact we should make it a word, 'endarken', because so many people go on endarkening each other. It is strange that the word does not exist although the reality is there. Enlightenment rarely happens and yet we have a word for that. We still don't have a word for that which goes beyond enlightenment, but perhaps there is a limit to everything. Something is always going to be beyond, far away, not within words but transcendental.

But 'endarken' should become a commonly used word. Everybody is endarkening everybody else. The husband is endarkening the wife; otherwise what is he doing in the dark? Just endarkening his wife. And what is the wife doing? He is a fool if he thinks only he is endarkening her. In the dark she is endarkening him more than he could ever manage. Anyway he needs glasses – she does not need them yet. He is only a poor head clerk, so of course he needs glasses. What is she? She is only a mother, a wife. She does not need glasses.

In darkness, be aware of the woman you love – particularly in darkness. Perhaps that's why man uses light. Men love the light while they are loving; they keep their eyes open when they make love. Women keep their eyes closed. They cannot look without giggling at the ugliness of the whole thing that is going on – the baboon sitting over them, and all that...etcetera, etcetera, etcetera.

I became a little sorry. I say a little, because for me just to be a little sorry is too much. Only one of my tears is enough. I need not cry for hours, and tear my hair out...which is no longer there. No one has ever heard of tearing out one's beard. I don't think in any language, not even Hebrew, such an expression exists: "tearing out one's beard." And you know the Hebrews and their biblical prophets – they all had beards. It is a natural law that if you have a beard you will become bald, because nature always keeps in balance.

Now I remember my grandmother again....

Although I was small, she used to say to me, "Listen, Raja, never grow a beard."

I would say, "Why do you mention it? I am only ten, my beard has not yet even started. Why mention it?"

She said, "One has to dig a well before the house is on fire."

My God! She was really digging a well before the house was on fire. She was really a beautiful woman. I never understood her answer and said, "Okay, go on, say what you want to say."

She said, "Never, never grow a beard...although I know you will."

I said, "This is strange. If you know already, then why are you trying to prevent it?"

She said, "I am trying my best, but I know you will grow a beard. People like you always grow beards. I have known you for eleven years; there must be some reason for it." And she started to ponder over it.

There is nothing much in it; it is just that one does not want to waste one's time every day looking in the mirror like a fool, shaving one's beard. Just think of a woman with a beard, looking in the mirror – how would she look? A man without a beard looks exactly like that. It is simple: it saves time, and it saves you from looking like a fool, at least in your own mirror.

But one thing is certain: the moment you start growing a beard you start getting bald. Nature always remembers to keep in balance. It can only give you so many hairs. If you start growing a beard, then of course the budget has to be cut from somewhere. It is simple economics, ask any bookkeeper.

I was just a little bit concerned about Devageet, feeling as if I had hurt him. Perhaps I had done it...perhaps it was needed. So don't worry about my sleep. If something is needed, I am always ready to lose my life at any moment – not for any national cause, not for any state, nor any race, but for any individual, for anyone whose heart still beats, who still feels, and is capable of all childish things. Remember, I am saying "childish things." I mean one who is still a child. I am ready to give my life if he can grow, mature, and become integrated. Whenever I use the word 'integration', I always mean intelligence plus love; that is equal to integration.

Now, this has been a long footnote. If George Bernard Shaw can be forgiven, and not only forgiven but given a Nobel Prize, then you can forgive me too. And I don't ask for a Nobel Prize. Even if they gave me the prize, I would refuse it. It is not for me – it is too full of blood.

The money given with the Nobel Prize is soaked in blood, because the man, Nobel, was a manufacturer of bombs. He earned his immeasurable money in the first world war selling arms to both camps. I would not even like to touch his money. In fact I have not touched money for many years, because I don't have to. Somebody always takes care of money for me – and money is always dirty, not only Nobel Prize money.

The man who founded the Nobel Prize was really feeling guilty, and just to get rid of his guilt he founded the Nobel Prize. It was a good gesture, but only like killing a man and then saying to him, "Sorry, sir, please excuse me." I would not accept that blood money.

George Bernard Shaw was not only respected but given a Nobel Prize, and his small books have such long introductions that you wonder whether the book was written for the introduction, or the introduction for the book. As far as I can see the book was written for the introduction, and that's what I appreciate.

So this has been a long introductory note. Don't be worried about my sleep, but remember not to get disturbed if I am hard. Although you know, and everybody knows, that nothing can make any change in me, many things can certainly change in my body and even my mind. Of course I am neither my body nor my mind, but I have to function through them.

Right now I can see that my lips are dry. Now, that much can be done by anything from the outside. I am speaking, but the dry lips are creating trouble. I will manage, but they are a hindrance. Deva-geet, you can help – do your trick. That will be a good break from this introductory note and then I can start. Thank you....

Now the story.

Death is not the end but only the culmination of one's whole life, a climax. It is not that you are finished, but you are transported to another body. That is what the Easterners call "the wheel." It goes on turning and turning. Yes, it can be stopped, but the way to stop it is not when you are dying.

That is one of the lessons, the greatest lesson I learned from my grandfather's death. He was crying, with tears in his eyes, and asking us to stop the wheel. We were at a loss what to do: how to stop the wheel?

His wheel was his wheel; it was not even visible to us. It was his own consciousness, and only he could do it. Since he was asking us to stop it, it was obvious that he could not do it himself; hence the tears and his constant insistence on asking us again and again, as if we were deaf. We told him, "We have heard you, Nana, and we understand. Please be silent."

In that moment something great happened. I have never revealed it to anybody; perhaps before this moment was not the time. I was saying to him, "Please be silent" – the bullock cart was rattling on the rough, ugly road. It was not even a road, just a track, and he was insisting, "Stop the wheel, Raja, do you hear? Stop the wheel."

Again and again I told him, "Yes, I do hear you. I understand what you mean. You know that nobody except you can stop the wheel, so please be silent. I will try to help you."

My grandmother was amazed. She looked at me with such big, amazing eyes: what was I saying? How could I help?

I said, "Yes. Don't look so amazed. I have suddenly remembered one of my past lives. Seeing his death I have remembered one of my own deaths." That life and death happened in Tibet. That is the only country which knows, very scientifically, how to stop the wheel. Then I started chanting something.

Neither my grandmother could understand, nor my dying grandfather, nor my servant Bhoora, who was listening intently from the outside. And what is more, neither could I understand a single word of what I was chanting. It was only after twelve or thirteen years that I came to understand what it was. It took that much time to discover it. It was *Bardo Thodal,* a Tibetan ritual.

When a man dies in Tibet, they repeat a certain mantra. That mantra is called *bardo*. The mantra says to him, "Relax, be silent. Go to your center, just be there; don't leave it whatsoever happens to the body. Just be a witness. Let it happen, don't interfere. Remember, remember, remember that you are only a witness; that is your true nature. If you can die remembering, the wheel is stopped."

I repeated the *Bardo Thodal* for my dying grandfather without even knowing what I was doing. It was strange – not only that I repeated it, but also that he became utterly silent listening to it. Perhaps Tibetan was such a strange thing to hear. He may never have heard a single word in Tibetan before; he may not even have known that there was a country called Tibet. Even in his death he became utterly attentive and silent. The *bardo* worked although he could not understand it. Sometimes things you don't understand work; they work just because you don't understand.

No great surgeon can operate on his own child. Why? No great surgeon can operate on his own beloved. I don't mean his wife – anyone can operate on his wife – I mean his beloved, who certainly is not his wife and can never be. To reduce your beloved into your wife is a crime. It is of course unpunished by law, but nature itself punishes, so there is no need for any law.

No lover can be reduced into a husband. It is so ugly to have a husband. The very word is ugly. It comes from the same root as 'husbandry'; the husband is one who uses the woman as a field, a farm, to sow his seed. The word 'husband' has to be completely erased from every language in the world. It is inhuman. A lover is understandable but not a husband!

I was repeating the *bardo* though I did not understand its meaning, nor did I know where it was coming from, because I had not read it yet. But when I repeated it just the shock of those strange words made my grandfather silent. He died in that silence.

To live in silence is beautiful, but to die in silence is far more beautiful, because death is like an Everest, the highest peak in the Himalayas. Although nobody taught me, I learned much in that moment of his silence. I saw myself repeating something absolutely strange. It shocked me to a new plane of being and pushed me into a new dimension. I started on a new search, a pilgrimage.

On this pilgrimage I have met many more remarkable men than Gurdjieff recounts in his book *Meetings with Remarkable Men*. By and by, as and when it happens, I will talk about them. Today I can talk about one of those remarkable men.

His real name is not known, nor his real age, but he was called "Magga Baba." *Magga* simply means "big cup." He always used to keep his magga, his cup, in his hand. He used it for everything – for his tea, his milk, his food, for the money people gave him, or whatsoever the moment demanded. All he possessed was his magga and that is why he was known as Magga Baba. *Baba* is a respectful word. It simply means grandfather, your father's father. In Hindi your mother's father is nana, your father's father is baba.

Magga Baba was certainly one of the most remarkable men that may ever have lived on this planet. He was really one of the chosen ones. You can count him with Jesus, Buddha, Lao Tzu. I know nothing about his childhood or his parents. Nobody knows from where he came – one day suddenly he appeared in the town.

He did not speak. People persisted in asking questions of all kinds. He either remained silent, or if they nagged too much he started shouting gibberish, rubbish, just meaningless sounds. Those poor people thought he was speaking in a language that perhaps they didn't understand. He was not using language at all. He was just making sounds. For example, *"Higgalal hoo hoo hoo guloo higga hee hee."* Then he would wait and again ask, *"Hee hee hee?"* It seemed as if he was asking, "Have you understood?"

And the poor people would say, "Yes, Baba, yes."

Then he would show his magga and make the sign. This sign in India means money. It comes from the old days when there were real gold and silver coins. People used to check whether it was real gold or not by throwing the coin to the ground and listening to its sound. Real gold has its own sound, and nobody can fake it. So Magga Baba would show his magga with one hand and with the other give the sign for money, meaning, "If you have understood then give something to me." And people would give.

I would laugh myself to tears because he had not said anything. But he was not greedy for money. He would take from one person and give it to another. His magga was always empty. Once in a while

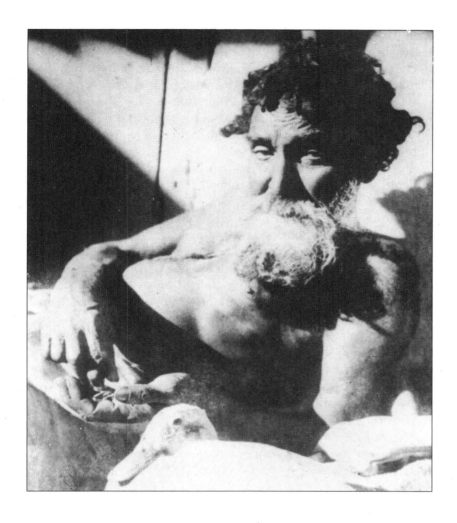

MAGGA BABA

there would be something in it, but rarely. It was a passage: money would come into it and go; food would come into it and go; and it always remained empty. He was always cleaning it. I have seen him morning, evening and afternoon, always cleaning it.

I want to confess to you – 'you' means the world – that I was the only person to whom he used to speak, but only in privacy, when nobody else was present. I would go to him deep in the night, perhaps two o'clock in the morning, because that was the most likely time to find him alone. He would be hugged up in his old blanket, on a winter's night, by the side of a fire. I would sit at his side for a while. I never disturbed him; that was the one reason why he loved me. Once in a while it would happen that he would turn on his side, open his eyes and see me sitting there and start talking of his own accord.

He was not a Hindi-speaking person, so people thought it was difficult to communicate with him, but that is not true. He was certainly not a Hindi-oriented person, but he knew not only Hindi but many other languages too. Of course he knew the language of silence the most; he remained silent almost all his life. In the day he would not speak to anybody, but in the night he would speak to me, only when I was alone. It was such a blessing to hear his few words.

Magga Baba never said anything about his own life, but he said many things about life. He was the first man who told me, "Life is more than what it appears to be. Don't judge by its appearances but go deep down into the valleys where the roots of life are." He would suddenly speak, and suddenly he would be silent. That was his way. There was no way to persuade him to speak: either he spoke or not. He would not answer any questions, and the conversations between us two were an absolute secret. Nobody knew about it. This is for the first time that I am saying it.

I have heard many great speakers, and he was just a poor man, but his words were pure honey, so sweet and nourishing, and so pregnant with meaning. "But," he told me, "you are not to tell anybody that I have been speaking to you until I die, because many people think I am deaf. It is good for me that they think so. Many think that I am mad – that is even better as far as I am concerned. Many who are very intellectual try to figure out what I say, and it is just gibberish. I wonder, when I hear the meaning that they have derived from it. I say to myself, 'My God! If these people are the intellectuals, the professors, the pundits, the scholars, then what about the poor crowd? I had not said anything, yet they have made up so many things out of nothing, just like soap bubbles.'"

For some reason, or maybe for no reason at all, he loved me.

I have had the fortune to be loved by many strange people. Magga Baba is the first on my list.

The whole day he was surrounded by people. He was really a free man, yet not even free to move a single inch because people were holding on to him. They would put him into a rickshaw and take him away wherever they wanted. Of course he would not say no, because he was pretending to be either deaf or dumb or mad. And he never uttered any word that could be found in any dictionary. Obviously he could not say yes or no; he would simply go.

Once or twice he was stolen. He disappeared for months because people from another town had stolen him. When the police found him and asked him whether he wanted to return, of course he did his thing again. He said some nonsense, *"Yuddle fuddle shuddle...."*

The police said, "This man is mad. What are we going to write in our reports: *'Yuddle fuddle shuddle'*? What does it mean? Can anyone make any sense out of it?" So he remained there until he was stolen back again by a crowd from the original town. That was my town where I was living soon after the death of my grandfather.

I visited him almost every night without fail, under his neem tree, where he used to sleep and live. Even when I was sick and my grandmother would not allow me to go out, even then, during the night when she was asleep, I would escape. But I had to go; Magga Baba had to be visited at least once each day. He was a kind of spiritual nourishment.

He helped me tremendously although he never gave any directions except by his very being. Just by his very presence he triggered unknown forces in me, unknown to me. I am most grateful to this man Magga Baba, and the greatest blessing of all was that I, a small child, was the only one to whom he used to speak. Those moments of privacy, knowing that he spoke to no one else in the whole world, were tremendously strengthening, vitalizing.

If sometimes I would go to him and somebody else was present, he would do something so terrible that the other person would escape. For example he would throw things, or jump, or dance like a madman, in the middle of the night. Anybody was bound to become afraid – after all, you have a wife, children, and a job, and this man seems to be just mad; he could do anything. Then, when the person had gone, we would both laugh together.

I have never laughed like that with anybody else, and I don't think it is going to happen again in this lifetime...and I don't have any other life. The wheel has stopped. Yes, it is running a little bit, but that is only past momentum; no new energy is being fed into it.

Magga Baba was so beautiful that I have not seen any other man who can be put by his side. He was just like a Roman sculpture, just perfect – even more perfect than any sculpture can be, because he was alive, so full of life I mean. I don't know whether it is possible to meet a man like Magga Baba again, and I don't want to either because one Magga Baba is enough, more than enough. He was so satisfying – and who cares for repetition? And I know perfectly, one cannot be higher than that.

I myself have come to the point where you cannot go any higher. Howsoever high you go, you are still on the same height. In other words, there comes a moment in spiritual growth which is untranscendable. That moment is called, paradoxically, the transcendental.

The day he left for the Himalayas was the first time he called me. During the night somebody came to my house and knocked on the door. My father opened it and the man said that Magga Baba wanted me.

My father said, "Magga Baba? What has he to do with my son? Moreover he never speaks, so how could he call for him?"

The man said, "I am not concerned about anything else. This was all I had to convey. Please tell the person concerned. If it happens to be your son, that is not my business." And the man disappeared.

My father woke me in the middle of the night and said, "Listen, this is something: Magga Baba wants you. In the first place he does not speak...."

I laughed because I knew he spoke to me, but I did not tell my father.

He went on, "He wants you right now, in the middle of the night. What do you want to do? Do you want to go to this madman?"

I said, "I have to go."

He said, "Sometimes I think that you are a little mad too. Okay, go, and lock the door from the outside so that you don't disturb me again when you come in."

I rushed, I ran. This was the first time he had called me. When I got to him I said, "What's the matter?"

He said, "This is my last night here. I am leaving perhaps forever. You are the only one I have spoken to. Forgive me, I had to speak to that man I sent to you, but he knows nothing. He does not know me as a spiritual man. He was a stranger and I bribed him simply by giving him one rupee, and told him to deliver the message to your house."

In those days, one gold rupee was so much. Forty years ago in India one gold rupee was almost enough to live on, in perfect comfort, for one month. Do you know the English word 'rupee' comes from the Hindi word *rupaiya* which means "the golden"? In fact the paper note should not be called a rupee; it is not golden. At least the fools could have painted it in golden colors, but they didn't even do that. One rupee of those days is almost seven hundred rupees of today. So much has changed in just forty years. Things have become seven hundred times costlier.

He said, "I just gave him one rupee and told him to deliver the message. He was so bewildered by the rupee that he did not even look at me. He was a stranger – I have never seen him before."

I said, "I can also say the same. I have never seen the man either in this town; perhaps he is a passer-by. But there is no need to be worried about it. Why did you have to call me?"

Magga Baba said, "I am leaving and there is nobody whom I could call to say goodbye to. You are the only one." He hugged me, kissed my forehead, said goodbye and went away, just like that.

Magga Baba had disappeared many times in his life – people had taken him and brought him back again – so when he disappeared last, nobody bothered much. Only after a few months did people become aware that he had really disappeared, that he had not come back for many months. They started looking around the places he had been before but nobody knew about him.

That night, before he disappeared he told me, "I may not be able to see you blossom to a flower but my blessings will be with you. It may not be possible for me to return. I am going to the Himalayas.

Don't say anything to anybody about my whereabouts." He was so happy when he was saying this to me, so blissful that he was going to the Himalayas. The Himalayas have always been the home of all those who have searched and found.

I didn't know where he had gone because the Himalayas is the biggest range of mountains in the world, but once while traveling in the Himalayas I came to a place which seemed to be his grave. Strange to say it was by the side of Moses and Jesus. Those two persons are also buried deep in the Himalayas. I had gone there to see the grave of Jesus; it was just a coincidence that I found Moses and Magga Baba too. It was a surprise of course. I could never have imagined that Magga Baba had anything to do with Moses or Jesus, but seeing his grave there I understood immediately why his face was so beautiful; why he looked more like Moses than any other Hindu. Perhaps he belonged to the lost tribe. Moses had lost a tribe while he was on the way to Israel. That tribe settled in Kashmir in the Himalayas. And I say it authoritatively, that that tribe was more correct in finding Israel than Moses himself. What Moses found in Israel was just a desert, utterly useless. What they had found in Kashmir was really the garden of God.

Moses went there in search of his lost tribe. Jesus also went there after his so-called crucifixion. I'm calling it so-called because it did not really happen, he remained alive. After six hours on the cross Jesus was not dead. The way Jews used to crucify people was such a crude method that it took almost thirty-six hours for a person to die.

It was arranged by a very rich disciple of Jesus that the crucifixion should happen on a Friday. It was an arrangement...because on Saturday Jews don't allow any work to be continued; it is their holy day. Jesus had to be put down off the cross into a cave temporarily, until the coming Monday. Meanwhile he was stolen from the cave.

That's the story Christians tell. The real fact is that on the night he was in the cave, after having been taken down from the cross, he was taken away from Israel. He was alive although he had lost much blood. It took a few days to heal him, but he was healed and he lived up to the age of one hundred and twelve in a small village called Pahalgam in the Kashmiri Himalayas.

He chose the place, Pahalgam, because he found the grave of

Moses there. Moses had gone before him to search for his lost tribe. He found it, but also found that Israel is nothing compared to Kashmir. There is no other place to be compared to Kashmir. He lived and died there – I mean Moses. And when Jesus went to Kashmir with Thomas, his beloved disciple, he sent Thomas to show India his way. He himself lived in Kashmir, near the grave of Moses, for his remaining life.

Magga Baba is buried in the same small village of Pahalgam. When I was in Pahalgam I discovered a strange relationship running from Moses to Jesus to Magga Baba and to me.

Before Magga Baba left my village he gave me his blanket saying, "This is my only possession and you are the only one I would like to give it to."

I said, "That's okay, but my father will not allow me to bring this blanket inside the house."

He laughed, I laughed…we both enjoyed. He knew perfectly well that my father would not allow such a dirty blanket in his house. But I was sad and sorry not to have preserved that blanket. It was nothing much – a dirty old rag – but it belonged to a man of the category of Buddha and Jesus. I could not take it to my house because my father was a clothes merchant and very careful about clothes. I knew perfectly well that he would not allow it. I could not take it to my grandmother's house either. She would not allow it because she was very fussy about cleanliness.

I have got my fussiness about cleanliness from her. It is her fault, not my responsibility at all. I cannot tolerate anything used or dirty – impossible. I used to say to her, laughingly of course, "You are spoiling me."

But it is a truth. She has spoiled me forever, but I am grateful to her. She spoiled me in favor of purity, cleanliness and beauty.

To me Magga Baba was important, but if I had to choose between my Nani and him I would still choose my Nani. Although she was not enlightened then and Magga Baba was, sometimes an unenlightened person is so beautiful that one would choose them, even though the enlightened one is available as an alternative.

Of course if I could choose both I would. Or, if I had a choice of two among the whole world of millions of people, then I would

135

have them both. Magga Baba on the outside…he wouldn't enter my grandmother's house; he would remain outside under his neem tree. And of course my Nani could not sit at the side of Magga Baba. "That fellow!" she used to call him. "That fellow! Forget about him and never go close to him. Even when you just pass by him, always take a shower." She was always afraid he had lice, because nobody had ever seen him take a bath.

Perhaps she was right: he had never taken a bath as long as I had known him. They could not exist together, that too is true. Coexistence could not be possible in this case – but we could always make arrangements. Magga Baba could always be under the neem tree outside in the courtyard, and Nani could be the queen in the house. And I could have the love of them both, without having to choose this or that. I hate "either/or."

What is the time?

"Sixteen minutes past ten, Osho."

Five minutes for me. Be kind to a poor man, and after five minutes you can stop.

Session 16   ...

T HERE ARE SIX GREAT RELIGIONS in the world. They can be divided into two categories: one consists of Judaism, Christianity and Islam. They believe in only one life. You are just between birth and death, there is nothing beyond birth and death – life is all. Although they believe in heaven and hell and God, they are the earnings from one life, a single life. The other category consists of Hinduism, Jainism and Buddhism. They believe in the theory of reincarnation. One is born again and again, eternally – unless one becomes enlightened, and then the wheel stops.

That was what my grandfather was asking while he was dying, but I was not aware of the whole significance of it...although I repeated the *bardo* just like a machine, without even understanding what I was saying or doing. Now I can understand the poor man's concern. You can call it "the ultimate concern." If it becomes diseased, as it has in the East, then it is an obsession, then I condemn it. Then it is more of a disease; it is not something to be praised but really condemned.

Obsession is a psychological way of condemning something; hence I have used the word. As far as the masses in the East are concerned, it has been a disease for thousands of years. It has stopped them from being rich, prosperous and affluent, because their whole concern was how to stop the wheel. Who then is going to grease it and who is going to run it smoothly?

Of course I need my sannyasins to keep the wheels of the Rolls rolling. Just a little noise and they are in trouble...even a sweet noise. For two days one of the Rolls Royces was making a little noise – it happens once in a while – very sweet, like a small bird singing in the trees. But it should not be so; a Rolls is not supposed to be a bird. And where is the noise coming from? From the steering wheel. I cannot tolerate it. As you know, I am not an intolerant man – but a new Rolls Royce starting to sing, and that too in the steering wheel?

In fact, I don't know anything about what is under the bonnet. I have never looked and I don't ever want to. That is not my business. But I must say the noise is sweet, just like a very tiny bird whistling. But it has to be stopped. A Rolls Royce is not meant to whistle, sweetly or not. And what are the guys doing? Their whole function is – and their meditation too – just to keep the Rolls Royces in perfect working order. Even if the other two guys, Rolls and Royce, were to be born again, they would be jealous because we have been trying to improve on what they have done. Of course the Rolls is the best car in the world, but it is not unimprovable. It can be, and should be, improved…and I don't want its wheels to be stopped.

Indians are obsessed. It has become a disease of the soul to stop the wheel of life and death. Of course to them, the wheel always reminds them of the bullock cart. If they want to stop it I am in perfect agreement. But there are better wheels; one need not stop all of them. In fact the very idea not to be born again simply shows that you have not lived. It may seem contradictory to you, but let me say it: only one who has totally lived stops the wheel of life and death. Yet those who want to stop it are those who have lived not at all. They will die a dog's death.

I am not against dogs – please note it – I am just using a metaphor. And it must be significant, because in Hindi there is also the same metaphor. It is the only metaphor which is similar in both Hindi and English. In fact, not similar but the same: *kutte ki maut* – "a dog's death." It is exactly the same. There must be something in it. To discover what it is I will have to tell you a story.

It is said that when God made the world – remember it is only a story – when God made the world, men and women, animals and trees and everything, he gave everybody the same age limit: twenty years.

I wonder why twenty? Perhaps God also counted on his fingers, and not only on his hands but his feet too: that makes it twenty.

I do my own research. Once in a while in your bath tub, while cleaning your fingers and toes, you must have counted them. Perhaps one day he counted his, and an idea may have struck him: to give everybody twenty years of life. He seems to be a poet. He also seems to be a communist. Now the Americans will be very offended. Let them be – I don't care. If I have not cared about anybody else in the world; why should I care about Yankees? And in this phase of my life I want to remain as outrageous, or even more so, than I was before.

I certainly know that if Jesus was allowed to teach a little longer, he would not have been so outrageous, he would have come to his senses. After all, he was a Jew. He would have understood, and then he would not have talked such nonsense – "the kingdom of God" – and those twelve fools that he or they themselves thought were apostles! He must have given them some hint; otherwise being such fools they could not have thought of it themselves.

Jesus was so outrageous that even the greatest revolutionary of the day, John the Baptist, who was also the master of Jesus and who was imprisoned – in jail, even from his cell he sent a message to Jesus. He said, "Listening to your statements I wonder, are you really the messiah we have been waiting for? – because your statements are so outrageous."

Now I call this a certification. John the Baptist was one of the greatest revolutionaries in the world; Jesus was only one of his disciples. It is an accident of history that John the Baptist is forgotten and Jesus is remembered.

John the Baptist was real fire. His head was cut off. The queen had ordered his head to be presented to her on a plate; only then would she feel that the country would remain at ease. And that's what was done. John the Baptist's head was cut off, put on a beautiful golden plate and presented to the queen. This man, John the Baptist, had also become a little worried when he heard the outrageous remarks of Jesus. And I say that once in a while they need to be edited – yes, even I say so – not because they were outrageous, but because they start becoming foolish. Outrageous is okay, but foolish? No.

Just think of Jesus cursing the fig tree because he and his disciples were hungry and the tree had no fruit. It was not the season. It was not the fault of the tree, yet he became so angry that he cursed the fig tree that it would remain ugly forever.

Now, this I call foolishness. I don't care whether it was said by Jesus or anybody else. Outrageousness is part of religiousness, but foolishness is not. Perhaps if Jesus had taught a little longer – he was only thirty-three when he was crucified – I think, being a real Jew, he would have become pacified by the time he was seventy. There would have been no need to crucify him at all. The Jews were in a hurry.

I think it was not only the Jews who were in a hurry – because Jews know better – perhaps the crucifixion of Jesus came from the Romans, who have always been childish and stupid. I don't know of anyone like a Jesus, or a Buddha, or a Lao Tzu, who has ever happened to their race and to their history.

Only one man comes to me; he was the Emperor Aurelius. He wrote the famous book, *Meditations*. Of course it is not what I call meditation, but meditations. My meditation is always singular; there can be no plural to it. His meditations are really contemplations; there can be no singular to it. Marcus Aurelius is the only name I can remember in the whole Roman history worth mentioning – but that not too much. Any poor Basho could defeat Marcus Aurelius. Any Kabir could hit the emperor and bring him beyond his senses.

I don't know whether this is permitted in your language or not, to "bring someone beyond their senses." Bringing him to his senses is certainly permitted – but that is not my work, anybody could do that. Even a good hit could do it, a stone in the road could do it. A buddha is not needed for that; a buddha is needed to bring you beyond your senses. Basho, Kabir, or even a woman like Lalla or Rabiya could really have brought this poor emperor to that beyond.

But this is all that has come from the Romans – nothing much, but still something. One should not reject anybody totally. Just by way of courtesy I accept Marcus Aurelius, not as an enlightened one but as a good man. He could have been enlightened if, by chance, he had come across a man like Bodhidharma. Just a look from Bodhidharma into the eyes of Marcus Aurelius would have been enough. Then he would have known, for the first time, what medi-tation is.

He would have gone home and burned what he had written so far. Perhaps then he would have left a collection of sketches – a bird on the wing, a rose withering away, or just a cloud floating in the sky – a few sentences here and there, not saying much, but enough to provoke, enough to trigger a process in the person who comes across it. That would have been a real notebook on meditation, but not on meditations.... There is no plural possible.

The East, and particularly India, can be called by the psycholo-gists not only obsessive about death, but really possessed by the idea of suicide. In a way the psychologist would not be wrong. One should live while one is alive; there is no need to think of death. And when death comes one should die, and die totally; then there is no need to look backwards. And every moment being total in living, in loving, in dying – that's how one comes to know. To know what? There is no what. One simply comes to know – not what, but that: the knower. "What" is the object, "that" is one's subjectivity.

The moment my Nana died, my grandmother was still laughing the last flicker of her laughter. Then she controlled herself. She was certainly a woman who can control herself. But I was not impressed by her control, I was impressed by her laughter in the very face of death.

Again and again I asked her, "Nani, can you tell me why you laughed so loudly when death was so imminent? If even a child like me was aware of it, it is not possible that you were not aware."

She said, "I was aware, that is why I laughed. I laughed at the poor man trying to stop the wheel unnecessarily, because neither birth nor death mean anything in the ultimate sense."

I had to wait for the time when I could ask and argue with her. When I myself become enlightened, I thought, then I will ask her. And that's what I did.

The first thing I did after my enlightenment, at the age of twenty-one, was to rush to the village where my grandmother was, my father's village. She never left that place where her husband had been burned. That very place became her home. She forgot all the luxuries that she had been accustomed to. She forgot all the gardens, the fields, and the lake that she had possessed. She simply never went back, even to settle things.

She said, "What is the point? All is settled. My husband is dead, and the child I love is not there; all is settled."

Immediately after my enlightenment I rushed to the village to meet two people: first, Magga Baba, the man I was talking about before. You will certainly wonder why.... Because I wanted somebody to say to me, "You are enlightened." I knew it, but I wanted to hear it from the outside too. Magga Baba was the only man I could ask at that time. I had heard that he had recently returned to the village.

I rushed to him. The village was two miles from the station. You cannot believe how I rushed to see him. I reached the neem tree....

The word 'neem' cannot be translated because I don't think anything like the neem tree exists in the West at all. The neem tree is something strange: if you taste the leaves they are very bitter; you cannot believe that poison could taste more poisonous. In fact it is just the opposite, it is not poisonous. If you eat a few leaves from the neem tree every day...which is a difficult thing. I have done it for years; fifty leaves in the morning and fifty again in the evening. Now, to eat fifty leaves of the neem tree really needs someone who is determined to kill himself!

It is so bitter, but it purifies the blood and keeps you absolutely free from any infection – even in India, which is a miracle! Even the wind passing through the leaves of a neem tree is thought to be purer than any other. People plant neem trees around their houses just to keep the air pure and unpolluted. It is a scientifically proven fact that the neem tree keeps away all kinds of infection by creating a wall of protection.

I rushed to the neem tree where Magga Baba sat, and the moment he saw me do you know what he did? I could not believe it myself – he touched my feet and wept. I felt very embarrassed because a crowd had gathered and they all thought Magga Baba had now really gone mad. Up till then he had been a little mad, but now he was totally gone, gone forever...*gate, gate* – gone, and gone forever. But Magga Baba laughed, and for the first time, in front of the people, he said to me, "My boy, you have done it! But I knew that one day you would do it."

I touched his feet. For the first time he tried to prevent me from doing it, saying, "No, no, don't touch my feet anymore."

But I still touched them, even though he insisted. I didn't care and said, "Shut up! You look after your business and let me do mine. If I am enlightened as you say, please don't prevent an enlightened man from touching your feet."

He started laughing again and said, "You rascal! You are enlightened, but still a rascal."

I then rushed to my home – that is, my Nani's home, not my father's – because she was the woman I wanted to tell what had happened. But strange are the ways of existence: she was standing at the door, looking at me, a little amazed. She said, "What has happened to you? You are no longer the same." She was not enlightened, but intelligent enough to see the difference in me.

I said, "Yes, I am no longer the same, and I have come to share the experience that has happened to me."

She said, "Please, as far as I am concerned, always remain my Raja, my little child."

So I didn't say anything to her. One day passed, then in the middle of the night she woke me up. With tears in her eyes she said, "Forgive me. You are no longer the same. You may pretend but I can see through your pretense. There is no need to pretend. You can tell me what has happened to you. The child I used to know is dead, but someone far better and luminous has taken his place. I cannot call you my own anymore, but that does not matter. Now you will be able to be called by millions as theirs, and everybody will be able to feel you as his or hers. I withdraw my claim – but teach me also the way."

This is the first time I have told anybody. My Nani was my first disciple. I taught her the way. My way is simple: to be silent, to experience in one's self that which is always the observer, and never the observed; to know the knower, and forget the known.

My way is simple, as simple as Lao Tzu's, Chuang Tzu's, Krishna's, Christ's, Moses', Zarathustra's...because only the names differ, the way is the same. Only pilgrims are different; the pilgrimage is the same. And the truth, the process, is very simple.

I was fortunate to have had my own grandmother as my first

disciple, because I have never found anybody else to be so simple. I have found many very simple people, very close to her simplicity, but the profoundness of her simplicity was such that nobody has ever been able to transcend it, not even my father. He was simple, utterly simple, and very profound, but not in comparison to her. I am sorry to say, he was far away, and my mother is very very far away; she is not even close to my father's simplicity.

You will be surprised to know – and I am declaring it for the first time – my Nani was not only my first disciple, she was my first enlightened disciple too, and she became enlightened long before I started initiating people into sannyas. She was never a sannyasin.

She died in 1970, the year when I started initiating people into sannyas. She was on her deathbed when she heard about my movement. Although I did not hear it myself, one of my brothers reported to me that these were her last words.... "It was as if she were talking to you," my brother told me. "She said, 'Raja, now you have started a movement of sannyas, but it is too late. I cannot be your sannyasin because by the time you reach here I will not be in this body, but let it be reported to you that I wanted to be your sannyasin.'"

She died before I reached her, exactly twelve hours before. It was a long journey from Bombay to that small village, but she had insisted that nobody should touch her body until I arrived; then whatever I decided should be done. If I wanted her body to be buried, then it would be okay. If I wanted her body to be burned, that too would be okay. If I wanted something else to happen, then that too would be okay.

When I reached home I could not believe my eyes: she was eighty years of age and yet looked so young. She had died twelve hours before, but still there was no sign of deterioration. I said to her, "Nani, I have come. I know you will not be able to answer me this time. I'm just telling you so that you can hear. There is no need to answer." Suddenly, almost a miracle! Not only I was present, but my father too, and the whole family, were there. In fact the whole neighborhood had gathered. They all saw one thing: a tear rolled down from her left eye – after twelve hours!

Doctors – please note it, Devaraj – had declared her dead. Now,

OSHO'S NANI IN OLD AGE

dead men don't weep; even real men rarely do, what to say about dead men! But there was a tear rolling from her eye. I took it as an answer, and what more could be expected? I gave fire to her funeral, as was her wish. I did not do that even to my father's body.

In India it is almost an absolute law that the eldest son should begin the fire for his father's funeral pyre. I did not do it. As far as my father's body was concerned, I did not even go to his funeral. The last funeral I attended was my Nani's.

That day I told my father, "Listen, Dada, I will not be able to come to your funeral."

He said, "What nonsense are you saying? I am still alive."

I said, "I know you are still alive, but for how long? Just the other day Nani was alive; tomorrow you may not be. I don't want to take any chances. I want to say right now that I have decided I will not attend any other funeral after my Nani's. So please forgive me, I will not be coming to your funeral. Of course you will not be there so I am asking your forgiveness today."

He understood and was a little shocked of course, but he said, "Okay, if this is your decision, but who then is going to give fire at my funeral?"

This is a very significant question in India. In that context it would normally be the eldest son. I said to him, "You already know I am a hobo, I don't possess anything."

Magga Baba, although utterly poor, had two possessions: his blanket and his magga – the cup. I don't have any possessions. Although I live like a king, I don't possess anything. Nothing is mine. If one day someone comes and says to me, "Leave this place at once," I will leave immediately. I will not even have to pack anything. Nothing is mine. That's how one day I left Bombay. Nobody could believe that I would leave so easily without looking back even once.

I could not go to my father's funeral, but I had asked his permission beforehand, a long time before, at my Nani's funeral. My Nani was not a sannyasin, but she was a sannyasin in other ways, in every other way except that I had not given her a name. She died in orange. Although I had not asked her to wear orange, but on the day she became enlightened she stopped wearing her white dress.

In India a widow has to wear white. And why only a widow? So that she does not look beautiful – a natural logic. And she has to shave her head! Look...what to call these bastards! Just to make a woman ugly they cut off her hair and don't allow her to use any other color than white. They take all the colorfulness from her life. She cannot attend any celebration, not even the marriage of her own son or daughter! Celebration as such is prohibited for her.

The day my Nani became enlightened, I remember – I have noted it down, it will be somewhere – it was the sixteenth of January, 1967. I say without hesitation that she was my first sannyasin; and not only that, she was my first enlightened sannyasin.

You are both doctors, and you know Doctor Ajit Saraswati well. He has been with me for almost twenty years, and I don't know anybody else who has been so sincerely with me. You will be surprised to know he is waiting outside...and there is every possibility that he is almost ready to be enlightened. He has come to live here in the commune; it must have been difficult for him, particularly as an Indian, leaving his wife, his children, and his profession. But he could not live without me. He is ready to renounce all. He is waiting outside. This will be his first interview, and I can feel that this is going to be his enlightenment too. He has earned it, and earned it with great difficulty. To be an Indian, and to be totally with me is not an easy job.

What is the time?

"Quarter to nine, Osho."

Five minutes for me. It is so immensely beautiful.... No, this is just great. No, one should not be greedy. No, I am a consistent man ...consistently, no...and remember that I am not saying "no" as a negative. To me 'no' is the most beautiful word in your language. I love it. I don't know if anybody else does or not, but I love it.

You are both patient...and I am the doctor. It is time. Everything has to come to a full stop.

Session 17

O KAY. THE FIRST WORDS THAT Ajit Saraswati uttered to me last night were, "Osho, I never expected that I would ever make it." Of course those who were present thought he was talking about coming to live in the commune. And that too is in a way true, relevant, because I remember the first day he came to see me twenty years ago. He had had to ask permission from his wife just to see me for a few minutes. So those who were present must have understood, naturally, that he had never expected to move in, leaving his wife and children and a very good business. Renouncing all, just to be here with me...in a true sense of renunciation. But that was not what he meant, and I understood.

I said to him, "Ajit, I am also surprised. Not that I never expected it; I had always expected it, hoped and longed for this moment, and I am happy that you have come."

Again, the others must have thought I was talking about his coming here to live. I was talking about something else – but he understood. I could see it in his eyes, which have been becoming more and more childlike. I saw that he had understood what coming to a master really means. It means coming to one's self. It cannot mean anything else other than self-realization. His smile was absolutely new.

I had been worried about him: he was becoming more serious every day. I was really concerned, because to me seriousness has always been a dirty word, a disease, something far more cancerous than cancer can ever be, and certainly far more infectious than any disease. But I breathed a great sigh of unburdening; a load disappeared from my heart.

He is one of those few people that if I had to die without them becoming enlightened, then I would have had to turn the wheel again, I would have had to be born again. Although it is impossible to turn the wheel...and I know nothing of the mechanics of turning a wheel, particularly the wheel of time. I am not a mechanic, I am not a technician, so it would have been very difficult for me to turn the wheel again...and it has not moved since I was twenty-one.

Thirty-one years ago the wheel stopped. Now everything must be rusted. Even if you poured oil onto it, it would not help. Even my sannyasins could do nothing about it – it is not the wheel of a Rolls Royce. It is the wheel of karma, of action, and the consciousness implied in every action. I am finished with it. But for a man like Ajit, I would have tried to come back again whatever the cost.

I am determined that I will leave this body only when at least one thousand and one of my disciples are enlightened, not before that. Devaraj, remember it! It is not going to be difficult – the basic work has been done – it is just a question of a little patience.

Gudia just said as I was coming in, on hearing that Ajit had become enlightened, "It is strange, enlightenment is popping up everywhere." It has to pop up everywhere, that's my work. And those one thousand and one people are almost ready to pop at any moment. Just a little breeze and the flower opens...or the first ray of the sun and the bud opens her heart to it – just anything.

Now, what was it that helped Ajit? In these twenty years that I have known him, I have always been loving towards him. I have never hit him – there has never been a need. Even before I said anything to him, he received it already. Before saying, he heard it. In these twenty years he has been following me as closely as it is possible. He is my Mahakashyapa.

What caused the thing last night? It was just because he had been thinking of me every moment. The moment he saw me, all that thinking disappeared – and that was the only thinking that had been surrounding him, like a cloud. And I don't think that he understood the exact meaning of his words! It takes time, and the words come so suddenly. He just said, as if in spite of himself, "I had never expected that I would be able to make it."

I said, "Don't be worried. I was always certain it was going to happen sooner or later, but it was going to happen."

He looked a little puzzled. He was talking about coming and I was talking about happening. Then, just as if a window opened and you see – just like that – a window opened and he saw. He touched my feet with tears in his eyes and a smile on his face. To see tears and smiles mixing and merging is beautiful. It is an experience in itself.

Because of Ajit Saraswati I could not complete the story that I had begun. He had been, somehow, just around the corner for so long that I had become accustomed to him. You remember that day when I was talking of Ajit Mukherjee, the famous tantra writer, the author of *Tantra Art* and *Tantra Paintings*? I said, and you can check your notes...when I said "Ajit" I could not say "Mukherjee." To me "Ajit" has always meant "Ajit Saraswati." So when I talked about Ajit Mukherjee, first I said "Ajit Sarasw...," then I corrected myself. I had started to say "Saraswati" and got as far as "Sarasw...," then said, "Mukherjee."

He has been, without interfering in any way, present, just around the corner, waiting, only waiting. Such trust is rare, although with me there are thousands of sannyasins with the same kind of reverence. Knowing it or not, that does not matter; what matters is the presence of reverence.

Ajit Saraswati has a Hindu background, so naturally it is easier for him to have that kind of reverence, trust. But he was educated in the West; perhaps that is why he could come close to me. A Hindu background and a Western scientific mind – having these two things together is a rare phenomenon, and he is a unique man.

And, Gudia, more are to follow. Yes, they are going to pop! Here, there, and everywhere. They have to pop quickly because I don't have much time. But the sound of a man popping into existence is not the sound of pop music, it is not even classical music; it is pure music, not capable of being classified...not even to be heard but only to be felt.

Now, do you see the nonsense? I am talking of a music that has to be felt and not heard. Yes, that's what I am talking about; that's what enlightenment is. All becomes silent, as if Basho's frog had never jumped into the ancient pond...never, never...as if the pond has remained without any ripples, forever reflecting the sky, undisturbed.

This haiku of Basho is beautiful. I repeat it so many times because it is always so new, and always pregnant with a new meaning. It is for the first time that I am saying that the frog has not jumped, and there is no plop. The ancient pond is neither ancient nor new; it knows nothing of time. There are no ripples on its surface. In it you can see all the stars more glorified, more magnificent, than they are in the sky above. The depth of the pond contributes immensely to their richness. They become more of the same stuff dreams are made of.

When one pops into enlightenment, then one knows the frog had not jumped...the ancient pond was not ancient. Then one knows what is.

This is all by the way. But before I again forget...the poor story that I started yesterday. You may not have thought that I would remember it, but I can forget anything except a beautiful story. Even when I am dead, if you want me to speak, ask me something about a story – perhaps just a fable by Aesop, *Panchtantra*, *Jataka Tales*, or just the parables of Jesus.

I was saying yesterday...it all began with the metaphor "dog's death." I said that the poor dog had nothing to do with it. But there is a story behind that metaphor, and because millions of people are going to die a dog's death, it is worth understanding. Perhaps you have already heard the story. I think every child has heard it; it is so simple.

God created the world: man, woman, animals, trees, birds, mountains – everything. Perhaps he was a communist. Now, this is not good; at least God should not be a communist. It would not look good to be called "Comrade God": "Comrade God, how are you?" It just doesn't sound good. But the story says he gave everybody twenty years of life. Everybody was given the same. As could be expected, man immediately stood up and said, "Only twenty years? It is not enough."

That shows something about man: nothing is enough. It is never enough. Woman did not stand up. That also shows something about women. She is satisfied with small things. Her desires are very human; she is not asking for the stars. In fact she giggles at man for all his efforts to reach Everest, or the moon or Mars. She cannot understand what all this nonsense is about. Why don't we just go and see what is on television right now? As far as I know, watching television....

Ashu is looking downwards. Don't be ashamed. I am not saying anything against women watching television. I am talking about myself. I think that women only watch television for the advertisements, not for anything else; a new soap, or shampoo, or new car... the new, anything new.

In advertising everything is always new. It is really the old stuff packaged again and again. Yes, the package is new, the label is new, the name is new. But a woman is interested in a new washing machine, refrigerator or bicycle. A woman's interest is immediate.

In this story she did not stand up and say to God, "What! Only twenty years?" In fact when man stood up, the woman must have been pulling him down saying, "Sit down, man. Why are you grumbling, always grumbling? You grumpy old fellow, sit down."

But man stuck to his ground and said, "I resist in every possible way this imposition of just twenty years. More is needed."

God was at a loss. Being a communist God, what could he do? He had distributed the years equally. But the animals were more understanding than this communist fellow.

The elephant laughed and said, "Don't be worried. You can take ten years from my life, because twenty years is too long. What am I going to do with twenty years? – ten years will do." So man got ten years of the elephant's life. These are the years between twenty and thirty when a man behaves like an elephant. These are the years when hippies and yippies and other similar tribes are born. Everywhere in the world they should be called "the elephants"...thinking too much of themselves.

Then the lion stood up and said, "Please accept ten years from my life. For me ten years are more than enough." Between thirty and forty man roars like a lion, as if he were Alexander the Great. Even Alexander was not a real lion, so what about the others? Between thirty and forty, every man in his own way behaves like a lion.

Then the tiger stood up saying, "When everybody is contributing to poor man, then my contribution is also ten years from my life." Between forty and fifty man behaves like a tiger – much reduced in comparison to the lion, very much shaved, no more than a big cat, but the old habit of bragging continues.

Then up stood the horse and contributed ten years also. Between fifty and sixty a man carries all kinds of loads. He is just a horse. Not an ordinary horse either, a very extra-ordinary horse, loaded with a mountain of worries, but somehow his will is such that he pulls through, and goes on and on.

At sixty the dog contributed his ten years, and that is why it is called "a dog's death." This story is one of the most beautiful parables. Between sixty and seventy man lives like a dog, barking at everything that moves. He just finds every excuse to bark.

The story does not go beyond seventy because it was originally told before man could expect to live more than seventy years. Seventy is the conventional age. If you are a conventional man then consult a calendar and die at exactly seventy. Any more than that is a little modern. Living till eighty, ninety, or even a hundred, that is ultra-modern, that is rebellious. That is going astray.

Do you know that in America there are people frozen in tanks because they were suffering from incurable diseases? Incurable at least today – perhaps in twenty years' time we may have found the cure. So even though they could have lived a few more years with the disease, they decided to be frozen – at their own expense, remember. In America it is always at your own expense. Even though they are frozen, almost dead, they are paying. They had to pay beforehand, in advance, for the coming twenty years, so that their bodies can be kept continuously frozen. It is, of course, an expensive affair. Only the very rich can afford it. I think the upkeep for a frozen body costs almost one thousand dollars per day. They are hoping, or rather they had hoped, that when a cure is found they could be unfrozen and brought back to life again, cured.

They are waiting – poor, rich fellows; there are at least a few hundred people all over America, waiting. This gives 'waiting' a new meaning. This is a new kind of waiting – not breathing, and yet waiting. This is really waiting for Godot, and paying too.

The story is old, hence the proverbial seventy years. "The dog's death" simply means the death of a man who has lived like a dog. Again, don't be offended if you are a dog lover. It has nothing to do with dogs. Dogs are nice people. But "to live like a dog" means to live just for barking, enjoying the bark, shouting at each and every opportunity. Living like a dog simply means not living a human life but something subhuman, something less than human. And one who lives like a dog is bound to die like a dog.

Obviously you cannot have a death that you have not earned. I repeat: you cannot have a death that you have not earned, for which you have not been working your whole life. Death is either a punishment or a reward; it all depends on you. If you live superficially, then your death will be just a dog's death. Dogs are heady people, very intellectual. If you live intensely, intuitively, from the heart, intelligently, not intellectually; if you allow your whole being to be involved in everything you do, then you can die a god's death.

Let me coin another phrase, opposite to a "dog's death": "a god's death." As you can see, 'dog' and 'god' are made of the same letters, just written differently. The same stuff put backwards becomes 'dog'; put rightly, becomes 'god'. The substance of existence, your being, is the same; whether you stand on your head or your feet it does not matter. In one way it matters: if you stand on your head you will suffer. And if you start walking on your head, then you can visualize yourself to be in the seventh hell. But you can jump up and stand on your feet – there is nobody preventing you!

This has been my whole teaching: Jump up! Don't do a headstand, stand on your feet. Be natural! Then you will be living like a god. And, of course, a god dies like a god. He lives like a god, and dies like a god. And by god I mean simply a master of one's self.

Session 18

SIGMUND FREUD WAS INTERVIEWING ONE of his patients. He asked the man lying on the couch, "Look through the window – can you see the flagpole on the office building across the street?"

The old man said, "Of course. Do you think I am blind? I may be old but I can see the pole, the flag and everything. What kind of question is this? Am I paying you to ask such stupid questions?"

Freud said, "Just wait, this is how psychoanalysis works. Tell me what the pole reminds you of."

The old man started giggling. Freud was immensely happy. Very shyly the old man said, "It reminds me of sex."

Freud wanted everybody to prove his new theory, and this was a confirmation. He said, "I understand. The pole is nothing but a phallic symbol. You need not be worried, it is absolutely true."

The old man was still giggling, and then Freud asked him, "What does this couch remind you of?"

The old man started laughing and said, "This is some psychoanalysis! I have come for this? Have I paid you in advance for this?" Remember, Freud used to take his fee in advance, because when you are dealing with all kinds of crazy people you cannot depend on them to pay you later on. It has to be taken before the treatment begins.

In fact nobody in the whole world, including Sigmund Freud himself, is ever totally psychoanalyzed, for the simple reason that it cannot be done. You can just go on and on and on ad nauseam. Why? – because it is nothing but thoughts, insubstantial. One thought leads to another, and so on and so forth; there is no end to it. Not a single psychoanalyst has existed ever who can claim to be totally psychoanalyzed. Something always remains, and that something is far bigger than the small fragment that you have been playing with in the name of psychoanalysis.

The old man was getting a little angry too. Freud said, "Just this last question, so don't get angry. Of course the couch reminds you of sex; it reminds everybody of sex, so there is no problem in it – don't feel angry. Just this last question: what do you think of when you see a camel?"

Now the old man was really in an uproar, laughing so loudly that he had to hold his stomach with his hands. He said, "My God! I had never thought psychoanalysis had anything to do with camels. But by a strange coincidence I went to the zoo just the other day, and for the first time in my life saw a camel, and here is this old guy asking me what a camel reminds me of! The camel reminds me of sex of course, you sonofabitch."

Now it was Freud's turn to be taken aback. Camel? – he could not figure out how a camel could remind anyone of sex! A camel? Even he, Sigmund Freud, had never thought that about a camel. It was just a question. He had been hoping the man would say, "It reminds me of nothing in particular. It is simply a camel. Should it remind me of anything?"

Freud said, "You have shattered my whole joy. I was thinking that you were confirming my beloved theory – but I cannot figure out how a camel can remind you of sex."

The man laughed even more loudly and said, "You fool! Don't you understand anything? Don't worry about that stupid camel. Everything reminds me of sex, even you! So what can I do? That is my problem. That's why I came here. It is my obsession."

I told you this story to explain what I mean by the word 'obsession'. And the whole world can be divided into two categories: people who are obsessed with sex, and the people who are obsessed with death. That is the real demarcation line between East and West. It is not a geographical division, but far more important than geography.

I told you that the English language goes on taking words from other languages. 'Geography' is a word, like many others, borrowed from Arabic. In Arabic it is beautiful, it is *jugrafia,* not 'geography'. But whether it is geography or jugrafia, it cannot be the dividing line. Something psychological has to be understood.

The East is obsessed with death, the West with sex. A materialist is bound to be obsessed with sex, and the spiritualist obsessed with death – and both are obsessions. And to live a life with any obsession, Western or Eastern, is to live almost without living...it is to miss the whole opportunity. The East and West are two sides of the same coin, and so are death and sex. Sex is the energy, the beginning of life; and death is the culmination of life.

It is no coincidence that millions of people never know what real orgasm is. It is for the simple reason that unless you are ready to go into a sort of death, you cannot know what orgasm is. And nobody wants to die, everybody wants to live, to renew life again and again.

In the East science could not gain any foothold, because when people are trying to stop the wheel, who is ready to study science? Or ready to listen? Who bothers? For what? The wheel has to be stopped. Yet that can be done by any fool, just by putting a rock in its path. You don't need much technology to stop a wheel, but to move it, you need science.

The most constant inquiry in science is to find the cause of the very movement of existence, or in other words to find some mechanism that moves perpetually on its own, without needing any fuel, without any gas – a perpetual, constant movement unsupported by any energy, because every energy source sooner or later runs dry, and then the wheel will stop. Science is in search of a way to keep the wheel moving forever, to find a movement that is independent of any source of energy.

In the East science could never get started; the car never started. Nobody was interested in getting it started either; they were too worried about how to stop it, because it was rolling downhill. In the East a totally different thing happened, that certainly had not ever happened in the West – tantra. The East could explore the deepest core of sexual energy without any inhibition, without any fear. It was not at all worried about sex. In fact I don't think that the story I told you was true.

157

My own feeling is that Sigmund Freud must have been in his bathroom facing the mirror, talking to himself. That old man on the couch is no one but Sigmund Freud himself. If you look into his book you will be convinced of what I am saying. Freud's whole concern was sex; everything had to be reduced to sex. He was the most sex-obsessed person in the whole history of man, and unfortunately he dominated the so-called psychology, psychoanalysis, and many other kinds of therapies. He has become a father-figure.

Strange, that a man like Sigmund Freud, who suffered all kinds of fears and phobias, could become the key figure for this whole century. He was so afraid. Naturally, remember, if you are obsessed with anything, whether sex or death – those are the two main categories.... There are thousands of things in the world, but they will fall into these categories. If you are obsessed with either of these two, you are utterly ignorant, and you will remain afraid – in fact, afraid of light, because in your darkness you have created your own imaginary world of theories, dogmas and all that. You will be afraid of light, of a man bringing a lamp...a man like Diogenes entering naked with a lamp even in the full sunlight of day.

I sometimes think it would have been good, good for Sigmund Freud, if Diogenes had entered his so-called psychoanalyst's office, with his lamp still burning bright – of course naked, because he was always naked. The meeting would have produced something of immense value. People like Sigmund Freud are afraid of light; that's why Diogenes used to carry his lamp. Whenever anybody would ask why he carried the lamp in daylight, he would answer, "I am searching for a man, and I have not found him yet."

Just a moment before he died somebody asked him, "Diogenes, before you leave the body, please tell us: Have you found the man yet?"

Diogenes laughed and said, "I am sorry to say that I could not find him. But I must say one thing: I still have my lamp with me, nobody has stolen it – and that is great."

Sigmund Freud was obsessed, but continues to represent the whole Western attitude. That is why Carl Gustav Jung could not stay with him for long. The reason is simple: Jung's obsession was not sex but death. He needed a master in the East not the West. Yet such is the complexity of things that he was very proud of the West, so much so that when he visited India somebody suggested he should go and see Maharshi Raman, who was still alive, but Jung did not go. It was only one hour's flight away…and he went everywhere else. He was in India for months, but he had no time to go and see Maharshi Raman. Again, the reason is simple: it needs guts to face a man like Raman. He is a mirror. He will show you your real face. He will take away all your masks.

I really hate this man Jung. I may condemn Sigmund Freud, but I don't hate him. He may have been wrong but he was a genius. He was a genius, even though he was doing something which I cannot support because I know it is not right. But this man Jung was just a pygmy; compared to Freud he stands nowhere. Moreover he was also a Judas: he betrayed his master.

The master himself was wrong, but that is another matter. Wrong or right, Freud had chosen Jung to be his chief disciple, and still he proved to be just a Judas. He is not of the same caliber as Freud. The real reason why they had to part – and I have never seen it mentioned by any Freudian or Jungian, I am telling it for the first time – was that Jung's obsession was with death, and Freud's was with sex. They could not stay together for long, they had to part.

The East, for thousands of years, has been morbidly engaged in somehow getting rid of life. Yes, I call it morbid. I love to call a thing what it is. A spade is just a spade, neither more nor less. I want simply to state the fact. The East has suffered much just because of this morbidity, continuously thinking from the very moment of birth how to get rid of life. I think this is the oldest obsession in the world. Thousands of the same caliber as Sigmund Freud have lived under it, and strengthened it and nourished it.

I don't recall a single man who stood against it. They all agreed, even though they disagreed about everything else: Mahavira, Manu, Kanad, Gautama, Shankara, Nagarjuna – the list is almost infinite. And they are all far superior to Sigmund Freud, C.G. Jung or Adler, and the many bastards that they left behind.

But just to be a genius, even a great genius, does not necessarily mean that you are right. Sometimes a simple farmer may be more right than a great scholar. A gardener may be more right than a professor. Life is really strange; it always visits the simplest, the loving. The East has missed, and the West is missing too. Both are lopsided.

I had to talk about it because this is one of my basic contributions, that man should not be worried about either sex or death. He should be free from both obsessions; only then does he know, and he knows that, strangely enough, they are not different. Each moment of deep love is also a moment of deep death. Each orgasm is also an end, a full stop. Something reaches to a height, touches a star, and will never be the same again whatsoever you do. In fact, the more you do, the farther away it is.

But man lives almost like a rat, hidden in his hole. You may call it Western, Eastern, Christian, Hindu; there are thousands of holes available for all kinds of rats. But to be in a hole, howsoever decorated, painted, almost like a cathedral, a beautiful temple or a mosque, still it is a hole. And to live in it is to go on committing slow suicide – because you are not meant to be a rat. Be a man. Be a woman.

Up till now everything has been happening unconsciously, by nature, but now nature cannot do anything anymore. Can't you see it simply? Darwin says that man is born of the monkey. Perhaps he is right. I don't think so, that's why I said *perhaps* he is right. But what happened then? Monkeys are not becoming men...you don't suddenly see a monkey turning into a man and proving Darwin's theory.

No monkey is interested in Charles Darwin. I don't think they have even read his very unpoetic books. In fact they are – they must be, I assume – angry, because Darwin thinks that man has evolved. No monkey can believe that man is more evolved than him. All monkeys – and believe me, I have been in touch with all kinds of people, monkeys included – believe that man is a fallen monkey... fallen from the trees. They cannot think it is evolution. You will have to agree with me on a new word: involution. Perhaps Darwin was right – but then what happened? Forget monkeys, we have nothing to do with them.

What happened to man? Millions of years have passed and man is still the same. Has evolution stopped? For what reason? I don't think that any Darwinian is capable of answering, and know well I have studied Darwin and his followers as deeply as possible. I say "possible" because there is not much depth. What can I do? But not a single Darwinian answers the basic question: If evolution is the rule of existence, then why has man not evolved into superman? or at least something better? Don't call it super; it sounds a little too grand a word to be attached to a man. Why is man not just a little better?

But there has been no change at all for centuries. As far as historians know, man has always been the same, as ugly as today. In fact, if anything can be said to have changed, he has become even uglier. Yes, I am saying what nobody seems to say. Politicians cannot say it because the votes belong to the monkeys. The so-called philosophers cannot say it because they are waiting for their Nobel Prize, and the committee consists of monkeys. If you tell the truth you will be in the same trouble as I am. I have not known a single day without trouble since I became aware. Inside there is no trouble; all trouble has ceased. But outside there is trouble every moment. Even if you associate with me you will be in trouble.

Just the other day I had the message that one of our centers has been attacked. All the windows were broken in a crowd attack. People took away whatsoever they wanted. And just after that a whole center has been burned.

Now, my people have not harmed anybody; they were just meeting there, meditating there. Even the policemen made the statement, "It is strange, because for two years we have been observing these people, and they are utterly innocent. They are neither political nor in any ideology – they just enjoy themselves. Why their houses should be burned is unexplainable." The police may not find the explanation, because the explanation is here, lying down in this dental chair.

I have not known a single day when there was not some trouble or other; and it is the strangest thing to comprehend, because we have been doing harm to nobody. I have not harmed anybody; my people have not harmed anybody...but perhaps that is their crime. The mafia is okay; I am not, you are not. This world, either obsessed with sex or obsessed with death, is going to remain morbid, sick. If

161

we want to have a healthy, wholesome humanity, then we will have to think in totally different terms.

The first thing I want to say is: accept that which is already there. Sex is not your creation, thank God; otherwise everybody would be using a different kind of mechanism, and there would be tremendous frustration because those mechanisms won't fit together at all. They don't even fit when they are exactly the same, when they are meant to be in harmony, they don't harmonize. If everybody was inventing his own sexuality then there would be real chaos. You cannot conceive of it. It is good that you came ready-equipped, already what you are potentially going to be.

And death too is such a natural thing. Just think for a moment: if you were to live forever, what would you do? Remember, you would not be able to commit suicide. I have always loved Alexander's search for the secret of eternal life.... He finally found it in the desert in Arabia. What joy! What ecstasy! He must have danced. But just then the crow said, "Wait, wait just a moment before you drink the water. That water is not ordinary water. I drank of it, alas! Now I cannot die. I have tried all the methods but nothing works. Poison cannot kill me. I hit my head against a rock, but the rock broke and I am unhurt. Before you decide to drink that water, think twice." The story goes that Alexander ran away from the cave so he would not be tempted to drink the water.

Alexander's teacher was none other than the great Aristotle, the father of European philosophy and logic. In fact, Aristotle was the father of the whole of Western thinking. A great father! Without him there would have been no science, and of course no Hiroshima or Nagasaki. Without Aristotle you could not conceive of the West. Aristotle was Alexander's teacher, and I have always found teachers to be very poor.

In my childhood I remember seeing a book – I can't remember which, or perhaps it was in a film – in which Aristotle was teaching Alexander, and the boy said, "Right now I don't want to learn anything; I want to ride a horse. You become a horse for me." So poor Aristotle became a horse. He got down on all fours while Alexander sat on his back and rode him. And this was the man who became the father of Western philosophy! What kind of father...?

Socrates is never called the father of Western philosophy. Socrates, of course, was the master of Plato, and Plato was the master of Aristotle. But Socrates was poisoned because he wasn't palatable – not easy to digest. The West wanted to forget all about him. He might have created the synthesis I am talking about. If he had not been poisoned, and was listened to; if his inquiry into truth had become the very base, we would be living in a totally different world. Nor is Plato thought to be the father, because he was too closely associated with the dangerous Socrates. In fact we know nothing of Socrates except what Plato wrote about him.

Just as Devageet is taking notes, so Plato must have continuously been taking notes from his master. Plato is not accepted because he is only a shadow of Socrates. Aristotle is Plato's disciple, but a Judas. He was a disciple in the beginning, and learned what his master had to teach, and then he became a master in his own right. But what a poor master he was, salaried by the king as a tutor to his son. It is so ugly to know that he was ready to become a horse for Alexander! Who is teaching who? Who is really the master?

I was a teacher in the university. I know that Alexander riding on Aristotle disproves that he was the father of Western philosophy. If he is the father then the whole philosophy in the West is just an orphan, a child adopted by the Christian missionaries, perhaps by Mother Teresa of Calcutta. That great lady can do anything! I pity Aristotle. I cannot find any other word for him. I am ashamed because I was also a professor.

The first thing I used to say to my class each day was, "Remember, here I am the master. If you don't want to listen to me, simply get lost. If you want to listen to me, then just listen. I am ready to answer all your questions, but I will not tolerate any noise, even whispering. If you have a girlfriend here, then get out immediately and I allow you to go with your girlfriend. When I am speaking, only I am speaking, and you are listening. If you want to say something then raise your hand and keep it raised, because it does not mean that when you want to ask I necessarily have to answer at that time. I am not here as your servant. I am not Aristotle. Even Alexander could not make a horse out of me."

This was my introduction every day, and I am happy that they understood it. They had to. That's why I sometimes get hard with you, Devageet, knowing perfectly well that you have to use your buttons, and the noise of them is bound to be there. What can you do? I know it perfectly well. It is just an old habit of mine.

I have never spoken except in utter silence. You know, for years you have heard me. You know the silence in Buddha Hall. Only in that silence.... Your English phrase is meaningful: that the silence is so profound that you can hear even a needle drop on the floor. So I know, but I am just accustomed to silence.

The other day, when I left the room, you were not looking very happy. Later that day I felt bad, it really hurt me. I never wanted in any way to hurt you, it was just my old habit, and you cannot teach me new tricks anymore. I have gone beyond the possibility of being taught.

When I came to America I started to drive again, and sitting with me in the car people would feel annoyed once in a while. I am not a driver, what to say of a good driver – so naturally I did everything that was wrong. Although they tried not to interfere, I could understand their difficulty. They kept control of themselves. I was driving and they were controlling themselves – that was a great scene. But still, once in a while they forgot and started saying something to me in which they were often right. About that I have nothing to say. But right or wrong it does not matter – when I am driving, I am driving. If I am going wrong then I am going wrong. How long could they control themselves? It was dangerous, and they were not concerned about their own life. They were concerned about my life, but what could I do? I could simply state the fact that if I was driving wrongly I would continue to do so. At that moment particularly I did not want to be taught. It was not any egoism.

I am simple in that way. You can always tell me where I am wrong, and I am open to listen. But when I am doing something, I hate interference. Even though the intention may be good, I don't want it even for my own good. I would rather die driving wrongly than be saved by somebody's advice. That's the way I am and it is too late to change.

You will be surprised to know that it has always been too late. Even when I was only a child it was too late. I can only do a thing the way I want to do it; right and wrong are irrelevant. If it happens to be right, good; if it does not happen to be right, that is far out.

Sometimes I may be hard on you, but I don't want to be. It is just a long, long habit from more than thirty years of teaching in utter silence. I cannot forget it.

I was making only one point, and was going to discuss it tomorrow. The point is that I am not against getting rid of the wheel, but I am against being obsessed with stopping it. It stops by itself, but not by you stopping it. It can stop only by you doing something else. That something else I call meditation.

Session 19

O KAY. I SAID "OKAY" A little early, just because I was becoming concerned about your worry. At least in the beginning don't be worried; in the beginning let me have my say. If you are worried, obviously I will say "Okay" but that will not be okay at all.

After my grandfather died I was again away from my Nani, but I soon returned to my father's village. Not that I wanted to – it was just like this "Okay" that I said at the beginning...not that I wanted to say "Okay" but even I cannot ignore the concern of others, and my parents would not allow me to go to my dead grandfather's home. My grandmother herself was not willing to go with me, and being just a seven-year-old child, I could not see any future in it.

Again and again I pictured myself going back to the old house, alone in the bullock cart...Bhoora talking to the bullocks. He at least would have had some kind of company. I would be alone inside the bullock cart, just thinking of the future. What would I do there? Yes, my horses would be there, but who would feed them? In fact, who would feed me? I have never learned even the art of making a single cup of tea.

One day Gudia went for a holiday and Chetana was doing her duty here, serving me. In the morning, when I wake up, I push the button for my tea. Chetana brought it, and put the cup by the side of my bed, then went to the bathroom to prepare my towel and toothbrush, and everything that I need. Meanwhile, for the first time in ten years, do you know – one has to learn small things – I tried to pick the cup up from the floor, and it fell down!

Chetana came running, naturally, afraid. I said, "Don't be

worried – it was my responsibility. I should not have done such a thing. I have never needed to pick up my cup from the floor. Gudia has been spoiling me for ten years. Now you cannot unspoil me in just one day."

I had so many years of spoiling. Yes, I call it spoiling because they never allowed me to do anything for myself. My grandmother was even greater than Gudia could conceive: she would even brush my teeth! I would say to her, "Nani, I can brush my own teeth."

She would say, "Shut up, Raja! Keep quiet. Don't disturb me when I am doing something."

I would shake my head and say, "This is something! You are doing something to me; I can't even tell you that I can do it myself."

I cannot remember a single thing that I was required to do except just to be myself – and that meant the source of all mischief. Because when you don't require a child to do anything at all he has so much energy, he has to invest it somewhere – right or wrong does not matter. What matters is the investment, and mischief is the nicest investment possible. So I did all kinds of mischief to everybody around.

I used to carry a small suitcase, just like the doctors'. Once I had seen a doctor passing through the village, and I had said to my Nani, "Unless I get that suitcase I will not eat!" Where did I get the idea not to eat? I had seen my grandfather not eating for days, particularly in the rainy season when the Jainas have their festival; the very orthodox do not eat at all for ten days. That is why I had said, "I will not eat unless I get that suitcase."

You know what she did? That's why I still love her. She told Bhoora, "Take your gun and run after that doctor and snatch his bag. Even if you have to shoot the man, get his bag. Don't worry, we will take care of you in court."

Bhoora ran with his gun; I ran behind to see what would actually happen. Seeing Bhoora with the gun – a European with a gun in India in those days was the last thing one wanted to see – the doctor started trembling like a leaf in a strong wind. Bhoora said to him, "There is no need to tremble; just hand over your case and go to hell, or wherever else you want to go." The doctor, still trembling, handed over his case. I don't know how you call this doctor's case,

Devaraj. Is it a suitcase or something? A doctor's case? Devageet, what do you call it?

"A visiting bag perhaps?"

A visiting bag? It does not look like a bag. Devaraj, can you suggest a name? A visiting bag? Okay...can you find a better word?

"The original bag was called a Gladstone bag. That was the original black bag."

What is it? A Gladstone's bag? Yes, that was what I was thinking of and could not remember – of course, a Gladstone's bag. Good, but I still don't like that name for the bag. I will continue to call it the doctor's suitcase, although I know it is not a suitcase. It does not matter; by now everybody has understood what I mean.

Seeing the doctor tremble, I saw, for the first time, that all education was useless. If it cannot make you fearless then what is it for? Just to earn bread and butter you will tremble? You will be a bag full of bread and butter, trembling. This is wonderful. It suddenly reminds me of Doctor Eichling.

I have heard – just a gossip, and I love gossips more than gospels…. Anyway those gospels are nothing but gossips, just not said rightly, not told juicily. I have heard – that's the way buddha gospels begin, I mean buddha gossips begin. I have heard – what a beautiful phrase! – that Doctor Eichling's beloved, who by the way I would rather call Inkling, but I heard that his name is not Inkling but Eichling….

I don't know this man. I thought he had died, because I gave him sannyas and called him Shunyo. I don't know what happened to Shunyo or how Doctor Eichling became resurrected, but if Jesus could manage it, why not Eichling? Anyway, he is still there – either he survived, or he resurrected, it is not very significant which. The gossip is that his beloved went off with another sannyasin and she fell in love with this new guy.

When they came back Doctor Eichling had a "love attack." I'm surprised he could manage it, because to have a love attack you first need to have a heart. A heart attack is not necessarily a love attack. A heart attack is physiological, a love attack is psychological, from the deeper part of the heart. But first you have to have a heart.

Now, Doctor Eichling having a heart attack, or love attack, is impossible. They should have consulted me. Of course I am not a doctor, but I am certainly a physician in the same sense Buddha was. Buddha used to call himself a physician, not a philosopher.

Poor Doctor Eichling…there was nothing wrong. When there is nothing there, how can there be anything wrong? Physiologically he was found to be absolutely in order. Psychologically the problem still exists: his beloved is now somebody else's beloved. That hurts – but where?

Nobody knows where it hurts. In the lungs? In the chest? That's where Doctor Eichling was showing his pain, in the chest. Doctor Eichling, it is not in your chest, it is in your mind, in your jealousy. And the center of jealousy is certainly not in the chest; in fact everything has its center in the mind.

If you are a follower of B.F. Skinner, or Pavlov, the grandfather or maybe the great-grandfather of Skinner and contemporary of Freud, his greatest opponent too – then 'mind' is not the right word; you can read 'brain' instead. But the brain is only the body of the mind, the mechanism through which the mind functions. Whether you call it the mind or the brain does not matter; what matters is that everything has its center there.

Doctor Eichling – I cannot call him Shunyo because in front of his office in Madras, on his sign he has written "Doctor Eichling's Office." If you phone him, his assistant says, "Doctor Eichling? He is not available. He is at a meeting." I will call him Shunyo again when he makes that board disappear, and his stupid assistant asks, "Who is this fellow Eichling? We have never heard of him. Yes, once he was here, then he went to India and died there. A fellow called Shunyo returned in his place." I will call him Shunyo only when he buries his board deep down and jumps on it and disappears.

But the story, or rather the gossip, was only to tell you that everything exists first in the mind; only then in the body. The body is an extension of the mind, in matter. Brain is the beginning of that extension, and the body its full manifestation, but the seed is in the mind. The mind carries not only this body's seed, but it also has the potentiality to become almost anything. Its potential is infinite. Humanity's whole past is contained in it – and not only humanity's past but even the prehuman past.

During the nine months in the mother's womb the child passes through almost three million years of evolution...very quickly of course, as if you see a film run so fast that you can hardly see it – just glimpses. But in nine months the child certainly passes through the whole of life from its very beginning. In the beginning – and I am not quoting the Bible, I am simply stating the facts of every child's life – in the beginning every child is a fish, just as once the whole of life began in the ocean. Man still carries the same quantity of salt in his body as ocean water. Man's mind plays the drama again and again: the whole drama of birth, from the fish to the old man gasping for his last breath.

I wanted to go back to the village, but it was next to impossible to regain that which had been lost. That is where I learned that it is better never to go back to anything. Since then I have been to so many places but I have never gone back. Once I have left a place I have left it forever. That childhood episode forever determined a certain pattern, a structure, a system. Although I wanted to go, there was no support. My grandmother simply said, "No, I cannot go back to that village. If my husband is not there then why should I go back? I only went there for his sake, not for the village. If I have to go anywhere I would like to go to Khajuraho."

But that too was impossible because her parents were dead. Later on I visited her house, where she had been born. It was only a ruin. There was no possibility of going back there. And Bhoora, who was the only person who would have been ready to go back, died just after the death of his master, just twenty-four hours after.

Nobody was prepared to see two deaths happen so quickly, particularly me, to whom they both meant such a lot. Bhoora may have been just an obedient servant to my grandfather, but to me he was a friend. Most of the time we were together – in the fields, in the forest, on the lake, everywhere. Bhoora followed me like a shadow, not interfering, always ready to help, and with such a great heart... so poor and yet so rich, together.

He never invited me to his house. Once I asked him, "Bhoora, why do you never invite me to your house?"

He said, "I am so poor that although I want to invite you, my poverty prevents me. I don't want you to see that ugly house in all its dirtiness. In this life I cannot see a time when I will be able to invite you. I really have dropped the very idea."

He was very poor. In that village there were two parts: one for the higher castes, and the other for the poorer ones, on the other side of the lake. That's where Bhoora lived. Although I tried many times to reach his house I could not manage it because he was always following me like a shadow. He would prevent me before I even stepped in that direction.

Even my horse used to listen to him. When it came to going towards his house, Bhoora would say, "No! Don't go." Of course he had brought the horse up from its very childhood; they understood each other, and the horse would stop. There would be no way to get the horse to move either towards Bhoora's house, or even towards the poorer part of the village. I had only seen it from the other side, the richer, where the brahmins and the Jainas lived, and all those who are by birth, pure. Bhoora was a sudra. The word 'sudra' means "impure by birth," and there is no way for a sudra to purify himself.

This is the work of Manu. That's why I condemn him and hate him. I denounce him, and want the world to know of this man, Manu, because unless we know of such people we will never be able to be free of them. They will continue to influence us in some form or another. Either it is race – even in America, if you are a negro, you are a sudra, a "nigger," untouchable.

Whether you are a negro or a white man, both need to be acquainted with the insane philosophy of Manu. It is Manu who has influenced the two world wars in a very subtle way. And perhaps he will be the cause of the third, and last…a really influential man!

Even before Dale Carnegie wrote his book, *How to Win Friends and Influence People,* Manu knew all the secrets. In fact, one wonders how many friends Dale Carnegie has got, and how many people he has influenced. He is certainly not like Karl Marx, Sigmund Freud, Mahatma Gandhi. And all these people were absolutely unacquainted with the science of influencing people. They did not need to know, they had it in their very guts.

I don't think any man has influenced humanity more than Manu. Even today, whether you know his name or not, he influences you. If you think yourself superior just because you are white or black, or just because you are a man or a woman, somehow Manu is pulling your strings. Manu has to be absolutely discarded.

I wanted to say something else, but I started with a wrong step. My Nani was very insistent: "Always step out of bed with your right foot." And you will be surprised to know, today I did not follow her advice, and everything is going wrong. I started with a wrong "okay"; now, when in the very beginning you are not okay, naturally, everything that follows on goes berserk.

Is there still time for me to say something right? Good. Let's begin again.

I wanted to go to the village but nobody was ready to support me. I could not conceive how I could exist there alone, without my grandfather, my grandmother, or Bhoora. No, it was not possible, so I reluctantly said, "Okay, I will stay in my father's village." But my mother naturally wanted me to stay with her and not with my grandmother, who from the very beginning had made it clear that she would stay in the same village, but separately. A little house was found for her in a very beautiful place near the river.

My mother insisted that I stay with her. For over seven years I had not been living with my family. But my family was not a small affair, it was a whole jumbo-set – so many people, all kinds of people: my uncles, my aunts, their children and my uncle's relatives, and so on and so forth.

In India the family is not the same as in the West. In the West it is just singular: the husband, the wife, one, two or three children. At the most there may be five people in the family. In India people would laugh – five? Only five? In India the family is uncountable. There are hundreds of people. Guests come and visit and never leave, and nobody says to them, "Please, it is time for you to go," because in fact nobody knows whose guests they are.

The father thinks, "Perhaps they are my wife's relatives so it is better to keep quiet." The mother thinks, "Perhaps they are my husband's relatives...." In India it is possible to enter a home where you are not related at all, and if you keep your mouth shut, you can live there forever. Nobody will tell you to get out; everybody will think somebody else invited you. You have only to keep quiet and keep smiling.

It was a big family. My grandfather – I mean my father's father – was a man I never liked very much, to say the least. He was so different from my other grandfather, just the opposite; very restless, ready to jump on anyone at any time, ready to take up any excuse to fight. He was a real fighter, cause or no cause. The fight itself was his exercise, and he was continually fighting. It was rare to see him when he was not fighting somebody, and, strange to relate, there were people who loved him too.

My father had a small clothes shop. Once in a while I used to sit there just to watch people, and to see what was going on, and sometimes it was really interesting. The most interesting thing was that a few people would ask my father, "Where is Baba?" – that was my grandfather. "We want to do business with him, and not with anybody else."

I was puzzled, because my father was so simple, so true and honest. He would simply tell people the price of an item like this: "This is my cost price. Now it is up to you how much profit you want to give us. I leave it to you. I cannot reduce the cost price of course, but you can decide how much you want to pay." He would tell his customers, "Twenty rupees is the cost price; you can give me one or two rupees more. Two rupees means ten percent profit, and that's enough for me."

But people would ask, "Where is Baba? – because unless he is here there is no joy in doing business." I could not believe it at first, but later on I did see their point. The joy of bargaining, shopping, or – what do you call it – higgling?

"Haggling, Osho."

Haggling? Good. It must have been a great joy to the customers, because if the item was twenty rupees, my Baba would first start at fifty rupees, and after a long session of haggling, which they both would enjoy, they would settle somewhere near thirty rupees.

I used to laugh; and when the customer had gone, my Baba used to say to me, "You are not supposed to laugh at such moments. You should be serious, as if we were losing money. Of course, we cannot lose," he used to tell me. "Whether the watermelon falls on the knife, or the knife falls on the watermelon, in any case it is the watermelon which gets cut, and not the knife. So don't laugh when you see that I am charging a person thirty rupees for a thing which he could have bought for only twenty rupees from your father. Your father is a fool."

And of course it looked like my father was a fool – the same kind of fool as Devageet. Now it is up to him to attain to the same ultimate foolishness that my father attained. For the fools everything is possible, even enlightenment. Yes, my father was a fool, and my Baba was a very cunning man, a cunning old man. The moment I remember him, it is as a fox. He must have once been born as a fox; he *was* a fox.

Everything Baba did was very calculated. He would have been a good chess player because he could have conceived at least five steps ahead. He was really the most cunning man I have ever come across. I have seen many cunning men, but nobody to compare with my Baba. I always used to wonder where my father got his simplicity from. Perhaps it is nature that does not allow things to become out of balance, so it gives a very simple child to a very complex man.

Baba was a genius in cunningness. The whole village would tremble. Nobody was able to conceive what his plans were. In fact, he was such a man – and I have observed it myself – that we would be going to the river, my Baba and me, and somebody would ask, "Where are you going, Baba?" The whole town used to call him Baba; it just means grandfather. We were going to the river, and it was clear to everybody where we were going, but this man with his quality would say, "To the station." I would look at him, and he would look at me and wink.

I was puzzled. What was the point? No business was being done, and you are not supposed to lie just for no reason at all. When the man had passed by, I asked him, "Why did you wink, Baba? And why did you lie to that man without any reason? Why could you not say 'to the river,' when we are going to the river? He knows, everybody knows, that this road leads to the river and not to the station. You know it and still you said, 'to the station.'"

He said, "You don't understand – one has to practice continuously."

"Practice what?" I asked him.

He said, "One has to continuously practice one's business. I cannot just tell the simple truth because then, one day, doing business, I may simply say the right price. And it is none of your business at all; that's why I winked at you, so you would keep quiet. As far as I am concerned, we are going to the station; whether this road leads there or not is nobody else's business. Even if that man had said that this road does not lead to the station, I would have just said I am going to the station via the river. It is up to me. One can go anywhere from anywhere. It may take a little longer, that's all."

Baba was that kind of man. He lived there with all his children, my father and his brothers and sisters, and their husbands...and one could not know all the people who had gathered there. I saw people coming and never leaving. We were not rich, yet there was enough to eat for everybody.

I did not want to enter this family, and I told my mother, "Either I will go back to the village alone – the bullock cart is ready, and I know the way; I will get there somehow. And I know the villagers: they will help support a child. And it is only a question of a few years, then I will repay them as much as I can. But I cannot live in this family. This is not a family, it's a bazaar."

And it was a bazaar, continuously buzzing with so many people, no space at all, no silence. Even if an elephant had jumped into that ancient pond, nobody would have heard the plop; there was too much going on. I simply refused, saying, "If I have to stay then the only alternative is for me to live with my Nani."

My mother was, of course, hurt. I am sorry, because since then I have been hurting her again and again. I could not help it. In fact I was not responsible; the situation was such that I could not live in that family after so many years of absolute freedom, silence, space. In fact, in my Nana's house I was the only one who was ever heard. My Nana was mostly silently chanting his mantra, and of course my grandmother had no one else to talk to.

I was the only one who was ever heard; otherwise there was silence. After years of such beautitude, then to live in that so-called family, full of unfamiliar faces, uncles, and their fathers-in-law, cousins – what a lot! One could not even figure out who was who! Later I used to think somebody ought to publish a small booklet about my family, a *Who's Who*.

When I was a professor people used to come up to me and say something like, "Don't you know me? I am your mother's brother."

I would look into the man's face, then say, "Please be somebody else, because my mother has no brothers – that much I know about my family."

This particular man then said, "Yes, you are right. I mean I am really a cousin."

I said, "Then it is okay. So what do you want? I mean how much do you want? You must have come to borrow money."

He said, "Great! But it is strange, how could you read my mind?"

I said, "It is very easy. Just tell me how much you want."

He took twenty rupees, and I said, "Thank God. At least I have lost one relative. Now he will never show his face again."

And that's what actually happened: I never saw his face again, anywhere. Hundreds of people borrowed money from me and nobody ever returned it. I was happy that they didn't, because if they had they would only have asked for more.

I wanted to return to the village but could not. I had to come to a compromise just not to hurt my mother. But I know I have been hurting her, really wounding her. Whatsoever she wanted I have never done; in fact, just the opposite. Naturally, slowly slowly she accepted me as one who was lost to her.

It used to happen that I would be sitting just in front of her, and she would ask, "Have you seen anybody about? – because I want to send somebody to fetch vegetables from the market." The market was not far away – the village was small, it was just two minutes away – and she was asking, "Have you seen anybody?"

I would say, "No, I have not seen anybody at all. The house seems to be completely empty. Strange, where have all the relatives gone? They always disappear when there is some work to be done." But she would not ask me to go and fetch vegetables for her. She tried once or twice, and then dropped the idea forever.

Once she asked me to purchase bananas, and I brought tomatoes because on the way I forgot. I tried hard; that was the trouble. I repeated to myself, "Banana...banana...banana...banana..." and then a dog barked, or somebody asked where I was going, and I went on saying, "Banana...banana...banana...."

They said, "Hey! Have you gone mad?"

I said, "Shut up! I have not gone mad. *You* must be mad. What nonsense is this, interrupting people who are silently doing their work?" But by that time I had forgotten what it was I was going to purchase, so I brought anything that I could manage to get. But tomatoes were the last thing to bring, because they are not allowed in a Jaina household. My mother beat her head saying, "Are these bananas? When will you understand?"

I said, "My God! Did you ask for bananas? I forgot – I'm sorry."

She said, "Even if you had forgotten, could you not have bought anything else other than tomatoes? You know that tomatoes are not allowed in our house" – because they look so red, like meat, and in a Jaina household, even a similarity to meat…just the color red could remind you of blood or meat. Even a tomato is enough to make a Jaina feel sick.

Poor tomatoes! They are such simple fellows, and so meditative too. If you see them sitting – they sit exactly like Buddhist monks with their shaven heads, and they look so centered too, as if they have been doing centering for their whole life, so grounded…but Jainas don't like them.

So I had to take those tomatoes back and distribute them to the beggars. They were always glad to see me. The beggars were the only ones who used to be happy to see me, because it was always an occasion when I had been sent to throw something out of the house. I never threw it, I would give it to the beggars.

I could not manage to live in the family according to them. Everybody was giving birth; every woman was almost always pregnant. Whenever I remember my family I suddenly think of freaking out – although I cannot freak out; I just enjoy the idea of freaking out. All the women were always with big bellies. One pregnancy over, another starts – and so many children….

"No," I said to my mother, "I know it hurts you, and I am sorry, but I will live with my grandmother. She is the only one who can understand me and allow me not only love but freedom too."

Once I had asked my Nani, "Why did you only give birth to my mother?"

She said, "What a question!"

I said, "...Because in this family every woman is always carrying a load in her belly. Why did you only give birth to my mother and not have another child – at least a brother for her?"

She then said something I cannot forget: "That too was because of your Nana. He wanted a child, so we compromised. I told him, 'Only one child, then it is your fate whether it is a boy or a girl' – because he wanted a boy." She laughed, "And it was good that a girl was born; otherwise where would I have got you from? Yes, it is good," she said, "that I did not give birth to any other children; otherwise you would not have liked this place either. It would have been too crowded."

I remained in my father's village for eleven years, and I was forced almost violently to go to school. And it was not a one-day affair, it was an everyday routine. Every morning I had to be forced to go to school. One of my uncles, or whosoever, would take me there, would wait outside until the master had taken possession of me – as if I was a piece of property to be passed from one hand to another, or a prisoner passed from one hand to another. But that's what education is still: a forced and violent phenomenon.

Each generation tries to corrupt the new generation. It is certainly a kind of rape, a spiritual rape – and naturally the more powerful, stronger and bigger father and mother can force the small child. I was a rebel from the very first day that I was taken to school. The moment I saw the gates I asked my father, "Is it a jail or a school?"

My father said, "What a question! It is a school. Don't be afraid."

I said, "I am not afraid, I am simply inquiring about what attitude I should take. What is the need for this big gate?"

The gate was closed when all the children, the prisoners, were inside. It was only opened again in the evening when the children were released for the night. I can still see that gate. I can still see myself standing with my father ready to register at that ugly school.

The school was ugly, but the gate was even uglier. It was big, and it was called "The Elephant Gate," *Hathi Dwar*. An elephant could have passed through it, it was so large. Perhaps it would have been good for elephants from a circus – and it was a circus – but for small children it was too big.

I will have to tell you many things about these nine years....

THE ELEPHANT GATE WITH THE PRIMARY SCHOOL BEHIND

Session 20

. . .

WAIT FOR MY "OKAY...."

I am standing before the Elephant Gate of my primary school...and that gate started many things in my life. I was not standing alone of course; my father was standing with me. He had come to enroll me at the school. I looked at the tall gates and said to him, "No."

I can still hear that word. A small child who has lost everything.... I can see on the child's face a question mark as he wonders what is going to happen.

I stood looking at the gates, and my father just asked me, "Are you impressed by this great gate?"

Now I take the story into my own hands:

I said to my father, "No." That was my first word before entering primary school, and you will be surprised, it was also my last word on leaving the university. In the first case, my own father was standing with me. He was not very old but to me, a small child, he was old. In the second case, a really old man was standing by my side, and we were again standing at an even larger gate....

The old university gate is now dismantled forever, but it remains in my memory. I can still see it – the old gate, not the new one; I have no relationship with the new one – and on seeing it, I wept, because the old gate was really grand, simple but grand. The new one is just ugly. It is modern perhaps, but the whole of modern art has taken up ugliness, just because it has been rejected for centuries. Perhaps taking up ugliness is a revolutionary step. But revolution, if ugly, is not revolution at all, it is only reaction. I saw the new gate only once. Since then I have passed that road many times but always closed my eyes. With closed eyes I could again see the old gate.

The old university gate was poor, really poor. It was made when the university was just beginning and they were not able to create a monumental structure. We all lived in military barracks, because the university had started so suddenly and there had been no time to make hostels or libraries. It was just an abandoned military barracks. But the place itself was beautiful, situated on a small hill.

The military had abandoned it because it had only been meaningful during the second world war. It was at a height they had needed for their radar, to look around for the enemy. Now there was no need, so they abandoned it. It was a blessing, at least for me, because I would not have been able to read and study in any university other than that.

Its name was the University of Sagar. *Sagar* means "ocean." Sagar has a tremendously beautiful lake, so big that it is not called a lake, but sagar, an ocean. It really looks like an ocean, with waves rising on it. One cannot believe that it is only a lake. I have seen only two lakes with such big waves. Not that I have only seen two lakes; I have seen many. I have seen the most beautiful lakes of Kashmir, the Himalayas, Darjeeling, Nainital, and many others in the south of India, in the Nandi Hills, but I have seen only two with waves which resemble the ocean: the lake of Sagar and the lake of Bhopal.

Compared to Bhopal, of course the lake of Sagar is small. The lake of Bhopal is perhaps the greatest in the whole world. In that lake I have seen waves that can only be described as tidal waves, rising maybe twelve or fifteen feet high. No other lake can claim that. It is so vast. I once tried to go around it in a boat, and it took seventeen days. I was going as fast as you can imagine – more so, because there were no policemen around, and no speed limit. By the time I had ended the tour I simply said to myself, "My God, what a beautiful lake!" And it was hundreds of feet deep.

The same is true on a smaller scale of the lake of Sagar. But in another sense it has a beauty which the lake of Bhopal does not possess. It is surrounded by beautiful mountains, not so vast but tremendously beautiful...particularly in the early morning at sunrise, and in the evening at sunset. And if it is a full-moon night you really know what beauty is. In a small boat on that lake, on a full-moon night, one simply feels that nothing more is needed.

It is a beautiful place...but I still feel bad because the old gate is no longer there. It was bound to be dismantled. I am absolutely aware of that, not only now; even then everyone was aware that it needed to be dismantled. It was only temporary, made just to inaugurate the university.

This was the second gate I remember. When I left the university I was standing by the gate with my old professor, Sri Krishna Saxena. The poor man died just a few years ago, and he had sent a message saying he wanted to see me. I would have loved to see him, but now nothing can be done unless he is born quickly, and to a sannyasin, so that he can reach me. I will recognize him immediately, that much I can promise.

He was a man of exceptional qualities. He was the only professor out of the whole lot that I came across – teachers, lecturers, readers, professors and whatnot – he was the only one who was able to understand that he had a student who should rather have been his master.

He was standing at the gate persuading me not to leave the university. He was saying, "You should not leave, particularly when the university has granted you a Ph.D. scholarship. You should not lose this opportunity." He was trying in thousands of ways to tell me that I was his most loved student. He said, "I have had many students all over the world, particularly in America" – because he had been teaching in America most of the time – "but I can say," he said to me, "I would not have bothered to convince any of them to remain. Why should I care? – it had nothing to do with me, it was their future. But as far as you are concerned" – and I remember his words with tears in my eyes – he said, "as far as you are concerned, it is my future." I cannot forget those words. Let me repeat them. He said, "Those other students' future was their own concern; your future is my future."

I said to him, "Why? Why should my future be your future?"

He said, "That is something I would rather not talk about to you," and he started crying.

I said, "I understand. Please don't cry. But I cannot be persuaded to do anything against my own mind, and it is set in a totally different dimension. I am sorry to disappoint you. I know perfectly well how much you had hoped, how happy you were that I topped the whole university. I have seen you, just like a child, so joyous about the gold medal that was given not even to you, but to me."

I didn't care a bit about that gold medal. I threw it down a very deep well, so deep that I don't think anybody is going to find it again; and I did it in front of Doctor Sri Krishna Saxena.

He said, "What are you doing? What have you done?" – because I had already thrown it down the well. And he had been so happy that I had been chosen for a scholarship. It was for an indefinite period, from two to five years.

He said, "Please reconsider again."

The first gate was the Elephant Gate, and I was standing with my father not wanting to enter. And the last gate was also an Elephant Gate, and I was standing with my old professor, not wanting to enter again. Once was enough; twice would have been too much.

The argument that had begun at the first gate lasted up till the second gate. The no that I had said to my father was the same no that I had said to my professor, who was really a father to me. I can feel its quality. He cared for me as much as my own father had cared, or perhaps even more. When I was ill he would not sleep; he would sit at my bedside the whole night. I would say to him, "You are old, doctor" – I used to call him doctor – "please go to sleep."

He used to say, "I'm not going to sleep unless you promise that by tomorrow you will be perfectly well."

And I had to promise – as if being sick or not depended on my promise. But somehow, once I had promised him, it worked. That's why I say there is something like magic in the world.

That 'no' became my tone, the very stuff of my whole existence. I said to my father, "No, I don't want to enter this gate. This is not a school, it's a prison." The very gate, and the color of the building.... It is strange, particularly in India, the jails and the schools are painted the same color, and they are both made of red brick. It is very difficult to know whether the building is a prison or a school. Perhaps once a practical joker had managed to play a joke, but he did it perfectly.

I said, "Look at this school – you call it a school? Look at this gate! And you are here to force me to enter for at least four years." That was the beginning of a dialogue that lasted for many years; and you will come across it many times, because it runs criss-cross through the story.

My father said, "I was always afraid..." and we were standing at the gate, on the outside of course, because I had not yet allowed him to take me in. He went on "...I was always afraid that your grandfather, and particularly this woman, your grandmother, were going to spoil you."

I said, "Your suspicion, or fear, was right, but the work has been done and nobody can undo it now, so please let us go home."

He said, "What! You have to be educated."

I said, "What kind of a beginning is this? I am not even free to say yes or no. You call it education? But if you want it, please don't ask me: here is my hand, drag me in. At least I will have the satisfaction that I never entered this ugly institution on my own. Please, at least do me this favor."

Of course, my father was getting very upset, so he dragged me in. Although he was a very simple man he immediately understood that it was not right. He said to me, "Although I am your father it does not feel right for me to drag you in."

I said, "Don't feel guilty at all. What you have done is perfectly right, because unless someone drags me in I am not going to go of my own decision. My decision is 'no.' You can impose your decision on me because I have to depend on you for food, clothes, shelter and everything. Naturally you are in a privileged position."

What an entry! – being dragged into school. My father never forgave himself. The day he took sannyas, do you know the first thing he said to me? "Forgive me, because I have done so many wrong things to you. There are so many I cannot count, and there must be more which I don't know at all. Just forgive me."

The entry into school was the beginning of a new life. For years I had lived just like a wild animal. Yes, I cannot say a wild human being, because there are no wild human beings. Only once in a while a man becomes a wild human being. I am now; Buddha was, Zarathustra was, Jesus was. But at that time it was perfectly true to say that for years I had lived like a wild animal. But it is far superior to Adolf Hitler, Benito Mussolini, Napoleon, or Alexander the Great. I am only naming the worst – worst in the sense that they thought they were the most civilized.

Alexander the Great thought himself to be the most civilized man of his time, of course. Adolf Hitler, in his autobiography, *My Struggle*…. I don't know how Germans pronounce the title – all I can remember is, *Mein Kampf*. It must be wrong, it has to be. Firstly it is German: M-e-i-n K-a-m-p-f.

Whatever the pronunciation, it does not matter to me. What matters to me is that in his book he tries to prove that he has attained the status of "superman," for which man has been preparing for thousands of years. And Hitler's party, the Nazis, and his race, the Nordic Aryans, were going to be the "rulers of the world," and this rule was going to last for one thousand years! Just a madman talking – but a very powerful madman. When he spoke you had to listen, even to his nonsense. He thought he was the only real Aryan, and the Nordics were the only pure-blooded race. But he was seeing a dream.

Man has rarely become a superman, and the word 'super' has nothing to do with 'higher'. The true superman is one who is conscious of all his acts, thoughts and feelings, of all that he is made of – of love, of life, of death.

A great dialogue started with my father on that day, and it continued on and off, and ended only when he became a sannyasin. After that there was no question of any argument, he had surrendered. The day he took sannyas, he was crying and holding my feet. I was standing, and can you believe it…like a flash, the old school, the Elephant Gate, the small child resisting, not ready to go in, and my father pulling him – it all flashed by. I smiled.

My father asked, "Why are you smiling?"

I said, "I am just happy that a conflict has ended at last."

But that is what was happening. My father dragged me; I never went to school willingly.

Devageet, moisten my lips….

I am happy that I was dragged in, that I never went on my own, willingly. The school was really ugly – all schools are ugly, in fact. It is good to create a situation where children learn, but it is not good to educate them. Education is bound to be ugly.

And what did I see as the first thing in the school? The first thing was an encounter with the teacher of my first class. I have seen beautiful people and ugly people, but I have never seen *something* like that again! – and underline something; I cannot call that something someone. He did not look like a man. I looked at my father and said, "This is what you have dragged me into?"

My father said, "Shut up!" Very quietly, so that the "thing" did not hear. He was the master, and he was going to teach me. I could not even look at the man. God must have created his face in a tremendous hurry. Perhaps his bladder was full, and just to finish the job he did this man and then rushed to the bathroom. What a man he created! He had only one eye, and a crooked nose. That one eye was enough! But the crooked nose really added great ugliness to the face. And he was huge! – seven feet in height – and he must have weighed at least four hundred pounds, not less than that.

Devaraj, how do these people defy medical research? Four hundred pounds, and he was always healthy. He never took a single day off, he never went to a doctor. All over the town it was said that this man was made of steel. Perhaps he was, but not very good steel – more like barbed wire! He was so ugly that I don't want to say anything about him, although I will have to say a few things, but at least not about him directly.

He was my first master, I mean teacher. Because in India school-teachers are called "masters"; that's why I said he was my first master. Even now if I saw that man I would certainly start trembling. He was not a man at all, he was a horse!

I said to my father, "First look at this man before you sign."

He said, "What is wrong with him? He taught me, he taught my father – he has been teaching here for generations."

Yes, that was true. That's why nobody could complain about him. If you complained your father would say, "I cannot do anything, he was my teacher too. If I go to him to complain, he could even punish me."

So my father said, "Nothing is wrong with him, he is okay." Then he signed the papers.

I then told my father, "You are signing your own troubles, so don't blame me."

He said, "You are a strange boy."

I said, "Certainly we are strangers to each other. I have lived away from you for many years, and I have been friends with the mango trees and the pines and the mountains, the oceans and the rivers. I am not a businessman, and you are. Money means everything to you; I cannot even count it."

Even today...I have not touched money for years. The occasion never arises. That helps me tremendously because I don't know how things go in the world of economics. I go my own way; they have to follow me. I don't follow them, I can't.

I told my father, "You understand money, and I don't. Our languages are different; and remember, you have stopped me from going back to the village, so now if there is a conflict, don't blame me. I understand something you don't, and you understand something that I neither understand nor want to. We are incompatible. Dada, we are not made for each other."

And it took nearly his whole life to cover the distance between us, but of course, it was him who had to travel. That's what I mean when I say that I am stubborn. I could not budge even a single inch, and everything started at that Elephant Gate.

The first teacher – I don't know his real name, and nobody in the school knew it either, particularly the children; they just called him Kantar Master. *Kantar* means "one-eyed"; that was enough for the children, and also it was a condemnation of the man. In Hindi kantar not only means "one-eyed," it is also used as a curse. It cannot be translated in that way because the nuance is lost in the translation. So we all called him Kantar Master in his presence, and when he was not there we called him just Kantar – that one-eyed fellow.

He was not only ugly; everything he did was ugly. And of course on my very first day something was bound to happen. He used to punish the children mercilessly. I have never seen or heard of anybody else doing such things to children. I knew of many people who had left school because of this fellow, and they remained uneducated. He was too much. You would not believe what he used to

187

do, or that any man could do that. I will explain to you what happened to me on that very first day – and much more was to follow.

He was teaching arithmetic. I knew a little because my grandmother used to teach me a little at home – particularly a little language and some arithmetic. So I was looking out of the window at the beautiful pipal tree shining in the sun. There is no other tree which shines so beautifully in the sun, because each leaf dances separately, and the whole tree becomes almost a chorus – thousands of shining dancers and singers together, but also independent.

The pipal tree is a very strange tree because all other trees inhale carbon dioxide, and exhale oxygen during the day.... Whatever it is you can put it right, because you know that I am not a tree, nor am I a chemist or a scientist. But the pipal tree exhales oxygen twenty-four hours a day. You can sleep under a pipal tree, and not any other because they are dangerous to health. I looked at the tree with its leaves dancing in the breeze, and the sun shining on each leaf, and hundreds of parrots just jumping from one branch to another, enjoying, for no reason. Alas, they didn't have to go to school.

I was looking out of the window and Kantar Master jumped on me.

He said, "It is better to get things right from the very beginning."

I said, "I absolutely agree about that. I also want to put everything as it should be from the very beginning."

He said, "Why were you looking out of the window when I was teaching arithmetic?"

I said, "Arithmetic has to be heard, not seen. I don't have to see your beautiful face. I was looking out of the window to avoid it. As far as the arithmetic is concerned, you can ask me; I heard it and I know it."

He asked me, and that was the beginning of a very long trouble – not for me but for him. The trouble was that I answered correctly. He could not believe it and said, "Whether you are right or wrong I am still going to punish you, because it is not right to look out of the window when the teacher is teaching."

I was called in front of him. I had heard about his punishment techniques – he was a man like the Marquis de Sade. From his desk he took out a box of pencils. I had heard of these famous pencils. He used to put one of those pencils between each of your fingers, and then squeeze your hands tight, asking, "Do you want a little more? Do you need more?" – to small children! He was certainly a fascist. I am making this statement so it is at least on record: people who choose to be teachers have something wrong with them. Perhaps it is the desire to dominate or a lust for power; perhaps they are all a little bit fascist.

I looked at the pencils and said, "I have heard of these pencils, but before you put them between my fingers, remember, it will cost you very dearly, perhaps even your job."

He laughed. I can tell you it was like a monster in a nightmare laughing at you. He said, "Who can prevent me?"

I said, "That is not the point. I want to ask: is it illegal to look out of the window when arithmetic is being taught? And if I am able to answer the questions on what was being taught and am ready to repeat it word for word, then is it wrong in any way to look out of the window? Then why has the window been created in this classroom? For what purpose? – because for the whole day somebody is teaching something, and a window is not needed during the night when there is nobody to look out of it."

He said, "You are a troublemaker."

I said, "That's exactly true, and I am going to the headmaster to find out whether it is legitimate for you to punish me when I have answered you correctly."

He became a little more mellow. I was surprised because I had heard that he was not a man who could be subdued in any way.

I then said, "And then I am going to the president of the munic- ipal committee who runs this school. Tomorrow I will come with a police commissioner so that he can see with his own eyes what kind of practices are going on here."

He trembled. It was not visible to others, but I can see such things which other people may miss. I may not see walls but I cannot miss small things, almost microscopic. I told him, "You are trembling, although you will not be able to accept it. But we will see. First let me go to the headmaster."

I went and the headmaster said, "I know this man tortures chil- dren. It is illegal, but I cannot say anything about it because he is the oldest schoolteacher in the town, and almost everybody's father and grandfather has been his pupil once at least. So no one can raise a finger against him."

I said, "I don't care. My father has been his student and also my grandfather. I don't care about either my father or my grandfather; in fact I don't really belong to that family. I have been living away from them. I am a foreigner here."

The headmaster said, "I could see immediately that you must be a stranger, but, my boy, don't get into unnecessary trouble. He will torture you."

I said, "It is not easy. Let this be the beginning of my struggle against all torture. I will fight."

And I hit with my fist – of course just a small child's fist – on his table, and told him, "I don't care about education or anything, but I must care about my freedom. Nobody can harass me unnecessarily. You have to show me the educational code. I cannot read, and you will have to show me whether it is unlawful to look out of the window even though I could answer all the questions correctly."

He said, "If you answered correctly then there is no question at all about where you were looking."

I said, "Come along with me."

He came with his educational code, an ancient book that he always carried. I don't think anybody had ever read it. The headmaster told Kantar Master, "It is better not to harass this child because it seems that it may bounce back on you. He won't give up easily."

But Kantar Master was not that type of man. Afraid, he became even more aggressive and violent. He said, "I will show this child – you need not worry. And who cares about that code? I have been a teacher here my whole life, and is this child going to teach me the code?"

I said, "Tomorrow, either I will be in this building or you, but we cannot both exist here together. Just wait until tomorrow."

I rushed home and told my father. He said, "I was worried whether I had entered you in school just to bring trouble upon others and upon yourself, and to also drag me into it."

I said, "No, I am simply reporting so that later you don't say you were kept in the dark."

I went to the police commissioner. He was a lovely man; I had not expected that a policeman could be so nice. He said, "I have heard about this man. In fact my own son has been tortured by him. But nobody complained. It is illegal to torture, but unless you complain nothing can be done, and I cannot complain myself because I am worried that he may fail my child. So it is better to let him go on torturing. It is only a question of a few months, then my child will go into another class."

I said, "I am here to complain, and I am not concerned about going into another class at all. I am ready to stay in this class my whole life."

He looked at me, patted me on the back and said, "I appreciate what you are doing. I will come tomorrow."

I then rushed to see the president of the municipal committee, who proved to be just cow dung. Yes, just cow dung, and not even dry – so ugly! He said to me, "I know. Nothing can be done about it. You have to live with it, you will have to learn how to tolerate it."

I said to him, and I remember my words exactly, "I am not going to tolerate anything that is wrong to my conscience."

He said, "If that is the case, I cannot take it in hand. Go to the vice president, perhaps he may be more helpful."

And for that I must thank that cow dung, because the vice president of that village, Shambhu Dube, proved to be the only man of any worth in that whole village, in my experience. When I knocked on his door – I was only eight or nine years old, and he was the vice president – he called, "Yes, come in." He was expecting to see some gentleman, and on seeing me he looked a little embarrassed.

I said, "I am sorry that I am not a little older – please excuse me. Moreover, I am not educated at all, but I have to complain about this man, Kantar Master."

The moment he heard my story – that this man tortures little children in the first grade by putting pencils between their fingers and then squeezing, and that he has pins which he forces under the nails, and he is a man seven feet tall, weighing four hundred pounds – he could not believe it.

He said, "I have heard rumors, but why has nobody complained?"

I said, "Because people are afraid that their children will be tortured even more."

He said, "Are you not afraid?"

I said, "No, because I am ready to fail. That's all he can do." I said I was ready to fail and I was not insisting on success, but I would fight to the last: "It is either this man or me – we both cannot be there in the same building."

Shambhu Dube called me close to him. Holding my hand he said, "I always love rebellious people, but I never thought a child of your age could be a rebel. I congratulate you."

We became friends, and this friendship lasted until he died. That village had a population of twenty thousand people, but in India it is still a village. In India, unless the town has one hundred thousand people it is not considered a town. When there are more than fifteen hundred thousand people then it is a city. In my whole life I never came across another in that village of the same caliber, quality or talent as Shambhu Dube. If you ask me, it will look like an exaggeration, but in fact, in the whole of India I never found another Shambhu Dube. He was just rare.

When I was traveling all over India he would wait for months for me to come and visit the village just for one day. He was the only person who ever came to see me when my train would pass through the village. Of course I am not including my father nor my mother; they had to come. But Shambhu Dube was not my relative. He just loved me, and this love started at that meeting, on that day when I had gone to protest against Kantar Master.

Shambhu Dube was the vice president of the municipal committee, and he said to me, "Don't be worried. That fellow should be punished. In fact, his service is finished. He has applied for an extension but we will not give it to him. From tomorrow you will not see him in that school again."

I said, "Is that a promise?"

We looked into each other's eyes. He laughed and said, "Yes, it is a promise."

The next day Kantar Master was gone. He was never able to look at me after that. I tried to contact him, knocked at his door many times just to say goodbye, but he was really a coward, a sheep under a lion's skin. But that first day in school turned out to be the beginning of many, many things.

Session 21

OKAY.... THE MAN I WAS talking about, his full name was Pandit Shambhuratan Dube. We all used to call him Shambhu Babu. He was a poet, and rare in that he was not eager to be published. That is very rare in a poet. I have come across hundreds of the tribe, and they are all so eager to be published that poetry becomes secondary. I call any ambitious person a politician, and Shambhu Dube was not ambitious.

He was not an elected vice president either, because to be elected you have to at least stand for election. He was nominated by the president, who was just holy cow dung as I have said before, and he wanted some men with intelligence to do his work. The president was an absolute cow dung, and he had been in office for years. Again and again he had been chosen by other cow dungs.

In India, to be a holy cow dung is a great thing – you become a mahatma. This president was almost a mahatma, and as bogus as they all are, otherwise they would not be mahatmas in the first place. Why should a man of creativity and intelligence choose to be a cow dung? Why should he be at all interested in being worshipped? I will not even mention the name of the holy cow dung; it is filthy. He had nominated Shambhu Babu as his vice president, and I think that was the only good thing that he did in his whole life. Perhaps he did not know what he was doing – cow dungs are not conscious people.

The moment Shambhu Babu and I saw each other, something happened: what Carl Gustav Jung calls "synchronicity." I was just a child; not only that, wild too. I was fresh from the woods, uneducated and undisciplined. We had nothing in common. He was a man of power and very respected by the people, not because he was a cow dung but because he was such a strong man, and if you were not respectful to him, some day you might suffer for it. And his memory was very very good. Everybody was really afraid of him and so they were all respectful, and I was just a child.

Apparently there was nothing in common between us. He was the vice president of the whole village, the president of the lawyers' association, the president of the Rotary Club, and so on and so forth. He was either the president or the vice president of many committees. He was everywhere, and he was a well-educated man. He had the highest degrees in law, but he did not practice law in that village.

Don't be worried about the noisy devils working outside – after all they are my disciples. If I initiate devils into sannyas what can you expect? I have been taking all the disciples from Beelzebub. That was the name Gurdjieff used to call the devil, Beelzebub. But I would like to tell Gurdjieff that Beelzebub is losing hundreds of disciples every day. But they have been with Beelzebub for so long that they have learned his technology. I am not against technology, I love it. That is why Beelzebub's disciples find it easy to become my disciples, very easy, because they continue the same work under me that they used to do for ugly Beelzebub.

So don't be worried if I am not. In fact all their noises give such a beautiful background to what I am saying to you...of course, a sort of Picasso background, a little nightmarish. But sometimes nightmares can be beautiful, and one can feel sorry when they are ended. And what they are doing may not sound beautiful, but they are doing my work. Naturally Beelzebub is very angry...they are his disciples and using all his technology for me.

Science is a little devilish. You are medically trained, so in a way you are part of Beelzebub's technology. Forgive those poor fellows – they are doing their best, and as far as I am concerned, when I am speaking nothing matters.

I was saying – look at the background, and the silence: if one knows, then one can use Beelzebub as a servant.

I was telling you about Shambhu Dube, Shambhu Babu. He was a poet, but never published his poetry while he was still alive. He was a great story writer too, and by chance a famous film director became acquainted with him and his stories. Now Shambhu Babu is dead but a great film has been made using one of his stories, *Jhansi ki rani* – "The Queen of Jhansi." It won many awards, both national and international. Alas he is no more. He was my only friend in that place.

Once it was decided that I would live there...it was planned for only seven years but I actually lived there for eleven years. Perhaps they said only seven years to persuade me to stay; perhaps it was their intention from the beginning.

In India in those days, the educational structure began with four years of primary education – it was a separate phenomenon, under the local authorities – then three years more if you wanted to continue in the same direction. That is seven years; and then you would get a certificate.

Perhaps that was their intention and they were not lying to me. But there was another way too, and that is what actually happened. After four years you could either continue in the same line or change: you could go to the middle school. If you continued in the same line you never learned English. Primary education ended after seven years, and you were fully educated in only the local language – and in India there are thirty recognized languages. But after the fourth year there was an opening and you could change gear. You could go to the English school; you could join the middle school as it was called.

Again it was a four-year course, and if you continued in that line then after another three years later you became a matriculate. My God! What a wastage of life! All those beautiful days wasted so mercilessly, crushed! And by the time you were a matriculate, you were then capable of going to university. Again it was a six-year course! In all, I had to waste four years in primary school, four years in middle school, three years in high school, and six years in university – seventeen years of my life!

I think, if I can make any sense out of it, the only word that comes to me, in spite of Beelzebub and his disciples doing great work – ex-disciples, I mean – the only word that comes to me is 'nonsense'. Seventeen years! And I was eight or nine when I started this whole nonsense, so the day I left the university I was twenty-six, and so happy – not because I was a gold medalist but because I was free at last. Free again.

I was in such a hurry that I told my professor, "Don't waste my time. Nobody can convince me to enter these gates again. Even when I was nine years old my father had to drag me in, but now nobody can drag me. If anyone tries then I will drag him out." And of course I was able to drag the poor old man who was trying to persuade me not to leave.

He said, "Listen to me: it is rare to receive a scholarship for a Ph.D. Do your Ph.D., and I promise you that you will one day be able to have a D.Litt."

I said, "Don't waste my time, because my bus is leaving." The bus was standing there at the gate. I had to rush to catch it, and I am sorry that I could not even thank him. I had no time – the bus was leaving, and my luggage was already on it, and the driver – as drivers do – was honking like mad. I was the only passenger not yet on the bus, and my old professor was almost on his knees persuading me not to leave.

Shambhu Babu was well-educated, I was uneducated, when the friendship began. He had a glorious past; I had none. The whole town was shocked by our friendship, but he was not even embarrassed. I respect that quality. We used to walk hand in hand. He was my father's age, and his children were older than me. He died ten years before my father. I think he must have been about fifty at that time. This would have been the right time for us to be friends. But he was the only man to recognize me. He was a man of authority in the village, and his recognition was of immense help to me.

Kantar Master was never seen at the school again. He was immediately sent on leave, because there was only one month before his retirement, and his application for an extension had been canceled. This created a great celebration in the village. Kantar Master had been a great man in that village, yet I had had him thrown out in just a single day. That was something. People started respecting me. I would say, "What nonsense is this? I have not done anything – I simply brought the man and his wrongdoing to the light."

I am surprised how he continued torturing small children his

SHAMBHU BABU

whole life. But that is what was thought to be education. It was thought then, and many Indians still think, that unless you torture a child he cannot be taught – although they may not say so clearly.

So I said, "There is no question of respect, and as far as my friendship with Shambhu Babu is concerned, it is not a matter of age. He is my father's friend really. Even my father is amazed."

My father used to ask Shambhu Babu, "Why are you so friendly to that troublesome boy?"

And Shambhu Babu would laugh and say, "One day you will understand why. I cannot tell you now." I was always amazed at the beauty of the man. It was part of his beauty that he could answer by saying, "I cannot answer. One day you will understand."

One day he said to my father, "Perhaps I should not be friendly to him, but respectful."

It shocked me too. When we were alone, I said to him, "Shambhu Babu, what nonsense were you telling to my father? What do you mean by saying that you should respect me?"

He said, "I do respect you because I can see, but not very clearly, as if hidden behind a smokescreen, what you are going to be one day."

Even I had to shrug my shoulders. I said, "You are just talking rubbish. What can I be? I am already it."

He said, "There! That's what amazes me in you. You are a child; the whole village laughs at our friendship and they wonder what we talk about together, but they don't know what they are all missing. I know" – he emphasized it – "I *know* what I am missing. I can feel it a little, but I can't see it clearly. Perhaps one day when you are really grown up, I may be able to see you."

And, I have to confess, after Magga Baba he was the second man who recognized that something immeasurable had happened to me. Of course he was not a mystic, but a poet has the capacity, once in a while, to be a mystic, and he was a great poet. He was also great because he never bothered to publish his work. He never bothered to read at any gathering of poets. It looked strange that he would read his poetry to a nine-year-old child, and he would ask me, "Is it of any worth, or just worthless?"

Now his poetry is published, but he is no more. It was published in his memory. It does not contain his best work because the people who chose it, none of them were even poets, and it needs a mystic to choose from Shambhu Babu's poetry. I know everything he wrote. There was not much – a few articles, and very few poems, and a few stories, but in a strange way they all connect with a single theme.

The theme is life, not as a philosophical concept but as it is lived moment to moment. Life with a small 'l' will do, because he would never forgive me if you wrote life with a capital 'L'. He was against capital letters. He never wrote any word with capitals. Even the beginning of a sentence would always be written with small letters. He would even write his own name in small letters. I asked him, "What is wrong with capital letters? Why are you so against them, Shambhu Babu?"

He said, "I am not against them, but I am in love with the immediate, not the faraway. I am in love with small things: a cup of tea, a swim in the river, a sunbath.... I am in love with little things, and they cannot be written with capital letters."

I understand him, so when I say that although he was not an enlightened master, not a master in any way, I still count him as number two, after Magga Baba, because he recognized me when it was impossible to do so, absolutely impossible. I may not even have recognized myself, but he recognized me.

When I entered his vice president's office for the first time and we looked at each other eye to eye, for a moment there was just silence. Then he stood up and said to me, "Please sit down."

I said, "There is no need for you to stand up."

He said, "It is not a question of need, and it makes me so happy to stand up for you. I have never felt that before – and I have stood before the governor and all the so-called powerful people. I have seen the viceroy in New Delhi, but I was not mystified as I am by you, I confess. Please don't tell anybody."

And this is for the first time that I have ever told it. I have kept it a secret all these years, forty years. It feels like a relief.

This morning Gudia said, "You slept so late."

Yes, last night I slept, for the first time in many years, as I would like to sleep every night. During the whole night I was not disturbed even for a single moment. Usually I have to look at my watch once in a while just to see whether it is time to get up. But last night, after many years, I did not look at my watch at all. I even had to miss Devaraj's concoction. That's what I call his special breakfast mixture. It is a concoction but it is really good. It is difficult to eat because it takes half an hour just to chew it, but it is really healthy and nourishing. We should make it available to everybody – Devaraj's concoction for breakfast. Of course it is not fast, it is slow, very very slow. Can we call it a "break-slow"? But then it would not sound right.

I had to miss breakfast today for two reasons: first, I had to keep Devageet's time, and still I was five minutes late, and I don't like to be late. Secondly, if I had started that concoction it would have taken so much time to eat that by the time I had finished, it would have been lunch time. There would have been no gap, which is needed. So I thought I would miss it. But I really enjoy it, and in missing it, I really miss it.

Last night was one of the rarest for the simple reason that yesterday I spoke to you about Shambhu Babu, and it relieved me of a weight. I also talked about my father and the continuous struggle and how it ended. I felt so unburdened.

Shambhu Babu was a man who could have become a realized one, but missed it. He missed because of too much intellectuality. He was an intellectual giant. He could not sit silently even for a single moment. I was present when he died. It is a strange destiny that I have to see everyone I love die.

I was not very far away when he was dying. He phoned just before to say, "Come quickly if you can, because I don't think that I can last long. I mean," he said, "that I can't last even a few days."

I immediately rushed to the village. It was only eighty miles from Jabalpur, and I got there within two hours. He was so happy. He again looked at me with the same look as when we had first met, when I had been about nine years old. There was a very eloquent silence. Nothing was said, but everything was heard.

Holding his hands I told him, "Please close your eyes, don't strain."

He said, "No. The eyes are going to close very soon of their own accord, and then I won't be able to open them. So please don't ask me to close my eyes. I want to see you. Perhaps I may not be able to see you again. One thing is certain," he said, "that you are not coming back to life. Alas, had I listened to you! You always insisted on being silent but I continued to postpone. Now there is no time even to postpone."

Tears came to his eyes. I remained without saying anything, just with him. He closed his eyes and died.

He had such beautiful eyes, and such an intelligent face. I know many beautiful people but it is very rare to have the beauty of that man. It is not man-made, certainly not made in India. He was, and still is, one of my most loved ones. Although he has not yet entered into a body again, I am waiting for him.

This is a multipurpose commune. A few purposes are known to you, and a few are known only to me. This is one of the purposes unknown to the organizers of the commune, that I am awaiting a few souls. I am even preparing couples to receive them. Shambhu Babu will be here before long. There are so many memories concerning this man that I will have to refer to him again and again. But today, just his death.

Strange that I should talk about his death first and the other things later on. No, as far as I am concerned it is not strange, because to me the moment of death opens a man as nothing else does. Not even love can do that miracle. It tries to but lovers prevent it, because in love two people are needed; in death only one is enough unto oneself. That's because there is no disturbance from the other. I saw Shambhu Babu dying with such a relaxed joyous attitude that I cannot forget his face.

You will be surprised to know that he had the face of – guess who? – almost the same face as the ex-president of America, Richard Nixon! But without the ugliness hidden in every cell and fiber of Nixon...! Otherwise Shambhu Babu would have been the president of India. He was far more intelligent than the so-called president of India, Sanjiva. But I mean photographically he looked very similar to Nixon in his younger days. Of course, when a different soul is there even the same face has a different aura, a different – how to say it – a different, altogether different significance. So please don't misunderstand me, because you all know Richard

Nixon while only I knew Shambhu Babu, so misunderstanding is bound to happen.

Please forget that I said that they looked alike, just forget it. It is better that you don't know Shambhu Babu's face at all rather than you start thinking of him as Richard Nixon. But I must confess that I have a soft spot for Richard Nixon, just because he resembles Shambhu Babu. You have to forgive me that; I know he does not deserve it, but I cannot help it either. Whenever I see his picture all I see is Shambhu Babu, and not Nixon at all.

When Nixon became president of America, I said to myself, "Aha! So at least a man resembling Shambhu Babu has become president of America." I would have loved Shambhu Babu to be the president of America; of course that was not possible, but the resemblance consoles me. When Nixon did what he did, I felt ashamed, again because he resembles Shambhu Babu. And when he had to resign the presidency I was sad, not because of him – I had nothing to do with him – but because now I would not see Shambhu Babu's face again in the newspapers.

Now there is no problem because I don't read the newspapers anymore. I have not read them for years. I used to finish reading four newspapers within one minute, but for more than two years I have not even looked at one. And I don't read any books – I simply don't read. I have become uneducated again, just as I always wanted to be if my father had not dragged me into that school...but he did drag me. And what all those schools and colleges and university did to me took so much energy to undo, but I have succeeded in undoing it all.

I have undone everything that society did to me. I am again just an uneducated, wild boy from – you don't use the word in English.... In Hindi, a man from a village is called a *gamar*. A village is called a *gam*, and the villager is called a gamar. But gamar also means "fool" and they have become intermixed, so much so that nobody now thinks that the word 'gamar' means villager; everybody thinks it means fool.

I came from the village utterly blank, with nothing written on me. Even while I was away from that village I had remained a wild boy. I have never allowed anybody to write anything on me. People are always ready...not only ready but insistent that they write some-thing on you. I had come from the village empty, and I can say now that all that has been written in between I have erased, and erased completely. In fact I have demolished the wall itself so you cannot write anything on it ever again.

Shambhu Babu could have done this too. I know he was capable of it, of becoming a buddha, but it didn't happen. Perhaps his very profession – he was a lawyer – prevented it. I have heard of all kinds of people becoming buddhas, but I have never heard of any lawyer becoming a buddha. I don't think anybody from that profession could become a buddha unless he really renounced all that he had learned. Shambhu Babu could not gather that courage, and I feel sorry for him. I don't feel sorry for anybody else because I have never come across anybody else who was so capable and yet did not take the jump.

I used to ask him, "Shambhu Babu, what is the hitch?"

And he would always say the same thing: "How can I explain it? I don't know exactly what the hitch is, but there must be something preventing me."

I know what it was, but he also knew it although he never recog-nized that he knew it. And he knew that I knew that he knew it. He would always close his eyes whenever I would ask the question – and I am a stubborn man; again and again I would ask him, "What is the hitch?"

He would close his eyes, just not to face me eye to eye, because that was the one situation where he could not lie. I mean he could not be a lawyer...liar. But now that he is dead I can say that even though he was not a buddha, he was almost a buddha, which I will never say about anybody else again. I will keep this special category, of almost-a-buddha, for Shambhu Babu.

Session 22

I WAS JUST GOING TO SAY "Okay," but no. One day I said it lightly, just to be polite, and suffered much. Then everything went wrong. So now I'm going to say okay only when it is really okay; otherwise silence is better....

Okay.

I am reminded again of poor Sigmund Freud. He was waiting in his office for a rich, and of course Jewish, patient. How can you be rich without being a Jew? And psychoanalysis is the greatest business that any Jew ever founded. They missed Jesus, they could not afford to miss Sigmund Freud. Of course he is no comparison.

Freud was waiting and waiting, walking up and down his room. The patient was really rich, and psychoanalysis is a treatment which goes on for years, unless the patient finds a far more articulate Jew, but he never gets out of the vicious circle.

Freud looked again and again at his gold watch, and then at the last moment, when he was really thinking of giving up, the patient appeared. His big car appeared on the horizon, and Freud was, of course, furious. Finally the car came to his porch, the Jew got out, and when he entered the office Sigmund Freud was really angry because he was fifty seconds late.

Freud said, "It's good that I heard your car at the porch at the right time; otherwise I was going to begin the session alone."

It is a professional joke. Only those who are in the profession of psychoanalysis will understand it. I will have to explain it to you because none of you is a psychoanalyst.

The joke is that Freud said, "I would have started even without you" – without the patient. Do you see the point? Let me be clearer

– the joke has to be put aside. At a certain point, I have to begin.

Exactly at the time to say "okay" I'll say it – and not like Sigmund Freud, but fully knowing the joke. Still, I cannot disappoint you. This is only an introductory note; now we take up the unending story.

Yes, it is unending. How can it end before I end? Somebody else will have to write the afterword. I cannot write it – please excuse me for that – but I am preparing my people: Devageet, Devaraj, Ashu... this trinity will do it. And remember, in my trinity there is a woman who will keep both the fellows fighting forever. But still they will manage to write the afterword. If they cannot manage, then Ashu can let them fight, and meanwhile she herself can write it.

This morning, by the way, I referred to Carl Gustav Jung's word 'synchronicity'. I don't like the man, but I like the word that he introduced. For that he should be given all possible credit. In no other language is there a word like 'synchronicity', because it is an invented word, invented by Carl Gustav Jung.

But all words are invented by somebody or other, so there is nothing wrong in inventing a word, particularly when it really indicates an experience which has remained unlabeled for centuries. Just for this single word, 'synchronicity', Jung should have received the Nobel Prize, although he is a mediocrity. But so many mediocre people have received the Nobel Prize; if one more receives it, what is wrong? And they also award the prize posthumously, so please, give this poor fellow Carl Gustav Jung a Nobel Prize. I'm not joking. I am really thankful for this word, because this is what has always eluded the grasp of the human intellect.

I was talking to you about my strange friendship with Shambhu Babu. It was strange on many counts. First, he was older than my father, or perhaps the same age – but as far as I remember, he looked older – and I was only nine years old. Now, what kind of friendship is possible? He was a successful legal expert, not only in that small place, but he practiced in the high court and in the supreme court. He was one of the topmost legal authorities. And he was a friend of a wild, unruly, undisciplined, illiterate child. When he said, on that first meeting, "Please be seated," I was amazed.

I had not hoped that the vice president would stand to receive me and would say, "Please be seated."

I said to him, "First, you be seated. I feel a little embarrassed to sit before you do. You are old, perhaps even older than my father."

He said, "Don't be worried. I am a friend of your father. But relax and tell me what you have come for."

I said, "I will tell you later on why I have come here. First...." He looked at me, I looked at him; and what transpired in that small fragment of a moment became my first question. I asked him, "First, tell me what happened just now, between your eyes and mine."

He closed his eyes. I think perhaps ten minutes must have passed before he opened them again. He said, "Forgive me, I cannot figure it out – but *something* happened."

We became friends; that was sometime in 1940. Only later on, years afterwards, just one year before he died – he died in 1960, after twenty years of friendship, strange friendship – only then was I able to tell him that the word he had been searching for had been invented by Carl Gustav Jung. That word is 'synchronicity'; that is what was happening between us. He knew it, I knew it, but the word was missing.

Synchronicity can mean many things all together, it is multi-dimensional. It can mean a certain rhythmic feeling; it can mean what people have always called love; it can mean friendship; it can simply mean two hearts beating together without rhyme or reason... it is a mystery. Only once in a while one finds someone with whom things fit; the jigsaw just disappears. All the pieces that were not fitting suddenly fit on their own accord.

When I told my grandmother, "I have become friends with the vice president of this town," she said, "You mean Pandit Shambhu-ratan Dube?"

I said, "You look a little shocked by it. What's the matter with you, Nani?"

Tears rolled down from her eyes. She said, "Then you will not find many friends in the world, that's why I am worried. If Shambhu Babu has become your friend then you will not find many friends in the world. Not only that: perhaps you may find friends, because you are young, but Shambhu Babu will certainly not find another friend in the world, because he is too old."

Again and again my grandmother will come into my story with

her tremendous insight. Yes, I can see it now. Recapitulating, I can see what she had seen and wept over. I know now that Shambhu Babu never had any other friend; except for me he was friendless.

I used to visit my village once in a while, perhaps once a year, or twice, not more than that. And as I became more and more involved in my own activity – or you can call it inactivity…as I became more and more involved with the sannyasins, and the movement of meditation, my visits to the village became even rarer. In fact, the last few years before he died my only visits were when I passed through the village on the train.

The stationmaster was my sannyasin, so of course the train would stay as long as I wanted it to. They – and by "they" I mean my father, my mother, Shambhu Babu, and many others who loved me – would come to the station. That would be my only visit: ten, twenty, at the most thirty minutes. The train could not be delayed any longer because other trains had to come. They would be waiting outside the station.

But I can understand his loneliness. He had no other friends. Almost every day he wrote a letter to me – that is very rare – and there was nothing to write. Sometimes he would just send the empty paper inside an envelope. I would understand even that. He was feeling very lonely, and would like to have my company. I tried my best to be there as much as it was practical, because to me it was really a drag to be in that village. It was just for him that I suffered that village.

After he died I rarely, very rarely went there. I now had an excuse – that I could not come because it reminded me of Shambhu Babu. But really there was no point in going there. When he was there, there was a point. He was just a small oasis in a desert.

He was absolutely unafraid about all kinds of condemnation that came to him because of me. To be associated with me, even in those days, was not a good thing. It was dangerous. They told him, "You will lose all the respect of the community, and it is the community that made you from vice president into the president."

I said to him, "You can choose, Shambhu Babu: be the president of this stupid village or be my friend."

He resigned his mayorship, and his presidency. He didn't say a single word to me; he simply wrote his letter of resignation there, in front of me. He said, "I love something in you which is indefinable. The presidency of this stupid town means nothing to me. I am ready to lose everything, if it comes to that. Yes, I am ready to lose everything."

They tried to persuade him not to resign, but he would not take it back.

I told him, "Shambhu Babu, you know perfectly well I hate all these presidencies, vice presidencies, whether they are municipal or national. I cannot say to you, 'Take back your resignation,' because I could not commit that crime. If you want to take it back you are free to do so."

He said, "The seal is closed. There is no point in going back, and I am happy that you did not try to persuade me."

He remained a lonely man. He had enough money to live like a rich man, so when he resigned his presidency he also resigned from the bar. He said, "I have enough money, why bother? And why law? – with all the legalities and continuous lying in the name of truth."

He stopped his profession. These were the qualities I loved in him. Without thinking for a single moment, he resigned, and the next day he dropped out of the bar association. For him, I had to visit the village once in a while, or call him to my place, just to be with me for a few days. Once in a while he used to come.

He was a real man, not afraid of any consequences. He once asked me, "What are you going to do? – because I don't think that you can remain in the university as a professor for long."

I said, "Shambhu Babu, I never plan. If I drop out of this work I hope some other work will be there waiting for me. If God..." and remember the "if," because he was not a theist, that was another quality I loved in him; he used to say, "Unless I know, how can I believe?"

I said to him, "If God can find work for all kinds of people, animals, trees, I think he will be able to find some kind of work for me too. And if he cannot find any it is his problem, not mine."

He laughed and said, "Yes, that is perfectly right. Yes, it is his problem if he is there – but the point is: if he is not there, then what?"

I said, "I don't see any problem for me then either. If there is no work I can take a deep breath and say goodbye to existence. It is enough proof that I am not needed. And if I am not needed then I am not going to impose myself on this poor existence."

Our talks, could they all be recapitulated, our arguments, could they all be again reproduced, would make even better dialogues than Plato. He was a very logical man, just as logical as I am illogical. And that is the most baffling thing: that we were the only friends for each other in the town.

Everybody asked, "He is a logician, you are utterly illogical. What is the bridge between you both?"

I said, "It will be difficult for you to understand because you are neither. His very logic brings him to its very brink. I am illogical, not because I was born illogical – nobody is born illogical; I am illogical because I have seen the futility of logic. So I can go with him according to his logic and yet, at a certain point, go ahead of him and then he becomes afraid and stops. And that is keeping our friendship, because he knows he has to go beyond that point, and he knows nobody else who can be of any help to him. You all" – I meant the people of the town – "think that he is a help to me. You are wrong. You can ask him. I am a help to him."

You will be surprised but one day a few people went to his house to inquire, "Is it true that this small boy is some sort of guide or help to you?"

He said, "Certainly. There is no doubt about it. Why have you come to ask me? Why don't you ask him? – he lives next door to your house."

The quality is very rare, and my grandmother was right when she said, "I am afraid that Shambhu Babu is going to be without a friend. And," she said, "as far as you are concerned, my fears are there.... But you are still young; perhaps you may find a few friends."

Her insight was really so clear. You will be surprised to know that in my whole life I have not had any friend except for Shambhu Babu. If he had not been there I would never have known what it means to have a friend. Yes, I have had many acquaintances – in school, in college, at university, there were hundreds. You might have thought they were all friends, they may even have thought the same – but except for this man, I have not known a single person whom I could call a friend.

To be acquainted is very easy; acquaintance is very ordinary. But friendship is not part of the ordinary world. You will be surprised to know that whenever I became ill – and I was eighty miles away from the town – I would immediately receive a phone call from Shambhu Babu, very much concerned.

He would ask, "Are you okay?"

I would say, "What's the matter? Why are you so worried? You sound sick."

He said, "I am not sick but I felt that you were, and now I know that you are. You cannot hide it from me."

It happened many times. You will not believe it, but it was just for him that I had to take a private number. Of course there was a phone for my secretary to take care of all my arrangements around the country. But I had a secret, private phone just for Shambhu Babu, so that he could inquire if he felt concerned, even in the middle of the night. I even made it a point that if I was not in the house, perhaps traveling somewhere in India, and I was sick, I would phone him myself just to say, "Please don't be worried because I am sick." This is synchronicity.

Somehow a deep, deep connection existed. The day he died I went to him without hesitation. I did not even inquire. I simply drove to the town. I never liked that road, and I like driving, but that road from Jabalpur to Gadarwara was really a sonofabitch! You will not find a worse road anywhere. Our road connecting the ranch to Antelope is a superhighway by comparison. What do they call them in Germany? Autobahn?

"Yes, Osho."

Okay, if Devageet says it is right, then it must be right. Our road is an autobahn compared to the road from the university to Shambhu Babu's house. I just rushed...a feeling in the guts.

I am a speedy driver. I love speed, but on that road you cannot go more than twenty miles an hour; that's the maximum possible, so you can conceive of what kind of a road it must be. By the time you arrive, if you are not dead then you are something close to it! There is just one good thing: before you enter the town you come across the river. That is its saving grace: you can take a good bath, you can swim for half an hour to refresh yourself, and give your car a good bath too. Then, when you reach the town, nobody thinks you are a holy ghost.

I rushed. Never in my life have I been in such a hurry. Not even now, although now I should be in a hurry because time is slipping out of my hands and the day is not far off when I will have to say goodbye to you all, although I may have liked to linger a little longer. Nothing is in my hands except the arms of this chair, and you can see how I am clinging onto them, feeling them to see whether I am still in the body. There is no need to worry…there is still a little time.

That day I had to hurry, and it proved true because if I had been just a few minutes later I would never have seen Shambhu Babu's eyes again. Alive, I mean – I mean looking at me just the way he had looked that first time. I wanted to see that first look for the last time…that synchronicity. And in that half hour before he died there was nothing but pure communion. I told him he could say whatever he wanted to say.

He sent everybody else away. Of course they were offended. His wife and sons and his brothers did not like it. But he clearly said, "Whether you like it or not, I want you all to leave immediately because I don't have much time to waste."

Naturally afraid, they all left. We both laughed. I said, "Anything you want to say to me, you can say."

He said, "I have nothing to say to you. Just hold my hands. Let me feel you. Fill me with your presence, I beg you." He went on, "I cannot go on my knees and touch your feet. It is not that I would not like to do it, just that my body is not in a position to get out of bed. I cannot even move. I have just a few minutes longer."

I could see that death was almost on his doorstep. I took his hands, and said a few things to him, to which he listened very attentively.

In my childhood I have known only two people who really made me aware what real attention is. The first, of course, was my Nani. I am even feeling a little sad to put her alongside Shambhu Babu, because her attention, although similar, possessed many more dimensions. In fact I should not have said two people. But I have already said it; now let me explain to you as clearly as possible.

With my Nani, every night it was almost a ritual, just as you all are waiting every night and every morning....

Do you know that every morning I wake up and hurry to my bathroom to take a bath and get ready because I know everybody must be waiting? Today I did not have my breakfast simply because I knew it would delay you all. I had slept a little longer than usual. Every evening I know you all must be getting ready, taking your shower, and the moment I see the light in your small room, I know the devils have arrived and now I must hurry.

And the whole day you are busy. Your time is packed the whole day. You could say that I am a completely retired man – not tired, retired...and not retired by anybody else. That is my way of life – to live relaxedly, not doing anything from morning to evening, from evening to morning. Keeping everybody else busy without business, that is my whole work. I don't think there is anybody in the world – or has ever been before, or will ever be after – who is so without business of any kind, like me. And yet, just to keep me breathing I need thousands of sannyasins to be continuously working. Can you think of a greater joke?

Just today I was telling Chetana that Vivek has gone on holiday. After ten years the poor girl certainly deserves it. It is not much to ask in ten years. Mathematically it is one day every two years.

I said to her, "You can go, happily."

She has gone to California. I said to her, "I will be happy for you to enjoy these few days."

I was telling Chetana, "Next year perhaps I too can go on holiday for a few days." But the problem is, I cannot go alone. I need my whole staff, and cannot do without any one of them. My whole staff is far bigger than the president of America's. It is a poor man's staff; it has to be bigger than his. And not the president of any country, but of the richest country. Why? – because my staff does not consist of servants, it consists of my lovers, and I cannot do without any of them.

That's the only problem, and I told Chetana. But she was happy. She was so happy that I don't think she even bothered about my problem. Of course she was happy, because if my staff is going on holiday with me then she is bound to be there. And Chetana...once there was a time when I used to do my own laundry, but it certainly wasn't as good as yours. I cannot give you a better recommendation than that, because although I did the best that I could, it was just a job to be done and finished as soon as possible. To you it is a prayer, a love affair, not just work to be done. I don't think there is anybody in the whole world who has better laundered clothes than mine.

So Chetana was happy, thinking, "Great, we are all going on holiday." But I have to take so many people that Vivek was right. When we were leaving Poona, there was so much preparation – particularly for her, because she had to be concerned with my body, my food, and small details like that. I don't think she could sleep the whole time, she was so concerned that nothing should be left behind, and that everything should be available on the journey. Vivek was right when she told me, "Osho, you are like a huge mountain of gold which has to be taken from one place to another."

I said to her, "That is true, exactly true. Just one thing has to be remembered: that the mountain, although golden, is alive and conscious too. So be very careful."

You see my difficulty, Chetana? Now, if I go on holiday even for a week, or for a weekend, how much will you have to prepare? We would have to make everything exactly as it is here in Lao Tzu House – it is a huge task. But because you were so happy I thought it would be worth doing. Just to make even a single person happy I can do anything whatsoever. That has been my whole life's very substance.

Session 23

OW, MY WORK UPON YOU....
I was telling you about a certain relationship that happened between a child of about nine years of age and an old man of perhaps fifty. The difference in age was great, but love can transcend all barriers. If it can happen even between a man and a woman, then what other barrier could be bigger? But it was not, and cannot be described as just love. He could have loved me like a son, or like his grandson, but that was not it.

What happened was friendliness – and let it be on record: I value friendliness higher than love. There is nothing higher than friendliness. I know you must have noticed that I have not used the word 'friendship'. Up till yesterday I was using it, but now is the time to tell you of something greater than friendship – friendliness.

Friendship can also be binding, in its own way, like love. It can also be jealous, possessive, afraid that it may be lost, and because of that fear, so much agony and so much struggle. In fact people are continuously fighting those whom they love – strange, just strange ...unbelievably strange.

Friendliness rises higher, to all that man knows and feels. It is more a fragrance of being, or you can say a flowering of being. Something transpires between two souls, and suddenly there are two bodies, but one being – that is what I call flowering. Friendliness is freedom from all that is small and mediocre, from all that we are acquainted with – in fact, too acquainted with.

I can understand why my Nani shed tears for my being friendly with Shambhu Babu. She was right when she said to me, "I am not bothered for Shambhu Babu – he is old enough, soon death will overtake him." And it is strange, but he died before my grandmother, exactly ten years before, and yet my grandmother was older than him.

I am still amazed at that woman's intuition. She had said, "He will die before long; then what about you? My tears are for you. You have to live a long life. You will not find many people of such quality as Shambhu Babu. Please don't make his friendship your criterion; otherwise you will have to live a very lonely life."

I said, "Nani, even Shambhu Babu is below my criterion, so you need not worry. I am going to live a life according to my vision, wherever it may lead – perhaps nowhere. But one thing is certain," I told her, "that I absolutely agree with you that I will not find many friends."

And it was true. In my schooldays I had no friends. In my college days I was thought to be a stranger. In the university, yes, people always respected me, but that is not friendship, what to say of friendliness. It is a strange fate to have always been respected from my very childhood. But if my Nani were alive now she could have seen my friends, my sannyasins. She would see thousands of people with whom I have a synchronicity. But she is dead; Shambhu Babu is dead. The flowering has come at a moment when all those who were really concerned about me are no more.

She was right in saying that I would live a lonely life, but she was wrong too, because just like everybody else, she thought loneliness and aloneness are synonymous; they are not. Not only are they not synonymous, they are poles apart.

Loneliness is a negative state. When you cannot be with yourself and beg the company of the other, then it is loneliness. Whether you get the company or not will not make any difference at all; you will remain lonely. All over the world, in every house, you can see the truth of what I am saying. I cannot say every home, I say every house. A home very rarely exists. A home is where loneliness has been transformed into aloneness, not into togetherness.

People think that if two people are together, then loneliness is finished. It is not so easy. Remember it, it is not so easy; in fact it becomes more difficult. When two lonely people meet loneliness is multiplied; not only doubled, remember, it is a multiplication, and very ugly. It is like an octopus, a continuous fight in different names, for different reasons. But if you put all these covers aside, underneath you will see nothing but naked loneliness. It is not aloneness. Aloneness is the discovery of one's self.

Many times I told my grandmother that being alone is the most beautiful state one can dream of. She would laugh and say, "Shut up! Nonsense. I know what it is – I am living a lonely life. Your Nana is dead. He deceived me: he died without even telling me that he was going to die. He died without even communicating to me where he was going, and to what. He betrayed me." She was bitter about it. She then told me, "You left me too. You went to university, and you only visit once or twice each year. I wait for months just for the day you will be back home. And those one or two days are over so quickly. You don't know what loneliness is – I know."

Although she was crying, I laughed. I wanted to cry with her but could not. Instead of crying, I laughed.

She said, "Look! You don't understand me at all."

I said, "I do understand, that's why I am laughing. Again and again you go on insisting that loneliness and aloneness are one, and I say definitely and absolutely, they are not the same. And you will have to understand aloneness if you want to get rid of your loneliness. You cannot get rid of it just by being sorry for yourself. And don't be angry with my grandfather...."

This was the only time I defended my Nana against her. "What could he do? He has not betrayed you – although you may feel betrayed. That's another matter. Death or life are in nobody's hands. He died as helplessly as he was born...and don't you remember how helpless he was? He was calling again and again, 'Stop the wheel, Raja, can't you stop the wheel?' In that constant asking us to stop the wheel what was he asking? He was asking for his freedom.

"He was saying, 'I don't want to be born against my will, and I don't want to die against my will.' He wanted to *be*. He may not have been able to say it correctly, but that's exactly how I translate what he said. He just wanted to be – without any interference, without being forced into birth or being forced into death. That's what he was against. He was only asking for freedom."

And do you know, the Indian word for the ultimate is *moksha*.

216

Moksha means "absolute freedom." There is no word in any language exactly like moksha – particularly not in English, because English is so dominated by Christianity.

Just the other day I received a photo album from one of the German centers. The album consists of all the pictures of that beautiful place and its opening ceremony. Even the Christian priest from the nearby church participated in the ceremony. I liked what he said: "These people are beautiful. I have been watching them working harder than anybody works nowadays, and so joyously that it is a joy to see them…but they are a little bit crazy."

What he said was right, but why he said, "They are a little bit crazy," is not right. Yes, they are crazy – far more than he could conceive. But the reason why he said it was ugly: the "why" not the "what." He called them crazy because they believe that there are many lives, lives after lives. That was his reason for calling them crazy.

In fact, if anyone is crazy then it is not my people but those who think that my people are crazy. I reserve that right for myself. I can call them crazy, because when I say it, I say it out of love and understanding. It is not a condemnatory word for me; for me it is an appreciation. All the poets are crazy, all the painters are crazy, all the musicians are crazy; otherwise they would not be the poets, the musicians and the painters. If this is so about the painters, the musicians and the dancers, then what about the mystics? They must be the craziest. And my sannyasins are on the way to being the craziest, because I know no other way to be really sane in this insane world.

My grandmother was right in saying I would not have friends, and she was also right in saying that Shambhu Babu would not have friends. About Shambhu Babu she was absolutely right; about me, only to the point when I started initiating people into sannyas. She was alive for just a few days after I initiated the first group of sannyasins in the Himalayas. I had particularly chosen the most beautiful part of the Himalayas, Kulu Manali – "the valley of the gods" as it is called. And certainly it is a valley of gods. It is so beautiful that one cannot believe it, even when one is standing in the valley itself. It is unbelievably true. I had chosen Kulu Manali for the first initiation of twenty-one sannyasins.

That was just a few days before my mother...my grandmother died. Excuse me again, because I go on again and again calling her "mother" and then correcting it. What can I do? I had known her as my mother. My whole life I have tried to correct it and not been able to. I still don't call my mother "mother"; I still call her "bhabhi," not mother, and *bhabhi* only means "elder brother's wife." All my brothers laugh at me. They say, "Why do you go on calling mother 'bhabhi'? – because bhabhi means elder brother's wife. Certainly your father is not your elder brother." But what can I do? I knew my grandmother as my mother from my earliest years, and those early years are the most important years of life. It is what I think the scientists call an "imprint."

When a bird comes out of its egg and looks at its mother, with that first look he is imprinted. But if the bird comes out and you have removed the mother and replaced her with something else, a different imprint happens.

It actually happened this way that the word 'imprint' came into use. A scientist was working on what happens when a bird first comes out of the egg. He removed everything from the surroundings but he completely forgot that he himself was there. The bird came out, looked around and could see only the boots of the scientist who was standing there watching.

The bird came to the boots and very lovingly started playing with them. The scientist was amazed but later on he was in trouble because the bird was continuously knocking on his door, not for him, but for his boots. He had to keep his boots near the bird's house. And the strangest thing you can imagine happened: when the bird became mature he first made love with the boots. He could not fall in love with a girl bird – and there were many available – but he had a certain imprint of how his love-object should be. He could only love a beautiful pair of boots.

I lived with my grandmother for years and thought of her as my mother. And it was not a loss. I would have liked her to be my mother. If there were any possibility of my being born again, although there is none, I would choose her to be my mother. I am simply emphasizing the point. There is no possibility of my being born again; the wheel has stopped long ago. But she was right when she said that I would not have friends. I did not have friends in school, high school, college or at university. Although many thought they were my friends, they were just admirers, at the most acquaintances, or at the very most followers, but not friends.

The day I started initiating, my only fear was, "Will I be able to someday change my followers into my friends?" The night before, I could not sleep. Again and again I thought, "How am I going to manage it? A follower is not supposed to be a friend." I said to myself that night in Kulu Manali in the Himalayas, "Don't be serious. You can manage anything, although you don't know the ABC of managerial science."

I recall a book by Bern, *The Managerial Revolution*. I read it, not because the title contained the word 'revolution', but because the title contained the word 'managerial'. Although I loved the book, naturally I was disappointed because it was not what I was looking for. I was never able to manage anything. So that night in Kulu Manali I laughed.

One man – I will not tell you his name because he betrayed me, and it is better not to mention somebody who betrayed me and is still alive – was sleeping in my room. He was awakened by my laughter, and I said to him, "Don't be worried. I cannot be more mad than I already am. You go to sleep."

"But," he said, "just one question; otherwise I cannot go to sleep: Why did you laugh?"

I said, "I was just telling myself a joke."

He laughed and went to sleep without even asking what the joke was.

I knew that very moment what kind of seeker he was. In fact, like a flash of lightning I saw that this man was not going to be with me very long. So I did not initiate him into sannyas, although he insisted. Everybody wondered, because I was insisting for others to "take the jump" yet resisting all persuasion from that man. He wanted to take the jump and I said, "Please wait."

Within two months it was clear to everybody why I had not given sannyas to him. Within two months he had left. Leaving is not a problem, but he became my enemy. To be my enemy is inconceivable to me – yes, even to me. I cannot believe how anybody can be an enemy to me. I have not harmed anybody in my life. You cannot find a more harmless creature. Why should anybody be my enemy? Must be something to do with the person himself. He must be using me as a screen.

I would have liked to initiate my grandmother, but she was in the village of Gadarwara. I even tried to contact her, but Kulu Manali is nearly two thousand miles from Gadarwara.

'Gadarwara' is a strange name. I wanted to avoid it, but it had to come anyway, this way or that, so it is better to be finished with it. It means 'the village of the shepherd'; it is even stranger because the place in Kashmir where Jesus is buried is called Pahalgam, which also means the village of the shepherd. In the case of Pahalgam it is understandable, but why my village? I have never seen any sheep there, nor any shepherds. Why is it called the village of the shepherd? There are not many Christians there either; in fact, only one. You will be surprised: he is the priest of a small church, and I used to be his only listener.

He once asked me, "It is strange: you are not a Christian so why do you come exactly on time, every Sunday without fail?" He went on, "Whether it rains or there is a hailstorm, I have to come because I think that you must be waiting – and you are always here. Why?"

I said, "You don't know me. I just love to torture people, and to listen to you torturing yourself for one hour, saying things you don't mean, and not saying things that you do mean, is such a joy to me. I would come even if the whole village were burning. You can rely on me: I would still be here exactly on time."

So certainly Christians have nothing to do with that village. Only one Christian lived there and his church was not much of a church either – just a small house. Of course a cross had been placed on it, and under it was written: "This is a Christian Church." I had always wondered why that village was called the village of the shepherd, and when I went to Jesus' grave in Pahalgam, in Kashmir, the question became even more pertinent.

Strangely, Pahalgam has almost the same structure as my village. It may be just a coincidence. When you cannot figure something out you say, "Perhaps it is a coincidence" – but I am not the type of man to leave a thing so easily. I looked into the matter as far as I could at that time, but now I can look as far as I want.

Gadarwara was also visited by Jesus, and outside the village is the place where he stayed. Its ruins are still honored. Nobody remembers why it is honored. There is a stone on which it says that at one time a man called Isu visited this place, and stayed there. He converted the people of the village and the surrounding area, then he returned to Pahalgam. The archeological department of India placed that stone there, so it is not very old.

I had to work really hard on that stone just to clean it. It was difficult because nobody had cared for it. The stone was inside a small castle. The castle was no longer habitable, and it was dangerous to even enter. My grandmother used to try to prevent me from going inside because it could collapse at any moment. She was right. Even with just a small wind the walls would start swaying. The last time I saw it, it had collapsed. That was when I had gone to Gadarwara for my grandmother's funeral. I also went to pay a visit to the place where a man called Isu had once stayed.

Isu is certainly nothing but another form of the Aramaic Yeshu, from the Hebrew Joshua. In Hindi Jesus is called Isa, and lovingly, Isu. Perhaps one of the men whom I love the most had been there, in that village. Just the idea that Jesus too had walked those streets was so exhilarating, was such an ecstasy. This is just by the way. I cannot prove it in any historical way, whether it is so or not. But if you ask me in confidence, I can whisper in your ear, "Yes, it is true. But please don't ask me more...."

Session 24

I WAS SAYING TO YOU THAT friendship is a higher value than love. Nobody has said it before. And I also say that friendliness is even higher than friendship. Nobody has even mentioned that. I will certainly have to explain.

Love, howsoever beautiful, remains earthbound. It is something like the roots of a tree. Love tries to rise above the earth and all that it implies – the body – but it falls again and again. It is no wonder that people say somebody has "fallen in love." This phrase exists in all languages, as far as I know.

I have tried to explore the matter by asking many people from various countries. I wrote to all the embassies asking whether they have a phrase in their language which is exactly the equivalent of "falling in love." They all replied, "Of course."

And when I asked, "Do you have a phrase or something similar to what I call 'rising in love'?" they either laughed, giggled, or started talking about something else. If I asked by letter, then they never replied. Certainly nobody replies to a madman who is asking, "Is there a word in your language for 'rising in love'?"

No language has that kind of word, and it cannot be just coincidence. In one language maybe, even two perhaps, but it cannot be a coincidence in three thousand languages. It is not just by chance that all languages have conspired together to make the phrase in three thousand ways always to mean "fall in love." No, the reason is, love is basically of the earth. It can jump a little bit, or rather you could call it jogging....

I have heard that jogging is in fashion, particularly in America, and so much so that just the other night I received a gift from a lady who loves my books. She sent me a jogging suit. Great idea! I loved it. I told Chetana, "Wash it, and I will use it."

She said, "Are you going to jog?"

I said, "In my sleep! I will use it as my sleeping robe." And, by the way, you probably know that all my sleeping robes are jogging suits already. I like them, because in my sleep I can still jog and exercise, or wrestle with Muhammad Ali the great, and do all kinds of things – but only in my sleep, under my blanket, in absolute privacy.

I was telling you that love, once in a while, jumps and feels as if it is free from the earth; but the earth knows better: soon he comes back to his senses with a thump, if not with broken bones. Love cannot fly. It is a peacock, with beautiful feathers – but remember, they are not able to fly. Yes, the peacock can jog....

Love is very earthly. Friendship is a little higher; it has wings – not just feathers, but the wings of a parrot. You know how parrots fly? – from one tree to another, or maybe from one garden to another, from one grove to another, but they don't fly towards the stars. They are poor flyers. Friendliness is the highest value, because friendliness has no gravitation at all. It is just levitation, if you allow me to use that word. I don't know whether the pundits of English will allow 'levitation'; it only means 'against gravity'. Gravitation pulls downwards, levitation pulls upwards. But who cares about the pundits? – they are very grave, they are already in their graves.

Friendliness is a seagull – yes, like Jonathan, it soars beyond the clouds. This is just to connect with what I was saying to you....

My grandmother wept because she thought I would not have friends. In a way she was right, in another way she was wrong. She was right as far as my school, college, and university days were concerned, but wrong as far as I am concerned, because even in my schooldays – although I did not have friends in the ordinary sense, I had friends in a very extraordinary sense. I told you about Shambhu Babu. I have told you about Nani herself. In fact these two people spoiled me, and spoiled me in such a way that there was no going back. What was their strategy?

My Nani comes first, chronologically too; she was so attentive to me. She listened to all my nonsense, my gossip, with such rapt attention that even I believed I must be saying the very truth.

The second was Shambhu Babu. He again listened with unblinking eyes. I had never seen anyone listen without blinking; in fact I know of only one other person, and that is me. I cannot watch a film for the simple reason that when I do I forget to blink. I cannot do two things together, particularly if they are so divergent as looking at a film, and blinking. Even now it is impossible for me. I don't watch films because two hours without blinking gives me a headache and tired eyes, so tired that they cannot even sleep. Yes, tiredness can be so great that even sleep seems to be too much effort. But Shambhu Babu used to listen to me without blinking. Once in a while I would tell him, "Shambhu Babu, please blink. Unless you blink I will not say anything more."

Then he would blink quickly two or three times and say, "Okay, now continue and don't disturb me."

Bertrand Russell once wrote that there would come a time when psychoanalysis would become the greatest profession. Why? Because they are the only people who listen attentively, and everybody needs someone to listen to them at least once in a while. But to pay a psychoanalyst to listen to you – just think of the absurdity of it, paying a person to listen to you! Of course he doesn't really listen at all, he pretends. That is why I was the first man in India to ask people to pay to listen to me. That is just the opposite to psychoanalysis, and that makes sense. If you want to understand me then pay for it. And in the West people are paying just to be listened to.

Sigmund Freud, being the perfect Jew, created one of the greatest inventions in the world – the psychoanalyst's couch. It is really a great invention. The poor patient lies on the couch, just like me here – but I am not the patient, that's the difficulty.

The patient is writing the notes: Doctor Devageet, he is called. He is called doctor, but he is not like Sigmund Freud. He is not here as a doctor. Strangely – with me everything is strange – the doctor is lying on the couch, and the patient is sitting in the doctor's seat. My own doctor is sitting here, just by my feet. Have you ever seen any doctor sitting at his patient's feet?

Here, it is a totally different world. With me everything goes rightside up – I cannot say upside down.

I am not a patient, although very patient; and my doctors are not doctors, although perfectly qualified as doctors. They are my sannyasins, my friends. That's what I am talking about, what friendliness can do – a miracle. It is alchemy. The patient becomes the doctor, the doctor becomes the patient; this is alchemy.

Love cannot do it. Love, although good, is not enough. And eating too much of even a good thing is bad for you; it gives you diarrhea or cramps in the stomach, and whatnot. Love can do everything except go beyond itself. It goes lower and lower. It becomes bickering, nagging, fighting. Every love, if naturally followed to its logical end, is bound to end in divorce. If you don't follow logically, that's another matter; then you are stuck. To see any person stuck is really terrible; you should do something about it. But these stuck people, if you do something about it, they will both fight you together, tooth and nail.

I remember just a few weeks ago, a friend of Anthony's came from England to take sannyas, and you know an English gentleman – he was so stuck, as you say, up to his very neck. You could not see anything, he was so stuck in the mud. You could only see a few of his hairs – only a few because he was a bald man, just like me. If he had been completely bald it would have been far better; at least nobody would notice him. I tried to pull him out, but how can you pull out a man with only a few hairs showing from the mud? I have my own ways.

I asked Anthony and Uttama to help the poor man. They said to me, "He wants to separate from his wife." I had seen his wife too, because she had insisted that she had to be present when he took sannyas. She wanted to see how he was being hypnotized. I had allowed her to be present because there is no hypnotism practiced here. In fact she even became interested herself. I invited her too, saying, "Why don't you become a sannyasin?"

She said, "I will think about it."

I told her, "My own principle is 'Jump before you think,' but I cannot help, so you think about it. If I am still around by the time you have thought about it, I will be ready to help you."

But I told Anthony and Uttama – who are both my sannyasins, and are of those few who are really close to me – to help their friend. I told them to make every arrangement for his wife and her children so she should not be at a loss, but spiritually her husband should not suffer any more. Even if he has to leave everything to his wife, let it be so. I alone am enough for him.

I had seen the man, and had seen his beauty. He had a very simple, childlike quality, the same fragrance you find when it rains for the first time and the earth rejoices – the fragrance and the joy. He was happy to be a sannyasin.

Just the other day I received a message saying that he is continuously sleeping, just because of his fear of his wife. He does not want to wake up. The moment he wakes up, he again takes sleeping pills. I told Anthony to tell him, "This sleeping is not going to help. It may even kill him, but it will not help him or his wife either. He must face the truth."

Very few people face the truth, that what they call love is only biological – and ninety-nine percent of love *is* biological. Friendship is ninety-nine percent psychological; friendliness is ninety-nine percent spiritual. The one percent left in love is for friendship; the one percent left in friendship is for friendliness. And the one percent left in friendliness is just for that which has no name. In fact the Upanishads have called it exactly that: *"Tattvamasi* – thou art that." *Tat*...what am I going to call it? No, I am not going to give it any name. All names have betrayed man. All names without exception have proved to be enemies of man, so I don't want to give it a name.

I simply indicate with my finger towards that. And whether I give it a name or not, it has no name. It is namelessness. All names are our inventions. When are we going to understand a simple thing? A rose is a rose is a rose; whatsoever name you call it, it makes no difference at all because even the word 'rose' is not its name. It is simply there. When you drop the language between you and existence, suddenly the explosion...the ecstasy!

Love can help, hence I am not against love. That would be as if I am against using a staircase. No, a staircase is good, but walk carefully, particularly on an old staircase. And remember: love is the oldest. Adam and Eve fell from it; but there was no need to fall, no necessity, I mean. If they had chosen – and once in a while one wants to fall too, then it is just your choice. But to fall out of free-dom is one thing, and to fall as a punishment is totally another.

If I were to write the Bible again...I would not do such a stupid thing, believe me. I am saying *if* I were to write it, then I would make Adam and Eve fall, not as a punishment but as a choice, out of their own freedom.

What is the time?

"Five past eight, Osho."

That's good, because I have not even begun. The beginning takes a long time.

Love is good, just good, but not enough, not enough to give you wings. For that, friendship is needed, and love does not allow it. So-called love, I mean, is very much against friendship. It is very afraid of friendship because anything higher is a danger, and friendship is higher.

When you can enjoy the friendship of either a man or a woman, then you know for the first time that love is a cheat, a deception. Alas, then you realize how much time was wasted. But friendship is only a bridge. One should pass over it; one should not start living on it. A bridge is not for living on. This bridge leads to friendliness.

Friendliness is pure fragrance. If love is the root, and friendship the flower, then friendliness is the fragrance, unseen by the eye. You cannot even touch it; you cannot hold it in your hand, particularly if you want to keep it in your closed fist. Yes, you can have it on your open hand, but not in your closed hand.

Friendliness is almost what, in the past, mystics have called prayer. I don't want to call it prayer for the simple reason that the word is associated with wrong people. It is a beautiful word, but to be in the wrong company contaminates; you start stinking of your company. The moment you say "prayer" everybody becomes alert, afraid, attentive – as if a general had called his soldiers to attention, and they have all suddenly become statues.

What happens when somebody mentions a word like 'prayer', 'god' or 'heaven'? Why do you become closed? I am not condemning you, I am simply saying – or rather bringing to your notice – that these beau-tiful words have been immensely dirtied by the so-called "holy ones." They have done such an unholy job, I cannot forgive them.

Jesus says, "Forgive your enemies" – that I can do – but he does not say, "Forgive your priests." And even if he did say it I would say to him, "Shut up! I cannot forgive the priests. I can neither forgive them nor forget them, because if I forget them then who is going to demolish them? And if I forgive them, then who is going to undo what they have done to humanity? No, Jesus, no! Enemies I can understand – yes, they should be forgiven, they don't understand what they are doing. But priests? Please don't say that they don't understand what they are doing. They understand exactly what they are doing. That is why I cannot forgive, nor can I forget. I have to fight to my very last breath."

Love takes you; it is a step – but only if it takes you towards friendship is it love. If it does not take you towards friendship, then it is lust, not love. If it takes you to friendship, be thankful to it but don't allow it to encroach upon your freedom. Yes, it has helped; that does not mean that now it has to hinder too. Don't carry the boat on your shoulders just because it carried you to the other shore.

Don't be foolish! I mean – excuse me, Devageet, that word I have reserved for you; I mean, don't be idiotic. But I go on forgetting. Again and again I use the wrong word, 'foolish', for others, when it is a special word for Devageet. Particularly in this Noah's Ark – that's my name for this cabin.

Love is good. Transcend it, because it can lead you to something better: friendship. And when two lovers become friends, it is a rare phenomenon. One wants to cry just out of joy, or celebrate, or if one is a musician, play on the guitar, or if one is a poet, then write a haiku, a *rubaiyat*. But if one is not a musician or a poet, one can still dance, one can still paint, one can sit silently and look at the sky. What more can be done? Existence has done it already.

Ashu, now look at the time....

"Eight twenty-five, Osho."

Look at your watch.

"Eight twenty-seven, Osho."

Eight twenty-seven? Look, I am a Jew – I still saved a few minutes. I believe your watch, but I will speak just a few minutes longer.

From love to friendship, and from friendship to friendliness – that can be said to be my whole religion. Friendship is again a "ship," a relation-ship, a certain bondage...very subtle, more subtle than love, but it is there; and with it all the jealousies and all the diseases of love also. They have come in a very subtle form. But friendliness is freedom from the other; hence there is no question of relationship.

Love is towards the other, so is friendship. Friendliness is only an opening of your heart to existence. Suddenly, at a particular moment, you may be opening it to a man, to a woman, a tree, to a star ...at the beginning you cannot just open it to the whole of existence. Of course in the end you have to open your heart to the whole, simultaneously, unaddressed to anybody. That is the moment ...let us just call it *the moment*.

Let us forget the words enlightenment, buddhahood, Christ-consciousness, just let us call it

THE MOMENT

– write it in capitals.

It has been so good. I know there is time, but it has been so beautiful, and with anything beautiful, more should never be asked for. The more destroys.

Session 25

O KAY. I WAS QUOTING Bertrand Russell – this quotation
will help like a nail. He said, "Sooner or later everybody
will need psychoanalysis, because it is so difficult to find
anyone to listen to you, to be attentive to you."

Attention is such a need that if the worst came to the worst one
would even pay for it, but at least one would have the joy of having
somebody listening attentively to you. The listener may have
plugged his ears with wool, that's another matter. No psychoanalyst
can listen to all that nonsense day in and day out. Moreover he
himself needs somebody to listen to him.

You will be surprised that all psychoanalysts go to each other. Of
course they don't charge each other, out of professional courtesy, but
there is a great need to unwind, to unload, to simply say whatever
comes into your mind and not to go on piling it up, because then
those piles torture you.

I quoted Bertrand Russell as a link. I called it a nail just so that I
could continue my story. Bertrand Russell himself, though he lived a
long life, never knew what life was. But sometimes the words of
those who have not known can be used significantly by those who
can see. They can put those words in a proper context.

You may not have come across this quotation because it is in a
book that nobody reads at all. You will not believe Bertrand Russell
even wrote such a book. It is a book of short stories. He has written
hundreds of books, many of them well known, well read and well
recognized, but this book is rare in a sense because it is only a
collection of short stories, and he was very reluctant to publish it.
He was not a short-story writer, and his stories are, of course, third-

rate, but here and there in those third-rate stories one comes across a sentence that only Bertrand Russell could have written. This quotation is from that book.

I love stories, and all this started with my Nani. She was a lover of stories too. Not that she used to tell me stories; just the contrary, she used to provoke me to tell her stories, all kinds of stories and gossips. She listened so attentively that she made me into a story teller. Just for her I would find something interesting, because she would wait the whole day just to listen to my story. If I could not find anything, then I would invent. She is responsible: all credit or blame, whatsoever you call it, goes to her. I invented stories to tell her just so she would not be disappointed, and I can promise you that I became a successful story teller just for her sake.

I started winning in competitions when I was just a child in primary school, and that continued to the very end, when I left university. I collected so many prizes, medals and cups and shields and whatnot, that my grandmother became just a young girl again. Whenever she would bring someone to show them my prizes and awards, she was no longer an old woman, she became almost young again. Her whole house became almost a museum because I went on sending her my prizes. Up till high school, of course, I was almost a resident in her house. It was just for courtesy's sake that I used to visit my parents in the daytime; but the night was hers, because that was the time to tell the stories.

I can still see myself by the side of her bed, with her listening so attentively to what I was saying. Each word uttered by me was absorbed by her as if it were of immense value. And it became valuable just because she took it in with so much love and respect. When it had knocked on my door it was just a beggar, but when it entered into her house, it was no longer the same person. The moment she called me, saying, "Raja! Now tell me what happened to you today – the whole thing. Promise me you will not leave out anything at all," the beggar dropped all that made him look like a beggar; now he was a king. Every day I had to promise her, and even though I told her everything that happened, she would insist, "Tell me something more," or "Tell me that one again."

Many times I said to her, "You will spoil me; both you and

Shambhu Babu are spoiling me forever." And they really did their job well. I collected hundreds of awards. There was not a single high school in the whole state where I had not spoken and won – except once. Only once had I not been the winner, and the reason was simple. Everybody was amazed, even the girl who had won, "because," she said to me, "it is impossible to think I could win against you."

The whole hall – and there must have been at least two thousand students – became full of a great humming, and everybody was saying that it was unfair, even the principal who was presiding over the contest. Losing that cup became very significant to me; in fact, if I had not lost that cup, I would have been in great trouble. Of that I will tell you when the time comes.

The principal called me and said, "I am sorry, you are certainly the winner" – and he gave his own watch to me saying, "This is far more costly than the cup which was given to that girl." And it certainly was. It was a gold watch. I have received thousands of watches, but I have never again received such a beautiful one; it was a real masterpiece. That principal was very interested in rare things, and his watch was a rare piece. I can still see it.

I have received so many watches, but I have forgotten them. One of those watches is behaving strangely. When I need it, it stops. All the time it runs perfectly; it stops only at night between three and five. Is that not strange behavior? – because that is the only time when I sometimes wake up, just an old habit. In my younger days I used to wake up at three in the morning. I did it for so many years that even if I don't get up, I have to turn in my bed and then go back to sleep. That is the time when I need to see whether I should really get up, or I can still have a little more sleep; and strangely, that is when the watch stops.

Today it stopped exactly at four. I looked at it and went back to sleep; four is too early. After sleeping for almost one hour, I again looked at the watch: it was still four. I said to myself, "Great, so tonight is never going to end." I went to sleep again, not thinking – you know me, I am not a thinker – not thinking that the watch may have stopped. I thought, "This night seems to be the last. I can sleep forever. Great! Just far out!" And I felt so good that it was never going to end that I fell asleep again. After two hours I again looked at the watch, and it was still four! I said, "Great! Not only is the night long, but even time has stopped too!"

The principal gave me his watch and said, "Forgive me, because you certainly were the winner, and I must tell you that the man who was the judge is in love with the girl who won the prize. He is a fool. I say it even though he is one of my professors and a colleague. This is the last straw. I am throwing him out right now. This is the end of his service in this college. This is too much. I was in the presidential chair, and the whole auditorium laughed. It seems everybody knew the girl was not even able to speak, and I think nobody except her lover, the professor, even understood what she was saying. But you know, love is blind."

I said, "Absolutely right – love *is* blind. But why had you chosen a blind person to be the judge, particularly when his girl was a competitor? I am going to expose the whole thing." And I exposed it to the newspapers, telling them the whole story. It was really troublesome for the poor professor – so much so that his love affair finished. He lost everything, his service, his reputation, and the girl for whose love he had staked everything – all was lost. He is still alive. Once, as an old man, he came to see me, and confessed, "I am sorry, I certainly did something wrong, but I never thought that it was going to take such a shape."

I said to him, "Nobody knows what an ordinary action is going to bring to the world. And don't feel sorry. You lost your service and your beloved. What did I lose? Nothing at all, just one more shield, and I have so many that I don't care."

In fact my grandmother's house had become, by and by, just a museum for my shields, cups and medals. But she was very happy, immensely happy. It was a small house to be cluttered with all this rubbish, but she was happy that I went on sending her all my prizes, from college and from the university. I went on and on, and every year I won dozens of cups, either for debate or for eloquence or for story-telling competitions.

But I tell you one thing: both she and Shambhu Babu spoiled me by their being so attentive. They taught me, without teaching, the art of speaking. When somebody listens so attentively, you immediately start saying something you had not planned or even imagined; it simply flows. It is as if attention becomes magnetic and attracts that which is hidden in you.

My own experience is that this world will not become a beautiful place to live in unless everybody learns how to be attentive. Right now, nobody is attentive. Even when people are showing that they are listening; they are not listening, they are doing a thousand other things. Hypocrites just pretending...but not the way an attentive listener should be – just all attention, just attention and nothing else, just open. Attention is a feminine quality, and everybody who knows the art of attention, of being attentive, becomes, in a certain sense, very feminine, very fragile, soft; so soft that you could scratch him with just your nails.

My Nani would wait the whole day for the time when I would come back home to tell her stories. And you will be surprised how, unknowingly, she prepared me for the job that I was going to do. It was she who first heard many of the stories that I have told you. It was her to whom I could tell any nonsense without any fear.

The other person, Shambhu Babu, was totally different from my Nani. My Nani was very intuitive, but not intellectual. Shambhu Babu was also intuitive, but intellectual too. He was an intellectual of the first grade. I have come across many intellectuals, some famous and some very famous, but none of them came close to Shambhu Babu. He was really a great synthesis. Assagioli would have loved the man. He had intuition plus intellect, and both not in small measure, but high peaks. He also used to listen to me, and would wait all day until school had finished. Every day after school was his.

The moment I was released from the prison, my school, I would first go to Shambhu Babu. He would be ready with tea and a few sweets that he knew I liked. I mention it because people rarely think of the other person. He always arranged things with the other person in mind. I have never seen anybody bother about the other as he did. Most people, although they prepare for others, they do it according to themselves really, forcing the other person to like what they themselves like.

That was not Shambhu Babu's way. His thinking of the other

was one of the things I loved and respected in him. He always purchased things only after asking the shopkeepers what my Nani used to buy. I came to know this only after he died. Then the shop-keepers told me, the sweetmakers too, that "Shambhu Babu always used to ask a strange question: 'What does that old woman, who lives there alone near the river – what does she purchase from you?' We never bothered why he asked, but now we know: he was inquiring about what you liked."

I was also amazed that he was always ready with the very things that I liked. He was a man of the law, so naturally he found a way. From school I would rush to his house, take my tea and sweets that he had bought; then he was ready. Even before I had finished, he was ready to listen to what I had to tell him. He would say, "Just tell me anything you like. It's not a question of what you say, but that you say it."

His emphasis was very clear. I was left absolutely free, with not even a subject to talk about, free to say anything I wanted. He always added, "If you want to remain silent, you can. I will listen to your silence." And once in a while it would happen that I would not say a single thing. There was nothing to say.

And when I closed my eyes he too would close his eyes, and we would sit like the Quakers, just in silence. There were so many times, day after day, when I either spoke or else we stayed in silence. I once said to him, "Shambhu Babu, it looks a little strange for you to listen to a child. It would be more appropriate if you spoke and I listened."

He laughed and said, "That is impossible. I cannot say anything to you, and will not say anything ever, for the simple reason that I don't know. And I am grateful to you for making me aware of my ignorance."

Those two people gave me so much attention that in my early childhood I became aware of the fact, which only now psychologists are talking about, that attention is a kind of food, a nourishment. A child can be perfectly taken care of, but if he is not paid any attention there is every possibility that he will not survive. Attention seems to be the most important ingredient in one's nourishment.

I have been fortunate in that way. My Nani and Shambhu Babu

started the ball rolling, and as it rolled on, it gathered more and more moss. Without ever learning how to speak, I became a speaker. I still don't know how to speak, and I have reached thousands of people – without even knowing how to begin. Can you see the amusing part of it? I must have spoken more than any man in the whole of history, although I am still only fifty-one.

I started speaking so early, yet I was not in any way what you call a speaker in the Western world. Not a speaker who says, "Ladies and Gentlemen," and all that nonsense – all borrowed and nothing experienced. I was not a speaker in that sense, but I spoke with my whole heart aflame, afire. I spoke not as an art but as my very life. And from my early schooldays it was recognized, not by one but by many, that my speaking seemed to be coming from my heart, that I was not trying parrotlike to repeat something I had prepared. Something spontaneous was being born, then and there.

The principal who gave me his watch and brought this whole trouble about for you, his name was B.S. Audholia. I hope he is still alive. As far as I know he is, and I know far enough. I don't hope against hope; when I hope, that means that it is so.

That night he said, "I am sorry" – and he really was sorry; he threw the professor out of service. B.S. Audholia also told me that whenever I needed anything, I had only to inform him, and if it was within his capacity at all he would do it. Later, whenever I required anything, I just sent a note to him and it was fulfilled. He never asked why.

Once I asked him myself, "Why don't you ever ask me why I need this?"

He said, "I know you: if you have asked for it, my asking why would be foolish. You could provide so many reasons, even if you didn't need it. One more thing," he said: "if you have asked for it, it is impossible to believe that you would have asked unless you really had a need. I know you, and knowing you is enough to give me all the reasons I need."

I looked at the man. I did not expect that a principal of a very famous college could be so understanding. He laughed and said, "It is just a coincidence that I happen to be the principal; in fact, I should not be. It was just a mistake on the part of the governors."

I had not asked that much, but he must have read it on my face. From that day I started growing a beard. You cannot read much from behind a beard. It is dangerous if things can be read so easily. You have to create something so that you are not just a newspaper.

Six months later when he met me again, he said, "Why have you started growing a beard?"

I said, "You are the cause. You said you had read my face; now my face will not be so easy to read."

He laughed and said, "You cannot hide it – it is in your eyes. Why don't you start wearing sunglasses if you really want to hide?"

I said, "I cannot wear sunglasses, for the simple reason that I cannot create any barrier between my eyes and existence. That is the only bridge where we meet, there is no other."

That is why a blind man is given sympathy by everybody everywhere. He is a man without a bridge; he has lost his contact. Researchers now are saying that eighty percent of our contact with existence is through the eyes. Perhaps they are right – perhaps it is more than they think, but eighty percent is certain. It may ultimately prove to be far more, perhaps ninety percent or even ninety-nine percent. The eye is the man.

The Buddha cannot have the same eyes as Adolf Hitler...or do you think he can? Forget them both; they are not contemporaries. Jesus and Judas were contemporaries, and not only contemporaries but master and disciple. Still I say they cannot have the same eyes, the same quality. Judas would have had very cunning eyes, really Jewish. Jesus would have had the eyes of a child; although physically he was no longer a child, but psychologically he was. Even on the cross he died as if he were in the womb, still in the womb – so fresh, as if the flower had never opened but remained a bud. It never knew all the ugliness that exists everywhere. Jesus and Judas lived together, moved together, but I don't think that Judas had ever looked into Jesus' eyes; otherwise things would have been different.

If Judas had even once gathered courage enough to look into the eyes of Jesus, there would have been no crucifixion and no Crossianity – I mean Christianity. That is my name for Christianity. Judas was cunning.

Jesus was so simple that you could almost call him "the fool."

That's what Fyodor Dostoevski said in one of his most creative novels, *The Idiot*.

Although it was not written for or about Jesus, Dostoevski was so filled with the spirit of Jesus that somehow Jesus comes in. The main character of the novel, *The Idiot*, is nobody but Jesus. He is not mentioned, nor can you find any reference to him, nor any resemblance, but if you read it something will start resounding in your very heart, and you will agree with me. It will be an agreement not through the head; it will be an agreement deeper than imagination can penetrate, in the very beat of your heart – a real agreement.

Session 26

I WILL HAVE TO GO IN circles, circles within circles within circles, for that's how life is. And more so in my case. In fifty years, I must have lived at least fifty lives. In fact, I have not done anything else other than living. Other people have many occupations, but from my very childhood I have remained a vagabond, not doing anything, just living. When you don't do anything except live, then of course life takes on a totally different dimension. It is no longer horizontal, it has depth.

Devageet, it is good that you were never my student; otherwise you would never have been a dentist. I would have been the last person to allow you any certificate. But here you can laugh and giggle thinking I am so relaxed, there is no problem. But remember, even if I am dead, I can come out of my grave to shout at you. That has been my whole business, my whole life.

I have not done anything in the sense of earning, of having a great bank balance, of becoming a powerful person politically. I have lived in my own way, and in that living, teaching has been an essential part. So, even here, forgive me, I cannot forget it: I am always the master. You know, I know, everybody else in this room knows, that you are under me, and I am in the dental chair – you are not. If I giggle, that can be forgiven: "Aha! The old man is enjoying himself!" Even Ashu is enjoying the idea; otherwise she is a serious woman, very serious. Women, once they are teachers, typists, nurses, something goes wrong in their scheme. They suddenly become so serious.

Yet it was Eve who was not serious, Adam was. The serpent could never have persuaded him. In fact, he tried many times; that's what the Egyptian story tells, and that is far more authentic than the biblical version. It is more ancient too. It says that the serpent tried with Adam, but could not get him hooked. Then finally, as a last resort, he tried Eve. It is better to call her Eva, just as the Egyptians do, it sounds more feminine – Eva. The serpent succeeded at the very first attempt. Since then, all salesmen and advertisers have been aiming at Eva. They don't take any notice of the poor man who has to pay for everything Eva purchases. That is his problem, so why should they bother about it?

Eve, or Eva as I would like to call her – I always like the beautiful, wherever it is. Eve does not sound very musical, and seems to be cut short, pruned, looks more like an English garden, not like a Zen garden. Eva has unlimited potential, just the sound of it, so let's call her Eva. Why did the devil succeed with her at his first attempt? For the simple reason that she was not business-minded. She was not serious, must have laughed at the devil's jokes, must have talked joyously – gossiped I mean. And when you gossip with the devil, he is going to get the upper hand. If you laugh at his jokes, then he knows he has a way, he can approach your very being. That is how he persuaded poor Eva.

Since then, I think women have lost their very quality of being joyous. Even if they laugh, it is a muffled laugh. Even when they laugh they put their hands up to their face, as if somebody may see the great work their dentist has done on them. But here, in this room, there is no need to be serious. And it is good that today, for the first time, Ashu is laughing so clearly that I can hear. And why is she laughing? She is laughing because poor Devageet is being beaten. Naturally she laughs and says to me – I can hear what she is thinking – "Give him a good slap, one more!" No, this is enough; otherwise I will go astray.

That's what I was saying: that life is a circle within a circle within a circle – and more so in my life. I have not lived in the way one is expected to live. I have not done anything else. Yes, I have just lived and done nothing else, but then it is too much: a single moment is almost an eternity! Just think of it....

So I will have to go on in the same way that I have lived. You will have to cope with me, there is no other way. I never coped with anybody, so I don't know how to, and even if I tried to learn now, it is too late. But you have been coping with every kind of person throughout your life.

I did not cope with my father, my mother, my uncles, who were all loving and helpful to me; nor my teachers, who were not my enemies; nor my professors, who always wanted, in spite of me, to help. But I could not cope with anybody, they all had to cope with me. Now it is too late. Things cannot be changed now. It was, and still is, a one-way affair.

You can cope with me, I am available. But I cannot cope with you, for two reasons: one, you are not available, not present. Even if I knock at your door, there's nobody inside – and the neighbors inform me that the fellow has never been seen. The door is locked. Who locked it? – nobody knows. Where is the key? – perhaps lost. And even if I could find the key or break the lock – which is far easier – what would be the point? The fellow is not inside the house. I would not find you there; you are always somewhere else. Now, how to find you and cope with you? It is impossible.

Secondly, even if it were possible, just for argument's sake, I cannot do it. I have never done it. I don't know its mechanism. I am still simply a wild boy from the village.

Just the other night my secretary was crying and saying to me, "Why do you trust me, Osho? I am not worthy. I am not even worthy to show you my face."

I said, "Who is bothered about worthiness and unworthiness? And who is to decide? I, at least, am not going to decide. Why are you crying?"

She said, "Just the idea that you have chosen me to do your work …it is such a big task."

I said, "Forget all about the bigness of it, and just listen to what I say."

I have never done anything myself, so naturally I never bother about whether she will be able to do it or not. I simply say to her "Listen," and of course, when I say something she has to listen. Now, how she manages to do it is not my problem, nor is it her problem. She manages because I have said so. I have said it because I don't know anything about management.

Do you see how perfectly I have chosen her? She fits. I am a misfit.

My grandmother was always worried. Again and again she would say, "Raja, you will be a misfit. I tell you, you will always be a misfit."

I used to laugh and tell her, "The very word 'misfit' is so beautiful that I have fallen in love with it. Now, if I fit, remember, I will hit your head – and when I say that, you know I mean it. I will really hit your head, if you are alive. If you are not alive then I will come to your grave, but I will certainly do something nasty. You can trust me."

She laughed even more, and said, "I take the challenge. I again say you will remain a misfit forever, whether I am alive or dead. And you will never be able to hit my head because you will never be able to fit."

And she was certainly right. I was *the* misfit, everywhere. At the university where I was teaching I never joined in the annual staff photograph. The vice-chancellor once asked me, "I have noticed that you are the only staff member who never comes for our annual photograph. Everybody else comes, because the photo is published, and who doesn't want his photo to be published?"

I said, "I certainly don't want to have my photograph published – not along with so many donkeys. And that photograph would remain forever a blemish on my name, knowing that once I was associated with this company."

He was shocked and said, "You call all these people donkeys? Including me?"

I said, "Of course including you. That's what I think," I told him. "And if you want to hear something nice, you have called the wrong man. Call one of the donkeys."

Not a single photograph exists in which I even participated while I was in service. I was such a misfit, I thought it was better not to be associated with those people with whom I had nothing in common. At the university I associated only with a tree, a *gulmohar* tree.

I don't know whether this kind of tree exists in the West or not, but it is one of the most beautiful trees in the East. Its shade is really cool. It does not grow high; it spreads its branches all around. Sometimes the branches of a single old gulmohar tree can cover enough land that five hundred people can easily sit beneath it. And when it flowers in the summer, thousands of flowers blossom simultaneously. It is not a miserly tree, producing one flower then another, no. Suddenly, one night, all the buds open, and in the morning you cannot believe your eyes – thousands of blossoms! And they are the color of sannyasins. I had only that tree as my friend.

I used to park my car beneath it for so many years that slowly everybody became aware not to park there; it was my place. I did not have to tell them, but by and by, slowly it became accepted. Nobody would disturb that tree. If I was not coming, that tree waited for me. For years I parked under that tree. When I left the university, I said good-bye to the vice-chancellor, and then I said, "I must go now, it is getting dark and my tree may go to sleep before the sun sets. I have to say goodbye to the gulmohar."

The vice-chancellor looked at me as if I was mad, but anybody would have looked just the same. That's the way to look at a misfit. But he still could not believe that I would do it. So he watched from his window while I said goodbye to the gulmohar.

I hugged the tree, and we remained together for a moment. The vice-chancellor rushed out, and came running to me saying, "Forgive me, just forgive me. I have never seen anybody hugging a tree, but now I know how much everybody is missing. I have never seen anybody say goodbye or good morning to a tree, but you have not only taught me a lesson, it has really sunk in."

After two months he phoned me, just to inform me, saying, "It is sad and very strange, but the day you left, something happened to your tree" – it had now become my tree.

I said, "What has happened?"

He said, "It started dying. If you come now you will just see a dead tree, with no flowers or leaves. What has happened? That's why I phoned you."

I said, "You should have phoned the tree. How can I answer for the tree?"

For a moment there was silence. Then he said, "It is as I always thought: you are mad!"

I said, "You are still not convinced; otherwise who phones a madman? You should have called the tree. And the tree is just outside your window – no phone is needed."

He simply hung up. I laughed, but the next day in the early morning, before any of the idiots at the university were there, I went to see the tree. Yes, all its flowers were gone, and yet it was in season. All had gone – not only the flowers but the leaves too. There were just naked branches standing against the sky. I again hugged the tree and knew it was dead. At the first hug there was a response; at the second hug there was nobody to respond. The tree had left; only its body was standing there, and may stand for years. Perhaps it is still standing, but it is just dead wood.

I could never manage to fit anywhere. As a student I was a nuisance. Every professor who taught me looked on me as a punishment that God had sent for him. I enjoyed being a messenger of God; I enjoyed it to the fullest. Who would not have enjoyed it? And if they thought I was a punishment, I proved to be exactly – or more than – what they expected.

Only a few have met me lately. Their first question was, "We cannot yet believe that you could have become enlightened. You were such a troublemaker. We have forgotten all the students that studied with you, but even now we see you once in a while, in our nightmares."

I can understand it. I could not fit in with anything. Whatsoever they taught me was so mediocre that I had to fight against it. I had to tell them, "This is very mediocre...." Now, you can imagine saying this to a professor who had been hoping that you would appreciate his lecture – which he has been preparing for days – and at the end of it a student stands up.... And I was a strange student, to say the least.

The first thing to be remembered is that I had long hair – and that long hair had an even longer history. I will come to it some day in some circle. That is the beauty of going in circles. You can come to the same point again and again, on a different level – like going round and round towards the peak of a mountain: you come to the same view many times, on different levels. Each time is a little different because you are not standing in the same spot, but still the view is the same, perhaps more beautiful, perhaps far more beautiful, because you can see more....

I will come to this point sometime, but not today.

What is the time?

"One minute past eight, Osho."

Good. Just moisten my lips.

Today particularly I wanted to say that attention is a double-edged sword – double-edged because it cuts both the listener and the speaker. It also joins them together. It is a very significant process. Gurdjieff had the right word for it, 'crystallization'.

If a man is really attentive, it does not matter what to – to XYZ, to anything – in that very process of being attentive he will become integrated, crystallized. By focusing himself on one thing he will become focused within his being.

But that is only half the story. The person who is listening attentively certainly attains crystallization. It is a well-known fact in all the Eastern schools of meditation. Just being attentive to anything, even nonsense, will do. Just a bottle of Coca-Cola will help immensely, particularly the Americans. Just looking at the bottle of Coca-Cola attentively, and you have the secret of Maharishi Mahesh Yogi's transcendental meditation. But it is only half the truth, and a half truth can be more dangerous than a complete lie.

The other half is possible only if you are not just reading a book, or chanting a mantra, or looking at a statue; the other half is possible only if you are in deep synchronicity with a living person. I am not calling it love, because that can misguide you; not even friendship, because you will think you know it already. I will call it "synchronicity," just so you have to think about it and give it a little of your being.

When you feel really attentive, synchronicity happens. It may be just a sunset you are watching, or just a flower, or children playing on a lawn and you are enjoying their joyousness…but a certain harmony is needed. If it happens, there is attention. If it happens between a master and a disciple, then certainly you have the most precious diamond possible in your hands.

I have told you that I have been fortunate, although I don't know why. There are things which one can only state; they are, and there is no reason why they are. The stars are, the roses are, the universe is – or perhaps, far better: the universes are. It is better to call existence a multiverse rather than a universe. The idea of multiple dimensions has to be introduced.

Man has been dominated by the idea of "one" for too long. And I am a pagan: I don't believe in God, I believe in gods. To me a tree is a god, a mountain is a god, a man is a god – but not always. He has the potential. A woman is a god, but not always; more often she is a bitch – but that is her choice. She need not have chosen it; nobody has forced her.

Ordinarily, man is just a husband, which is an ugly word in every language. The word 'husband' comes from 'husbandry'. That's what our sannyasins are doing – gardening, agriculture…. From the word 'agro' meaning industry…that is husbandry. And when you introduce someone as your husband, do you know what you are saying? Does that poor fellow know that he is being reduced to a farmer? But that's the whole idea; that man is the farmer, and woman is the field! Great ideas!

Man ordinarily remains very much tethered to the mundane, and woman even more so. She defeats man in every possible way. Of course she is the back-seat driver, but she is the driver.

A man was stopped for speeding, and the cop was very angry because he was not only speeding, but he had no license, and what he showed as his license was just a ticket for a picture show they were going to. This was too much!

The cop said, "Now I am going to give you a real ticket!"

The wife shouted at the husband, "I have been telling you from the very beginning, but you never listen to me!" And she shouted so loudly that even the cop stopped writing the ticket and listened to what was happening. She said, "Where are your specs in the first place? You cannot see, and you are driving! Moreover you're so drunk that I have been continuously kicking you, yet I don't see any effect at all! It seems you have lost all sensitivity!" Then she turned to the cop and said, "Officer, send him to jail! He deserves at least six months' hard labor; less than that won't teach him anything!"

Even the cop could not understand that much punishment for just a little speeding. He said to the man, "Sir, you can go. God has already punished you enough by giving you this woman as a wife. That is enough. Even I feel sorry for you. I know why you lost your eyesight. Who would like to see this woman? And I know you are speeding because she is continuously kicking you. I'm really sorry for you." He said, "You go on speeding, but she will always be there. Speed so fast that she is left behind, really behind."

Man and woman both live such a mundane and ugly, really ugly life. I once pointed out to my grandmother the wife of one of my professors as she was passing through my village. I had told her, "My grandmother and my whole family live there and they would be happy to meet you."

I introduced her to my grandmother, and when she had left we both laughed. Neither of us said anything for a few moments. I laughed because my grandmother had had to tolerate the woman. She laughed, saying, "That's nothing – you have to tolerate her husband. If she is terrible, he must be even more so."

I said, "I can only say this much: he certainly looks uglier than any passport photograph."

I have been teaching my whole life. I was rarely present in my schooldays either. They had to give me a seventy-five percent attendance record just to get rid of me. Even that was an absolute lie. I was absent ninety-nine percent of the time. That was the case throughout my schooldays, in high school and college.

In college, I even had an agreement with the principal, B.S. Audholia. He was a beautiful man. He was the principal of a college in Jabalpur, in the very center of India. Jabalpur has many colleges, and his was one of the most prominent. I had been expelled from one college because a professor was not prepared to remain in service if I was not expelled. That was his condition – and he was a respected professor. I may come to the details of that story later.

I had been expelled, naturally. Who cares about a poor student? And the professor was a Ph.D., D.Litt. etcetera, etcetera, and he had served in that college for almost his whole life. Now, to throw him out because of me – whether I was right or wrong was not the question. That's what the principal said to me before he expelled me. He had to give me an explanation, so he called me. He must have thought I was just like any other student, trembling because I was about to be expelled. He had not expected that I would enter his office like an earthquake.

I shouted at him before he had a chance to say anything. I said, "You have proved yourself to be just a holy cow dung." I used the

Hindi word *gobar ganesh,* which actually means "a statue made from cow dung," and I hit on his table with my fist so hard that he stood up. I said, "Is there a spring in your table? I hit it, and you stood up! Sit down!" I said it so loudly that he sat down silently. He was afraid that others may hear, and perhaps rush in, particularly the man who was guarding the door.

He said, "Okay, I will sit down. What do you have to say?"

I said, "You call me here and you are asking me what do I have to say? I say that you should expel this other fellow, Doctor S.N.L. Shrivastava. He is just stupid, even with his Ph.D. and D.Litt. – which makes it worse. I did not harm him, I simply asked questions which were completely legitimate. He teaches us logic, and if I am not allowed to use logic in his class, where am I to be logical? You tell me."

He said, "That sounds right. Obviously if he teaches you logic, you have to be logical."

I said, "Then call him, and just see who is logical."

The moment Doctor Shrivastava heard that I was in the principal's office and that he was being called, he escaped to his house. He didn't turn up for three days. I sat there for three days continuously, from the time the office opened till it closed. He finally wrote a letter to the principal, saying, "This cannot go on any longer, and," he wrote, "I don't want to face that boy. Either you expel him or you must relieve me of my duty."

The principal showed me the letter. I said, "Now it is okay. He is not capable of even encountering me in your presence, just once, so that you see who is logical. A taste of logic at least would not have been bad for you. But if he is not able to face me – and this letter is enough proof that he is a coward – I don't want him thrown out. I cannot be so heartless, because I know his wife and children and his responsibilities. Please expel me right now, and give it to me in writing that I am expelled."

He looked at me and said, "If I expel you it may be difficult for you to get admission in any other college."

I said, "That is my problem. I am a misfit – I have to face these things."

It was after this had happened that I knocked on all the doors of all the principals in the city – it is a city of colleges – and all of them said, "If you were expelled then we cannot take the risk. We have heard the rumors that you have been arguing continuously for eight months with Doctor Shrivastava, and that you did not allow him to teach at all."

When I told the whole story to B.S. Audholia, he said, "I will take the risk, but with a condition." He was a good man, generous, but limited. I don't expect anybody to have unlimited generosity, but unless you have unlimited generosity you have missed the most beautiful experience of life. Yes, it was generous of him to even admit me, but the condition canceled much of it. The condition was good for me, but not for him. For him, it was a crime; for me it was an opportunity to be free.

He made me sign an agreement that I would not attend the philosophy class. I said, "This is perfectly good; in fact, what more could I ask? This is what I would love to do, not attend these idiots' lectures. I am willing to sign it, but remember, you also have to sign an agreement saying that you will give me seventy-five percent attendance."

He said, "That is a promise. I cannot give it in writing because it would create complications, but it's a promise."

I said, "I take your word, and I trust you."

And he kept his word. He gave me ninety percent attendance although I never attended the philosophy class in his college even once.

I really did not attend primary school much, because the river was so attractive and its call was irresistible. So I was always at the river – not alone of course, but with many other students. Then there was the forest beyond the river. And there was so much real geography to explore – who bothered about the dirty map that they had in the school? I was not concerned where Constantinople was, I was exploring on my own: the jungle, the river – there were so many other things to do.

For example, as my grandmother had slowly taught me to read, I started reading books. I don't think anybody before or after me had ever been so involved in the library of that town. Now they show everybody the place where I used to sit, and the place where I used to read and write notes. But in fact they should show people that this was the place from where they wanted to throw me out. They threatened me again and again.

But once I started reading, a new dimension opened. I swallowed the whole library, and I started reading the books that I love most to my grandmother at night. You will not believe it, but the first book I read to her was *The Book of Mirdad*. That began a long series.

Of course once in a while, she used to ask, in the middle of a book, the meaning of a certain sentence, or passage, or a whole chapter – just the gist of it. I would say to her, "Nani, I have been reading it to you, and you have not heard it?"

She said, "You know, when you read I become so interested in your voice that I completely forget what you are reading. To me, you are my Mirdad. Unless you explain it to me, Mirdad will remain absolutely unknown as far as I am concerned."

So I had to explain to her, but that was a great discipline to me. To explain, to help the other person who is willing to go a little deeper than he could go on his own, to hold him by the hand, slowly slowly, that became my whole life. I have not chosen it, not in the way it was chosen for J. Krishnamurti. It was imposed upon him by others. In the beginning even his speeches were written either by Annie Besant or Leadbeater; he simply repeated them. He was not on his own. It was all preplanned, and done methodically.

I am an unplanned man, that is why I stay still wild. Sometimes I wonder what I am doing here, teaching people to be enlightened. And once they become enlightened, I immediately start teaching them how to become unenlightened again. What am I doing?

I know now the time is coming closer when many of my sannyasins will just pop up into enlightenment. And I have started preparing, and working on the ground and the science of how to unenlighten so many enlightened souls again. This is what I have been doing. A strange kind of work, but I have enjoyed it to the fullest, and still I am enjoying it. I am going to enjoy to the very last breath, or even after it. I'm a little crazy you know, so I can do that, although no crazy man has done that yet. But somebody has to do it someday. Somebody has to break the ice.

Session 27

OKAY. DO YOU SEE THE synchronicity? Simultaneously, I and Devageet said, "Okay." Of course he said it for one thing, I for something else – but the lines cross.

The moment before I came in I was listening to one of the greatest flutists, Hariprasad. It stirred many memories in me.

There are many types of flute in the world. The most important is the Arabic; the most beautiful, the Japanese; and there are many others. But there is nothing comparable to the small Indian bamboo flute for its sweetness. And Hariprasad is certainly a master as far as the flute is concerned. He played before me, not just once but many times. Whenever he felt he had to play really to his utmost, he would rush to me wherever I was – sometimes even thousands of miles, just to play his flute for one hour alone with me.

I asked him, "Hariprasad, you could have played anywhere – why make such a long journey?"

And in India, one thousand miles is almost like twenty thousand miles in the West. The Indian trains – they still walk, they don't run. In Japan the trains run at four hundred miles per hour; and in India forty miles an hour is a great speed; and the buses, and the rickshaws…. Just to play the flute for one hour alone in my bedroom…I asked him, "Why?"

He said, "Because I have thousands of admirers, but nobody understands particularly the soundless sound. Unless one understands the soundless sound he cannot really appreciate. So I come to you; and just that one hour is enough to enable me to play my flute for months before all kinds of idiots – governors, chief ministers, and the so-called "great ones." When I feel utterly tired and exhausted and fed up with the idiots, I run to you. Please don't deny me just this one hour."

I said, "It is a joy to hear you, your flute, your song. In themselves they are great, but particularly so because they remind me of the man who introduced us. Do you remember that man?"

He had completely forgotten who had introduced him to me, and I can understand...it must have been forty years ago. I was a small child, he was a young man. He tried hard to remember but could not, and said, "Excuse me but it seems my memory is not functioning well. I cannot even remember the man who introduced me to you. Even if I forget everything else, at least I should remember him."

I reminded him of the man, and he became just tears. That is the man I would like to talk to you about today.

Pagal Baba was one of those remarkable men whom I am going to talk about. He was of the same category as Magga Baba. He was known just as Pagal Baba; *pagal* means "the mad." He came like a wind, always suddenly, and then disappeared as suddenly as he had come.

I did not discover him, he discovered me. By that I mean I was just swimming in the river when he passed by: he looked at me, I looked at him, and he jumped in the river and we swam together. I don't know how long we swam but I was not the one to say "enough." He was already an established saint. I had seen him before, but not so closely. At a gathering, doing *bhajan* and singing songs of God, I had seen him and had a certain feeling towards him, but I had kept it to myself. I had not even uttered a single word about it. There are things which are better kept in the heart; there they grow faster. That's the right soil.

At this time he was an old man; I was not more than twelve. Obviously he was the one to say, "Let us stop. I am feeling tired."

I said, "You could have told me any time and I would have stopped, but as far as I am concerned I am a fish in the river."

Yes, that's how I was known in my town. Who else swims six hours every morning from four till ten? When everybody was asleep, fast asleep, I would be already in the river. And when everybody had gone to work I would still be in the river. Of course at ten o'clock every day my grandmother would come, and then I would have to come out of the water because it was school time, I had to go to school. But immediately after school I was back in the river.

When I first came across *Siddhartha*, Herman Hesse's novel, I could not believe that what he had written about the river I had known so many times. And I knew perfectly well that Hesse was only imagining – a good imagination – because he died without being a buddha. He was able to create *Siddhartha*, but could not become a Siddhartha. But when I came across his description of the river, and the moods, and the changes, and the feelings of the river, I was overwhelmed. I was more impressed by his description of the river than by anything else. I cannot recall how long I had loved the river – it seemed as if I had been born in its waters.

In my Nani's village I was continuously either in the lake or in the river. The river was a little too far away, perhaps two miles, so I had to choose the lake more often. But once in a while I used to go to the river, because the quality of a river and a lake are totally different. A lake, in a certain way, is dead, closed, not flowing, not going anywhere at all, static. That's the meaning of death: it is not dynamic.

The river is always on the go, rushing to some unknown goal, perhaps not knowing at all what that goal is, but it reaches, knowing or unknowing – it reaches the goal. The lake never moves. It remains where it is, dormant, simply dying, every day dying; there is no resurrection. But the river, howsoever small, is as big as the ocean, because sooner or later it is going to become the ocean.

I have always loved the feel of the flow: just going, that flux, that continuous movement...aliveness. So, even though the river was two miles away, I used once in a while to go just to have the taste.

But in my father's town the river was very close. It was just two minutes' walk from my Nani's house. Standing on the top floor you could see it; it was there with all its grandeur and invitation... irresistible.

I used to rush back from school to the river. Yes, just for a moment I would stop to throw my books in at my Nani's house. She would persuade me to at least have a cup of tea, saying, "Don't be in such a hurry. The river is not going to leave, it's not a train." That's exactly what she used to say again and again: "Remember, it is not a train. You cannot miss it. So please drink your cup of tea, then go. And don't throw your books down like that."

I didn't say anything because that would have meant further delay. She was always amazed, saying, "At any other time you are ready to argue. But when you are going to the river, even if I say anything – whether it is nonsense, illogical, absurd – you simply listen as if you were such an obedient child. What happens to you when you are going to the river?"

I said, "Nani, you know me. You know perfectly well that I don't want to waste time. The river is calling. I can even hear the sound of its waves while I am drinking my tea."

I have burned my lips many times just by drinking tea which was too hot. But I was in a hurry, and the cup had to be emptied. My Nani was there; she wouldn't allow me to go before I drank my tea.

She was not like Gudia. Gudia is special in that way; she always tells me, "Wait. The tea is too hot." Perhaps it is my old habit. I again start taking the cup and so she says, "Wait! It's too hot." I know she is right, so I wait until she does not object, then I drink the tea. Perhaps the old habit of just drinking tea and rushing to the river is still there.

Although my grandmother knew that I wanted to reach the waters as soon as possible, she would try to persuade me to have a little something to eat – this or that. I would say to her, "Just give everything to me. I will keep it in my pockets and eat it on the way." I have always liked cashew nuts, particularly salted ones, and for years I used to fill all my pockets with them. All my pockets meant two in my pants – meaning shorts, because I never liked long trousers, perhaps because all my teachers wore them, and I hated teachers, and a certain association must have arisen. So I only wore shorts.

In India shorts are far better, climatically, than long trousers. Both my pants pockets were full of cashew nuts. And you will be surprised: just because of those cashew nuts I had to tell the tailor to make two pockets in my shirts. I always had two pockets in my shirts. I never understood the reason why just one pocket was put on shirts. Why not only one pocket in trousers too? or just one pocket in shorts? Why only one in shirts? The reason is not obvious, but I know why. The single shirt pocket is always on the left side so that the right hand can take things out and put things in, and naturally no pocket is needed for the poor left hand. What would a poor man do with a pocket?

The left hand is one of the repressed parts of the human body. If you try, you will understand what I am saying. You can do everything with the left hand that you can do with the right, even writing, and perhaps better. After thirty or forty years of habit, in the beginning you would certainly find it difficult to use your left hand, because the left hand has been ignored and kept ignorant.

The left hand is really the most important part of your body because it represents the right side of your brain. Your left hand is connected to your right brain, and your right hand with the left brain, just like a cross. The right is really left, and the left is really right.

To ignore the left hand is to ignore the right side of your brain – and the right side of your brain contains all that is valuable, all the diamonds, emeralds, sapphires, and rubies…all that is valuable – all the rainbows and the flowers, and the stars. The right side of the brain contains the intuition, the instincts; in short it contains the feminine. The right hand is a male chauvinist.

You will be surprised to know that when I started writing, being such a nuisance I started writing with my left hand. Of course everybody was against me; again, of course, except my Nani. She was the only one who said, "If he wants to write with his left hand what is wrong with it?" She went on, "The question is to write. Why are you all so concerned which hand he uses? He can hold the pen in his left hand, and you can hold the pen in your right hand. What is the problem?"

But nobody would allow me to use my left hand, and she could not be everywhere with me. In school, every teacher and every student was against me using my left hand: right is right, and left is wrong. Even now I cannot understand why. Why should the left side of the body be denied and kept imprisoned? And do you know, ten percent of people would love to write with their left hand; in fact they had started writing like that but were stopped.

It is one of the most ancient calamities that has happened to man, that half of his being is not even available to him. A strange kind of man we have created! It is like a bullock cart with only one wheel: the other wheel is there but kept invisible; used, but only in an underground way. It is ugly. I resisted from the very beginning.

I asked the teacher and the headmaster, "Show me the reason why I should write with my right hand."

They just shrugged their shoulders. I then said, "Your shrugging will not help; you have to answer me. You would not accept me if I shrugged my shoulders; then why should I accept you? I don't take any notice of it. Please explain properly."

I was sent to the school board because the teachers would not understand me, or explain to me. In fact they understood me perfectly. What I was saying was plain: "What was wrong in writing with the left hand? And if I write the right answer with my left hand, can that answer be wrong – just because it has been written with the left hand?"

They said, "You are crazy and you will drive everybody else crazy. It is better that you go to see the school board."

The board was the municipal committee which directed all the schools. In the town there were four primary schools and two high schools, one for girls and one for boys. What a town – where boys and girls are kept so absolutely apart. It was this board that made decisions about almost everything, so naturally I was sent there.

The board members listened to me very seriously, as if I were a murderer and they were sitting like judges to hang me. I said to them, "Don't be so serious, relax. Just tell me what is wrong if I write with my left hand?" They looked at each other. I then said, "That won't help. You have to answer me, and I am not easy to deal with. You will have to give it in writing because I don't trust you. The way you are looking at each other appears so cunning and political that it is better to have your answer in writing. Write what is wrong in writing a right answer with the left hand."

They sat there almost like statues. Nobody even tried to say anything to me. Nobody was ready to write either. They simply said, "We will have to consider it."

I said, "Consider. I am standing here. Who is preventing you from considering in front of me? Is it something private like a love affair? And you are all respected citizens: at least six people should not be in a love affair – that would be like group sex."

They shouted at me, "Shut up! Don't use such words!"

I said, "I have to use such words just to provoke you; otherwise you would just sit there like statues. At least now you have moved and said something. Now consider, and I will help you and not hinder you at all."

They said, "Please go out. We cannot consider it in front of you; you are bound to interfere. We know about you, and so does everybody else in the town. If you don't leave then we will leave."

I said, "You can leave first, that is gentlemanly."

They had to leave their own committee room before me. The decision came the next day. The decision was simply that "The teachers were right, and everybody should write with their right hand."

This phoniness is dominant everywhere. I cannot even comprehend what kind of stupidity it is. And these are the people who are in power! The rightists! They are powerful – the male chauvinists are powerful. The poets are not powerful, nor the musicians....

Now look at this man Hariprasad Chaurasia – such a beautiful bamboo flute player, but he lived his whole life in utter poverty. He could not remember Pagal Baba, who had introduced him to me – or is it better to say, "me to him"? – because I was only a child, and Hariprasad was a world-recognized authority as far as the bamboo flute is concerned.

There were other flutists also introduced to me by Pagal Baba, particularly Pannalal Ghosh. But I had heard his playing and he was nothing compared to Hariprasad. Why did Pagal Baba introduce me to these people? He himself was the greatest flutist, but he would not play before the crowd. Yes, he played before me, a child, or before Hariprasad, or before Pannalal Ghosh, but he made it a point that we should not mention it to anyone. He kept his flute hidden in his bag.

The last time I saw him he gave me his flute and said, "We will not meet again – not that I don't want to meet you, but because this body is not capable of carrying itself any longer." He must have been about ninety. "But as a memento I give you this flute, and I say to you, if you practice you can become one of the greatest flutists."

I said, "But I don't want to become even *the* greatest flutist. To be a flutist is not what can fulfill me; it is one-dimensional."

He understood and said, "Then it is up to you."

I asked him many times why he tried to contact me whenever he came to the village – because that was the first thing he would do.

He said, "Why? You should ask it the other way around: why do I come to the village? Just to contact you – I don't come to this village for any other reason."

For a moment I could not say a word, not even "thank you." In fact in Hindi there is no word which is really equivalent to "thank you." Yes, there is a word which is used, but it has a totally different flavor: *dhanyavad*. It means "God bless you." Now, a child cannot say "God bless you" to a ninety-year-old man. I said, "Baba, don't give me trouble. I cannot even thank you." To say that I had to use an Urdu word, *shukriya*, which comes closer to the English, but it is still not exactly the same. *Shukriya* means "gratitude," but it comes very close.

I said to him, "You have given me this flute. I will keep it in your memory, and I will try to practice too. Who knows? – you, you know better than me; perhaps that is my future, but I don't see any future in it."

He laughed and said, "It is difficult to talk to you. Keep the flute with you and try to play with it. If something happens, good; if nothing happens then just keep it in my memory."

I started playing on it, and I loved it. I played it for years and became really proficient. I used to play the flute, and one of my friends – not really a friend, but an acquaintance – used to play on the tabla. We both came to know each other because we both loved swimming.

One year when the river was in flood and we were both trying to swim across – that was my joy, to cross the river in the rainy season when it used to become really enlarged; flowing with such force that it used to carry us at least two or three miles downstream. Just crossing meant we had to be ready to travel three miles back, and to cross back meant traveling three miles further, so it was a six-mile journey! And in the rainy season…! But that was one of my joys.

This boy, Hari was his name too. Hari is a very common name in India; it means "god." But it is a very strange name. I don't think any language has a name for God like Hari because it really means "the thief" – God the thief! Why should God be called a thief? Because sooner or later he steals your heart…and the sooner the better. The boy's name was Hari.

We were both trying to cross the river in full flood. It must have been almost a mile wide. He did not survive; he drowned somewhere on the way across. I searched and looked, but it was impossible: the river was flooding too fast. If he had drowned, it would have been impossible to find him; perhaps someone further down the river would find his body.

I called as loudly as I could, but the river was roaring. I went to the river every day, and tried the best that a child could do. The police tried, the fishermen's association tried, but not even a trace was found. He must have been taken by the river long before they heard about it. In his memory I threw the bamboo flute that Pagal Baba had given me into the river.

I said, "I would have liked to throw myself but I have other work to do. This is the most precious thing that I have next to myself, so I throw it. I will never play this flute again without Hari playing on the tabla. I cannot conceive of myself ever playing again. Take it, please!"

It was a beautiful flute, perhaps carved by a very skillful flute-maker. Perhaps it had been made specially for Pagal Baba by one of his devotees. I will talk more about Pagal Baba because so many things have to be said about him.

What is the time?

"Ten twenty-three, Osho."

Good. The time today will not suffice, so we will have to leave Pagal Baba for some other time. But one thing perhaps I may forget later on: that is about the boy Hari, who died…. Nobody knows whether he died or escaped from his home, because his dead body was never found. But I think for certain that he died, because I was swimming with him, and suddenly at a certain point in the middle of the river I saw him disappearing. I shouted, "Hari! What's the problem?" but there was nobody to answer.

To me, India itself is dead; I don't think of India as a living part of humanity. It is a dead land, dead for so many centuries that even the dead have forgotten that they are dead. They have been dead so long, somebody has to remind them. That's what I am trying to do, but it is a very thankless task, reminding somebody, saying, "Sir, you are dead. Don't believe that you are alive."

That's what I have been doing continuously for these twenty-five years, day in, day out. It hurts that a country that has given birth to Buddha, Mahavira and Nagarjuna is dead.

Poor Devageet – just to hide his giggle, he had to cough. Sometimes I wonder who is taking the notes. Coughing is okay, giggling is also forgiven, but what about the notes? I used to deceive my teachers by just scribbling, pretending that I was taking notes, and fast. And I used to laugh when they were deceived. But it is impossible to deceive me, and it is good that you cannot. I am watching you, even though you think my eyes are closed. Yes, they are closed, but open enough to see what you are writing.

This is beautiful. I hit you so hard and yet you....

...Stop it now.

Session 28

O KAY. THIS NOISE THAT YOU are making is enough to make anybody say okay. Thank you. Now I can really say okay.

I was just listening again, not to Hariprasad Chaurasia, but another flutist. In India the flute has two dimensions: one, the southern; the other, the northern. Hariprasad Chaurasia was a northern flutist; I was listening to the polar opposite, the southern.

This man too was introduced to me by the same man, Pagal Baba. When he introduced me he said to the musician, "You may not understand why I'm introducing you to this boy; at least right now you will not understand, but perhaps one day, God willing, you may."

This man plays the same flute but in a totally different way. The southern flute is far more penetrating, piercing to be exact. It enters and stirs something in your very marrow. The northern flute is tremendously beautiful but a little flat – just as northern India is flat.

The man looked at me, puzzled. He thought for a moment, then said, "Baba, if you are introducing me to him then there must be something. I cannot understand; that is my mediocrity, and I am immensely grateful that you are so loving to me that you not only introduce me to the present, but even to the future."

I have only heard him a few times because we never became directly connected – it remained via Pagal Baba. The flutist used to visit him. If by chance I was there, then of course he said hello to me. Baba always laughed and said, "Touch his feet, you fool! 'Hello' is not the way to greet this boy."

He did it reluctantly, and I could see his reluctance, that's why

I am not mentioning his name. He is still alive and may feel offended, because it was not out of love for me that he touched my feet, but because Pagal Baba ordered him. He had to touch my feet.

I laughed and said, "Baba, can I hit this man?"

He said, "Of course."

And can you imagine it – as he was touching my feet, I slapped his face!

This reminds me of the letter Devageet wrote to me. I knew that he would cry and weep. I knew. How did I know even before he had written to me? Even if he hadn't written to me I would have known. I know my people. I know those who love me, whether they say it or not. And what really touched me were his words: "You can hit me as much as you want, that does not hurt; what hurts is that when I am not giggling you say, 'Devageet, don't try to deceive me....' This hurts. It is the apparent injustice of it that hurts." This is the word he used. Gudia, I think these are the words – 'apparent injustice'. Am I right, Gudia?

"Yes, Osho."

Okay, because Gudia had to read the letter to me.

I have not read anything for years because the doctors said that if I read I will have to wear glasses, and I hate glasses. I cannot think of myself wearing glasses. I would rather close my eyes. I don't want to create any barrier, even that of transparent glass, between me and that which surrounds me. So I have to depend on someone to read for me.

The words 'apparent injustice' exactly show his heart. He knows it is only apparent, but it certainly looks unjust when you are not giggling and suddenly I say, "Devageet, don't giggle!" Naturally he is taken aback – and poor Devageet is just taking his notes.

Again I am reminded of Pagal Baba, because I was talking about him this morning and I am going to continue. He used to say apparently meaningless sentences to people – and not only that, sometimes actually hitting them! Not like me, but literally, actually. I don't actually hit, not because I don't want to, but just because I am absolutely lazy. Once or twice I have tried; then my hand hurt. I don't know whether the person learned anything or not, but my hand said, "Please don't try this trick again."

But Pagal Baba used to hit for no reason at all. Somebody may have been just sitting silently by his side, and he would give the person a good slap. The person had not done anything, he had not even said anything. Sometimes people would object that it was unjust, and say to Pagal Baba, "Baba, why did you hit him?"

He would laugh and say, "You know I am *pagal*, a madman." That was enough of an explanation as far as he was concerned. That explanation won't do for me...so mad that even the most intelligent cannot decipher what kind of madness this is. Pagal Baba was a simple madman; I am a multidimensional madman.

So, if sometimes you feel that it is apparently unjust, then remember the word 'apparent'. I cannot do anything unjust, particularly to those who love me. How can love be unjust? But "apparently"...perhaps it has to be many times. One never knows the ways of people like me. I may be hitting Ashu and really aiming at Devaraj. It is a very complicated phenomenon. It cannot be computerized.

It is so complicated that I don't think any computer will become a master. He will become everything else – an engineer, a doctor, a dentist, everything possible – and be more efficient than any human being can be. But there are only two things that a computer can't do: one is, he cannot be alive. He can hum with mechanical noise but he cannot be alive. He cannot know what life is.

The second is a corollary of the first: he cannot become a master. To know life is to be a master. Just to be alive is one thing; everybody is. But to turn upon oneself, to one's own being, to see the seer, or to know the knower – this is what I mean by turning upon oneself – then one becomes a master. A computer cannot turn upon itself; that is not possible.

Devageet, your letter was beautiful – and you cried. I feel happy about it. Anything authentic is helpful on the way, and nothing can be as authentic as tears. Yes, there are professional weepers, but then they have to use tricks.

In India it happens when somebody dies – perhaps an old person nobody wanted and really everybody is happy, but nobody can show their happiness. Then the professional weepers are called in, particularly in big cities like Bombay, Calcutta, Madras, and New Delhi. They even have their own association. You just give them a call, tell them how many weepers you want, and they come – and they really weep. They can defeat any real weeper because they are technically trained people, and very efficient, and they know all the tricks. They use certain medicines, putting them just below the eyes, and that is enough for the tears to start flowing. And it is a very strange phenomenon: when tears start flowing the person suddenly feels sad.

In psychology there has been a long argument, yet undecided: "Which comes first...does a man run away because of fear, or does he feel fear because he runs away?" And there are contenders for both positions. "Fear creates running," is one position, "running creates fear," the other position. But in fact it is the same point; they are both together.

If you are sad, tears come. If tears come, for any reason, even chemical tears, let us call them artificial tears – then too, just because of an instinctive heritage, you will feel sad. I have seen these professional weepers really crying their hearts out, and you could not say that they are being deceitful; they may themselves be deceived.

Tears out of love are the most precious experience. You cried, I am happy...because you could have been angry, but you were not. You could have been annoyed, irritated, but you were not. You cried, that is as it should be. But remember, I will go on doing the same again and again; I have to do my work.

As a dentist you perfectly know how much it hurts, but still you have to do it. Not that you want to hurt, but you have anesthesia, you have certain gases; you can make a local part almost insensitive or you can make the whole person unconscious.

But I don't have anything; I have to do all my surgery without any anesthetics. Just opening somebody's stomach or brain, and without making the person unconscious, what would happen? The pain would be too much; it would kill the person, or at least drive him mad. He would jump off the table, perhaps leaving his skull behind, and run home as fast as possible; or he may even kill the doctor. But this is how my work is. There is no possibility ever to do my work in any other way.

It has to be "apparently unjust." But you mentioned the word 'apparent'; that's enough to satisfy me that although it hurts, you understand my love. Let me repeat again and again so that you do not forget: I will do it again and again!

You must have been really afraid, because you write a P.S. and a P.P.S. too, saying that, "I have never even dreamed that I would be so close to you, or that this work would be given to me. I love taking notes." And P.P.S., "Please don't stop this work, ever."

He must have become afraid that I may stop, thinking that it hurts him. It hurts Ashu too, although she has not written a letter – yet. But one day she will write, I predict, maybe tomorrow.

I simply go on hitting this side and that. Because you both happen to be on either side, naturally you get most of the hits. That has always been my way: those who are nearest to me have been hit the most. But they have also grown; they have become more integrated with each hit they absorbed. Either they ran away or they had to grow. Do or die. If you do – that's what I mean by integration, or crystallization – only then do you live. Or else – remember the dog's death – one dies; one is dying every moment.

The letter was beautiful in many senses. Gudia, later on give the letter back to him so that it can become a footnote in his notes, or a part of many appendices that are going to follow.

Pagal Baba again…this is what I call moving about in circles. He introduced me to not only these flutists but also to many other musicians. He was a musician of the musicians. Ordinarily the masses had no idea; only the great musicians knew that he could play music with anything. I have seen him play with anything possible – just a stone, and he would start by striking it on his *kamandala*. A kamandala is a pot that Hindu sannyasins carry for water and food etcetera. He would hit on the kamandala with just anything, but he had such a sense of music that even his kamandala would become a sitar.

Just in the marketplace he would purchase a flute meant only as a toy for children – you could have bought a dozen for just one rupee – and he would start playing. From that crude flute such notes would come out that even a musician would look at the whole thing with wide open eyes, shocked, thinking, "Is it possible?"

I have to tell you the name of that southern flutist I mentioned at the beginning; otherwise it will remain on my chest, and I want to unburden myself totally before I leave, so that I can leave just as I had come – with nothing, not even a memory. That's the whole purpose of these memoirs. The flutist's name was Sachdeva, one of the most well-known southern Indian flutists. I mentioned three flutists, all of them introduced to me by Pagal Baba. One man, Hariprasad Chaurasia, from north India where they play a different kind of flute music; another from Bengal, Pannalal Ghosh – he again plays a different kind of flute, very male, very loud and over-powering. Sachdeva's flute is almost silent, feminine, just the opposite of Pannalal Ghosh. I feel good that I have mentioned his name – now it is up to him what he makes out of it.

Devageet says in his letter, "Osho, I trust you...." I know – there is no question about it – otherwise why should I hit you so much? And remember, once I trust somebody I never mistrust them. It does not matter what that person does to me – my trust remains whatsoever that person does.

Trust is always unconditional. I know your love, and I trust you all; otherwise this work would not have been given to you. But remember, that does not mean that I will change in any way. Letter or no letter, P.S. or no P.P.S.; I am going to remain the same. Sometimes I will suddenly say, "Devageet, why are you giggling?" Right now you are giggling and I am not hitting you. Sometimes I will make you cry. That's my work.

You know your work, I know my work – and it's far more diffi-cult. It is not only drilling, it is drilling without anesthesia, not even a painkiller. It is not only drilling in the teeth, it is drilling into your very being. It hurts, really hurts. Forgive me, but never ask me to change my strategies. And in your letter you have not asked either. I am just saying it for the benefit of the others present.

Ashu, tomorrow I will wait for your letter. Let's see what hap-pens. Then Devageet will really giggle!

Beloved Master,
I am sitting here in the Noah's Ark weeping and wondering what to do.
When You are here, and I am empty of everything except Your words and presence pouring through me; it is the greatest fulfillment I have known.

Then You hit – from nowhere! You tell me I am giggling...when, for example, this morning I suppressed a sneeze. Other days sighs escape my lips.... What to do? I sigh when You are close...again You tell me I am giggling. When You accuse me of deceiving You by pretending not to write Your notes, it is too much.

I love writing these notes beyond any other thing in my life. The writing of them is a pleasure, a gift beyond any possibility my mind may have conceived.

You have called me a fool – and that is obviously so – perhaps never more than now. But I am Your fool through and through. I have never cheated You, betrayed You, never giggled or whispered to deceive You, and always give You the maximum.... And the pain from the hit is not from the blow but at the apparent injustice of it.

Beloved Master, I am Your fool and never more than at this moment. I love You,
Devageet

Beloved Master, P. S. Thank You for destroying me, it seems to allow me to love You even more deeply.
Devageet

P. P. S. Please, please keep up the good work...forever.

Session 29

T HE WHOLE NIGHT THE WIND went on blowing in the trees. The sound was so beautiful that I played Pannalal Ghosh, one of the flutists that Pagal Baba had introduced to me. Just now too I was playing his music, but he has a way of his own. His introduction is very long, so before Gudia called me it was still only the introduction; I mean he had not started playing his flute yet. The sitar and tabla were preparing the ground for him to play his flute. Last night I listened to his music again after perhaps two years.

Pagal Baba has to be talked about only in an indirect way; that was the quality of the man. He was always in brackets, very invisible. He introduced me to many musicians, and I always asked him why. He said, "One day you will be a musician."

I said, "Pagal Baba, sometimes it seems people are right: you are mad. I am not going to be a musician.

He laughed and said, "I know that. Still I say you will be a musician."

Now, what to make of it? I have not become a musician, but in a way he was right. I have not played on musical instruments, but I have played on thousands of hearts. I have created a far deeper music than any instrument can – noninstrumental, nontechnical.

I liked those three flutists – at least their music – but not all of them liked me. Hariprasad always loved me. He never bothered that I was a child and he was older, and a world-famous musician. He not only loved me, he respected me. Once I asked him, "Hari Baba, why do you respect me?"

He replied, "If Baba respects you, then there is no question. I trust Pagal Baba, and if he touches your feet, and you are just a child, I know he knows something that I am incapable of knowing right now. But that does not matter. He knows; that is enough for me." He was a devotee.

The musician I listened to last night, and was again trying to hear just now before I came in, Pannalal Ghosh, neither liked nor disliked me. He was not a man of strong likes or dislikes – a very flat man, no hills, no valleys, just a far stretching plain. But he played the flute in his own way as nobody else has ever done before, or can ever do again. With his flute he roared like a lion.

I once asked him, "In your life you are more like a sheep, a Bengali *babu*." He was from Bengal, and in India, Bengalis are the most unaggressive people, so anybody who is a coward is called a Bengali Babu. I told him, "You are an authentic Bengali Babu. What happens when you play the flute? You become a lion."

He said, "Something certainly happens. I am no more myself; otherwise I would be the same Bengali Babu, just the same cowardly man that I am. But something happens, I am possessed."

That's exactly the words he used. "I am taken over by it, I don't know what. Perhaps you know; otherwise why does Pagal Baba have so much respect for you? I have never seen him touch anybody's feet except yours. All the great musicians come to him just for his blessing, and to touch his feet."

Pagal Baba introduced me to many people, not only flutists. Perhaps in some circle of my story they will come in. But what Pannalal Ghosh said was very significant. He said, "I become possessed. Once I start playing, I am no more; something else is. It is not Pannalal Ghosh." I am quoting his words. He then said, "That's why it takes such a long introduction before I play. I am condemned everywhere because of my long introduction…because flutists are not known to have such long introductions."

He was the Bernard Shaw of the flute world. With George Bernard Shaw…his book may have been only ninety pages long but the introduction would be three hundred pages. Pannalal Ghosh said, "People cannot understand, but I can tell you, that I have to wait to become possessed; hence the long introduction. I cannot start playing until it comes."

These are truly the words of an authentic artist, but only the authentic artist, not the journalistic type, the third-rate artist. It is better not to call this type an artist at all. He writes about music, but knows nothing of the experience; he writes about poetry without ever composing a single poem; he writes about politics and has never been in the thick of the struggle. It is tooth and nail in the political world. Just sitting in his office, the journalistic type can manage to write everything. In fact it is the same person who one week writes about music, and another week about poetry, and another week about politics, using different names.

I have been a journalist once, out of sheer necessity; otherwise I would not have suffered it. I had no money and my father wanted me to go to a science college. I was not interested in science, neither then nor now. And he was so poor that I could understand that he would be risking too much. Nobody in my family had been well educated. One of my uncles, my father's brother, was sent to university by my father, but had to be called back because there was not enough money to keep him there.

My father was ready to send me to university. Naturally it was a sacrifice for him, and he wanted to do it in a businesslike way. It had to be an investment.

I said to him, "Listen, is it my education or your investment? You are thinking of making me an engineer or a doctor. Naturally I will earn more, but what I am planning to do is never earn anything, but to go on learning and never begin earning." I then told him, "I am going to remain a hobo."

He said, "What! A hobo?"

I said, "In respectable words – a sannyasin."

He was still shocked. "A sannyasin! Then why do you want to go to university?"

I said, "I hate those professors, but naturally, first I have to know their profession so that my whole life I can condemn them perfectly."

He said, "This is strange, going to university just to condemn it. I have to borrow money for you, mortgage my house for you, risk my business for you – and you are just going to condemn those professors? Why can't you condemn them without going to university?"

I left home, just writing a note to my father saying, "I can under-stand your feelings, and I can understand your economy. We belong to different worlds, and there is no bridge, at least right now. I don't see that you can understand me, or that I can understand you, and there is no need either. Thank you for the gesture of wanting to support me, but it was an investment, and I don't want to become your business partner. I am leaving without seeing you. Perhaps I will meet you only when I have arranged my own finances." That's why I went to work as a journalist.

It was the worst thing that one can be forced to do, and yes, I was forced to do it because no other job was available. And journal-ism in India is the third degree of the third-rate. It is not just third-rate, it is the worst in the world. I did it but could not do it very well. I cannot do anything very well, so that is not at all a complaint against myself, just an acceptance that I cannot do anything, what to say of doing it very well.

And the job ended very soon because I was fast asleep, with my legs on the table, just the way I am right now, when the owner, the chief editor entered. He saw me, shook me, and I opened my eyes and looked at him and said, "This is not gentlemanly. I was fast asleep and you disturbed my dream. I would give a fortune for that dream to continue again. I am ready to pay; now tell me how to continue it."

He said, "What do I care about your dream? I am not concerned with it. But this is my time and you are being paid for it. I have every right to wake you up."

I said, "Okay, then I have every right to walk out." And I walked out. Not that he was wrong, but it was not my place. I had entered into a wrong place. Journalists are the worst people, and I know them: I lived with them for three years. It was hell.

What was I saying? I just try to keep a check on you.

"You were talking about how you had to take up journalism because your father had no money to support you."

Before that?

"When you are truly an authentic artist you become possessed."

Right.

"Not the journalistic type."

Continue taking really exact notes. You have become a good writer.

My father was always amazed whenever Pagal Baba would come and touch my feet. He himself would touch Pagal Baba's feet. It was really hilarious. And just to make the circle whole I would touch my father's feet. Pagal Baba would start laughing so loudly that everybody became silent as if something really great was happening – and my father would look embarrassed.

Pagal tried again and again to convince me that my future was to be a musician. I said "No," and when I say no, I mean no.

From my very childhood my no has been very clear, and I rarely use yes. That word yes is so precious, almost holy, that it should be used only in the presence of the divine, whether it is love or beauty, or right now...orange blossom on the gulmohar, so thick it is as if the whole tree is aflame. When anything reminds you of the sacred, then you can use the word yes – it is full of prayer. No simply means that I cut myself off from the proposed activity. And I have been a no-sayer; it was very difficult to get a yes out of me.

Seeing Pagal Baba, a man who was known to be enlightened, I recognized that he was unique even in those days. I did not know anything of what enlightenment is. I was in just the same position as I am now, again utterly unknowing. But his presence was luminous. You could recognize him among thousands.

He was the first man who took me to a *Kumbha Mela*. It takes place every twelve years in Prayag, and is the biggest gathering in the whole world. For Hindus Kumbha Mela is one of their life's cherished dreams. A Hindu thinks that if you have not been to a Kumbha Mela at least once, you have missed your life. That's what a Hindu thinks. The minimum count is ten million people, the maximum is thirty million people.

It's the same with the Mohammedans. Unless you are a *haji*, unless you have been to Haj, to Mecca, you have missed. *Haj* means "journey to Mecca," where Mohammed lived and died. All over the world it is every Mohammedan's most precious dream; he has to go at least once to Mecca. The Hindu has to go to Prayag. These places are their Israels. The religions may look very different on the surface, but if you just scratch a little bit you will find the same rubbish; Hindu, Jew, Mohammedan, Christian, it does not matter.

But Kumbha Mela has a unique character. Just a gathering of thirty million people is in itself a rare experience. All the Hindu monks come there, and they are not a small minority. They number five hundred thousand, and they are very colorful people. You cannot imagine so many unique sects. You cannot believe that such people even exist, and they all gather there.

Pagal Baba took me to the first Kumbha Mela of my life. I was to attend once more, but this experience with Pagal Baba at the Kumbha Mela was immensely educating, because he took me to all the great, and the so-called great saints, and in front of them, and with thousands of people around, he would ask me, "Is this man a real saint?"

I would say, "No."

But Pagal Baba was also as stubborn as I am, he did not lose heart. He went on and on, taking me to every kind of saint possible, until I said to one man, "Yes."

Pagal Baba laughed and said, "I knew that you would recognize the true one. And this man" – he pointed to the man about whom I had said yes – "he is a realized one, not known to anybody."

The man was just sitting under a pipal tree, without any follow-ers. Perhaps he was the loneliest man in that great crowd of thirty million people. Baba first touched my feet, then his feet.

The man said, "But where did you find this child? I never thought a child would be able to recognize me. I have hidden myself so perfectly. You can recognize me, that's okay, but how could he do it?"

Baba said, "That's the puzzle. That's why I touch his feet. You touch his feet right now." And who could have disobeyed that ninety-year-old man? He was so majestic. The man immediately touched my feet.

That's how Pagal Baba used to introduce me to all kinds of people. In this circle I am mostly talking of the musicians, because they were his love affair. He wanted me to become a musician, but I could not fulfill his desire because for me music, at the most, can only be an entertainment. I told him exactly in those same words, saying, "Pagal Baba, music is a much lower kind of meditation. I am not interested in it."

He said, "I know it is. I wanted to hear it from you. But music is a good step to go higher; no need to cling to it, or to remain on it. A step is a step to something else."

That's how I have used music in all my meditations, as a step to something – which is really "the music" – soundless. Nanak says, "*Ek omkar sat nam*: there is only one name of God, or of truth, and that is the soundless sound of aum." Perhaps meditation came out of music, or perhaps music is the mother of meditation. But music itself is not meditation. It can only indicate, or be a hint....

> *The ancient pond,*
> *the frog jumps in,*
> *the soundless sound....*

It has been translated in many ways. This is one of them: 'the soundless sound'. A 'plop' is even better. But the Hindi word is even more significant. When a frog jumps into a pond it makes a sound – you can call it "plop," but in Hindi the word is exactly how it sounds: *chhapak*. Be a frog, jump into a pond, and you will know chhapak.

It will be difficult to write in English. It is better that I tell you; otherwise you will inevitably write something wrong. Chhapak has to be written c-h-h-a-p-a-k. In English there is no letter for 'chh' so we have to write it in that way.

The English alphabet has only twenty-six letters. You will be surprised that Hindi or Sanskrit has double that number: fifty-two letters. So many times it is difficult to translate, or even romanize words. 'Chh' does not exist at all in English, but without 'chh' there will be no frog, and there will be no chhapak, and thousands of other things will be missed.

Ek omkar sat nam, the real name of the truth, is the soundless sound. To write it in Sanskrit we have created a nonalphabetical symbol; it is aum. It is not part of the Sanskrit alphabet – ABC, XYZ. Aum is just a sound, and a very significant sound. It consists of a-u-m, and these are the three basic musical notes. The whole of music depends on these three sounds. If they all become one, there is silence. If they diverge there is sound. If they converge, there is silence. Aum is a silence.

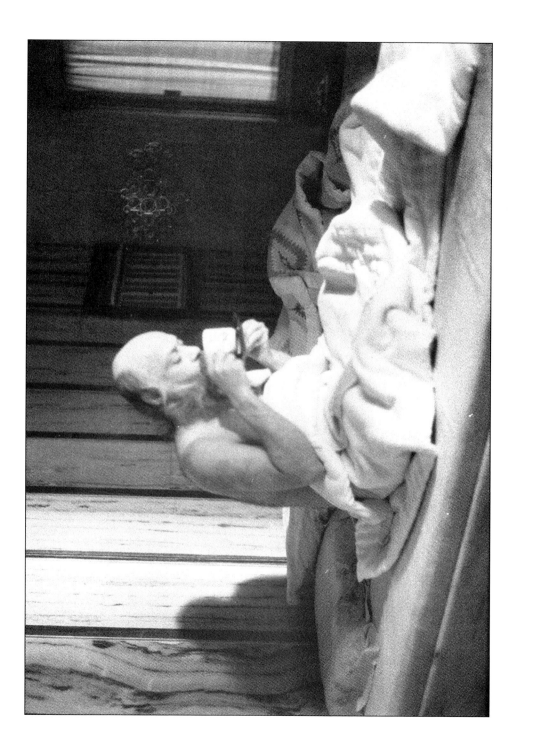

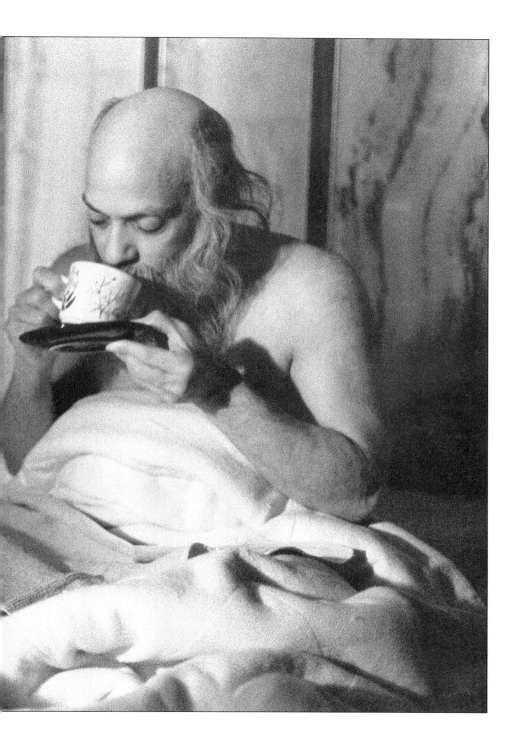

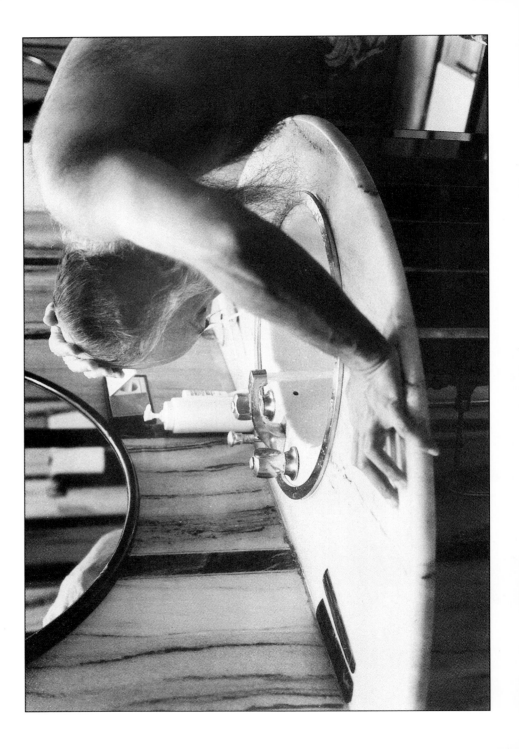

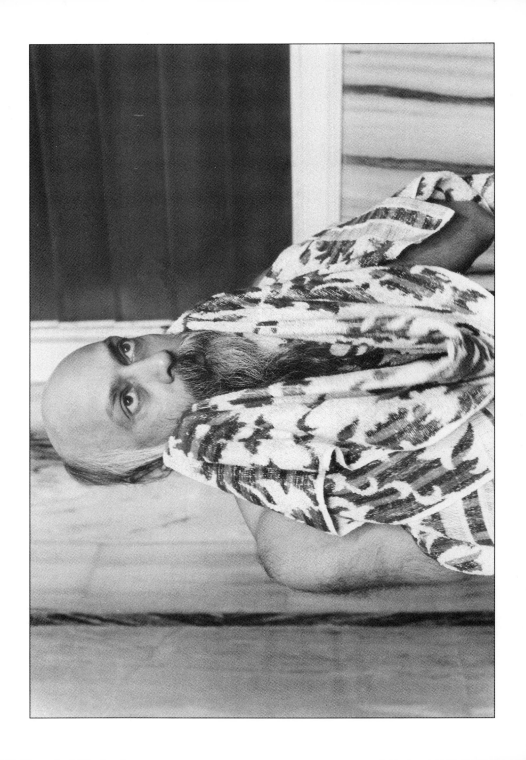

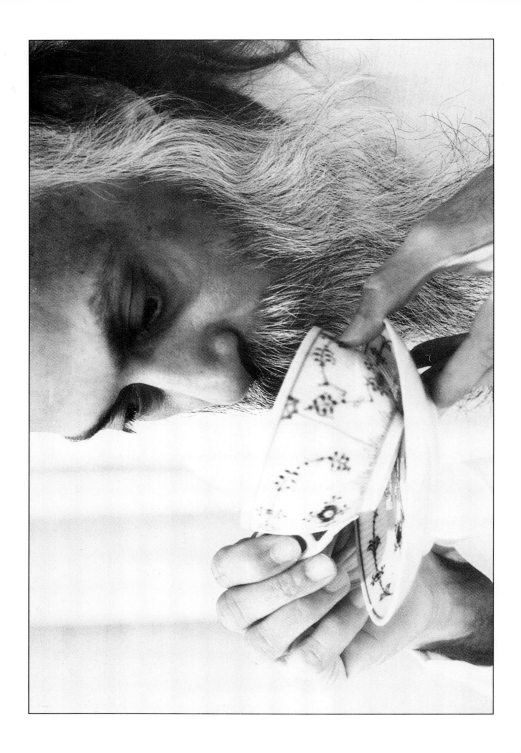

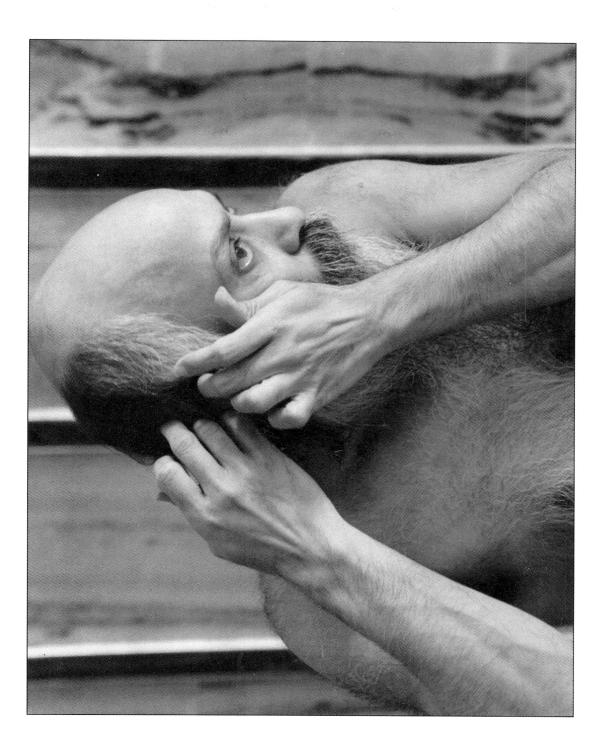

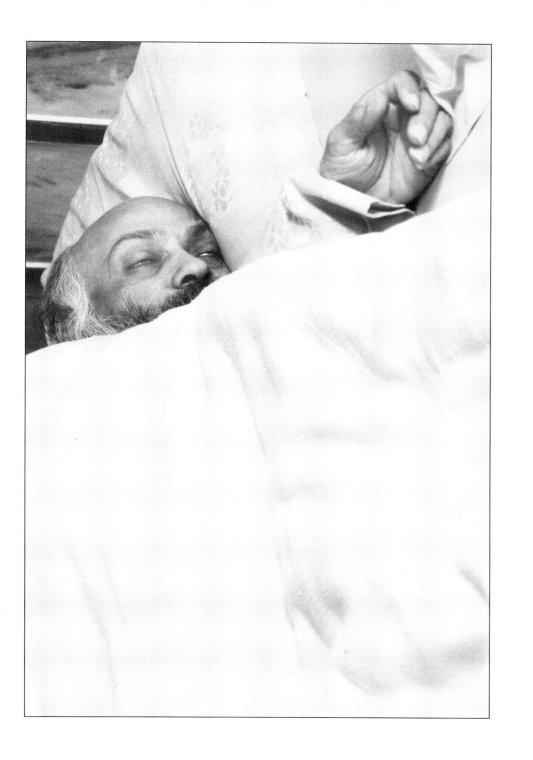

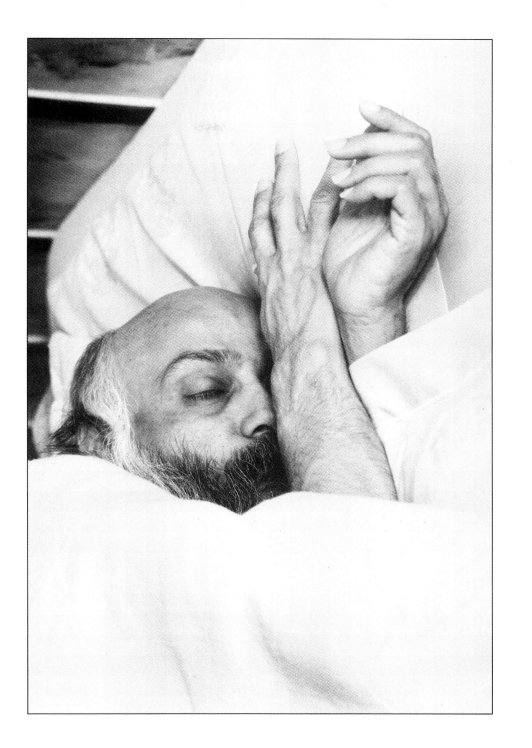

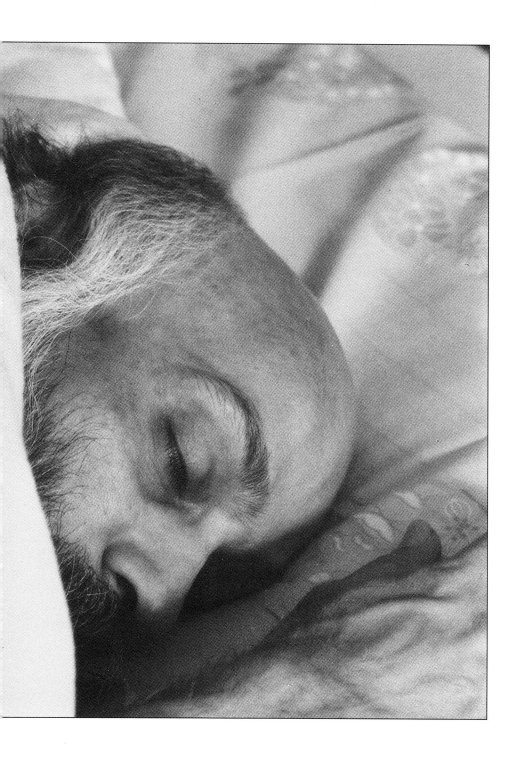

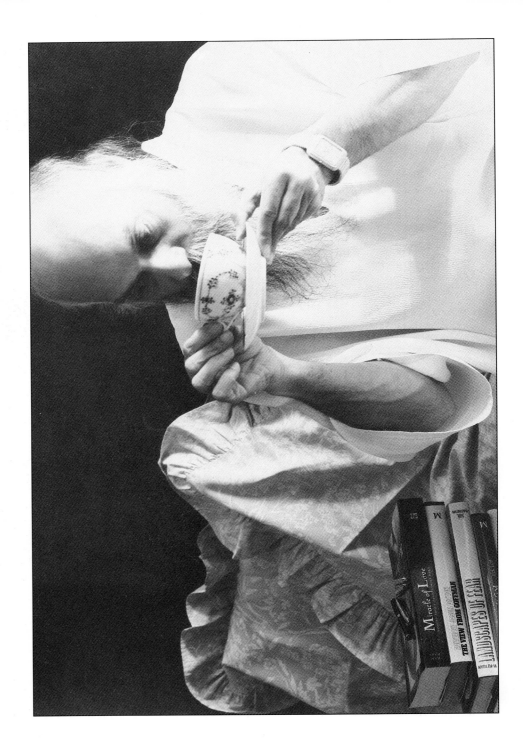

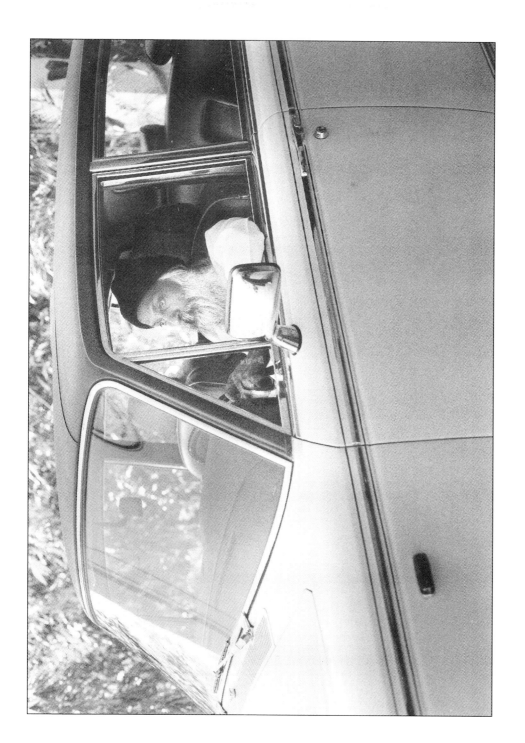

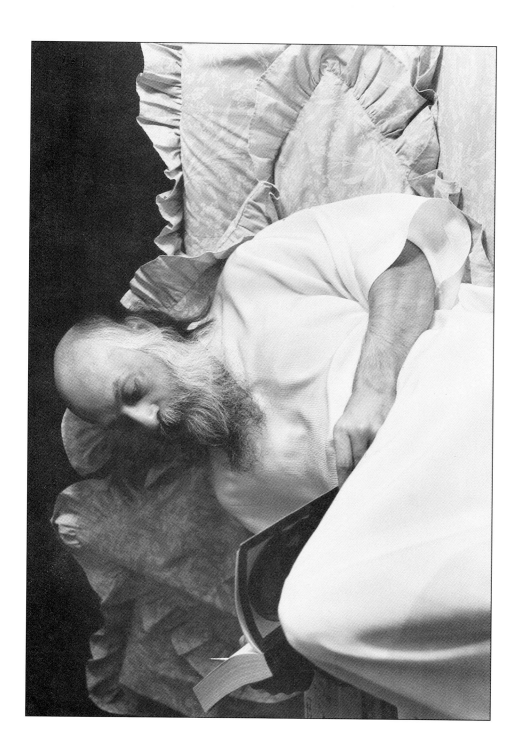

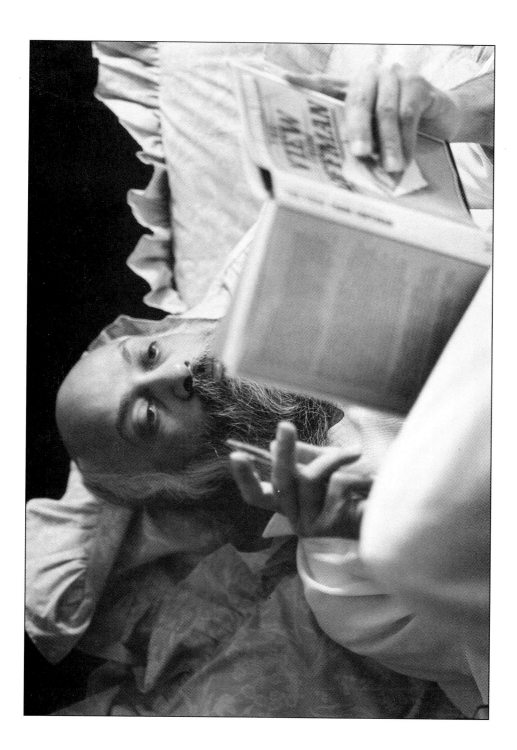

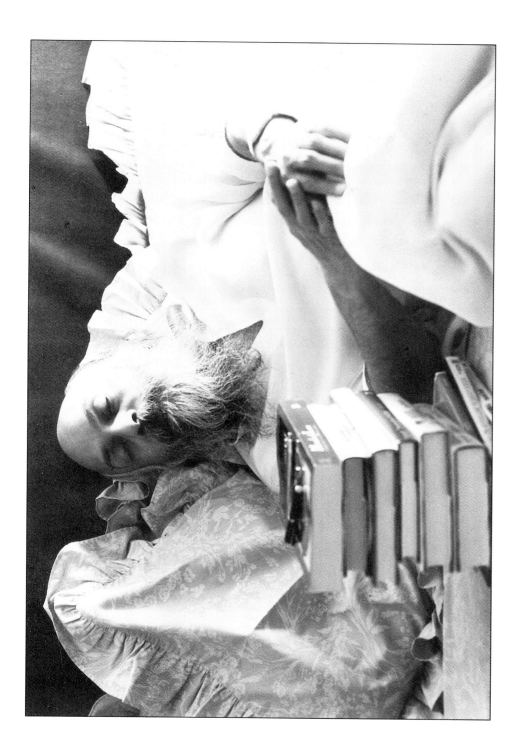

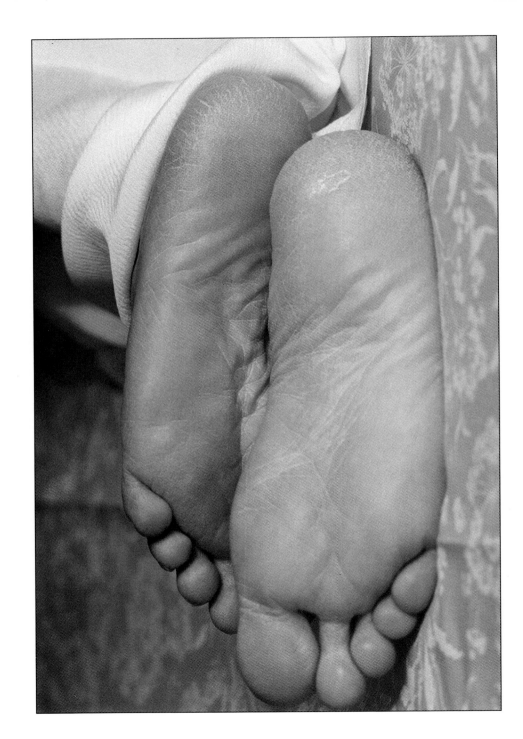

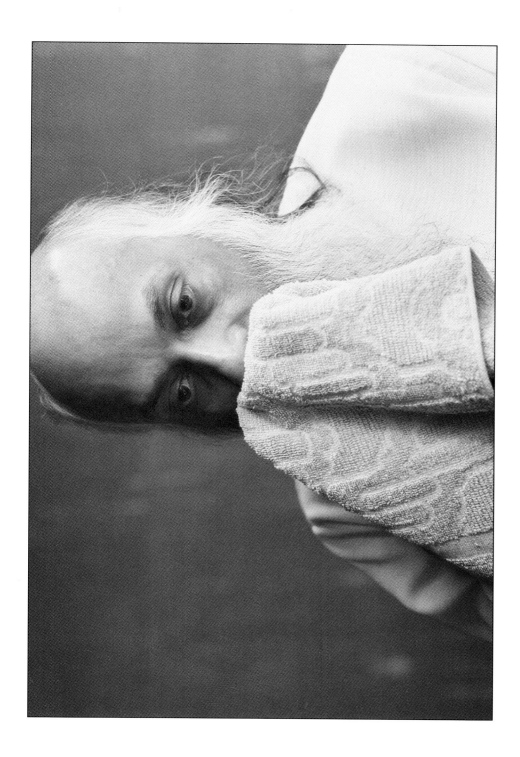

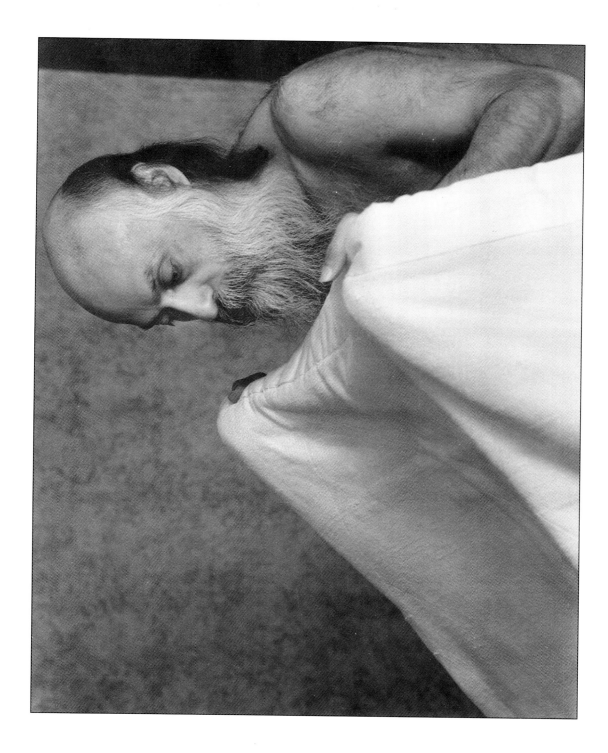

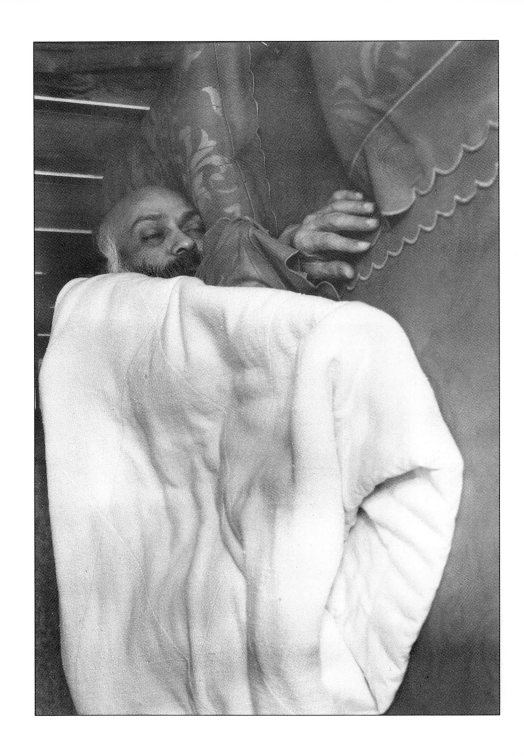

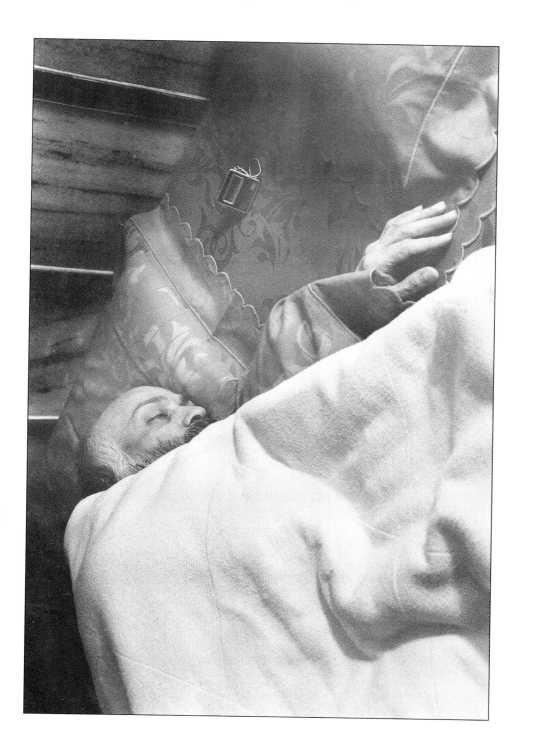

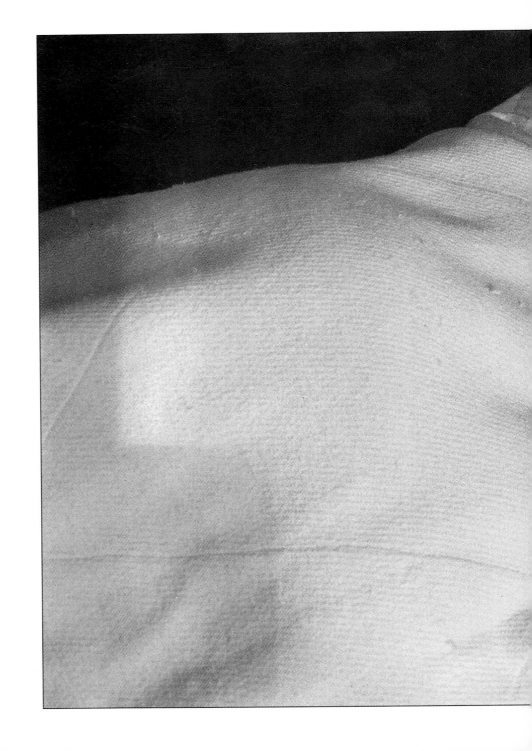

You must have seen the bell in every Hindu temple, but you may not have seen a really artistic one. For that you will have to look in the Tibetan section of some museum. The Tibetan bell is the most beautiful. It is a strange bell, like a cup made of many metals, and it has a wooden handle. You take the handle in your hand, and go round and round the inside of the cup. This is done a certain number of times, for example seventeen; then you hit the inside of the bell at a certain point which is marked. That is the beginning and the end.

From there you begin going around again, and then you strike at the end. And it is strange, the bell repeats the whole Tibetan mantra! When one hears it for the first time one cannot believe that the bell is repeating the Tibetan mantra exactly. But the bell was made for that purpose.

I was shown a bell of that kind by a Tibetan lama. It was just wonderful to hear the whole mantra being repeated by the bell. You know the mantra, I have told it to you. The mantra is not significant, it is meaningless, but musical, very musical; that's how the bell can create it. If it was meaningful it would be very difficult for a bell to do the job. A bell is just a dumb bell.

Om Mani Padme Hum – the bell repeats it so clearly that you suspect perhaps the Holy Ghost is hidden somewhere. But there is nobody, no Holy Ghost, nothing – just the bell. You have to go round and round with the stick; then at a certain point strike, and the bell resounds with the mantra.

The bell in every temple in India or Tibet or China or Burma, is meaningful in the sense that it reminds you that if you can become as silent as the bell slowly becomes after you have hit it: first it is all sound, then slowly the sound dies – then the soundlessness enters in. People hear only the sound; then they have not heard the bell. You should hear the other part too. When the sound is dying, disappearing, the soundless sound is appearing, coming in. When the sound has completely disappeared, there is utter soundlessness, and that is what meditation is.

I was not going to become a musician. Pagal Baba knew it, but he was in love with music, and he wanted me to at least be acquainted with the best of the musicians; perhaps I may become attracted. He introduced me to so many musicians, it was even difficult to remember all their names. But a few names are very famous and known all over the world, for example these three.

Pannalal Ghosh is thought to be the greatest flutist who has ever lived, and certainly it is not wrong, but he is not my choice. He roars like a lion, but the man is just a mouse, and that's what I don't like. A mouse roaring like a lion – that's what hypocrisy is. But still I must say he manages it well. It is a difficult affair but he manages it almost perfectly. I say "almost" because he could not deceive my eyes. I told him, and he said, "I know it." He is not my choice.

The second man is from south India. I never liked him from the very beginning. Of course I love his flute; perhaps nobody has the depth he has. But man to man, eye to eye, we could not stand each other. This man...I told you his name and I won't repeat it again; once is more than enough. I neither like the man nor his name. But his flute is just the best that has come out of centuries. Still he is not my choice, because of the man. If I don't like the man, howsoever beautifully he plays, I cannot choose him to be the first.

My choice is Hariprasad. He is very humble, neither like a mouse nor like a lion. He is exactly what is meant by the word, *majjhim*, the middle, the "golden mean." He has brought the balance which is lost in both Pannalal Ghosh and the south Indian man, whose name I am not going to say again. But Hariprasad has brought a balance, an immense balance, just like a tightrope walker.

This man Pagal Baba will be referred to many times, for the simple reason that he introduced so many people to me. Whenever I mention them, Pagal Baba will have to be mentioned too. Through him a world opened up. He was far more valuable to me than any university, because he introduced me to all that is best in every possible field.

He used to come to my village just like a whirlwind and he would take hold of me. My parents could not say no to him; not even my Nani could say no to him. In fact, the moment I mentioned Pagal Baba they all said, "Then it's okay," because they knew that if they denied me, Pagal Baba would come and create a nuisance in the house. He could break things, he could beat people, and he was so respected that nobody would prevent him from doing any damage. So it was best for everybody to say, "Yes...if Pagal Baba wants to take you with him, you can go. And we know," they said, "that with Pagal Baba you will be safe."

My other relatives in the town used to tell my father, "You are not doing the right thing in sending your boy along with that insane man."

My father replied, "My boy is such that I am more worried about that old insane man than about him. You need not bother."

I traveled many places with Pagal Baba. He took me not only to great artists and musicians, but also to the great places. It was with him that I first saw the Taj Mahal, and the caves of Ellora and Ajantas. He was the man with whom I first saw the Himalayas. I owe him too much, and I have never even thanked him. I could not because he used to touch my feet. If I would ever say anything to him in thanks, he would immediately put his hand to his lips and say, "Just be quiet. Never mention your thankfulness. I am thankful to you, not you to me."

One night when we were alone I asked him, "Why are you thankful to me? I have not done anything for you and you have done many things for me, yet you don't even allow me to say thank you."

He said, "One day you will understand, but right now go to sleep and don't mention it again at all, never, never. When the time comes you will know." By the time I came to know it was too late, he was no more. I came to know, but too late.

If he had been alive perhaps it would have been too difficult for him to realize that I had come to know that once, in a past life, he had poisoned me. Although I had survived, he was now just trying to compensate; he was trying to efface it. He was doing everything in his power to be good to me – and he was always good to me, more than I ever deserved – but now I know why: he was trying to bring balance.

In the East they call it *karma*, the "theory of action." Whatever you do, remember, you will have to bring a balance again to things disturbed by your action. Now I know why he was so good to a child. He was trying, and he succeeded, to bring about balance. Once your actions are totally balanced you can then disappear. Only then can you stop the wheel. In fact, the wheel stops by itself, you don't even have to stop it.

Session 30

I WAS TALKING ABOUT PAGAL BABA and the three flutists he introduced to me. It is still a beautiful memory, the way he introduced
me to people – particularly to those who were accustomed to
being received, respected and honored. The first thing he would say
to them was, "Touch the feet of this boy."

I remember how differently people reacted, and how we both
laughed later on. Pannalal Ghosh was introduced to me at his own
house in Calcutta. Pagal Baba was his guest, I was Pagal Baba's
guest. Pannalal Ghosh was really very famous, and when Baba said
to him, "Touch the feet of this boy first, then I can allow you to
touch my feet," he hesitated for a moment, then touched my feet
without really touching.

You can touch a thing without really touching it. You do it all
the time – shaking hands with people yet having no feeling, no
warmth, no receptivity, no joy to share. What are you shaking
hands for? It is unnecessary exercise. And what have your hands
done wrong? – why shake them?

And do you know, there is a Christian sect called the Shakers;
they shake their whole body. They are shaking hands with God. Of
course, when you shake hands with God the whole body has to be
shaken. And you know the Quakers; they go even a step further:
they don't only shake, they quake! These are the real origins of their
names. The Quakers used to roll around, jump up and down, and do
all kinds of things that you can see in any madhouse. I am not
against what they do, I'm simply describing them. In the same way,
Pannalal Ghosh touched my feet.

I said to Baba, "He has not touched them."

Baba said, "I know. Pannalal, do it again."

It was too much for the famous man, in his own house, and with so many people present. In fact, all the eminent people of Calcutta were there. The prime minister's son was there, the chief minister was there, and so on and so forth. "Do it again?" But that shows the quality of the man. He again touched my feet. This time it was even more dead than before.

I laughed. Baba roared. I said, "He needs training."

Baba said, "That is true. He will be born many times to get that training. In this life he has missed the train. I was giving him a last opportunity, but he has missed that too."

And you will be surprised, after only seven days Pannalal Ghosh was no longer in this world. Perhaps Baba was right; the last opportunity had been given and Pannalal Ghosh had missed it. He was not a bad man, remember. Note it: I don't say he was a good man, I only say he was not a bad man. He was just ordinary. To be good or to be bad needs some extraordinariness.

He had poured all his talent, intelligence, and his soul into his flute, and he was left barren, desertlike. His flute was beautiful, but it was better not to have known the man. Now, when I hear his flute on a record, I try to dispose of him. I tell him, "Pannalal Ghosh, please don't come in; let me listen to the flute."

But Baba wanted him to be introduced to me, and not me to him. It was not for me, because I had no name. I had not done anything, right or wrong, yet, and I was never going to do anything either.

Even now, I can say the same thing: I have not done anything right or wrong. I am a nondoer, and I have remained persistently so, just a nondoer. But Pannalal Ghosh was a great musician. To tell him to touch my feet in front of so many people was very humbling. It was good exercise for him – but twice was too much. But he was a real Bengali Babu.

This term, Bengali Babu, was invented by the British because their first capital in India was in Calcutta, not New Delhi, and obviously their first servants were Bengalis. All Bengalis are fish-eaters. They stink of fish. Chetana will understand, she is a fisherman's daughter. Fortunately she can understand exactly. She has the nose too because when I smell something and nobody else can smell it, I have to depend on her. I then ask her, and she certainly smells it.

Bengalis are all fish-eaters, and of course they all smell of fish. Every Bengali house has a pond. It happens nowhere else in India; it is special to Bengal. It is a beautiful country. Every house has, according to its capacity, a small or large pond to grow one's own fish.

You will be surprised to know that the English word 'bungalow' is the name for a Bengali house. Bengal is the English transformation of *bangla,* and the Britishers called the Bengali house "bungalow." Each bungalow – that is Bengali house – has a pond in which you grow your own food. The whole place stinks of nothing but fish. To talk to a Bengali, particularly for a man like me, is so difficult. Even when visiting Bengal I never used to speak to Bengalis because of the smell, but only to non-Bengalis who were living there. It was really fishy.

Pannalal Ghosh died just seven days after I had seen him, and Baba had said to him, "This is your last opportunity." I don't think he understood it – he looked a little stupid. Forgive me for that expression, but what can I do if someone looks stupid? Whether I say it or not, he still looks stupid. But as far as his playing the flute is concerned, he was a genius. Perhaps that is why, in all other ways, he had become stupid – sucked by the flute, a dangerous instrument. But at least he touched my feet, but without really touching. So Baba said to him, "Touch his feet again and *really* touch them."

Pannalal Ghosh said, "I have touched them twice. How does one really touch?"

And can you believe what Baba did? He touched my feet to show him how to do it – with tears in his eyes – and Baba was ninety years old!

Baba never allowed me to sit with other people. I had to sit on his pillow, above and behind him. You know that in India a particular round pillow is used only by very rich people or by very respected people. Baba used to carry very few things, but his pillow was always with him. He had told me, "Do you know, I don't need it, but to sleep on somebody else's pillow is so dirty. I should at least have my own private pillow, even though I have nothing else. So I carry this pillow everywhere I go."

Do you know, when I used to travel…Chetana will understand – because one pillow is not enough for me, I use three pillows, two for my sides and one for my head. That meant a very big suitcase for only the pillows, then another big suitcase only for the blankets, because I can't sleep under anybody else's blankets; they smell. And the way I sleep is so childlike, you will really laugh; I simply disappear under my blanket, head and all. So if it is smelling I cannot breathe, and I cannot keep my head out, because then it disturbs my sleep.

I can sleep only if I cover myself totally and forget the whole world. That is not possible if there is some smell. So I had to carry my own blanket, and one suitcase for my clothes. So I was carrying three big suitcases continuously for twenty-five years.

Baba was fortunate; he used to carry his round pillow under his arm. It was his only possession. He told me, "I carry it especially for you because when you come with me, where would I tell you to sit? I will be sitting on a higher platform than anybody else, but you have to sit a little higher than me."

I said, "You are mad, Pagal Baba."

He said, "You know, and everybody else knows, that I am mad. Does that have to be mentioned? But this is my decision, that you have to sit higher than I do."

That pillow was meant for me. I had to sit on it, reluctantly of course, embarrassed, sometimes even angry, because it made me look so awkward. But he was not the man to be bothered by anything. He would simply pat my head or back and say, "Cheer up, my son. Don't be so angry just because I have made you sit on the pillow. Cheer up."

This man, Pannalal Ghosh, I neither liked nor disliked him. I was almost indifferent to him. He had no salt, so to speak, he was just tasteless. But his flute…he brought the Indian bamboo flute to the world's notice, and raised it to be one of the greatest instruments of music. Because of him, the more beautiful flute, the Japanese, has completely faded out. Nobody bothers about the Arabic flute. But the Indian flute owes immensely to this very flat Bengali Babu, this fishy-smelling government servant.

You will be really surprised that the word *babu* has become a name of great respect in India. When you want to respect anybody, you call him Babu. But it simply means "one who stinks" – *ba* means "with" and *bu* means "stink." The word was created by the Britishers for the Bengalis. Slowly slowly it spread all over India. Naturally, they were the first British servants, and they rose to the highest posts. So the word 'babu', which cannot be in any way respectable, became respectable. It is a strange fate, but words do have strange fates. Now nobody thinks that it should be thought ugly; it is thought very beautiful.

Pannalal Ghosh was really a babu, I mean, stinking of fish, so I had to hold my nose.

He asked, "Baba, why is this boy of yours, whose feet I have to touch again and again, holding his breath?"

Baba said, "He is trying to do some yoga exercise. It has nothing to do with you or your fishy smell." He was such a beautiful man, this Pagal Baba.

The second musician, whose name I have been avoiding to even mention – although I did mention it once and I have to mention it again just to finish this chapter – was Sachdeva. His flute playing is totally different from Pannalal Ghosh, although they use the same type of flute. You could give them the same flute and you would be amazed at the difference in the music. What comes out of the flute is what matters, not the flute itself.

Sachdeva had a magical touch, whereas Pannalal Ghosh was technically perfect, but not a magician. Sachdeva was also technically perfect and had the art of music and magic together. Just listening to his flute is to be transported into another world. But I never liked the man. Not in the same sense as Pannalal Ghosh, which was indifference; this man I hated. It was pure and simple dislike, so total that I could not see any possibility whatsoever that we could even be acquaintances. And Baba knew it, Sachdeva knew it, but still he had to touch my feet.

I told Baba, "I cannot allow him to touch my feet again. The first time I was not aware of the ugliness of his vibe; now I know it."

And his vibe was not only ugly, it was nauseous, and so was his face. One felt sick. I was avoiding talking about it simply not to remember it. Why? Because I will have to see it again to describe it to you. But I have decided to unburden myself totally, so let it be so. He was really more ugly than his passport photograph.

I used to think that a passport photo was the most ugly thing possible; nobody could be that ugly. Sachdeva was. And what a beautiful name: Sachdeva, God of Truth – and yet he was so ugly. My God! Jesus!

But when he started playing on his bamboo flute, all his ugliness simply disappeared. He took you to some other world. His music is very penetrating, sharp as the edge of a sword. He cuts through and through, and so skillfully that you don't even know that the surgery has happened.

But the man was simply ugly. I don't bother about physical ugliness. What do I have to do with his physique? But psychologically he was ugly too. When he touched my feet for the first time, very reluctantly, it felt as if a reptile had crawled over them, the kind of feeling as if a snake has crawled over your feet. And I could not even jump and kill the snake then and there – he was not a snake, he was a man.

I looked at Baba and said, "What am I supposed to do about the snake?"

Baba said, "I knew that you would recognize it. Please be patient. First listen to his flute, then we will think about his being a snake." He went on, "I was afraid you would become aware of it. I knew he would not be able to deceive you, but we will talk about that later on. First, listen to his flute."

So I listened, and he was certainly a magician, reaching into you so deeply, just like a cuckoo calling from a distant hill. This phrase can be understood only in an Indian context.

In India, the cuckoo is not what you make of it. To be cuckoo in the West is to be in the madhouse. In the East, the name cuckoo is given only to the highest singers and poets. Sachdeva was called "the cuckoo of the flute world." And any cuckoo would find himself jealous, because the man's flute was far more beautiful – don't forget, I mean his music.

Pannalal Ghosh moves in a perfectly flat way, very sure of his ground, each step taken with care, prepared by long, long practice. You cannot find a single flaw. You cannot find a single flaw in

Sachdeva either, but he does not move on flat ground. He is a bird of the hills, flying high and low; a bird still wild, not yet tamed, but so perfect. Pannalal Ghosh seems to be very far away, something of the head – a technician really. But Sachdeva is a genius, a real artist. Innovators are very rare, and he is one of them. Particularly in a small field like the flute, he has innovated so much that for generations nobody is going to defeat him, to break his record.

You can also see that although I never liked the man I am very fair and just as far as his flute is concerned. And what does the man have to do with his flute? Neither he liked me nor did I like him. I disliked him so much that when he next came to see Baba, and inevitably Baba told him to touch my feet, I sat in the lotus posture, covering my feet with my robe.

Baba said, "Where did you practice the lotus posture? Today you are behaving like a great yogi." He then asked, "Where did you learn yoga?"

I said, "I had to learn it for all these creeping creatures, snakes and reptiles etcetera. For example, this man...I love his flute, but his flute is a totally different thing from his whole being. I don't want to be touched by him, and I knew you would say what you just said. Please tell me to touch his feet; that would be far easier."

Now I can explain to you something without which what I said will not be understood. When you touch the feet of somebody, you are pouring yourself, energy-wise, at his feet. It is an offering of whatsoever you are. Unless you are really worthy it would be better if you could be prevented from doing it. I could have touched his feet without any trouble. I could have poured whatsoever I had onto his feet. You can throw a flower on a rock, but don't throw a rock on the flower.

Baba said, "I understand, but he too has to be changed."

He did not tell him again to touch my feet. The few times we met again Sachdeva neither looked at me, nor I at him. I was afraid of Baba; Sachdeva was afraid of me. Whenever he came I would simply start pushing Baba to remind him not to tell Sachdeva to touch my feet. Baba would say, "I know, I know."

I said, "'I know, I know,' won't help. Unless he leaves I will go on reminding you. Either he plays his flute or tell him to go, because it is not only ugly the way he touches, but his face, his very presence, is something like a spiritual cancer."

So it became an agreement that if Sachdeva wanted to talk to Baba, I was freed, told to go somewhere, just to do something, just as an excuse so that I did not have to be present. Or else he was told to play his flute. Then he could bring stars to the earth; then he could transform stones into sermons. He was a magician, but only when he was playing. I like his flute, but I don't like the man.

The third man, Hariprasad, is both. His being is as beautiful as his music. He is not as famous as Pannalal Ghosh, and perhaps he never will be, because he does not care. He will not play his flute to order...he will not go after the politicians. His flute has its own flavor. The flavor of his flute can only be called balance, absolute balance, as if you were walking in a very strongly flowing stream.

The example I am giving you is from Lao Tzu. You are walking across a very strong, flowing, wild stream, and naturally you have to be very alert; otherwise you will go with the stream. Lao Tzu also says that you have to walk very fast because the stream is very cold, below zero, perhaps even colder. Fast, and yet balanced – that describes what Hariprasad Chaurasia does with his flute. Suddenly he starts and suddenly he ends; you were not expecting that he would start so suddenly.

Pannalal Ghosh takes half an hour over the preface, the foreword. In India that is the way of classical music. The tabla player will arrange his tabla. He will knock with his small hammer here and there, tuning it, finding the right key. The sitarist will tighten or loosen his strings, and try again and again to see whether all the strings have come into a synchronicity or not. This goes on for almost half an hour – but Indians are patient people. This is called the preparation. Why can't they do it before the people arrive? Or behind a screen, as they do in every drama? But strangely, the Indian classical musician has to prepare himself and his instruments in front of his audience. Why?

There must be some reason. My feeling is that classical music, particularly in the East, is so deep, that if you are not even ready to be patient for half an hour, you are not worthy to be present at all.

I am reminded of a very famous story: Gurdjieff used to call his disciples at very odd hours. His meetings were not like my meetings, where the time is fixed. You have to be there before I arrive and if I am five minutes late, remember it is never my fault.

My chauffeurs used to bring me a little late just so that the many people who were still coming in could get seated, because once I arrive I don't like people moving here and there, coming in and going out. I want everything to stop completely. Only in that full stop can I begin my work, or whatsoever I am going to say. A slight disturbance is enough to change what I am going to say. I will say something anyway, but it won't be the same, and I may never say the same thing again, ever.

You know my way; Gurdjieff's way was just the opposite. His disciples' phones would start ringing. He would call a meeting some-where, perhaps thirty miles away, and tell them to rush to be on time. Now, to travel thirty miles and arrive on time, in fact before time, without any preparation for it, you at least need a vehicle. You have to cancel other appointments. You do all these things and rush to the appointed place, only to find a notice there saying the meet-ing was canceled for today!

Next day again the phones would start ringing. If on the first day one hundred people turned up out of two hundred who had been called, then on the second day, only fifty would turn up. Again they would find a notice on the door: "Meeting postponed" – not even a "Sorry." There was nobody there to say sorry, just a board. And this would go on, and on the fourth day, or the seventh he would turn up. By he, I mean Gurdjieff.

Out of the original two hundred people, by now only four had turned up. He would look at them and say, "Now I can say what I wanted to say, and all the fellows that I never wanted to be here have dropped out by themselves. It is really great; only those remain who are worthy of listening to me."

Gurdjieff's way was different. That too is a way, but only one way; there are many. I always respect and love whatsoever brings results. I believe in Gautam Buddha's definition that "Truth is that which works." Now, this is a strange definition because sometimes a lie can work, and I know that many times truth does not work at all; the lie works.

But I agree with Buddha. Of course he would not agree with me, but I am more generous than Gautam Buddha himself. If something works, brings the right results, what does it matter whether it was a lie in the beginning or a truth? What matters is the end, the ultimate outcome. I may not use Gurdjieff's method, because I never use anybody else's methods, although people believe that I do. Yes, I pretend. I use only that which works; whose it is does not matter at all. Truth is neither mine nor yours.

This third man, I love him. From the very moment we saw each other, we recognized each other. He was the only one out of the three flutists who touched my feet before Baba told him to. When it happened Baba said, "This is something! Hariprasad, how could you touch the feet of a child?"

Hariprasad said, "Is there some law prohibiting it? Is it a crime to touch the feet of a child? I liked, I loved, hence I touched his feet. And it is none of your business, Baba."

Baba was really happy. He was always happy with such people. If Pannalal Ghosh was a sheep, Hariprasad is a lion. He is a beautiful man, a rare, beautiful man. The third fellow – I mean Sachdeva; I don't even like to say his name – has not done me any harm, but still, the very name and I start seeing his ugly face. And you know my respect for beauty. I can forgive anything but not ugliness. And when the ugliness is not only of the body but of the soul too, then it is too much. He was ugly through and through.

Hariprasad is my choice as far as these flutists are concerned. His flute has the beauty of both the others and yet is neither like that of Pannalal Ghosh – too loud and bombastic – nor so sharp that it cuts and hurts you. It is soft like a breeze, a cool breeze on a summer's night. It is like the moon; the light is there but not hot, cool. You can feel the coolness of it.

Hariprasad must be considered the greatest flutist ever born, but he is not very famous. He cannot be, he is very humble. To be famous you have to be aggressive. To be famous you have to fight in the ambitious world. He has not fought, and he is the last man to fight to be recognized.

But Hariprasad was recognized by men like Pagal Baba. Pagal Baba also recognized a few others whom I will describe later on, because they too came into my life through him.

It is a strange thing: Hariprasad was not at all known to me till Pagal Baba introduced him to me, and then he became so interested that he used to come to Pagal Baba just to visit me. One day Pagal Baba jokingly said to him, "Now you don't come for me. You know it, I know it, and the person for whom you come knows it."

I laughed, Hariprasad laughed and said, "Baba you are right."

I said, "I knew Baba was going to mention it sooner or later." And this was the beauty of the man. He brought many people to me, but prevented me from even thanking him. He said only one thing to me: "I have only done my duty. I ask just one favor: when I die, will you give the fire at my funeral?"

In India, it is thought to be of great importance. If a man is without a son he suffers his whole life, because who will give the fire at his funeral? It is called "giving the fire."

When he asked me, I said, "Baba, I have my own father, and he will be angry – and I don't know about your family; perhaps you have a son...."

He said, "Don't be bothered about anything, either about your father or about my family. This is my decision."

I had never seen him in that kind of mood. I knew then that his end was very close. He was not able to waste time even discussing it.

I said, "Okay, no argument. I will give you the fire. It does not matter whether my father objects or your family objects. I don't know your family."

By chance Pagal Baba died in my own village. But perhaps he arranged it – I think he arranged it. And when I started his funeral by giving fire to it, my father said, "What are you doing? This can be done only by the eldest son."

I said, "Dada, let me do it. I have promised him. And as far as you are concerned, I will not be able to do it; my younger brother will do it. In fact, he is your eldest son, not me. I am of no use to the family, and will never be. In fact, I will always prove to be a nuisance to the family. My younger brother, second to me, will give you the fire, and he will take care of the family."

I am very grateful to my brother, Vijay. He could not go to the university just because of me, because I was not earning, and somebody had to provide for the family. My other brothers went to university too, and their expenses had also to be paid, so Vijay stayed at home. He really sacrificed. It is worth a fortune to have such a beautiful brother. He sacrificed everything. I was not willing to marry, although my family was insistent.

Vijay told me, "Bhaiyya" – *bhaiyya* means brother – "if they are torturing you too much, I am ready to get married. Just promise me one thing: you will have to choose the girl." It was an arranged marriage as all marriages are in India.

I said, "I can do that." But his sacrifice touched me, and it helped me tremendously. Once he was married I was completely forgotten, because I have other brothers and sisters. Once he was married, then there were the others to be married. I was not ready to do any business.

Vijay said, "Don't be worried, I am ready to do any kind of work." And from a very young age he became involved in very mundane things. I feel for him immensely. My gratitude to him is great.

I told my father, "Pagal Baba asked me and I have promised him, so I have to give the fire. As far as your death is concerned, don't be worried, my younger brother will be there. I will also be present, but not as your son."

I don't know why I said this, and what he might have thought, but it proved true. I was present when he died. In fact I had called him to live with me, just so that I did not have to go up to the town where he lived. I never wanted to go there again after my grandmother's death. That was another promise. I have to fulfill so many promises, but up to now I have successfully fulfilled a major part of them. There are only a few promises which remain to be fulfilled.

I had told my father, and I was present at his funeral but could not give the fire. And certainly I was not present as his son. When he died he was my disciple, a sannyasin, and I was his master.

What is the time?

"Eight thirty-five, Osho."

Five minutes for me. When the time is over, it is over. I also have to laugh once in a while. A single moment at the climax is enough.

Stop.

Session 31

PAGAL BABA IN HIS LAST days was always a little bit worried. I could see it, although he had not said anything, nor had anybody else mentioned it. Perhaps nobody else was even aware that he was worried. It was certainly not about his illness, old age, or his oncoming death; those were absolutely immaterial to the man.

One night, when I was alone with him, I asked him. In fact, I had to wake him up in the middle of the night, because it was so difficult to find a moment when there was nobody else with him.

He said to me, "It must be something of great importance; otherwise you would not have awakened me. What's the matter?"

I said, "That's the question. I have been watching you – I feel a little shadow of worry around you. It has never been there before. Your aura has always been so clear, just like a bright sun, but now I see a little shadow. It cannot be death."

He laughed and said, "Yes, the shadow is there, and it is not death, that too is true. My concern is, I am waiting for a man so that I can hand over my responsibility for you to him. I am worried because he has not come yet. If I die it will be impossible for you to be able to find him."

I said, "If I really need somebody, I will find him. But I don't need anybody. You relax before death comes. I don't want to be the cause of this shadow. You should die as brilliantly radiant as you have lived."

He said, "It is not possible…. But I know the man will come – I am worrying unnecessarily. He is a man of his word; he has promised to reach me before I die."

I asked him, "How does he know when you are going to die?"

He laughed and said, "That is why I want you to be introduced to him. You are very young and I would like someone like me just to be around you." He said, "In fact, this is an old convention, that if a child is ever going to become awakened, then at least three awakened people should recognize him at an early age."

I said, "Baba, this is all nonsense. Nobody can prevent me from awakening."

He said, "I know, but I am an old, conventional man, so please, particularly at the time of my death, don't say anything against convention."

I said, "Okay, for your sake I will keep absolutely silent. I will not say anything, because whatsoever I say is somehow going to be against convention, tradition."

He said, "I am not saying that you should be silent, but just feel what I am feeling. I am an old man. I have nobody in the world for whom I care, except you. I don't know why, or how, you became so close to me. I want somebody in my place so you don't miss me."

I said, "Baba, nobody can replace you, but I promise you that I will try hard not to miss you."

But the man arrived the next morning.

The first awakened man who recognized me was Magga Baba. The second was Pagal Baba, and the third was more strange than even I could have imagined. Even Pagal Baba was not so mad. The man was called Masta Baba.

Baba is a respectful word; it simply means "the grandfather." But anybody who is recognized by the people as someone enlightened is also called Baba, because he is really the oldest man in the community. He may not be actually; he may be just a young man, but he has to be called Baba, the grandfather.

Masta Baba was superb, just superb, and just the way I like a man to be. He was exactly as if made for me. We became friends even before Pagal Baba introduced us.

I was standing outside the house. I don't know why I was standing there; at least now I can't remember the purpose, it was so long ago. Perhaps I was also waiting, because Pagal Baba had said the man would keep his word; he would come. And I was certainly curious like any child. I was a child, and I have remained a child in spite of everything else. Perhaps I was waiting, or pretending to do something else but actually waiting for the man, and looking up the road – and there he was! I had not expected him to arrive this way! He came running!

He was not very old, no more than thirty-five, just at the peak of his youth. He was a tall man, very thin, with beautiful long hair and a beautiful beard.

I asked him, "Are you Masta Baba?"

He was a little taken aback and said, "How did you know my name?"

I said, "There is nothing mysterious in it. Pagal Baba has been waiting for you; naturally he mentioned your name. But you are really the man I myself would have chosen to be with. You are as mad as Pagal Baba must have been when he was young. Perhaps you are just the young Pagal Baba come back again."

He said, "You seem to be madder than me. Where is Pagal Baba anyway?"

I showed him the way, and entered behind him. He touched the feet of Pagal Baba, who then said, "This is my last day, and Masto" – that was the way he used to call him – "I was waiting for you, and getting a little worried."

Masto replied, "Why? Death is nothing to you."

Baba replied, "Of course death is nothing to me, but look behind you. That boy means much to me; perhaps he will be able to do what I wanted to and could not. You touch his feet. I have been waiting so that I could introduce you to him."

Masta Baba looked into my eyes...and he was the only *real* man out of the many whom Pagal Baba had introduced to me and told to touch my feet.

It had become almost a cliché. Everybody knew that if you go to Pagal Baba you will have to touch the feet of that boy who is a nuisance in every possible way. And you have to touch his feet – what absurdity! But Pagal Baba is mad. This man, Masto, was certainly different. With tears in his eyes and folded hands he said, "From this moment onwards you will be my Pagal Baba. He is leaving his body, but he will live on as you."

I don't know how much time passed, because he would not let go of my feet. He was crying. His beautiful hair was spread all over the ground. Again and again I told him, "Masta Baba, it is enough."

He said, "Unless you call me Masto, I will not leave your feet."

Now, 'Masto' is a term used only by an older man to a child. How could I call him Masto? But there was no way out. I had to. Even Pagal Baba said, "Don't wait, call him Masto, so that I can die without any shadow around me."

Naturally, in such a situation I had to call him Masto. The moment I used the name, Masto said, "Say it thrice."

In the East, that too is a convention. Unless you say a thing thrice it does not mean much. So three times I said, "Masto, Masto, Masto. Now will you please leave my feet?" And I laughed, Pagal Baba laughed, Masto laughed – and that laughter from all three joined us together into something which is unbreakable.

That very day Pagal Baba died. But Masto did not stay, although I told him that death was very close.

He said, "For me now, you are the one. Whenever I need to, I will come to you. He is going to die anyway; in fact, to tell you the truth, he should have died three days ago. He has been hanging around just for you, so that he could introduce me to you. And it is not only for you, it is for me too."

I asked Pagal Baba before he died, "Why did you look so happy after Masta Baba had come here?"

He said, "Just a conventional mind, forgive me."

He was such a nice old man. To ask forgiveness, at the age of ninety, from a boy, and with so much love....

I said, "I am not asking why you waited for him. The question is not about you or him. He is a beautiful man, and worth waiting for. I am asking why you worried so much."

He said, "Again let me ask you not to argue at this moment. It is not that I am against argument, as you know. I particularly love the way you argue, and the strange turns you give to your arguments, but this is not the time. There is no time really. I am living on borrowed time. I can tell you only one thing: I am happy that he came, and happy that you both became friendly and loving as I wanted you to. Perhaps one day you will see the truth of this old, traditional idea."

The idea is that unless three enlightened people recognize a child as a future buddha, it is almost impossible for him to become one. Pagal Baba, you were right. Now I can see it is not just a convention. To recognize somebody as enlightened is to help him immeasurably. Particularly if a man like Pagal Baba recognizes you and touches your feet – or a man like Masto.

I continued to call him Masto because Pagal Baba had said, "Never call him Masta Baba again; he will be offended. I used to call him Masto, and from now on you have to do the same." And it was really a sight! – a child calling him, who was respected by hundreds of people, "Masto." And not only that, he would immediately do whatever I said to him.

Once, just as an example.... He was delivering a talk. I stood up and said, "Masto, stop immediately!" He was in the middle of a sentence. He did not even complete it; he stopped. People urged him to please finish what he was saying. He would not even answer. He pointed towards me. I had to go to the microphone and tell the people to please go to their homes, the lecture was over, and Masto had been taken into my custody.

He laughed hilariously, and touched my feet. And his way of touching my feet.... Thousands of people must have touched my feet, but he had a way of his own, just unique. He touched my feet almost – how to say it – as if he were confronting God himself. And he always became just tears, and his long hair.... I had such a job helping him to sit up again.

I would say, "Masto, enough! Enough is enough." But who was there to listen? He was crying, singing, or chanting a mantra. I had to wait until he had finished. Sometimes I was sitting there for even half an hour, just to say to him, "It is enough." But I could only say it when he had finished. After all, I too have some manners. I could not just say, "Stop!" or "Leave my feet!" when they were in his hands.

In fact I never wanted him to leave them, but I had other things to do, and so did he. It is a practical world, and although I am very impractical, as far as others are concerned, I am not; I am always pragmatic and practical. When I could get a single moment in which to interrupt, I would say, "Masto, stop. Enough. You are crying your eyes out, and your hair – I will have to wash it. It is becoming dirty in the mud."

You know the Indian dust: it is omnipresent, everywhere, particularly in a village. Everything is dusty. Even people's faces look dusty. What can they do? How many times can they wash? Even here, although in an air-conditioned room where there is no dust, just out of old habit, whenever I go to the bathroom – just to tell you a secret, don't tell anybody – I wash my face for no reason at all, many times each day...just an old Indian habit.

It was so dusty that I used to run to the bathroom again and again.

My mother used to say to me, "It seems we should make a bathroom in your room, so that you don't have to run through the house so many times. What do you do?"

I said, "I just wash my face – there is so much dust." I told Masto, "I will have to wash your hair." And I used to wash his hair. It was so beautiful, and I always love anything beautiful. This man Masto, about whom Pagal Baba worried so much, was the third enlightened man. He wanted three enlightened men to touch the feet of a small unenlightened boy, and he managed.

Madmen have their own ways. He managed perfectly. He even persuaded the enlightened ones to touch the feet of a boy who was certainly not enlightened.

I asked him, "Don't you think this is a little violent?"

He said, "Not at all. The present has to be offered to the future. And if an enlightened person cannot see into the future, he is not enlightened. It is not just a crazy man's idea," he said, "but one of the most ancient and respected ideas."

Buddha, even when he was only twenty-four hours old, was visited by an enlightened man, who cried and touched the feet of the child. The father of Gautam the Buddha could not believe what was happening, because the man was very famous; even Buddha's father used to go to him. Had he gone crazy or something? Touching the feet of a twenty-four-hour-old child?

Buddha's father asked, "Can I ask, sir, why are you touching the feet of this small child?"

The enlightened man said, "I am touching his feet because I can see what is possible. Right now he is a bud, but he will become a lotus." And Buddha's father – Shuddhodana was his name – asked, "Then why are you crying? Be happy if he is going to become a lotus."

The old man said, "I am crying because I will not be present at that moment."

Yes, even buddhas cry at particular moments – particularly at a moment like that one. Seeing a child who is going to become a buddha and knowing that one is going to die before it happens, is certainly hard. It is almost like a dark night: you can see, the birds have started singing, the sun will be rising soon; there is even a little light on the horizon already – and you have to die without seeing another morning.

Certainly, the old man who cried and touched Buddha's feet was right. I know from my own experience. These three people are the most important that I have ever met, and I don't think I am going to meet anybody who will be more important than those three. I have met other enlightened people too, after my enlightenment, but that is another story.

I have met my own disciples after they became enlightened; that too is a different story. But to be recognized when I was just a small child, and everybody else was against me, was a strange fate. My family was always against me. I exclude my father, my mother, my brothers – but it was a big family. They were all against me, for a simple reason – and I can understand them, they were right in a way – that I was behaving like a madman, and they were concerned.

Everybody in that small town was complaining against me to my poor father. I must say that he had infinite patience. He would listen to everybody. It was almost a twenty-four-hour job. Each day – day in, day out, sometimes even in the middle of the night – somebody would come, because I had done something which should not have been done. And I was doing only things which should not be done. In fact, I wondered how I knew which were the things which should not be done, because not even by accident did I do anything which should have been done.

Once I asked Pagal Baba, "Perhaps you can explain it to me. I could understand if fifty percent of the things I did were wrong, and fifty percent were right, but with me it is always one hundred percent wrong. How do I manage it? Can you explain it to me?"

Pagal Baba laughed and said, "You manage perfectly. That is the way to do things. And don't be bothered what others say; you go on in your own way. Listen to all the complaints, and if you are punished, enjoy."

I really did enjoy it, I must say – even the punishment. My father stopped punishing me the moment he found out that I enjoyed it. For example he once told me, "Run around the block seven times. Run fast, and then come back."

I asked, "Can I run seventy times? It is so beautiful in the morning." I could see his face. He thought he was punishing me. I really did run seventy times around the block. By and by he understood that it was difficult to punish me. I enjoyed it.

I always sympathized with my father because he suffered unnecessarily. I used to have long hair, and I loved it. Not only that, I used to wear Punjabi clothes, which were not worn in that area. I had fallen in love with Punjabi clothes after seeing them on a group of singers who had visited the town. I think that they are the most beautiful clothes in India. With my long hair, and wearing the *salwar* and *kurta*, people thought I was a girl. And I was always passing through my father's shop, coming and going into the house the whole day.

People would ask my father, "Whose girl is that? What kind of clothes is she wearing?" Of course my father was offended. I don't see that there is anything wrong if somebody thinks your boy is a girl. But in this male chauvinist society my father naturally came running after me saying, "Listen, you stop wearing this salwar and kurta. These clothes look like those of a woman. And moreover, cut your hair; otherwise I will cut it for you!"

I told him, "The moment you cut my hair you will repent."

He said, "What do you mean?"

I said, "I have said it. Now you can think it over, and find out what I mean. You will repent."

He became so angry. That is the only time I saw him so angry. He brought his scissors from the shop. It was a clothes shop, and so there were always scissors to cut the clothes. Then he cut my hair saying, "Now, you can go to the haircutter so that he can do it better; otherwise you will look like a cartoon."

I said, "I will go, but you will repent."

He said, "Again? What do you mean?"

I said, "It is your doing. You think it over. Why should I explain it to you? I don't owe any explanation to anybody. You cut my hair and you will repent."

I went to a haircutter who was an opium-eater. I chose him particularly because he was the only man who would do whatever I told him. No other haircutter would do anything unless he thought it was right. I will have to explain to you that in India, a child's head is completely shaved only when his father dies. I went to this opium-addicted fellow whom I loved anyway. His name was Natthu. I said to him, "Natthu, are you at least able to cut off all my hair?"

He said, "Yes, yes, yes" – thrice.

I said, "Great. That's the way of the Buddha – thrice. So please cut it." And he shaved my head completely.

When I came home, my father looked at me and could not believe it: I looked like a Buddhist monk. That is the difference between the Buddhist and the Hindu monks. The Hindu monk shaves his head leaving some hair on the top of the head, at the very point where the *sahasrar*, the seventh chakra is. It is to protect and to give it a little shade from the hot sun. The Buddhist monk is more daring; he cuts off everything, he shaves his whole head.

My father said, "What have you done? Do you know what this means? I will now be in more trouble than before. Everybody will ask, 'Why is this child completely shaved? Has his father died?'"

I said, "That is up to you now. I told you that you would repent." And he repented for months. People kept asking him, "What is the matter?"...because I did not allow my hair to grow.

Natthu was always there, and he was such a lovely man. Whenever I would go and his chair was empty, I would sit down and say, "Natthu, please do it again."

So whatever few hairs had grown he would shave them off. He said to me, "I love shaving heads. The fools come to me and say, 'Cut it this way, in this style, or that.' All nonsense. This is the best style: I don't have to worry, nor do you. It is simply plain, and very saintly."

I said, "You have said the word. This is very saintly. But do you realize that if my father comes to know you are the person who is doing all this, you will be in trouble?"

He said, "Don't you be worried. Everybody knows that I am an opium addict. I can do anything. If I have not cut off your head, that's enough." And he laughed.

I said, "That's good. Next time, if I feel like cutting off my head, I will come to you. I know I can rely on you."

He said, "Yes my boy, yes my boy, yes my boy."

Perhaps because of the opium, he had to repeat everything thrice. Perhaps only then he could hear what he was saying.

But my father had learned a lesson. He said to me, "I have repented enough. I will not do such a thing again." And he never did. He kept his word. That was his first and last punishment to me. It is even unbelievable to me, because I did so many troublesome things. But he listened patiently to all complaints, and never said anything to me. In fact, he tried his best to protect me.

Once I asked him, "You have promised not to punish me, but you did not promise to protect me. There is no need to protect me."

He said, "You are so mischievous that if I don't protect you, I don't think you will survive. Somebody, somewhere is bound to kill you. I have to protect you. Moreover, this Pagal Baba is always telling me to 'protect this child.' I love and respect him. If he says to protect you, then he must be right. Then I can believe the whole village to be wrong, myself included. But I can't think of Pagal Baba being wrong."

And I know Pagal Baba used to tell everybody, my teachers, my uncles, "Protect this child." Even my mother was told to protect me. I remember perfectly, the only person he never said it to was my Nani. It was such an absolutely clear exception that I had to ask him, "Why do you never tell my Nani 'Protect him'?"

He said, "There is no need: she will protect you even if she has to die for you. She would even fight with me. I can trust her. She is the only one in your family I don't need to say anything to about your protection."

His insight was crystal clear. Yes, there are eyes which can see beyond the fog which every human being creates around himself just to hide behind.

Session 32

I HAVE ALWAYS WONDERED THAT SOMETHING went right with me from the very beginning. Of course, there is no such phrase in any language. There is a phrase like "something going wrong," but not "something going right," but what can I do? It really has gone right from my very first breath – up to now at least, and I hope it won't change. It must have become accustomed to the routine.

I have been loved by so many people for no reason at all. People are respected for their talents; I have been loved for just being myself. It is not only now – that's why I say from the very beginning something must have gone right in the very scheme of things. Otherwise, how can something go right?

From the very beginning – and every moment I have lived – it went on going more and more right, righter and righter. One can only wonder....

Perhaps I can give a new meaning to the word 'god': when something goes right for no reason at all – you have not done it, you don't even deserve it, and it goes on and on; when everything goes right in spite of you.

Of course, I am not a right person, yet things went on being right with me. Even today, I cannot believe so many people around the globe love me for no reason at all. I have no achievement for which to claim any respect, neither outside nor in. I am a nonentity, just a zero.

The day I left university service, the first thing I did was to burn all my certificates and diplomas, and the whole nonsense that I had carried all along, neatly piled. I enjoyed the burning of it so much that my whole family gathered around, thinking that finally I had gone completely mad. They always had thought that I was partly mad. Seeing their faces, I started laughing even more loudly.

They said, "It has happened."

I said, "Yes, at last it has happened."

They said, "What do you mean by, 'It has happened'?"

I said, "My whole life I have been trying to burn these certificates, but I could not because they were always needed. Now there is no need: I can again be as uneducated as when I was born."

They said, "You are foolish, utterly mad. You have burned the most precious certificates. You threw the gold medal down the well; now you have burned even the last remnant showing that once you were the first in the whole university."

I said, "Now nobody can talk about that nonsense to me."

Even today I don't have any talent. I am not a musician like Hariprasad; I am not a man like so many Nobel Prize winners. I am just a nobody, yet thousands of people have given their love without any desire for any return.

Just the other day Gudia told me that when I was in this chair, Asheesh was fixing my other chair. She had never seen him crying before. He was just tears, and she asked, "What's the matter?"

He said, "Nothing is the matter. It is just that for five days Osho had not told anybody that his chair was smelling, and I am responsible because I made it. I should have checked. I should have smelled every part of it. Now who will forgive me?"

Asheesh is no ordinary carpenter. He has a Ph.D. in engineering; he is as qualified as anyone can be. And there is nothing wrong with the chair; if something is wrong, it is wrong with me. When I heard of his tears, I remembered the many, many people who have loved and wept for me, for no reason at all...and I am not a very good man either.

If you divide the good guys from the bad guys, I am certainly going to stand with the bad guys. I will be the last to stand with Mahatma Gandhi, Mao Zedong, Karl Marx, Mother Teresa, Martin Luther King, and the list is endless. As far as bad guys are concerned, I am alone.

At least I cannot count anybody as bad: Adolf Hitler, Mussolini, Joseph Stalin. Certainly they did what they believed to be good.

Maybe it was not, but that is not their fault. They were retarded, but not bad. I cannot count anybody as bad.

If I had to count anybody, then I only would remember people like Socrates, Jesus, Mansoor, Sarmad – people who were crucified, punished. But no, I cannot even count them either. They were different in their own ways.

People have tried to punish me, but have never succeeded. On the contrary, from Kantar Master to Morarji Desai, they have all gone down the drain, where they actually belonged in the first place.

But it is strange, I can simply say that from the very beginning I have really walked on a path of roses. They say, "Don't believe it"...but what can I do? I have walked, and I have known. I have seen and experienced bliss every moment of my life.

The first man to call me "the Blessed One" was the last person I mentioned yesterday. That's why I want to continue to talk about him this evening. Masta Baba...I will call him only Masto, because that's the way he wanted me to call him. I always called him Masto, although reluctantly, and I told him to remember it. Also, Pagal Baba had said to me, "If he wants to be called Masto by you, just as I call him, then don't create misery for him in any way. From the moment I die you will take my place for him."

And that day Pagal Baba died, and I had to call him Masto. I was not more than twelve years old, and Masto was at least thirty-five, or maybe more. It is difficult for a twelve-year-old boy to judge exactly, and thirty-five is a most deceptive age; the person could be thirty or forty, it all depends on his genetics.

Now, that is a complicated affair. I have seen men who still have all their hair, still black, even at the age of sixty. It is not something to brag about; every woman has it. Those men are really meant to be women, that's all. By mistake something went right. It is only a question of chemistry.

Women don't get white hair as early as men, they have a different chemistry – biochemistry to be exact. And women rarely go bald. It would be really beautiful to find a bald woman. I have come across only one woman in my whole life who could have been bald, and she was only on the way. Perhaps by now she is bald, because it is ten years since I have seen her.

Why are women bald? Nothing special – it is just because the body has to throw out dead cells in the form of hair. The woman cannot grow a beard or mustache; she has a limited area where hair can grow. Of course no man can grow hair as long as a woman because his capacity is divided. Moreover, a woman is by nature meant to live ten years longer than a man, on average.

One thing more: by the time a man is thirty-five years old, he has reached his sexual climax. In fact, I am just saying that not to hurt the feelings of poor men. In fact, he has reached his sexual climax by the age of eighteen; after that he starts declining. Thirty-five may be said to be the beginning of the end. It is then that a man realizes he is finished. That is the time a man becomes spiritual, between thirty-five and forty. At this age all kinds of nonsensical things impress him. The real reason is that he is losing his potency. Because he is losing potency, he becomes concerned about the omnipotency of God.

What a word they have found, omnipotence! It must have been the most impotent man in the world who first coined the word omnipotence. They start becoming members of the Theosophical Society, Witnesses of Jehovah, and whatnot. You can name anything and you will find a follower, but he will always be between the age of thirty-five and forty, because that is the time when he wants some support to stand by, to give him a sense that he still exists.

That is the time when people start doing all kinds of things like playing the guitar, sitar, flute, and if they are rich, golf. If they are not rich, just poor fellows, then they start drinking beer and playing cards. Thousands of people around the world are playing cards every moment.

What kind of a world are we living in? And they believe in their cards – the king, the queen, and the joker too. In fact, they are the only kings and queens in the world – except of course the queen of England, who is neither a real queen nor a real playing-card queen; she is worse.

What was I saying?

"You were talking about Masto...always calling him Masto."

Masto, good.

He was a king – not a playing-card king, not even a king of

England, but a real king. You could see. Nothing else was needed to prove it. It is strange that he was the first person to call me "the Blessed One," Bhagwan.

When he said it, I said to him, "Masto, have you also gone as mad as Pagal Baba, or even more?"

He said, "From this moment, remember, I will not call you other than what I have just called you. Please," he said, "let me be the first, because thousands will call you 'the Blessed One.' Poor Masto should at least be allowed to be the first. At least let me have that prestige."

We hugged each other, and cried together. That was our last meeting; just the day before I had had *the* experience. It was 22nd March, 1953, that we hugged each other without knowing that this was going to be our last meeting. Perhaps he knew, but I was not aware of it. He told me this with tears in his beautiful eyes.

The other day I asked Chetana, "Chetana, how is my face looking?"

She said, "What?"

I said, "I am asking because I have not eaten anything but fruit for months, except for a few days of Devaraj's concoction. I don't know what it consists of; all that I know is it needs immense will-power to eat it. You have to chew it for half an hour, but it is very good. By the time I am finished I am so tired, utterly tired, almost asleep. That's why I am asking."

She said, "Osho, you are asking me, can I tell you the truth?"

I said, "Only the truth."

She said, "When I look at you I can't see anything except your eyes, so please don't ask me. I don't know how you looked before, or how you look now. All I know is your eyes."

Alas, I cannot show you Masto. His whole body was beautiful. One could not believe that he had not come from the world of the gods. In India there are many beautiful stories. One of them from the *Rigveda,* is that of Pururva and Uruvashi.

Uruvashi is a goddess who becomes fed up with all the pleasures of paradise. I love the story because it is so true. If you have all the pleasures, how long can you endure them? One is bound to become bored. The story must have been written by someone who knew.

Uruvashi becomes bored with all the pleasures, and the gods and their love affairs. Finally, when she is in the hands of the head god, Indra, she uses the moment, as every woman uses such moments, to ask for a necklace or a watch or a diamond ring or anything you can imagine.

Ashu, what are you imagining? Do you know? Yes, you laugh because I know. Just tell me, otherwise I will tell it. Shall I tell it? No, it is not gentlemanly. And you are laughing so happily – I would not like to destroy it.

Uruvashi asks Indra, "Please, if you are so happy with me, will you grant me just a little gift? Not much, a very small gift."

Indra says, "Whatsoever it is, ask it, and it will be fulfilled."

She said, "I want to go to earth and to love an ordinary man."

Indra was completely drunk. You must realize that Indian gods are not like the Christian God – not even like Christian priests, what to say of the Christian God. Christianity is a dictatorial religion. The Hindu religion is more democratic, and more human too.

Indra is utterly drunk, and says, "Okay, but this will be the condition: the moment you tell a man you are a goddess, you will have to return to paradise immediately."

Uruvashi comes down to earth and falls in love with Pururva, who is an archer and also a poet, And she is so beautiful that naturally Pururva wants to marry her.

She said, "Please don't talk of marriage. Never mention it. Unless you promise me not to ever mention it again I will not be able to live with you."

And Pururva, as a poet, of course understands the beauty of a woman like Uruvashi. He has never known anything comparable to her, naturally; she is a goddess on earth. Under the influence of this intoxicating beauty, he promises. Then Uruvashi said, "One more thing. You must never ask me who I am; otherwise we should forget all about it right now. It is better not to even begin."

Pururva said, "I love you. I don't want to know who you are – I am not an investigator."

These two promises given, Uruvashi lies with Pururva. After a few days…. The Vedas in that way are really human; no other scripture is so human. All other scriptures are very bombastic. In other words, just bullshit. But the *Rigveda* is simply human, with all human limitations, frailties, weaknesses and imperfections. As every honeymoon comes to an end, perhaps a little quicker in the West than in India...so it took the lovers six months.

In America, a weekend is enough for the beginning and the end of the honeymoon – and when the honeymoon ends, then the marriage begins. Jesus! And you say that after death there is a hell for those who sin...it is after the honeymoon! In fact it is marriage! In India it takes six months – a bullock-cart way of ending things.

One night, Uruvashi was awakened by Pururva who was looking at her. This was not husbandly, looking at your own wife! What was he doing looking at her when she was asleep? If she had been someone else's wife, that would have been okay, but your own wife? But Uruvashi must have been, was bound to have been, a divine beauty, something from the beyond. Pururva could not contain himself.

He asked her, "Please tell me who you are."

Uruvashi said, "Pururva, you have broken your promise. I will tell you the truth, but now I will not be with you anymore." The moment she told him that she was a goddess, bored with paradise, who came to earth to have a little experience of real people because the gods were so phony – at that very moment she evaporated just like a beautiful dream. Pururva looked again and again at the empty bed; there was no one there.

It is one of the beautiful stories that I have always loved.

Masto must have been a god born in this world. That's the only way to say how beautiful he was. And it was not only the beauty of the body, which certainly was beautiful. I am not against the body, I am all for it. I loved his body. I used to touch his face, and he would say, "Why do you touch my face with closed eyes?"

I said, "You are so beautiful, and I don't want to see anything else that may perhaps disturb me, so I keep my eyes closed...so I can dream you as beautiful as you are."

Do you note my words? – "so I can dream you as beautiful as you are. I want you to be my dream." But it was not only his body which was beautiful, nor his hair – I have never seen such beautiful hair, particularly on a man's head. I used to touch and play with his hair, and he would laugh.

Once he said, "This is something. Baba was mad, and now he has given me a master who is even madder. He told me that you would take his place, so I cannot prevent you from doing anything. Even if you cut off my head, I will be ready and willing for it."

I said, "Don't be afraid, I will not cut even a hair. As far as your head is concerned, Baba has done the job already. Only the hair is left." Then we both laughed. This happened many times, in many ways.

But he was beautiful, bodily, and psychologically too. Whenever I was in need, without asking, so as not to offend me, he would leave money in my pockets during the night. You know that I don't have any pockets. Do you know the story of how I lost my pockets? It was Masto. He used to put money, gold, anything that he could manage, into my pockets. Finally I dropped the very idea of having pockets; it tempts people. Either they cut your pocket open and become pickpockets, or very rarely, with a man like me, they become a person like Masto.

He would wait until I went to sleep. Once in a while I would pretend, as if I was asleep. I would even have to snore to convince him – then I would catch him red-handed, his hand in my pocket. I said, "Masto! Is this the way of a sage?" And we both laughed.

Finally I dropped the idea of having pockets. I am the only person in the world who needs no pockets at all. In a way it is good, because nobody can cut open my pockets. It is also good that I don't have to carry any weight. Somebody else can always do it. I don't need to. I have not needed pockets for years; somebody has always managed for me.

Just this morning Gudia was giving me tea and I allowed the saucer to slip out of my hand. I cannot say I dropped it; that would be too much, because the saucer was really costly. It was inlaid with gold. And she would not forgive me if I said that I had dropped it, that I allowed it to slip out of my hand. So naturally it fell. It was not possible for it to fly; it had to fall.

In that moment I understood many things that I had always understood, but at that moment they all culminated in me. The fall...man could not fly – neither Adam nor Eve...naturally they had to fall. It was not the serpent's politics; it was just natural for man to fall. It was natural, very natural for Adam and Eve to fall, because there was no way for them to fly – no Lufthansa, no Pan Am, not even Air India. And poor Adam was really poor. But in a way it was good that he fell; otherwise he would be in the same situation as Uruvashi.

He would have enjoyed all the fruits of paradise, without any joy of course. He would have lived with Eve without love. In paradise nobody loves that much. I can say it without any fear of being expelled because I don't want to enter paradise, so who cares! Paradise is the last place I would like to enter; even hell is preferable. Why? Just because of good company. Paradise is just horrible. The company of the saints...my God! These gods must be imbeciles, or perhaps without minds at all, just robots; otherwise how do they continuously keep going on the merry-go-round? I don't want to be part of it.

But Masto looked like a god who had come to earth. I loved him – without any reason of course, because love cannot have any reason. I still love him. I don't know whether he is alive or not, because on 22nd March, 1953 he disappeared. He just told me he was going to the Himalayas.

He said, "My responsibility is fulfilled as far as I had promised Pagal Baba. Now you are what you potentially were. Now I am no longer needed."

I said, "No, Masto, I will need you still, for other reasons."

He said, "No. You will find ways for everything that you require. But I cannot wait."

Since then, once in a while I used to hear – perhaps from someone coming from the Himalayas, a sannyasin, a bhikkhu – that Masto was in Kalimpong, or that he was in Nainital, or here or there, but he never came back from the Himalayas. I asked everybody who was going to the Himalayas, "If you come across this man...." But it was difficult, because he was very reluctant to be photographed.

Once I had convinced him to be photographed, but the photographer in my village was a genius! His name was Munnu Mian, a poor man, but he had a camera. It must have been the oldest model in the world. His camera should have been preserved; it would be worth millions of dollars now. Out of the whole film, perhaps one photograph would turn out. That too was not certain. And when you looked at the photo you could not believe how he had managed it because it did not look like you. He was avant-garde! Really avant-garde. He did with photography what only Picasso would have liked...or I don't know, even he may not have liked it if Munnu Mian had done it of Picasso himself.

Somehow I convinced Masto to go to Munnu Mian. Munnu Mian was very happy. Masto reluctantly sat there in the villager's studio. I cannot really call it a studio; it was only a rusted chair without arms. People rarely came to be photographed, so there was no studio really.

You cannot know how it was done in Indian villages. You cannot even imagine it. It is still the same. As a background, there was a painting, a large curtain painted with a street scene of Bombay – huge buildings, motors, buses. And of course it was thought that the picture had been taken in Bombay. What more can you expect for one rupee for three pictures? But Masto managed...or, to be more correct, the idiocy of Munnu Mian undid everything that I had arranged. He forgot to put the plate in the camera!

I can still see the whole scene. I had prepared Munnu Mian by saying, "Be very exact, correct. It is with great difficulty that I managed to bring this man, and if you have his picture it will be great publicity for your studio."

He was convinced and said, "I will try. Just teach me two words in English. I have heard that in the bigger cities, before they click the shutter, they say, 'Please be ready.'" Of course he said it to me in Hindi, but he wanted to say it in English to impress this very respected man.

Then he wanted to know how to say "Thank you," for when it was finished. So he arranged everything, then he said, "Please be ready" – of course in English. Even Masto could not believe that Munnu Mian knew any English. Then he clicked his camera – a loud click of course. I can still see his camera. I can certainly say it would get a million dollars at least just because of its antiquity. It was huge.

He then said, "Thank you, sir." And we departed.

He came running behind us and said with tears in his eyes, "Forgive me, please come back. I forgot to put the plate in the camera!"

That was too much. Masto said, "You idiot! Just run away from here; otherwise I will lose my temper – and I am very temperamental!"

I knew that he was not at all temperamental, and I said to Munnu Mian, "Don't be worried. I will arrange it again." But he escaped, actually ran. I said, "Listen, don't run away..." but he would not listen.

I persuaded Masto to return, but when we reached the studio it was locked. Munnu Mian was so afraid that on seeing us coming he locked the studio and ran away.

So we don't have any picture of Masto. There are just three pictures I always wanted to have, just to show you. One was of Masto, a rare beauty. Another was a man I will talk about later on, and a woman who I will also talk about later on. But I don't have a picture of any of these people.

It's a strange thing: they were all reluctant to have their picture taken, utterly reluctant – perhaps because a picture invariably distorts the beauty, because beauty is a living phenomenon and a picture is static. When we take a picture of a flower, do you think it is the same flower that is still there? No, meanwhile it has grown. It is no longer the same, yet the picture will always remain the same. The picture never grows. It is dead from the very beginning. What do you call it? – stillborn? Is that right?

"Yes, Osho."

Okay, a picture is stillborn, dead, already dead before it has taken its first breath; it breathes not.

The only person whom I loved and knew as one of the most beautiful people, and who allowed me to take pictures, was my Nani. She allowed me, but with the condition that the album would be in her custody.

I said, "There is no problem in that – but why? Can't you trust me?"

She said, "I can trust you, but I can't trust these photographs. It is not that you can do any harm to me, but I want the photographs to be in my care. When I am dead they will be yours."

She allowed me to take as many photographs of her as I liked. But after she had died, when I opened her closet where she used to keep all those photographs, there was an empty album. She could not write, so she had told my father to write on it, "Please excuse me." She had signed it with her right thumb print.

The people I wanted you to be acquainted with, at least in their form, never allowed me to take their photographs. Only one allowed me to, but it seems my Nani only allowed me in order not to hurt me…and she always destroyed the pictures.

The album was empty. I looked minutely, and it had never been used. I searched the whole house. There was not a single picture to be found. I would have loved to show you her eyes, just her eyes. Her whole body was beautiful, but her eyes…it needs a poet to say something about them, or a painter – and I am neither. I can only say that they reflected something of the beyond.

Session 33 ...

OKAY. THE OTHER DAY I told you about Masto's disappearance. I think he is still alive. In fact I know he is. In the East, this has been one of the most ancient ways – to disappear in the Himalayas before you die. To die in that beautiful part is richer than to live anywhere else; even dying there has something of the eternal. Perhaps it is the vibe of the saints chanting for thousands of years. The Vedas were composed there, the Gita was written there, Buddha was born and died there, Lao Tzu in his last days disappeared in the Himalayas. And Masto did almost the same.

No one knows yet whether Lao Tzu died or not. How can one be decisive? Hence the legend that he is immortal. Nobody is. One who is born is bound to die. Lao Tzu must have died, but people never came to know of it. At least one should be able to have a completely private death if one wants it.

Masto took care of me more efficiently than Pagal Baba could ever have done. First, Baba was really the madman. Secondly, he would come only once in a while like a whirlwind to visit me, then disappear. This is not the way to take care. Once I even told him, saying, "Baba, you talk so much about how you are taking care of this child, but before you say it again, I must be heard."

He laughed and said, "I understand, you need not say it, but I will pass you on to the right hands. I am not really capable of taking care of you. Can you understand that I am ninety years old? It is time for me to leave the body. I am hanging around just to find the right person for you. Once I have found him I can relax into death."

I never knew then that he was really serious, but that's what he did. He handed over his charge to Masto, and died laughing. That was the last thing he did.

Zarathustra may have laughed when he was born...nobody is a witness, but he must have laughed; his whole life indicated towards it. It was that laughter which caught the attention of one of the most intelligent men in the West, Friedrich Nietzsche. But Pagal Baba really laughed as he died, before we could ask why. We could not have asked the question anyway. He was not a philosopher, and he would not have answered even if he had lived. But what a way to die! And remember, it was not just a smile. I really mean a laughter.

Everybody there looked at each other thinking, "What's the matter?" – until he laughed so loudly that everybody thought that up till then he had been only mildly mad, but now he had gone to the extreme. They all left. Naturally, nobody laughs when one is born, just as part of etiquette; and nobody laughs at death, again just nothing but a mannerism. Both are British.

Baba was always against manners and the people who believe in manners. That's why he loved me, that's why he loved Masto. And when he was looking for a man who could take care of me, naturally, he could not have found a better man than Masto.

Masto proved himself more than Baba could ever have thought. He did so much for me that even to say it hurts. It is something so private that it should not be said, so private that one should not even say it while one is alone.

I was just saying to Gudia, "Tell Devageet never to leave his notebooks in this Noah's Ark" – because last night the devil was typing from his notebooks. You will not believe it. In fact, I could not believe it when I first heard the story. Gudia said there was no light from the window. I wondered and said to myself, "Have they gone mad or what? Typing without a light?"

Gudia looked in the room and said, "This is really something! The machine is making a noise exactly like a typewriter."

Not only that: every once in a while it stopped, as if the typist was looking at the notebook, then again typing. Gudia asked Asheesh, "What could be the matter?"

He told her, "Nothing much, just the filter on the air conditioner has gathered too much dust and that makes such a noise."

But exactly like a typewriter...? I loved the story anyway, and I tell you to keep your notebooks away from the devil. He can even type without a typewriter, without a light.

The devil is always a perfectionist. He cannot be otherwise; it is part of his very function. Typing without a typewriter – in the dark? And I know Devageet would not leave his notebooks anywhere. But the devil can even type without notebooks too. He can read your minds. So don't bring your minds in, at least when you are working on my words. Don't bring your minds in, otherwise you open the door to the devil.

Masto was the best choice that Baba could have made. I cannot in any way conceive of a better man. Not only was he a meditator... of course he was; otherwise there would have been no communion possible between him and me. And meditation simply means not being a mind, at least for the time you are meditating.

But that was not all; he was many more things. He was a beautiful singer, but he never sang for the public. We both used to laugh at the phrase, "the public." It consists of only the most retarded children. It is a wonder how they manage to gather at a place at a certain appointed time. I cannot explain it. Masto said he could not explain it either. It just cannot be explained.

He never sang for the public, but only for a very few people who loved him, and they had to promise never to talk about it. His voice was really "his master's voice." Perhaps he was not singing, but only allowing the existence – that's the only proper word that I can use – he was allowing existence to flow through him. He was not preventing; that was his merit.

He was also a talented sitar player, but again, I have never seen him playing before a crowd. Often I was the only one present when he played, and he would tell me to lock the door, saying, "Please lock the door, and whatsoever happens, don't open it until I am dead." And he knew that if I wanted to open the door I would have to kill him first, and then open it. I would keep my promise. But his music was such.... He was not known to the world: the world missed.

He said, "These things are so intimate that it is prostitution to play before a crowd." That was his exact word, 'prostitution'. He was really a philosopher, a thinker, and very logical, not like me.

With Pagal Baba I had only one thing in common: that was the madness. Masto had many things in common with him. Pagal Baba was interested in many things. I certainly could not be a representative of Pagal Baba, but Masto was. I cannot be anybody's representative whosoever.

Masto did so much for me in every way that I could not believe how Baba had known that he would be the right person. And I was a child and needed much direction – and not an easy child either. Unless I was convinced I would not move an inch. In fact I would move back a little just to be safe.

I am reminded of a small anecdote. I used to use this anecdote as a joke. Many of my jokes are perhaps painted a little here and there to make them look like jokes, but many of them come from real life. And real life is far more of a joke book than any joke book could ever be. How do I know this joke comes from real life? Because it cannot be otherwise, there is no other way. I remember I used to tell this joke and this is the way I remember it.

A child comes to school late, very late. It is raining. The teacher looks with those stony eyes that are given specially only to teachers – and to wives. And if you marry a woman who is both, then God help you! We can only pray for you. Then that woman will have four stony eyes which look in all directions. Beware of schoolteachers! Never, never marry a schoolteacher. Whatsoever happens, escape before you stumble and fall. Fall anywhere, but not into a schoolteacher; otherwise you will have a real hell of a life. And if she is English then things are tripled!

The small boy, already very afraid, completely drenched with water, somehow had still reached the school. But a schoolteacher is a schoolteacher. She asked, "Why are you late?"

He had thought it was enough proof. It was raining so hard... cats and dogs were raining, and he was completely wet, dripping. And yet she was still asking, "Why are you late?"

He invented, just like any child would, saying, "Miss, it is so slippery that as I took one step forward, I slipped two steps back."

The woman looked even more stern and said, "How can that be? If you take one step forwards and then slip back two steps – you cheat – then you could never have got to school."

The small boy said, "Miss, please understand: I turned towards my house and started running away from school, that's how I got here."

I say it is not a joke. That schoolteacher is real, the boy is real, the rain is real. The schoolteacher's conclusion is real, and the small boy's conclusion could not be more real. I have told thousands of jokes and many of them came from real life. Those which don't come from real life also come from real life, but from the underground life, which is also real but never on the surface – it is not allowed.

Masto had real talent in many dimensions. He was a musician, a dancer, a singer, and whatnot, but always very shy of "those eyes." He used to call the people, "those ugly eyes." He would say, "People cannot see, but only believe that they see. I am not for them." Again and again he would remind me that I should not invite a single friend – although I had none – I mean a single acquaintance.

But once when I asked him, "Can I ever be allowed to bring someone?" he replied, "If you just want the joy of inviting somebody intimate, then your Nani is allowed. For her, you need not even ask. Of course if she does not want to come, then I cannot do anything about it." And that is what happened.

When I told my Nani, she said, "Tell Masto to come to my house and play his sitar here." And he was such a humble man he came to play his sitar for the old woman, and he was so happy playing for her, and I was so happy that he had come and did not refuse. I had been worried that he might.

And my grandmother, my Nani, the old woman, suddenly became as if she were young again. I saw what can only be called a transfiguration! As she became more and more attuned to the sitar, she became younger and younger. I saw a miracle happen. By the time Masto had finished playing his sitar, she was suddenly the old woman again.

I said, "This is not right, Nani. At least let poor Masto have one glimpse of what his music can do for a person like you."

She said, "It is not in my hands. If it happens it happens. If it does not happen, nothing can be done about it. I know that Masto will understand."

Masto said, "I do understand."

But what I saw was just unbelievable. I blinked my eyes again and again just to see whether it was only a dream, or I was really seeing her youth come back. Even today I cannot believe that it was just my imagination. Perhaps on that day...but today I don't have any imagination at all. I see things as they really are.

Masto remained unknown to the world at large for the simple reason that he never wanted to be among the crowd. And the moment his duty towards me, his promise to Pagal Baba, was finished, he disappeared in the Himalayas.

The Himalayas...the very word simply means "the home of ice." Scientists say that if all the ice in the Himalayas melts someday, then the world would really have a flood. The whole world – it would not be limited to any one part – every ocean would rise by forty feet. They have given it the right name, Himalaya. *Him* means "ice"; *alaya* means "the home."

There are hundreds of peaks with eternal ice which has never melted...and the silence that surrounds them, the undisturbed atmosphere.... It is not just old; it has a strange warmth, because thousands of people of immense depth have moved into those parts with a tremendous meditativeness, with immense love, prayer and chanting.

The Himalayas are still rare in the whole world. The Alps are just children compared to the Himalayas. Switzerland is beautiful, and more so because of all the conveniences available there. But I cannot forget the silent nights in the Himalayas: stars above and no one around.

I want to disappear there, just as Masto had. I can understand him, and it will not be a surprise if suddenly one day I disappear. The Himalayas are far bigger than India. Only part of the Himalayas belongs to India; another part belongs to Nepal, another to Burma, another to Pakistan – thousands of miles of purity, just purity. On the other side there is Russia, Tibet, Mongolia, China; they all have a part of the Himalayas.

It won't be a surprise if someday I disappear just to lie down by the side of a beautiful rock and be no longer in the body. One cannot find a better place to leave the body – but I may not do it, you know me. I will remain unpredictable as ever, even in my death.

Perhaps Masto wanted to go sooner, and was just fulfilling the last task given by his guru, Pagal Baba. He did so much for me, it is difficult to even list it. He introduced me to people so that whenever I might need money I just had to tell them and the money would arrive. I asked Masto, "Won't they ask why?"

He said, "Don't you be worried about it. I have answered all their questions already. But they are cowardly people; they can give you their money, but they cannot give you their hearts, so don't ask that."

I said, "I never ask anybody for his or her heart; it cannot be asked. Either you simply find that it is gone, or not. So I will not ask these people for anything except money, and that too only if it is needed."

And he certainly introduced me to many people who have always remained anonymous; but whenever I needed money, the money arrived. When I was at Jabalpur, where I was at the university and stayed more than nine years, the money was continuously coming. People wondered, because my salary was not very much. They could not believe how I could use such a beautiful car, a beautiful bungalow, a vast garden, acres of green. And the day somebody asked how such a beautiful car...that day, two more arrived. There were three cars then and nowhere to keep them.

The money was always coming. Masto had made every arrangement. Although I don't have anything, no money at all, but somehow it manages itself.

Masto...it is difficult to say goodbye to you, for the simple reason that I don't believe you are no more. You still exist. I may not be able to see you again; that is not very important. I have seen you so much, your very fragrance has become a part of me. But somewhere in this story I have to put a full stop as far as you are concerned. It is hard, and it hurts...forgive me for that.

Session 34

THIS MORNING I SAID A very abrupt goodbye to Masto, and I felt it the whole day. It simply cannot be done, at least in his case. It reminds me of when I was going to college and leaving my Nani after being so long together.

Since my grandfather died and left her, there had been no one in her life except me. It was not easy for her. It was not easy for me either. Except for her there was nothing to keep me in that village. I can see that day: the early morning – it was a beautiful winter's morning and people from the village had gathered.

Even today, in those parts of central India, things are not contemporary; they are at least two thousand years behind. Nobody has much to do. Everybody seems to have enough time to loaf around. I really mean that everybody is a loafer. I simply mean the literal meaning, not any association that has arisen about the word. So, all the "loafers" were there. Please write the word in inverted commas so nobody misunderstands.

My whole family was there, which was a big crowd. They had come because they had to come; otherwise I could see no point in seeing their faces, which were then, and are now, faceless, just names. But my poor father was there, my mother was there, my younger brothers and sisters were there, and they were all really weeping.

Even my father was weeping. I had never seen him tearful, never before and never afterwards. And I was not dying, just going a hundred miles away. But it was the very idea of going away for four years at least, to get a bachelor's degree. Then what if I decide – and nobody knows – to stay two more years for a master's degree? Then a minimum of two more years for a Ph.D.?

It was a long separation. Perhaps by that time, who knows, many of them would not be in the world. But I was only concerned about my Nani, because my mother and my father had lived so long without me when I was so small. Now I could live on my own, I could help myself; I needed no other help.

But for my Nani.... I can still see the early morning sun, the warm sun, the crowd, my father, my mother. I touched the feet of my Nani, and said to her, "Don't be worried. Whenever you call I will immediately rush. And don't think that I am going far away: it is only a hundred miles, just three hours by train."

In those days the fastest train did not stop at that poor village; otherwise the journey was only two hours. Now it stops there – but now it does not matter whether it stops or not.

I told her, "I will come running. Eighty or a hundred miles is nothing."

She said, "I know and I am not worried."

She tried to keep herself as collected as she could, but I could see the gathering of tears in her eyes. That was the moment when I turned away and left for the station. I didn't look back when I turned the corner of the street. I knew that if I looked back, either she would burst out crying, and then I would never go to college; or if she did not burst out crying she may even die, just stop breathing. I was so much to her. Her only existence was around me: my clothes, my toys, my room, my bed, my bed sheets, the whole day....

I used to say to her, "Nani, you are mad. Twenty-four hours a day you are engaged doing things just for me, who is never going to do anything for you in his life."

She said, "You have already done it."

I don't know what to make of it, and now there is no way to ask her. But the way she said, "You have already done it," was so powerful, with so much energy, that whether you understood it or not, you were overwhelmed. Even today remembering it I am overwhelmed.

Later on I came to know that when I turned the corner of the street, the whole neighborhood wondered, "What kind of boy is this? He didn't even look...."

And my Nani was very proud; she said to them, "Yes, he is my boy. I knew he would not look back, and not only on this street corner, he will never look back in his life. And I am also proud that he understood his poor Nani, knowing that if he had looked back I would have burst into tears, and he never wanted that. He knew perfectly well, better than I knew, that if I had burst into tears he would not have been able to go. Not because of me, but because of his love for me. He would have stayed his whole life just so that I would not have to weep and cry."

Saying an abrupt goodbye to Masto is just like that. No, I cannot do it. I will have to come to a natural end with no full stop just arbitrarily chosen, because my life is such that if I go on talking about it, there will be neither beginning nor end. In my life there will be neither beginning nor end.

The Bible at least says, "In the beginning...." You will have to publish this without a beginning or an end. It will be very difficult to publish that way. But Devageet can understand, he is a Jew. A Jewish scroll can be almost without beginning and end. Of course there seems to be a beginning, but it is only seemingly so. That's why all the ancient stories begin, "Once upon a time" – and then you can start anything. And once upon a time everything stops, without even saying, "The End." My life cannot be an ordinary autobiography.

Vasant Joshi is writing a biography of me. The biography is bound to be very superficial, so superficial that it is not worth reading at all. No biography can penetrate to the depths, particularly the psychological layers of a man – especially if the man has come to the point where the mind is no longer relevant to the nothingness hidden in the center of an onion. You can peel it layer by layer, of course with tears in your eyes, but finally nothing is left, and that is the center of the onion; that is from where it had come in the first place. No biography can penetrate to the depths, particularly of a man who has known the no-mind also. I say "also" consideredly, because unless you know the mind, you cannot know the no-mind. This is going to be my small contribution to the world.

The West has gone deep in search of the mind, and has discovered layers upon layers – the conscious, the unconscious, the subconscious, and so on and so forth. The East has simply put the whole thing aside and jumped into the pond...and the soundless sound, the no-mind. Hence East and West stand opposed.

In a way the opposition is understandable, and Rudyard Kipling was right in saying, "West is West, and East is East, and never the twain shall meet." He is right to a point. He really emphasizes a certain point that I am making.

The West has only looked into the mind, without looking into who is looking into the mind. It is very strange. The so-called great scientists are all trying to look into the mind, and nobody is bothered about who is looking into the mind.

H.G. Wells was not a bad man – a good man, just a goody-goody. In fact he is too sweet for my taste, a little too much white sugar. But still I should not consider my taste; you have your own tastes, and not everybody is a diabetic. I am not only a diabetic, I am also against white sugar. Even before I came to know about diabetes, I was against white sugar; I call it "the white poison." So perhaps I am a little prejudiced against white sugar.

But H.G. Wells, although very full of white sugar, is not just that. Once in a while he came up with an insight which was rare. For example, his idea of a time machine. He had the idea that one day a machine is discovered that goes back into time. Do you understand the meaning of it? It means you can go back into your childhood, into your mother's womb, or perhaps, if you are a Hindu, into your past lives – perhaps as an elephant, an ant, or whatnot. One could just go back, and one could go forward.

The idea itself is a great insight. I don't know whether there will ever be machines like that or not, but there have been people who could move back in time just as easily as you move. Do you have any difficulty in moving back to your yesterday? In the same way, the daring ones have moved into their yesterlives.

Perhaps that word may not be allowed, but I don't care. To me 'yesterlife' looks perfectly right. When anything looks right to a wrong man like me, then you can be certain it must be right. It has to be right.

I suddenly said full stop to Masto, but the whole day it tortured me in a way. You know I cannot be tortured, you know I cannot be unhappy either, but the idea that I had finished so abruptly again reminds me of one incident which is directly concerned with Masto.

He had come to take me to the station at Allahabad. Deep down we wanted never to separate, particularly on that day. The reason only became clear later on, but that had nothing to do with it. I will just mention it and give you the details later on. He had come to give me a send-off, because he said that perhaps for two or three months he may not be able to see me, so as long as he could be with me, he would like to be.

Masto said, "Let us hope the train is late."

I said, "What nonsense are you talking, Masto? Have you really gone mad? Indian trains and you have to *hope* for them to be late?"

The train came, of course six hours late, which is not much for an Indian passenger train – just usual. But we could not separate. We talked and talked, and got so involved in talking that the train was missed. We both laughed. We were happy that at least we could be together for a few hours more before another train came.

Listening to our talk and our laughter, and the reason for the laughter, the stationmaster said, "Why are you wasting your time on this platform? You can go to the other platform opposite."

I asked him, "Why?"

He said, "Only goods trains stop there, so you can talk, hug each other and enjoy yourselves, and there will be no need to worry that you may catch the train. You cannot catch it on that platform."

I told Masto that the idea sounded very spiritual. The station-master was thinking that we might hit him over the head, but when we both thanked him and went over to the other platform, he came running behind us saying, "Please don't take the idea seriously. I was just joking. Believe me, only goods trains stop here. You will never catch any train on this platform."

I said to him, "I don't want to catch any train. Nor does Masto want me to catch any train – but what to do?" The host where we were staying was very insistent that it was time for me to go back to the university hostel, saying that my time should not be wasted.

And Masto too wanted me to at least get a master's degree, according to the wishes of my dead friend Pagal Baba. So I had to go. You will not believe me, but I only remained at university because I had promised Pagal Baba to get a master's degree. The university gave me a scholarship for further studies, but I said no, because I had promised only up to this point.

They said, "Are you mad? Even if you go directly into service you cannot get more money than you will get with this scholarship. And the scholarship can extend from two to as many years as your professors recommend. Don't waste the opportunity."

I said, "Baba should have asked me to get a Ph.D. What can I do? He never asked me, and he died without knowing about it."

My professor tried hard to persuade me, but I said to him, "Simply forget it, because I only came here to fulfill a promise given to a madman."

Perhaps if Pagal Baba had known about the Ph.D. or D.Litt. then I would have been in a trap. But thank God he only knew about the master's degree. He thought that was the last word. I don't know whether he really wanted me to go for more scholarship. Now there is no way. One thing is certain: that if he had wanted it, I would have gone and wasted as many years as necessary. But it was not a fulfillment of my own being, nor was the master's degree. Somehow Pagal Baba got the idea that unless you had a master's degree, a post-graduate degree, you would not be able to get a good job.

I said, "Baba, do you think I will ever desire a job?"

He laughed and said, "I know you will not desire it, but just in case. I am just an old man, and I think of all the worst things possible." You have heard the proverb, "Hope for the best, but expect the worst." He added something more to it. Baba said, "Prepare for the worst too. It should not be met unprepared; otherwise, how are you going to face it?"

Masto cannot be given a farewell so easily, so I will drop the very idea. Wherever he pops up, it's okay. This is not going to be an orthodox, conventional autobiography. It is not an autobiography at all, just fragments of a life reflected in thousands of mirrors.

I was once a guest at a place called the Mirror Palace. It was made only of mirrors. It was horrible – to live in it was so difficult – but perhaps I was the only man who enjoyed it. The raja who owned the palace was puzzled. He said to me, "Whenever I put a guest there, after just a few hours they say to me, 'Please put me somewhere else, it is too much.' To see so many people just like yourself all around…and whatever you do, they all do. If you laugh, they all laugh; if you cry, they all cry; if you hug your girl, they all hug…. It is so horrible. You feel that you are just a mirror and nothing else, and all the mirrors seem to be doing even better than you are!"

I said to the raja, "I don't want to change anything. In fact, if you want to sell this palace I am ready to purchase it and make it a meditation center. It will be hilarious. People just sitting there looking at themselves from all directions – everywhere thousands of miniatures of themselves.

"They may go mad – which is not a calamity anyway. They will go mad sooner or later in some other life; it will just take a little longer. I will do it quickly. I believe in instant-coffee methods. But if they can relax with the whole crowd surrounding them and not be worried; if they can accept that and say, 'It is okay, thank you for surrounding me for so long,' and still remain centered, they will become enlightened. Either way they will be benefited."

Madness is falling below the mind. There is a madness that is falling above the mind; that madness is enlightenment. It is abnormal; hence it is not wrong that poor psychologists think that people like Jesus or Buddha are abnormal. But they should be a little sensitive about their words.

If they use the same word, 'abnormal', for the inmates of a madhouse, with what face can they use the same word for the buddha? They should say "supranormal." Buddhas and madmen are certainly not normal; about that we agree. One is below normal, one is above normal. Both are abnormal, we agree, but they need different classifications. And psychology has no place for what I call "the psychology of the buddhas."

Masto was certainly a buddha. I cannot just say, "Thank you, see you again," for the reason that he has done so much for me. "Thank you" is very small, and too inappropriate. Nobody does so much for anybody.

That's why there is no word for it – nobody needs it. And I cannot say, "See you again," because neither he is going to again be in this world, nor am I going to again be in this world. The meeting is, in the very nature of things, impossible. So the only way is to let him come whenever it happens. And in this way these memoirs will have their own flavor. Sudden abrupt arrivals and departures.

So I bring Masto in again. He was not the same type of man as

Pagal Baba. Pagal Baba was simply a mystic; Masto was a philosopher too. At night we would lie for hours by the banks of the Ganges discussing so many things. We enjoyed just being together, either discussing or being silent. That same Ganges, where the Upanishads were first sung, where Buddha delivered his first sermon, where Mahavira moved and preached.... One cannot think of Eastern mysticism without the Himalayas and the Ganges. In fact, both have contributed infinitely.

I remember the beauty of that silence.... We sat there for hours. Once in a while we even slept there, on the sand, because Masto had said, "It is so beautiful tonight that it would be insulting to go to bed. The stars are so close." That's his word, 'insulting'. I am simply quoting.

I said, "Masto, you know that I love the stars, and particularly when they are reflected in the river. Stars are beautiful, but their reflection is a miracle. What water does so simply is only possible to compare with dreams. I love the stars, the river, the reflection of the stars, and I love your company and your warmth. So there is no question about staying. Never consider me even for a single moment when you want to do something, because even that consideration will hurt me. It will show that I am being a burden to you."

He said, "What! I have not said anything about you being a burden to me."

I said, "You have not said it, nobody has. I was just saying it for the future. Remember, if you consider me for any reason, then tell me about it, because I feel very offended by any consideration."

I told him that day, and today I will tell you too, that Gurdjieff had a very strange idea. I don't think any master had ever entertained it. It is not that it could not have knocked on their doors, but I think nobody was the type to receive it and respond to it.

Gurdjieff used to say, "Please, never, never consider others. It is an insult." He had these words written over his door. It is a tremendously significant statement.

People force one another to consider each other. They say, "Please consider me." What could be more humiliating than to say to somebody, "Please consider me"? In my life I have never said that to anybody, not a single person.

I remember many situations where just those words would have helped me immensely – but they are so humiliating. It is not ego, remember. The egoist is always asking for consideration; in fact more so, because he is no ordinary person, he has to be considered first. A really humble person cannot ask for consideration – in fact, he will reject any consideration even if it is given to him.

I was at university, a poor student. I reached university somehow by working at different kinds of jobs. Again, just by coincidence, I participated in a national inter-university debate. One of the judges, who is now the head of the department of philosophy at Allahabad University, S.S. Roy, just fell in love with me. And the same was true from my side too.

He gave me ninety-nine marks out of a hundred – he was one of the judges in the debate. Naturally I won. It was a very important debate because the winner was going on a three months' tour of the Middle East as a government guest. He was to be treated almost as an ambassador. It was a great opportunity.

S.S. Roy gave me ninety-nine out of a hundred, and to everybody else he gave just zero – just to be sure that I would win. I asked him later, "Why were you so partial to me?"

He said, "The moment I looked into your eyes I became hypnotized. My wife also says that I am hypnotized by you; otherwise how could I do such a thing? If anybody sees your sheet the partiality will be apparent: ninety-nine out of a hundred and simply zero for all the other dozen participants!"

I said, "No, I have not asked why you have given me ninety-nine percent; that is your wife's question. Perhaps others may ask it too. I have come to ask why you didn't give me one hundred percent."

For a moment he looked at me astounded. Then he started laughing and said, "I was one of Masta Baba's devotees. He was right when he said to me, 'Once you see this man you will not need me.' And Masta Baba told me this almost two or three years before he disappeared. Now I can truthfully say to you I was not hypnotized: it was just that your eyes reminded me of his eyes. I have also seen Pagal Baba, and it is strange how your eyes are almost the same. How it happens I don't know."

I said, "It is not the eyes, it is the transparency which makes them appear to be the same. I am happy that you are reminded of Pagal Baba and Masta Baba for a reason which to me is the greatest reward in the world – that in my eyes you saw something of the same. Now I have nothing to ask you except: Why not one hundred percent?"

He said, "I am a poor professor. If I gave you one hundred percent and gave zero to all the remaining eleven participants, it would appear that I was not being fair. I am fair, but who would understand? Where would I find Masta Baba or Pagal Baba to understand it? I gave you ninety-nine percent just because of my cowardice."

I loved this man because he could say so simply that he was a coward, although he had really done an uncowardly act already, almost, so what difference would one percent have made? Ninety-nine percent for one person, and zero percent for the others? – it is the same. He could have given me one hundred percent, or even more.

But that debate, and his remembrance of Pagal Baba and Masta Baba, was the reason I stayed at the university of Sagar. He was there at that time. I said, "If I have to be a postgraduate then let it be under you."

It was Pagal Baba's desire, and also Masta Baba's, that I should be prepared in case I was ever in need. I have never needed anything. Not only have I never needed anything ever, but I have been showered constantly by things from all sides. That's why I told you something went right for me from the very beginning.

S.S. Roy was one of my most loved teachers, for the simple reason that he was capable of asking me to stand up in class and explain something to him that he could not understand. And I had to do it. Once I said to him, "Roy Sahib" – that's what I used to call him – "it does not look good that you ask me, your student."

He said, "If Pagal Baba could touch your feet, and if Masta Baba could not only touch your feet but had to fulfill every rational and irrational demand made by you" – and I have been irrational from the very beginning, just irrational – "then why could I not ask? I am just a small man."

I have known hundreds of professors as teachers, as colleagues and acquaintances, but S.S. Roy stands apart. He was so authentic that you could not find more authenticity in any teacher. And he

PROFESSOR S.S. ROY, 1990

was so much in love with what I used to say to him that he used to quote me in his lectures – and not just use it, but he referred to it as my statement. Of course the other students were jealous. Even the other professors in the philosophy department were jealous. You will be surprised to know that even his wife was jealous.

I came to know just by chance. One day I went to his house and she said to me, "What! You have even started coming here? He is mad about you. Since you have been in his department our love life is shattered. It's on the rocks."

I said, "I will never come to this house again, but remember, that will not put it right. One day you will have to come to me." And I never went to his house again.

After a year or so his wife had to come to me, and she said, "Forgive me. Please come; only you can reconcile us."

I said, "My work of separating or reconciling couples has not begun yet. You will have to wait."

She cried and so I had to go. I didn't say anything to S. S. Roy. I just sat by his side holding his hand, and after an hour left, without saying a single word. And that did it; the alchemy worked. There is magic in silence.

How much time is left?

"Three minutes, Osho."

Good, because maximus – the maximum – is my principle. The whole trinity is available...we can do miracles.

Is the time over? Then it is over.

Session 35

KAY. I HAVE HEARD RAVI SHANKAR play on the sitar. He has everything one can imagine: the personality of a singer, the mastery of his instrument, and the gift of innovation, which is rare in classical musicians. He is immensely interested in the new. He has played with Yehudi Menuhin; no other Indian sitar player would be ready to do it, because no such thing has ever happened before. Sitar with a violin? Are you mad? But innovators are a little mad; that's why they are capable of innovation.

The so-called sane people live orthodox lives from breakfast till bed. Between bed and breakfast, nothing should be said – not that I am afraid of saying it. I am talking about "them." They live according to the rules; they follow lines.

But innovators have to go outside the rules. Sometimes one should insist on not following the lines, just for not following's sake – and it pays, believe me. It pays because it always brings you to a new territory, perhaps of your own being. The medium may be different but the person inside you, playing the sitar or the violin or the flute, is the same: different routes leading to the same point, different lines from the circle leading to the same center. Innovators are bound to be a little crazy, unconventional...and Ravi Shankar has been unconventional.

First: he is a pandit, a brahmin, and he married a Mohammedan girl. In India one cannot even dream of it – a brahmin marrying a Mohammedan girl! Ravi Shankar did it. But it was not just any Mohammedan girl, it was the daughter of his master. That was even more unconventional. That means for years he had been hiding it from his master. Of course the master immediately allowed the marriage, the moment he came to know. He not only allowed, he arranged the marriage.

He too was a revolutionary, and of a far greater range than Ravi Shankar. Allauddin Khan was his name. I had gone to see him with Masto. Masto used to take me to rare people. Allauddin Khan was certainly one of the most unique people I have seen. He was very old; he died only after completing the century.

When I met him he was looking towards the ground. Masto didn't say anything either. I was a little puzzled. I pinched Masto, but he remained as if I had not pinched him. I pinched him harder, but still he remained as if nothing had happened. Then I really pinched him, and he said, "Ouch!"

Then I saw those eyes of Allauddin Khan – although he was so old you could read history in the lines of his face. He had seen the first revolution in India. That was in 1857, and he remembered it, so he must have been at least old enough to remember. He had seen a whole century pass by, and all that he did this whole time was practice the sitar. Eight hours, ten hours, twelve hours each day; that's the classical Indian way. It's a discipline, and unless you practice it you soon lose the grip over it. It is so subtle.... It is there only if you are in a certain state of preparedness; otherwise it is gone.

A master is reported to have once said, "If I don't practice for three days, the crowd notices it. If I don't practice for two days, the experts notice it. If I don't practice for one day, my disciples notice it. As far as I am concerned, I cannot stop for a single moment. I have to practice and practice; otherwise I immediately notice. Even in the morning, after a good sleep, I notice something is lost."

Indian classical music is a hard discipline, but if you impose it upon yourself it gives you immense freedom. Of course, if you want to swim in the ocean you have to practice. And if you want to fly in the sky, then naturally it is apparent that immense discipline is required. But it cannot be imposed by somebody else. Anything imposed becomes ugly. That's how the word 'discipline' became ugly – because it has become associated with the father, the mother, the teacher, and all kinds of people who don't understand a single thing about discipline. They don't know the taste of it.

The master was saying, "If I don't practice even for a few hours nobody notices, but of course I notice the difference." One has to continuously practice, and the more you practice, the more you become practiced in practice; it becomes easier. Slowly slowly a moment comes when discipline is no longer a practice but enjoyment.

I am talking about classical music, not about my discipline. My discipline is enjoyment from the very beginning, or from the beginning of enjoyment. I will tell you about it later on....

I have heard Ravi Shankar many times. He has the touch, the magic touch, which very few people have in the world. It was by accident that he touched the sitar; whatsoever he touched would have become his instrument. It is not the instrument, it is always the man. He fell in love with Allauddin's vibe, and Allauddin was of a far greater height – thousands of Ravi Shankars joined together, stitched together rather, could not reach to his height. Allauddin was certainly a rebel – and not only an innovator but an original source of music. He brought many things to music.

Today almost all the great musicians in India are his disciples. It is not without reason. All kinds of musicians would come just to touch Baba's feet: sitarists, dancers, flutists, actors, and whatnot. That's how he was known, just as "Baba," because who would use his name, Allauddin?

When I saw him, he was already beyond ninety. Naturally he was a Baba; that simply became his name. And he was teaching all kinds of instruments to so many kinds of musicians. You could have brought any instrument and you would have seen him play it as if he had done nothing else but play that instrument for his whole life.

He lived very close to the university where I was, just a few hours' journey away. I used to visit him once in a while, whenever there was no festival. I make this point because there were always festivals. I must have been the only one to ask him, "Baba, can you give me the dates when there are no festivals here?"

He looked at me and said, "So now you have come to take even those away too?" And with a smile he gave me three dates. There were only three days in the whole year when there was not a festival. The reason was, there were all kinds of musicians with him – Hindus, Mohammedans, Christians – and every festival happened there, and he allowed them all. He was, in a real sense, a patriarch, a patron saint.

I used to visit him on those three days, when he was alone and there was no crowd around. I told him, "I don't want to disturb you. You can sit silently. If you want to play your veena it is up to you, or whatsoever. If you want to recite the Koran, I would love it. I have come here just to be part of your milieu." He wept like a child. It took me a little time to wipe his tears away and ask, "Have I hurt you?"

He said, "No, not at all. It just touched my heart so deeply that I could not find anything else to do but cry. And I know that I should not cry: I am so old and it is inappropriate – but has one to be appropriate all the time?"

I said, "No, at least not when I'm here." He started laughing, and the tears in his eyes, and the laughter on his face...both together were such a joy.

Masto had brought me to him. Why? I will just say a few more things before I can answer it....

I have heard Vilayat Khan, another great sitarist – perhaps a little greater than Ravi Shankar, but not an innovator. He is utterly classical, but listening to him even I loved classical music. Ordinarily I don't love anything classical, but he plays so perfectly you cannot help yourself. You have to love it, it is not in your hands. Once a sitar is in his hands, you are not in your own hands. Vilayat Khan is pure classical music. He will not allow any pollution; he will not allow anything popular. I mean "pop," because in the West, unless you say pop nobody will understand what is popular. It is just the old "popular" cut short – badly cut, bleeding.

I have heard Vilayat Khan, and I would like to tell you a story about one of my very rich disciples. That is circa 1970, because since then I have not heard anything of them. They are still there – I have inquired about their well-being – but sannyas has made so many people afraid, particularly the rich ones.

This family was one of the richest in India. I was amazed when the wife told me, "You are the only man to whom I can say it: for ten years I have been in love with Vilayat Khan."

I said, "What is wrong with that? Vilayat Khan? – nothing is wrong."

She said, "You don't understand. I don't mean his sitar; I mean him."

I said, "Of course! What would you do with his sitar without him?"

She hit her head with her hand and said, "Can't you understand anything at all?"

I said, "Looking at you, it seems not. But I do understand that you love Vilayat Khan. It is perfectly good. I am just saying that there is nothing wrong in it."

At first she looked at me in disbelief, because in India, if you say such a thing to a religious man – a Hindu wife falling in love with a Mohammedan musician, singer or dancer – you cannot have his blessing, that much is certain. He may not curse you, but most likely he will; even if he can forgive you, even that is too modern, ultra-modern.

"And," I said to her, "there is nothing wrong in it. Love, love whomsoever you want to love. And love knows no barriers of caste or creed."

She looked at me as if I were the one who had fallen in love, and she was the saint I was talking to. I said, "You are looking at me as if I have fallen in love with him. That too is true. I also love the way he plays – but not the man." The man is arrogant, which is very common in artists.

Ravi Shankar is even more arrogant, perhaps because he is a brahmin too. That is like having two diseases together: classical music and being a brahmin. And he has a third dimension to his disease too, because he married the great Allauddin's daughter; he is his son-in-law.

Alauddin was so respected that just to be his son-in-law was enough proof that you are great, a genius. But unfortunately for them, I had also heard Masto. And the moment I heard him I said, "If the world knew about you they would forget and also forgive all these Ravi Shankars and Vilayat Khans."

Masto said, "The world will never know about me. You will be my only listener."

You will be surprised to know that Masto played many instruments. He was really a versatile genius, a very fertile mind, and he could make anything beautiful out of anything. He painted and as meaninglessly as even Picasso could not do, and as beautifully as certainly Picasso could not do. But he simply destroyed his paintings saying, "I don't want to leave any footprints on the sands of time."

But sometimes he used to play music with Pagal Baba, so I asked him, "What about Baba?"

He said, "My sitar is reserved for you; not even Baba has heard it. Something else is reserved for Baba, so please don't ask me. You may not hear it."

Naturally I wanted to know what it was. I was curious, but I said to him, "I will keep my curiosity to myself. I will not ask anybody – although I could ask Baba and he cannot lie to me, but I will not ask, that much I will promise you."

He laughed and said, "In that case, when Baba is no longer in the world, then I will also play that instrument for you, because only then can I play it to you or anybody, and not before."

And the day that Pagal Baba was no more, the first thing that came into my mind was, "What is that instrument? Now is the time...." I condemned myself, cursed myself, but what did it matter? The only thing that kept coming up for me again and again was, "What is Masto's instrument?"

Curiosity is something very deep in man. It was not the serpent who persuaded Eve; it was curiosity that persuaded her, and also Adam, and so on and so forth...up until now. I think it is going to go on forever persuading people. They pursue curiosity. It is a strange phenomenon. Of course it was not a big deal. I had heard Masto play other instruments; perhaps he may be even more proficient on this one, but so what? A man has died and you are thinking about the instrument that Masto will now have to play for you...it's human.

It is good that people don't have windows in the top of their heads; otherwise everybody could see what is going on. Then there would be real trouble, because what they pretend to be on their face is totally different; it is only a persona, a mask. What are they within? – a current of a thousand things.

If we had windows in our heads it would be very difficult to live. But I entertained the idea.... It would help tremendously for people to become silent, so that anybody else could look into their head and see that there is nothing to see. The silent ones could smile looking at their neighbors and say, "Look on, boys, look on. Look

on as much as you want." But the head has no windows. It is completely sealed.

At Baba's death I thought only of Masto's instrument. Forgive
me, but I have decided to tell the whole truth whatsoever it is. And
mind you all, I am going to tell it howsoever long it takes. Devageet, Devaraj, and Ashu – it may take years for me to tell it and
then I will tell you that you have to finish the book quickly, so don't
go on piling it up.

Don't in any way depend upon tomorrows. Just do it today; only
then will you be able to do it. Unknowingly you have fallen into a
trap. And you think that I am caught in a mousetrap? Forget it,
man. I have got all three of you, and now the trap will become
tighter every day; there is no escape.

Yes, one woman – who will come somewhere in the story because she means much to me – she told me something similar. She is
strange in a way; everything she gave me was a first: the first watch,
the first typewriter, the first car, the first tape recorder, the first
camera. I cannot believe how she managed it, but everything was
the first. I will tell you about her later on. Remind me when the
time comes.

She told me that the only thing heavy on her heart is that when
her husband's mother died she felt hungry.

I said, "What is wrong with feeling hungry?"

She said, "Do you think it is okay? My husband's mother is dead,
lying dead in front of me, and I just felt so hungry, and was thinking
only of good food: *paratha, bhajia, pulau, rasogulla.* I have never told
anybody," she said to me, "because I thought nobody would forgive
me."

I said, "There is nothing wrong in it. What can you do? You did
not kill her. Anyway, one has to start eating sooner or later – the
sooner the better. And when one is about to eat, one thinks of what
one would like."

She said, "Are you sure?"

I said, "How many times do I have to say it?"

At the time she told me I again remembered how she must be
feeling, because I remembered Baba dying and the first thought that
came to me. Thoughts are really strange people…. I had thought to

myself, "What is the instrument that Masto plays?" Of course the moment I saw Masto I said, "Now...."

He said, "Okay."

No other word passed between us. He understood, and for the first time he played the veena for me. He had never played it to me before. It is a sort of guitar, but more complicated, and of course reaching to heights which even the sitar cannot reach, and also to depths which sitars leave only halfway.

I said, "The veena! Masto, you wanted to hide this experience from me?"

He said, "No, no, never. But when I was with Baba, and I had not yet known you, I had promised him on my own that I would not play this instrument for anybody else while he was alive. Now to me you are Pagal Baba; that's the way I will think of you always. Now I can play for you. I was not hiding anything from you, but you were not known to me at all when this promise was given. Now it is over."

For a moment I could not believe my own ears at how much he had been hiding. I said, "Masto, you know that it was not a good thing between two friends."

He looked down towards the earth and did not say anything. It was the first time in my life that I had seen him in that mood.

I said to him, "No. No need to be sorry, and no need to feel sad. What has happened has happened; it has nothing to do with us anymore."

He said, "I was not sorry, I was ashamed. I know being sorry is very easy to wash away, but to be ashamed...you can wash it but again it is still there. You can wash it again, and it is there."

The feeling of shame only happens to those who are really great. It does not happen to ordinary people; they don't know what it means to be ashamed. I am suddenly reminded of one thing.... What is the time?

"Ten twenty-two, Osho."

Okay.

I was not reminded of the time. I am never reminded of the time, and you know it. Sometimes it becomes really too much. You are hungry, ready to run to Magdalena...and I am still talking. Obviously you cannot stop me. Only I can stop myself. Not only that, I even tell you only to stop when I say "Stop." It is just an old habit. No, I was reminded of something else, not the time.

Masto was staying at my Nani's house. That was my guest house. In my father's house there was not even a place for the host, what to say of the guest. It was so overcrowded – I cannot believe that Noah's Ark was more overcrowded. All kinds of creatures were there. What a world! Yes, it was almost a world. But my Nani's house was almost empty: the way I like things, empty.

The English word 'empty' is not the way to express what I want to say. The word is *shunya* – and please don't think of Doctor Eichling, because his name, the name given by me, is Shunyo. But poor Eichling seems to be Chinese or something. What kind of name is that: I-kling? He can't be an American, and when he shaved his beard off he looked exactly like a Chinese. Just by chance I came across him. I could not even recognize him.

I said, "What happened to you?"

Gudia reminded me, saying, "It is Shunyo."

I said, "It is good that you reminded me; otherwise I would have hit him. He looks exactly like a Chinese. Why have you cut off your beard?" I asked him.

He said, "Because I am going to practice in Madras."

I said, "My God! Does one need to shave off one's beard to practice in Madras?"

In fact if you look into the history of medicine, all the great doctors for some unknown reason had beards. Perhaps they had no time to shave, or perhaps they had no wives, so who cares? I asked him, "Who gave you the idea that to be a doctor in America you have to cut off your beard? And from Shunyo you have become Doctor Eichling again? Are you a cat or something? They say a cat has nine lives, how many lives have you got, Mister Eichling?"

My Nani's house was really shunyo. It was so empty, as a temple should be, and she kept it so clean. I like Gudia for many reasons; one is that she keeps everything so clean. She even finds fault with me! And naturally, if she finds a fault – as far as cleanliness is concerned – I always agree with her. She has the same sensitivity as my Nani. Perhaps a man cannot have that quality which a woman has naturally. To see a woman unclean is very terrible. To see a man unclean is okay, one can tolerate it – after all, he is just a man. But a woman unknowingly keeps herself and her surroundings clean. And Gudia is English, proper English. There are only two proper English people, Gudia and Sagar...in the whole world I mean.

My Nani was so concerned with cleanliness that as far as she was concerned, God was next to cleanliness. The whole day she was cleaning...for whom? Only I was there. I came in the evenings; by the morning I was gone. And the whole day the poor woman kept herself occupied with cleaning.

Once I asked her, "Don't you get tired? And nobody is telling you to do it all."

She said, "Cleaning has helped me so much. It has become almost a prayer. You are my guest. You don't live here anymore, do you? – you are a guest. I have to prepare my house for the guest." In India they say, "The guest is the god...." She said, "You are my god."

I said, "Nani, are you mad? I am your god? You have never believed in any god."

She said, "I only believe in love, and I have found it. Now you are the only guest in my temple of love. I have to keep it as clean as I can."

Her house became a guest house, not only for me, but also for my guests. Whenever Masto would come, he used to stay in her house. And my Nani would serve whosoever I brought to her house as a guest, as if the person really meant a lot to her.

I said to her, "You need not be so concerned."

She said, "They are your guests, and so I have to take care, more care than I would take of my own guests."

I never saw my Nani talking to Masto. Once in a while I would see them sitting together, but I have never seen them talking. It was strange.

I asked her, "Why don't you talk with him? Don't you like him?"

She said, "I like him very much but there is nothing to say. I have nothing to ask; he has nothing to ask either. We simply nod heads and sit silently. It is so beautiful to sit silently. With you I talk. I have to ask so many things, and you have so many things to tell me. With you talking is beautiful."

I understood that they related in a different way. The way she and I related was different, and certainly not the only way. Since that day talking became less and less between us until it finally stopped. Then we used to sit for hours. Her house was really beautiful. It was just by the river, and the moment I say "river," something in my heart immediately starts singing songs.

I will never see that river again, but there is no need, because whenever I close my eyes I can see it. I hear that now it is no longer the same beautiful place. Just near it many houses have arisen, shops have opened up; it has become a marketplace. No, I would not like to go. Even if I had to go there I would close my eyes just to see the beautiful place that it was – tall trees and a small temple...I can still hear the bell ringing.

Just the other day someone brought me a few bells, strange bells, the kind that are not known in most parts of the world. They are Tibetan. Although made in California, the design is Tibetan. Not only that, but even though they have been made in California they have certainly been improved. Tibetan bells are ordinarily crude, but these are very refined and made of glass. Let me describe them to you.

They are not like any bells you can conceive of. They are like plates, many plates strung together so that when the wind moves them they hit each other, and the sound is really worth hearing. They are beautiful bells. Once in a while California certainly makes some beautiful things; otherwise they are all Californiacs. But once in a while they do something really nice.

I have seen many kinds of bells. One Tibetan lama in Kalimpong showed me a Tibetan bell which I will never forget. It is worth mentioning to you. Perhaps you may never see such a thing because those bells are part of the disappearing Tibet. Soon they will disappear completely. The bell I saw was certainly a strange one.

I had only seen bells in India and had always associated the word 'bell' with the Indian bell. It is hung from the ceiling and there is a small stick inside which you strike against the side of the bell. It is to wake up the god who goes on falling asleep. I can understand the beauty of it – that even God has to be woken up, what to say of man. But this Tibetan bell was totally different. It had to be placed on the floor, not hung from the ceiling.

I said, "Is it a bell? It does not look like one."

The lama laughed, "Wait and see," he said. "It is not only a bell but a special bell."

And he brought a small round wooden handle from his bag. Then he started rubbing the handle around and around the inside of the so-called bell, which looked like a pot. After going round for a few times he hit the bell at a certain point which was marked, and strange, the bell repeated the whole Tibetan mantra, Om Mani Padme Hum. I could not believe it when I heard it for the first time. It repeated the mantra so clearly.

He said, "You will find this type of bell in every Tibetan monastery, because we cannot repeat the mantra as often as we should, but we can at least make the bell repeat the mantra."

I said, "Great, so this is not a dumb bell."

He said, "Not at all. And if you hit it in the wrong place you will know that it also shouts. It will only repeat the mantra when you hit it in the right spot; otherwise it shrieks and screams, and makes all kinds of noise, but never the mantra."

I have been to Ladakh, a country between India and Tibet. Perhaps now Ladakh will become the most important religious country in the world, as Tibet once was. Tibet is finished, murdered, massacred. In Ladakh I saw those same bells, but much bigger, houselike. You could go inside them and by holding the hanging rod and then hitting with it at certain points, you could create any mantra you liked. It is only a question of knowing the language of the bell. It is almost like a computer.

What was I saying, Devageet?

"You were talking about how Nani never used to talk with Masto, they just used to sit silently...."

Right, so we should sit silently now...ten minutes for me. For God's sake – whether he exists or not – just relax.

Satyam Shivam Sundaram...I am not, and you are trying to reach me. Everybody can see. Do you see? I am not. Continue for just a few minutes, just two minutes, because I am waiting for something, so be alert. Yes.... Good....

No, Devageet. You would have been such a good wife, even I would laugh, but I am not supposed to.

Stop.

Session 36

Just now I was thinking of a story. I don't know who created the story or why, and I don't agree with his conclusions either, but I still love it. The story is simple. You may have heard it, but perhaps not understood it because it is so simple. Everybody thinks he understands simplicity. It's a strange world. People try to understand complexity, yet they ignore simplicity thinking it's not worth paying attention to. Perhaps you may not have paid attention to the story, but when I tell it, it is bound to come back to you.

Stories are strange creatures; they never die. They are never born either. They are as old as man; that's why I love them. If a truth is not contained in a story, it is not a story. Then it may be philosophy, theosophy, anthroposophy; and no matter how many "sophies" there are, they are all nonsense – write nonsense, without a hyphen – pure nonsense. ...Because ordinarily the word is written with a hyphen, dividing "non" from "sense." I don't see any point in the hyphen. At least remove it from my words except when I say that Zen is non-sense; then of course the hyphen needs to be there.

I had first told this story to Masto, who must have heard it before, but not in the way I distort things or create them.

The story is – and I am telling it to Masto – "God created the world, Masto."

Masto said, "Great. You have always been against philosophy and religion; what happened? This is the very first enigma all religions begin with."

I said, "Wait, before you conclude. Don't be foolish in concluding without having heard the whole story."

Masto said, "I know the story."

I said, "You cannot know it."

He looked amazed and said, "This is something. I can repeat it if you want me to."

I said, "You can repeat it, but that does not mean that you know it. Is repetition knowing? Is the parrot repeating the sutras of Buddha, a buddha or at least a *bodhisattva*?"

He looked really thoughtful. I waited, but then I said, "Before you start thinking, listen to the story. What you know cannot be the same as I know, because we are not the same. God created the world. Naturally, the question arises, and the Vedas ask it exactly: Why did he create the world? The Vedas, in that sense, are just great. They say, 'Perhaps even he does not know why' – and by 'he' they meant God."

And I can see the beauty of it. Perhaps it all came out of innocence, not knowledge. Perhaps he was not creating; perhaps he was just playing, like a child making houses in the sand. Do children know for whom the houses are being made? Do they know the ant who will crawl in during the night and will feel warm?

In Hindi, ants are always "she" – I don't know why. They are never thought to be male. The truth is that only one ant, the queen, is female; all other ants are male. It is strange, or perhaps not so strange, but to hide the truth they call the ant "she." Perhaps because the ant is so small, to call it "he" would be against the male ego. They call the elephant "he." They call the lion "he." If they specifically want to indicate the female elephant they call it a she-elephant, or a female lion a she-lion, but otherwise the term in general use is the male. But the poor ant...and unfortunately I have chosen it for the story.

He, or she, whoever the ant is, philosophizes – perhaps the ant cannot be a "she"; otherwise where will the philosophy come from? I have never come across a woman who philosophizes. I have known many women professors of philosophy, but strangely, even these professors talk only of clothes and pictures. If somebody is present then they praise her; if she is absent, then they condemn her. Philosophy is the last thing they think of. How they manage to become professors is not strange to me, although you may have thought it should have been. No, they can teach because it needs no thinking; in fact, that is its most basic requirement. If you think, you cannot teach.

One of my professors was the strangest man I ever came across in the university world. For years not a single student enrolled in his class, the simple reason being that he would always start his lectures on time, but nobody ever knew when he was going to end.

At the very beginning he would say, "Please don't expect the end, because nothing in the world ends. If you want to leave, you can, because in the world many leave, and the world still continues. Just don't disturb me. Do not ask me, 'Can I leave, sir?' Nobody asks that, even when one has to die, so why should you ask a poor professor of philosophy? Dear one, can I ask you why you came in the first place? You can leave whenever you want, and I will speak for as long as I feel the words are coming."

When I reached university everybody told me, "Avoid that man, Doctor Dasgupta. He is just mad."

I said, "That means I have to meet him first. I have come in search of really mad men. Is he really mad?"

They said, "Really mad. He is absolutely mad, and we are not joking."

I said, "It gives me great ecstasy to know that you are not joking. I can do that for myself. Whenever I need to, I just tell myself beautiful jokes and laugh hilariously saying, 'Great! Never heard that one before.'"

They said, "This guy seems to be mad himself."

I said, "Absolutely right. Now tell me where Doctor Dasgupta lives."

I went to his house and knocked on the door. There was not even a servant. He lived like a god: no wife, no servant, no children, just alone. He said to me, "You must have knocked on the wrong door. Do you know I am Doctor Dasgupta?"

I said, "I know. Do you know who I am?"

He was an old man, and he just looked at me through his thick glasses and then said, "How can I know you?"

I said, "I have come to find out."

He said, "Do you mean that you don't know either?"

I said, "No."

He said, "My God! Two madmen in one house! And you are far madder than I am. Come in, sir, and be seated."

He was really respectful. Without joking he said, "In this university nobody has turned up for my classes for three years. In fact, I have stopped going myself. What is the point? I deliver my lectures in this room, exactly where you are sitting."

I said, "That's really beautiful, but to whom?"

He said, "That's the point. Once in a while I also ask, 'to whom?'"

I said, "I will enroll in your class, and you still need not bother to come to the classroom. It is almost one mile from your house. I can come here."

He said, "No, no, I will come – that is part of my duty. Just one thing, forgive me, but although I can start my lecture on time – if it is eleven, I can start at eleven – I cannot guarantee that I can finish when the bell rings forty minutes later."

I said, "I can understand that. How can the poor man who rings the bell every forty minutes understand what you are doing? And not only you, what are all the professors in the whole university doing? If they stop, then they are stupid. The bell does not know; the man who rings the bell does not know – so why should you stop? If you make it a point that you will not stop, then listen, I will also make it a point, man to man, that if you stop I will hit you so hard you may not survive."

He said, "What? You will hit me?" He was a Bengali man.

I said, "I simply meant metaphorically. I will touch your head slightly, just to remind you that you need not bother about the bell."

He said, "Then it is okay. You need not go to the hostel, you can live in my house. It is very big, and I am alone."

That day I thought of Masto. He would have enjoyed that house, and that man with his contemplative eyes. That day too, I remembered this story. I will tell it again so that you can follow:

God created the world. He finished it in six days. The last thing he created was the woman. Naturally, the question arises: Why? Why did he create the woman last? Of course, the feminists will say, "Because woman is the most perfect creation of God." Obviously he created her after his experience of creating man. Man is a little older model; naturally God refined it and made it better.

But the male chauvinists have another reply. They say God created man as the last of his creations, but then man started asking questions such as, "Why did you create the world?" and, "Why did you create me?" And God became so puzzled that he created woman to puzzle man. Since then God has heard nothing from man.

Man comes home tail between his legs, goes out to purchase bananas, and by and by he has become a banana: Mr. Banana, Ph.D., M.A., D.Litt., and whatnot. But basically Mr. Banana is utterly rotten. Please don't eat it. Don't even look inside the skin; otherwise you will repent and immediately start saying, "Stop the wheel!" – the wheel of birth and death – because who wants to be a banana? But bananas may be well dressed, with beautiful clothes, perhaps made in Paris. Mr. Banana can do anything. He wears a beautiful tie, so that he cannot even breathe...shoes so tight that if you see Mr. Banana's feet you would never look at his face.

I have never liked shoes, but everybody insisted that I wear them. I said, "Whatsoever happens I am not going to use shoes."

What I use are called *chappals* in India. They are not really shoes, not even sandals; they are the least possible covering. And I have chosen the ultimate chappal – you could not reduce it any more. My chappal-maker, Arpita, knows that there is no way to make them more perfectly. Even just a little less and my feet would be nude. It is just the most minimal: just a strap somehow holding my feet in the chappal. You could not cut it down any more.

Why do I hate shoes? For the simple reason that they make you into a banana. Of course Mr. Banana, Doctor Banana, Professor Banana, all kinds of bananas; lady bananas, gentleman bananas... you can find all varieties, but they always start from the shoes.

Have you ever seen Victorian ladies with their high heels? – so high that any tightrope walker would fall off if he tried to walk in them. Why were they chosen? They were chosen by a very religious society, for a very irreligious reason – pornographic – because when the heels are high, the buttocks stand out.

Now nobody bothers about the reason; even ladies go on doing it, and thinking they are being ladylike. It is very unladylike. They are simply parading their buttocks around for free, and enjoying it. And with their tight clothes, obviously they look better than they ever could naked, because the skin is, after all, just skin. If you are thirty years old, the skin is thirty years old. It has seen thirty years go by, and it cannot be as tight as a newly bought dress. And now the manufacturers are doing miracles: they are making women look so tempting that God himself would have eaten the apple!

Do you recognize what I am saying? It may take you a little time. Even Ashu has not laughed. It will take a little time for it to sink in. Yes, a snake would not have been needed, just a clothes salesman would have done. Just a tight dress for Mrs. Eve, and God himself would have eaten the apple, and driven out with Mrs. Eve – for the evening, I mean.

Why did God create woman after man? The male chauvinist says man is the perfect creation. You must have seen men in Greek and Roman sculpture, but you rarely come across a woman's naked body sculpted, just men. Strange. What was the matter with those people? Could they not see any beauty in women?

They were male chauvinists, so much so that they praised homosexuality more than heterosexuality. It will sound very strange, because almost twenty-five centuries have passed since Socrates, but Socrates himself was in love with men, not women. Perhaps his wife Xanthippe created so much trouble for him that he overreacted and forgot all about women, and started loving men. Perhaps there were other reasons.

If some day I have to go into the psychoanalysis of Socrates, then I may uncover things which no one else would even think to uncover. But the male chauvinist says God created man, and just because man was alone and needed company, God created Eve.

This is not the original story. The original woman's name was not Eve, her name was Lilith. God created Lilith, but Lilith created, from the very first moment, *the* problem.

It started like this: Night was coming on, the sun was setting, and they had only one bed, this was the problem. They were not as fortunate as me in having Asheesh; otherwise he would have prepared – even though he may have been suffering from a migraine – still he would have created a perfect bed. But Asheesh was not there. In fact no other human being was there....

My watch has stopped, and just the other day I was talking about it, and it stopped. You know watches are temperamental. It stopped exactly at that same moment. And I was talking about another watch, a metaphorical watch, but who is going to explain to this watch that I was not talking about her? During the night I tell her many times again and again, "Listen, you need not stop. I was not talking about you – you are such a beautiful watch…" but she won't listen.

What was I saying?

"You were talking about Eve not having a bed…or Lilith not having a bed, Osho."

Yes. The fight started even before going to bed. Lilith was certainly the originator of the Women's Liberation Movement, whether they know it or not. She fought. She threw Adam out of bed. What a great woman! Adam tried again and again to throw her out, but what was the point? Even if he succeeded, she was back again, throwing him out.

She said, "Only one can sleep in this bed. It is not meant for two." Of course it was not made for two by God; it was not a double bed.

They fought the whole night, and in the morning Adam said to God, "I was perfectly happy…" although he was not, but the whole night's unhappiness had helped him to see his past as very happy. He said, "I was so happy before this woman came."

And Lilith said, "I was also happy. I don't want to exist." She must have been the originator of many things. Perhaps she was the first real Zen patriarch, because she said, "I don't want to exist. One night is enough for one life, because I know it is going to be almost the same every night, again and again. And even if you give me a double bed, what difference does it make? We are still going to fight, because the question is, 'Who is the master?' I cannot allow this brute to be my master."

God said, "Okay." In those days – and they were the days just at the very beginning; in fact it was the first day after the creation. It must have been a Sunday, according to the Christians. God must have been in a Sunday mood, because he said, "Okay, I will make you disappear." Lilith disappeared, and then God created Eve from Adam's rib.

It was the first operation, Devaraj, please take note. God was the first surgeon, whether the Royal Society recognizes him or not does not matter. He did a great job. No other surgeon has been able to do the same since then. From just a rib, he created woman. But it is insulting, and I hate the story. It is not the way God should behave. Just a rib...!

And then there is the rest of the story. Every night, Eve counts Adam's ribs before she goes to sleep, to be certain that all the other ribs are still there and that there is no other woman in the world. Then she can sleep well.

Strange...if other women are there, why can't she sleep well? But I don't like that ending to the story. In the first place it is male chauvinistic; in the second place, very ungodly; in the third place, very unimaginative and too factual. Things should only be indicated.

Masto asked me, "What is your conclusion?"

I then said, "My conclusion is that God created man first because he did not want any interference while he was creating." This is a well-known saying in the East. It has nothing to do with me, but I loved it so much that I can almost claim that it is mine. If love can make anything one's own, then it is mine. I don't know who said it in the first place, and I don't need to know either.

I also told Masto, "Since then, nothing has been heard of God. Have you any news about the poor old man? Has he retired? Has he forgotten his creation? Has he no love and compassion for those whom he has made?"

Masto said, "You always create such strange questions out of such absurd stories, and then you make them sound sensible. I wonder if one day you will become a story writer."

I said, "Never. Far more talented people are engaged in that work. I am needed somewhere else where nobody else seems to be interested, because I am thinking to be interested only in God."

Masto was shocked. He said, "In God? I thought you don't believe in him."

I said, "I don't believe, because I know, and I know so deeply that even if you cut off my head I will still say, 'I know.' I may not be...once before I was not.... He was, and he will be."

In fact, to say "he" is not right. In the East we say "it," and that sounds perfect. IT written in capital letters gives a real meaning to Buddha's words, Lao Tzu's sayings, Jesus' prayers. "He" is again male-oriented, and "he" is not "she" either.

I have heard…you may not have heard yet, because it belongs to the future. It's a future story. The Polack pope dies, and goes to heaven, of course. He rushes in to see God, and as fast as he goes in, he comes out even faster – crying and weeping. Saints Peter, Paul, Thomas, and all the other saints gather and say, "Don't cry, don't weep. You are a good man, and we understand your feelings."

The pope shouted, "What do you understand? Did you know that in the first place he is not even a white man, he is a nigger? And in the second place, even worse: he is not even a he, he is a she!"

God is neither he nor she – but Polacks are Polacks. You can make them popes, but that does not make any difference. God created the world, not according to the male chauvinists' or the feminists' points of view. Their views are just opposite.

He created woman as the perfect model, and certainly every artist believes she is the perfect model. If you see their paintings, you will also believe that she is the perfect model. But please stop there. Don't touch a real woman. Paintings are okay, statues too, but a real woman is as imperfect as she should be.

I don't mean anything derogatory by that. Imperfection is life's very law. Only dead things are perfect. Life is, necessarily, imperfect. Women are imperfect, men are imperfect; and when two imperfections meet, you can imagine what the outcome will be.

"That's what my conclusions are," I told Masto, "that God created man, and man started asking philosophical questions. God created woman to keep man occupied." Since then man has been purchasing bananas, and by the time he reaches home he is so tired that although his wife wants to discuss great things, he just wants to hide himself behind *The Times* or any other newspaper. He is kept continuously on the run by the woman: "Do this, do that."

It is strange that women are given the job of teacher, although they are not allowed many other jobs. Perhaps there is a logic in it. It is good to catch hold of the poor boys before it is too late, and after that they are always trembling before the woman, continuously afraid. Since then God has been enjoying looking at the whole non-sense going on in the world he created in six days.

Buddhas are trying in some way to give you a glimpse of that world of relaxation that existed before the world and all its troubles began. Even now it is possible to just step aside. In stepping outside the stream you suddenly start laughing; God or no God, it was just a story. I told Masto, "Unless somebody steps outside the mundane stream of life...."

I wanted to say goodbye to this man, but it is good that I could not. So many things are still related to him, and anything may reflect many other things. Life is always simple and complex, both – simple as a dewdrop, and as complex also as a dewdrop, because the dewdrop can reflect the whole sky, and it contains all the oceans. And certainly it is not going to be there forever...maybe just a few minutes, and then gone forever. I emphasize *forever*. Then there is no way to get it back, with all those stars and oceans.

So much is involved with Masto....

Whenever I wanted to cry I would ask Masto to play his veena. It was easy, no explanation needed; nobody asks why you are crying. The veena is such that it simply stirs your depths. But it was his stubbornness that made me tell you that story, because he used to say to me, "Unless you tell me a story I will not play." I have told him the story, and now is the time for him to play...but only I can hear. It is better that still only I can hear.

Just ten minutes for me to hear it. I am enjoying it in the sense that Adam must have.

How many minutes have we been in this ancient bullock-cart procedure? Can anyone figure it out?

"Forever, Osho."

Then just one minute, and you can stop.

This is good. One should never want to continue anything so beautiful; one should be capable of ending it too. I know that you can continue, but no – my doctor prohibits me from eating too much of anything. He wants me to reduce my weight, and if I eat your diet, then Jesus...!

You can end it now.

Session 37

O KAY. WE ARE ONLY AT the second day of my primary school. It is going to be like that. Every day opens up so many things. I have not finished even the second day yet. Today I will do my best to finish it.

Life is interlinked; you cannot cut it into neat pieces. It is not a piece of cloth. You cannot cut it at all, because the moment you cut it from all its connections it is no longer the same. It becomes something dead, not breathing. I want it to take its own course, not even to direct it, because I have not directed it in the first place. It took its own course, unguided.

In fact, I hated guides and still do because they prevent you from flowing with that which is. They direct, their business is to hurry you up to the next point. Their work is to make you feel as if you have come to know. Neither they know, nor you. Knowing only comes through living unguided, undirected. That is the way I have lived and am still living.

It's a strange fate. Even from my very childhood I knew this was not my home. It was my Nana's house, and my father and mother were far away. I had hoped that perhaps my home would be there, but no, it was just a big guest house, with my poor mother and father serving the guests continuously, for no reason – at least to me there seemed to be none.

Again I said to myself, "This is not the home I was looking for. Now where do I go? My grandfather is dead, so I cannot go back to that house." It was his house, and without him, just the house is meaningless. If my Nani had gone back it would have meant something, ninety-nine percent at least, but she refused to go.

She said, "I went there for him, and if he is not there then there is no other reason for me to return. Of course if he comes back, I am ready, but if he is not coming back, if he cannot keep his promise, why should I bother about his house and property? They were never mine. There is always somebody who can take care of these things. I am not meant for them. I did not go for them in the first place, and I will not return for them."

She refused so totally that I learned how to refuse...and I learned how to love. After leaving that house, we stayed a few days with my father's family. It was certainly not just a family, but more a gathering of tribes, many families; perhaps a kind of *mela*, a fair. But we only stayed for a few days. That too was not my house. I stayed there just to have a look at it, then moved.

Since then, how many houses have I lived in? It is almost impossible for you to imagine that in almost fifty years of life I have been just moving houses, and doing nothing else. Of course, the grass was growing – I was moving house, and doing nothing, and the grass was growing. But the whole credit goes to "nothing," not to my moving house.

After that I moved to my Nani's house, and then to one of my uncles' – my father's sister's husband's house – where I had gone to study after matriculation. They had thought it would be only for a few days, but those days proved longer than they had thought. No hostel was ready to take me in because my records were so beautiful! The remarks given by all my teachers, and particularly by the principal, were really worth preserving. Everybody condemned me as much as was allowed on a certificate.

I had told them to their faces, "This is not a character certificate, this is a character assassination. Please write as a P.S. that, 'I call this document a character assassination.' Unless you write it, I will not take it." They had to.

They said to me, "You are not only mischievous but dangerous too, because now you can sue us."

I said, "Don't be afraid. In my life many will sue me in the courts; I will never sue anybody."

I have not sued anybody although I could have done it very easily, and hundreds would have been punished.

I was saying I have never had a house. Even this house, I cannot call it my house. From the first one to the last – perhaps this is not the last, but whichever is the last, I cannot call it *my* house. Just to hide the fact, I call it Lao Tzu House. Lao Tzu has nothing to do with it.

And I know the man. I know that if he meets me – and someday a meeting is bound to happen – the first thing he will ask will be, "Why did you name your house 'Lao Tzu House'?" Naturally, the curiosity of a child – and nobody could be more childlike than Lao Tzu, neither Buddha, nor Jesus, nor Mohammed, and certainly not Moses. A Jew being childlike? Impossible!

A Jew is born a businessman, with a business suit, just leaving the house and going to the shop. He comes ready-made. Moses? – certainly not. But Lao Tzu, or if you want someone even more childlike than Lao Tzu, then his disciple, Chuang Tzu…. To be a disciple of Lao Tzu one needed to be more innocent than Lao Tzu himself. There is no other way.

Confucius was just refused. In short, he was told to "Get out, and get lost forever – and remember, do not return to this place again." Not actually in these words, but that was the very essence of what Lao Tzu said to Confucius, the most scholarly man of that day. Confucius could not be accepted. But Chuang Tzu was even crazier than Lao Tzu, his master. When Chuang Tzu came, Lao Tzu said, "Great! Are you here to be my master? You can choose: either you can be my master, or I can be your master."

Chuang Tzu replied, "Forget all about that! Why can't we just be?"

And that was the way they remained. Of course Chuang Tzu was a disciple and very respectful to the master; nobody could compete with him. But that's the way they started – with him saying, "Can't we forget all about that rot?" I add the word 'rot' to make it exactly what it would have been. But that does not mean that he was not respectful. Even after this, Lao Tzu laughed and said, "Just great! I was waiting for you." And Chuang Tzu touched the master's feet.

Lao Tzu said, "What!"

Chuang Tzu said, "Don't bring anything in between us. If I feel like touching your feet, then nobody can prevent me, neither you nor I. We have just to watch it happen."

And I had to watch it happen, moving from one house to another. I can remember hundreds of houses, but not a single one where I could have said, "This is my house." I was hoping, perhaps this one...that's been the way for my whole life: "Perhaps the next one."

Still...I will tell you a secret. I am still hoping to have a house somewhere, perhaps.... "Perhaps" *is* the house. My whole life I waited and waited in so many houses for the real one to come. It always seemed just around the corner. But the distance remained the same: it remained always just around the corner. I can again see it....

I know that no house is ever going to be mine. But knowing is one thing: once in a while, something which can only be called "being" covers it. I call that "all-knowing"; and in those moments, again I am searching for "the home." I said it can be named only "perhaps"; I mean that is the name of the home. It is always going to happen, but never really happens...always just about to happen.

From my Nani's house I moved to my father's sister's house. The husband, I mean my father's brother-in-law, was not very willing. Naturally, why should he be? I was in perfect agreement with him.

Even if I had been in his place I would not have been willing either. Not only unwilling, but stubbornly unwilling, because who would accept a troublemaker unnecessarily? They were childless, so really living happily – although in fact they were very unhappy, not knowing how "happy" those who have children are. But they had no way of knowing either.

They had a beautiful bungalow, with more room than for just one couple. It was big enough to have many people in it. But they were rich people, they could afford it. It was not a problem for them to just give me a small room, although the husband was, without saying a word, unwilling. I refused to move in.

I stood outside their house with my small suitcase, and told my father's sister that, "Your husband is unwilling to have me here, and unless he is willing it would be better for me to live on the street than to be in his house. I cannot enter unless I am convinced that he will be happy to have me. And I cannot promise that I will not be a trouble to you. It is against my nature to not be in trouble. I am just helpless."

The husband was hidden behind a curtain, listening to everything. He understood one thing at least, that the boy was worth trying.

He came out and said, "I will give you a try."

I said, "Rather you learn from the very beginning that I am giving you a try."

He said, "What!"

I said, "The meaning will become clearer slowly. It enters thick skulls very slowly."

The wife was shocked. Later on she said to me, "You should not say such a thing to my husband, because he can throw you out. I cannot prevent him; I am only a wife, and a childless one."

OSHO (FAR RIGHT) WITH HIS FATHER'S SISTER (2ND FROM RIGHT) AND HER HUSBAND (FAR LEFT)

Now, you cannot understand.... In India, a childless wife is thought to be a curse. She may not be responsible herself – and I know perfectly well that this fellow was responsible, because the doctors told me that he was impotent. But in India, if you are a childless woman.... First, just to be a woman in India, and then to be childless! Nothing worse can happen to anybody. Now if a woman is childless, what can she do about it? She can go to a gyne-cologist…but not in India! The husband would rather marry another woman.

And the Indian law, made of course by men, allows a husband to marry another woman if the first wife remains childless. Strange, if two people are involved in conceiving a child, then naturally two people are involved in not-conceiving too. In India, two people are involved in conceiving, but in not-conceiving only one – the woman.

I lived in that house, and naturally, from the very beginning, a conflict, a subtle current arose between me and the husband, and it continued to grow. It erupted in many ways. First, each and every thing he said in my presence, I immediately contradicted it, whatso-ever it was. What he said was immaterial. It was not a question of right or wrong: it was him or me.

From the beginning the way he looked at me decided how I had to look at him – as an enemy. Now, Dale Carnegie may have written *How to Win Friends and Influence People*, but I don't think that he really knows. He cannot. Unless you know the art of creating ene-mies, you cannot know the art of creating friends. In that, I am immensely fortunate.

I have created so many enemies that you can depend on it, that I must have made a few friends at least. Without creating friends, you cannot create enemies; that is a basic law. If you want friends, get ready for the enemies too. That's why many, the majority of people, decide to have neither friends nor enemies, but just acquaintances. These are thought to be common-sense people; in fact they really have uncommon sense. But I don't have that, whatsoever it is called. I created as many friends as I created enemies; in fact, in the same proportion. I can count on them both. They are both reliable.

The first, of course, was his guru. The moment he entered the house I told my father's sister, "This man is the worst I have ever seen."

She said, "Shut up. Keep quiet. He is my husband's guru."

I said, "Let him be, but tell me: am I right or not?"

She said, "Unfortunately you are, but keep quiet."

I said, "I cannot keep quiet. We have to come to a confrontation."

She said, "I knew that once this man comes there is going to be trouble."

I said, "He is not responsible; I am the trouble. The day you accepted me, remember, I told your husband, 'Remember, you can accept me, but you are accepting trouble.' Now he will know what I meant. There are things which only time can reveal; a dictionary is useless."

The moment he seated himself, pompously of course, I touched his head. Now, that was the beginning, just the beginning. My relatives all gathered and said, "What are you doing? Do you know who he is?"

I said, "I did it just to know who he is. I was trying to measure him, but he is very shallow. He does not even reach up to his feet, that's why I touched his head."

But he was all fire, jumping and crying and shouting, "This is an insult!"

I said, "I am simply quoting from your book." He had recently published a book in which he had said, "When somebody insults you, be silent, be quiet, don't be disturbed."

He then said, "What about my book?"

That helped me a little, and I then said, "Sit down in your chair, although you don't deserve it."

He said, "Again! Are you bent on insulting me?"

I said, "I am not bent on insulting anybody. I am just thinking of the chair."

He was so fat that the poor chair was somehow just managing to hold him up. The poor chair was actually crying and making noises.

I said, "I'm just talking about the chair. I am not concerned about you, but I am concerned about the chair because later on I will have to use it. In fact it is my chair. If you don't behave, you will have to vacate it."

This was almost like setting light under a bomb. He jumped up, shouting vulgarities, and said, "I always knew the moment this child entered this house it would no longer be the same."

I said, "At least that is true. Whenever there is truth I will always agree, even with an enemy. The house is no longer the same, that is true. Go ahead, tell us why it is not the same."

He said, "Because you are godless."

In India, the word for godless is *nastika*, which is a beautiful word. It cannot be translated as "godless," although that is the only available translation. Nastika simply means "one who does not believe." It does not say anything about the object of belief or disbelief. It is tremendously significant, at least for me. I would like to be called nastika, "one who does not believe," because only the blind ones believe. Those who can see, they need not believe.

The Indian word for the believer is *astika*; like "theist" it exactly gives you the sense of "the believer." In the Indian language a theist is called astika – one who believes, the believer.

I have never been a believer, and nobody who has any intelligence can ever be a believer. Belief is for the imbeciles, the retarded, the idiots, and that lot – and it is a big company; in fact it is the majority.

He called me nastika.

I said, "I again agree, because it describes my attitude towards life. Perhaps it will always describe my attitude towards life, because to believe is to limit. To believe is to be arrogant; to believe is to believe that you know."

To be nastika simply says, "I do not know." It is exactly the English word 'agnostic', "one who does not believe." Nor can he say that he does not believe; in fact he simply remains with a question mark. A man with a question mark, that is an agnostic.

Carrying one's cross is not very difficult, particularly if it is made of gold and studded with diamonds, and hanging around your neck. It is so easy. It was difficult for Jesus. It was not a drama; it was a real cross. And Jesus was not a Christian – and the Jews were really angry. Ordinarily they are good people, and when good people get angry then something nasty is bound to happen, because all good people repress their nastiness. When it explodes, it is an atomic explosion! Jews are always nice people; that is their only fault.

If they had been a little less nice, Jesus need not have gone to the cross. But they were so nice, they had to crucify him. They were really crucifying themselves. Their own son, their very blood – and not an ordinary son, their very best. Jews have not produced, neither before nor after, anyone who even resembles, or even comes close to Jesus. They should have loved the man, but they were nice guys, that was the trouble. They could not forgive him.

I have been with many saints, so-called of course, and a few really saintly, but I will not call them saints. The word has fallen into wrong company and become foul. I will not call Pagal Baba a saint, nor call Magga Baba a saint, nor Masta Baba a saint – just sages. Saintly certainly, but not in the ordinary way people think of saints.

My uncle's guru, Hari Baba, was thought to be a saint. I said to him, "You are neither a Baba, nor a Hari. Hari is the name of God; please change your name to something that applies to you. Baba has no reference to you either. Just look in the dictionary and find something that makes some sense." The conflict started and continued. I will tell you about it later on.

From this house I moved to a university hostel, then to a small house when I went into service. But the house was small, and the family so good that I felt continuously embarrassed, because I could even hear what they were saying in their bed. Now, it is not right, but in the middle of one night I had to say, "Please excuse me, I can hear you."

They were, of course, very shocked. In the morning they said, "You have to leave the house."

I said, "I know. Look, I have already packed everything." I had packed. In fact I had brought a vehicle, and my things were already being loaded.

They said, "This is strange, we had not yet said anything to you."

I said, "You may not have said anything to me, but I heard everything that you were saying to your wife in bed. The wall is so thin. It is not your fault. What can you do? But what can I do either? I tried hard not to hear you."

And do you know that even today I have to sleep with ear plugs. Those ear plugs started after that night. It was long ago – it must have been somewhere in 1958, or perhaps the end of 1957, but somewhere around there. I started using ear plugs just so as not to hear what was not meant for me. It had cost me a house, but I left immediately.

I have been continuously leaving, always packing for the new house. In a way it was good; otherwise I would have had nothing else to do, just packing and then unpacking, then again packing and unpacking. It kept me more occupied than any other buddha before, and more harmlessly. They too were occupied, but their occupation implied others.

My occupation has always been, in a certain sense, personal. Even if thousands of people are with me it is still a one-to-one relationship between you and me. It is not an organization, and it can never be. Certainly for managerial purposes it has to function as an organization, but as far as my sannyasins are concerned, each single sannyasin is related to me, and only to me, not via anybody else.

I am a very unoccupied man. I cannot say unemployed, hence I have used the word 'unoccupied', because I rejoice in it. I am not applying for any employment. I am finished with all employment; I am just enjoying. But to enjoy a certain milieu is needed. That's what I am creating.

The whole of my life I have been creating it, gradually, in steps. I have spoken again and again about the new commune. It is just to remind myself, not you, so that I don't forget the new commune – because the moment I forget it, I may not wake up the next morning.

Gudia will wait.... You will run; yes, I have seen you coming, almost running. You will wait, but I will not be coming because I will have lost the only small thread with which I was holding myself.

And this was going on and on. From Gadarwara I moved to Jabalpur. In Jabalpur I changed houses so many times that everybody wondered if it was my hobby, changing houses.

I said, "Yes, it helps you to become acquainted with so many people in different localities, and I love to be acquainted."

They said, "It is a strange hobby, and very difficult too. Only twenty days have passed and you are moving again."

In Bombay too I moved from one locality to another. This went on until I ended it here. Nobody knows where next.

It started with my school, and it is just the second day. Life is so multidimensional. When I say so multidimensional, it may look absurd because just multidimensional covers it. Why call it so multi-dimensional? Life is multi-multidimensional.

You must be feeling hungry, and hungry ghosts are dangerous people. Just two minutes for me....

Just end it now.

Session 38

O KAY. I WANTED TO TELL you a simple truth, perhaps forgotten for its simplicity; and no religion can practice it because the moment you become part of a religion you are no longer simple nor religious. I wanted to tell you just a very simple thing which I have learned the hard way. Perhaps you are getting it too cheap, and the simple is generally mistaken for the cheap. It is not cheap at all; it is the costliest thing possible because one has to pay for this simple truth with one's own life. It is surrender, trust.

Naturally you will misunderstand trust. How many times have I told you? Yes, I must have told you millions of times, but have you listened even once? Just the other night my secretary was crying, and I asked why.

She said, "The reason for my tears is that you trust me so much, and I am not worthy of it. It is too unbearable."

I said, "I trust you. Now if you want to cry again, you can cry. If you want to laugh, you can laugh."

Now, this is certainly difficult for her. She understands me, but her tears were not against me, they were for me. I said to her, "What can you do? At the most you can tell me to leave this house. Anyone who wants to come with me from this house will come; otherwise I will go alone. Alone I have come, alone I will have to go. Nobody can accompany me on the real journey. In the meantime you can play all kinds of games just to pass the time."

She looked at me. Her tears had dried but were still there on her cheeks. For a moment I knew what was in her mind.

I said to her, "You are thinking that now you can cheat me. Okay, you will not find a better opportunity."

She started crying again and falling at my feet saying, "No, no. I don't want to cheat you. That's why I was crying. I don't want to cheat you."

I said, "Then why the idea? If you don't want to, and I don't want you to either, then why are we wasting our time? If you want to cheat me, I am willing. In fact I should cry for you because from the very beginning I have been nothing but a problem. And still I am a problem, not to myself – myself, I am not at all, so the question does not arise. But to others who are, and are very much so... the more they are, the more problematic is their life. But you are with a man who is not, and as far as he is concerned he has no problem. And if he can trust you, existence is enough to take care of you."

But nobody seems to be at all interested in existence – in everything except existence.

That brings Masto back again. This Masto is such a fellow he would enter anywhere – asked, unasked, invited, uninvited. He was so interesting that whether he was invited or not, everybody would stand to receive him. Masto comes in again and again. It is just an old habit which is very difficult to cure.

Now poor Devageet simply writes his notes, and he does it perfectly. Once in a while I check by asking, "What was I saying?" and he reminds me exactly what it was that I was saying. He does his work, and because he is so full of love for me he cannot resist sighing, and breathing as if something he could never believe would happen has at last happened – and he cannot believe it still. And my difficulty is that I think that he is giggling! He is not giggling, just the sound of his excited breathing makes me feel that he is giggling.

He has written to me about it. I know it, but whenever he does it – I am also a diehard – immediately the word that comes to me is giggling. So again he is giggling. This too is an old habit from when I was a professor. And you can understand: a professor is, after all, a professor, and he cannot allow giggling in his class. I don't mind it now, I enjoy it.

In my class there were more girls than boys, so there was much giggling. And you know me: whether they are boys or girls it does not matter; I still share the jokes. But if the giggling is out of place, then the person is bound to be in trouble. Just after the joke there is a moment when I would allow it, but not out of place. If the giggling came out of place then I would catch the person red-handed. Such giggling was not because of any joke, it was just because of boys and girls together – the old story of Adam and Eve. "Just get out, both of you!" That's what God said. "Get out of the garden of Eden!"

He must have been the old kind of teacher. And this serpent must have been just an old servant who had served many Adams and Eves, helping in every possible way, perhaps sending their letters to each other, etcetera. It is better not to mention the other things. Of course there are no ladies here, and no gentlemen either. But just in case somebody is a gentleman pretending not to be, or a lady pretending not to be, then there would be unnecessary pain. I don't want to cause pain to anybody.

I remember my first lecture.... See how things happen in this series? It was in high school. All the high schools in the district had sent a speaker there. I was chosen to be the representative of my school, not because I was the best – I cannot say that – but only because I was the most troublesome. If I had not been chosen there would have been trouble, that much was certain. So they decided to choose me, but they were not aware that wherever I am, trouble starts anyway.

I started the speech without the normal address to "Mister President, Ladies and Gentlemen...." I looked the president up and down, and said to myself, "No, he does not look like a president." Then I looked around and said to myself, "No, nobody here seems to be either a lady or a gentleman, so unfortunately I have to begin my speech without addressing anybody in particular. I can only say, 'To whom it may concern.'"

Later on my principal called me, because I had still won the prize, even after this.

He said, "What happened to you? You behaved strangely. We prepared you but you never said a single word that you were taught. Not only you completely forgot the prepared lecture, you did not even address the president or the ladies or gentlemen."

I said, "I looked around, and there were no gentlemen. I knew all those fellows very well, and not one is a gentleman. As far as the ladies are concerned, they are even worse because they are the wives of these same fellows. And the president…he seems to have been sent by God to preside over all the meetings in this town. I am tired of him. I cannot call him 'Mister President' when in fact I would rather have hit him."

On that day, when the president had called me for my prize, I said, "Okay, but remember you will have to come down here and shake hands with me."

He said, "What! Shake hands with you! I will never even look at you. You insulted me."

I said, "I will show you."

Since that day he became my enemy. I know the art of how to make enemies. His name was Shrinath Bhatt, a prominent politician in the town. Of course he was the leader of the most influential Gandhian political party. Those were the days when India was under the British Raj. Perhaps as far as freedom is concerned India is still not free. It may be free from the British Raj, but not free from the bureaucracy which the British Raj created.

I have really always been talking about trust, and I have never been able to explain it. Perhaps it is not my fault. Trust: perhaps it cannot be talked about, only indicated. I have been trying hard to say something very definite, but everything fails. Either it becomes your experience, then you don't need to know what it is; or it does not become your experience, then you may know everything under the heading "trust," but still you know nothing.

I was again trying to tell you – in fact giving myself one more try, perhaps; and it is always alluring to talk about all the attempts, even those that failed. Just knowing that they were made in the right direction one feels proud. It is a question of direction.

Yes, trust is many things, but first a question towards oneself – a change of direction.

We are born looking outwardly. To look inside is not part of the body organism. The body functions well; if you want to go somewhere else, it can take you. But the moment you ask "Who am I?" it flops, simply flops on the ground, not knowing what to do now because the relevant direction is not part of the so-called world.

The world consists of ten dimensions, or ten directions, rather.

Dimension is a bigger word and should not be used for direction. These ten directions are: two, upwards and downwards; and the four we know as east, west, north, and south; the remaining four are just the corners. When you draw the east-west line, the north-south line, there are corners between the north and the east, and between the east and the south, and so on – the four corners.

I should not have used the word dimension. It is totally different, as different as Devageet's sneeze. He tries to suppress it, and it is one of the most impossible things to suppress. I will suggest to him to allow it. It comes anyway; why suffer? Next time when you hear the knock, open the door and say, "Madam, come in." Perhaps it may not happen at all. Sneezes are strange things. If you try to bring one on then you will have to do all the tricks of yoga. Then too, it is only a probability. But try to suppress it and it will come on with tremendous force. It is a woman you know; and when a woman takes possession of you it is better to sneeze her out and escape, rather than suppress.

Direction and dimension are as different as his sneeze and my understanding that he is giggling. He is trying to suppress his sneeze and I was just starting to talk about the untalkable, and at that exact moment he sneezed. This is what Carl Gustav Jung calls synchronicity. Not a very great example – not exemplary I mean, but just a little example.

It is strange, but particularly in India, whenever such things are talked about – and I don't think people have talked about such things anywhere else for thousands of years – sneezing at a meeting with the master is prohibited. Why? I don't understand how you can prohibit a sneeze. A sneeze is not afraid of your cops, nor your guns. How can you prohibit it? – unless you do plastic surgery on the nose, which would not be good because a sneeze simply informs you that something wrong has entered. It should not be prevented in any way.

So I say to you, Devageet, you are my disciple, and my disciples have to be different in every way, even in sneezing. They can sneeze exactly when the master is talking about trust; there is no harm in it. But sometimes when you start repressing it, naturally it affects your breathing. It affects everything in you, and then I think that you are giggling. Then you are very shocked. In fact you should be happy that "My master, even if he misunderstands once in a while, always interprets it as a giggle."

Laughter – that can be said to be my creed, if it is allowed. I mean if the word 'creed' is allowed to be used, I don't mean a loud laughter allowed. That will be okay with me. But people are such fanatics about their creeds, they don't laugh. At least in church they have such long faces that you cannot believe they have come there to understand the man whose only message if reduced to one word would be, "Rejoice!" They are not the people to rejoice.

They must have been the people who killed the man, and are still putting fresh nails into his coffin – who knows, he may come out! They must be the people who are still hanging him, and he has been dead for two thousand years. Now there is no need to hang him, although he was intelligent enough not to be crucified. He managed to escape just in time. Of course he played the role of being crucified for the masses, and when the masses went home he also went home. I don't mean he went to God. Please don't misunderstand; he really went to his home.

The cave which is still shown to Christians, where Jesus' body was kept, is all nonsense. Yes, it was there for a few hours, perhaps a night at the most, but he was still alive. This is proved by the Bible itself. It says that a soldier pierced Jesus' side with a spear after they thought he was dead, but blood came out. Blood never comes out of a dead man. The moment a man dies his blood starts disintegrating. If the Bible had said only water had come out then I would have believed that they were writing truly, but it would have looked so stupid to write that water came out of his body. In fact Jesus never died in Jerusalem; he died in Pahalgam, which at least as far as the meaning of the word is concerned means exactly the same as the name of my village.

Pahalgam is one of the most beautiful places in the world. That is where Jesus died, and he died at the age of one hundred and twelve. But he got so fed up with his own people that he simply spread the story that he had died on the cross.

Of course he was crucified – but you have to understand that the Jewish way of crucifixion was not the American way. It was not sitting in a chair, and with just a push of a button you were no more – not even time to say, "God forgive these people who are pushing the button, they don't know what they are doing." They know what they are doing! They are pushing the button! And *you* don't know what *they* are doing!

Jesus would not have had any time if he had been crucified in the scientific way. No, it is a very crude way that the Jews followed. Naturally it sometimes even took twenty-four hours or more to die. There have been cases of people having survived for three days on the cross – the Jewish cross I mean – because they simply nailed the man by his hands and his feet.

Blood has the capacity to clot; it flows for a while, then it clots. The man is, of course, in immense pain. In fact he prays to God, "Please let it be finished." Perhaps that is what Jesus was saying when he said, "They don't know what they are doing. Why have you forsaken me?" But the pain must have been too much, for he finally said, "Let thy will be done."

I don't think that he died on the cross. No, I should not say that "I don't think…," I *know* that he didn't die on the cross. He had said, "Let thy will be done"; that's his freedom. He could say anything he wanted to say. In fact, the Roman governor, Pontius Pilate, had fallen in love with the man. Who would not? – it is irresistible if you have eyes.

But Jesus' own people were busy counting money; they had no time to look into the eyes of this man who had no money at all. Pontius Pilate for one moment had even thought to release Jesus. It was in his power to order his release, but he was afraid of the crowd. Pilate said, "It is better that I should keep out of their business. He is a Jew, they are Jews – let them decide for themselves. But if they cannot decide in his favor then I will find a way."

And he found a way, politicians always do. Their ways are always roundabout; they never go directly. If they want to go to A, they first go to B; that's how politics works. And it really works. Only once in a while it does not work. I mean, only when there is a nonpolitical man, then it does not work. In Jesus' case also, Pontius Pilate managed perfectly well without getting involved.

Jesus was crucified on the afternoon of Friday; hence "Good Friday." Strange world! Such a good man is crucified, and you call

369

it "Good Friday." But there was a reason, because Jews have…. I think, Devageet, you can help me again – not with a sneeze, of course! Is Saturday their religious day?

"Yes, Osho."

Right…because on Saturday nothing is done. Saturday is a holiday for the Jews; all action has to be stopped. That's why the Friday was chosen…and late afternoon, so by the time the sun sets the body has to be brought down, because to keep it hanging on Saturday would be "action." That's how politics functions, not religion. During that night, a rich follower of Jesus removed the body from the cave. Of course, then comes Sunday, a holiday for everybody. By the time Monday comes, Jesus is very far away.

Israel is a small country; you can cross it on foot in twenty-four hours very easily. Jesus escaped, and there was no better place than the Himalayas. Pahalgam is just a small village, just a few cottages. He must have chosen it for its beauty. Jesus chose a place which I would have loved myself.

I tried continuously for twenty years to get into Kashmir. But Kashmir has a strange law: only Kashmiris can live there, not even other Indians. That is strange. But I know ninety percent of Kashmiris are Mohammedan and they are afraid that once Indians are allowed to live there, then Hindus would soon become the majority, because it is part of India. So now it is a game of votes just to prevent the Hindus.

I am not a Hindu, but bureaucrats everywhere are delinquents. They really need to be in mental hospitals. They would not allow me to live there. I even met the chief minister of Kashmir, who was known before as the prime minister of Kashmir.

It was such a great struggle to bring him down from prime ministership to chief ministership. And naturally, in one country how could there be two prime ministers? But he was a very reluctant man, this Sheikh Abdullah. He had to be imprisoned for years. Meanwhile the whole constitution of Kashmir was changed, but that strange clause remained in it. Perhaps all the committee members were Mohammedans and none of them wanted anybody else to enter Kashmir. I tried hard, but there was no way. You cannot enter into the thick skulls of politicians.

I said to the sheikh, "Are you mad? I am not a Hindu; you need not be afraid of me. And my people come from all over the world – they will not influence your politics in any way, for or against."

He said, "One has to be cautious."

I said, "Okay, be cautious and lose me and my people."

Poor Kashmir could have gained so much, but politicians are born deaf. He listened, or at least pretended to, but he did not hear.

I said to him, "You know that I have known you for many years, and I love Kashmir."

He said, "I know you, that's why I am even more afraid. You are not a politician; you belong to a totally different category. We always distrust such people as you." He used this word, distrust – and I was talking to you about trust.

At this moment I cannot forget Masto. It was he who introduced me to Sheikh Abdullah, a very long time before. Later on, when I wanted to enter Kashmir, particularly Pahalgam, I reminded the sheikh of this introduction.

The sheikh said, "I remember that this man was also dangerous, and you are even more so. In fact it is because you were introduced to me by Masta Baba that I cannot allow you to become a permanent resident in this valley."

Masto introduced me to many people. He thought perhaps I might need them; and I certainly did need them – not for myself but for my work. But except for very few people, the majority turned out to be very cowardly. They all said, "We know you are enlightened...."

I said, "Stop, then and there. That word, from your mouth, immediately becomes unenlightened. Either you do what I say, or simply say no, but don't talk any nonsense to me."

They were very polite. They remembered Masta Baba, and a few of them even remembered Pagal Baba, but they were not ready to do anything at all for me. I am talking about the majority. Yes, a few were helpful, perhaps one percent of the hundreds of people that Masto introduced me to. Poor Masto – his desire was that I should never be in any difficulty or need, and that I could always depend on the people he had introduced me to.

I said to him, "Masto, you are trying your best, and I am even doing better than that by keeping quiet when you introduce me to these fools. If you were not there I would have caused real trouble. That man, for instance, would never have forgotten me. I control myself just because of you – although I don't believe in control, but I do it just for your sake."

Masto laughed and said, "I know. When I look at you as I am introducing you to a bigwig, I laugh inside myself thinking, 'My God, how much effort you must be making not to hit that idiot.'"

Sheikh Abdullah took so much effort, and yet he said to me, "I would have even allowed you to live in Kashmir if you had not been introduced to me by Masta Baba."

I asked the sheikh, "Why?...when you appeared to be such an admirer."

He said, "We are no one's admirer, we admire only ourselves. But because he had a following – particularly among rich people in Kashmir – I had to admire him. I used to receive him at the airport, and give him a send-off, put all my work aside and just run after him. But that man was dangerous. And if he introduced you to me, then you cannot live in Kashmir, at least while I am in power. Yes, you can come and go, but only as a visitor."

It is good that Jesus entered Kashmir before Sheikh Abdullah. He did well by coming two thousand years before. He must have been really afraid of Sheikh Abdullah. Jesus' grave is still there, preserved by the descendants of those who had followed him from Israel. Of course men like me cannot go alone, you can understand. A few people must have followed him there. Even though he went far away from Israel, they must have gone with him.

In fact the Kashmiris are the lost tribe of Hebrews of which the Jews and Christians both talk so much. The Kashmiris are not Hindu, nor of Indian origin. They are Jewish. You can see by looking at Indira Gandhi's nose; she is a Kashmiri.

She is imposing emergency rule in India – not in name but in fact. Hundreds of political leaders are behind bars. I had been telling her from the very beginning that those people should not be in parliament or assemblies or in the legislature.

There are many kinds of idiots, but politicians are the worst, because they also have power. Journalists are number two. In fact they are even worse than politicians, but because they have no power they can only write – and who cares what they write! Without power in your hands then you may have as much idiocy as possible, it cannot do anything.

I was introduced to Indira too by Masto, but in an indirect way. Basically Masto was a friend of Indira's father, Jawaharlal Nehru, the first prime minister of India. He was really a beautiful man, and a rare one too, because to be in politics and yet remain beautiful is not easy.

When Helen Keller met him, because she was blind, deaf and dumb, she had to touch his face. She gave the message to someone who could interpret her sign language: "Touching this man's face I feel as if I am touching a marble statue."

Many other people have written about Jawaharlal, but I don't think anything more needs to be said. This woman with no eyes, no ears and no tongue to speak with, still managed to say the most poignant statement, and in a very simple way.

It was my feeling also, when I was introduced by Masto. I was only twenty. After only one more year Masto was to leave me, so he was in a hurry to introduce me to everybody that he could. He rushed me to the prime minister's house. It was a beautiful meeting. I had not expected it to be beautiful because I had been disappointed so many times. How could I have expected that the prime minister would not just be a mean politician? He was not.

It was only by chance that, in the corridor as we were leaving and he was coming with us to say goodbye, Indira came in. At that time she was nobody, just a young girl. She was introduced to me by her father. Masto was present, of course, and it was through him that we met. But Indira may not have known Masto, or who knows? – maybe she did. The meeting with Jawaharlal turned out to be so significant that it changed my whole attitude, not only to him, but to his family too.

He talked with me about freedom, about truth. I could not believe it. I said, "Do you recognize the fact that I am only twenty years old, just a young man?"

He said, "Don't be bothered about age, because my experience is that a donkey, even if it is very old, still remains a donkey. An old donkey does not necessarily become a horse – nor even a mule, what to say of a horse. So don't you bother about age." He continued, "We can forget completely for a moment how old I am and how old you are, and let us discuss without any barriers of age, caste, creed, or position." He then said to Masto, "Baba, would you please close the door so that nobody enters. I don't even want my own private secretary."

And we talked of such great things! It was I who was surprised, because he listened to me with as much attention as you. And he had such a beautiful face as only the Kashmiris can have. Indians are certainly a little dark, and the more you move downwards towards the south the darker they become, until finally you come to a point when you see, for the first time in your life, what black means.

But Kashmiris are really beautiful. Jawaharlal certainly was, for two reasons. My own feeling is that the white man, just a white man, looks a little shallow, because whiteness has no depth. That's why all the Californian girls are trying to get their skins a little suntanned. They understand that when the skin is suntanned it starts having a certain depth which white skin cannot have. But black is too suntanned, burned. There is no question of depth, it is death. But Kashmiris are exactly in the middle: they are white people, very beautiful people, suntanned from their very birth, and they are Jews.

I have seen Jesus' grave in Kashmir, where he escaped to after his so-called crucifixion. I say so-called because it was managed so well. The whole credit goes to Pontius Pilate. And when Jesus was allowed to escape from the cave, naturally the whole question was, "Where to go?" The only place outside Israel where he could be at ease was Kashmir, because it was a small Israel. And it is not only Jesus who is buried in Kashmir, but Moses too.

That will shock you even more. I have been to his grave too. I am a grave-digger. Moses had been nagged, naturally, by other Jews asking, "Where is the lost tribe?"

One tribe was missing after their forty years' long journey in the desert. Moses mismanaged that too: if he had gone to the left instead of to the right, the Jews would have been the oil kings now.

But Jews are Jews; you cannot predict what they will do. Moses traveled for forty years from Egypt to Israel.

I am neither a Jew nor a Christian, and it is none of my concern. But still, just out of curiosity, I wonder why he chose Israel. Why did Moses search for Israel? In fact he must have been searching for a beautiful place, but old age comes, and after a tedious journey, forty years in the desert....

I could not have done it. Forty years! I cannot do it for even forty hours. I cannot. I would rather commit hara-kiri. You know hara-kiri? It is the Japanese way of disappearing; in ordinary language, suicide.

Moses traveled for forty years and ultimately came to Israel, and that dusty, ugly place, Jerusalem. And after all this – Jews are Jews – they nagged him to travel again in search of the lost tribe. My own feeling is that he went just to get rid of these fellows. But where to look? The most beautiful place that was close was the Himalayas, and he reached the same valley.

It is good that Moses and Jesus both died in India. India is neither Christian, and certainly not Jewish. But the man – or the families to be exact – who take care of the two graves, are Jewish, and both graves are made in the Jewish way. Hindus do not make graves, as you know. Mohammedans do, but in a different way. A Mohammedan grave has to point towards Mecca; the head has to be towards Mecca. These are the only two graves in Kashmir which are not made according to the Mohammedan rules.

But the names are certainly not exactly what you might expect. In Arabic, Moses is called Mosha, and the name on his grave is Mosha. Jesus in Arabic is just the same in Aramaic, Yeshu, from the Hebrew, Joshua; and it is written in the same way. It may mislead you. You might not think Yeshu is Jesus, nor that Mosha is Moses. Moses is only an English – what to say – mispronunciation of the original, just as Jesus is.

Joshua will certainly slowly become Yeshu. Joshua is too much; Yeshu will do, and that is exactly how we call Jesus in India: Isu – pronounced Eesu. We have added something to the beauty of the name. "Jesus" is good, but you know what has been made out of it. When one wants to curse, one says "Jesus!" The sound certainly has something cursing in it. Try to curse somebody by saying "Joshua!" and you will find difficulty. The word itself prevents you. It is so feminine, so beautiful, and so round that you cannot hit anybody with it.

What's the time?

"Twenty past eleven, Osho."

That's good, finish it.

Session 39

DEVAGEET, I THINK YOU ARE being affected by something. You have to be unaffected, right?

"Right."

...Otherwise who is going to write the notes? The writer has to be, at least, the writer.

Okay. These tears are for you, that's why they are on the right side. Ashu missed. A little one is coming on the left for her also. I cannot be too hard. Unfortunately I have only got two eyes, and there is Devaraj, for whom I will weep from both eyes together. He is of those few for whom I have been waiting, and not in vain. That is not my way. When I wait, it has to happen. If it does not happen, that only means that I was not really waiting, nothing else. Now, back to the story.

I never wanted to meet Pandit Jawaharlal Nehru, the father of Indira Gandhi, for two reasons. I had told Masto, but he would not listen. He was just the right man for me. Pagal Baba had really chosen the right man for a wrong man. I have never been right in anybody's eyes, but Masto was. Except for me, nobody knew he was laughing like a child. But that was a private affair, and there were many private things which I have to make public now.

We argued for days whether I should go to see the first prime minister of India. I was as reluctant as ever. The moment you ask me to go anywhere, even to God's house, I will say, "We will think it over," or, "We could invite him for tea."

We argued to no end, but he not only understood the arguments, but who was arguing, and he was more concerned with that.

He said, "You can say whatever you like, but," as he always said when he could not convince me with rational argument, "Pagal Baba has told me to do this, so now it is up to you."

I said, "If you say that Pagal Baba told you, then let it be so. If he was alive I would not leave him in peace so easily, but he is no more, and one does not argue with a dead man, particularly a loved one."

He used to laugh and say, "What happened to your argument?"

I said, "Now, you shut your mouth up. The moment you bring Pagal Baba in, a dead man out of his grave, just to win an argument.... And you have not won either; I have simply given up. Do what you have been arguing about with me for these last three days."

But those arguments were tremendously beautiful, very minute, subtle and far reaching – but that is not the point, at least not for today. Perhaps in some other circle....

The thing Masto was insisting upon was that I should see the prime minister, because one never knows, perhaps someday I might need his help. "And," I added, "perhaps...." *(rattling noise from the air conditioner)*

This is the devil I was telling you about who types poor Devageet's notes during the night. Look, now he is typing directly. Even Ashu is laughing because she does not know what to do. Perhaps nobody knows.

(the noise stops) Great! I had to stop talking myself, that's why he has stopped. If I speak again, unless something is done, he will start again. *(rattling noise again)* This is too much! Typing during the night, in the dark, is okay....

What was I saying?

"That Masto insisted you should meet the prime minister, because one never knows, you may need his help one day."

I said to Masto, "Please make a small addition to it, that perhaps someday the prime minister may need my help. I am willing to go, because if Baba told you, then it is not so much trouble as having to disappoint the poor old Baba. Okay. But Masto, have you got the guts to also make the addition?"

Although a little hesitantly, he rose to his full height and said, "Yes, one day, not only perhaps but certainly, he or somebody else who occupies that chair is going to need your help. Now come with me."

I was only twenty at that time, and I asked Masto, "Have you told Jawaharlal my age? He is old, and the prime minister of one of the biggest democracies in the world, and of course he must have thousands of things on his mind. Has he got time for a boy like me? I mean a boy who is not even conventional – I mean, from a convent."

I was really unconventional. First, I used to wear wooden sandals, which were a nuisance everywhere. In fact, they were a good declaration that I was coming, coming closer; the louder the noise, the closer I was.

My headmaster used to say, "Do whatsoever you want to do. Go and eat the apple again" – he was a Christian, that's why he said that – "or, if you want to, eat the snake too! But for God's sake don't use those wooden sandals!"

I said to him, "Show me your rule book, the one you show me every time I do anything wrong. Is there any mention of wooden sandals in it?"

He said, "My God! Who would have thought that a student would turn up wearing wooden sandals? Of course there's no mention of it in my book."

I said, "Then you will have to inquire at the Ministry of Education, but until they pass a bill against using wooden sandals in school and let the whole world laugh at the foolishness of it, I'm not going to change. I am a very law-abiding person."

The headmaster said, "I know you are very law-abiding, at least in this matter you are. It is good that you don't insist that I should wear these wooden monsters too."

I said, "No. I am a very democratic man too; I never force anything on anybody. You could come naked, and I would not even ask, 'Sir, where are your pants?'"

He said, "What!"

I said, "I am just saying 'suppose,' the way you do when you come into class and say, 'Suppose, just suppose....' I'm not saying that you should actually come naked...you don't have the guts to actually do it."

(*rattling noise again*) Only Asheesh can help, because perhaps the devil may understand Italian, and no other language. That's good. What was I saying?

"You were telling the headmaster that he didn't have the guts to come without his pants."

Yes. I said to him, "It's only a supposition, just the way you say to the class 'Suppose....' We never ask whether it is real or not, so don't ask me. Suppose you come without your pants. Now I make some more additions: without a shirt, or even without your underwear...."

He said, "You! Simply get out of here!"

I said, "I cannot, unless you tell me that I may use my wooden sandals. Wood is natural, and I am a nonviolent man so I cannot use leather. So either I have to follow you, and use leather as you do – although you call yourself a brahmin, but with those shoes, with what face can you call yourself a brahmin? – or I have to use the wooden sandals."

He said, "Do whatsoever you want to do. Just go away as far as you can, as quickly as possible, because I may do something which I may repent my whole life."

I asked him, "Do you think you could kill me just because of my wooden sandals?"

He said, "No more questions, don't provoke me. But I must tell you that when I hear the sound" – because all the floors in the school were paved with stone – "I can hear you from anywhere in the building. In fact it is impossible not to hear you because you are continuously moving – I don't know why – and that noise just knocks me out of my senses."

I said, "That is your problem. I am going to use the sandals." And I used them until I left the university. For my whole life, from high school to university, I used wooden sandals. Anybody could have told you about me because I was the only person with wooden sandals. Everybody used to say, "You can hear him from miles away."

I loved those wooden sandals. As far as I was concerned I loved them because I used to go for long walks for miles, in the morning and at night, and with a wooden sandal.... I don't think any of you has the experience of wooden sandals, but it sounds as if somebody is walking behind you, and although you know it is only your sandals making the noise, who knows – perhaps, maybe…why take a chance? Just have a look. One wants to look back to see who is following. It took me years to train myself not to do such a stupid thing, and even longer not to even think of doing such a stupid thing.

I told Masto, "I have always been reluctant, even about things which anybody else would agree to easily."

But to say yes came to me very late. I went on saying no, no, until all the no's turned into a YES – but I was not waiting for it.

Now, this has become a distraction. In fact, everything in this series is going to be a distraction of some sort, but I will try to come back again and again to the same point from where we were distracted.

I agreed. Masto and I went to the prime minister's house. I didn't know how many people respected Masto, because I did not know much of the world anyway. I asked him on the way there, "Have you made an appointment?"

He laughed and didn't say anything. I thought to myself, "If he isn't worried, why should I be concerned? It is none of my business; I am only going with him."

But he needed no appointment, it became clear as we entered the gate. The policeman fell at his feet saying, "Masta Baba, you have not been for months, and we love to see you. Once in a while the prime minister needs your blessing."

Masto laughed but didn't say anything. We entered. The secretary touched his feet and said, "You should have just phoned and we would have sent you the prime minister's car. And who is this boy?"

Masto said, "I have brought this boy to be introduced only to Jawaharlal and to nobody else. And please remember, nothing about him is to be mentioned in any way."

Although he took every care, still my principle worked. I have told you the moment you create a friend, immediately you create an enemy. If you don't want the enemy then forget about the friends. That is the way of the monk, Buddhist and Christian: forgetting all about relationship, friendship and everything, so that you don't create enemies. But to just not create enemies is not the purpose of life.

You will be surprised as I was – but not that day, only after many years.... That day it was not possible for me to recognize the man sitting in the secretary's office waiting for his appointment. I had not heard of him then, but he looked very arrogant. I thought he must be somebody powerful. I asked Masto, "Who is this man?"

Masto said, "Forget all about him; he is nothing of much value. He is Morarji Desai."

I said, "He is of no value?"

Masto said, "I mean, of any real value. He is just hocus-pocus. Of course he is a cabinet minister – and look at him: he is very angry because it is his time to be with the prime minister."

But Masto was known, and the prime minister called him first and told Morarji Desai to wait. That was an insult, unintended on the part of Jawaharlal, but Morarji perhaps has not forgotten it even to this day. He may not remember the young boy, but he must be able to remember Masto. Masto was very impressive in every way.

We went in, and it was not just for five minutes; it took us exactly one hour and thirty minutes. And Morarji Desai had to wait. Now, that was too much for him. It was his appointment, and somebody else, a sannyasin with a young boy, entered before him...and then he had to wait for ninety minutes!

And for the first time in my life I was surprised, because I was not there to meet a poet, but a politician. I met a poet.

Jawaharlal was not a politician. Alas, he could not succeed in bringing his dreams to reality. But whether one says "alas" or "aha," a poet is always a failure. Even in his poetry he is a failure. To be a failure is his destiny, because he longs for the stars. He cannot be satisfied with the small, the finite. He wants to have the whole sky in his hands.

I was completely taken aback. Even Jawaharlal could see it, and he said, "What happened? The boy looks as if he has had a shock."

Masto, without even looking at me, said, "I know that boy. That's why I have brought him to you. In fact if it had been in my power, I would have taken you to him."

Now it was the turn for Jawaharlal to be taken aback. But he was a man of tremendous culture; he looked at me again so that he could measure the meaning of Masto's words. For a moment we looked into each other's eyes, and we both laughed. And his laughter was not that of an old man; it was still that of a child. He was immensely beautiful, and when I say this I mean it, because I have seen thousands of beautiful people, but I can say without hesitation that he was the most beautiful of them all, and not only in his body.

It is strange: we talked of poetry, and Morarji was waiting outside. We talked of meditation, and Morarji was waiting outside. I can still see the scene – he must have been fuming. In fact that day decided and sealed our enmity. Not from my side, of course; I have nothing against him. All his concerns are just stupid, not worth being against. Yes, once in a while he is good to laugh at. That's what I have done with his name, and his urine therapy – drinking your own urine. He was in America preaching it. Nobody asks whether he drinks his own or somebody else's, because when a person drinks urine he is already out of his senses, so that now he could drink anything – what to say of somebody else's urine. And he was teaching there, sermonizing.

That day he became an enemy to me, but on my part at least, it was unknowingly. It was just because he had to wait for one and a half hours. He must have come to know who I was from the secretary, perhaps asking, "Who is that boy? And why is he being introduced to the prime minister? What is the purpose of it? And why is Masta Baba taking an interest in him?"

Of course, sitting there for one and a half hours you have to talk about something. I can understand it, but it was the most difficult thing for him to swallow – even him, who can swallow his own urine. That's a great feat, but a greater thing to swallow than that was when he saw Jawaharlal come out to the porch just to say goodbye to this twenty-year-old boy.

At that moment he saw that it was not Masta Baba with whom the prime minister was speaking, but this strange, unknown boy with wooden sandals, making a noise all over the veranda – it was a beautiful marble veranda. And I had long hair and a strange robe that I had made myself, because my sannyasins who now make my clothes were not there yet. Nobody was there....

I had made a very simple long robe, with just two holes for the hands to come out whenever they were needed, and they could go in whenever you wanted them in. I had made it myself. There was nothing artful in it; all that had been needed was just to sew a piece of cloth on two sides, and to cut a small neck hole.

Masto liked it, so he had somebody make one for him too.

I told him, "You should have asked me."

He said, "No, that would be too much. I would not be able to use it, because I would rather preserve it."

We came out of the house which was later to become famous as "Trimurti." It is now a museum to the memory of Jawaharlal. Jawaharlal was really great, in the sense that he need not have come out to give a send-off to a young boy, and to then stand there and close the door of the car and wait until the car had left.

And all this was watched by this poor fellow, Morarji Desai. He is a cartoon, but that cartoon became my enemy for my whole life. Although he could not harm me in any way, he tried his best, I must say.

What's the time?

"Eight twenty-one, Osho."

Ten minutes for me, then I have to go to work. My office starts after this.

Session 40

          . . .

I AM STANDING – STRANGE, BECAUSE I am supposed to be relaxing
– I mean in my memory, I am standing with Masto. Of course
there is nobody with whom I would rather stand. After Masto,
with anybody else it would be poor, bound to be.

That man was really rich in every cell of his being, and in every
fiber of his vast net of relationships that he slowly made me aware
of. He never introduced me to the whole; that was not possible. I
was in a hurry to do what I call not-doing. He was in a hurry to do
what he called his responsibility towards me, as he had promised
Pagal Baba. We were both in a hurry, so as much as he wanted to he
could not make all his relationships available to me. There were
other reasons also.

He was a traditional sannyasin – at least on the surface, but I
knew him underneath. He was not traditional, but only pretending
to be because the crowds wanted that pretense. And only today can
I understand how much he must have suffered. I have never suffered
like that because I simply refused to pretend.

You cannot believe, but thousands of people were expecting
from me something of their own imaginations. I had nothing to do
with it. The Hindus, among my millions of followers – I am talking
about the days before I started my work – they believed that I was
Kalki. Kalki is the Hindu *avatara*, the last.

I have to explain it a little, because it will help you to understand many things. In India, the ancient Hindus believed in only
ten incarnations of God. Naturally – those were the days when people used to count on their fingers – ten was the ultimate. You could
not go beyond ten; you had to begin again from one. That's why the

Hindus believed that each cycle of existence has ten avataras. The word 'avatara' means literally "descending of the divine." Ten, because after the tenth, one cycle, or circle, ends. Another immediately begins, but then there is again a first avatara, and the story continues up to the tenth.

You will be able to understand me easily if you have seen poor Indian farmers counting. They count on their fingers up to the tenth; then they start again from one, two.... Ten must have been the primitive ultimate. It is strange that as far as languages are concerned, it still is. Beyond ten there isn't anything; eleven is a repetition. Eleven is just putting one behind one, making them married, putting them in trouble, that's all. After ten, all your numbers are just repetitions.

Why are the numbers up to ten so original? – because everywhere man has counted on his fingers.

I should mention, by the way, before I go on – just a little distraction before I settle – your words in English for one, two, three, four, five, six, seven, eight, nine, ten, are all borrowed from Sanskrit.

Mathematics owes much to Sanskrit, because without these numbers there would have been no Albert Einstein, no atomic bomb either; no *Principia Mathematica* by Bertrand Russell and Whitehead. These numbers are the basic bricks.

And the foundations were laid down nowhere else but in the valleys of the Himalayas. Perhaps they encountered the immeasurable beauty and tried to measure it. Perhaps there was some other reason, but one thing is certain: that the Sanskrit word *tri* becomes three in English. It has just traveled the long, dusty journey of a word. The Sanskrit *sasth* becomes six in English; the Sanskrit *asth* becomes eight, and so on and so forth.

What was I saying?

"You were talking about the Hindus thinking you were the tenth incarnation of the avatara Kalki."

Yes. You are doing well.

Kalki is the tenth and the last Hindu incarnation of God. After him the world ends – and of course begins again, just as you demolish a house made of playing cards, then start afresh. Perhaps before starting you reshuffle the cards just to create a little enthusiasm in yourself; otherwise, what does it matter to the cards? But by reshuffling them you feel good.

Exactly like that, God reshuffles and starts thinking, "Perhaps this time I will do a little better." But every time, whatever he does, out comes Richard Nixon, Adolf Hitler, Morarji Desai.... I mean God fails every moment.

Yes, once in a while he does not fail – but perhaps the credit should go to man, because he succeeds in a world where everything is failing. Certainly the credit cannot be given to God. The world is enough proof that God is utterly discredited.

Hindus have continued to use ten as the ultimate since before the time of the *Rigveda* – that is about ten thousand years ago. But Jainas, who are far more mathematical and logical and also older than the Hindus, never believed in the sanctity of ten. They had their own idea. Of course they also derived it from some source. If you cannot derive it from your own fingers, somebody must have done it some other way, from some other source.

What the Jainas did has never been discussed clearly, and I cannot support it from any scripture because I am mentioning it perhaps for the first time. I am adding "perhaps," in case somebody may have done it before and I do not know about it. But I know almost all the scriptures that are worth knowing. I simply ignored the others. But still, I may have ignored somebody in the crowd who should not have been ignored; hence I used the word 'perhaps', otherwise I am certain that nobody has said it before. So let us say it now.

The Jainas believe in twenty-four masters, *tirthankaras* as they call them. Tirthankara is a beautiful word; it means "one who makes a place for your boat from where it can take you towards the other shore." That is the meaning of *tirth,* and tirthankara means "one who makes such a place from which many, many people can go to the other shore, the further shore." But they believe in twenty-four. Their creation is also a circle, but a bigger one, naturally. Hindus have a small circle of ten; Jainas have a bigger circle of twenty-four. The radius is bigger.

Even Hindus, without knowing what they were doing, became impressed by the number twenty-four, because Jainas would tell them, "You have only ten? – we have twenty-four." Just like a child's psychology: "How big is your daddy? Only five feet? My daddy is six feet. Nobody is bigger than my daddy" – and this "god" is nothing but a form of daddy.

Jesus was exactly right; he used to call him *Abba,* which can only be translated as "daddy," not "god." You can understand it: abba is just a word of love and respect; father is not.

The moment you say "father," something serious immediately happens to you, and even to the person you are calling father, because he has to be a father. Perhaps that is why the Christians call their priests father; daddy would not fit, and abba makes children laugh – nobody would take him seriously.

The Hindus came from outside India. They are not original to the country; they are foreigners, without passports. And for centuries they went on coming from central Asia, from where all the European races have also come: the French, the English, the German, the Russian, the Scandinavian, the Lithuanian...and so on. All the "ians" came from Mongolia, which today is almost a desert. Nobody bothers about Mongolia. Nobody even thinks it is a country. Part of it belongs to China, most of it belongs to Russia, and they are continuously fighting a cold war about where to draw the line, because Mongolia is just a desert.

But all these people, particularly the Aryans, came from Mongolia. They came to India because Mongolia had suddenly started turning into a desert, and they were growing in population in the Indian way. They had to move in every direction. It was good. That's how all these countries came into existence.

But before the Aryans reached India it was already a very cultured country. It was not like Europe. When the Aryans reached Germany or England, they had nobody to fight there; they found beautiful land without anybody to be afraid of. But in India the story was different. The people who lived in India before the Aryans entered must have been really civilized. I mean really, not just living in cities.

Two cities of those days have been excavated: Mohenjodaro in Pakistan, which was once part of India, and Harappa. These cities show strange things: they had wide streets, sixty feet wide; three-storied buildings; bathrooms – yes, attached to the bedroom. Even today millions in India are not aware that such a thing exists. In fact, if you told them they would laugh, they would think you were a little insane – having a bathroom attached to your bedroom? Are you mad?

The latest designer would certainly look a little mad, even to you, because the latest design from Scandinavia is a bathroom with a bedroom included in it. The whole thing takes on a different meaning. It is basically a bathroom, and the bedroom is just in the corner, not even separated. The bathroom is more basic; it has a small swimming pool, and everything you need, and also a bed…but the bathroom is not attached to the bedroom, the bed is inside the bathroom.

Perhaps this may be the future shape of things, but if you tell it to the millions in India…! I was the only one in the whole village – my grandfather's village where I lived for so long – who had a bathroom attached to his bedroom, and people made jokes about it. They used to ask me, "Do you really have a bathroom attached to your bedroom?" And they would say it in a whisper.

I would say, "There is no need to hide it. Yes – so what?"

They said, "We cannot believe it, because nobody in these parts has ever heard of a bathroom attached to a bedroom. This must be your grandmother. That woman is dangerous. She must have brought this idea. She does not belong to us, of course; she came from some faraway place. We have heard stories about her birthplace which we would not tell to a child. We should not tell them to you."

I said to them, "You need not worry. You can tell me, because she herself tells me."

They would say, "Look, we told you so! She is a strange woman from Khajuraho. That place cannot produce right people."

Perhaps something of my Nani has created in me what they called "wrong," and I call "right."

The Hindus are not, as they claim, the oldest religion in the world. The Jainas are, but they are a very small minority, and very cowardly. But they brought the idea of twenty-four. Why twenty-four? I have wondered. I discussed it with Masto, with my mother, and with my so-called mother-in-law, about whom I will talk sometime later. Nobody called her my mother-in-law in front of me, because both were dangerous. After my Nani, she was certainly the most daring woman I have known. Of course I cannot give her the first place.

It was a joke that she was called my mother-in-law, but if you look at the words, mother-in-law...she was almost a mother to me, if not by nature, then by law. It was not that I was married to her daughter, although her daughter was in love with me. Of that in some other circle, because that is a very vicious circle, and I don't want to start it right now.

What is the time?

"Ten-thirty, Osho."

That's great. Just ten minutes for me. It has been beautiful.

(Osho begins to chuckle. He tries to explain what He is laughing at... but He is laughing too much.)

Session 41

OKAY. I COULD NOT EVEN begin to tell you what I wanted to tell you. Perhaps it was not meant to be, because I tried so many times to bring myself to the point, but in vain, and then everything went sane. But it was a most fruitful session, although nothing was said, and nothing was heard either. There was so much laughter, but I felt imprisoned.

You must have been wondering why I laughed. It is good that there is no mirror in front of me. You must arrange a mirror; at least that will make this place what it is meant to be. But it was really good. I am relieved. I have not laughed perhaps for years. Something in me must have waited for this morning, but I was not making any effort in that direction, at least not today – perhaps someday.

Sometimes these circles overlap each other, and they are going to do that again and again. I try my best to keep clear-cut directions, but those circles, they just go on trying to encircle everything they can. They are mad people, or who knows – perhaps they are buddhas again trying to have a glimpse of the old world, to see how things are going now. But that is not my purpose. I could not get where I was trying to go, and I laughed instead of continuing in spite of your laughter.

Now, these are just the introductions, but I became aware of one thing this morning – not that I was not aware of it before, but I was not aware that it needed to be told. But now it needs to be told.

On the 21st of March 1953, a strange thing happened. Many strange things happened, but I am only talking about one thing. The others will come in their own time. It is, in fact, a little early in my story to tell you, but I was reminded this morning of this peculiar thing. After that night I lost all sense of time. Howsoever hard I may try, I cannot – as everybody else can at least approximately – remember what time it is.

Not only that, in the morning, every morning I mean, I have to look out of the window to see whether it was my afternoon sleep or the night sleep, because I sleep twice each day. And every afternoon too, when I wake up, the first thing I do is to look at my clock. Once in a while the clock plays a joke on me; it stops working. It is showing only six, so it must have stopped in the morning. That's why I have two watches and a clock, just to keep checking to see whether any of them is playing a joke.

And one of the other clocks is more dangerous, better not to mention it. I want to give it to somebody as a present, but I have not found the right man to whom I would like to give this clock, because it is going to be a real punishment, not a present. It is electronic, so whenever the electricity goes off, even for a single moment, the clock goes back to twelve and flashes it: 12...12...12...simply to show that the electricity has gone off.

Sometimes I want to throw it out, but somebody has presented it to me, and I don't throw things away easily. It is disrespectful. So I am waiting for the right person.

I have got not only one, but two such clocks, one in each room. Sometimes they have deceived me when I go for my afternoon sleep. I usually go at eleven-thirty exactly, or at the most twelve, but very rarely. Once or twice I have looked out from a peep hole in my blanket, and the clock is showing twelve, and I say to myself, "That means I have just come to bed." And I go to sleep again.

After one or two hours I again look. "Twelve," I say to myself. "Strange...today time seems to have finally stopped. Better to go to sleep rather than to find everybody else asleep." So I go to sleep again.

I have now instructed Gudia that if I am not awake by two-fifteen, she should wake me up.

She asked, "Why?"

I said, "Because if nobody wakes me I may go on sleeping forever."

Every morning I have to decide whether it is morning or

evening, because I don't know – I don't have that sense. It was lost on that date I told you.

This morning when I asked you, "What is the time?" you said, "Ten-thirty." I thought, "Jesus! This is too much. My poor secretary must have been waiting one and a half hours already, and I have not even begun my story." So I said, just to finish it, "Give me ten minutes." The real reason was that I was thinking it was night.

And Devaraj also knows; now he can understand it exactly. One morning when he accompanied me to my bathroom, I asked him, "Is my secretary waiting?" He looked puzzled. I had to close the door just so that he could be himself again. If I went on standing there in the doorway, waiting – and you know Devaraj: nobody can be so loving to me. He could not say to me that it was not nighttime. If I was asking for my secretary, then there must be some reason; and of course she was not there and it was not the time for her to come, so what should he say?

He didn't say anything. He simply kept silent. I laughed. The question must have embarrassed him, but I am telling you the truth, just because time is always a problem for me. Somehow I go on managing, by using strange devices. Just look at this device: has any buddha spoken like this?

I was telling you that Jainism is the most ancient religion. It is not a value to me, remember it, it is a *dis*value. But a fact is a fact; value or disvalue, that is our attitude. Jainism is rarely known in the West, and not only in the West, but even in the East, except for a few parts of India. The reason is that the Jaina monks are naked. They cannot move into communities which are not already Jaina. They would be stoned, killed, even in the twentieth century.

The British government, which remained in India until 1947, had a special law for Jaina monks, that before they enter a city, their followers had to ask for permission. Without a permit they can't enter. And even with a permit they cannot enter great cities like Bombay, New Delhi or Calcutta. Their followers should surround them in such a way that nobody can see that they are naked.

I am using "they" because a Jaina monk is not allowed to travel alone. He has to travel with a group of monks, at least five; that is the minimum limit. The limit is placed so that they can spy on each other. It is a very what you would call "suspicious" religion – suspicious naturally, because everything it prescribes to be done is unnatural.

It is winter and one is shivering, and would like to sit by the side of a fire – but a Jaina monk cannot sit by the side of a fire, because fire is violence. Fire kills, because trees are needed for it, so they are killed. The ecologists perhaps may agree. And when you are burning a fire, many very small creatures, alive but invisible to the naked eye, are burned. And sometimes even the wood carries ants within it, and other kinds of insects which have made their houses in it.

So, in short, the Jaina monk is not allowed to come close to a fire. Of course he cannot use a blanket – it is made of wool; that is again violence. Of course something else could be found, but because he cannot possess anything.... Nonpossessiveness is very fundamental, and the Jainas are extremists. They have taken the logic of nonpossessing to its very extreme.

It is really a sight to see a Jaina monk: one can see what logic can do to a man. He is ugly, because he is undernourished: just bones, almost dead; just his belly is big, though his whole body is shrunken. That is strange, but you can understand. It happens wherever there is famine and people are starving. You must have seen pictures of children with big bellies – such big bellies, and all their limbs, hands and legs, are just bones covered by skin, and that too not very beautiful...almost dead skin. The same happens to a Jaina monk.

Why? I can understand because I have known both. The bellies of both starving children and Jaina monks immediately became my interest. Why? – because they both have the same kind of bellies, and also their bodies are similar. Their faces too are similar. Forgive me for saying it, but their faces are faceless; they don't say anything, they don't show anything. They are not only empty pages, but pages which have waited and waited for something to be written on them, to make them significant...but they became sore because nobody ever came.

They became so bitter against the world that they turned over – rolled over rather, because I am using the page as a symbol – they rolled over and closed themselves against any future possibilities.

The starving child has to be helped; the Jaina monk has to be helped more, because he thinks that what he is doing is right.

But an ancient religion is bound to be very stupid. This very stupidity is a proof of its ancientness. *Rigveda* mentions the first Jaina master, Rishabhdeva. He is thought to be the founder of the religion. I can't say for sure because I don't want to blame anybody, particularly Rishabhdeva, whom I have never met – and I don't think that I will ever meet him either.

If he was really the founder of this stupid cult, then I am the last person he would like to meet. But that is not the point; the point is that the Jainas have a different calendar. They count their days not by the sun, but by the moon, naturally, because their year is divided into twenty-four parts, so they have twenty-four tirthankaras. Their whole creation is the circle in the image of a year but moon-oriented, just as there are sun-oriented people. It is all arbitrary. In fact the whole thing, at this moment, according to me, is stupid.

Just look at the English calendar and see the stupidity, then you will understand me. It is easy to laugh at the Jainas because you don't know anything about them. They must be idiots. But what about the English calendar? How come one month has thirty days, another month has thirty-one days, one month twenty-nine days, another month twenty-eight days? What is all this nonsense? And the year has three hundred and sixty-five days, not because you have made a calendar according to the sun – it is not because of the sun.

Three hundred and sixty-five days is only the time it takes the earth to complete its journey around the sun. How you divide it is up to you – but three hundred and sixty-five…? Three hundred and sixty-five days has created trouble, because it is not exactly three hundred and sixty-five; there is also lingering behind a small part which becomes one day every fourth year. That means three hundred and sixty-five and one-fourth days should be the whole year. A very strange year!

But what can you do about it? You just have to manage, so you divide the different months into different numbers of days, and February has to be one day more every four years. A strange calendar! I think no computer would allow this kind of nonsense.

There are, just like sun-oriented fools, moon-oriented fools too.

They are really lunatics because they believe in the lunar. Then, of course, the year is divided into twelve parts, and each month has two divisions. And these fools are always great philosophers; they go on building up strange hypotheses. This was their hypothesis in the Jaina tradition of fools. I mean all traditions are foolish, this is only one tradition of fools.

The Jainas believe that there are twenty-four tirthankaras, and each cycle will again and again have twenty-four tirthankaras. Now, Hindus felt belittled. People started asking, "You have only ten, not twenty-four?"

Naturally the Hindu priests started talking of twenty-four *avataras*. It is a borrowed foolishness. In the first place, foolishness; in the second place, borrowed. That is the worst thing that can happen to anybody. And this has happened to a great country of millions of people.

This disease was so infectious that when Buddha died the Buddhists felt naturally very deceived, or what do you say? – put down, belittled, humiliated. Why had he not told them about the figure twenty-four? "Jainas have it, Hindus have it...and we have only one buddha." So they created twenty-four buddhas who preceded Gautam the Buddha.

Now, you can see how far nonsense can go. Yes, it can go on and on.... That's what I mean, but I have to end the sentence. Remember, that does not mean that I am putting a full stop on nonsense; it has no end.

If you are stupid, you are as infinitely stupid as they say God is wise. I don't know anything about God and his wisdom, but I know about your foolishness. That's what I am here to do: just to help you get rid of the stupidity you are now carrying. First the Jainas carried it, then Hindus borrowed it, then Buddhists borrowed it, then the number twenty-four became an absolute necessity.

I have seen one man, Swami Satyabhakta. He is one of those rare people whom I always have wondered why existence tolerated at all. He thought that he was the twenty-fifth tirthankara. Mahavira was the twenty-fourth. Of course Jainas could not forgive Satyabhakta and they expelled him.

I told him, "Satyabhakta, if you want to be a tirthankara, why can't you be the first? Why stand in a queue just trying hard for your whole life to be the twenty-fifth, the last? Just look behind you: there is nobody there."

He made great effort, and worked very hard writing hundreds of books – and he was very scholarly. That also proves that he is a fool – but not an ordinary fool, an extraordinary fool.

I told him, "Why don't you create your own religion if you have known the truth?"

He said, "That's the problem, I'm not certain."

I said, "Then at least don't bother others. First be certain. Wait, let me call your wife."

He said, "No, no!"

I said, "Wait. I am calling your wife. You cannot stop me."

But I need not have called; she had come already. In fact I had seen her coming, that's why I had said, "Don't stop me." Nobody could have stopped her; she was already coming. I don't mean the word 'coming' as you Westerners mean it. She was really coming, and she came with great force.

I mean that she really came in with great force, and she asked me, "Why are you wasting time with this fool? I have wasted my whole life, and not only lost everything, but even my religion. Just because he has been expelled, naturally I am expelled too. One is born a Jaina only after millions of lives, and this fool has not only fallen himself, he has degraded me. It is good that he is impotent and we don't have any children; otherwise they would have been expelled too."

I was the only one who laughed, and I told them, "Laugh. This is wonderful. You are impotent. I am not saying it, your wife is. I don't know how much she knows about gynecology, but if she is saying it, and you are listening without even raising your eyes, it is proof enough that she is a gynecologist. You are impotent, great! You are not even able to make your wife your follower, and yet you are trying to prove to be the twenty-fifth tirthankara! This is really amusing, Satyabhakta."

He never forgave me, just because I found him exactly at the right moment. Satyabhakta is still an enemy, although I sympathize with him. At least he can say that he has an enemy. As far as a friend is concerned, he has none – and the credit goes to his wife.

In the same way Morarji Desai became my enemy. I have nothing against him, but just because he had to wait ninety minutes for a young boy of no political importance at all, naturally he was immensely offended. When he saw the prime minister opening the door of the car for the boy.... I can still see the scene – how to describe it? There was something very slimy, slippery, about the man. You could not catch hold of it. It slips again and again, and every time it slips it becomes more and more dirty. There was something slimy and slippery in his eyes, I remember. I saw him later, on three other occasions. Some other circle may cover them.

Very good. After such an experience only "no" can be any good, because there is nothing like no.

Very good.

Devageet, stop it. I have other things to do. Gudia has opened the door to remind me.

Session 42

OKAY. WHAT WAS I TELLING you? I cannot remember it, remind me.

"We were talking about how Morarji Desai and Satyabhakta became your enemies, and the last thing you said was that Morarji Desai had something in his eyes that was slimy and slippery, which you remember."

Good. It is better to not remember it. Perhaps that's why I cannot remember; otherwise my memory is not bad, at least nobody has told me that. Even those who don't agree with me say that my memory is just impossible to believe. When I was moving around the country, I remembered thousands of people's names, their faces; and not only that, but when I met them again I immediately remembered where we had last met, what I had said to them, what they had said to me – it may have been ten or fifteen years before. Naturally the man would be astonished. It is good that at least my memory fails exactly where it should, at Morarji Desai, that is.

You cannot believe that even God makes caricatures. I have heard he made creatures, but caricatures? Specially made for cartoonists? Morarji is a walking cartoon. But I had not laughed at him; I was so full of the strange meeting between a boy and the prime minister, and the way they talked together. I still cannot believe that a prime minister could talk that way. He was almost just a listener, only asking questions so that the conversation would continue. It seemed he wanted it to continue forever, because many times the door opened and his personal secretary looked in. But Jawaharlal was really a good man. He had turned his chair away from the door; the personal secretary could only see his back.

Only later on did I understand, when Masto told me that this was the first time he had seen Jawaharlal put his chair this way. He said the personal secretary is meant to open the door to announce that the time for the visitor is now over, and another visitor is ready to enter.

But Jawaharlal was not bothered by anything in the world. It was as if all that he wanted to know about was *vipassana*. I was a little hesitant to tell him what vipassana is because of the situation. I will have to tell you the meaning of the word 'vipassana'. It means "looking back." *Passan* means "looking"; vipassana means "looking back."

What I am doing at this moment is vipassana.

I was knocking Masto with my leg, but he was sitting like a yogi. He was afraid I would do something like that, so he was prepared, in a way prepared for anything to happen. And I really hit him hard.

He said, "Aargh!"

Jawaharlal said, "What is the matter?"

Masto said, "Nothing."

I said, "He is lying."

Masto said, "This is too much. You hit me, and you hit me so hard that I forget that I have to keep quiet and not become a football in your hands, and now you are telling Jawaharlal that I am lying."

I said, "Now he is not lying but telling you how you can forget, because vipassana means not forgetting." And I said to Masto, "I am explaining vipassana to Jawaharlal so I hit you hard. Please excuse me, and don't take it for granted that it was the last."

Jawaharlal really laughed...he laughed so much that tears came to his eyes. That is always the quality of a real poet, not an ordinary one. You can buy ordinary poets: perhaps in the West they are a little more costly, otherwise a dollar-a-dozen will do. He was not a poet of that type – a dollar-a-dozen. He was really one of those few rare souls whom Buddha has called *bodhisattvas*. I will call him a bodhisattva.

I was, and still am, amazed how he could become the prime minister. But the first prime minister of India was of a totally different quality from any other prime minister who was to follow. He was not chosen by the crowd; he was not, in fact, a chosen candidate. He was Mahatma Gandhi's choice.

Gandhi, whatsoever his faults, at least did one thing that even I can appreciate. This is the only thing; otherwise I am against Mahatma Gandhi point by point. But why he had to choose Jawaharlal is another story, perhaps not meant to be part of my circle. What matters to me is that at least he must have been sensitive to a poetic person. He was certainly ascetic; yet with all his nonsense he was still sensible enough to choose Jawaharlal.

That's how a poet became the prime minister; otherwise there is no possibility for a poet to become a prime minister – unless a prime minister goes mad, and becomes a poet, but that will not be the same thing.

We talked of poetry. I had thought that he would talk of politics. Even Masto, who had known him for years, was astounded that he was talking about poetry and the meaning of the poetic experience. He looked at me as if I knew the answer.

I said, "Masto, you should know better. You have known Jawaharlal for years. I did not know him at all until just now. We are still only in the process of introducing ourselves. So don't look with a questioning eye, although I understand your question: 'What has happened to the politician? Has he gone mad?' No, I say it to you, and to him also, that he is not a politician – perhaps by accident, but not by his intrinsic nature."

And Jawaharlal nodded and said, "At least one person in my life has said it exactly, as I was not able to formulate it clearly. It was vague…but now I know what has happened. It is an accident."

"And," I added, "a fatal one." And we all laughed. But I said, "The accident has been fatal, but your poet is unharmed, and I don't care about anything else. You can still see the stars as a child does."

He said, "Again! …Because I love to see the stars – but how did you come to know about it?"

I said, "I have nothing to do with it. I know what being a poet is, so I can describe you in every detail. So please, from this moment, don't be astonished. Just take it easy." And he certainly relaxed. Otherwise, for a politician to relax is impossible.

In India, the mythology is that when an ordinary person dies, only one devil comes to take him, but when a politician dies, a crowd of devils have to come because he won't relax even in death. He won't allow it. He has never allowed anything to happen of its own accord. He does not know the meaning of those simple words, 'let go'.

But this man Jawaharlal immediately relaxed. He said, "With you I can relax. And Masto has never been a source of tension to me, so he can also relax – I am not preventing him – unless being a swami, a sannyasin, a monk, prevents him."

We all laughed. And this was not the last meeting, it was only the first. Masto and I had thought it was the last, but when we were departing, Jawaharlal said, "Can you come again tomorrow at this same time? And I will keep this fellow," he said, pointing towards Morarji Desai, "away from here. Even his presence stinks, and you know of what. I am sorry, but I have to keep him in the cabinet because he has a certain political importance. And what does it matter if he drinks his own urine? It is not my business." We laughed again, and departed.

That evening, he reminded us again on the phone saying, "Don't forget. I have canceled all my other appointments and I will be waiting for you both."

We had no work to do at all. Masto had come just to make me acquainted with the prime minister, and that was done. Masto said, "If the prime minister wants it, we have to stay. We cannot say no, that would not be helpful to your future."

I said, "Don't be worried about my future. Will it be helpful to Jawaharlal or not?"

Masto said, "You are impossible." And he was right, but I came to know it too late, when it was difficult to change.

I have become so accustomed to being what I am that even in small things it is difficult for me to change. Gudia knows; she tries to teach me in every possible way not to splash water all over the bathroom. But can you teach me anything? I cannot stop. Not that I want to torture the girls, or that they have to be tortured twice every day – because I take two baths, so naturally they have to clean twice.

Of course Gudia thinks I can take a bath in such a way that they don't have to remove water from everywhere. But finally she dropped the idea of teaching me. It is impossible for me to change. When I take my shower I enjoy it so much that I forget and splash the water all over. And without splashing it I would have to remain controlled even in my bathroom.

Now look at Gudia: she is enjoying the idea because she knows exactly what I am saying. When I take a shower I really take a shower, and I splash not only the floor, but even the walls, and if you have to clean, then of course it is a problem for you. But if you clean with love, as my cleaners do, then it is better than psychoanalysis, and far better than transcendental meditation. I cannot change anything now.

Now, what Masto was talking about has happened. What was future then is now past. But I am the same, and I have remained the same. In fact to me it seems that death happens not the moment when you stop breathing, but when you stop being yourself. I have never for any reason allowed any compromise.

We went the next day, and Jawaharlal had invited his son-in-law, Indira Gandhi's husband. I wondered why he had not invited his daughter. Later on Masto said to me, "Indira takes care of Jawaharlal. His wife died young, and he has only one-child, his daughter Indira, and she has been both a daughter and a son to him."

In India, when the daughter marries she has to go to her husband's house. She becomes part of another family. Indira never went. She simply refused. She said, "My mother is dead, and I cannot leave my father alone."

This created the beginning of the end in their marriage. They remained husband and wife, but Indira was never part of Feroze Gandhi's family. Even their two sons, Sanjay and Rajiv, came to belong naturally, because of their mother, to her family.

Masto told me, "Jawaharlal cannot invite them together; they would start fighting then and there."

I said, "That's strange. Even for one hour can't they forget that they are husband and wife?"

Masto said, "It is impossible to forget even for a single moment. To be a husband or a wife means a declaration of war." Although people call it love, it is really a cold war. And it is better to have a hot war, particularly in a cold winter, than to have a cold war twenty-four hours a day. It even starts freezing your being.

We were again surprised when he invited us the third day. We had been thinking of leaving, and he had not said anything the second day. The morning of the third day Jawaharlal phoned. He had a private number which was not listed in the directory. Only a few people, those who were very close, could call him on that number.

I asked Masto, "He called us himself; can't he just tell his secretary to call us?"

Masto said, "No, this is his private number; even the secretary has no knowledge that he is inviting us. The secretary will come to know only when we reach the porch."

And that third day Jawaharlal introduced me to Indira Gandhi. He simply said to her, "Don't ask who he is, because right now he is no one, but someday he could be really somebody."

I know he was wrong. I'm still no one, and I am going to remain no one to the very end. To be a no one is so tremendously blissful; one gets really spaced. I must be one of the most spaced-out people in the world. But still, try to be no one. It is far out – just faaar out.

But nobody wants to be no one, nobody, nothing, and naturally that's why Jawaharlal was saying to Indira, "Now he is no one, but I can predict one day he certainly will be someone."

Jawaharlal, you are dead, but I am sorry to say I could not fulfill your prediction. It failed, fortunately.

And that started my friendship with Indira. She already had a high post, and soon became the president of the ruling party in India, and then a minister in Jawaharlal's cabinet, and finally prime minister. Indira is the only woman I have known who could manage these idiots, the politicians, and she managed well.

How she managed it I cannot say. Perhaps she had learned all their faults while she was a nobody, just a caretaker for old Jawaharlal. But she knew their faults so well that they were afraid of her, trembling. Even Jawaharlal could not throw this perfect idiot, Morarji Desai, out of his cabinet.

I told this to Indira in a later meeting. It may come sometime, or may not, so better that I mention it right now. These circles are not dependable. I told her in our last meeting – that was years after Jawaharlal had died; it must have been somewhere around 1968. She told me, "What you are saying is absolutely right, and I would like to do it, but what to do with people like Morarji? They are in my cabinet, and they are the majority. Although they belong to my party, they would not be able to understand if I try to implement anything you are saying. I agree, but I feel helpless."

I said, "Why don't you throw out this fellow? Who is preventing you? And if you cannot throw him out, then resign, because it does not suit a person of your caliber to work with these fools. Put them right – that is right side up, because they are doing *shirshasana*, standing on their heads. Either put them right or resign, but do something."

I have always liked Indira Gandhi. I still like her, although she has not done anything to help my work – but that's another matter. I liked her from the moment she told me, or rather whispered in my ear, although there was nobody to hear, but who knows – politicians are careful people. She whispered, "I will do something or other."

I could not figure out at that moment what she meant – "something or other." But after seven days I read in the newspaper that Morarji Desai had been suddenly thrown out. I was far away, perhaps thousands of miles.

He had just returned from a tour of his constituency to visit the prime minister, and this was his welcome – a rather strange welcome, or I should say a "well-go." Can I make a word, 'well-go'? Then they are giving a good well-go. That will be exactly what people do – who welcomes?

But I was not surprised. In fact, every day I was looking in the newspapers to see what was happening, because I had to figure out her meaning – "something or other." But she did something. She did the right thing. This man had been the most obstructive, obscurantist, orthodox, and whatnot, and anything wrong that you can think of.

What is the time, Devageet?

"Ten twenty-four, Osho."

Ten minutes for me. This is good but it can be improved. Unless you come to your perfection today I am going to be a hard taskmaster.

Go for perfection. Don't ask for continuation; perfection is the word. Although it is not heard, but still perfection is the word, heard or unheard.

Yes, unless I know that you have come to your ultimate capacity I am not going to stop – so be quick!

Good.

The moment I say good, you become afraid. I immediately see your fear and trembling. That's why, once in a while, I have to address Ashu, saying, "Don't be bothered about Devageet's fear. Just be a simple woman, without knowledge, and go to the heights. Let poor Devageet run behind." He will try hard. I can see him running to get ahead of you, that's why I laugh. Who can be behind one's own assistant?

Don't be worried: today at twelve the world is going to stop anyway. So Ashu, be quick! Before the world ends at least let me have my lunch.

Good. Stop.

Session 43

O KAY. I HAVE ALWAYS WONDERED how God could manage to make this world in only six days. And *this* world! Perhaps that's why he called his son Jesus! What a name to give to your own son! He had to punish somebody for what he had done, and there was nobody else available. The Holy Ghost is always absent; he is sitting there on the horse seat. That's why I told Chetana to vacate it, because to ride a horse with somebody already riding on it is not good – I mean not good for the horse, and not good for Chetana either. As for the Holy Ghost, I don't care a bit. I don't feel for the Holy Ghost or any other type of ghost. I'm always for the living.

A ghost is a shadow of the dead, and even if holy, what is the use? And it is ugly too. Chetana, I was not worried about the Holy Ghost. If you ride on him, it is okay as far as I am concerned. Ride on the Holy Ghost. But this poor chair is not even meant for a full person. It is not meant to be sat on. It is meant only for half a person, so that you don't fall asleep. That's why it is made in such a way.

In that chair you cannot even sit, what to say of sleeping! And even that chair could not fit in this small Noah's Ark. It is so small that Noah himself has to stand outside, just to make space for all you creatures.

What was I saying, Devageet?

"The Holy Ghost is always absent; he is now sitting on the horse seat." *(laughter)*

That I remember. I knew you could not take notes. Concentrate. But I will manage. I managed my whole life without notes.

What Jawaharlal asked me on that last day was certainly strange.

He asked, "Do you think it is okay to be in the political world?"

I said, "I don't think, I *know* it is not okay at all. It is a curse, a karma. You must have done something wrong in your past lives; otherwise you could not be the prime minister of India."

He said, "I agree."

Masto could not believe that I could answer the prime minister in such a way, nor, even more, that the prime minister would agree.

I said, "That finishes a long argument between me and Masto, in my favor. Masto, do you agree?"

He said, "Now I have to."

I said, "I never like anything that 'had to'; it is better to disagree. At least in that disagreement there will be some life. Don't give me this dead rat! In the first place, a rat – and then too, dead! Do you think I am an eagle, a vulture, or what?"

Even Jawaharlal looked at both of us in turn.

I said, "You have decided. I am thankful to you. Masto, for years, has been in a dilemma. He could not decide whether a good man should be in politics or not."

We talked of many things. I did not think in that house – I mean the prime minister's house – that any meeting would have lasted so long. By the time we ended it was nine-thirty – three hours! Even Jawaharlal said, "This must be my life's longest meeting, and the most fruitful."

I said, "What fruitfulness has it brought you?"

He said, "Just the friendship of a man who does not belong to this world, and will never belong to this world. I will cherish it as a sacred memory." And in his beautiful eyes I could see the first gathering of tears.

I rushed out, just not to embarrass him, but he followed me and said, "There was no need to rush so fast."

I said, "Tears were coming faster." He laughed and wept together.

It very rarely happens, and only either to madmen or to the really intelligent ones. He was not a madman, but superbly intelligent. We – I mean Masto and I – talked again and again about that meeting, particularly the tears and the laughter. Why? Naturally we, as always, did not agree. That had become a routine thing. If I had agreed, he would not have believed it. It would have been such a shock.

I said, "He wept for himself, and laughed for the freedom I had."

Of course, Masto's interpretation was, "He wept for you, not for himself, because he could see that you could become an important political force, and he laughed at his own idea."

That was Masto's interpretation. Now, there was no way to decide, but fortunately Jawaharlal decided it himself, accidentally. Masto told me, so there is no problem.

Before Masto left me forever to disappear in the Himalayas, and before I died the way everybody has to die to be resurrected, he told me, "Do you know, Jawaharlal has been remembering you again and again, and particularly in my last meeting with him he said, 'If you see that strange boy, and if you are in any way concerned about him, keep him out of politics, because I wasted my life with these stupid people. I don't want that boy begging votes from utterly stupid, mediocre, unintelligent masses. No, if you have any say in his life, please protect him from politics.'"

Masto said, "That decided our argument in your favor, and I'm happy because although I argued with you, and against you, deep down I always agreed with you."

I never saw Jawaharlal again, although he lived many years. But, just as he wanted it – and I had already decided it; his advice only became a confirmation of my own decision – I have never voted in my life and never been a member of any political party, never even dreamed of it. In fact, for almost thirty years I have not dreamed at all. I cannot.

I can manage a sort of rehearsal. The word will seem strange – a 'rehearsal' dream – but the actual drama never happens, cannot happen; it needs unconsciousness, and that ingredient is missing. You can make me unconscious, but still you will not make me dream. And to make me unconscious needs not much technology; just a hit over my head and I will be unconscious. But that is not the unconsciousness I am talking about.

You are unconscious when you go on doing things without knowing why – during the day, during the night – the awareness is missing. Once awareness happens, dreaming disappears. Both cannot exist together. There is no coexistence possible between these two things, and nobody can make it. Either you dream, then you are unconscious; or you are awake, aware, pretending to dream – but that is not a dream. You know and everybody else knows too.

What was I saying?

"For almost thirty years you haven't dreamed. 'I never saw Jawaharlal again, even though he lived many years.'"

Good.

There was no need to see him again, although many people approached me. Somehow they came to know through various sources, from Jawaharlal's house, secretaries or others, that I knew him and he loved me. Naturally they wanted something to be done for them, and asked if I would recommend it to him.

I said, "Are you mad? I don't know him at all."

They said, "We have solid proofs."

I said, "You can keep your solid proofs. Perhaps in some dream we have met, but not in reality."

They said, "We always thought that you were a little mad; now we know."

I said, "Spread it, please, as far and wide as possible, and don't be so conservative – just a little mad? Be generous – I am absolutely mad!"

They left without even saying thank you to me. I had to give them a thank-you, so I said, "I am a madman. At least I can give you a good thank-you."

They said to each other, "Look! A good thank-you? He *is* mad."

I loved to be known as mad. I still love it. There is nothing more beautiful than the madness I have come to know.

Masto said before he left, "Jawaharlal has given me this man's name, Ghanshyam Das Birla. He is the richest man in India, and very close to the family of Jawaharlal. In any kind of need he can be approached. And when he was giving me this address Jawaharlal said, 'That boy haunts me. I predict he can become…'" and Masto remained silent.

I said, "What is the matter? Complete the sentence at least."

Masto said, "I am going to. This silence is also his. I am simply imitating him. What you are asking me, I had asked him. Then

Jawaharlal completed the sentence. And I will tell you," Masto said, "what the reason was. Jawaharlal said, 'He may become one day...' and then came the silence. Perhaps he was weighing something inside, or was not very clear about what to say. Then he said, 'a Mahatma Gandhi.'"

Jawaharlal was giving me the greatest respect that he could. Mahatma Gandhi had been his master, and also the man who decided that Jawaharlal would be the first prime minister of India. Naturally, when Mahatma Gandhi was shot dead, Jawaharlal wept. Speaking on the radio, weeping, he said, "The light has gone out. I don't want to say anything more. He was our light; now we will have to live in darkness."

If he had said it to Masto with hesitation, then either he was thinking whether to compare this unknown boy with the world-famous mahatma, or he was perhaps weighing between the mahatma and a few other names...and I think that is more probable, because Masto told him, "If I tell that boy, he will immediately say, 'Gandhi! He is the last person in the world I would like to be. I would rather go to hell than be Mahatma Gandhi.' So it is better to let you know how he will react. I know him very deeply. He will not be able to tolerate this comparison – and he loves you; just because of this name don't destroy your lover."

I said to Masto, "This is too much, Masto. You need not have said that to him. He is old, and as far as I am concerned, he has compared me to the greatest man in his way of thinking."

Masto said, "Wait. When I said this, Jawaharlal said, 'I had suspected, that's why I waited, weighing whether to say it or not. Then don't say it to him, change it. Perhaps he may become a Gautam Buddha!'"

Rabindranath, the great Indian poet, has written that Jawaharlal very secretly loved Gautam Buddha. Why secretly? Because he never liked any organized religion, and he did not believe in God either, and Jawaharlal was the prime minister of India.

Masto said, "I then said to Jawaharlal, 'Forgive me. You have come very close, but to tell you the truth he will not like any comparison.' And do you know," Masto then asked me, "what Jawaharlal said? He said 'That is the kind of man I love and respect. But protect him by every possible means so that he does not get caught into politics, which destroyed me. I don't want that same calamity to happen again to him.' "

Masto disappeared after that. I also disappeared, so nobody is there to complain. But the memory is not consciousness, and memory can function even without consciousness, in fact more efficiently. After all, what is a computer? A memory system. The ego has died; that which is behind the ego is eternal. That which is part of the brain is temporal and will die.

Even after death I will be available to my people as much, or as little, as I am now. It all depends on them. That's why I am, by and by, disappearing from their world, so that it becomes more and more their thing.

I may be just one percent, and their love, their trust, their surrender are ninety-nine percent. But when I am gone even more will be needed – one hundred percent. Then I will be available, perhaps more, to those who can afford – write "who can afford" in capital letters – because the richest man is one WHO CAN AFFORD a one-hundred-percent surrender in love and trust.

And I have got those people. So I don't want, even after death, in any way to disappoint them. I would like them to be the most fulfilled people on earth. Whether I am here or not, I will rejoice.

Session 44

I WAS WONDERING YESTERDAY HOW GOD created this world in six days. I was wondering, because I have not yet been able to even go beyond the second day of my primary school. And what a world he created! Perhaps he was a Jew, because only Jews have circulated the idea.

Hindus don't believe in a God; they believe in many gods. In fact, when they first conceived the idea, they counted exactly as many gods as there were Indians – at that time I mean. At that time too they were not a small population: thirty-three crores, that means three hundred and thirty million – or it may not be so, but it will give you some idea of the Hindus. They believed that each single individual had to have a god of his own. They were not dictatorial, but very democratic; in fact too much so – I mean the previous Hindus.

Thousands of years have passed since they conceived the idea of a parallel divine world, with as many beings as there were on earth. And they did a great job. Even to count three hundred and thirty million gods…and you don't know the Hindu gods! They are everything that a human being can be – very cunning, mean, political, in every way exploitative. But somehow, somebody at least managed to have a census.

Hindus are not theistic in the Western sense. They are pagans, but they are not pagans as Christians want to use the word. Pagan is a valuable word; it should not be allowed to be misused by the Christians, Jews and Mohammedans. These three religions are all basically Jewish. Whatsoever they say, their foundations were laid down long before Jesus was born and Mohammed was heard. They are all Judaic.

Of course the God you have heard about is a Jew; he cannot be otherwise. That's where the secret lies. If he were a Hindu, he himself would have fallen into three hundred and thirty million pieces, what to say of creating a world. Even if there was already a world, these three hundred and thirty million gods would have been enough to destroy it.

The Hindu 'God' – no such word can be used because there are only "gods" in Hinduism, not a God – is not a creator. He himself is part of the universe. By he I mean the three hundred and thirty-three million gods. I have to use your word 'he', but Hindus always use 'that'. 'That' is a big umbrella; you can hide as many gods in it as you want. Even the unwanted ones can have a little space at the back. It is almost like a circus tent – vast, big and capable of having every kind of god that can be imagined.

The Jewish God really did a great job. Of course he was a good Jew, and he created the world in only six days. This whole mess is what Albert Einstein, another Jew, calls "the expanding universe." It is expanding every second, becoming bigger and bigger like a pregnant woman's belly, and of course faster than that. It is expanding at the same speed as light, and that is the greatest speed yet conceived of.

Perhaps someday we may discover more speedy things, but right now it still remains the highest as far as speed is concerned. The world is expanding with the speed of light, and it has been expanding forever. There is no beginning and no end, at least in the scientific approach.

But the Christians say it not only began, but was finished within six days. And of course Jews are there, and the Mohammedans are there, and they are all branches of the same nonsense. Perhaps just one idiot created the possibility for all three religions. Don't ask me his name; idiots, particularly perfect ones, don't have names, so nobody knows who created the idea of creating the world in six days. At the most it is just worth laughing at. But listen to a Christian priest or a rabbi, and see the seriousness with which they are talking about the genesis, the very beginning.

I was wondering only because I cannot even finish my story in six days. I'm only on the second day, and that too because I have left so much unsaid, thinking that it is not important – but who knows, it may be. But if I start saying everything without choosing, then what about poor Devageet? I can see that he will have so many notebooks he will go crazy looking at them. It will be as if he is standing by the side of the Empire State Building in New York looking at his own notebooks thinking, "Now who is going to read them?"

And then I think of Devaraj who has to edit them. Whether anybody reads them or not, at least you will have one reader; that is Devaraj. Another, that is Ashu; she has to type them.

In the story of God's creation there is no editor, no typist. He just created it in six days, and was so finished that nothing has been heard of him since then. What happened to him? Some think he has gone to Florida, where every retired person goes. Some think he is enjoying himself at Miami Beach...but this is all guesswork.

God does not exist at all. That's why existence is possible; otherwise he would have poked his nose in – and a Jewish nose is meant for that. Rather than thinking of God, it is better to forget him, and forgive him also; it is time. It may sound a little strange to forget and forgive God, but only then do you begin: his death is your birth.

Only a madman, Friedrich Nietzsche, had the idea – but who listens to madmen, particularly when they are talking real sense. Then it is even more difficult to listen to them. Nobody ever took Nietzsche seriously, but I think his declaration was one of the greatest moments in the history of consciousness: "God is dead!" He had to declare it, not because God died – he had never been there, never been born in the first place, how could he be dead? Before you can be dead you have to suffer at least seventy years of so-called life. God has never been. It is good, because existence is enough unto itself. No outside agency is needed to create it.

But I was not going to talk about it. You see, each moment opens up so many ways, and you have to walk. Whichever you choose you will repent, because who knows what was on the other paths that you have not chosen.

That's why nobody is happy in the world. There are hundreds of successful people, rich people, powerful people, but you don't find a crowd of happy people unless you meet my people. They are a different kind altogether.

Ordinarily everybody is going to be frustrated sooner or later.

The more intelligent, the sooner; the more stupid, the later; and if utterly stupid, then never. Then he will die sitting on the merry-go-round in Dinseyland.

How do you pronounce it, Ashu?

"Disneyland, Osho."

Disnay? Disney. Disney. Good. No woman can hide her feelings from me. A man can do that. I immediately became aware I had said something wrong. But you need not have worried about it; I am a wrong type of man. It is only rarely, by accident, that I will say something right; otherwise, I am always wise.

Now let us continue the story. This was a little diversion, and this is going to be a collection of thousands of diversions, because that's what life is....

Masto was not present to convince Indira Gandhi to work for me, but he tried his best with the first prime minister of India. Perhaps he did succeed, but only in convincing him that here is a man who should not in any way be in the political life of the country. Perhaps Jawaharlal was thinking for my sake, or for the country's sake, but he was not a cunning man, so the second cannot be the case. I have seen him so I know. Not just seen, but really have felt in deep empathy, a deep harmony, synchronicity with him.

He was old. He had lived his life and succeeded, and was frustrated. That was enough for me not to want to succeed in any worldly sense, and I can say I have kept myself intact from any success. In a strange way I have remained as if I have not been in the world at all.

Kabir has a beautiful song which describes what I am saying in a far more poetic way. He was a weaver, so of course his song is that of a weaver, remember.

He says, "*Jhini jhini bini chadariya*: I have prepared a beautiful cover for the night.... *Jhini jhini bini chadariya, ramnam ras bhini*: but I have not used it. I have not in any way made it second-hand. It is as fresh at my death as it was at my birth."

And can you believe, he sang the song and died. People were thinking he was singing the song to them – he was singing the song to existence itself. But those words were from a poor man, and yet so rich that even the whole of life had not been able to make a single scratch on him. And he has given back to existence what had been given to him by existence, exactly as it was given.

Many times I am surprised at how the body has grown old, but as far as I am concerned I don't feel old age or the aging process. Not even for a single moment have I felt different. I am the same, and so many things have happened but they have happened only on the periphery. So I can tell you what happened, but remember always, nothing has happened to me. I am just as innocent and as ignorant as I was before my birth.

The Zen people say, "Unless you know how you were, what was your face before you were born, you cannot understand us."

Naturally you will think, "These people are mad and they are trying to drive me mad too. Perhaps they are trying to convince me to look at my navel, or do something stupid like that." And there are people who are doing things like that, and with great success, and have thousands of followers.

To be with me is not to be on any trodden path. It is, in a strange way, not to be on any path at all…and then suddenly, you are home. This happened to me, but around it thousands of other things also happened. And who knows who will trigger what?

Look at Devageet. Now something is triggered in him. Nobody knows, anything can start a process that can lead you to yourself. It is not far away, nor close by; it is just where you are. That's why sometimes the buddhas have laughed, seeing the utter stupidity of all effort; the stupidity of all that they have been doing. But to see it they had to pass through many things.

What is the time?

"Seven minutes past ten, Osho."

Seven past ten?

"Yes."

Good.

Masto, at our last meeting, said many things; perhaps some of it may be helpful to somebody somewhere. He was about to leave, so he was saying everything that he wanted to say to me. Of course, he had to be very, very brief. He used maxims. That was strange, because the man was a prolific orator – and using maxims?

He said, "You don't understand, I am in a hurry. Just listen, don't argue, because if we start arguing I will not be able to fulfill my promise to Pagal Baba."

Of course, when he said, "Pagal Baba," he knew that name meant so much for me that I never argued against him. Then he could say even two plus two is five, and I would listen, and not only listen but believe, trust. "Two plus two is four" needs no trust; but "two plus two equals five" certainly needs a love that goes beyond arithmetic. If Baba had said it, then it must be so.

So I listened. These were his few words. They were not many, but very significant.

He said, "First, never enter into any organization."

I said, "Okay." And I have not entered into any organization. I have kept my promise. I am not even a part, I mean a member, of neo-sannyas. I cannot be, because of a promise given to someone whom I loved. I can only be amongst you. But howsoever I hide myself, I am a foreigner, even amongst you, just because of a promise that I'm going to fulfill to the very end.

"Second," he said, "you should not speak against the establishment."

I said, "Listen Masto, this is your own, and not Pagal Baba's, and I am absolutely sure of that."

He laughed, and said, "Yes, this is mine. I was just trying to check whether you could sort out the wheat from the chaff."

I said, "Masto, there is no need to bother about that. You just tell me what you want to say, because you said there is a very great hurry. I don't see the hurry, but if you say it – I love you too – I believe it. You just tell me what is absolutely necessary; otherwise we can sit silently for as long as you allow."

He remained silent for a while, and then said, "Okay, it is better that we sit silently, because you know what Baba has told me; he must have told you already."

I said, "I have known him so deeply that there is no need to tell me. Even if he came back I would say, 'Don't bother, just be with me.' So it is good that you decided, but keep to your promise."

He said, "What promise?"

I said, "It is just a simple promise: being silent with me as long as you want to be here."

He was there for six hours more, and he kept his promise. Not a single word passed through us, but much more than words can convey. The only thing that he said to me when he left for the station was, "Can I now say the last thing? – because I may not see you again." And he knew he was going forever.

I said, "Certainly."

He said, "Only this, that if you need any help from me you can always inform this address. If I am alive they will immediately tell me." And he gave me an address which I would not have believed had anything to do with Masto.

I said, "Masto!"

He said, "Don't ask, just inform this man."

"But," I said, "this man is Morarji Desai. I cannot inform him, and you know it."

He said, "I know it, but this is the only man who soon will be in power, and will be able to reach me anywhere in the Himalayas."

I said, "Do you think this is the man to succeed Jawaharlal?"

He said, "No. Another man should succeed him, but that man will not live long, and then Indira will succeed, and after that, this man. I'm giving you this address because these are the years when you will need me most; otherwise if Jawaharlal is there, or Indira is there...."

And between the two, Jawaharlal and Indira, there was another prime minister, a very beautiful man; very small as far as the body is concerned, but very great: Lal Bahadur Shastri. But he was there only for a few months. It was strange, the moment he became prime minister he informed me that he wanted to see me saying, "Come to see me as soon as you can manage."

I reached Delhi because I knew Masto's hand must be there behind him. In fact I went to find the hand behind. I loved Masto so much I would have gone to hell – and New Delhi is a hell. But I went because the prime minister had called, and it was a good time to find out where Masto was, and whether he was alive or not.

But, as fate would have it, the date that he had given me.... He was due to arrive in New Delhi from Tashkent, in Soviet Russia, where he had been for a summit conference of India, Russia, and Pakistan, but only his dead body came. He had died in Tashkent.

I had come all the way to Delhi to ask him about Masto, and he came, but dead.

I said, "This is really a joke, a practical joke. Now I cannot ask." And this address of Morarji Desai that Masto gave me, he knew, and if Masto is alive he knows that even if there is a need I will not ask Morarji Desai. I will not. Not that I am against his policies, his philosophy – that is superficial, I am against his very structure. He is not a man with whom I could have a dialogue, not even a discussion.

It had to happen a few times, just by the configuration of circumstances, but I was not the initiator, and I never approached him about Masto. I never asked, although I have met him in his own home, and there was absolute privacy, but somehow – how to say it – the very man is sickening; one feels like throwing up. And the feeling is so strong that although he had given me one hour, I left after two minutes. Even he was surprised. He asked, "Why?"

I said, "Forgive me. There is some urgency and I have to leave, and forever, because we may not see each other again."

He was shocked, because at that time he was just coming close to being the prime minister of the country, very close. But you know me: particularly if a person's very presence is sickening, I am the last person to stay there. Even my staying there for two minutes was just out of courtesy, because it would have been too discourteous just to enter the room, smell around a little, then take off.

But in fact that's what I did. Two minutes...just because he had been waiting for me and he was an old man, and certainly of political importance, which means nothing to me, but to him it meant too much. That's what repulsed me. He was too political.

I loved Jawaharlal because he never talked about politics. For three days continuously we met, without a single word about politics, and within just two minutes the first question Morarji Desai asked was, "What do you think about that woman, Indira Gandhi?" The way he said, "that woman" was so ugly. I can still hear his voice ..."that woman." I cannot believe that a man can use words in such an ugly way.

Session 45

. . .

OKAY. THE STORY OF MAHATMA GANDHI'S death, and Jawaharlal's bursting into tears on the radio, stunned the whole world. It was not a prepared speech; he was just speaking out of his own heart, and if tears came, what could he do? And if there was a pause, it was not his fault but his greatness. No stupid politician could have done it even if he had wanted to, because their secretaries would even have to write in the prepared speech: "Now please start weeping, cry and leave a pause so that everybody believes that it is for real."

Jawaharlal was not reading; in fact, his secretaries were very worried. One of his secretaries, later on, after many years, became a sannyasin. He confessed that, "We had prepared a speech but in fact he threw it exactly in our faces and said, 'You fools! Do you think I am going to read your speech?'"

This man, Jawaharlal, I immediately recognized as one of those very few people in the world at any moment who are so sensitive and yet in a position to be useful, not just to exploit and oppress but to serve.

I told Masto, "I'm not a politician and will never be one, but I respect Jawaharlal, not because he is the prime minister but because he can still recognize me although I am just a potentiality. Perhaps it may happen, or it may not happen at all, who knows. But his emphasis to you, to protect me from the politicians, shows that he knows more than is apparent."

This incident of Masto's disappearance, with this as his last statement, has opened many doors. I will enter at random, that is my way.

The first was Mahatma Gandhi. He was just mentioned by

Jawaharlal, who wanted to compare me – and naturally – to the man he respected most. But he hesitated, because he knew a little bit of me too, just a little bit, but enough to make me a presence while he was making the statement. Hence he hesitated. He felt as if something was not as it should be, but could not immediately find any other name. So he finally blurted out, "One day he can be another Mahatma Gandhi."

Masto protested on my behalf. He knew me far better than Jawaharlal. Hundreds of times we had discussed Mahatma Gandhi and his philosophy, and I was always against. Even Masto was a little bit puzzled why I was so insistent against a man I had only seen twice, when I was just a child. I will tell you the story of that second meeting. It was suddenly interrupted…. And then one never knows what comes: I never knew that this was going to come in.

I can see the train. Gandhi was traveling, and of course he traveled third class. But his "third class" was far better than any first class possible. In a sixty-man compartment there was just him and his secretary and his wife; I think these three were the only people. The whole compartment was reserved. And it was not even an ordinary first-class compartment, because I have never seen such a compartment again. It must have been a first-class compartment, and not only first class, but a special first class. Just the name plate had been changed and it became "third class" so Mahatma Gandhi's philosophy was saved.

I was just ten. My mother – again I mean my grandmother – had given me three rupees. She said, "The station is too far and you may not be back in time for lunch, and one never knows with these trains: it may come ten hours, twelve hours late, so please keep these three rupees." In India in those days, three rupees was almost a treasure. One could live comfortably for three months on them.

She had made a really beautiful robe for me. She knew I did not like long pants; at the most I wore pajama pants and a *kurta*. A kurta is a long robe which I have always loved, and slowly slowly the pajama has disappeared, only the robe remains. Otherwise one has not only divided the upper body and the lower body, but even made different clothes for each. Of course the higher body should have something better, and the lower body is just to be covered, that's all.

She had made a beautiful kurta for me. It was summer and in

those parts of central India summer is really difficult because the hot air going into the nostrils feels as if it's on fire. In fact, only in the middle of the night can people find a little rest. It is so hot in central India that you are continuously asking for some cold water, and if some ice is available then it is just paradise. Ice is the costliest thing in those parts, naturally, because by the time it comes from the factory, a hundred miles away, it is almost gone. It has to be rushed as quickly as possible.

My Nani said I should go to see Mahatma Gandhi if I wanted to and she prepared a very thin muslin robe. Muslin is the most artistic and the most ancient fabric too, as far as clothes are concerned. She found the best muslin. It was so thin that it was almost transparent. At that time gold rupees had disappeared and silver rupees had taken their place. Those silver rupees were too heavy for the poor muslin pocket. Why am I saying it? – because something I'm going to say would not be possible to understand without it.

The train came as usual, thirteen hours late. Almost everybody was gone except me. You know me, I'm stubborn. Even the stationmaster said, "Boy, you are something. Everybody has gone but you seem ready to stay the whole night. There is no sign of the train and you have been waiting since early this morning."

To come to the station at four o'clock that morning I had to leave my house in the middle of the night. But I had not yet used those three rupees because everybody had brought so many things with them, and they were all so generous to a little boy who had come so far. They were offering me fruits, sweets, cakes and everything, so there was no question of feeling hungry. When the train finally arrived, I was the only person there – and what a person! Just a ten-year-old boy, standing by the side of the stationmaster.

He introduced me to Mahatma Gandhi and said, "Don't think of him as just a boy. The whole day I have watched him, and I have discussed many things with him, because there was no other work. And he is the only one who has remained. Many had come but they left long ago. I respect him because I know he would have stayed here till the last day of existence; he would not leave until the train arrived. And if the train had not arrived, I don't think he would ever have left. He would have lived here."

Mahatma Gandhi was an old man; he called me close and looked at me. But rather than looking at me, he looked at my pocket – and that put me off him forever. And he said, "What is that?"

I said, "Three rupees."

He said, "Donate them." He used to have a box with a hole in it by his side. When you donated, you put the rupees in the hole and they disappeared. Of course he had the key, so they would appear again, but for you they had disappeared.

I said, "If you have the courage you can take them. The pocket is there, the rupees are there, but may I ask you for what purpose you are collecting these rupees?"

He said, "For poor people."

I said, "Then it is perfectly okay." And I myself dropped those three rupees into his box. But he was the one to be surprised, for when I started leaving I took the whole box with me.

He said, "For God's sake, what are you doing? That is for the poor!"

I said, "I have heard you already, you need not bother repeating it again. I am taking this box for the poor. There are many in my village. Please give me the key; otherwise I will have to find a thief so that he can open the lock. He is the only expert in that art."

He said, "This is strange...." He looked at his secretary. The secretary was dumb, as secretaries always are; otherwise why should they be secretaries? He looked at Kasturba, his wife, who said, "You have met your equal. You cheat everybody, now he is taking your whole box. Good! It is good, because I am tired of seeing that box always there, just like a wife!"

I felt sorry for that man and left the box, saying, "No, you are the poorest man, it seems. Your secretary does not have any intelligence, nor does your wife seem to have any love for you. I cannot take this box away – you keep it. But remember, I had come to see a mahatma, but I saw only a businessman."

That was his caste. In India, *baniya*, businessman, is exactly what you mean by a Jew. India has its own Jews; they are not Jews, they are baniyas. To me, at that age, Mahatma Gandhi appeared to be only a businessman. I have spoken against him thousands of times because I don't agree with anything in his philosophy of life. But the day he was shot dead – I was seventeen – my father caught me weeping.

He said, "You, and weeping for Mahatma Gandhi? You have always been arguing against him." My whole family was Gandhian, they had all gone to jail for following his politics. I was the only black sheep, and they were, of course, all pure white. Naturally he asked, "Why are you weeping?"

I said, "I am not only weeping but I want to participate in the funeral. Don't waste my time because I have to catch the train, and this is the last one that will get there on time."

He was even more astonished. He said, "I can't believe it! Have you gone mad?"

I said, "We will discuss that later on. Don't be worried, I will be coming back."

And do you know that when I reached Delhi, Masto was on the platform waiting for me. He said, "I thought that however much you are against Gandhi, you still have a certain regard for the man. That is only my feeling…." He then said, "It may or may not be so, but I depended on it. And this is the only train that passes through your village. If you were to come, I knew you would have to be on this train; otherwise you would not be coming. So I came to receive you, and my feeling was right."

I said to him, "If you had spoken before about my feeling for Gandhi, I would not have argued with you, but you were always trying to convince me, and then it is not a question of feeling, it is pure argument. Either *you* win, or the other fellow wins. If you had mentioned only once that it is a question of feeling, I would not have even touched that subject at all, because then there would have been no argument."

Particularly – just so that it is on the record – I want to say to you that there were many things about Mahatma Gandhi that I loved and liked, but his whole philosophy of life was absolutely disagreeable to me. So many things about him that I would have appreciated remained neglected. Let us put the record right.

I loved his truthfulness. He never lied; even though in the very midst of all kinds of lies, he remained rooted in his truth. I may not agree with his truth, but I cannot say that he was not truthful. Whatsoever was truth to him, he was full of it.

It is a totally different matter that I don't think his truth to be of any worth, but that is my problem, not his. He never lied. I respect his truthfulness, although he knows nothing of the truth – which I am continuously forcing you to take a jump into.

He was not a man who could agree with me: "Jump before you think." No, he was a businessman. He would think a hundred times before taking a single step out of his door, what to say of a jump. He couldn't understand meditation, but that was not his fault. He never came across a single master who could have told him something about no-mind, and there were such people alive at the time.

Even Meher Baba once wrote a letter to Gandhi. It was not exactly that he himself wrote; somebody must have written it for him, because he never spoke, never wrote, just made signs with his hands. Only a few people were able to understand what Meher Baba meant. His letter was laughed at by Mahatma Gandhi and his followers, because Meher Baba had said, "Don't waste your time in chanting 'Hare Krishna, Hare Rama.' That is not going to help at all. If you really want to know, then inform me and I will call you."

They all laughed; they thought it was arrogance. That's how ordinary people think, and naturally it looks like arrogance. But it is not, it is just compassion – in fact, too much compassion. Because it is too much, it looks like arrogance. But Gandhi refused by telegram saying, "Thank you for your offer, but I will follow my own way"...as if he had a way. He had none.

But there are a few things about him that I respect and love – like his cleanliness. Now, you will say, "Respect for such small things...?" No, they are not small, particularly in India, where saints, so-called saints, are expected to live in all kinds of filth. Gandhi tried to be clean. He was the cleanest ignorant man in the world. I love his cleanliness.

I also love that he respected all religions. Of course, my reasons and his are different. But at least he respected all religions – of course for the wrong reasons, because he did not know what truth is, so how could he judge what was right, or whether any religions were right, whether all were right, or whether any ever could be right? There was no way. Again, he was a businessman, so why irritate anybody? Why annoy them?

They are all saying the same thing, the Koran, the Talmud, the Bible, the Gita, and he was intelligent enough – remember the "enough," don't forget it – to find similarities in them, which is not a difficult thing for any intelligent, clever person. That's why I say "intelligent enough," but not truly intelligent. True intelligence is always rebellious, and he could not rebel against the conventional, the traditional, the Hindu or the Christian or the Buddhist.

You will be surprised to know that there was a time when Gandhi contemplated becoming a Christian, because they serve the poor more than any other religion. But he soon became aware that their service is just a façade for the real business to hide behind. The real business is converting people. Why? – because they bring power. The more people you have, the more power you have. If you can convert the whole world to be either Christian or Jew or Hindu, then of course, those people will have more power than anybody ever had before. Alexanders will fade out in comparison. It is a power struggle.

The moment Gandhi saw it – and I say again, he was intelligent enough to see it – he changed his idea of becoming a Christian. In fact, being a Hindu was far more profitable in India than being a Christian. In India, Christians are only one percent, so what political power could he have? It was good that he remained a Hindu, I mean for his mahatmahood. But he was clever enough to manage and even influence Christians like C.F. Andrews, and Jainas, Buddhists, and Mohammedans like the man who became known as "the Frontier Gandhi."

This man, who is still alive, belongs to a special tribe, Pakhtoons, who live in the frontier province of India. Pakhtoons are really beautiful people, dangerous too. They are Mohammedans, and when their leader became a follower of Gandhi, naturally they followed. Mohammedans of India never forgave "Frontier Gandhi" because they thought he had betrayed their religion.

I'm not concerned whether he fulfilled or betrayed; what I am saying is that Gandhi himself had first thought of becoming a Jaina. His first guru was a Jaina, Shrimad Rajchandra, and Hindus still feel hurt that he touched the feet of a Jaina.

Gandhi's second master – and Hindus will be even more offended – was Ruskin. It was Ruskin's great book, *Unto This Last*, that changed Gandhi's life. Books can do miracles. You may not have heard of the book, *Unto This Last*. It is a small pamphlet, and Gandhi was going on a journey when a friend gave it to him to read on the way because he had liked it very much. Gandhi kept it, not really thinking to read it, but when there was time enough he thought, "Why not at least look into the book?" And that book transformed him. That book gave him his whole philosophy.

I am against his philosophy, but the book is great. Its philosophy is not of any worth – but Gandhi was a junk collector; he would find junk even in beautiful places. There is a type of person, you know, who even if you take them to a beautiful garden they suddenly come upon a place and show you something that should not be. Their approach is negative. And then there is a type of person who will collect only thorns – junk collectors; they call themselves collectors of art.

If I had read that book as Gandhi did, I would not have come to the same conclusion. It is not the book that matters, it is the man who reads, chooses and collects. His collection would be totally different although we may have visited the same place. To me, his collection would be just worthless. I don't know, and nobody knows, what he would think about my collection. As far as I know he was a very sincere man. That's why I cannot say whether he would say, the way I am saying, "All his collection is junk." Perhaps he may, or perhaps he may not have said it – that's what I love in the man. He could appreciate even that which was alien to him and tried his best to remain open, to absorb.

He was not a man like Morarji Desai, who is completely closed. I sometimes wonder how he breathes, because at least your nose has to be open. But Mahatma Gandhi was not the same type of man as Morarji Desai. I disagree with him, and yet I know he has a few small qualities worth millions.

His simplicity...nobody could write so simply and nobody could make so much effort just to be simple in his writing. He would try for hours to make a sentence more simple, more telegraphic. He would reduce it as much as possible, and whatsoever he thought true, he tried to live it sincerely. That it was not true is another matter, but about that what could he do? He thought it was true.

I pay him respect for his sincerity, and that he lived it whatsoever the consequences. He lost his life just because of that sincerity.

With Mahatma Gandhi, India lost its whole past, because never before was anybody in India shot dead or crucified. That had not been the way of this country. Not that they are very tolerant people, but just so snobbish, they don't think anybody is worth crucifying... they are far higher.

With Mahatma Gandhi India ended a chapter, and also began a chapter. I wept, not because he had been killed – because everybody has to die, there is not much in it. And it is better to die the way he died, rather than dying on a hospital bed – particularly in India. It was a clean and beautiful death in that way. And I am not protecting the murderer, Nathuram Godse. He is a murderer, and about him I cannot say, "Forgive him because he did not know what he was doing." He knew exactly what he was doing. He cannot be forgiven. Not that I am hard on him, just factual.

I had to explain all this to my father later on, after I came back. And it took me many days, because it is really a complicated relationship between me and Mahatma Gandhi. Ordinarily, either you appreciate somebody or you don't. It is not so with me – and not only with Mahatma Gandhi.

I'm really a stranger. I feel it every moment. I can like a certain thing about a person, but at the same time there may be something standing by the side of it which I hate, and I have to decide, because I cannot cut the person in two.

I decided to be against Mahatma Gandhi, not because there was nothing in him that I could have loved – there was much, but much more was there which had far-reaching implications for the whole world. I had to decide to be against a man I may have loved if – and that "if" is almost unbridgeable – if he had not been against progress, against prosperity, against science, against technology. In fact, he was against almost everything for which I stand: more technology and more science, and more richness and affluence.

I am not for poverty, he was. I am not for primitiveness, he was. But still, whenever I see even a small ingredient of beauty, I appreciate it. And there were a few things in that man which are worth understanding.

He had an immense capacity to feel the pulse of millions of people together. No doctor can do it; even to feel the pulse of one person is very difficult, particularly a person like me. You can try feeling my pulse; you will even lose your pulse, or if not the pulse then at least the purse, which is even better!

Gandhi had the capacity to know the pulse of the people. Of course, I am not interested in those people, but that is another thing. I'm not interested in thousands of things; that does not mean that those who are genuinely working, intelligently reaching to some depth, are not to be appreciated. Gandhi had that capacity, and I appreciate it. I would have loved to meet him now, because when I was only a ten-year-old lad, all that he could get from me were those three rupees. Now I could have given him the whole paradise – but that was not to happen, at least in this life.

Session 46

OKAY. I CAN BEGIN WITH the second day in my primary school. How long can it wait? It has already waited too long. The second day was my real entry into the school, because Kantar Master had been thrown out and everybody was joyous. Almost all the children were dancing. I could not believe it, but they told me, "You did not know Kantar Master. If he dies we will distribute sweets for the whole town, and burn thousands of candles in our houses." I was received as if I had done a great deed.

In fact I felt a little sorry for Kantar Master. He may have been very violent, but after all he was human too, and with all the weaknesses a human being is prone to. It was not at all his fault that he had only one eye and an ugly face. And I would even like to say something which I have never said before because I never thought anybody would believe it...but I am not seeking believers, believe it or not.

Even his cruelty was not his fault – I emphasize *his* fault – it was natural to him. Just as he had only one eye, he had anger, and very violent anger. He could not tolerate anything that went against him in any way. Even the silence of the children was enough to provoke him.

He would look around and say, "Why so much silence? What is going on? There must be a reason for you to be so silent. I will teach you all a lesson, so that you will never do this thing again to me."

The children were all amazed. They had just been keeping quiet so as not to disturb him. But what could he do? – even that disturbed him. He needed medical treatment, and not only physical, but psychological too. He was, in every way, sick. I felt sorry for him because I was, apparently at least, the cause of his removal.

But everybody was enjoying the occasion, even the teachers. I could not believe it when the headmaster also said to me, "Thank you, my boy. You have started your school life by doing something beautiful. That man was a pain in the neck."

I looked at him and said, "Perhaps I should remove the neck too."

Immediately he became serious, and said, "Go and do your work."

I said, "Look, you are happy, rejoicing, because one of your colleagues has been thrown out – and you call yourself a colleague? What kind of friendship is this? You never told him to his face how you felt. You could not have done it; he would have crushed you."

The headmaster was a small man, not more than five feet tall, or perhaps even less. And that seven-foot giant, weighing four hundred pounds, could easily have crushed him without any weapon, just with his fingers. "In front of him why did you always behave like a husband before his wife?" Yes, these were the exact words.

I remember saying, "You behaved like a henpecked husband. And remember, I may by chance have been the cause of his removal, but I was not planning anything against him. I had only just entered school; there was no time for setting up a planning commission. And you have been planning against him your whole life. He should at least have been sent to another school" – there were four schools in that town.

But Kantar Master was a strong man, and the president particularly was under his thumb. The president of that town was ready to be under anybody's thumb. Perhaps he liked thumbs, I don't know, but soon the whole town realized that this holy cow dung was not going to help.

In a town of twenty thousand, there was no road worth calling a road, no electricity, no park, nothing. Soon the people realized that it was because of this cow dung. He had to resign, so that at least for the remaining two and a half years his vice president took his place.

Shambhu Babu transformed almost the whole face of that town. One thing I must say to you: that through me he came to know that even a small child could not only remove a teacher, but could create a situation in which the president of the town had to resign.

He used to say laughingly, "You have made me president." But there were times afterwards when we disagreed. He remained president for many years. Once the town saw his work during those two and a half years he was elected unanimously again and again. He did almost miracles in changing that town.

He made the first paved roads in the whole province, and brought electricity to our twenty thousand people. That was very rare; no other town of that size had electricity. He planted trees at the side of the roads to give a little beauty to an ugly town. He did much. What I am preparing you for is that there were times when I did not agree with his policies. Then I was his opponent.

You cannot believe how a young child of perhaps twelve could be an opponent. I had my strategies. I could persuade people very easily – just because I was a child, and what interest could I have in politics? And certainly I had no interest at all.

For example, Shambhu Babu imposed the *octroi* tax. I can understand that: without money how could he manage all his beautifying projects and roads and electricity? Naturally he needed money. Some form of taxation was necessary.

I was not against taxation, I was against the octroi tax, because it goes on the head of the poorest. The rich get richer and the poor get poorer. I am not against the rich becoming richer, but I am certainly against the poor becoming poorer. You will not believe it, and even he was surprised when I said, "I will go from house to house telling people not to vote for Shambhu Babu again. If the octroi remains then Shambhu Babu has to go. Or if Shambhu Babu wants to remain, then the octroi has to go. We will not allow both together."

I not only went from house to house, I even spoke at my first public meeting. People enjoyed seeing just a small boy speaking so logically. Even Shambhu Babu was sitting nearby in a shop. I can still see him sitting there. That was his place; he used to sit there every day. It was a strange place for him to sit, but the shop was in a very prominent place, at the very center of the town. That's why all the meetings used to be held there, and he could pretend that he was just sitting at his friend's shop and had nothing to do with the meeting.

When he heard me – and you know me, I have always been the

same. I pointed to Shambhu Babu sitting in that small shop, and said, "Look! He is sitting there. He has come to listen to what I am going to say. But, Shambhu Babu, remember: friendship is one thing, but I am not going to support your octroi tax. I will oppose it even if I have to lose your friendship. I will know that it was not worth much. If we can still remain friends although we may not agree on some points, or may even come to public conflict, only then will our friendship have any significance."

He was really a good man. He came out of the shop, patted me on the back and said, "Your arguments are worth considering. And as far as our friendship is concerned, this conflict has nothing to do with it." He never mentioned it again. I had thought that someday he would bring it up and say to me, "You were hitting me very hard and it was wrong." But he never even mentioned it. The most wonderful thing was that he withdrew the tax.

I asked him, "Why? I may oppose it, but I'm not even a voter yet. It was the public who voted you in."

He said, "That is not the point. If even you can oppose it, then there must be something wrong with what I am doing. I am withdrawing it. I have no fear of the public, but when a person like you disagrees...although you are very young, I respect you. And your argument is right that whatsoever taxation one applies, it has finally to be paid by the poor, because the rich are clever enough to shift it."

The octroi tax is taxation on any goods that enter the town. Now when those goods are sold they will be sold at a higher price. You cannot prevent the taxation that the shopkeeper has paid being taken out of the pocket of a poor farmer. Of course the shopkeeper will not call it taxation; it will just become part of the price.

Shambhu Babu said, "I understand the point and I have withdrawn the tax." As long as he was president the taxation was never again brought up, or even discussed. But he never felt offended; rather he became more respectful towards me. I felt awkward that I had to oppose somebody who I can say was the only person in that town I loved.

Even my father was surprised, and said, "You do some strange things. I heard you speaking in public. I knew you would do something like that, but not so soon. You were speaking so convincingly, and against your own friend. Everybody was shocked that you were speaking against Shambhu Babu."

The whole town knew that I had no friend other than this old man, Shambhu Babu – he must have been around fifty. This would have been the time for us to have been friends -- but the gap was not in our hands, so we did not take any notice of it. And he too had no other friends. He could not afford to lose me, nor could I afford to lose him. My father said, "I could not believe that you would speak against him."

I said, "I never said a single word against him. I was speaking against the taxation that he is trying to bring about. My friendship certainly does not include that; octroi is excluded. And I had told Shambhu Babu beforehand, by way of making him aware, that if anything is disagreeable to me I will fight it, even against him. That's why he was present in that shop, just to listen to what I was saying against his tax. But I did not say a single word against Shambhu Babu."

The second day at school was as if I had done something great. I could not believe that people had been so oppressed by Kantar Master. It was not that they were rejoicing for me; even then I could see the distinction clearly. Today too, I can remember perfectly that they were rejoicing because Kantar Master was no longer on their backs.

They had nothing to do with me, although they were acting as if they were rejoicing for me. But I had come to school the day before and nobody had even said, "Hello." Yet now the whole school had gathered at the Elephant Gate to receive me. I had become almost a hero on just my second day.

But I told them then and there, "Please disperse. If you want to rejoice go to Kantar Master. Dance in front of his house, rejoice there. Or go to Shambhu Babu, who is the real cause of his removal. I am nobody. I did not go with any expectation, but things happen in life that you had never expected, nor deserved. This is one of those things, so please forget about it."

But it was never forgotten in my whole school life. I was never accepted as just another child. Of course, I was not very concerned with school at all. Ninety percent of the time I was absent. I would appear only once in a while for my own reason, but not to attend school.

I was learning many things, but not in school. I was learning strange things. My interests were a little uncommon, to say the least. For example I was learning how to catch snakes. In those days so many people used to come to the village with beautiful snakes, and the snakes would dance to their flute. It really impressed me.

All those people have almost disappeared, for the simple reason that they were all Mohammedan. They have either gone to Pakistan or been killed by the Hindus, or perhaps changed their profession because it was too much of a public declaration that they were Mo-hammedan. No Hindu practiced that art.

I would follow any snake charmer all day asking him, "Just tell me the secret of how you catch snakes." And slowly slowly they understood that I was not one who could be prevented from doing anything. They said among themselves, "If we don't tell him he is going to try on his own."

When I said to one snake charmer, "Either you tell me or else I am going to try on my own; if I die you will be responsible" – he knew me because for days I had been bothering him and bugging him – he said, "Wait, I will teach you."

He took me outside the town and started to teach me how to catch snakes; how to teach them to dance when you play the flute. It was he who told me for the first time that snakes don't have ears, they cannot hear – and almost everybody believes that they are influenced by the snake charmer's flute.

He told me, "The truth is they can't hear at all."

I then asked him, "But how do they start swaying then when you play your flute?"

He said, "It is nothing but training. When I play my flute, have you ever noticed that I sway my head? That is the trick. I sway my head and the snake starts swaying, and unless he sways he remains hungry. So the sooner he starts swaying, the better. Hunger is the secret, not the music."

I learned from these snake charmers how to catch snakes. In the first place, ninety-seven percent of snakes are harmless, nonpoison-ous; you can catch them without any problem. Of course they will bite, but because they don't have any poison it will just be a bite, you will not die. Ninety-seven percent don't have poison glands. And the three percent who do have a strange habit: they bite just enough to make a place available for their poison, then they turn over. The poison gland is upside down in their throat, so first they make the wound, then they turn over and pour in the poison. You can catch them either before they make the wound...and the best way is to grasp their mouth really tight.

I had not known that you need to grasp the mouth, but that has to be the first thing. If you miss and they make a wound in you, don't be worried: keep a tight hold and just don't let them turn over. The wound will heal and you won't die. I was learning, and this is just an example.

Unfortunately all those snake charmers had to leave India. There were magicians doing all kinds of unbelievable things, and I was certainly more interested in the magicians than in my poor teacher and his geography or history. I followed these magicians like a servant. I would not leave them unless they taught me a little trick.

I was continuously amazed that what appeared so unbelievable was nothing but a small trick. But unless you knew the trick you had to accept the greatness of the phenomenon. Once you knew the trick – it is like a balloon losing its air: it becomes smaller and smaller, just a punctured balloon. Soon you have just a little piece of rubber in your hand and nothing else. That great balloon was simply hot air.

I was learning in my own ways things which were really going to help me. That's why I can say that Satya Sai Baba and people like him are just street magicians – and not even very good ones, just ordinary. But these magicians have disappeared from the streets of India because they also were Mohammedans.

In India you have to understand one thing, that people for thousands of years have followed a certain structure. One's profession is almost always given by the parents; it is a heritage, you cannot change it. It will be difficult for a Westerner to understand; hence so many problems arise in understanding, in communicating with the Easterner.

I was learning, but not in school, and I never repented for it.

I learned from all kinds of strange people. You cannot find them working in schools as teachers; that is not possible. I was with Jaina monks, Hindu *sadhus,* Buddhist *bhikkhus,* and all kinds of people one is not expected to associate with.

The moment I became aware that I was not supposed to associate with somebody, that was enough for me to associate with that person, because he must be an outsider. Because he was an outsider, hence the prohibition – and I am a lover of outsiders.

I hate the insiders. They have done so much harm that it is time to call the game off. The outsiders I have always found a little crazy, but beautiful – crazy yet intelligent. Not the intelligence of Mahatma Gandhi – he was a perfect insider – nor is it the intelligence of the so-called intellectuals: Jean-Paul Sartre, Bertrand Russell, Karl Marx, Hugh Bach...the list is endless.

The first intellectual was the serpent who started this whole thing; otherwise there would have been no trouble. He was the first intellectual. I don't call him a devil, I call you the devils – this company. You may not follow the meaning I give to the word. To me "the devil" always means "divine." It comes from the Sanskrit root *deva,* meaning "divine." So I have named your company "the devils."

But the serpent was an intellectual, and he played the trick that all intellectuals do. He persuaded the woman to purchase something while her husband was at the office, or maybe somewhere else, because offices came later – must have been fishing, hunting, or you can imagine what the husband was doing. At least he was not fooling around, that much was certain, because there was nobody to fool around with. It all had to come, but later on.

The serpent argued that, "God has told you not to eat the fruit of the tree of life..." and it was nothing more than an apple tree. Sometimes I think nobody could have sinned more than me, because I must be eating more apples than anybody in the world. And apples are so innocent that I wonder why the apple had to be chosen – what wrong had the apple done to God? I cannot figure it out.

But one thing I can say: the man called "serpent" must have been a great intellectual, so great that he proved eating apples to be a sin.

But intelligence to me is never of the mind....

Session 47

I WAS TALKING ABOUT MY PRIMARY school. I rarely went, and it was such a relief to everybody that I wanted to give it to them as much as possible. Why could I not give them one hundred percent relief? For the simple reason that I loved them too – I mean the people: the teachers, the servants, the gardeners. Once in a while I wanted to visit them, particularly when I wanted to show them something. A little boy, anxious to show everything he has to those he loves...but those things were sometimes dangerous. Even now I cannot resist laughing.

I remember one day very vividly. It has always been waiting there for its moment. Perhaps the moment has come, and it has to be told and shared. It is a series of events....

I had just learned how to catch snakes. Snakes are poor people, innocent too, and beautiful, very alive. You cannot believe what I am saying unless you have seen two snakes in love. You may wonder how snakes make love. They don't make it – it is only man who makes everything – they do it. And when they are in love they are just flames. And the reason that I am saying it is surprising, is because they have no bones, yet they still stand up to kiss each other! Stand on what? They have no legs either, they just stand on their tails. If you see two snakes standing on their tails kissing each other, you will never bother to see any Hollywood film again.

I had just learned how to catch a snake and how to make the distinction between the poisonous snake and the nonpoisonous. A few are absolutely so poisonless that you can perhaps call them another kind of fish, because many of them live in water. The water snakes are the most innocent, even more than fish. Fish are cunning, but water snakes are not. I had tried my hand at all kinds of snakes, so when I say it, I am not just telling somebody else's story, it is my story.

I had just caught a snake. Now, this was the day to go to the school. You will say, "Strange...?" Otherwise I was so busy, there was no time to waste with stupid questions, answers, foolish maps. Even then I could see that maps are all nonsense, because on the earth I don't see lines anywhere, either for the district or the municipality. So all the nations are just cow dung, and not holy either – unholy cow dung. If anything like that exists it is politics – unholy and cow dung, both together. It is politics that has created the maps.

I was not the one to waste my time there. I was exploring real geography: going to the mountains, disappearing for days. Only my Nani knew when I would come. And for days I would not be heard or seen, because I was not there. And everybody, I think, except my Nani, was happy. You will come to know why...and they were right, about that I have no doubt.

I had caught a snake, my first success. Naturally, I wanted to go to school immediately. And I didn't bother to wear the uniform, and nobody can expect me to; I never did even in primary school. I said, "I have come to learn, not to be destroyed. If I can learn anything, good, but I won't allow you to destroy me, and the uniform – chosen by you who don't know a thing about beauty and form – I cannot accept. I will create great trouble if you try to impose it on me."

They said, "Keep it ready just in case the inspector comes; otherwise we will be in trouble. We don't want to trouble you because we don't want trouble ourselves. It is a costly affair," my teacher said, "to create trouble for you. We know what happened to Kantar Master; it can happen to anybody. But please keep the uniform just for our sakes."

And you will be surprised that my uniform was supplied by our school. I don't know who contributed its cost, nor do I care. I kept it, knowing perfectly well that it was almost a mathematical impossibility that my visit to the school and the inspector's visit to the school could fall on the same date. It was not possible, that's what I thought, but I kept the uniform. It was beautiful: they had done their best and they were not insisting that I should come wearing it.

I was always a foreigner. Even now among my own people I am not wearing the uniform. I just cannot. I cannot even be in a uniform that I have chosen for you. Why? That day there was the same question. Today again it is the same question. I just cannot conform. You can think of it as a whim; it is not whimsical at all, it is very existential. But we will not go into that; otherwise what I was saying to you will be missed. I will never come to it again.

I had caught my first snake. It was such a joy, and the snake was so beautiful: just to touch it was to touch something really alive. It was not like touching your wife, your husband, your son, or even your son-in-law, where you touch and bless them, and you don't have any feeling – you just want to go and watch TV, particularly if you are in America, or if you are in England go to the cricket match or the football match. People are crazy in different ways, but crazy all the same.

That snake was a real snake, not a plastic snake that you could purchase in any store. Of course, the plastic snake may be made perfectly but it does not breathe; that's the only trouble with it, otherwise it is perfect. God could not have improved upon it. Just one thing is missing – the breathing – and for just one thing why complain? But that one thing is all. I had just caught a *real* snake, so beautiful and so clever that I had to put my whole intelligence into catching him...because I was not in any way interested in killing him.

The man who was teaching me was an ordinary street magician; in India we call them *madari*. They do all kinds of tricks without any charge. But they do so well that in the end they simply spread their handkerchief on the ground and say, "Now something for my stomach." And people may be poor, but when they see something so beautifully done they always give.

So this man was an ordinary madari, a street magician. That is the closest translation I can manage, because I don't think that anything like the madaris exist in the West. In the first place, they won't allow a crowd to gather on the street; the police car will immediately arrive saying that you are blocking the traffic.

In India there is no question of blocking the traffic; there are no traffic laws! You can walk in the middle of the road, you can follow the golden mean – literally. You can follow the American way, you can go to the extreme right, or to the very extreme left. The extreme right is the American way, the extreme left is the Russian way: you can choose – or you can choose any position anywhere in between. The whole road is yours; you can make your house there. You will be surprised to know that in India you can do anything imaginable, or unimaginable, on the street. I include even the unimaginable, because one never knows.

The madaris were certainly causing a traffic jam, but who was to object? Even the policeman was one of the admirers, clapping at the tricks the madari was playing. I have seen all kinds of people gathered there blocking the whole road. No, madaris could not exist in the West in the same sense – and they're really beautiful people; simple, ordinary, but they "know something," as they say.

The man who was teaching me told me, "Remember, this is a dangerous snake. These snakes should not be caught."

I said, "You are freed. These are the only snakes I am going to catch." I had never seen such a beautiful snake, so colorful, so alive in every fiber of his being. Naturally I could not resist – I was just a little boy – I rushed to the school. I wanted to avoid relating what happened there, but I will just because I can see it again.

The whole school, as many as were possible, gathered in my classroom, and the others were standing on the verandah outside looking through the windows and the doors. Others were standing even farther away just in case the snake escaped or something went wrong – and this boy, from the very first day, had been a trouble-maker. But my class, just thirty or forty little boys, were all afraid, standing and shouting, and I really enjoyed it.

The thing that you will also enjoy and I could not believe, was that the teacher stood on his chair! Even today I can see him standing on his chair and saying, "Get out! Get out! Leave us alone! Get out!"

I said, "First you get down."

He became quiet, because the question of getting down was dangerous with such a big snake. The snake must have been six or seven feet long, and I was dragging it in a bag, so that I could suddenly expose it to everybody. And when I exposed it there was chaos! I can still see the teacher jumping on his chair. I could not believe my eyes. I said, "This is just wonderful."

He said, "What is wonderful?"

I said, "You jumping up and standing on the chair. You will break it!"

First the children were not afraid, but when they saw him so afraid – just see how children are being impressed by stupid and wrong people. When they had seen me coming in with the snake, they were just joy, "Alleluia!" But when they saw the teacher standing on his chair...for a moment there was complete silence, only the teacher was jumping and shouting, "Help!"

I said, "I don't see the point. The snake is in my hands. I am in danger, you are not. You are standing on your chair. You are too far away for the poor snake to reach. I would like him to reach, and have a little talk with you."

I can still see that man and his face. He met me only once after that experience. By that time I had renounced my professorship and become a beggar...although I never begged. But the truth is I am a beggar, but a special type of beggar who does not beg.

You will have to find a word for it. I don't think a word exists in any language that can explain my situation, simply because I have not been here before – in this way, this style. Neither has anybody else been this way, with this style: having nothing and living as if you own the whole universe.

I remember him saying, "I cannot forget when you brought that snake into my class. It still comes into my dreams, and I cannot believe that that kind of boy has become a buddha. Impossible!"

I said, "You are right. 'That kind of boy' has died, and what is after the death of that boy, you may call buddha, or you may choose something else, or you may choose not to call it anything. I simply don't exist the way you knew me. I would have loved to, but what can I do? I died."

He said, "See? I'm talking seriously and you are making a joke out of it."

"I am doing my best, but," I told him, "it is not only you who remembers. Whenever I have a bad day or the weather is not good, or something – the tea was not hot enough, the food was as if prepared for food poisoning – then I remember you jumping on your chair and calling for help, and that cheers me up again. Although I am dead, it still helps. I am tremendously grateful to you."

I used to go to school only for such moments. There were certainly only a few…"occasions" I should call them. It was necessary for everybody's happiness that I should not be present there regularly every day. You will be surprised that the peon, the man whose duty was…. What do you call him? Peon? – or don't you have any word for it: p-e-o-n, peon? But we in India call him peon. Whatsoever the word is, it is the lowest servant in every office.

Devaraj, what is it?

"Janitor?"

No, that is a different thing, but comes close to it. I thought 'peon' must be an English word; it is not of Hindi origin. I may not be pronouncing it rightly. We will find out, but it is spelled p-e-o-n.

The peon was the only person who was unhappy when I was not there…because everybody else was happy about it. He loved me. I have never seen an older man than him: he was ninety or perhaps more. Perhaps he had made the century. In fact he may have been even more, because he tried to reduce his age as much as possible so that he could continue in service a little longer…and he continued.

In India you don't know your birth date, and particularly if you were born one hundred years ago, I don't think there would be any certificate or record – impossible. But I have never seen a man older than him and yet full of juice, really juicy.

He was the only man in that whole school for whom I had some respect – but he was the lowest, nobody even looked at him. Once in a while, just for his sake, I used to visit the school, but I only went to his place.

His place was just by the corner of the Elephant Gate. His work was to open and close the gate, and he had a bell hanging in front of his cabin to hit every forty minutes, leaving just ten minutes twice each day for tea breaks, and one hour for lunch. That was his only work; otherwise he was a completely free man.

I would go into his cabin, and he would close the door so that nobody disturbed us, and so that I could not escape easily. Then he would say, "Now tell me everything since we met last time." And he was such a lovely old man. His face had so many lines that I had even tried to count them, of course not telling him. I was pretending to listen to him while I was counting how many lines his forehead had – and it was all forehead because all his hair had gone – and how many lines were on his cheeks. In fact his whole face, howsoever you divided it, was nothing but lines. But behind those lines was a man of infinite love and understanding.

If I did not visit the school for many days, then it was certain that the day was coming closer when if I didn't go, then he would come to find me. That meant my father would know everything: that I never went to school, that attendance was given to me just to keep me out. That was the agreement. I had said, "Okay, I will keep myself out, but what about my attendance…because who is going to answer my father?"

They said, "Don't be worried about your attendance. We will give you one hundred percent attendance, even on holidays, so don't be worried at all."

So I was always aware that before he came to visit my house, it was better to go to his cabin, and somehow – again I have to use the word 'synchronicity' – he knew when I was coming. I knew that if I didn't go that day he would be coming to inquire what had happened to me – and it became almost mathematically accurate.

I would start from the very morning with the feeling, "Listen" – I am not saying it to you, I am just telling you how I used to get up – "Listen, if you don't go today, Mannulal" – that was his name – "is going to visit by the evening. Before that happens, somehow at least make an appearance before him."

And except once I always followed my inner voice – I mean in reference to Mannulal. Only once…and I was getting a little tired of the whole thing. It was a kind of torture: I *had* to go, I went out of fear; otherwise he would tell my father and mother and would create havoc. I said, "No. Today I'm not going. Whatsoever happens I'm not going."

And who did I see? – nobody but Mannulal, the old man, coming. Perhaps he was more than a hundred and just pretending he was not. To me he always looked, and I still insist that he was, more than a hundred – perhaps a hundred and ten, or even a hundred and twenty. He was so ancient-looking you would not believe it. I have never seen anything so ancient. I have visited museums, all kinds of collections of old objects, but I have never come across anything more prehistoric than Mannulal.

He was coming! I ran out just in time to prevent him from entering the house. He said to me, "I had to come to find you, because you were trying not to come to see me. And you know that I am an old man. I may die tomorrow, who knows. I just wanted to see you. I am happy that you are healthy and as alive as ever." Saying that, he blessed me, turned, and went away. I can see his back, with the strange uniform that the peon had to wear.

Now this will be really difficult for me to describe. First the color: it was khaki – I think you call it khaki, am I right? Second: up to his knees there was a strap running around his leg, also khaki, but a separate thing. It was just to make the man look more alive, alert, or better to say "on alert." In fact it was so tight, what else could you do other than be alert!

It is strange but your dress can even change your behavior. For example, wearing a very tight robe, or tight dress I mean, not robe, or tight pants like the teenagers are using – so tight that one wonders how they got into them…. I could not get into them, that much is certain. And even if they were born into them from the very beginning, then how will they get out of them? But these are philosophical questions. They are not worried. They just sing pop songs and eat popcorn – what else to do in the world! But dress can certainly change your behavior.

Soldiers cannot have loose uniforms; otherwise they cannot be fighters. When you wear something tight, so tight that you want to get out of it, then naturally you want to fight with everybody. You are simply angry. It is not objective – directed to anybody in particular – it is simply a subjective feeling. You simply want to get out of it. What to do? – have a good fight. It certainly makes people feel a little relaxed. Then, naturally, the tight clothes get a little looser.

That's why every lover, before making love, first has to go through the ritual pillow fight, argument, and say nasty things to the other. Then of course it is a comedy: everything in it ends well. Alas, can't people start loving from the very beginning? But no, their very tightness prevents it. They cannot loosen up.

Just three minutes for me.... There was much to say, but I have something else to do. You can see the tear...please remove it. But it was beautiful, thank you.

This is great.... *(chuckle)* You go on, Ashu, you are doing well. You go on your way, he goes on his way. Ways differ and I don't think they will meet anywhere.

It is finished? Good! *(chuckling)*

Session 48

I WAS TALKING ABOUT MY VISITS to school. Yes, I call them visits because they were certainly not attendance. I was only there to create some mischief. In a strange way I have always loved to be involved in some mischievous act. Perhaps it was the beginning of how I was to be for my whole life.

I have never taken anything seriously. I cannot, even now. Even at my own death I will, if allowed, still have a good laugh. But in India for the last twenty-five years I have had to play the role of a serious man. It has been my most difficult role, and the longest drawn. But I did it in such a way that although I have remained serious, I have never allowed anybody around me to be serious. That has kept me above water; otherwise those serious people are far more poisonous than snakes.

You can catch snakes, but serious people catch you. You have to run away from them as fast as possible. But I am fortunate that no serious person will even try to approach me. I quickly made myself notorious enough, and it all began when I was not even thinking where it was going to land me.

Whenever they saw me coming, everybody was alerted, as if I was going to create some danger. At least to them it must have looked dangerous. For me it was just fun – and that word summarizes my whole life.

For example, another incident from my primary school. I must have been in the last class, the fourth. They never failed me, for the simple reason that no teacher wanted me in his class again. Naturally, the only way to get rid of me was to pass me on to somebody else. At least for one whole year let him have the trouble too. That's how they called me, "the trouble." On my part I could not see what trouble I created for anybody.

I was going to give you an example. The station was two miles from my town and divides it from another small village called Cheechli, six miles away.

By the way, Cheechli was the birthplace of Maharishi Mahesh Yogi. He never mentions it, and there are reasons why he does not mention where he was born – because he belongs to the sudra class in India. Just to mention that you come from a certain village, certain caste, or profession – and Indians are very uncultured about that. They may just stop you on the road and ask you, "What is your caste?" Nobody thinks that this is an interference.

Maharishi Mahesh Yogi was born on the other side of the station, but because he is a sudra, he can neither mention the village – because it is a village of only sudras, the lowest caste in the Indian hierarchy – nor can he use his surname. That too will immediately reveal who he is.

His full name is Mahesh Kumar Shrivastava, but "Shrivastava" would put a stop to all his pretensions, at least in India, and that would affect others too. He is not an initiated sannyasin in any of the old orders, because again, there are only ten sannyasin orders in India. I have been trying to destroy them; that is why they are all angry with me.

These orders are again castes, but of sannyasins. Maharishi Mahesh Yogi cannot be a sannyasin because no sudra can become an initiate. That's why he does not write "Swami" before his name. He cannot; nobody has given him that name. He does not write behind his name, as Hindu sannyasins do, Bharti, Saraswati, Giri etcetera; they have their ten names.

He has created his own name – "Yogi." It does not mean anything. Anybody trying to stand on his head, and of course falling again and again, can call himself a yogi; there is no restriction on it.

A sudra can be a yogi, and the name Maharishi is something to replace "Swami," because in India things are such that if the name "Swami" is missing, then people would suspect something is wrong. You have to put something else there just to cover up the gap.

He invented "Maharishi." He is not even a *rishi*. Rishi means "seer," and maharishi means "great seer." He can't even see beyond his nose. All he can do when you ask him relevant questions is giggle. In fact, I will call him "Swami Gigglananda"; that will fit him perfectly. That giggling is not something respectable, it is really a strategy to avoid questions. He cannot answer any question.

I have met him, just by chance, and in a strange place – Pahalgam. He was leading a meditation camp there, and so was I. Naturally my people and his were meeting each other. They first tried to bring him to my camp, but he made so many excuses that he had no time, he wanted to but it would not be possible.

But he said, "One thing can be done: you can bring him here so that my time and my scheduled work is not disturbed. He can speak with me from my stage." And they agreed.

When they told me I said, "This is stupid of you. Now I will be in unnecessary trouble. I will be in front of his crowd. I don't have to worry about the questions; the only problem is that it will not be right for the guest to hit his host, especially before his own crowd. And once I see him I cannot refrain from hitting him. Any decision I make not to hit him will be gone."

But they said, "We have promised."

I said, "Okay. I'm not bothered, and I am ready to come." It was not very far, just a two-minutes' walk away. You just had to get in the car and then get out again, that was the distance. So I said, "Okay, I will come."

I went there, and as I had expected he was not there. But I don't care about anything. I started the camp – and it was his camp! He was not there; he was just trying to avoid me as much as he could. Somebody must have told him…. Because he was staying in the hotel just nearby, he must have heard what I was saying from his room. I started hitting him hard, because when I saw that he was not there, I could hit him as much as I wanted to and enjoy doing it. Perhaps I hit him too hard and he could not stay away. He came out giggling.

I said, "Stop giggling! That is okay on American television; it won't do here with me!" And his smile disappeared. I have never seen such anger. It was as if that giggling was a curtain, and hiding behind it was all that was not supposed to be there.

Naturally it was too much for him, and he said, "I have other things to do, please excuse me."

I said, "There is no need. As far as I am concerned you never came here. You came for the wrong reasons, and I don't come into it at all. But remember, I have got plenty of time."

Then I really hit him, because I knew he had gone back into his hotel room. I could even see his face watching from the window. I even told his people: "Look! This man says he has much work to do. Is this his work? – watching somebody else work from his window? He should at least hide himself, just as he hides behind his giggle."

Maharishi Mahesh Yogi is the most cunning of all the so-called spiritual gurus. But cunningness succeeds; nothing succeeds like cunningness. If you fail, it simply means you have come across somebody who is more cunning than you. But cunningness still succeeds.

He never mentions his village, but I remembered because I was going to tell you about an incident. This incident had some concern with his village, and my story is always going in all directions.

Cheechli was a small state; it was not part of the British Raj. It was a very small state, but the king, after all, was a king even though he could only afford one elephant. That's how they used to measure how much kingliness you had – by the number of elephants you owned.

Now, I have told you about the Elephant Gate that stood in front of the school. One day, for no reason, I approached the maharaja of Cheechli and asked, "I would like to have your elephant for just one hour."

He said, "What! What will you do with my elephant?"

I said, "I don't want your elephant, I only want to make the gate feel good. You must have seen that gate: perhaps you even studied there yourself!"

He said, "Yes. In my day it was the only primary school. Now there are four."

I said, "I want to make that gate feel good, at least once. It is called the Elephant Gate but not even a donkey ever passes through it."

He said, "You are a strange boy, but I like the idea."

His secretary said, "What do you mean, you like the idea? He is crazy!"

I said, "You are both right, but crazy or not, I have come to ask for your elephant for just one hour. I want to ride it into the school."

He liked the idea so much he said, "You ride on the elephant, and I will follow in my old Ford."

He owned a very ancient Ford, perhaps a T-model – I think it was the T-model which was the most ancient one. He wanted to come just to see what happened.

Of course, as I passed through the town on the elephant everybody wondered, and people gathered saying to themselves, "What's the matter? And how did this boy get the elephant?"

When I reached the school there was a big crowd. Even the elephant found it difficult to enter because of all the people. And the children were jumping – do you know where? – on the roof of the school! They were shouting, "He has come! We knew he would bring some trick, but this one is so big!"

The headmaster had to tell the peon to ring the bell signaling that the school was closed; otherwise the crowd would destroy the garden, or even the roof may give way with so many children on it. Even my own teachers were on the roof! And the strange thing is that even I, foolishly, felt like going up on the roof to see what was happening.

The school was closed. The elephant had entered and passed through, and I made the gate relevant. At least it could now say to the other gates: "Once upon a time a boy passed through me on an elephant, and there was such a crowd to see it happen…." Of course the gate will say "…to see me, the gate."

The raja also came. When he saw the crowd he could not believe it. He asked me, "How did you manage to gather so many people so quickly?"

I said, "I did nothing. Just my entry into school was enough. Don't think it was your elephant; if you think that, tomorrow you go on the elephant, and I will see that not a single soul reaches here."

He said, "I don't want to look like a fool. Whether they come or not, I would look foolish if I was sitting on my elephant for no reason in front of a primary school. You at least belong to the school. I know about you – I have heard many stories. Now, when are you going to ask for my Ford?"

I said, "Just you wait."

I never went, although he had invited me himself, and it would have been a great occasion, because in the whole town there was no other car. But this car was too...what to say about it? Every twenty yards you had to get out and push it; that's the reason I never went.

I said to him, "What kind of car is this?"

He said, "I am a poor man, a king of a small state. I have to have a car, and this is the only one I can afford."

It was absolutely worthless. I still wonder how it managed to even move for a few yards. The whole town used to enjoy it, and laughed when the raja came past in his car – and of course everybody had to push!

I said to him, "No. Right now I am not in a position to take your car, but someday, maybe." I said it just not to hurt his feelings. But I still remember that car: it must still be there in that house.

In India they have such antique cars.... What do you call them? – vintage? The government of India had to make a law that no vintage car can be taken outside India. There is no need to make any law; the cars could not go anyway. But Americans are ready to purchase them at any price. In India you can find even the first model of all kinds of cars. In fact in Bombay or Calcutta you will still see such ancient cars that you cannot believe that you are still in the twentieth century.

Once, by the way, the raja and I accidentally met in a train, and his first question to me was, "Why didn't you come?"

I could not immediately remember what he meant by "did not come"...so I said, "I don't remember that I had to come."

He said, "Yes, it must have been forty years ago. You promised to come and take my car to the school." Then I remembered! He was right.

I said, "Wonderful!"...because he must have been about ninety-five and he still had such a good memory. After forty years, "Why did you not come?" I said, "You are a miracle."

I think if we meet somewhere in the other world the first question he will ask me will be the same: "Why didn't you come?" –

because I again promised saying, "Okay, I forgot. Forgive me. I will come."

He said, "When?"

I said, "You want me to give you a date? For that car? After forty years! Even forty years ago it was a car in name only. What can have happened to it after another forty years?"

He said, "It is in perfect order."

I said, "Great! Why don't you say it is just like new, as if it had just come from the showroom? But I will come; I would love a ride in that car." But unfortunately by the time I got there, the raja had died...or fortunately, because I saw the car! Forty years before it used to go at least a few feet; now, even if the raja had been alive, the car was dead.

His old servant said, "You came a little late. The raja is dead."

I said, "Thank God! Otherwise that fool would have made me sit in this car, and it could not possibly move."

He said, "That's true. I have never seen it move, but I have only been in his service for fifteen years, and it has not moved in that time. It just stands there in the porch to show that the maharaja has a car."

I said, "The ride would have been really great, and very quick too. You would enter from one door and get out the other, no time wasted."

But these visits to the school are still remembered by the few teachers still alive. And none of them believed that I could have been first in the whole university, because they all knew how I had passed from their class. It was all due to their favor, or fear, or whatsoever. They simply could not believe how I could get to be the first in the whole university. When I came home, all the newspapers reported it with my picture saying, "This schoolboy has won the gold medal." My teachers were astounded. They all looked at me as if I were from some other planet.

I said to them, "Why are you looking like that?"

They said, "We don't believe it even now, seeing you. You must have played some trick."

I said, "In a way you are right; it certainly was a trick." And they knew, because all that I ever did with them was to play tricks.

Once a man came to the town with a horse. You may have heard about a very famous horse in Germany; I think his name was Hans.

Devageet, how do you pronounce it? Hands? H-a-n-s.

"Hunts, Osho."

Okay, "Hands."

Hans had become world-famous at that time, so much so that great mathematicians, scientists, and all kinds of thinkers and philosophers went to see this horse. And what was all the fuss about? I know, but I came to know about this "Hans affair" only very late, because in my village there was a man with a horse which did the same trick. I bugged him so much that finally he gave in and agreed to tell me how he did it.

His horse...but first let me tell you about this famous horse in Germany, so you can understand how even great scientists can be fooled by a horse. This horse, Hans, was able to do any small mathematical problem. You could ask him how much two plus four is, and he would tap six times with his right foot.

What the horse was doing was really something, although the problem was very small: How much is two plus four? – but the horse solved it without any mistake. Slowly he began to solve bigger problems involving greater figures. Nobody was able to figure out what the secret was. Even biologists started saying that perhaps horses have intelligence just like man, and all they need is training.

I too have seen this type of horse in my village. He was not world-famous; he belonged to a poor man, but he could do the same trick. The horse was the man's only income. He would move with his horse from village to village, and people would ask it questions. Sometimes the horse would say yes, sometimes the horse would say no, by just moving its head – not like the Japanese, but like everybody else in the world. Only the Japanese are strange.

When I used to give sannyas to a Japanese, that was a problem. They move their heads oppositely to the way everybody else does. When they nod up and down, they mean no, and vice versa. Although I knew it, again and again I got so involved talking to them that when they said yes I thought they were saying no.

For a moment I was shocked; then Nartan, who translated for me, said, "They are doing their thing. Neither they learn, nor do you. And I am in such a difficulty. I know it is going to happen. I even push them, pinch them to remind them. They even tell me that they will remember, and yet when you ask them a question...."

The habit becomes so much part of your structure. Why did it only happen to the Japanese? Perhaps they belonged to a different kind of monkey; that can be the only explanation. In the beginning there were two monkeys, and one of them was Japanese.

I was always asking this man with the horse to tell me the trick. His horse could also do what the famous Hans was known to do. But the man was poor; I knew it was his whole livelihood – but finally the man had to give up. I promised him saying, "I will never tell anybody your secret, but there is just one favor you will have to do for me: let me have your horse for one hour so I can take it to school. That's all. Then I will keep completely mum."

He said, "That's okay."

He wanted to get rid of me somehow, so he told me the trick. It was very simple: he had trained the horse so that when he moved his head one way, the horse also moved his head in the same way. And of course everybody would be watching the horse, and nobody would be watching the owner who would be standing in the corner. And he moved his head so slightly that even if you watched you may not have noticed – but the horse sensed it. When the owner did not move his head, the horse had been trained to move his head from side to side. The same was true about tapping.

The horse did not know any figures, what to say about arithmetic. When asked, "What is two plus two?" he would tap four times, then stop. The whole trick was that when the owner closed his eyes, the horse stopped tapping – while the eyes were open, the horse went on tapping.

And this was the same trick that was found out about the famous Hans. But this was a poor man, living in a poor village, whereas Hans was really a famous horse, and German. When the Germans do something, they do it thoroughly. A German mathematician researched for three years to find out these secrets that I am telling you.

After he had shown me the tricks, I took the horse to school. Of course there was great festivity among the children, but the head-master said to me, "How do you manage to find these strange things? I have lived in this village my whole life, yet I never knew about this horse."

I said, "One needs a certain insight, and one has to be on the lookout continuously. That's why I cannot come to school every day."

He said, "That's very good. Don't come. Searching is good for everybody. Because when you do come it means that the whole day is disturbed. You are bound to do something disturbing. I have never seen you sitting doing your work as everybody else does."

I said, "The work is not worth doing. The fact that everybody else is doing it is enough proof that it is not worth doing. In this school everybody is doing this work. In India there are seven million villages, and in every village everybody is doing the same work. It is not worth doing. I try to find something which nobody else is doing, and I bring it to you free of charge. Whenever I come it is almost a carnival, and yet you are looking at me so sadly. I am perfectly okay."

He said, "I am not sad about you; I am sad about myself – that I have to be the headmaster of this school."

He was not a bad man. My last days in the primary school were in his class. That was the fourth class. I never brought him any big troubles, but small ones I can't help; they just come my way on their own. But just looking at his sad eyes, I said, "Okay, so now I will not bring you anything that disturbs you; that means that I will not be coming here anymore. I will just come to take my certificate at the end. If you can give it to the peon, I will take it from him, and I won't enter this school again."

And I did not enter to get my certificate. I sent the peon for it. He told the headmaster, "The boy says, 'Why should I go in for my certificate when I was never appreciated for my visits? You can bring it and give it to me at the Elephant Gate.'"

I loved that peon. He was such a beautiful soul. He died in 1960. Just by chance I was in the town, but to me it was as if I was only there for him, so that I could see him die. And that has been my deep interest from my very childhood: death is such a mystery, far deeper than life can ever be.

I am not saying that you should commit suicide, but remember that death is not the enemy, and not the end either. It is not a film which finishes with "The End." There is no end. Birth and death, both are events in the stream of life, just waves. And certainly death is richer than birth, because birth is empty. Death is one's whole life's experience. It depends on you how much you make your death significant. It depends on how much you live, not in terms of time but in terms of depth.

I went back to the primary school years later. I could not believe that everything had disappeared except the Elephant Gate. All the trees – and there were so many trees – had been cut. And there had been so many beautiful flowering trees, but not a single one was there.

I had gone only for that old man, the peon, who had just died. He lived by the side of the gate, next to the school. But it would have been better if I had not gone, because in my memory it was beautiful, and I would have remembered it that way, but now it is difficult. It looked like a faded picture, all colors gone – perhaps even the lines are disappearing – just an old picture, only the frame is intact.

Only one man had come to visit me in Poona who had been my teacher in that school. Then too he had been very loving towards me, but I never thought that he would come to Poona to see me. It is a long and costly journey for a poor man.

I asked him, "What prompted you to come?"

He said, "I just wanted to see what deep down I had always dreamed – that you are not what you appeared to be. You are somebody else."

I said, "Strange that you never told me before."

He said, "I myself thought it strange to tell somebody that they are somebody else other than who they appeared to be, so I kept it to myself. But it came again and again – and now I am old, and I wanted to see whether it had happened, or was I just a fool wasting my time in thinking about it."

By the time he left he was a sannyasin. He said, "Now there is no point in not becoming a sannyasin. I have seen you, and I have seen your people. I am old and will not live long, but even a few days as a sannyasin and I will feel that my life has not been in vain."

Just ten minutes for me....

It is beautiful, but no more. I know there is time but I have something else to do.

Session 49

O KAY. I WAS JUST TRYING to remember the man. I can see his face, but perhaps I never bothered about his name so I don't remember it. I will tell you the whole story.

My Nani, seeing that I was unteachable and sending me to school was just creating trouble, tried to convince my family, my father and mother, but nobody was ready to listen to her. But she was right in saying, "This boy is an unnecessary nuisance for one thousand other boys" – that was when I entered high school – "and every day he is up to something. It would be better to have a private tutor for him. Let him 'visit' the school, as he calls it, once in a while, but that is not going to help him learn anything worthwhile, because he is always creating trouble for others and for himself. There is no time left."

She tried as hard as she could to teach me the basics, but nobody in my family was ready to get a private tutor for me. In that town, even today, I don't think anybody has a private tutor. What for? The whole family was saying, "Then why are these schools here if we have to have private tutors?"

She said, "But this boy should not be counted with others – not because I love him, but because he is real trouble. I live with him, and I have lived for so many years that I know he will do everything that is possible to create trouble. And no punishment can prevent it."

But my father and mother, my father's brothers and sisters – and I mean the whole Noah's Ark, all the creatures – disagreed with her. But they were all shocked when I agreed.

I said, "She is right. I will never learn anything in those third-rate schools. In fact the moment I see those teachers I want to teach them a lesson that they will never forget in their whole life. And the boys, so many boys sitting silently…it is unnatural. So I just do some small thing and immediately nature takes over, and nurture is left far behind with all its culture. She is right: if you want me to at least know language, mathematics, something of geography or history, then listen to her."

They were more shocked than if I had exploded a firecracker… because that was absolutely expected. People of my family and neighborhood, everybody expected trouble, so much so that they even started asking me, "What is up your sleeve today?"

I said, "Can't I even have a holiday? What is up *your* sleeves? Are you paying for it? The whole town should pay me if you feel it is of any value. I can produce every possible thing in the world."

Only my Nani was really interested, and I told my family, "I should know the basics. Listen to her. I am going to have a tutor whether you listen or not. All that she needs is my agreement, and I totally agree with her."

She said, "Have you heard what you were expecting? You were not expecting this, but this is his very quality – the unexpected. So don't be shocked or feel insulted. If you feel shocked or insulted he will do more on the same lines. Just do what I say: fix up a private tutor for him."

My poor father – poor because everybody laughed at him – said, "I wanted to agree with you, but I was afraid of everybody else in the family, even of your daughter, my wife. I was afraid that they would all jump upon me. You are right, he needs some basic training. And the real problem is not whether he needs it or not; the real problem is, can we find a tutor who will be ready to teach him? We are ready to pay; you find him a tutor."

She had somebody in mind. She had already asked me what I felt about the man. I said, "The man looks good, just a little henpecked."

She said, "That is not your business. Why should a child be worried about that? He is a good teacher. He has been given the governor's certificate as the best teacher of the province. You can depend on him."

I said, "He depends on his wife; his wife depends on his servant;

his servant is just a fool – and I have to depend on him? A great chain! But the man is good; just don't ask me to depend on him. Instead ask that I should remain available to him; that's enough for teaching. Why dependence? He is not my boss; in fact, I am his boss."

She said, "Look, if you say this to him he will leave immediately."

I said, "You don't know anything about him. I know him. Even if I actually hit him on the head, he will not go anywhere because I know who has his ears in their hands."

In India, donkeys are caught by their ears. Of course they have long ears; that is the easiest thing to hold to catch them. "He is a donkey. He may be educated, but I know his wife, and she is a real woman. She has many donkeys under her like him. If he creates any trouble I will take care of him, don't be worried. And remember, the monthly payment that you have to make to him has to go via me to his wife."

She said, "I know you! Now I understand the whole logic of it."

I said, "Then go ahead."

I called the man. He was really henpecked – not just so-so, but multidimensionally. When I brought him to my Nani, first he tried to escape. I said, "Listen, if you try in any way to escape, I'm going directly to your wife."

He said, "What? No! Why to my wife?"

I said, "Then just keep quiet, and whatsoever salary my Nani is going to pay – because the envelope will be closed – I will deliver it to your wife. The arrangement is already made. I'm not interested in the money part, but the envelope has to reach your wife, not to you. So before escaping, think twice at least."

He was trying to bargain, this much or that, but that moment he immediately agreed. I winked at my Nani and said, "Look! This is the tutor you have found. Will he teach me, or will I have to teach him? Who is going to teach whom? His salary is fixed; now the second question is far more important to me."

The man said, "What does it mean, Who is going to teach? Are you going to teach me?"

I said, "Why not? I am paying you; obviously I should teach and you should learn. Money can do everything."

My Nani said to the man, "Don't be afraid, he's not that bad. He won't create any trouble for you if you promise not to provoke him in any way. Once provoked, then I cannot do anything to prevent him, because he is not under any salary. In fact I have to persuade him to accept some money for sweets, toys and clothes, and he is very reluctant about that. So remember, don't provoke him; otherwise you will be in trouble." And the fool did, the very first day.

He came early in the morning. He was a retired headmaster, but I don't think that he ever had a head. But that's how people are divided in the whole world: into heads and hands. Laborers are called "hands," just hands, as if there is nobody behind the hands. And the intellectuals, those who call themselves intelligentsia, are known as "heads" – whether they have any heads or not. I have seen so many so-called heads of departments that I have always wondered whether this was a law: that anybody who has no head will be made the head of a department.

When this man came to start, he did what my grandmother had warned him not to. What he did I can understand now. At that time of course I could not have understood the whole psychology of it, but now I can see why he behaved the way he did.

The more I have known myself, the more I have understood the "robotness" of people. They function like machines. They are really nuts and bolts – sometimes nuts and sometimes bolts, but both. If nuts are needed, they will be nuts; if bolts are needed they will be bolts. You know the nuts, but who are the bolts?

Now, this will be difficult, and will take me into a long diversion and I may forget the poor man who is standing before me with folded hands. So in some other circle we will talk about the bolts. But first, about this man....

He came into my room, in my Nani's house. In fact the whole house was mine, except for her room, and the house had many rooms. It was not a big house, but it had at least six rooms, and she needed only one; the other five belonged to me, naturally. Nobody else was there.

I divided those rooms according to my different kinds of activities. One room I kept for learning; I used to learn all kinds of things in that room, like snakes and how to catch them, how to teach them to dance to your music, which is not much to do with music at all. I learned all kinds of magical tricks. That was my room. Even my grandmother was not allowed to enter, because it was a sacred place of learning, and she knew that everything except the sacred went on in there. But nobody was allowed in. I put a notice on the door: NO ADMISSION WITHOUT PERMISSION.

I had found exactly the right notice in Shambhu Babu's office. I just told him, "I'm taking it away."

He said, "What?"

I said, "On this notice there is nothing written saying that you have to pay for it. It is free. Shambhu Babu, do you understand?"

Then he burst into laughter and said, "For years this notice has been up right in front of my eyes, and nobody pointed out to me that the price was not written on the board. Anybody could have taken it away. And it was just hanging on a nail; nothing needed to be done. You can just take it away."

I said, "You are a friend, but in these matters don't bring your friendship in."

I had that notice on the door of my room. Perhaps it may still be hanging there.

That man, whose name I cannot remember all this time.... I have been trying all kinds of memory exercises while talking to you. Nobody can help either, so we will just forget what his name was. What matters is not his name but the material that he was made of – just rubber. You could not find another man like that. But he came with tie and suit, and it was a hot summer's day! From the very beginning he showed his stupidity.

In central India during the hot summer you start perspiring even before the sun rises. And he came dressed in socks, tie, long pants – and you know I always disliked long pants. Perhaps this very kind of person has created in me a sort of seasickness about long pants. He is still standing before me: I can describe him in very minute detail.

He coughed when he entered the room, fixed his tie, tried to stand upright, and said, "Listen, boy, I have heard many stories about you, so I want to tell you from the very beginning that I am not a coward." He looked here and there in case somebody might be listening and may tell his wife, and he was not aware that I was very friendly with his wife. He continuously looked from side to side.

I always think that is the way all cowards behave. Generalizations are not absolute truths, including this one, but they certainly contain some truth. Otherwise, what is the need to look from side to side when there is only one child sitting there in front of you? Yet he was looking everywhere except at me: the door, the window, and yet talking to me. It was so hilarious and so pitiable that I told him, "You listen too. You are saying that you are not a coward. Do you believe in ghosts?"

He said, "What?" – and he looked all around, even behind his chair. He said, "Ghosts? Where did ghosts come into this? I am introducing myself to you, and you introduce ghosts."

I said, "I am not introducing them yet. Tonight I will see you with a ghost."

He said, "Really?" And he looked so afraid, he started perspiring. It was a hot summer morning, and he was so tied up, even more than I am right now.

I told him, "You simply start teaching. Don't waste time, because I have many things to do."

He looked at me absolutely unable to believe what I was saying – that I have many things to do. But he was not concerned with me, or the things I had to do or not do. He said, "Yes, I will start teaching – but what about the ghosts?"

I said, "Forget about them. Tonight I will introduce you."

He now realized that I was serious. He started trembling so much I could not hear what he was saying, I could only see his long pants shaking. After one hour of teaching me nonsense, I said, "Sir, something is wrong with your long pants."

He said, "What is wrong?" Then he looked down and saw that they were shaking, and then they started shaking even more.

I said, "I feel that there is something inside them. I cannot see from my side, but you must know. But why are you shaking? And it is not just your long pants, it is you."

He left without finishing the lesson he had begun, saying, "I have another appointment. I will finish the lesson tomorrow."

I said, "Tomorrow please come in shorts because then we can be certain whether it is the pants shaking or you. It will be in the service of truth – because right now it is a mystery. I am also wondering what kind of pants these are."

He had a beautiful pair of pants – at least it looked as if they were his, but I don't know whether they were his or not, because that night finished everything; he never came again. That's how my private tutor, as he was called, left. I had told my grandmother, "Do you think anybody, at any salary you are ready to give, will be able to stand me?"

She said, "Don't disturb things. Somehow I have managed to persuade your family, and you agreed. In fact it is only because of you that I succeeded."

"No," I said, "I am not going to do anything, but if something happens what can I do? And I ought to tell you this because tonight will decide whether you pay him or not."

She said, "What? Is he going to die or something? And so soon? He only started this morning, and he has only worked one hour."

I said, "He provoked me."

She said, "I warned him not to provoke you."

In the courtyard of my grandmother's old house there was a big neem tree. That house still belonged to us after my grandmother's death. It was really a huge, ancient tree, so big that the whole house was covered by it. When it was in season, when the neem flowers came, the fragrance was everywhere.

I don't know whether any tree like the neem exists anywhere else, because it needs a very hot climate. Its flowers have a very sharp – that's the only word I can find, 'sharp' – edge to their fragrance. I should not call it fragrance because it is bitter. The moment you smell it, it is brisk and crisp, but it leaves a bitter taste in the mouth. It is bound to, because neem tea must be the most bitter tea in the whole world. But if you start liking it, it is just like coffee. You have to practice a little; otherwise it is not such that you can like it instantly.

Although instant coffee is available on the market you still have to learn the taste. The same is true about alcohol, and a thousand other things. You have to imbibe the taste slowly. If you have lived in a neem grove, and known the fragrance from your very first breath, then it is not bitter to you, or even if bitter it is sweet too.

In India it is thought to be a religious duty that one should plant as many neem trees as possible. Very strange! – but if you know the neem tree, its crisp freshness, its purifying power, then you will not laugh at it. India is poor and cannot afford many purifying devices, but the neem tree is a natural thing and it grows easily.

This neem tree was behind my house. I used to call my Nani's house "my" house. The other house was for everybody else, all kinds of creatures; I was not part of it. Once in a while I would go to see my father and my mother, but rush out as quickly as was humanly possible. I mean that just as soon as the formalities were over I was gone. And they knew that I did not want to come to their house. They knew I called it "that house." So my house, with that big neem tree, was a really beautiful place, but I don't know who created the world, nor do I know who created this story about the neem tree either.

The story was – and it made the neem tree a real beauty – the story was that the neem tree had the power to catch hold of ghosts. How the neem tree did it I don't know, nor did my enlightenment help either. In fact the first thing that I wanted to know after enlightenment was how the neem tree did it, but no answer came. Perhaps it did not do anything at all. In India any story becomes a truth, and soon the ultimate truth.

But the story was that if any ghost has taken possession of you, just go to the neem tree, sit underneath it, take a nail with you, the bigger the better; then say to the neem tree, "I am nailing my ghost." Also take a hammer, or use any large stone lying around, and hit the nail hard. Once the ghost is nailed you are free of it. There were at least one thousand nails in that tree. I really still feel sorry for it, although it is no more.

Every day people were coming and a small shop had even opened on the other side of the street to sell nails, because they were in such demand. What is more significant is that the ghost almost always disappeared. The natural conclusion was that the ghost had been nailed to the tree. Nobody ever took a nail out, because if you did the ghost would be released, and perhaps finding you close by would get possession of you.

My family was very worried about me and that tree. They told my Nani that, "It's good that he sleeps at your place. We have nothing against it. He eats there and that too is perfectly okay. He rarely comes to see his family; that too is okay – we know he is taken care of – but remember that tree, and this boy. If he takes a nail out, he will have much misery throughout his whole life."

And the story goes on to say that once a ghost is released from the tree you can't nail it again because it knows the trick, and it won't be deceived twice.

So my Nani was constantly alert that I did not go near the neem tree. But she was not aware that I was removing as many nails as possible; otherwise who was supplying the shopkeeper on the other side of the street? I had a great business going. At first even the shopkeeper was very much afraid. He said to me, "What! You have brought these nails from the tree itself?"

I said, "Yes, and no ghosts. We are friendly, very friendly." I did not want to get him disturbed, because once my grandmother knew there would be trouble. So I told him, "The ghosts love me very much. We are very friendly."

He said, "That's very strange. I have never heard that ghosts love small children like you. But business is business…."

I was giving him nails at half the price he could get them from the market. It was a real bargain. He thought that if I could take the nails out, and the ghosts had not disturbed me at all, then they must be very friendly to me, and he thought that it is good not to antagonize the boy. The boy himself is a nuisance, and if the ghosts are helping him, then nobody is safe from him.

He used to give me money, I used to give him nails. I told my grandmother, "To tell you the truth, it's all hocus-pocus. There are no ghosts. I have been selling nails from that tree for almost one year now."

She could not believe it. For a moment she could not breathe. Then she said, "What! Selling the nails! You are not even supposed to come close to that tree. If your mother and father find out they will take you away."

I said, "Don't be worried, I am friendly with the ghosts."

She said, "Tell me the truth. What is really happening?" She was a simple woman in that way. She was utterly innocent.

I said, "The whole thing is true, and that is what is happening. But don't be against the poor shopkeeper, because it's a question of business. My whole business will be finished if he escapes or becomes afraid. If you really want to protect my small business you could just mention to him, just by the way, something like, 'It is strange how these ghosts somehow love this boy. I have never seen them be friendly to anybody else. Even I cannot go near the tree.' Just tell him when you pass by."

In India they make a small platform of bricks around a tree, just to sit on. This tree had a big platform. It was a big tree: at least one hundred people could easily manage to sit underneath it on the platform, and at least one thousand under the shade of the whole tree. It was huge.

I said to my Nani, "Don't disturb that poor shopkeeper. He is my only source of income."

She said, "Income? What income? What kind of thing is happening? And I am not even told about it!"

I said, "I was afraid that you would get worried, but now I can assure you that there are no ghosts. Come with me and I will take a nail out and show you."

She said, "No. I believe you." That's how people believe.

I said, "No, Nani, that is not right. Come with me. I will take the nail out. If anything wrong happens it will happen to me, and I am going to take the nails out anyway, whether you come or not. I have taken out hundreds of nails already."

She thought for a moment and then said, "Right, I will come. I would have preferred not to, but then you will always think of me as a coward, and I could not accept that association in your mind. I am coming."

She came. Of course in the beginning she watched from a little distance. It was a big courtyard. The house had once belonged to a small estate. It had really beautiful statues beneath the neem tree, and a few in the house too. The doors were old but beautifully carved. Asheesh would have loved those doors. They made a great noise – but that is another matter. Some ancient architect must have planned the house. The reason we could get it very cheap for my grandmother was because of the ghosts. Who wanted to live in the house with so many ghosts already living there in the tree? We got it almost free of cost, for almost nothing, just token money. The owner was happy to get rid of it.

My father had told my Nani, "You will be alone there with, at the most, this small boy who is more trouble than any ghost. With so many ghosts and this boy too, you will be in trouble. But I know you love the river, the view, and the silence of the place."

It was almost a temple. Nobody had lived there for years except the ghosts. I told my Nani, "Don't be worried. Come with me but remember not to disturb the poor shopkeeper. He lives off it, I live off it; in fact many poor boys in my school are supported by me because of these ghosts, so please don't disturb it."

But she still stood a little way away. I told her, "Come on...." That's what I have been doing since then, telling everybody, "Come on, come a little closer. Don't be worried, don't be afraid."

Somehow she came and saw that the whole thing was all invention. She then asked, "But how does it work? – because I have seen thousands of people, not just one.... They come from faraway places and their ghosts disappear. When they come they are mad; when they go, after the nail has been stuck into the poor tree, they are perfectly sane. How does it work?"

I said, "Right now I don't know how it works, but I will find out. I'm on the way to finding out. I cannot leave the ghosts alone."

That tree was between my house and the rest of the neighborhood, overlooking a small street. During the night, of course, nobody passed along that street. It was very good for me; there was no disturbance at night at all. In fact, just before sunset people started rushing back to their houses before it got dark. Who knows, with so many ghosts....

The poor tutor lived just a few houses behind my Nani's house. He had to pass along that street; there was no other way for him. I arranged it that night. It was difficult because during the day everybody passed along the street, and in the daytime it was difficult for me to persuade the ghosts to do something, but at night I could arrange it.

I just sent a boy to the tutor's house. The boy had to go because in my neighborhood, any boy who was not ready to follow my advice, or whatsoever, was going to be in constant trouble, twenty-four hours a day, day in, day out. So whatsoever I said, they did it, knowing perfectly well that it was dangerous – because they too believed in the ghosts.

I told him, "You go to the tutor's house and tell him that his father" – who lived in another street – "is very seriously ill, and perhaps may not survive. And say it really seriously."

Naturally, when your father is dying who thinks of ghosts? The tutor immediately rushed out. And I had made every arrangement: I was sitting in the tree. It was my tree, nobody could object. The tutor came past with his kerosene lamp – of course he must have thought he should at least take a kerosene lamp so that the ghosts wouldn't come too near, or if they did he would see them and escape in time.

I simply jumped out of the tree, on top of the tutor! What happened next was really great, just great! Something I never expected.... *(laughing out loud)* His pants gave way! He ran away without his pants! I can still see him.... *(roaring with laughter)*

Session 50

I T IS GOOD THAT I cannot see...but I know what is going on. But what can you do? – you have to follow your own technology, and with a man like me, naturally you are in a great difficulty. I am tied and can't help you.

Ashu, can you do something? Just a little laughter on your side will help him keep quiet. It is a very strange thing: when somebody else starts laughing the other person stops. The reason is clear, not to them, but to me. The person who was laughing immediately thinks that he is doing something wrong, and of course becomes serious.

So when you see Devageet is going a little off the road, laugh, defeat him. It is a question of female liberation. And if you give a good laugh he will immediately start taking his notes. You have not even started yet, and he has come to his senses.

I was telling you yesterday that I jumped from the tree that night, not to hurt the poor teacher but to let him know what kind of student he had. But it went too far. Even I was surprised when I saw him so terrified. He was just fear. The man disappeared.

For a moment I even thought to put an end to it, thinking, "He is an old man; perhaps he may die or something, may go mad, or may never return to his house," because he could not reach his house without again passing that tree – there was no other way. But it was too late. He had run away leaving his pants behind.

I collected them and went to my grandmother and said, "These are the pants, and you thought he was going to teach me? This pair of pants?"

She said, "What happened?"

I said, "Everything has happened. The man has run away naked, and I don't know how he will manage to reach his home. And I am in a hurry – I will tell you the whole story later on. You keep the pants. If he comes here, give them to him."

But strange, he never came back to our house to collect his pants which remained there. I even nailed them to the neem tree so that if he wanted to take them, there would be no need to ask me. But to take his pants from the neem tree meant releasing the ghost that he thought had jumped on him.

Thousands of people as they passed the neem tree must have seen those pants. People came there as a kind of psychoanalysis, an effective – what do you call it, Devaraj? Plassbo?

"Placebo, Osho."

Plassba?

"Plas-see-bo."

Okay, but I will continue to call it "plassbo." You can correct it in your book. "Plasseebo" is right, but my whole life I have called it "plassbo," and it is better to stick to your own whether it is right or wrong. At least it is your own. Devaraj must be right, and I must be wrong about it, but I'm right in still calling it "plassbo" – not the name, but to give it the flavor of how I have behaved.

Right and wrong have never been my consideration. What I happen to like is right – and I don't say that it is right for everybody. I'm not a fanatic; I'm just a madman. At the most...I cannot claim more than that.

What was I saying?

"You were talking about people coming to the tree as a kind of placebo for psychoanalysis, Osho."

Marriage is a placebo. It works, that's the weird thing. Whether it is true or not does not matter. I am always for the result; what brings it about is immaterial. I am a pragmatist.

I told my grandmother, "Don't be worried. I will hang these pants on the neem tree, and you can be certain of its effect."

She said, "I know you and your strange ideas. Now the whole town will know whose pants these are. Even if the man were to come for his pants he could never come here again." Those pants were famous because he used them for special occasions.

But what happened to the man? I even searched everywhere in the town, but naturally he was not to be found in the town because he was naked. So I thought, "Better wait. Perhaps late at night he may come. He may have gone to the other side of the river." That was the closest place where one would not be seen by anybody.

But the man never returned. That's how my tutor disappeared. I still wonder what happened to him without his pants. I'm not very interested in him, but how did he manage without pants? And where did he go? Naturally certain ideas came to me. Perhaps he died of a heart attack — but still the body, without pants, would have been discovered. And even though he was dead, anybody who would have seen him would have laughed. Because his pants were so famous, he was even called "Mister Pants." I don't even remember his name. And he had so many pairs of pants — the story in the town was that he had three hundred sixty-five pairs, one for every day. I don't think that is true, just gossip. But what happened to him?

I asked his family; they said, "We are waiting, but he has not been seen since that night."

I said, "Strange…." To my Nani I said, "Certainly his disappearance sometimes makes even me suspect that perhaps ghosts exist. …Because I was simply introducing him to the ghosts. And it is good that his pants should hang on the tree."

My father became so angry that I could do such a nasty thing. I had never seen him so angry.

I said, "But I had not planned it that way. I had not even thought that the man would simply evaporate. It is too much even for me. I just did a simple thing. I sat in the tree with a drum, struck it loudly just so that he would take notice of what was happening and forget everything else in the world — and then I jumped to the ground."

And it was my usual practice. I had made many people run. In fact my grandmother used to say, "Perhaps this street is the only street in the town where nobody walks at night, except you."

The other day someone was showing me a few car-stickers. One was beautiful; it said, "Believe me, this road really belongs to me." While reading that sticker I remembered the road that passed near my house. At least during the night I owned it. During the day it was a government road, but at night absolutely my own. Even today I cannot see that any road could be as silent as that road used to be at night.

But my father was so angry that he said, "Whatsoever happens I'm going to cut down this neem tree, and I'm going to finish this whole business that you have been doing."

I said, "What business?" I was afraid about the nails, because that was my only income. He was not aware of that as he was saying, "This nasty business that you have been doing, making people afraid.... And now that man's family continuously haunts me. Every day somebody or other comes and asks me to do something. What can I do?"

I said, "I can at least give you the pants; that's all that is left. And as far as the tree is concerned, I tell you nobody will be willing to cut it down."

He said, "You don't have to worry about that."

I said, "I am not worrying. I am just making you aware so that you don't waste your time."

And after three days he called me to say, "You are really something. You told me nobody would cut down the tree. It is strange: I have asked all the people who might be able to cut the tree down – there are not many in this town, only a few woodcutters – but nobody is ready to do it. They all said, 'No. What about the ghosts?'"

I said to him, "I told you before, I don't know anybody in this town who will even touch the tree unless I decide to cut it down myself. But if you want I can find someone, but you will have to depend on me."

He said, "I cannot depend on you because one never knows what you are planning. You may tell me you are going to cut down the tree but you could do something else. No, I cannot ask you to do it."

That tree remained without anybody being ready to cut it down. I used to harass my poor father saying, "Dada, what about the tree? It is still standing – I saw it this morning. Have you not found a woodcutter yet?"

And he would look everywhere to see that nobody was listening, then say to me, "Can't you leave me alone?"

I said, "I rarely visit you. I come once in a while just to ask about that tree. You say that you cannot find a person to cut it down. I know you have been asking people, and I know that they have been refusing. I have also been asking them."

He said, "What for?"

I said, "No, not to cut the tree down, just to make them aware what the tree contains – the ghosts. I don't think anybody will agree to cut it down unless you ask me to do it." And of course he was reluctant to do that. So I said, "Okay, the tree will remain."

And that tree remained while I was in the town. It was only when I left that my father managed to get a Mohammedan from another village to cut the tree down. But a strange thing happened: the tree was cut down – but because it may have grown again, and to remove it completely, he made a well in its place. But he suffered unnecessarily because the tree and its roots had gone so deep that they made the water as bitter as you can imagine. Nobody was ready to drink the water from that well.

When I finally came home I told my father, "You never listened to me. You destroyed a beautiful tree and created this ugly hole, and now what use is it? You wasted money in making the well and even you cannot drink the water."

He said, "Perhaps once in a while you are right. I realize it, but nothing can be done now."

He had to cover that well with stones. It is still there, covered. If you remove a few stones, just slabs, you will find the well. By this time the water will be really bitter.

Why did I want to tell you this story? – because the tutor, on his first day, tried to impress me that he was a man of great courage, fearless, saying he did not believe in ghosts.

I said, "Really? You don't believe in ghosts?"

He said, "Of course I don't believe." I could see he was already afraid when he said it.

I had said, "Believe it or not, but tonight I will introduce you." I had never thought that the introduction would make the man simply disappear. What happened to him? Whenever I went to the town I always visited his house to inquire, "Has he come home yet?"

They said, "Why are you so interested in it? We have forgotten the whole idea of his coming."

I said, "I cannot forget, because what I saw had such great beauty, and I was only introducing him to somebody."

They said, "To whom?"

I said, "Just somebody – and I could not even finish the introduction. And," I told his son, "what your father did was not at all gentlemanly: he just ran out of his pants."

The wife, who was cooking something, laughed and she said, "I always used to tell him to hold his pants tight, but he would not listen. Now his pants are gone and so is he."

I said, "Why did you tell him to keep a tight hold of his pants?"

She said, "You don't understand. It is simple. He had all his pants made when he was young, and now they were all loose because he had lost weight. So I was always afraid someday or other he would create an embarrassing situation where his pants would suddenly fall down."

I then remembered that he always kept his hands in his pants pockets. But naturally when you meet ghosts you cannot remember to keep your hands in your pockets and to hold on tightly to your pants. Who cares about pants when there are so many ghosts jumping out on you!

He did one more thing before he left.... I don't know where he went; in this world there are many things which are unanswerable, and this can be counted among them. I don't know why, but before he left he put out his kerosene lamp. That is another question about that tutor which has remained unanswered.

He was a great man in a way. I often wondered why he put out the lamp; then one day I came across a small story, and it was solved. I don't mean that the man returned, but the second question was answered.

His little boy would not go to the bathroom without his mother standing at the door, and if it was night-time, then naturally she had to keep a lamp there. I was visiting the house and heard the mother say to the boy, "Can't you take the lamp yourself?"

He said, "Okay, I will take the lamp because I have to go. I can't wait any longer."

I said, "Why use the lamp in the daytime? I have heard the story of Diogenes; is he another Diogenes? Why the lamp?"

The mother laughed and said, "Ask him."

I said, "Why do you want the lamp during the day, Raju?"

He said, "Day or night, it does not matter; ghosts are every-where. When you have a lamp you can avoid clashing with them."

That day I understood why the tutor had put out the lamp before running away. Perhaps he thought if he kept the lamp on, the ghost would find him. But if he put it out – and it is only my logic – if he put it out, at least they could not see him and he could dodge and escape.

But he really did a great job. To tell you the truth, it seems he always wanted to escape from his wife, and this opportunity was his last. He used it to the fullest. This man would not have come to such an end if he had not started with his fearlessness, and by saying, "I'm not even afraid of ghosts."

"But," I said, "I am not asking you." And his pants were trem-bling when he said the word 'ghosts'.

I said, "Sir, you have very strange pants. I have never seen anything tremble like that. They look so alive."

He looked down at his pants – I can still see him – and the legs were going completely berserk.

In fact my primary school days had ended. Of course thousands of things happened that cannot be talked about...not that they are worthless – nothing in life is worthless – but just because there is no time. So just a few examples will do.

The primary school was just the beginning of middle school. I entered middle school, and the first thing that I remember – you know me, I see strange things....

My secretary collects all kinds of crazy car-stickers. One was: "Warning – I brake for hallucinations." I liked it. Really great!

The first thing that I remember is this man who – fortunately or unfortunately, because it's difficult to know which – was not at all sane. He was not even insane like me; he was genuinely insane. In the village he was known as Khakki Master. The meaning of *khakki* is something very close to what you mean by cuckoo, crazy. He was my first teacher in the middle school. Perhaps because he was genuinely insane we immediately became friends.

I have rarely been friendly towards teachers. There are a few tribes like politicians, journalists, and teachers whom I simply cannot like, although I would like to like them too. Jesus says: "Love your enemies." Okay, but he never went to any school so he does not know about teachers, that much is certain; otherwise he would have said, "Love your enemies, except for teachers."

Of course there were no journalists or politicians, no people whose whole work it was to somehow suck your blood. Jesus was talking about enemies – but what about friends? He said nothing about love your friends. ...Because I don't think an enemy can do you much harm; the real harm is done by the friend.

I simply hate journalists, and when I hate I don't mean anything else; no interpretations, simply hate! I hate teachers! I don't want teachers in the world...not teachers in the old sense. Perhaps a different kind of elderly friend will have to be found.

But this man who was known as a madman immediately became my friend. His full name was Rajaram, but he was known as Raju-Khakki, "Raju, the mad." I had expected that he would be what he was known to be.

When I saw the man – you will not believe it, but that day for the first time I realized it is not good to be really sane in an insane world. Looking at him, just for a moment it was as if time had stopped. How long it lasted is difficult to say, but he had to finish writing my name and address and registering things, so he asked these questions.

I said, "Can't we remain silent?"

He said, "I would love to be silent with you, but let us finish this dirty job first, then we can sit silently."

The way he said, "Let us finish this dirty job first..." was enough to show me that here is a man who at least knows what is dirty: the bureaucracy, and the endless red-tape-ism. He quickly finished, closed the register and said, "Okay, now we can sit silently. Can I hold your hand?"

I was not expecting that from a teacher, so I said, "Either what people say is right – that you are mad – or perhaps what I am feeling is right: that you are the only sane teacher in the whole town."

He said, "It is better to be mad; it saves you from many troubles."

We laughed and became friends. For thirty years continuously, until he died, I used to visit him, just to sit. His wife used to say, "I thought my husband was the only madman in the town. That's not right; you are mad too. I wonder," she said, "why you come to see this madman." And he was a madman in every way.

For example, you would see him going to school on a horse. That was not a bad thing in those parts, but sitting backwards...! I loved that about him. To sit on a horse, not as everybody else sits but looking backwards, is a strange experience.

It was only later on I told him the story about Mulla Nasruddin, how he used to ride on his donkey also sitting backwards. When his students used to go out of town, naturally they felt embarrassed, to say the least. Finally one of the students asked, "Mulla, everybody sits on a donkey, there is nothing wrong in that. You can sit on a donkey, but backwards...! The donkey is going in one direction, and you are looking in the opposite direction, so people laugh and say, 'Look at that crazy Mulla!' – and we feel embarrassed because we are your students."

Mulla said, "I will explain it to you. I cannot sit keeping you at my back, that would be insulting to you. I cannot insult my own students, so that is out of the question. Other ways can be found. Perhaps you could all walk backwards in front of the donkey, but it would be very difficult, and you would feel even more embarrassed. Of course you would then be facing me, and there would be no question of disrespect. But it would be very difficult for you to walk backwards, and we are going a long way. So the only natural and also the easiest solution is that I should sit facing backwards on the donkey. The donkey has no objection to not seeing you. He can see where we are going and reach the destination. I don't want to be disrespectful to you, so the best way is for me to sit backwards on the donkey."

It is strange, but Lao Tzu also used to sit backwards on his buffalo, perhaps for the same reason. But nothing is known about his answer. The Chinese don't answer such questions, and they don't ask them either. They are very polite people, always bowing down to each other.

I was determined to do everything that was not allowed. For example, when I was in college I wore a robe without buttons, and pajama pants. One of my professors, Indrabahadur Khare...I remember his name although he died long ago, but because of this story I am about to tell you I cannot forget it.

He was in charge of all celebrations in the college. Of course, because of all the awards I was bringing to the college, he decided that my picture should be taken with all the medals, shields and cups, so we went to the studio. But a great problem arose there when he said, "Do up your buttons."

I said, "That is not possible."

He said, "What? You cannot close your buttons?"

I said, "Look, you can see, the buttons are false. I don't have any button holes; they cannot be closed. I don't like to do up buttons, so I instructed my tailor to not make any button holes in my clothes. The buttons are there, you can see them, so the picture will show the buttons."

He was so angry because he was very much — what do you say, concerned? — concerned about clothes and things like that, so he said, "Then the picture cannot be taken."

I said, "Okay, then I will go."

He said, "I don't mean that" — because he was afraid I would cause trouble and perhaps go to the principal. He knew perfectly well that there was no law saying that your buttons should be closed when you are being photographed.

I reminded him by saying, "Know well that tomorrow you will be in trouble. There is no law against it. Read all night, find out, do homework, and tomorrow face me in the principal's office. Prove to me that a photograph may not be taken without closed buttons."

He said, "You are certainly a strange student. I know that I will not be able to prove it, so please just get the photo finished. I will leave, but your photograph has to be taken."

That photograph still exists. One of my brothers, my fourth brother, Niklanka, has been collecting everything concerning me from his very childhood. Everybody laughed at him. Even I asked him, "Niklanka, why do you bother to collect everything about me?"

He said, "I don't know, but somehow there is a deep feeling in me that someday these things will be needed."

OSHO IN THE ROBE WITHOUT BUTTONS

I said, "Then go ahead. If you feel like that, go ahead, do it." And it is because of Niklanka that a few pictures of my childhood have been saved. He has collected things which now have significance.

He was always collecting things. Even if I threw something away in the wastepaper basket, he would search to see if I had thrown away something I had written. Whatsoever it was, he would collect it because of my handwriting. The whole town thought he was mad.

People even said to me, "You are mad, and he seems to be even more mad!"

But he loved me as nobody in my whole family did – although they all loved me, but nobody like him. He may well have the photograph because he was always collecting. I remember having seen it in his collection – with the buttons open. And I can still see the irritation on Indrabahadur's face. He was a man very particular about everything, but I too was a man of my own type.

I said to him, "Forget about the photograph. Is it going to be my photo or yours? You can have your photo taken with your buttons closed, but I never close my buttons as you know. If I closed them for this photo, it would be false. Either take my photo or else forget all about it!"

It was good, beautiful...but be vertical. With me, horizontal is not applicable. Good. When things are going so good it is better to stop. And Devageet, it is beautiful, but enough. Devaraj, help him. Ashu, do your best. I would love to continue but the time has gone. One has to withdraw somewhere.

Stop.

Appendix

YOU CAN ASK MY MOTHER something – because she happens to be here…. After my birth, for three days I didn't take any milk, and they were all worried, concerned. The doctors were concerned, because how was this child going to survive if he simply refused to take milk? But they had no idea of my difficulty, of what difficulty they were creating for me. They were trying to force me in every possible way. And there was no way I could explain to them, or that they could find out by themselves.

In my past life, before I died, I was on a fast. I wanted to complete a twenty-one day fast, but I was murdered before my fast was complete, three days before. Those three days remained in my awareness even in this birth; I had to complete my fast. I am really stubborn! Otherwise, people don't carry things from one life to another life; once a chapter is closed, it is closed.

But for three days they could not manage to put anything in my mouth; I simply rejected it. But after three days I was perfectly okay and they were all surprised: "Why was he refusing for three days? There was no sickness, no problem – and after three days he is perfectly normal." It remained a mystery to them.

I have not done anything, I have simply continued what I was doing in my past life. And that's why in my childhood I was thought to be crazy, eccentric – because I would not give any explanation of why I wanted to do something. I would simply say, "I want to do it. There are reasons for me, why I am doing it, but I cannot give you those reasons because you cannot understand."

My father would say, "I cannot understand and you can?"

I said, "Yes, it is something that belongs to my inner experience.

It has nothing to do with your age, your being my father. You, of course can understand much more than I can understand, but this is something which is inside me – only I can approach there, you cannot."

And he would simply say, "You are impossible."

I said, "If everybody accepted this it would be a great relief. Just accept me as impossible, so I am no longer a problem for you and I have not to trouble explaining all kinds of things. I am going to do whatever I am going to do. There is no way to change it. For me it is absolute. It is not a question of your giving me permission or not."

So this was my usual practice: whatever I wanted to do I would do.

I cannot forget one day.... There are a few things which make no logical sense and have no relevance but somehow remain hanging in your memory. You cannot understand for what reason they are there because millions of things have happened which are far more important, far more significant, and they have all disappeared. But a few insignificant things – you cannot find any reason why, but they have remained; they have left a trace behind.

One such thing I remember. I was coming home from school – my school was almost one mile away from home. Just halfway there was a huge bo tree. I had passed that bo tree every day at least four times: going to school, then in the middle of the day coming home for lunch, then going to school again, then coming back home. So many thousands of times I had passed that tree, but that day something happened.

It was a hot day, and as I came close to the tree, I was perspiring. I passed under the tree; and it was so cool that without having any deliberate thought I stopped for a while, not knowing why. I simply went close to the tree trunk, sat there and felt the tree trunk. I cannot explain what happened but I felt so immensely happy, as if something was transpiring between me and the tree. Just the coolness could not be the cause, because many times when I had been perspiring, I had passed through the coolness of the tree. I had also stopped before, but never before had I gone and touched the tree and sat there as if meeting an old friend.

That moment has remained shining like a star. So much has happened in my life, but I don't see that moment diminishing in any way: it is still there. Whenever I look back it is still there. Neither that day was I clearly aware what had happened, nor can I say today – but something *had* happened. And from that day there was a certain relatedness with the tree which I had not felt before, even with any human being. I became more intimate with that tree than with anybody else in the whole world. It became a routine thing to me: whenever I passed the tree, I would sit for a few seconds or a few minutes and just feel the tree. I can still see – something went on growing between us.

The day I left school and moved to another city to join the university, I took leave of my father, of my mother, of my uncles and my whole family. I was not the type who easily cries or weeps. Even when I was punished badly, the blood might have been oozing from my hands, but tears would not come to my eyes.

My father used to say, "Do you have tears in your eyes or not?"

I said, "You can make my hands bleed but you cannot force me to cry and weep. And why should I? – because whatsoever you are doing is absolutely right. I have done something, knowing well that this is going to be the consequence. I never lie, so there is no way to escape from the punishment. What is the point of tears?"

But when I went to the tree to say goodbye, I started crying. That is the only time that I remember in my whole life; otherwise tears were absolutely unknown to me. In my childhood one of my sisters, whom I had loved more than any other of my brothers and sisters, died. And in India you have brothers and sisters by the dozen. I used to tease my father, "How did you miss making the dozen whole? – because you have only eleven children. You should be a little mathematical, just one child more."

And he said, "You are my son but you even try to joke with me."

I said, "I am not joking; I am simply saying that it is so easy to tell somebody 'one dozen' – and exactly that is what I have been doing. If anybody asks me how many children you have, I say, 'One dozen.' It is simpler. You have made it unnecessarily complicated: eleven! Either you should have stopped at ten – that seems to be complete – or twelve; that too is complete. But eleven? – what kind of number is that?"

Out of these ten sisters and brothers, I loved most one of my sisters who died when I was very young. I must have been five years old and she must have been three years old. But even then I had not cried. I was surprised and shocked. Everybody was crying, and they all thought that I was in shock because I loved my sister the most. In my whole family everybody knew it, that I loved her the most, and she loved me the most. They thought perhaps it was just because of the shock that tears were not coming, but that was not the case.

When my maternal grandfather died I did not weep – and he had brought me up. On my birthday he used to bring an elephant from a nearby town.... Elephants in India, in those days, were kept either by kings – because it is very costly, the maintenance, the food and the service that the elephant requires – or by saints.

Two types of people used to have them. The saints could have elephants because they had so many followers; just as the followers looked after the saint, they looked after the elephant. Nearby there was a saint who had an elephant, so for my birthday my maternal grandfather used to bring the elephant. He would put me on the elephant with two bags, one on either side, full of silver coins.

In my childhood, in India, notes had not yet appeared; pure silver was still used for the rupee. My grandfather would fill two bags, big bags, hanging on either side, with silver coins, and I would go around the village throwing the silver coins. That's how he used to celebrate my birthday. Once I started, he would come in his bullock cart behind me with more rupees, and he would go on telling me, "Don't be miserly – I am keeping enough. You cannot throw more than I have. Go on throwing!"

Naturally, the whole village followed the elephant. It was not a big village either, not more than two or three hundred people in the whole village, so I would go around the village, the only street in the village. He managed in every possible way to give me the idea that I belonged to some royal family.

He loved me so much that it was impossible for me to fall sick. Now, you have no power over sickness but you can manage not to say anything about it. He would get in such a panic if I had just a slight headache. He would get in such a panic that he would take his horse and ride to the closest doctor and bring the doctor back.

It was so much trouble, more than the headache was, so I would simply remain silent, not saying anything about it. Even when he died in my lap there were no tears. Even I suspected that perhaps I didn't have tear glands.

But on that day, taking leave of the bo tree, I wept for the first and the last time. It remains a very lighted spot. And when I was crying I had an absolute certainty that there were tears in the eyes of the tree too, although I could not see the eyes, and I could not see the tears. But I could feel – when I touched the tree I could feel the sadness, and I could feel a blessing, a goodbye. And it was certainly my last meeting, because when I came back after one year, for some stupid reason the tree had been cut down and removed.

The stupid reason was that they were making a small memorial pillar, and that was the most beautiful spot in the middle of the city. It was for an idiot who was rich enough to win all the elections and become the president of the municipal committee. He had been president for at least thirty-five years – the longest time anybody had been president in the town. Everybody was happy with his presidency because he was such an idiot; you could do anything and he was not going to create any interference.

You could make your house just in the middle of the street; he would not bother, you just had to vote for him. So the whole town was happy with him because everybody had such freedom. The municipal committee, the members, the clerks and the head clerks – all were happy with him. Everybody wanted him to remain eternally the president; but even idiots have to die, fortunately. But his death was unfortunate because they looked for a place to make a memorial for him, and they destroyed the bo tree. Now his marble stone stands there instead of a living bo tree.

I do not forget things, but there are so many things to be said; and language is one-dimensional. It is linear – you can go only in one line – and experience is multidimensional, it moves in thousands of lines. The problem with so-called orators is what to say. My problem is what *not* to say, because there is so much waiting to be said, knocking from all sides and asking, "Let me in." So I drift away…but don't be shy in reminding me.

. . .

ONE ASTROLOGER HAD PROMISED to work on my life's birth chart. He died before he had done it, so his son had to prepare the chart. But he was also puzzled. He said, "It is almost certain that this child is going to die at the age of twenty-one. Every seven years he will have to face death."

So my parents, my family, were always worried about my death. Whenever I would come to the beginning of a new seven-year cycle, they would become afraid. And he was right. At the age of seven I survived, but I had a deep experience of death – not of my own, but of the death of my maternal grandfather. And I was so much attached to him that his death appeared to be my own death. In my own childish way I imitated his death. I would not eat for three days continuously, would not drink water, because I felt that if I did so it would be a betrayal.

I loved him so much, he loved me so much, that when he was alive I was never allowed to go to my parents. I was with my maternal grandfather. He said, "When I die, only then can you go." He lived in a very small village, so I couldn't go to any school because there was no school. He would never leave me, but then the time came when he died. He was part and parcel of me. I had grown with his presence, his love.

When he died I felt that it would be a betrayal to eat: "Now I don't want to live...." It was childish, but through it something very deep happened. For three days I remained lying down; I would not come out of the bed. I said, "When he is dead, I do not want to live." I survived, but those three days became a death experience. I died in a way, and I came to realize – now I can tell about it, though at that time it was just a vague experience – I came to feel that death is impossible. This was a feeling.

Then at the age of fourteen, my family again became disturbed that I would die. I again survived, but then I again tried consciously. I said to them, "If death is going to occur as the astrologer has said, then it is better to be prepared. And why give a chance to death?

Why should I not go and meet it halfway? If I am going to die, then it is better to die consciously."

So I took leave from my school for seven days. I went to my principal and I told him, "I am going to die."

He said, "What nonsense you are talking! Are you committing suicide? What do you mean you are going to die?"

I told him about the astrologer's prediction that the possibility of death would confront me every seven years. I told him, "I am going into retreat for seven days to wait for death. If death comes, it is good to meet it consciously so that it becomes an experience."

I went to a temple just outside of my village. I arranged with the priest that he should not disturb me. It was a very lonely, unvisited temple – old, in ruins. No one ever came to it. So I told him, "I will remain in the temple. You just give me once a day something to eat and something to drink, and the whole day I will be lying there waiting for death."

For seven days I waited. Those seven days became a beautiful experience. Death never came, but on my part I tried in every way to be dead. Strange, weird feelings happened. Many things happened, but the basic note was this – that if you are feeling you are going to die you become calm and silent. Nothing creates any worry then because all worries are concerned with life. Life is the base of all worries. When you are going to die anyway one day, why worry?

I was lying there. On the third or fourth day a snake entered the temple. It was in view; I was seeing the snake, but there was no fear. Suddenly I felt very strange. The snake was coming nearer and nearer, and I felt very strange. There was no fear. So I thought, "When death is coming, it may be coming through this snake, so why be afraid? Wait!"

The snake crossed over me and went away. Fear had disappeared. If you accept death, there is no fear. If you cling to life, then every fear is there.

Many times flies came around me. They would fly around, they would creep over me, on my face. Sometimes I felt irritated and would have liked to throw them off, but then I thought, "What is the use? Sooner or later I am going to die, and then no one will be here to protect the body. So let them have their way."

The moment I decided to let them have their way, the irritation disappeared. They were still on the body, but it was as if I was not concerned. They were as if moving, as if creeping on someone else's body. There was a distance immediately. If you accept death, a distance is created. Life moves far away with all its worries, irritations, everything.

I died in a way, but I came to know that something deathless is there. Once you accept death totally you become aware of it.

Then again, at the age of twenty-one, my family was waiting. So I told them, "Why do you go on waiting? Do not wait. Now I am not going to die."

Physically, someday I will die, of course. However, this prediction of the astrologer helped me very much because he made me aware very early on about death. Continuously, I could meditate and could accept that it was coming.

. . .

ONE DAY MY FATHER PUT all my *salwars* and my *kurtas* and my three Turkish caps in a bundle and went into the godown, the basement, and put them there somewhere where many kinds of things were – broken, useless. I could not find anything, so when I came out of the bathroom I simply went naked, with my eyes closed into the shop. As I was going out my father said, "Wait! Just come in. Take your clothes."

I said, "You bring them, wherever they are."

He said, "I had never thought you would do this. I thought you would look around and search for the clothes, and you would not find them – because I had put them in such a place that you wouldn't find them. Then naturally you would wear the normal clothes that you are supposed to wear. I never thought that this would be your action."

I said, "I take direct action. I don't believe in unnecessary talk;

I didn't even ask anybody where my clothes were. Why should I ask? My nakedness will serve the same purpose."

He said, "You have your clothes, and nobody is going to bother you about your clothes, but please, don't start walking naked because that will create more trouble – that a cloth merchant's son has no clothes to wear. You are notorious and you will make us notorious also with you: 'Look at the poor child!' Everybody will think that we are not giving you clothes."

Since they had stopped, by the time I passed matriculation I dropped that dress. As I left the town I changed my dress to be more suited to my college life. I had found that in the first college I went to, the cap was compulsory – you could not come without a cap. That was a great idea! You have to come very properly dressed: shoes, buttons closed, with a cap. I went there with no buttons, with no cap, with my wooden sandals – and immediately I became a celebrity.

The principal immediately called me. He said, "What is this?"

I said, "This is just a way to get introduced to you, otherwise it may take years. Who bothers about a first-year student?"

He said, "You have some idea behind it, but it is not allowed; you will have to wear a cap, and buttons have to be closed."

I said, "You will have to prove to me what the scientific grounds are for wearing a cap. Does it help in any way to increase your intelligence? Then I can even use a turban – why a cap? – if it increases your brain power. But the fact is that the most idiots in India are in Punjab, and they use a turban, tied tightly. Perhaps they are the only people in the whole world who use the turban so tightly; their mind is completely imprisoned, finished. And the most intelligent people in India are the Bengalis, who don't use caps." I said, "You just tell me what are the fundamental, scientific reasons that I have to wear a cap."

He said, "This is strange – nobody ever asked the fundamental, scientific reasons about caps. This is simply our convention in this college."

I said, "I don't bother about convention. If the convention is unscientific and destroys people's intelligence, I am the first to rebel against it. And soon you will see caps disappearing from the college because I am going to tell people, 'Look – Bengalis have the best intelligence and they don't use caps.'

"In India, two Nobel Prizes have gone to Bengalis. To Punjabis, I don't think ever in the future there is going to be given a single Nobel Prize. I am going to spread this movement, but if you keep silent and allow me the way I am, I won't create a nuisance; otherwise there will be a movement. You will see bonfires, caps burning, in front of your office."

He looked at me and he said, "Okay, don't create any nuisance, just go on the way you are. But I will be in trouble because sooner or later others are going to ask, 'Why did you allow him?'"

I said, "The fact is that if you are an honest man, you should stop wearing the cap yourself, because you don't have any scientific grounds for it. Otherwise, whosoever comes, tell him to find scientific, fundamental reasons for it – that in some way it helps intelligence. The college is meant to help people's intelligence; it should be sharpened. In what way does the cap help? It imprisons."

But he said, "At least buttons...."

I said, "I don't like them. I like the air going directly to my chest, I enjoy it; I don't like buttons. And nowhere in your college code is a cap mentioned, so for the cap I need scientific reasons. Nowhere is it mentioned that you have to have buttons."

But nobody there had ever thought that people would come to college without buttons.

. . .

MY MOTHER WAS JUST TELLING me yesterday...and Vivek listened to her talking so animatedly for the first time in so long; otherwise whatever she has to ask is answered in one or two sentences; yes or no, and the conversation is over. But yesterday she was talking for a long time and she was very animated, so Vivek asked me, "What was your mother telling you?"

I told her she was remembering a few things. I have not told her yet what she was telling me, because it was a long story. She was telling me that when I was five months old in her womb, a miracle happened.

She was going from my father's house to her father's house; and it was the rainy season. It is customary in India for the first child to be born at the maternal father's home, so although it was the rainy season and very difficult – no roads, and she had to go on a horse – the sooner she went, the better; if she waited longer then it would have become more difficult, so she went with one of her cousin-brothers.

In the middle of the journey was a big river, the Narmada. It was in flood. When they reached the boat, the boatman saw that my mother was pregnant, and he asked my mother's cousin-brother, "What is your relationship?"

He was not aware that he would get into trouble so he simply said, "We are brother and sister."

The boatman refused; he said, "I cannot take you because your sister is pregnant – that means you are not two, you are three."

In India, this is a custom, an old custom – perhaps it started in the days of Krishna – that one should not travel on water, particularly in a boat, with one's sister's son. There is a danger of the boat sinking.

The boatman said, "What guarantee is there that the child in your sister's womb is a girl and not a boy? If he is a boy I don't want to take the risk – because it is not a question only of my life, sixty other people are going in the boat. Either you can come or your sister can come; both I won't take."

On both sides there were hills and jungle, and the boat used to go only one time a day. In the morning it would go – and the river is really vast at that point – and then it would come back by the evening. The next morning it would go again, the same boat. So either my mother had to remain on this side, which was dangerous, or go on that side alone, which was just as dangerous. So for three days they continued to ask him, beg him, saying that she was pregnant and he should be kind.

He said, "I can't help it – this is not done. If you can give me a guarantee that it is not a boy then I can take you; but how can you give me a guarantee?"

So for three days they had to stay in a temple there. In that temple lived a saint, very famous in those days in that area. Now, around that temple there has arisen a city in the memory of that saint, Saikheda. Saikheda means "the village of the saint." *Sai* means the saint; he was known as Sai Baba. It is not the same Sai Baba who became world-famous – Sai Baba of Shirdi – but they were contemporaries.

Sai Baba of Shirdi became world-famous because of the simple coincidence that Shirdi is near Bombay, and all the celebrities of Bombay and the rich people of Bombay started going to Sai Baba of Shirdi. And because of Bombay being a world center, soon Sai Baba of Shirdi's name started reaching outside India, and so many miracles were created around him.

The same was the situation with this Sai Baba who lived in that temple. Finally my mother had to ask Sai Baba, "Can you do something? For three days we have been here. I am pregnant and my cousin-brother has told the boatman that he is my brother, and he won't take us in the boat. Now, unless you do something, say something to that boatman, we are in a fix. What to do? My brother cannot leave me here alone; I cannot go alone to the other side. On both sides are wild jungles and forests, and for at least twenty-four hours I will have to wait alone."

I never met Sai Baba, but in a way I did meet him; I was five months old. He just touched my mother's belly. My mother said, "What are you doing?"

He said, "I am touching the feet of your child."

The boatman saw this and said, "What are you doing, Baba? You have never touched anybody's feet."

And Baba said, "This is not *anybody*; and you are a fool – you should take them to the other side. Don't be worried. The soul that is within this womb is capable of saving thousands of people, so don't be worried about your sixty people – take her."

So my mother was saying, "At that time I became aware that I was carrying someone special."

I said, "As far as I understand, Sai Baba was a wise man: he really befooled the boatman! There is no miracle, there is nothing. And boats don't sink just because somebody is traveling with their sister's son. There is no rationality in the idea, it is just absurd. Perhaps sometime accidentally it may have happened and then it became a routine idea."

My own understanding is that because in Krishna's life his mother's brother was told by the astrologers that "one of the children of your sister will kill you," he kept his sister and his brother-in-law in prison. She gave birth to seven children, seven boys, and he killed them all. The eighth was Krishna, and of course when God himself was born, the locks of the prison opened up, and the guards fell fast asleep, and Krishna's father took him out.

The river Yamuna was the boundary of Kansa's kingdom. Kansa was the person who was killing his sister's sons in the fear that one of the sons was going to kill him. The Yamuna was in flood – and it is one of the biggest rivers in India. The father of Krishna was very much afraid, but somehow the child had to be taken to the other side, to a friend's house whose wife had given birth to a girl – so he could exchange them. He could bring the girl back with him because the next morning Kansa would be there asking, "Where is the child?" and planning to kill him. A girl he wouldn't kill – it had to be a boy.

But how to cross this river? There was no boat in the night, but it had to be crossed. But when God can open locks without keys, without anybody opening them – they simply opened up, the doors opened up, the guards fell asleep – God would do something.

So he put the child in a bucket on his head and passed through the river – something like what happened to Moses when the ocean parted. This time it happened in an Indian way. It could not have happened to Moses because that ocean was not Indian, but this river was.

As he entered the river, the river started rising higher. He was very much afraid: what was happening? He was hoping the river would subside, but it started rising. It went to the point where it touched the feet of Krishna, then it receded. This is the Indian way; it cannot happen anywhere else. How can the river miss such a point? When God is born and passing through her, just giving way is not enough, not mannerly.

Since that time there has been this idea that there is a certain antagonism between a person and his sister's son, because Krishna killed Kansa. The river was crossed, it subsided; it favored the child. Since then rivers are angry against maternal uncles – all the rivers of India. And that superstition is carried even today.

I told my mother, "One thing is certain – that Sai Baba must have been a wise man and had some sense of humor." But she wouldn't listen. And it became known in the village what had happened, and to support it, after one month another thing happened which.... In life there are so many coincidences out of which you can make miracles. Once you are bent upon making a miracle then any coincidence can be turned into a miracle.

After one month there was a very great flood, and in front of my mother's house in the rainy season it was almost like a river. There was a lake, and a small road between the lake and the house, but in the rainy season so much water came that the road was completely like a river, and the lake and the road became merged into one. It was almost oceanic; as far as you could see it was all water. And that year perhaps India had the biggest floods ever.

Floods ordinarily happen every year in India, but that year a strange thing was noted, that floods started reversing the rivers' flow of water. The rains were so heavy that the ocean was not able to take the water as quickly as it was coming, so the water at the ocean front was stuck; it started flowing backwards. Where small rivers fall into big rivers, the big rivers refused to take the water, because they were not able even to contain their own water. The small rivers started moving backwards.

I have never seen it – that one also I missed – but my mother says that it was a strange phenomenon to see the water moving backwards. And it started entering houses; it entered my mother's house. It was a double-storied house, and the first story was completely full of water. Then it started entering the second story. Now, there was nowhere to go, so they were all sitting on the beds, the highest place that was possible there. But my mother said, "If Sai Baba was right, then something will happen." And it must have been a coincidence that the water came up to my mother's stomach and then receded!

These two miracles happened before I was born, so I have nothing to do with them. But they became known; when I was born I was almost a saint in the village! Everybody was so respectful; people were touching my feet, even old people. I was told later on that "the whole village had accepted you as a saint."

When I must have been nearabout four, I was the only child in the house – nothing to do, no school, no place to go. My maternal grandfather had a multipurpose shop, of all kinds of things. That was the only shop in the village so every kind of thing…a very miniature market it was, rather than a shop. So I started playing with sweets and things, and I don't know how it occurred to me… but soon people were continuously coming who were sick; and there was no doctor, no physician, no hospital, even for hundreds of miles, no hospital.

Somehow it came to me that if people think of me as a saint, and they touch my feet, I would start giving them medicines. And the medicines were nothing but mixtures of a few sweets, ground well, powdered, and kept in bottles of different colors. And of course, people who get fever or a headache or a stomachache don't die. And they started getting cured. They were going to be cured anyway – that was not a miracle, but it became a miracle.

My Nana started saying, "You will spoil my shop – now it is a hospital! The whole day people are coming and sometimes *I* even have to give your medicines, and I have no idea what those medicines are! You are destroying my sweets and my shop. But they are getting cured, so no harm, you continue."

When I moved after seven years to my father's house I dropped that business of giving medicines, but people from that village, whenever they used to come, would remind me. They had already started calling me Doctor Sahib, and I would say, "Please don't use that word here, because I have stopped that profession completely. In the first place there are no sweets here; my father has a shop of cloth, I cannot make medicines out of cloth. And here nobody knows that I can do miracles. First people have to know, then you can do them, otherwise you cannot."

. . .

ONE DAY I WAS JUST playing; I must have been four or five years old, not more than that. My father was shaving his beard when somebody knocked on the door; my father said to me, "Just go and tell him, 'My father is not at home.'"

I went out and I said, "My father is shaving and he says to tell you, 'My father is not at home.'"

The man said, "What? He is inside?"

I said, "Yes, but this is what he has told me. I have told you the whole truth."

The man came in and my father looked at me: what had happened? And the man was very angry, he said, "This is something! You had called me to come at this time, and you send a message with the boy that you have gone out."

My father asked him, "But how did you find out that I was in?"

He said, "This boy has said the whole thing, that 'My father is in. He is shaving his beard, and he has told me to tell you that he is out.'"

My father looked at me. I could understand; he was saying, "Just wait! Let this man go, and I will show you."

And I told him, "I am going before this man leaves."

He said, "But I have not said anything to you."

I said, "I have understood everything!"

I told the man, "Just stay here. First let me get out, because there is going to be trouble for me." But on departing I said to my father, "You insist with me, 'Be truthful....' So," I said, "this is a chance to be truthful, and to check whether you really mean me to be truthful – or is it just that you're trying to teach me cunningness?"

Of course he understood that it was better to keep quiet, not to quarrel with me then, because when the man was gone, I would have to come home. I came after two or three hours so that he would cool down or other people would be there and no problem would arise. He was alone. I went in, and he said, "Don't be worried – I will never tell you anything like that again. You have to forgive me." He was in this way a fair man, otherwise who bothers about a four or five-year-old child, and asks – being a father – "Forgive me"?

And he never said anything like it again his whole life. He knew that with me he had to be different than with other children.

. . .

M Y GRANDFATHER LOVED ME VERY much, just because of my mischief. Even in his old age he was mischievous. He never liked my father or my uncles because they were all against this old man's mischievousness. They all said to him, "You are now seventy and you should behave. Now your sons are fifty, fifty-five, your daughters are fifty, their children are married, their children's children are there – and you go on doing such things that we feel ashamed."

I was the only one with whom he was intimate, because I loved the old man for the simple reason that he had not lost his childhood even at the age of seventy. He was as mischievous as any child. And he would play his mischief even on his own sons and daughters and sons-in-law, and they would be just shocked.

I was his only confidant, because we conspired together. Of course many things he could not do – I had to do them. For example, his son-in-law was sleeping in the room and my grandfather could not go up onto the roof, but I could go. So we conspired together; he would help me, he would become a ladder for me to go onto the roof and remove a tile. And with just a bamboo and a brush attached to it, in the night, touching the face of the son-in-law…. He would scream, and the whole house would run there…. "What is the matter?" But by that time we had disappeared, and he would say, "There was some ghost or somebody just touching my face. I tried to catch him but I could not; it was dark."

My grandfather remained utterly innocent, and I saw the great freedom that he had. In my whole family he was the eldest. He should have been the most serious and most burdened with so many problems and so many anxieties, but nothing affected him. Everybody was serious and worried when there were problems; only he was not worried. But one thing I never liked – that's why I remembered him this moment – and that was sleeping with him. He had the habit of sleeping with his face covered and I would have to sleep with my face also covered, and that was suffocating.

I told him clearly, "About everything I agree, but this I cannot tolerate. You cannot sleep with your face uncovered; I cannot sleep with my face covered – it suffocates me. You do it lovingly" – he would keep me close to his heart and cover me completely – "that's perfectly good, but in the morning my heart will not be beating. Your intention is good, but you will be alive in the morning and I will be gone. So our friendship is out of the bed."

He wanted me there because he loved me and he had said, "Why don't you come and sleep with me?"

I said, "You know perfectly well that I don't want to be suffocated by anybody, even if his intention is good. You love me and you would like to keep me close to your heart even in the night." Also, we used to go for a long walk in the mornings, and sometimes, when there was a moon, in the night. But I never allowed him to hold my hand. And he would say, "But why? You may fall, you may stumble upon a stone or anything."

I said, "That's better. Let me stumble, it is not going to kill me. It will teach me how not to stumble, how to be alert, how to remember where the rocks are. But you holding my hand – how long can you hold my hand? How long are you going to be with me? If you can guarantee that you will always be with me, then of course I am willing."

He was a very sincere man; he said, "That I cannot guarantee. I cannot even say about tomorrow. And one thing is certain, you will live long, and I will be dead, so I will not be here forever to hold your hand."

"Then," I said, "it is better for me to learn from now, because one day you will leave me in the middle, helpless. And if you have trained me to hold your hand…then there are only two ways: either I start living in a fiction: God the father – who is invisible of course – is holding your hand and he is leading you…."

I told my grandfather, "I don't want to be left in the situation where I have to create a fiction to live in. I want to live a real life, not a fictitious life. I am not a character in a novel. So you leave me alone, let me fall. I will try to get up. You wait; just watch and that will be more compassionate towards me than holding my hand."

And he understood it; he said, "You are right – one day I will not be there."

. . .

MY GRANDFATHER WAS ALWAYS FAVORABLE to me about anything. He was ready to participate if he could; of course he never punished me, he always rewarded me.
I used to come home every night and the first thing my grandfather would ask was, "What did you do today? How did things go? Was there any trouble?" We always used to have a good meeting in the night in his bed, sitting together, and he enjoyed everything. I used to tell him everything that had happened in the day, and he would say, "It was really a good day!"

My father only punished me once because I had gone to a fair which used to happen a few miles away from the city every year. There flows one of the holy rivers of the Hindus, the Narmada, and on the bank of the Narmada there used to be a big fair for one month. So I simply went there without asking him.

There was so much going on in the fair…. I had gone only for one day and I was thinking I would be back by the night, but there were so many things: magicians, a circus, drama. It was not possible to come back in one day, so three days…. The whole family was in a panic: where had I gone?

It had never happened before. At the most I had come back late in the night but I had never been away for three days continuously…and with no message. They inquired at every friend's house; nobody knew about me. And on the fourth day, when I came home, my father was really angry. Before asking me anything, he slapped me. I didn't say anything.

I said, "Do you want to slap me more? You can, because I have enjoyed enough in three days. You cannot slap me more than I have enjoyed, so you can do a few more slaps. It will cool you down, and to me it is just balancing. I have enjoyed myself."

He said, "You are really impossible. Slapping you is meaningless. You are not hurt by it; you are asking for more. Can't you make a distinction between punishment and reward?"

I said, "No, to me everything is a reward of some kind. There are different kinds of reward, but everything is a reward of some kind."

He asked me, "Where have you been for these three days?"

I said, "This you should have asked before you slapped me. Now you have lost the right to ask me. I have been slapped without even being asked. It is a full stop – close the chapter. If you wanted to know, you should have asked before, but you don't have any patience. Just a minute would have been enough. But I will not keep you continuously worrying where I have been, so I will tell you that I went to the fair."

He asked, "Why didn't you ask me?"

I said, "Because I wanted to go. Be truthful: if I had asked, would you have allowed me? Be truthful."

He said, "No."

I said, "That explains everything, why I did not ask you – because I wanted to go, and then it would have been more difficult for you. If I had asked you and you had said no, I still would have gone, and that would have been more difficult for you. Just to make it easier for you, I didn't ask, and I am rewarded for it. And I am ready to take any more reward you want to give me. But I have enjoyed the fair so much that I am going there every year. So you can... whenever I disappear, you know where I am. Don't be worried."

He said, "This is the last time that I punish you; the first and last time. Perhaps you are right: if you really wanted to go then this was the only way, because I was not going to allow you. In that fair every kind of thing happens: prostitutes are there, intoxicants are available, drugs are sold there" – and at that time in India there was no illegality about drugs, every drug was freely available. And in a fair all kinds of monks gather, and Hindu monks all use drugs – "so I would not have allowed you to go. And if you really wanted to go then perhaps you were right not to ask."

I told him, "But I did not bother about the prostitutes or the monks or the drugs. You know me: if I am interested in drugs, then in this very city...." Just by the side of my house there was a shop where all drugs were available, "And the man is so friendly to me that he will not take any money if I want any drug. So there is no problem. Prostitutes are available in the town; if I am interested in seeing their dances I can go there. Who can prevent me? Monks come continuously in the city. But I was interested in the magicians."

And my interest in magic is related to my interest in miracles. In India, before the partition, I have seen every kind of miracle being done on the streets by magicians, poor magicians. Perhaps after the whole show they may get a one-rupee collection. How can I believe that these people are messiahs? For one rupee, for three hours they are doing almost impossible things. Of course everything has a trick to it, but if you don't know the trick then it is a miracle.

You have simply heard – I have *seen* them throwing a rope up, and the rope stands by itself. They have a boy with them they call *jamura*; every magician has a jamura. I don't know how to translate it...just "my boy." And he goes on talking with the jamura, "Jamura, will you go up the rope?"

And he will say, "Yes, I will go." And this continuous conversation has something to do with the trick; it keeps people's mind on the conversation, and the conversation is funny in many ways. I have seen that boy climbing up the rope and disappearing!

And the man calls from down below, "Jamura?"

And from far above comes the voice, "Yes, master."

And he says, "Now I will bring you down part by part." Then he throws a knife up, and the head of the boy comes down! He throws the knife up, and a leg comes down! Part by part the boy comes down, and the magician goes on putting the parts together, covers them with a bed sheet and says, "Jamura, now be together."

And the jamura says, "Yes, master." The magician removes the bed sheet and the boy stands up! He pulls down the rope, winds it up, puts it in the bag and starts asking for money.

At the most he would get one rupee – because in those days sixty paise was equivalent to one rupee, and nobody was going to give him more than one paise, two paise at the most; a very rich person would give him four paise. If he could gather one rupee for his miracle he was fortunate.

I have seen all kinds of things, and the people who are doing them are just beggars.

. . .

I N MY CHILDHOOD – BECAUSE FROM there I can speak to you more authoritatively; I don't know your childhood, I know only my childhood – it was an everyday question. I was continuously asked to be truthful. And I said to my father, "Whenever you say to me to be truthful, you have to remember one thing, that truth has to be rewarded; otherwise *you* are forcing me not to be truthful. I am willing."

Very easily I figured out that truth does not pay: you are punished. Lies pay: you are rewarded. Now it was a question of very decisive, very great importance. So I made it clear to my parents that it had to be understood clearly: "If you want me to be truthful then truth has to be rewarded, and not in a future life but here and now, because I am being truthful here and now. And if truth is not rewarded, if I am punished for it, then you are forcing me to lie. So let this be clearly understood; then there is no problem for me, I will always be truthful."

What had happened was that, living two or three blocks away from my family was a brahmin family, very orthodox brahmins. Brahmins cut all their hair and just leave a small part on the seventh chakra on the head uncut, so that part goes on growing. They go on tying it and keeping it inside their cap or inside their turban. And what I had done was, I had cut the father's hair. In summertime in India, people sleep outside the house, on the street.

They bring their beds, cots, on the streets. The whole town sleeps on the streets in the night, it is so hot inside.

So this brahmin was sleeping – and it was not my fault…he had such a long *choti*; it is called a choti, that bunch of hair. I had never seen it because it was always hidden inside his turban. While he was sleeping, it was hanging down and touching the street. From his cot it was so long that I was tempted, I could not resist; I rushed home, brought the scissors, cut it of completely and took it and kept it in my room.

In the morning he must have found that it was gone. He could not believe it because his whole purity was in it, his whole religion was in it – his whole spirituality was destroyed. But everybody in the neighborhood knew that if anything goes wrong…first they would rush to me. And he came immediately. I was sitting outside knowing well that he would come in the morning. He looked at me. I also looked at him. He said to me, "What are you looking at?"

I said, "What are *you* looking at? Same thing."

He said, "Same thing?"

I said, "Yes. The same thing. You name it."

He asked, "Where is your father? I don't want to talk to you at all."

He went in. He brought my father out and my father said, "Have you done anything to this man?"

I said, "I have not done anything to this *man*, but I have cut a choti which certainly cannot belong to this man, because when I was cutting it, what was he doing? He could have prevented it."

The man said, "I was asleep."

I said, "If I had cut your finger while you were asleep, would you have remained asleep?"

He said, "How could I remain asleep if somebody was cutting my finger?"

I said, "That certainly shows that hairs are dead. You can cut them but a person is not hurt, no blood comes out. So what is the fuss about? A dead thing was hanging there…and I thought that you are unnecessarily carrying this dead thing inside your turban for your whole life – why not relieve you? It is in my room. And with my father I have the contract to be true."

So I brought out his choti and said, "If you are so interested in it, you can take it back. If it is your spirituality, your brahmanism, you can keep it tied and put it inside your turban. It is dead anyway; it was dead when it was attached to you, it was dead when I detached it. You can keep it inside your turban."

And I asked my father, "My reward?" – in front of that man.

That man said, "What reward is he asking for?"

My father said, "This is the trouble. Yesterday he proposed a contract that if he speaks the truth...and sincerely; he is not only speaking the truth, he is even giving the proof. He has told the whole story – and even has logic behind it – that it was a dead thing so why be bothered with a dead thing? And he is not hiding anything."

He rewarded me with five rupees. In those days, in that small village, five rupees was a great reward. The man was mad at my father. He said, "You will spoil this child. You should beat him rather than giving him five rupees. Now he will cut other people's chotis. If he gets five rupees per choti, all the brahmins of the town are finished, because they are all sleeping outside in the night; and when you are sleeping you cannot go on holding your choti in your hand. And what are you doing? – this will become a precedent."

My father said, "But this is my contract. If you want to punish him, that is your business; I will not come into it. I am not rewarding him for his mischief, I am rewarding him for his truth – and for my whole life I will go on rewarding him for his truth. As far as mischief is concerned, you are free to do anything with him."

That man told my father, "You are getting me into more trouble. If I do something to this boy, do you think things will stop there? I am a family man: I have my wife, my children, my house – tomorrow my house will be burned down." He was very angry, and he said, "Especially now it's a problem, because tomorrow I am going to perform a ceremony in the next village, and people seeing me without my choti...."

I said, "There is no need to worry – the choti I am giving you back. You can also reward me with something for giving your choti back. Just don't ever take off your turban in the other village; even in the night keep your turban on. That's all. It is not a big problem, it is only a question of one night. And in the night who is going to look for you choti? Everybody will be asleep."

He said, "Don't you give me advice. I feel like beating you but I know better, because that will create a whole chain of things."

I said, "It has already been created. You have come to complain; you are not rewarding me for my being so absolutely honest and sincere and telling you that I could not resist the temptation. And I have not done any harm to anybody; no violence has happened – not a single drop of blood came from your choti. Just by complaining to my father you have already created a chain of reaction."

He said to my father, "Look...!"

My father said, "It is not my business."

And I said to my father, "That's what the whole brahmanism teaches – the chain of reactions."

My father said, "You keep your philosophy to yourself. And stop going to these lectures of the sadhus and the monks and mahatmas, because from whatsoever you get from them you somehow manage to conclude such strange things."

I said, "But this is what I am saying, and it is not strange. That's exactly what the theory of karma is: you do one act, the reaction will follow. He has done an act of complaining against me, now the reaction will follow."

And the reaction followed, because he had told me that he was going to the other village.... He was very angry with me, but when you are angry, you are angry – and he was really completely freaked out. So he was angry with his wife, with the children.... I watched everything, and he somehow managed to get his things together and went off in a horse buggy.

The moment he left, I told his wife, "Do you understand where he is going? He is going forever – and you don't know! He had come to say this to my father, that he is going forever and he is never coming back again."

The wife suddenly started crying and screaming, "Stop him!" Other people ran and they stopped his buggy.

He said, "Why are you stopping me? I have to catch the train!"

They said, "Not today. Your wife is crying and beating her heart – she will die!"

He said, "But this is strange. Why should she beat herself, and why should she cry?"

But the people would not allow him to go, and they were pulling at his bag and suitcase.

The man who was driving the buggy said, "I will not take you. If this is the situation, that you are leaving your wife and small children forever, I will not do such an act."

The brahmin said, "I am not leaving, I will come back, but I don't have time to convince you. The train will be missed – the station is two miles away from my house."

But nobody was listening to him, and I was provoking people: "Stop him, otherwise his wife, his children...you will have to look after them – who is going to feed them?"

They brought him back with his bags, and of course he was angry and threw his bag at his wife. His wife asked, "What have we done? Why are you...?" And I was there outside in the crowd.

He said, "Nobody has done anything. That boy told me there would be a reaction. The reason is that three days before, in the temple, I was teaching the philosophy of action and reaction and this boy was present there. Now he is teaching me."

He told me, "Forgive me and I will never say a single word about this action and reaction. And you can cut anybody's choti if you want, I will not complain. You can cut off my head and I will not complain – because I want to stop this chain completely. My train is gone."

Then everybody asked, "What is the matter? We don't understand. Who has cut your choti?"

I said, "Look! The chain is impossible to stop. These people are asking, 'Whose choti? Who has cut it? Where is the choti?'" I said, "Just look inside his turban, on his head!" And a man who was considered to be a wrestler in the town came up and took off his turban and the choti fell out.

My father was also there, and saw it. When we were returning home he said to me, "I will reward you but don't take advantage of our contract."

I said, "I am not. That is not a contract between me and you. My contract is that I will always speak the truth to you, and you will reward me for it." And he remained consistent. Whatsoever I had done, howsoever wrong in his eyes, he continuously rewarded me.

But it is difficult to find a father like that – the father has to forcibly impose his ideals on you.

My father was condemned by my whole city: "You are spoiling the child."

He said, "If that is his destiny, to be spoiled, let him be spoiled. I will not be responsible for interfering in his destiny; he will never be able to say, 'My father spoiled me.' And if he is happy in being spoiled, then what is the wrong in being spoiled? Wherever, and whatsoever happens in his life, I don't want to interfere. My father has interfered with my life, and I know that I would have been a different person if he hadn't.

"And I know that he is right, that every father turns the child into a hypocrite, because I have been turned into a hypocrite. When I want to laugh, I am serious. When I want to be serious I have to laugh. At least let one person laugh at the time when he wants to laugh. And let him be serious when he wants to be serious."

He said, "I have eleven children but I will think of myself as having only ten." And he always thought that he had only ten. Me he never counted among his children because, he said, "I have given him total freedom to be himself. Why should he carry any image of me?"

. . .

WHEN I WAS IN MY primary school, my house was very close to the school. So when the school bell would ring, that was the time for me to go into the bathroom. My whole family would be knocking on the door, and I would remain silent – not even answering anything.

It was a daily routine that the headmaster used to come to pick me up, because I was not going on my own. And he would come, and my father would say, "What to do? You stop ringing this bell, because the moment you ring it, he immediately goes into the bathroom and locks the door! And then it is absolutely pointless, because whatever you say, he does not answer."

Finally, the school decided not to ring the bell, and the head-master used to come – first to catch hold of me – and then the bell was rung for all other children.

Every child has to be forced into many things for his own sake. I am grateful to the headmaster. He was really generous – just for a single student he changed the whole routine of the school!

I am grateful to my parents – their patience with me. The whole family was standing before the bathroom and persuading me, "You come out! If you don't want to go to school, there is no need. We will ask the headmaster to give you leave for today." But I remained silent.

And I am also grateful because those moments of silence have given me so much. And everybody shouting and running around – amidst that cyclone I was the center, simply sitting under the shower and enjoying it.

In my village, where I was born, there was a colony of potters. And the potters in India carry their pots on donkeys. That is the only thing in India that donkeys are used for. The colony was just near my house, and there were so many beautiful donkeys, but they were engaged the whole day in carrying things. Only in the night were they free, and I was also free, so I would catch hold of a donkey.

Nobody rides on a donkey in India, because a donkey is thought to be something untouchable. Riding on a donkey.... My whole family was embarrassed, because the neighbors were telling them, "We have seen your son going towards the market, sitting on a donkey. Don't let him in till he goes to the river and takes a bath."

My father used to persuade me, "We can arrange and buy a horse for you, if you are so much interested."

I said, "I am not interested in horses at all. My interest is in the donkeys. They are very philosophical people, unpredictable. A donkey may stop at any point, and whatever you do he will not move. You cannot figure out why he has stopped – and against the common knowledge that donkeys are idiots, my experience is that they are very cunning, clever politicians."

My father said, "Do you want to write a thesis on donkeys, or what?"

I said, "I can write one, because my experience with donkeys perhaps is more than anybody else's."

Riding on a donkey is a difficult job; riding on a horse is not. The donkeys are so cunning, they will never go in the middle of the road. They will always go on rubbing your leg on the side of a wall. Naturally, you will jump!

It was so difficult to keep them in the middle of the road. Either left or right, but they would never be in the middle. So I told my father, "Donkeys are rightists or leftists, but they are not Buddhists."

Buddha used to teach his disciples, "Follow the middle way." Donkeys are the only people Buddha has not been able to convince. And I don't think that they are stupid people, because when nobody is riding then, they walk in the middle. They are clever. And on a hot day, you can see them standing under a tree.

And the very face of a donkey is philosophic, as if they are brooding upon great things. Just look at the face of a donkey, and you will always feel that he is thinking so much.

Finally, my family decided that I should not be allowed to enter the kitchen – "because we don't know exactly whether you have been riding on a donkey or not." So I was always sitting outside the kitchen. I was not allowed to enter the kitchen; particularly my grandmother would not...I was an outcast!

. . .

LISTENING TO THE BIRDS, I remember.... Just outside my classroom in the high school there were beautiful mango trees. And mango trees are where cuckoos make their nests. This is the cuckoo that is calling, and there is nothing sweeter than the sound of a cuckoo.

So I used to sit by the window, looking out at the birds, at the trees, and my teachers were very much annoyed. They said, "You have to look at the blackboard."

I said, "It is my life, and I have every right to choose where to look. Outside is so beautiful – the birds singing, and the flowers, and the trees, and the sun coming through the trees – that I don't think your blackboard can be a competitor."

The teacher was so angry that he told me, "Then you can go out and stand there outside the window unless you are ready to look at the blackboard – because I am teaching you mathematics, and you are looking at the trees and the birds."

I said, "This is a great reward you are giving me, not a punishment." And I said goodbye to him.

He said, "What do you mean?"

I said, "I will never come in, I will be standing every day outside the window."

He said, "You must be crazy. I will report to your father, to your family: 'You are wasting money on him, and he's standing outside.'"

I said, "You can do anything you want to do. I know how to manage things with my father. And he knows perfectly well that if I have decided then I will remain outside the window – nothing can change it."

The principal used to see me standing outside the window every day when he came for a round. He was puzzled at what I was doing there every day. On the third or fourth day he came to me, and he said, "What are you doing? Why do you go on standing here?"

I said, "I have been rewarded."

He said, "Rewarded? For what?"

I said, "You just stand by my side and listen to the songs of the birds. And the beauty of the trees.... Do you think looking at the blackboard and that stupid teacher...because only stupid people become teachers; they cannot find any other employment. Mostly they are third-class graduates. So neither do I want to look at that teacher, nor do I want to look at the blackboard. As far as mathematics is concerned, you need not be worried – I will manage it. But I cannot miss this beauty."

He stood by my side, and he said, "Certainly it is beautiful. I have been a principal for twenty years in this school, and I never came here. And I agree with you that this is a reward. As far as mathematics is concerned, I am an M.Sc. in mathematics. You can come to my house anytime, and I will teach you mathematics – but you continue to stand outside."

So I got a better teacher, the principal of the school, who was a better mathematician. And my mathematics teacher was very much puzzled. He thought that I would get tired after a few days, but the whole month passed. Then he came out, and he said, "I am sorry, because it hurts me continuously the whole time I am in the class that I have forced you to stand out here. And you have not done any harm. You can sit inside and look wherever you want."

I said, "Now it is too late."

He said, "What do you mean?"

I said, "I mean that now I enjoy being outside. Sitting behind the window only a very small portion of the trees and the birds is available; here all the thousands of mango trees are available. And as far as mathematics is concerned, the principal is teaching me himself; every evening I go to him."

He said, "What?"

I said, "Yes, because he agreed with me that this is a reward."

He went directly to the principal and said, "This is not good. I had punished him and you are encouraging him."

The principal said, "Forget punishment and encouragement – you should also stand outside sometime. Now I cannot wait; otherwise I used to go for the round as a routine, but now I cannot wait…. The first thing I have to do is to go for the round and stay with that boy and look at the trees.

"For the first time, I have learned that there are better things than mathematics – the sounds of the birds, the flowers, the green trees, the sunrays coming through the trees, the wind blowing, singing its song through the trees. Once in a while you should also go and accompany him."

He came back very sorry and said, "The principal told me what has happened, so what should I do?" He asked me, "Should I take the whole class out?"

I said, "That would be great. We can sit under these trees, and you can teach your mathematics. But I am not going to come in the class, even if you make me fail – which you cannot do, because I now know more mathematics than any student in the class. And I have a better teacher. You are a third-class B. Sc., and he is a first-class gold medalist M. Sc."

For a few days he thought about it, and one morning when I went there I saw that the whole class was sitting under the trees. I said, "Your heart is still alive; mathematics has not killed it."

. . .

ONE OF MY TEACHERS IN the primary school, when I was in the fourth grade.... It was my first day in his class, and I had not done anything very wrong, I was just doing what you do in meditation: "Om, Om..." but inside, with closed mouth. I had a few of my friends, and I told them to sit in different places so he could not figure out from where the sound was coming. One time it was coming from here, another time it was coming from there, another time it was coming from here; he went on looking from where the sound was coming. So I told them, "Keep your mouths shut and do the 'Om' inside."

For a moment he could not figure it out. I was sitting at the very back. All teachers wanted me to sit in the front so they could keep an eye on me, and I always wanted to sit at the back from where you can do many more things; it is more feasible. He came directly to me. He must have heard from the third-grade teacher, "You keep an eye on this boy!" So he said, "Although I cannot figure out who the people are who are doing it, you must be doing it."

I said, "What? What am I doing? You have to tell me. Just saying, 'You must be doing it' does not make sense. What...?"

Now it was difficult for him to do what I was doing, because that would have looked foolish, and everybody would have started laughing. He said, "Whatsoever it is, hold both your ears in your hands and sit down, stand up, sit down, stand up – five times."

I said, "Perfectly okay." I asked him, "Can I do it fifty times?"

He said, "This is not a reward, this is a punishment."

I said, "This morning I have not done any exercise so I thought that this was a good chance, and you would be very happy. Instead of five I will do fifty. And always remember, whenever you give me any kind of reward" – that's exactly the word I told him – "whenever you give me any kind of reward, be generous." And I started doing fifty.

He went on, "Stop! It is enough. I have never seen such a boy. You should be ashamed that you have been punished."

I said, "No, I am doing my morning exercise. You helped me, you have rewarded me; this is a good exercise. In fact, you should do it too."

· · ·

IN MY HIGH SCHOOL, THERE were two buildings, and between the two buildings there was at least a twenty-foot distance. I had found a piece of wood, twenty feet long. First, I would put it on the ground and ask my friends, "Can you walk on it?" And everybody was able to walk on it without falling. And then I would put the same piece of wood on the two buildings, and except me, nobody was ready even to try.

I said, "This is strange, because you have walked on the same wood and you did not fall."

They said, "That was a different situation. Now it is so dangerous that if a little fear comes, if just one step goes wrong, you will fall nearabout thirty feet down."

I persuaded them by saying, "You can watch me; you should just not look this side or that side. You have walked on the wood...and this is my strategy: not to look here and there, just to keep totally concentrated on the wood, and go on. And I can go on for miles."

When one day I was persuading a few students, one new teacher, a chemistry teacher, who used to brag that he was a very brave man, just came by. I said, "You are a very brave man, perhaps you can try."

He said, "I can try." But then he looked down, there were thirty feet. He went two feet at the most, fell down, and had multiple fractures.

I went to see him in the hospital. He told me, "I have never seen such a dangerous fellow. What was the idea?"

I said, "You have been bragging so much…. Once you get well we will try a few more ideas."

He said, "What do you mean?"

I said, "You have just to say that you have been bragging because basically you are a man who is very much afraid. To cover it up, you are bragging: 'In the middle of the night, in the darkest forest, I can go alone. I am not afraid of any ghosts or any thieves, or any murderers.'

"It was you who provoked me to find something. And I had walked ahead of you, so it was not that I was not taking the risk. You thought that because I had walked, you would also be able to walk. That's where you were wrong.

"You started trembling from the first foot, but you could not go back. There was time, you could have jumped back, you had just taken two steps, but it was against your ego, so you went on and fell. It is not a multiple fracture to your body, it is a multiple fracture to your ego. Your body will be better within two or three weeks, but about your ego…never mention about your bravery again; otherwise …I have found a few other things."

He said, "I am going to resign from this school. This is enough. I don't want it!"

I said, "That is up to you. You can resign, but still we will try something."

And we managed to try. He resigned, and he took his luggage – he had no wife, no children, nothing. He had just come out of the university…a young man. I and a few of my friends got hold of him, and we made so much fuss, a great crowd gathered.

We said, "He's leaving his wife."

And he was trying to persuade the crowd, "I don't have any wife. These people are all lying, I am simply resigning and going."

I said to the crowd, "Just take him back to his home. He has a wife and three children."

The man said, "Leave me, because my train will be missed. I can't go back."

But then the crowd took over, and said, "You cannot go. First you come back home. Why should these children be telling lies?" And we were not just one, I had at least ten boys lined up who were saying, "Your wife is crying, your children are crying, and you are leaving them. This is not good."

The crowd caught hold of him – we all disappeared. He was shouting and screaming and saying, "I am not married, I don't have a child, I don't have any wife."

The crowd said, "First you come back home."

He said, "But my train will be gone."

They said, "We are not concerned about the train. The train you can pick up tomorrow" – because there was only one train every day. "So it is only a question of twenty-four hours. First you come home."

And we had managed to find a very poor woman who had three children, and we had told her, "We are going to give you five rupees for just a little act."

She said, "But this is not a good act."

I said, "What is the harm? You just cover your face so nobody knows...." And in India, with the *ghoonghat* you cover your head, and you cry. And I told the children, "You say, 'Papa, why are you leaving us?'"

He could not believe his eyes: there was a woman who was crying and holding his feet, saying, "Don't leave me, you have married me!" And the three children were crying, "Papa!"

And the crowd said, "Now, what do you say?"

He said, "Now, what can I say? I have never seen these children, I have never seen this woman, and they are sitting in my house."

We were all present there behind the crowd. Finally I told him, "The train is late, don't be worried." I took him aside and I told him, "This is just one of the devices. You will have to give five rupees to the woman, then you can go. Then I will take care."

He had to give five rupees to the woman. The crowd asked, "What is happening?"

I said, "They have compromised. He is going just for two days, and he has given money for two days expenses; then he will be coming back."

So they allowed him to go. And the woman told me later on, "If you have more of this kind of act...for just a five-minute act, five rupees!" And in those days five rupees was a lot of money. One could live for one month on five rupees.

We went with the teacher, and he was so angry, he would not talk with us. And I said, "Don't be angry, because we can still try some other devices."

He said, "No more devices; I am fractured all over my body, my five rupees are gone, and I don't think that I am going to catch the train."

I said, "You don't be worried, the train has gone. You will have to wait in the waiting room, but we have made every arrangement... you will be comfortable there. In the night just be a little alert, be watchful." I said, "We don't have much time, only one night. We tried many ghosts...only one ghost is ready."

He said, "My God!"

So in the night, in the waiting room...because in the night there is no train, and the stationmaster goes away, and the waiting room is empty, and the whole platform is empty. He said, "Then I am not going to the station. I will lie down anywhere on the street, in the market, but I am not going to the station, to that empty place in the night."

I said, "You used to say that you don't believe in ghosts."

He said, "I used to say that, but seeing your devices...whether ghosts exist or not, some ghost will appear, and I don't want to get into any more trouble."

That man met me after twenty or twenty-five years. I asked him, "How are you?"

He said, "How am I? You made me so afraid that I decided never to get married, and never to have children, and never to be employed in any school; it is dangerous. My whole body has been destroyed, and that day you could have done even more harm, because the whole crowd was believing you."

I said, "That woman was ready to go with you, those children were ready to go with you. You yourself bribed them."

He said, "I bribed them? You suggested five rupees, and you managed to find those people. And I know that woman and those three children; they were just living in the neighborhood."

But I said, "Why were you trembling?"

He said, "Why was I trembling? I was trembling because that crowd might have forced that woman and those children on my head. My service was gone, and I would have had a family which was not concerned with me at all. That woman was so ugly, and you were so tricky that you told her to keep her face hidden behind the sari. But I have become so much afraid since then, I have not served in any school, and I have never said to anybody, 'I am a brave man.' I have accepted that I am a coward."

I said, "If you had accepted it before, this tragedy would have been avoided."

. . .

IN MY NEIGHBORHOOD THERE WAS a temple, a temple of Krishna, just a few houses away from my house. The temple was on the other side of the road, my house was on this side of the road. In front of the temple lived the man who had made the temple; he was a great devotee.

The temple was of Krishna in his childhood – because when Krishna became a young man he created many troubles and many questions, so there are many people who worship Krishna as a child – hence the temple was called, the temple of *Balaji*.

This Balaji's mandir was just in front of the house of the man who had made it. Because of the temple and the man's devotion, continuous devotion…. He would take a bath – just in front of the temple was a well – he would take a bath there first thing. Then he would do his prayers for hours; and he was thought to be very religious. By and by people started also calling him Balaji. It became so associated that I don't remember his real name myself, because by the time I had any idea that he existed, I only heard his name as Balaji. But that cannot be his name; that name must have come because he made the temple.

I used to go to the temple because the temple was very beautiful and very silent – except for this Balaji who was a disturbance there. And for hours – he was a rich man so there was no need for him to be worried about time – three hours in the morning, three hours in the evening, he was constantly torturing the god of the temple. Nobody used to go there, although the temple was so beautiful that many people would have gone there; they would go to a temple further away because this Balaji was too much. And his noise – it can only be called noise, it was not music – his singing was such that it would make you an enemy of singing for your whole life.

But I used to go there and we became friendly. He was an old man. I said, "Balaji, three hours in the morning, three hours in the evening – what are you asking for? And every day? – and he has not given it to you?"

He said, "I am not asking for any material things. I ask for spiritual things. And it is not a matter of one day; you have to continue your whole life and they will be given after death. But it is certain they will be given: I have made the temple, I serve the Lord, I pray; you can see even in winter, with wet clothes...." It is thought to be a special quality of devotion, to be shivering with wet clothes. My own idea is that with shivering, singing comes easier. You start shouting to forget the shivering.

I said, "My idea about it is different, but I will not tell you. Just one thing I want, because my grandfather goes on saying, 'These are only cowards; this Balaji is a coward. Six hours a day he is wasting, and it is such a small life; and he is a coward.'"

He said, "Your grandfather said that I am a coward?"

I said, "I can bring him."

He said, "No, don't bring him to the temple because it will be an unnecessary trouble – but I am not a coward."

I said, "Okay, we will see whether you are a coward or not."

Behind his temple there was what in India is called an *akhara*, where people learn to wrestle, do exercises, and the Indian type of wrestling. I used to go there – it was just behind the temple, by the side of the temple – so I had all the wrestlers there as my friends. I asked three of them, "Tonight you have to help me."

They said, "What has to be done?"

I said, "We have to take Balaji's cot – he sleeps outside his house – we have just to take his cot and put it over the well."

They said, "If he jumps or something happens he may fall into the well."

I said, "Don't worry, the well is not that deep. I have jumped into it many times – it is not that deep nor is it that dangerous. And as far as I know, Balaji is not going to jump. He will shout from the cot; sitting in the cot, he will call to his Balaji, 'Save me!'"

With difficulty I could convince three persons: "You have nothing really to do with it. Just alone I cannot carry his cot, and I am asking you because you are all strong people. If he wakes up in the middle it will be difficult to reach to the well. I will wait for you. He goes to sleep at nine o'clock, by ten the street is empty and eleven is the right time, not to take any chances. At eleven we can move him."

Only two persons turned up; one didn't turn up, so we were only three. I said, "This is difficult. One side of the cot…and if Balaji wakes up…." I said, "Just wait, I will have to call my grandfather."

And I told my grandfather, "This is what we are going to do. You have to give us a little help."

He said, "This is a little too much. You have some nerve to ask your own grandfather to do this to that poor man who does no harm to anybody, except that he shouts six hours a day…but we have become accustomed to it."

I said, "I have not come to argue about it. You just come, and anything that you want, anytime, I will owe it to you; you just say, and I will do it. But you have to come for this thing. And it is not much – just a twelve-foot road has to be crossed without waking up Balaji."

So he came. That's why I say he was a very rare man – he was seventy-five! He came. He said, "Okay, let us have this experience also and see what happens."

The two wrestlers started escaping, seeing my grandfather. I said, "Wait, where are you going?"

They said, "Your grandfather is coming."

I said, "I am bringing him. He is the fourth person. If you escape then I will be at a loss. My grandfather and I will not be able to manage. We can carry him, but he will wake up. You need not be worried."

They said, "Are you sure of your grandfather? – because they are almost of the same age; they may be friends and some trouble may arise. He may tell on us."

I said, "I am there, he cannot get me into any trouble. So don't you be afraid; you will not be in any trouble, and he does not know your names or anything."

We carried Balaji and put his cot over his small well. Only he used to take a bath there, and once in a while I used to jump into it, which he was very much against – but what can you do? Once I had jumped in, he had to arrange to take me out. I said, "What can you do now? The only thing is to take me out. And if you harass me, I will jump in every day. And if you talk about it to my family, then you know I will start bringing my friends to jump into it. So right now, keep it a secret between us. You take your bath outside, I take my bath inside; there is no harm."

It was a very small well, so the cot could completely fit over it. Then I told my grandfather, "You go away because if you are caught then the whole city will think that this is going too far."

And then, from far away we started throwing stones to wake him up...because if he did not wake up the whole night, he might turn and fall into the well, and something would go wrong. The moment he woke up he gave such a scream! We had heard his voice, but this...! The whole neighborhood gathered. He was sitting in his cot and he said, "Who has done it?" He was trembling and shaking and afraid.

People said, "Please get out of the cot at least. Then we will find out what has happened."

I was there in the crowd, and I said, "What is the matter? You could have called your Balaji. But you didn't call him, you gave a scream and you forgot all about Balaji. Six hours training every day for your whole life...."

He looked at me and he said, "Is that too a secret?"

I said, "Now there are two secrets you have to keep. One you have already kept for many years. This is now the second."

But from that day he stopped that three hours shouting in the temple. I was puzzled. Everybody was puzzled. He stopped taking a bath in that well, and those three hours every evening and morning he just forgot. He arranged a servant priest to come every morning to do a little worship and that was all.

I asked him, "Balaji, what has happened?"

He said, "I had told you a lie that I am not afraid. But that night, waking up over the well – that shriek was not mine." You can call it the primal scream. It was not his, that is certainly true. It must have come from his deepest unconscious. He said, "That scream made me aware that I am really an afraid man, and all my prayers are nothing but trying to persuade God to save me, to help me, to protect me.

"But you have destroyed all that, and what you have done was good for me. I am finished with all that nonsense. I tortured the whole neighborhood my whole life, and if you had not done that, I may have continued. I am aware now that I am afraid. And I feel that it is better to accept my fear because my whole life has been meaningless and my fear is the same."

Only in 1970 I went for the last time to my city. I had a promise with my mother's mother that when she dies – she had taken it as a promise – I would come. So I had gone. I just went around the town to meet people and I saw Balaji. He was looking a totally different man. I asked him, "What has happened?"

He said, "That scream changed me completely. I started to live the fear. Okay, if I am a coward, then I am a coward: I am not responsible for it. If there is fear, there is fear; I was born with it. But slowly slowly, as my acceptance grew deeper, that fear has disappeared, that cowardliness has disappeared.

"In fact I have disposed of the servant in the temple, because if my prayers have not been heard, then how is a servant's prayer going to be heard...a servant who goes to thirty temples the whole day?" – because he gets two rupees from each temple. "He is praying for two rupees. So I have disposed of him, and I am perfectly at ease, and I don't bother a bit whether God exists or not. That is his problem, why should I be bothered?

"But I am feeling very fresh and very young in my old age. I wanted to see you, but I could not come. I am too old. I wanted to

thank you that you did that mischief; otherwise, I would have continuously prayed and died, and it was all just meaningless, useless.
Now I will be dying more like a man freed, completely freed." He
took me into his house. I had been there before; all the religious
books were removed. He said, "I am no longer interested in all that."

. . .

MY FATHER WOULD TAKE ME with him if he was going to
some ceremony, some marriage, some birthday party, anywhere. He would take me on the condition that I should
remain absolutely silent, "Otherwise, you please remain at home."

I would say, "But why? Everybody is allowed to talk, except me!"

He said, "You know, I know, and everybody knows why you are
not allowed to talk – because you are a disturbance."

"But," I said, "in things which concern me, you promise me that
you will not interfere with me, and I promise you that I will remain
silent."

And many times it happened that he had to interfere. For example, if some elderly man was there – a faraway relative, but in India
it doesn't matter – my father would touch his feet, and would say,
"Touch his feet."

I said, "You are interfering with me, and our contract is finished.
Why should I touch this old man's feet? If you want to touch them,
you can touch them twice, thrice; I will not interfere. But why
should I touch his feet? Why not his head?"

And that was enough disturbance. Everybody would explain to me
that he was old. I said, "I have seen many old people. Just in front of
my house there is an old elephant; I never touch his feet. That
elephant belongs to a priest; it is a very old elephant. I never touch
his feet, and he is very wise – I think more wise than this old man.

"Just old age does not give him any quality. A fool remains a fool
– perhaps becomes more foolish as he becomes older. An idiot

becomes more idiotic as he grows old, because you cannot remain the same, you are going to grow. And the idiot, when he becomes senile...then his idiocy is multiplied. And that is the time when he becomes very respectable. I am not going to touch the feet of this old man unless it is proved to me why I should."

Once I went to a funeral; one of my teachers had died. He was my Sanskrit teacher – a very fat man, funny looking, and funnily dressed in the way of old brahmins, ancient brahmins, with a very big turban. He was a laughingstock in the whole school but he was very innocent too. The Hindi word for innocent is *bhole*, so we used to call him Bhole. As he entered the class, the whole class would recite loudly, "Jai Bhole" – long live Bhole. And of course he could not punish all the students; otherwise, how was he going to teach, whom was he going to teach?

He died. So naturally, thinking that as he was my teacher I would behave, my father didn't ask for the contract. But I could not, because what happened there I had not expected – nobody had expected it. His dead body was lying there when we arrived. His wife came running out and fell upon him and said, "Oh my Bhole!" Everybody remained silent but I could not. I tried hard, but the harder I tried, the more difficult it was. I burst out laughing and I said, "This is great!"

My father said, "I had not made a contract with you thinking that as he was your teacher you would be respectful."

I said, "I am not disrespectful, but I am surprised by the coincidence. Bhole was his nickname and he used to get angry about it. Now the poor fellow is dead and his wife is calling him Bhole and he cannot do anything. I am just feeling sorry for him!"

Every place I used to go with my father he always made the contract; but he was always the first party to break it because something or other would happen and he would have to say something. And that was enough, because that was the condition – that he was not to interfere with me.

One Jaina monk was in the town. Jaina monks sit on a very high pedestal, so that even standing you can touch their feet with your head...at least a five-foot, six-foot-high pedestal – and they sit on it. Jaina monks move in a group, they are not allowed to move alone;

five Jaina monks should move together. That is a strategy so that the four keep and eye on the fifth to see that nobody tries to get a Coca-Cola – unless they all conspire. And I have seen them conspiring and getting Coca-Cola, that's why I remember it.

They are not allowed even to drink in the night and I have seen them drinking Coca-Cola in the night. In fact, in the day it was dangerous to drink Coca-Cola – what if somebody saw it! – so only in the night.... I had supplied it myself so there was no problem about it. Who else would supply them? No Jaina would be ready to do it, but they knew me, and they knew that any outrageous thing, and I would be ready to do it.

So five pedestals were there, but one monk was sick, so when I went there with my father, I went to the fifth pedestal and sat on it. I can still remember my father and the way he looked at me...he could not even find words: "What to say to you?" And he could not interfere with me, because I had not done any wrong to anybody. Just sitting on a pedestal, a wooden pedestal, I was not hurting anybody or anything. He came close to me and he said, "It seems, contract or no contract, you are going to do whatsoever you are intending to do; so from now onwards we will not make the contract, because it is absolutely unnecessary."

And those four monks were in such uneasiness and they also could not say anything – what to say? One of them finally said, "This is not right. Nobody who is not a monk should sit on an equal level." So they told my father, "You bring him down."

I said, "You think twice. Remember the bottle!" – because I had supplied them with the Coca-Cola.

They said, "Yes, that's right, we remember the bottle. You sit on the pedestal as long as you please."

My father said, "What bottle?"

They said, "We are perfectly satisfied. You can sit here, there is no harm – but please keep silent about the bottle."

Now, many people were there, and they all became interested... what bottle? When I came out of the temple everybody gathered; they all said, "What is this bottle?"

I said, "This is a secret. And this is my power over these fools whose feet you go on touching. If I want, I can manage to tell them to touch my feet; otherwise – the bottle...." These fools!

My father, on the way home, asked me, "You can just tell me. I will not tell anybody: what is this bottle? Do they drink wine?"

I said, "No. Things have not gone that far, but if they remain here a few days more, I will manage that too. I can force them to drink wine...otherwise I will name the bottle."

The whole town was discussing the bottle, what the bottle was, and why they had become afraid: "We have always thought that they were such spiritual sages, and this boy made them afraid. And they all agreed that he could sit there, which is against the scriptures." Everybody was after me. They were ready to bribe me: "Ask whatsoever – you just tell us what is the secret of the bottle."

I said, "It is a very great secret, and I am not going to tell you about it. Why don't you go and ask your monks what the bottle is? I can be there, so they cannot lie – and then you will know what kind of people you are worshipping."

. . .

IN MY CHILDHOOD I USED to go early in the morning to the river. It is a small village. The river is very very lazy, as if not flowing at all. In the morning when the sun has not yet arisen, you cannot see whether the river is flowing; it is so lazy and silent. And in the morning when there is nobody, the bathers have not come yet, it is tremendously silent. Even the birds are not singing in the morning – early, no sound, just a soundlessness pervades. And the smell of the mango trees hangs all over the river.

I used to go there, to the furthest corner of the river, just to sit, just to be there. There was no need to do anything, just being there was enough; it was such a beautiful experience to be there. I would take a bath, I would swim, and when the sun would arise I would go to the other shore, to the vast expanse of sand, and dry myself there under the sun, and lie there, and sometimes even go to sleep.

When I would come back my mother used to ask, "What have you been doing the whole morning?"

I would say, "Nothing," because, actually, I had not been doing anything.

And she would say, "How is it possible that you have not been doing anything? You must have been doing something." And she was right, but I was also not wrong.

I was not doing anything at all. I was just being there with the river, not doing anything, allowing things to happen. If it felt like swimming, remember, if it *felt* like swimming, I would swim, but that was not a doing on my part, I was not forcing anything. If I felt like going into sleep, I would go. Things were happening, but there was no doer. And my first experiences of *satori* started near that river: not doing anything, simply being there, millions of things happened.

But she would insist that, "You must have been doing something."

So I would say, "Okay, I took a bath and I dried myself in the sun," and then she was satisfied. But I was not – because what happened there in the river is not expressed by words; "I took a bath" looks so poor and pale. Playing with the river, floating in the river, swimming in the river, was such a deep experience; to say simply, "I took a bath," makes no sense. To just say, "I went there, had a walk on the bank, sat there," conveys nothing.

. . .

I N MY VILLAGE THERE WAS a very beautiful, old, good man. Everybody loved him; he was so simple and so innocent, even though he was more than eighty. And by the side of my village flows a river. He had made a special spot of his own on the river, where he used to take his bath. As far as anybody could remember in the village, they had always seen him, day in, day out, year in, year out; whether it was rainy season, summer or winter, made no difference; whether he was sick or healthy made no difference. He would be there at exactly five o'clock in the morning, on his spot. And that was the deepest part of the river, so nobody ordinarily used to go there – and it was far away.

People used to go to the river; it was just half a furlong from my house, but that spot was almost two miles away. And just like our hills surrounding the river, you had to go and pass one mountain, then another, then another, then you would reach to that spot. But it was a beautiful spot. As I became aware of it, I started going there. And we immediately became friends because…you know me, what type of person I am. If he was going to be there at five, I was going to be there at three. One day, two days, three days…he said, "What is the matter? Have you decided to defeat me?"

I said, "No. That is not the point, but I am going to be here at three – just as you have decided to be here at five."

He said, "Do you know how to swim?"

I said, "I don't know, but you need not worry. If other people can swim, then I can swim. If you can swim, then what is the problem? One thing is certain: that it is humanly possible, that's enough. At the most I can be drowned – so what? One day everybody has to die. It does not matter."

He said, "You are dangerous. I will teach you how to swim."

I said, "No." I told him, "You simply sit here and I will jump. Don't try to save me if I am dying; even if I am calling you to save me, don't listen."

He said, "What kind of child are you? You will be crying, 'Save me!' and I am not to save you?"

I said, "Yes. I will not be crying. I am simply making it absolutely sure. Perhaps when I am drowning, dying or suffocating or water is going in my nose and mouth, I may start crying, 'Save me!' but I want to be clear: I don't want to be saved by anybody in any case. Either I will come out knowing what swimming is or I will go down, knowing that swimming is not for me."

And before he could stop me, I jumped. Certainly I had to go two or three times under the water and come up. And he was standing there, waiting, so that if I call him…but I simply waved my hand, that no, I am not going to call. Three or four times I went down, came up, threw my hands about haphazardly, because I had no idea how to swim – but what can you do? When you are drowning you try every possible way you can. And within five minutes I knew the knack.

And I came back and I told him, "You were offering to teach me this – which I can learn within five minutes? I just have to risk, and accept the fact: at the most it can mean death."

Swimming is a knack, it is not an art that anybody has to learn. You have just to be thrown in water. You are bound to start splashing and throwing your hands and your legs about, and soon you will find that if you throw your hands and legs about in a harmonious way, in synchronicity, then the water itself keeps you up.

I had told that old man, "I have seen dead bodies passing along the river. When a dead man can swim, do you mean to say to me that I am alive, and I cannot swim? Even the dead man knows the art."

In the rains, when there were floods, it would happen many times that whole villages would be taken by the river – many people, dead bodies, dead animals would pass by. So I said, "Even dead people go by, fast. And I am alive, so let me have the chance of learning it by myself, because my feeling is that it is only a knack. What art can there be? It is not craftmanship, or some difficult art to be understood. All that I see is that people are throwing their hands about – so I can throw mine about too."

. . .

I HAVE NOT DONE ANYTHING IN this life to be courageous or to be sharp and intelligent from the very beginning, and I have never thought about it as courage or sharpness or intelligence.
It was only later on that slowly I became aware of how stupid people are. It was only a later reflection; earlier I was not aware that I was courageous. I was thinking everybody must be the same. Only later

on it became clear to me that everybody is not the same.

This was one of my joys in my childhood – to go to the highest hill by the side of the river, and jump! Many neighborhood boys would come with me, and they would try it. But they would just go to the very brink and come back; seeing the height they would say, "Suddenly something happens." I used to show them again and again that "If I can jump – I don't have a steel body – and if I go on managing, surviving, why can't you?"

They said, "We try our hardest" – and they really did try. There was one brahmin boy living just next door who was very much humiliated by this, because he could not jump. So he must have asked his father, "What to do?...because it is very humiliating. He goes on top of the hill and jumps from there, and we just watch. We can see that if he can jump, we can jump; there is no problem in it. If the height cannot kill him, why should it kill us? But just when we gather courage, making all kinds of effort, and we rush, suddenly there comes the break.

"From where it comes we don't know, but just a break; something from our inside says, 'No, these rocks, and this river...if you fall on some rock, or...and the river is deep. And when you fall from a height, first you go to the very bottom of the river, *then* you come up; you cannot do anything else.'"

His father said, "This is not good" – because his father was a very good wrestler, one of the champions in the district. He used to run a gymnasium and teach other people how to fight, Indian free-style wrestling. That is more human, more skillful, and more artful than boxing.

If the child had belonged to somebody else he would have told him not to go there at all, but this man was not that type. He said, "If he can jump and you cannot, that is a disgrace to me. I will come with you, I will stand there. And don't be worried: when he jumps, you jump."

I had no idea that his father was going to be there. When I went there I saw the father, the son and a few other boys who had gathered to see. I had a look and I figured out what was the matter. I said to the boy, "Today you need not bother – let your father jump. He is a great wrestler and there will be no problem for him."

The father looked at me, because he had come just to encourage the boy so that he did not become a coward. He said, "So I have to jump?"

I said, "Yes. Get ready!"

He looked down, and he said, "I am a *wrestler*. These rocks and this river...and you have found some spot! You must have been rehearsing here. Anybody else trying to jump is going to break his neck or leg or anything."

I said, "You brought your son."

He said, "I had brought him not knowing what was the situation. I thought that if you can jump, he can jump; he is of the same age. But here, seeing the situation, I was worried and thinking that if you didn't turn up today it would be a great thing, because my boy is not going to survive. But you are clever: you simply dropped my boy out and caught hold of me. I will try."

And the same thing happened. Even that wrestler who was so courageous – in every way he had been fighting his whole life.... But coming to the brink, the sudden break – because the slope was such, at least fifty feet down, and the river was thirty feet deep, and the rocks were such that it was beyond your control where you would land, what would hit you. And standing on the top of the hill...the wind was so strong that you could be simply killed.

He just stopped there and he said, "Forgive me." And he told his son, "Son, come home. This is not our business. Let him do it – perhaps he knows something."

That day I felt strangely about myself: why doesn't that break come to me? – and I had tried on very strange places.

The railway bridge was the highest point on the river, naturally, because in the rains the river swells up so big that the bridge has always to remain above it, so it was made at the highest point. And there were always two guards moving on the bridge, for two reasons: firstly, so that nobody committed suicide, because that was the place for people to commit suicide.... Just falling from there into the river was enough. You never reached the river alive, you lost your breath somewhere in the middle. It was so high that just to look downwards was enough to give you a nauseous feeling.

And secondly, there was a fear of revolutionaries who were

planting bombs, blowing up bridges, burning trains. To cut a bridge was very significant for revolutionaries because those bridges were joining two parts of the province. If the bridge was broken then the army could not pass; then the revolutionaries could do something in the other part where there was no army headquarters. So these guards were there twenty-four hours a day. But they accepted me.

I explained to them, "I neither want to commit suicide, nor have I come to blow up your bridge. In fact I want the bridge to be guarded carefully because this is *my* place. If this bridge is gone then my highest point of jumping is gone."

THE RAILWAY BRIDGE OSHO USED TO JUMP FROM

They said, "This is your practice?"

I said, "This is my practice. You can watch, and once you have seen you will be convinced that I have no other desire."

They said, "Okay, we will watch."

I jumped. They could not believe it. When I came back I asked them, "Would you like to try?" They said, "No, but for you it is always free – you can come at any time. We have seen you going so easily, but we cannot jump – we know people have died from here."

That bridge was known as Death Bridge and that was the easiest, cheapest way to commit suicide. Even if you purchased poison, some money was wasted, but from that bridge it was simply easy. The river there was the deepest and it took you away. Nobody would even find your body because just after a few miles it met a bigger river, a huge river – and you were gone forever.

Seeing the fear on those two guards' faces, seeing the fear in this wrestler, I simply started wondering, "Perhaps I miss the breaks; perhaps they should be there because they *are* protective." But as I started growing up – and I have been growing up, I have not been growing older. From my very birth I have been growing up, growing up, growing up. Never think that I am growing older. Only idiots grow older, everybody else grows up.

As I started growing up I started becoming aware of my past life, and death, and I remembered how easily I had died – not only easily but enthusiastically. My interest was more in knowing the unknown that was ahead than in the known that I had seen.

I have never looked back. And this has been my whole life's way – not to look back. There is no point. You can't go back, so why waste time? I am always looking ahead. Even at the point of death I was looking ahead.

. . .

ONE OF MY TEACHERS USED to begin his class every day with this ritual: "First listen to my conditions. I don't accept a headache, I don't accept a stomachache. Things that I cannot find, I don't accept. Yes, if you have fever, I accept it because I can check that your temperature is high. So remember, nobody is to ask leave for things which are unprovable. Even a doctor cannot prove whether there is a headache or not." He prevented almost everything because you had to produce a visible disease, only then could you get out; but I had to find some way around it because this was unacceptable.

He was an old man, so all that I had to do was in the night.... He was old, but very strong and very particular about exercises, about walking, so he used to get up early, at five o'clock, and in the dark he would go for a long walk. So I just had to put a few banana peels in front of his door. In the morning he fell, and had a bad back. I was available immediately because I knew about it.

He said, "My back is hurting so much."

I said, "Don't mention anything which you cannot prove."

He said, "But whether I can prove it or not, I am not able to come to school today."

"Then," I said, "you will have to stop your conditions from tomorrow, because I am going to spread the whole thing to the whole school, that if a bad back is accepted.... What proof have you got? Then why not a headache? Why not a stomachache?"

He said, "I think you have something to do with these banana peels here."

I said, "Perhaps you are right, but you cannot prove it, and I believe only in things which can be proved."

He said, "You can at least do me one favor: you can take my application to the principal."

I said, "I will take your application, but remember, from tomorrow you stop those conditions, because sometimes I have a headache, sometimes I have a stomachache, because I am accustomed to eating all kinds of unripe fruits – when you are stealing from other people's gardens, you cannot ask that they should be ripe. And only before they are ripe can you get them; once they are ripe the people take them. So I suffer from stomachache." And certainly from that day he stopped those conditions. He just looked at me, smiled, and started his class.

The students were simply shocked: "What has happened to him? What about the conditions?" I stood up and said, "I have a lot of pain in my stomach."

He said, "You can go." That was the first time.... He told me in the evening when he came to see my father, "This is the first time I have given leave to anybody for a stomachache...because these people are just so imaginative and inventive." And he told my father, "Your boy is dangerous."

I said, "Again you are trying to do something which you cannot prove, you are just assuming. I was simply going for a morning walk and I saw you fall, and I just went to help you to get up. Do you think it is wrong to help somebody?"

He said, "No, it is not wrong to help somebody; but who put those banana peels there?"

I said, "That, you have to find out – it is *your* house. It was just coincidence that I was going for a morning walk; and my father knows that every day I go for a morning walk."

My father said, "That's true, he goes every day. But it is possible he may have done it. But unless you prove it, it is no use: we have to prove things to him. If argumentatively he wins, then even though we are right, he is the winner and we are the losers. He has told me the whole story about your bad back, and that since then you have stopped your two conditions."

My father had also been his student. He said, "This is strange, because you never began without those two conditions."

My teacher said, "Never before did I have this kind of student. I had to change my whole plan because it is dangerous to be in conflict with him; he could have killed me."

. . .

I WAS VERY YOUNG, PERHAPS TWELVE years old when a very strange human being visited our house. My father brought him because he was learned – and not only learned, he had some authentic experiences of his own. Perhaps he was not enlightened at this moment, it is impossible for me to remember exactly. I cannot even remember his face. I just know that he was a Sufi, a Mohammedan mystic, and my father had been listening to him.

He thought the mystic might be able to do something, suggest something, convince me of something, because everybody was worried about me. Although I was living in their house, they all felt I was a stranger. And they were not wrong. And finally, my presence was not as if somebody was present.

My father had brought this Sufi mystic, thinking perhaps he could be helpful. And my father was puzzled, my family was puzzled because what the man did.... They had given me a separate room so that I would not be a constant nuisance to them, because just sitting there, doing nothing, was enough to irritate them – they are all doing, everybody is working, and I am sitting with closed eyes, meditating.

So they had given me a separate room with an independent entrance to it. The Sufi came with my father and he went around smelling the walls, at this corner, on that corner. My father said, "My God, I brought him to bring you to your senses. He seems to be far gone."

My room was absolutely empty. I have always loved emptiness, because only emptiness can be absolutely clean. Whatever you go on collecting in your room, sooner or later becomes junk. So I had nothing in the room.

My father looked at him, looked at me and he said, "I have invited him, so I should see what he does."

Then he came and started smelling me. Now it was too much. My father said, "I had explained to you that my boy is a little eccentric – and you are confirming his eccentricities!"

"No," he said, "I can smell the room and I can smell him. It is the smell of silence, the fragrance of silence. You should feel blessed that you have got such a son. I had to smell both to see whether this fragrance belongs to his presence. It belongs to his presence, this room is full of his presence. Don't disturb him." And he asked my forgiveness, saying, "Forgive me; I have disturbed, coming into your room."

My father took him out and then he came back and said, "I used to think that only you were mad. There are even madder people – smelling the room!"

But I told him, "Your house is your extension: in a subtle way, it represents you. And the man you brought is certainly a great human being, a man of insight and understanding."

. . .

IN MY CHILDHOOD IN MY village.... Each time Mohammedans celebrate the holidays of Muharram, some people are "possessed by the holy spirit." The holy spirit is called *wali*. There are a few people who are thought to be very saintly – they are possessed by walis – and they dance and they shout, scream, and you can ask questions.

And they should not run away, so their hands are tied with ropes, and two persons keep them in control. There are many walis, and each wali has his own crowd, and people come with sweets and fruits – somebody has received a blessing last year and has got a boy, a child; somebody has got married, and somebody has come to get a blessing for the future.

Only Mohammedans participate in it. But I always enjoyed every kind of entertainment. My parents used to tell me, "Listen, that is the Mohammedans' festival, and you are not supposed to be there."

I said, "I am neither Hindu nor Mohammedan nor Jaina nor anybody. What do you mean – that I cannot enjoy anything? All festivals belong to some religion. In fact, I belong to *no* religion so I can participate in all festivals." So I would go there.

Once I managed to hold the rope of one wali who was just an ordinary man and a fraud. I had told him before, "I will expose you if you don't allow me to hold your rope."

He said, "You can hold my rope, and you can share a few sweets also, but don't say anything to anybody."

We both used to go to the same gymnasium – that's how we became friends, and he himself told me that it was all fake. So I said, "That means I am coming; if it is fake, you have to share it."

I went there with a long needle, so I could make him jump. He became the most famous wali because no other wali was jumping so high!

He could not say anything about what was happening – because he is possessed by the wali and the wali cannot be afraid of a needle. So he could not say anything, and I went on sticking him with the needle. He managed to get almost four times more sweets, more fruit, more rupees…more people came to get his blessing.

He said, "That is great, but you tortured me so much!"

I was in such demand from that day – every wali wanted his rope to be given to me, because whoever got me as his assistant would become the greatest wali – immediately, the very same day.

For ten days the function continued, and no wali wanted me again the next day! They would say, "I will escape from town if you come again!"

I said, "There is no need. I am in so much demand by other fools who don't know what is happening…. You just give me half your share – because you will still have double."

And I found that almost everybody was a fraud – because I could make everybody jump with my needle. Not a single one in the whole town was an authentic person who was possessed or anything. They were just pretending – shouting, screaming, saying things that you cannot understand, but you have to make sense out of it.

And the *maulvis*, the Mohammedan scholars, will explain to you what the meaning of it is: "You have been blessed, your desire will be fulfilled" – and who bothers about whose desire is fulfilled or not? If a hundred people come, at least fifty people's desires are going to be fulfilled. These fifty will come back, and these fifty people will spread the idea. The other fifty will also come back – not to the same wali, but to other walis who are there, because the first wali they went to doesn't seem to work: "Perhaps he was not powerful enough."

And my walis were the most powerful. Their power was decided by how high they jumped, how much they screamed, how much they shouted.

And everybody asked me why my walis were making such gestures towards me....

I said, "That is a spiritual language – you will not understand."

. . .

IN MY CHILDHOOD IT WAS an everyday problem with my parents. I told them again and again and again, "One thing you should understand is that if you want me to do something, don't tell me, because if you tell me that I have to do it then I am going to do just the opposite – whatsoever happens."

My father said, "You will do just the opposite?"

I said, "Exactly – just the opposite. I am ready for any punishment, but really you are responsible, not I, because I have made it clear from the very beginning that if you want something to be done please don't tell me. Let me find it myself.

"Once I am ordered, I am determined to disobey, even though I know that what you are saying is right; but that is not the question. This small thing and its rightness does not matter much. It is a question of my whole life. Who is going to be in control? These small rights and wrongs don't matter to me – what does it matter?

"What matters to me – it is a life and death question – is who is going to be in control. Are you going to be in control, or am I going to be in control? Is it my life or your life?"

A few times they tried and they found that I was determined. I would do just the opposite. Of course it was not right, what they wanted was certainly right. And there was no denial of the fact from my side. I said, "What you wanted was right. But that *you* wanted it was not right; you should have allowed me to want it. You were impatient; you forced me to take the opposite action. Now who is responsible that things have gone wrong?"

For example, my grandfather was sick. My father was going out and he told me, "You are here, and you are such a great friend to your grandfather, so just take a little care. This medicine has to be given at three o'clock, and that medicine has to be given at six o'clock."

I did just the reverse – I gave the medicine that was to be given at six o'clock at three, and gave the medicine at six o'clock that was to be given at three...changed the whole order. Of course my grandfather became more seriously ill. And when my father came he said, "This is too much. I had never imagined that you would do this."

I said, "You should have imagined. You should start imagining, visualizing. When I have said it, I have to do it even if it means putting my grandfather into danger. And I have told him that I have reversed the order because I have to do it this way. And he agreed with me."

My grandfather was a jewel of a man. He said, "You do exactly what you have said. Remain determined. My life I have lived, your life is ahead. Don't be controlled by anybody. Even if I die, never feel guilty about it."

He did not die, but I had taken a risky decision. My father stopped telling me to do things from that day. I said, "You can suggest, you cannot order. You have to learn to be polite to your own son, because as far as our beings are concerned, who is father and who is son? You don't possess me, I don't possess you; it is just an accidental meeting of two strangers. You had no idea to whom you were going to give birth. I had no idea who was going to be my father, my mother. It was just an accidental meeting on the road.

"Don't try to exploit the situation. Don't take advantage because you are powerful, you have money, and I don't have anything. And don't force me, because this is ugly. You suggest to me. You can always give me a suggestion: 'This is my suggestion – you can think over it. If you feel it is right, you do it; if you feel it isn't, don't.'"

And slowly it settled that my family started giving only suggestions. But they were in for a surprise, because I started giving suggestions too. My father said, "This is some new development. You had not told us about that."

I said, "It is simple. If you can give suggestions to me because you are experienced, mature, I can also give you suggestions because I am inexperienced. And that is not necessarily a disqualification, because all the great inventions in the world have happened through in-experienced people. Experienced people go on repeating the same thing – because of their experience they know the 'right' method; they cannot invent anything."

For invention you have to be ignorant of the "right" method that has always been done, only then can you break new ground. Only an inexperienced person will have the guts to go into the unknown.

So I said, "You have a qualification of experience, I have a quali-fication of inexperience. You are mature, but maturity also means that your mirror is no longer as clean as my mirror is; much dust has gathered over it. Yes, you have seen much of life – so that is your qualification.

"My qualification is, I have not seen any of life. No dust has gathered on my mirror – my mirror reflects more clearly, more accu-rately. Your mirror may simply imagine that it is reflecting. It may be just an old memory floating, not a real reflection of the objective reality.

"So this has to be: if you can give suggestions to me, I can also give suggestions to you. I am not telling you to follow them. It is not an order. You can think over it just as I think over your sugges-tions."

. . .

M Y FATHER USED TO GO at least three or four times a year to Bombay, and he would ask all the children, "What would you like?" And he would ask me also, "If you want any-thing I can note it down and bring it from Bombay."

I never asked him. Once I said, "I only want you to come back more human, less fatherly, more friendly, less dictatorial, more demo-cratic. Bring a little more freedom for me when you come back."

He said, "But these things are not available in the market."

I said, "I know they are not available in the market, but these are the things I would like: a little more freedom, a little bigger rope, fewer orders, fewer commandments, and a little respect."

No child has asked for respect. You ask for toys, sweets, clothes, a bicycle, and things like that. You get them, but these are not the real things which are going to make your life blissful.

I asked him for money only when I wanted to purchase more books; I never asked money for anything else. And I told him, "When I ask money for books you had better give it to me."

He said, "What do you mean?"

I said, "I simply mean that if you don't give it to me then I will have to steal it. I don't want to be a thief but if you force me then there is no way. You know I don't have money. I need these books and I am going to have them, that you know. So if money is not given to me, then I will take it; and remember in your mind that it was you who forced me to steal."

He said, "No need to steal. Whenever you need money you simply come and take it."

And I said, "You be assured it is only for the books," but there was no need for the assurance because he went on seeing my library growing in the house.

Slowly there was no place in the house for anything other than my books.

And my father said, "First we had a library in our house, now in the library we have a house! And we all have to take care of your books because if something goes wrong with any book you make so much fuss, you create so much trouble that everybody is afraid of your books. And they are everywhere; you cannot avoid stumbling on them. And there are small children...."

I said, "Small children are not a problem to me; the problem is the older children. The smaller children – I respect them so much that they are very protective of my books."

It was a strange thing to see in my house. My younger brothers and sister were all protective of my books when I was not there: nobody could touch my books. And they would clean them and they would keep them in the right place, wherever I had put them, so when I needed any book I could find it. And it was a simple matter because I was so respectful to them, and they could not show their respect in any other way than to be respectful to my books.

I said, "The real problems are the older children – my uncles, my aunts, my father's sisters, my father's brothers-in-law – these are the people who are the trouble. I don't want anybody else to mark my books, underline in my books, and these people go on doing that." I hated the very idea that somebody should underline in my books.

One of my father's brothers-in-law was a professor, so he must have been in the habit of underlining. And he found so many beautiful books, that whenever he used to come he would write notes on *my* books. I had to tell him, "This is simply not only unmannerly, uncivilized, it shows what kind of mind you have.

"I don't want books from libraries, I don't read books from libraries, for the simple reason that they are underlined, marked. Somebody else has emphasized something. I don't want that, because without your knowing, that emphasis enters your mind. If you are reading a book and something is underlined with red, that line stands out. You have read the whole page but that line stands out. It leaves a different impact on your mind.

"I have an aversion to reading somebody else's books, underlined, marked. To me it is just like somebody going to a prostitute. A prostitute is nothing but a woman underlined and marked – notes all over her from different people in different languages. You would like a woman fresh, not underlined by somebody else.

"To me a book is not just a book, it is a love affair. If you underline any book then you have to pay for it and take it. Then I don't want that book here, because one dirty fish can make the whole pond dirty. I don't want any book prostituted – you take it."

He was very angry because he could not understand. I said, "You don't understand me because you don't know me much. You just talk to my father."

And my father said to him, "It was your fault. Why did you underline his book? Why did you write a note in his book? What purpose did it serve to you? – because the book will remain in his library. In the first place you never asked his permission – that you wanted to read his book.

"Nothing happens here without his permission if it is his thing; because if you take *his* thing without permission then he starts taking everybody's things without permission. And that creates trouble. Just the other day one of my friends was going to catch the train and he took away his suitcase...."

My father's friend was going crazy: "Where is the suitcase?"

I said, "I know where it is, but in your suitcase there is one of my books. I am not interested in your suitcase, I am simply trying to save my book." I opened it – I had said, "Open the suitcase," but he was very reluctant because he had stolen the book – and the book was found. I said, "Now you pay the penalty, because this is simply barbarious.

"You were a guest here; we respected you, we served you. We did everything for you – and you steal a book of a poor boy who has no money; a boy who has to threaten his father that 'If you don't give me money then I am going to steal. And then don't ask, Why did I do it? – because then wherever I can steal, I will steal.'

"These books are not cheap – and you just kept it in your suitcase. You cannot deceive my eyes. When I enter my room I know whether my books are all there or not, whether something is missing."

So my father said to the professor who had underlined my book, "Never do that to him. Take this book and replace it with a fresh one."

. . .

IN MY HOMETOWN THERE WAS a monastery where a very famous follower of Kabir, Sahibdas, had lived long before me. But he had left a big monastery, a huge temple and many caves for meditators. They are very beautiful caves because his monastery is very close to the river. In small hills by the river he has made those caves, and inside the caves there are small ponds of water. You can go inside the cave, from one cave to another cave, although a few are blocked; either the water has filled them completely or the earth has fallen. But it is something beautiful to see.

And just to sit in those caves...they are so silent – not even the breeze comes there. They have made them exactly in the right proportion so that a man can live in those caves without being short of oxygen, because air will not be coming from the outside. But the size of the cave is enough to provide oxygen for you at least for three months. So people were sent to meditate in those caves.

I was very young; Sahibdas must have died twenty or thirty years before I was born. But his successor, Satyasahib, I knew very well, and he was an idiot. As it happens, for some particular reason, saints somehow attract idiots.

I am not a saint, so you need not be worried! But saints attract idiots; perhaps there is a certain balance nature has to keep, that if there is a saint then a certain number of idiots are needed to keep the balance. Nature believes in balance; it continuously goes on balancing everything.

This Satyasahib was an utter idiot, but he was a great friend of my father. So it is because of my father I started going there and moving around and looking in those caves. It was really a huge monastery and the man – his master – must have been of great influence.

Now there is nobody else there except Satyasahib, his successor; everybody has left. There are huge gardens, fields, and the monastery is in a very secluded spot, very green and with the river just by the side. Satyasahib's master was buried in the campus of the monastery.

In India many religions don't cremate their saints; everybody else is cremated. But a few religions – for example, Kabir panthis – don't cremate their saints because their bodies have been in contact with such a great soul. They have become associated with something so great that to destroy them is not right.

So their bodies have to be buried just as Christians and Mohammedans do: a *samadhi*, a grave, is made. It is not called a grave, it is called a samadhi – the same word that is used for the ultimate state of consciousness. Because the man had attained samadhi, his grave is no ordinary grave; it is a symbol of samadhi, of the ultimate consciousness.

The monastery was huge and only one person was living there.

And the samadhis of Kabir panthis are not completely closed; they have a sliding side so every year the body can be brought out and every year they can worship the saint again.

One of my teachers was an atheist. I said to him, "Your atheism is perfectly good, but do you believe in ghosts or not?"

He said, "Ghosts? I don't believe even in God, why should I believe in ghosts? They don't exist."

I said, "Before saying that, give me a chance to prove that they do, because I have been meeting a ghost – seeing, talking to him. And he is the ghost of such a great man, Sahibdas."

He said, "All nonsense! You must have got the idea from that idiot, Satyasahib. He goes on talking about his guru; nobody listens but he goes on talking. And I have seen that you have been going there."

I said, "It is right that you have seen me going there but you don't know that I have managed meetings with his master, which he himself has not been able to manage."

My teacher looked suspicious, but I sounded just the way I always sound – so certain. I said, "There is no problem, there is no need to discuss it. Discussion will come later on; first let the encounter...."

He started feeling a little fear. I said, "Don't be afraid, I will be with you, and three or four of my friends will be there, because we have to slide the door, which is heavy; then we have to pull out the body."

He said, "All these things will have to be done?"

I said, "Yes, they have to be done. The body has to be pulled out; only then can I ask Sahibdas to materialize. Just one thing you have to be aware of: don't make any noise, because if the successor, Satyasahib, gets up, then there will be trouble because this is very much against their religion. Only on one day in the year – the anniversary of the day he died – can they pull out the body. And this is absolutely against their religion. There will be great trouble.

"So be very quiet and be very silent. And if any situation arises where you have to run away, then don't wait for anybody and don't call anybody's name; simply run away. Just take care, because this is the trouble: the ghost sometimes catches hold of you, particularly your clothes. So just take care."

This teacher was a Bengali – wearing a long *kurta* and *dhoti* – and Bengalis use very loose clothes, so anybody who is of no use, who cannot run, who cannot do any hard work, is called "Bengali Babu." In India to be called "Bengali Babu" is an insult. These are the two extremes. If somebody calls you "Sardarji," that is an insult. That means you have no mind – not in the sense that you are a meditator but in the sense that you are an Ayatollah Khomeini. Or if somebody calls you "Bengali Babu," that means just useless.

And Bengalis have strange habits: their dhoti is so loose that if they run they are bound to fall. They continuously carry an umbrella, twelve months a year. Whether it is raining or not does not matter, whether it is hot or not does not matter. And in India, seasons are very fixed; you need not carry the umbrella all year round. In the whole of India nobody carries an umbrella the whole of the year, but Bengali babus – somehow it has become part of their style. They continuously carry the umbrella, unnecessary luggage, for no reason.

So I told my teacher – Bhattacharya was his surname – I said, "Sir, leave your umbrella, because if he catches hold of your umbrella – these ghosts *do* catch hold of things...."

He said, "I cannot leave my umbrella. Without my umbrella I feel as if I am naked or something is continuously missing."

"And," I said, "you have to make your dhoti tight, because if it falls open then you will have to run naked. And these ghosts are ghosts: they don't believe in your manners, your etiquette. He may catch hold of your dhoti and you will have to run without your dhoti."

He said, "But he is a saint!"

I said, "He *is* a saint but now he is a ghost too. But it is up to you: you can come the way you want."

He came. He had his dhoti as tight as he could. The fashion they wear...the dhoti can be worn in many fashions. The Maharashtrians wear it the best; then it functions almost like a pajama – parted in two ways. You can run, you can work in it.

The Bengalis wear it the worst. The one part that they tuck in at their back is so loose that it goes on touching the floor, and the other part that they tuck in front of them, that goes on touching the floor. They are just hodgepodge.

We went in the middle of the night. We had chosen a dark night when there was no moon, because if the successor saw us…. And I needed a dark night for ghosts – because I had made a young man ready to be a ghost, to catch hold of Bhattacharya's dhoti if he did not come with his umbrella.

The grave was big because the panthis had to pull out the body; it was in a casket which you have to pull out. But the grave was big enough so that by the side of the casket *my* ghost could be lying down. So this was the arrangement, that we would pull out our man, and at that very moment one of us would drop something and somebody would shriek and the running would start. And before Bhattacharya could see who the ghost was, the ghost would catch something of his. And that's what happened.

It went perfectly well. The ghost caught his dhoti, and Bhattacharya…. You cannot believe what a man can become when he is really in fear: he himself dropped his dhoti. He did not wait for the dhoti to drop by itself; he himself opened it up! Dhoti, umbrella…. The ghost did not even catch the umbrella because the ghost was lying down and the umbrella was up under Bhattacharya's arm. But Bhattacharya thought, "Who knows? – he may jump for the umbrella!" And when he started taking off his kurta, I said, "The ghost is satisfied – come on!"

Two days later I asked him, "What about your atheism?"

He said, "All that was nonsense; I was a fool. You are right – there *is* a God. But what a strange night!"

I said, "You should at least thank me – I saved your kurta."

He said, "That I remember. I was throwing it because if the ghost started holding onto anything then I would be caught. I thought, 'I will leave everything so I can at least reach my home. At the most, people will laugh and it will be embarrassing.' And it *was* embarrassing: when I got there in my kurta…."

We had made all the arrangements so that people should be there; otherwise in the middle of the night who would see? In a town, a small town, all the people go to sleep by nine, at the most ten. In those days there was no movie, "talkie," so by nine the town would be almost deserted. So we had arranged, "Something really great is going to happen: you just wait. Nearabout twelve you will see Bhattacharya coming home naked."

They said, "Naked!"

We said, "But don't tell anybody. He will be even without his umbrella!"

So people were really excited and they were waiting, everybody lying down on his bed. In summer, in India, people sleep with their beds on the streets. Everybody was lying down but awake, and as Bhattacharya came there was a great crowd: torches and lamps and people.

Bhattacharya was perspiring and just trembling, so we had to say to people, "This is not right – you should go. He has met a ghost and now you are bothering him. He may die, he has got such a shock."

We took him inside; we gave him a good cold bath, and poured as many buckets of water over him as possible to bring him to his senses. It was very difficult to bring him to his senses, but at last he said, "Yes, now I am feeling better, but where is that ghost?"

I said, "That ghost has gone. We have closed the casket."

"And my umbrella and dhoti?"

I said, "We have brought those, because we prayed to the ghost: 'Poor Bhattacharya is a very poor man and you are a saint. It is enough punishment for the atheist; more than that is not needed' – so he has given them back to you."

From that day we saw that every day Bhattacharya was going in the morning to put flowers on that samadhi and to pray and do some worship there.

I said, "Have you become a Kabir panthi?"

He said, "I have to become a Kabir panthi. I am reading the scriptures of Kabir panthis, the sayings of Kabir, the songs of Kabir – they are really beautiful. But I must thank you," he said to me. "If you had not arranged that encounter with the ghost I would have died an atheist."

About Osho

O SHO IS A MODERN-DAY BUDDHA WHOSE WISDOM, clarity and humor have touched the lives of millions of people around the world. He is creating the conditions for the emergence of what he calls the "New Man" – a qualitatively new kind of human being who is aware, life-affirmative and free.

According to Osho, the spiritual traditions of the past have made a deep split within the individual, and this is reflected in all the institutions of society. His way is to heal this split, to restore the unity of body and spirit, earth and sky.

After his enlightenment in 1953, the evolution of this New Man became his dream. In 1966, Osho left the academic world and his post as a philosophy professor at the University of Jabalpur and began touring India intensively and speaking to many hundreds of thousands of people. At the same time, Osho was developing practical tools for man's self-transformation.

By the late 1960s, Osho had begun to create his unique dynamic meditation techniques. He says that modern man is so burdened with the traditions from the past and the anxieties of modern-day living, that he must go through a deep cleansing process before he can begin to discover the thought-free, relaxed state of meditation.

By 1974, a commune had been established around Osho in Pune, India, and the trickle of visitors from the West had become a flood. Today, his Commune is the largest spiritual growth center in the world. Each year it attracts thousands of international visitors to its meditation, therapy, bodywork and creative programs.

Osho speaks on virtually every aspect of the development of human consciousness. His talks cover a staggering range – from the meaning of life and death to the struggles of power and politics, from the challenges of love and creativity to the significance of science and education. These talks, given over thirty years, have been recorded on audio cassette and videotape, and published in hundreds of books in every major language of the world. He belongs to no tradition and says, "My message is not a doctrine, not a philosophy. My message is a certain alchemy, a science of transformation."

Osho left his body in 1990 as a result of poisoning by U.S. government agents, while being held in custody for technical immigration violations in 1985. He asks always to be referred to in the present tense. The words on his Samadhi, which Osho himself dictated, read:

OSHO
Never Born – Never Died
Only Visited this Planet Earth between
December 11, 1931 – January 19, 1990

Osho Commune International

OSHO COMMUNE INTERNATIONAL in Pune, India, is a place to relax from the outward stresses of life and nourish the soul. Osho describes the Commune as a laboratory, an experiment in creating a "New Man" – a human being who lives in harmony with the inner and the outer, with himself and his environment, and who is free from all ideologies and conditionings that now divide humanity.

Set in thirty-one acres in the tree-lined suburb of Koregaon Park, this meditation resort receives thousands of visitors every year from all countries and from all walks of life. Visitors generally spend from three weeks to three months and stay in nearby hotels and apartments.

The Commune houses the unique Osho Multiversity, which offers hundreds of personal growth and self-discovery programs and professional trainings throughout the year, all of which are designed to help people find the knack of meditation: the passive witnessing of thoughts, emotions and actions, without judgment or identification.

Unlike many traditional Eastern disciplines, meditation at Osho Commune is an inseparable part of daily life, whether working, relating or just being. The result is that people do not renounce the world but bring to it a spirit of awareness, celebration, and a deep reverence for life.

At the center of the Commune is Gautama the Buddha Auditorium, where seven different one-hour-long meditations are offered every day. These include:

Osho Dynamic Meditation:* Osho's technique designed to release tensions and repressed emotions, opening the way to a new vitality and an experience of profound silence.

Osho Kundalini Meditation:* Shaking free dormant energies, and through spontaneous dance and silent sitting, allowing these energies to be redirected inward.

Osho Nataraj Meditation:* The inner alchemy of dancing so totally, that the dancer disappears and only the dance remains.

Osho Nadabrahma Meditation:* Based on an ancient Tibetan humming technique to harmonize the energy flow.

Osho No-Dimensions: A powerful method for centering the energy, based on a Gurdjieff technique.

Osho Vipassana Meditation: Gautam Buddha's technique of dissolving mental chatter through the awareness of breath.

Osho White Robe Brotherhood: The highlight of the day at the Commune is the evening meeting of the Osho White Robe Brotherhood. This two-hour celebration of music, dance and silence, followed by a videotaped talk by Osho, is unique – a deep and complete meditation where thousands of seekers, in Osho's words, "...dissolve into a sea of consciousness."

*Service mark Osho International Foundation

Further Reading

MEDITATION:
THE ART OF ECSTASY
A wonderful book for someone new to meditation, as well as those already on the path. Osho explains the difference between concentration and meditation, and emphasizes a playful, non-serious approach. Dynamic Meditation is described and he answers questions about this meditation and sannyas.
ISBN 81 7261 000 9

NOWHERE TO GO BUT IN
Osho talks on the nature of enlightenment, the seeking of spiritual powers, the relationship between meditation and love, meditation and sex, making love without a partner but with existence, and tantra.
ISBN 81 7261 017 3

SEEDS OF WISDOM
Seeds of Wisdom is a collection of 120 letters written by Osho to a beloved disciple.
The selections in this book are actually more like small stories and parables than letters. Using incidents in his daily life as a starting point, or recalling ancient teaching stories, Osho reflects on the nature of truth and the spiritual search, while at the same time giving the reader an intimate glimpse into his own life and search.
ISBN 81 7261 018 1

A CUP OF TEA
This unique book is a compilation of intimate letters written by Osho to his disciples and friends on subjects as diverse as solitude, love, meditation and receptivity, as well as our fruitless efforts to make our lives secure, the stupidity of the human mind, and the ability to laugh at oneself.
ISBN 81 7261 013 0

INDIA MY LOVE
FRAGMENTS OF A GOLDEN PAST
This beautifully illustrated volume is Osho's tribute to the India he describes in the following excerpt:

"...And down the centuries, seekers have been coming to this land from all over the world. The country is poor, the country has nothing to offer, but to those who are sensitive it is the richest place on the Earth. But the richness is of the inner. This poor country can give you the greatest treasure that is possible for human beings."
Treat your inner being to a journey into the mystic heart of India with an enlightened master as your guide. Osho's extraordinary gift for storytelling brings a uniquely contemporary freshness to the tales of India's golden past. His lively discourses animate the enchanted landscape of a land that even today continues to intrigue and attract the seeker and adventurer within us all.

ISBN 81 7261 006 8

TANTRA, THE SUPREME UNDERSTANDING
DISCOURSES ON THE TANTRIC WAY OF TILOPA'S SONG OF MAHAMUDRA

Nothing much is known about the Indian master, Tilopa, yet his mystical insight into Tantra in the form of a song passed on to his disciple Naropa, has lived on through the ages. In this series of discourses, Osho speaks on Tilopa's verses, which contain many significant meditation techniques suitable for the modern-day seeker.

"Mahamudra...is a total orgasm of the whole being.... This is a song of Mahamudra. And who will sing it? Tilopa is no more. The orgasmic feeling itself is vibrating and singing.... I am also here to sing a song, but it can be given to you only when you are ready."
Osho

ISBN 81 7261 009 2

THE EMPTY BOAT
TALKS ON STORIES OF CHUANG TZU

Osho revitalizes the 3000-year-old Taoist message of self-realization through the stories of the Chinese mystic, Chuang Tzu. He speaks about the state of egolessness – "the empty boat" – about spontaneity, dreams and wholeness; about living life choicelessly and meeting death with the same equanimity.

ISBN 3 89338 118 X

THE INNER JOURNEY

"Fearlessness is the total presence of fear, with the courage to face it." Osho

For the inner traveler, *The Inner Journey* describes what is needed for a seeker to clear the path that returns to the self. It is a precise manual for tuning the instrument - body, mind, hara - to an inner balance and harmony that will pave the way for the experience of meditation.

"Love is not something to be obtained from the outside," says Osho; "Love is the music of your inner being. Nobody can give you love. Love can arise within you, but it cannot be obtained from the outside. There is no shop, no market, no salesman from whom you can purchase love. Love is an inner flowering. It arises from some dormant energy within, yet all of us search for love on the outside, but all of us search for love in the beloved."

ISBN 81 7261 091 X

The Supreme Doctrine
DISCOURSES ON THE KENOPANISHAD

Speaking to his first Western disciples, Osho says of these ancient Vedic scriptures, "I have chosen to talk about the Upanishads because to me they represent one of the purest expressions of the ultimate that is possible, if it is possible at all." He also answers questions about using the intellect, transcending the duality of sex, the role of the master in the spiritual journey of the disciple, psychoanalysis, and his chaotic meditation techniques.

ISBN 81 7261 074 2

And the Flowers Showered
TALKS ON ZEN

Commenting on eleven Zen anecdotes, Osho explores the spiritual search – speaking on emptiness and no-mind, knowledge and being; on belief and trust, repression and truth; on philosophy and religion, love and divinity; on death and disease, on happiness and living in the here-and-now.

ISBN 81 7261 002 5

Vedanta: Seven Steps to Samadhi
TALKS ON THE AKSHYA UPANISHAD

These discourses were delivered mornings and evenings at an early meditation camp, with the day spent experiencing the meditations Osho describes. An incomparable opportunity to explore Osho's most powerful techniques.

ISBN 81 7261 012 0

Hsin Hsin Ming
VERSES OF THE FAITH-MIND OF SOSAN.

This book contains the quintessence of Zen, the path of awareness and meditation. "Sosan was a man of power, a man who has come to know.... With him enters the divine, a ray of light into the darkness of your mind."

ISBN 81 7261 003 3

The Goose is Out

Questions from seekers and friends, all attempting in so many ways – just as in the famous Zen koan – to free their goose from their bottle without either killing the goose or breaking the bottle. Full of jokes and humor.

ISBN 81 7261 014 9

Osho Media

OSHO IS THE WORLD'S MOST PROLIFIC AUTHOR in the vast arena of body, mind and spirit. He has spoken on almost all of the world's enlightened mystics and masters; on Buddha and Buddhist masters, Zen and Zen masters, Indian mystics, Jesus, Jewish mystics and Western mystics. He has also spoken extensively on Sufism, Tantra, Tao, Yoga, the Upanishads, and on the art of meditation.

Books: Virtually all of Osho's discourses, including many from the early days of his travels around India, have been transcribed and collected into many hundreds of volumes, not only in the original English and Hindi but also translated into all the major languages of the world.

Audio: Most of Osho's discourses are available on audiotape and cover every aspect of the development of human consciousness: from love and creativity to power and politics; from sex and death to science, education and humor.

Video: Approximately 1750 English discourses are available on videotape. There is also a wide selection of videotapes documenting significant milestones throughout the years of Osho's work, including a beautiful record of the celebration of his leaving the body in January 1990 (*I Leave You My Dream*), and Osho's vision for a new world and a new man (*The New Manifesto*).

Worldwide Web (www): Comprehensive information on Osho and his vision, including a tour of Osho Commune International as well as online audio, an online magazine and online shopping facilities for all publications, is available on http:// www.osho.com.

Further Information

For information about visiting the Commune,
your nearest Osho Meditation Center and general information, contact:

Osho Commune International
17 Koregaon Park,
Pune 411 001 (MS), India.
Tel: +91 (0) 20 628 562
Fax: +91 (0) 20 624 181
e-mail: osho-commune@osho.com

For publishing and copyright information
regarding Osho's books, contact:
Osho International
570 Lexington Ave,
New York, NY 10022, USA
Tel: +1 212 588 9888
Fax: +1 212 588 1977
e-mail: osho-int@osho.com

www.osho.com
A comprehensive website in many languages
featuring Osho's meditations, books and tapes,
an online tour of Osho Commune International
a list of Osho Information Centers worldwide,
and a selection of Osho's talks.